THE ZEN OF DIRECT3D GAME PROGRAMMING

PRIMA TECH'S

GAME DEVELOPMENT

CHECK THE WEB FOR UPDATES

To check for updates or corrections relevant to this book and/or CD-ROM, visit our updates page on the Web at **http://www.prima-tech.com/updates**.

SEND US YOUR COMMENTS

To comment on this book or any other PRIMA TECH title, visit our reader response page on the Web at **http://www.prima-tech.com/comments**.

HOW TO ORDER

For information on quantity discounts, contact the publisher: Prima Publishing, P.O. Box 1260BK, Rocklin, CA 95677-1260; (916) 787-7000. On your letterhead, include information concerning the intended use of the books and the number of books you want to purchase.

THE ZEN OF
DIRECT3D GAME
PROGRAMMING

PETER WALSH

PRIMA TECH'S

GAME DEVELOPMENT

P
PRIMA
TECH

A DIVISION OF PRIMA PUBLISHING

A Division of Prima Publishing

Prima Publishing and colophon are registered trademarks of Prima Communications, Inc. PRIMA TECH is a trademark of Prima Communications, Inc., Roseville, California 95661.

Publisher: Stacy L. Hiquet
Associate Marketing Manager: Jennifer Breece
Managing Editor: Sandy Doell
Acquisitions Editor: Jody Kennen
Project Editor: Estelle Manticas
Technical Reviewer: Greg Perry
Copy Editor: Laura R. Gabler
Interior Layout: LJ Graphics: Susan Honeywell, Julia Grosch. Illustrations: Patrick Cunningham
Cover Design: Prima Design Team
Indexer: Kelly Talbot

Microsoft, DirectX, Direct 3D, DirectDraw, DirectPlay, DirectInput, Windows, and Visual C++ are either registered trademarks or trademarks of Microsoft Corporation in the United States and/or other countries. *Alien vs. Predator* copyright Fox Interactive. *Incoming* copyright Rage Software. All other trademarks are the property of their respective owners.

Important: Prima Publishing cannot provide software support. Please contact the appropriate software manufacturer's technical support line or Web site for assistance.

Prima Publishing and the author have attempted throughout this book to distinguish proprietary trademarks from descriptive terms by following the capitalization style used by the manufacturer.

Information contained in this book has been obtained by Prima Publishing from sources believed to be reliable. However, because of the possibility of human or mechanical error by our sources, Prima Publishing, or others, the Publisher does not guarantee the accuracy, adequacy, or completeness of any information and is not responsible for any errors or omissions or the results obtained from use of such information. Readers should be particularly aware of the fact that the Internet is an ever-changing entity. Some facts may have changed since this book went to press.

ISBN: 0-7615-3429-6

Library of Congress Catalog Card Number: 2001-086795

Printed in the United States of America

00 01 02 03 04 II 10 9 8 7 6 5 4 3 2 1

To Simon and Joy Walsh.
Thanks for all of your support over the years.

Acknowledgments

Writing this book has been one of the largest experiences that I have undertaken. But it was a lot of fun, and I met so many great people that it was definitely one of the most interesting experiences, as well. First off, thanks to my Mom and Dad—without their help I wouldn't be in the position I'm in now. They always made sure that I had the latest technology when I was growing up, so that I could always push the limits of what I knew. They weren't quite sure what I was doing half the time, but I'm sure they thought it would eventually add up to something interesting.

Thanks to my high school English teacher, Conor Norton, in Sandford Park School, Dublin, Ireland, for showing me how to use a, comma in, a, sentence, properly. I bet I'm the last person he thought would be writing a book.

A damn big THANK YOU to André Lamothe, of Xtreme Games. His book, *The Black Art of 3D Game Programming,* was the first book that I ever read on game development many, many years ago. Not only did he alter my career by introducing me to the game industry, but years later he ended up getting me signed on to do my own book!

I couldn't leave out Jody Kennen, my acquisitions editor on the book. Jody is one of the nicest people that I have ever met—she put up with my excuses for being late with chapters and went out of her way to help me, for instance, by getting me that free press pass to the GDC. Thank you so much Jody—I will pay you back sometime. Thank you also to Estelle Manticas, my project editor. Estelle is fantastic, and really knew how to break it to me lightly that my messed-up sense of humor was best not printed, but kept in a more verbal form. Thanks Estelle—I enjoyed meeting you in San Jose. And thank you to the rest of the Prima team, including the artists, editors, marketing people, and everyone else who put in their two cents in order to convert a few trillion of my brain impulses into this book.

I've also got to say thanks to Abertay University, in Dundee, Scotland. During the time I was writing the book, they hooked me up with my own office, a slick computer with all the optionals, and gave me access to a lot of support. Thanks guys. In particular I would like to thank Louis Natanson, head of Computer Arts division and Peter Astheimer, head of IC-CAVE, as well as Henry Fortuna, and John Sutherland, of the Games Tech division. Keep up the good work – you are changing more people's lives than you realize!

Thanks to Jim Bulvan and Alex for writing Appendix A on C++ for me. I was just too busy to do it myself and after I met Jim at the XGDC he agreed to help me out.

Thanks to Mike Andrews, Jon Keatley, Clare Simms, Carolyn Kerr, and Joanna Hendry. A special thank you to Stewart Wright for promising to do the artwork for my book and providing...umm, oh wait, nothing! Well, thanks for all the valuable information you gave me on 3D modeling and Web design.

And finally, thank you to Microsoft for developing DirectX. And a bigger thank you to the DirectX documentation team for giving me a reason to write this book. I am truly in awe that Microsoft managed to pull off the DirectX philosophy and their dreams of device independence for interactive entertainment development. Don't take my endless sarcastic comments about Microsoft too seriously.

Author Bio

Peter Andrew Walsh was born in London, England, 20-something years ago. He has traveled widely and lived in places as normal as Boston, Massachusetts, and as exotic as Dhahran, Saudi Arabia. Peter has more than six years of experience in the creation of interactive-entertainment software, four of which were with DirectX. Recently he worked in the computer games research, development, and consultancy firm IC-CAVE, as well as in the University of Abertay, Dundee, a university at the forefront of computer-based entertainment degrees. The question he gets asked most is "Where the heck did you learn all this stuff?" The answer, duh, is the cerebral uplink that was implanted in his brain when he started breaking CIA codes in kindergarten.

If you have any questions or comments about the book, life, the universe, or anything else, Peter would love to hear from you. Reach him at peter_walsh@presidency.com.

CONTENTS

CHAPTER 7

GETTING JIGGY WITH WINDOWS 119

Chapter 9
Putting Direct3D to Work ▪▪▪▪▪▪▪▪▪▪▪▪305

CHAPTER 10

CALIFORNIA-STYLE CONSOLES 371

CHAPTER 12
GETTING TO KNOW DIRECT3D
IN A MORE 3D SORT OF WAY 475

CHAPTER 13

BUILDING THE ZEN 3D ENGINE ⋯⋯⋯⋯531

Chapter 16

Advanced Graphics Techniques 701

Appendix B

Direct 3D Advanced Reference 771

LETTER FROM THE SERIES EDITOR

Dear Reader,

I still remember the day when I was invited, along with a small group of developers, to hear about Microsoft's new Direct3D technology. I remember sitting at lunch and listening to how this new Direct3D engine would revolutionize the industry. I, and everyone else, disagreed. The problem was that 3D graphics was a complex procedure to pull off in software, and no generalized 3D software engine could possibly work for everyone. And we were right! Ultimately, I doubt if much of the original code still exists in Direct3D (though the overall COM-based scheme, and many of the original data structures, are intact in one way or another). Direct3D has a long heritage, but only within the last few years has it caught on—mostly due to the arrival of seriously powerful 3D accelerators that blow away any software engine you can think of.

Direct3D, along with all the other DirectX components, continue to change, rendering the SDK documents nearly useless. The public has been screaming for good books on DirectX/3D, and the DirectX pleas have been answered quite well, but still there's a big gap concerning Direct3D. Sure, a lot of books have been written on Direct3D, but they're all mediocre, as far as I'm concerned.

The Zen of Direct3D Game Programming is part of Prima's Game Development series' first wave of Direct3D books that push the envelope and cover the subject from the ground up—and don't include a single line of SDK code! *Zen* is what I needed years ago when I was figuring out Direct3D (back then, it had execution buffers—yuck!), but had nothing to go on except broken SDK demos. This book is for the C/C++ programmer who has some experience with graphics and Win32, but isn't an expert by any means. If you are new to Win32 programming, this book will give you enough to get going under Windows, along with foundation information on DirectX (DirectDraw and DirectInput specifically) that will prepare you for one of the most complete treatises on Direct3D that you will ever read.

Zen is the book you'll keep by your side as a reference, as well as a tutorial containing solid examples on everything Direct3D has to offer. Peter Walsh takes you on a mesmerizing journey through Direct3D, in the most concise and clearly-written prose on the subject to date. He explains a topic or action, and then shows you how to do it. And that's all anybody could ask!

What if you already know Direct3D and just want to learn more? Well, we didn't call it "Zen" of Direct3D for nothing! Part Four of the book is hardcore 3D, and I mean *hardcore*. Peter creates an entire 3D engine for you, piece by piece and step by step. The engine, when it's complete, is a full object-oriented 3D engine with support for everything you can imagine, including hierarchical animation, object frames, collision, and more.

In conclusion, this book is what Microsoft should be sending along with every single copy of the DirectX/3D SDK. It's that good and that complete.

Sincerely,

André LaMothe
Series Editor

1 INTRODUCTION

Welcome to *The Zen of Direct3D Game Programming*. You're in for one heck of a ride as you read through this on your path to becoming a Zen guru of DirectX graphics. This book is about one thing: learning to program amazing 3D computer graphics with Microsoft Direct3D 8.0. And that's the thing that sets this book apart from other books on 3D game programming, in which usually over half the content has nothing to do with learning about how to program the graphics, and which are concerned with input, sound, networking, and so on. This entire tome is dedicated to the explanation and implementation of 2D and 3D graphical techniques using the standard Windows GDI and Direct3D.

This book is also aimed at a wide market segment, ranging from the professional programmer trying to get his head around the incredible amount of changes in DirectX 8.0 to the programmer just coming to grips with the idea that programming games might be fun. With that in mind, I have structured the book so that it is easy to jump in at a point where you feel comfortable. Obviously, if you are new to programming, you can't just jump in and right off the bat create the next *Quake* killer 3D game without first understanding 3D theory and mathematics, and you can't get *that* without knowing 2D graphics, and it is hard to get 2D Direct3D if you don't get the GDI, and you definitely won't get the GDI if you don't know the Windows API. And that's basically the overall structure of the book.

Game Theory

⬇

Windows API

⬇

Windows GDI

⬇

2D Direct3D

⬇

3D Theory

⬇

3D Mathematics

⬇

3D Direct3D

⬇

Creating a 3D Engine

⬇

Advanced 3D Techniques

I'll cover absolutely everything that you need to know in order to get off the ground and start programming your own 3D engines—complete with all the optional extras like texture mapping, 3D object-oriented frame-based hierarchies, developing *Quake*-style programmable consoles, and so many other topics that I can't even summarize the book's gazillion or so pages into this one paragraph. By the time you finish this book you will feel confident programming with Direct3D. And not *just* Direct3D—I will also show you the techniques that professionals in the industry use for things like advanced synchronization topics, dealing with the vsync, object animation, and even how to design your own bitmap-based font engine.

The Layout of the Book

This book has traveled far to get to you. It was originally started in Dublin, Ireland, before being continued in Dundee, Scotland. Some of it was written on planes, some of it on trains. Later chapters were thought of in New York and written in San Francisco. Appendix A comes to you all the way from Chicago. And the book's content has sped through the Internet between Europe, Indianapolis, Sacramento, Oklahoma, and Chicago so many times that it would make you dizzy. Before even hitting the page, these words traveled a good 150,000 miles. But that is nothing compared to the distance your mind is going to travel as you peruse these pages.

This book is split into a number of parts—five, in fact.

- **Part One: Learning the Ropes.** This part will cover all of the introductory stuff for DirectX, such as how it is structured, how it fits in with Windows, and a little bit about the dreaded COM. I will also be discussing how to get Visual C++ up and running with DirectX, as well as how a game actually works under the hood. This is a must-read if you are new to programming games.

- **Part Two**: **Windows Programming.** This part is a necessary evil! You can't use Direct3D without understanding the underlying layers, and as unfortunate as that may be, this of course means Windows. However, I am not going to rush it. This section will cover all of the theory and code that goes into developing a stable Win32 application. I will also show you advanced topics in detail, such as how the GDI works and how to implement menus into your application, as well as fun stuff like asynchronous mouse and keyboard input. And you'll get the full rundown on how to create a real-time event loop, how to output debug messages, and a million other topics.

- **Part Three: 2D DirectX Graphics**. This part covers what used to be known in the good old days as DirectDraw but has now been simplified, in Microsoft fashion, to *2D graphics implemented with Direct3D*. This section has so much information in it that I don't think I could have written about anything else. I cover everything from accessing display memory, to rendering sprites, to writing your own font engine, to creating your own replica of a *Quake*-style console.

- **Part Four: 3D Fundamentals.** 3D graphics is an incredibly large subject with a lot of mathematics that you need to know in order to work with it efficiently. How's your knowledge on coordinate systems, vectors, matrices, and velocities? If you need a little refresher, then this is the section for you. I have created a lot of diagrams to make the chapters more interesting, so even if you get bored with the math, you can always look at the pictures!

- **Part Five: 3D Direct3D.** And finally you come to the guts of the book, which is, coincidentally the largest section as well. By the end you will have the knowledge to create an advanced 3D game engine that has an incredible amount of functionality—from a fully programmable camera, to external 3D model loading, to texturing, to lights, to materials, to…shut up now, Peter, they get the point!

What You Need to Have and Know

You don't need too much for this book. What you definitely need is a computer with a Windows 98 (or later) based OS or a Windows 2000 (or later) based OS. You also need the DirectX SDK version 8.0 or later, which is included on the companion CD. Plus you need a development environment. I highly recommend Microsoft Visual C++ 6.0 or later. You can use something else if you want, but don't ask me for the details of how to get it working. The book will be very VC++ specific. Although it is quite possible to get it working in other environments, why bother with the extra hassle? Finally, you will need a 3D accelerator that supports Direct3D. Without one, you will lose out on a lot of the advanced features that I am going to cover.

Now for the intellectual side—what you need to know. You actually don't need to know too much for this book. The one mandatory thing is that you just *have* to know how to program in C. Some of the code is C++ based, but there is a primer in Appendix A that covers C++ for those of you who know C. You don't have to be a NASA rocket scientist at C, but you should be fairly competent. I'm not going to assume that you know anything about game programming or Win32 development at all. Everything will be covered step by step, but I'm not going to spend ages on every topic, so don't even think about falling asleep!

This book is targeted at both the beginner and the more advanced programmer. If you are advanced, then you will probably want to skip past the first couple of sections. I have structured the book so that it should be easy to join in at the beginning of each section without worrying about information in the previous sections if you already know it.

What you really need for this book is an open mind that is ready to grasp new concepts, because there are a lot of them.

The Zen CD

The companion CD contains all sorts of cool stuff to help you become the best possible game developer. The DirectX SDK directory contains the DirectX SDK. See Chapter 2 for the details of installing this. The goodies directory contains a whole bunch of useful applications, kindly donated by companies, such as Paintshop Pro 7 and Fastgraph, which contains a lot of useful graphical technology that you may find useful. In the source directory you will find all the source code that is discussed in the book. It is organized like *Source / Chapter # / Example #*. You may also be interested in the eBook directory, where you can find an electronic hypertext version of the book. It is fully searchable and hyperlinked, which should be quite useful. I have also included some models from the Direct X SDK and some textures from 3D café (http://www.3dcafe.com).

A Final Note

The most important thing to do with this book is have fun! It makes it much easier to learn. Don't try and rush through the beginning chapters just to get to the good stuff. Everything you learn will help you later in life. And try not to get too psychologically damaged from my twisted sense of humor. I have taught myself like 90 percent of the stuff I know, so here is a small tip that will help your productivity: Don't try to force yourself to read more than your synaptic matrix can handle. Use this test: When you finish reading a page, just as you are about to turn to the next page, ask yourself if you can remember the main points covered on the page you just read. If you can't remember what you just read two minutes ago, then it is time to take a five-minute break and eat some junk food. Then come back and you will be ready to take over the world again!

I would love to hear from you about any questions, comments, or anything else that you have in mind. I will try my best to respond to you quickly. Reach me at peter_walsh@presidency.com.

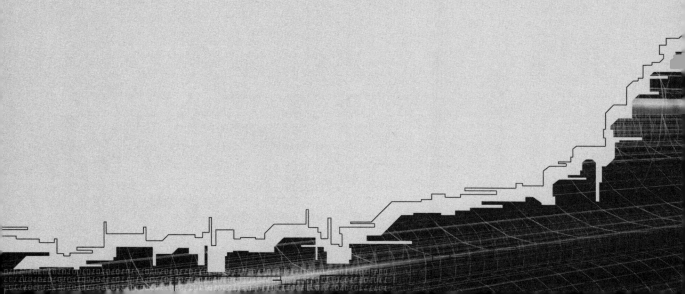

PART ONE

LEARNING THE ROPES

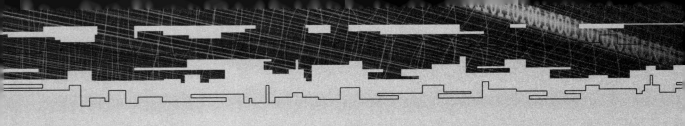

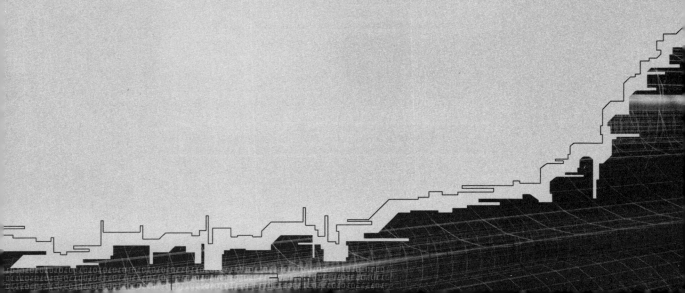

CHAPTER 1

INTRODUCTION TO DIRECT3D AND DIRECTX

Welcome to the *Zen of Direct3D Game Programming*. Before you is a journey into the dark realms of knowledge that only the most determined will complete. You will see and learn things that you never even dreamed of; your mind will acquire the power to shape and mold entire universes, and you will gain the powers of the supernatural elite known as the Zen gurus. Normally this knowledge and power is restricted to the few because there are not many of this world who can harness their potential. It will be a tough journey; however, if you stick with me, I think you will make it. To have reached this page means that you have the makings of a Great One within you.

Let's take some time to delve a little further into your future and see how much greater you can become. When you complete this book you will have gained a number of abilities. First off you will learn that which appears in the Table of Contents: Windows programming, 3D mathematics, and Direct3D. But there is more to game programming than just knowing what the tools of the trade are—you must also understand *how to use* these tools. You need to know all the intricacies of the development environment in which you will be working: what it is capable of, what its personality is, what kind of topping it likes on its hot dog, and so on. It is only when you have a complete understanding of your tools that you will be completely ready and able to take over the world. The *how* part is often lacking in other books that claim to teach programming subjects. And that is one thing that I will strive to write about in this book. If, by the time you finish reading it, you don't think I have adequately explained both the what *and* the how of DirectX graphics, then you have my permission to come to my house and throw eggs at me. I'm talking albatross eggs here.

Understanding is key to the title of this book. Let me tell you how the Zen philosophy relates to this book. *Zen* means to be one with your environment. In this book, that environment is DirectX. Since you can't actually be one with a piece of software, you must have a symbiotic relationship with it. In other words, if you help DirectX, it will help you. And you can live in endless peace and happiness. (If you're Buddhist, work with me here—don't send me hate mail.) But you can only help out your other half if you know what it needs, hence the necessity of achieving complete understanding.

With that out of the way, let's talk a little bit about what this chapter covers:

- what DirectX is exactly. I'll discuss what makes it up and also, most importantly, why it was created.
- the structure of Direct3D and how it fits into the bigger picture.
- a bit about COM. I'm not going to discuss too much code just yet; this chapter will deal with the concepts that go on behind the scenes of DirectX so that you will be better prepared for the code in subsequent chapters.

What Exactly Is DirectX?

DirectX is the key to your future happiness in life. (Well, probably *unhappiness* while you are learning, but that will be over quickly.) You could sum up what DirectX is as *a set of tools and technologies designed to hide the implementation details of the underlying hardware so that you can program in a device-independent manner.* In other words, DirectX brings device-independent programming to what used to be an incredibly device-dependent world. DirectX was developed by Microsoft to solve a number of problems and deficiencies that existed in the PC games market prior to its creation. Back then (before 1996) the technology for the creation of games was very different. So different, in fact, that games were forced to be controlled by the Evil One, also known as DOS. This section will examine the deficiencies that existed and then take a look at how DirectX remedies them.

But first let's run through some basic terminology, so that you'll know what I'm talking about. A *graphics card,* or *display adapter,* is a piece of hardware in your computer that transforms the digital information in your computer's memory into analog signals that your monitor can display (see Figure 1.1). Recent graphics cards contain hardware that accelerates the drawing of 2D and 3D images by performing calculations in parallel with the main CPU. If the graphics card helps the CPU to perform a task, it is said to be computing the task in hardware. Alternatively, if the main CPU computes the task, it is said to be processed in software.

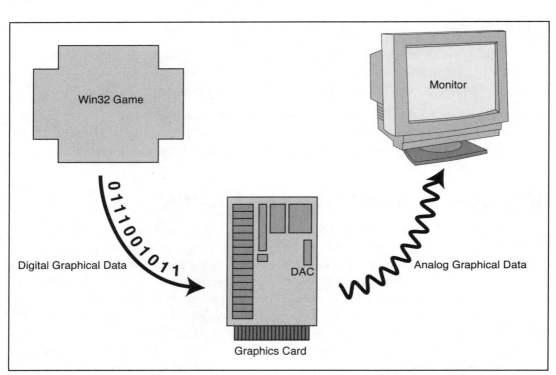

Figure 1.1

The relationship between an application, the graphics card, and the monitor

The term *pixel* comes from the two words *picture* and *element*. Your monitor is made of thousands of pixels that are illuminated by an electron beam to form the images that you see on screen. Each pixel is in fact made of three color-units, which are red, green, and blue. By varying the intensity of these three elements, a pixel can be turned into any color in the spectrum. If you look very closely at your screen with a magnifying glass, you will be able to pick out the individual red, green, and blue elements. See Figure 1.2 to see how the color components relate to a pixel.

Figure 1.2

Pixels on the monitor

Resolution is the number of pixels that make up the image. The more pixels, the better the definition of the image. When talking about monitors, resolution is normally specified in the number of horizontal pixels by the number of vertical pixels. For example, your graphics card can probably output images at resolutions of 640 x 480, 800 x 600, and higher. Figure 1.3 shows how the screen resolution relates to the monitor.

A *frame* is a word used to describe an update to the screen. So if the screen is updated 450 times a second then the *frame rate* will be 450. In other words, every second there are 450 new screens.

Figure 1.3

Screen resolution

The *frame rate* of a game is the number of times per second that the screen is updated with new visual information. Frame rates will usually be above 20. Anything less and the image will start to look jerky and cause eyestrain.

Each graphics card on the market has similar features, such as setting the display mode, accessing memory, and so on. However, the way in which you access these features is very different between manufacturers and even between hardware from the same manufacturer. A *display driver* is a piece of software that allows access to the features of a display card in a slightly more standard way.

In the Beginning

Now that you have the terminology assimilated into your neural net I can show you what the world was like for game developers before DirectX came onto the scene. While you're reading this keep an image of the world in *Terminator 2* after the nuclear strike.

- **Graphics.** Prior to DirectX, unless you wanted to use low-resolution display modes (such as 320 x 200), you were stuck. Even though computers could support higher resolutions at reasonable frame rates, there was just no way for the programmer to easily access the technology. Every single graphics card had a different way of implementing advanced features. So unless the programmer wanted to write a display driver for every single graphics card on the market, there was no option except to go with the lowest common denominator. Also, there was not even a remote hope of getting access to hardware acceleration such as support for blitting, let alone 3D acceleration. (Don't worry if you don't know what *blitting* means; by the end of this book you will be an expert on this stuff!)

- **Sound.** The good thing about graphics cards is that at least there is some standardization for low-resolution modes. There is no such thing as a standard in the sound card market. The only thing that comes close to a standard is the Sound Blaster from Creative Labs because of its high market penetration. So again game developers had to write drivers for every single sound card on the market. This is an incredibly time-consuming and boring process. One solution to the problem is to purchase third-party sound drivers from a company that had actually written all 20 bazillion drivers for every make and model of card out there. The disadvantage is that you usually have to pay royalties to the company that created the drivers and generally you can't modify the source code.

- **Multiplayer Games.** If there is one subject in game programming that really makes my skin crawl, it is multiplayer programming. Yuck, yuck, yuck! Trying to get modems, network cards, protocol stacks, and everything else working on different technology, on different computers, on different parts of the planet at the same time, and in synchronization is a painful experience.

- **Input Devices.** These are not particularly hard to get working, but again, taking advantage of new features becomes a pain. How do you know what the code for the 2,451st button on the second joystick (which is made by an obscure manufacturer in the depths of Taiwan), is going to look like when it comes flying down the joystick port? And what about these newfangled gizmos like USB force-feedback devices? You can't be expected to write drivers for them, can you? No, you can't. So, in the past, joystick support was generally limited to four-button, two-axis analog devices.

- **Operating Systems.** Let's face it: DOS is a pain. It has got to be one of the most user-unfriendly, mangled-messes-of-biblical-proportions that has ever been unleashed on the world. Have you ever seen a complete beginner (read: *middle-aged parent*) try to install a DOS game onto a PC? He reads the manual and actually types the following at the prompt:

```
C:\> "[CD Drive (eg d:) ]:\Setup.exe"
```

Let's call technical support and see what "Bad Command or File Name" means, shall we?

And Then There Was DirectX

Now that I've given you a small glimpse of the nightmare in which some game programmers once had to live, let's take a look at the slick new toys there are to play with today.

- **DirectX Graphics:** *Direct3D*. This probably should have been called DirectHolyGrailForProgrammers. Direct3D takes care of all the mess of dealing with thousands of different graphics cards and gives you one slick interface to work with. You get access to all the advanced features of cards, such as high-resolution display modes and hardware acceleration, without worrying about drivers. It's all taken care of for you. And if a feature isn't supported in hardware, you don't have to worry about that either—Direct3D will emulate it for you (most of the time). And most importantly, it is fast—very fast. Despite its name, Direct3D can be used for both 2D and 3D graphics. This ability is new; in the past, there were two technologies, DirectDraw, which handled 2D graphics, and Direct3D, which handled the 3D stuff. I will be discussing the "new" Direct3D in detail throughout the rest of the book.

- **DirectX Sound:** *DirectSound*. This little beauty does the same as DirectDraw and Direct3D, except it is obviously for the sound hardware. Again, a nice consistent interface is provided no matter what sound hardware you happen to be using. Whether it is a Diamond Monster card or a Sound Blaster Live, your code will run fine. DirectSound3D creates stunningly realistic 3D positional sound that actually works. If you're wearing headphones and you rotate a sound source around your head, you can audibly track it as it moves.

- **DirectX Multiplayer:** *DirectPlay.* I like it. I like it a lot. Here's that phrase again: *consistent interface.* You are going to hear that a lot when you are using DirectX. Although DirectPlay does not get the same coverage as the rest of DirectX, I think it is one of the most important developments for games after DirectDraw. Anything that gives assistance to multiplayer programming is good in my book (get it—*in my book*?). And this allows you to use modems, network cards, or smoke signals to communicate easily.

- **DirectX Input:** *DirectInput.* This little beauty gives programmers a simple and consistent way to interact with input devices such as the mouse, the keyboard, joysticks, VR bodysuits, or whatever. Also, there is now support for the new range of force-feedback devices. I will be discussing DirectInput and how you use it to interface with the mouse and keyboard in Chapter 14.

- **Operating Systems:** *Windows.* This is one of the major benefits of DirectX. It allows games to run on Windows with greater than or equal performance to DOS. Now when the novice user inserts the CD, it starts up, installs itself, and then runs automatically, without a single mouse click. Well, most of the time it's not actually that simple, but I have seen some titles that do come close. It is certainly light-years beyond the dark days of DOS.

So with all that good news in mind, have a look at Figure 1.4, which shows how the different parts of DirectX relate to each other and also how they relate to the different components within your PC.

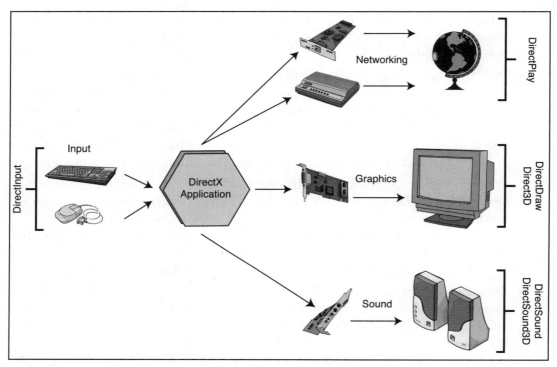

Figure 1.4

The major components of DirectX

How Does Direct3D Fit In?

Now that you've seen the overall structure of DirectX, it's time to take a more technical look at Direct3D. I like to think of Direct3D as a mysterious black box with two sides. One side, the input side, is for you to communicate with while you program. The other side is the output side, which communicates with the graphics hardware in the computer. So you could say, "Direct3D, would you mind changing the current texture to this picture of a wall?" to the input side. It will say, "Of course, anything I can do to help," and then it will output "*Est-ce que Direct3D, cela vous dérangerait de changer la texture actuelle en cette image d'un mur?*" to the graphics card. As you can see, the output has been converted to the language that the graphics card speaks. If a different card is being used, then the output would be "*Direct3D, würden Sie sich kümmern, die aktuelle Beschaffenheit zu dieser Abbildung einer*

Wand zu ändern?" Direct3D is able to translate your request to work with any number of display cards, even though behind the scenes they work in completely different ways. Handy, isn't it?

Direct3D is split into two sections; let's examine those now.

Immediate Mode vs. Retained Mode

Immediate Mode (IM) is the lowest level of Direct3D. By "lowest level" I mean that you are very close to dealing with the actual chip on the graphics card yourself. Direct3D Immediate Mode is the very thin layer that sits between your code and the graphics hardware and translates your requests. Because Immediate Mode is such a thin layer, it is very fast, but there are some disadvantages to it. One of the biggest is that you have to do everything yourself, and I mean *everything*. There's no such thing as requesting Direct3D to move that cube a bit to the left. Why? Because there is no cube. To Direct3D, there are only numbers that need to be transported to the graphics card. You need to perform all the mathematics on the cube to get it to the right place yourself, and then tell Direct3D to tell the graphics card to draw it. I will of course explain all of this in detail throughout the book.

The advantage to performing all the mathematics and everything else yourself is that you have complete control over your graphical technology and source code. You don't need to find workarounds for some other guy's code that was badly written. Also, because you write everything, you *understand* everything. Always remember the importance of understanding.

And then there is Retained Mode. Oh my. I think in a few years Microsoft may deny Retained Mode (RM) ever existed. People will shout in the media that they had personal experience with RM and will suspiciously go missing the next day, never to be seen again. And RM will be erased from the history books. It is already happening: Look up RM in the DirectX 3.0 documentation. Nice, isn't it? Now look up RM in the DirectX 8.0 documentation. Can't find it? Hmmm…

Retained Mode has a number of advantages, but it also has one big disadvantage: it is pathetic. It wasn't written to make games, even if Microsoft claimed it was. It was written to make budget 3D-modeling programs. That's about all you could do with it, anyway. So what is it? Well, RM is another layer that sits on top of IM. It contains a much easier-to-use interface that has a scene hierarchy, texture-wrapping functions, and many other features. And it *is* easy to use: RM will make a cube and move it around as easily as it will move around a million-polygon jet plane. But it is very, very slow and suffers from Microsoftitis—we all know the symptoms well, the main one being 45,897 million unneeded features. In fact, the only unnecessary thing RM is missing is a happy little paperclip to give you all the answers in the world except the one you're looking for!

Until now there has been very little published information on IM, while there was gallons of it on RM. That's unfortunate, because RM is about as useful as a lead life jacket and IM is brilliant. (I'm not aware of a single commercially released application or game that used RM.) Because of this information void, and because I'm a nice guy, I'm going to give you more information about Immediate Mode than has ever been published before.

Why Bother with 2D?

Ahh, good question, Grasshopper. The answer can be summed up with an ancient Chinese proverb: "Man who build skyscraper must build steel-reinforced foundations first, else get sinking feeling."

It all has to do with layers. The 3D technology in Direct3D is layered on top of the 2D Direct3D, or what used to be known as DirectDraw. So in order to understand 3D, you must know 2D. Have a look at Figure 1.5 to see how DirectDraw and Direct3D stack up. *Layered* means that some of the technology in Direct3D is based on technology used in DirectDraw. In Figure 1.5 you can see that your code uses some of Direct3D's code, which in turn uses DirectDraw's code, which then finally communicates with the hardware. I'll leave the details for later, when you start implementing Direct3D and DirectDraw, but just keep these concepts in mind as you go.

> **NOTE**
>
> By the way, the acronym *HAL* in the figure stands for Hardware Abstraction Layer. You don't need to worry too much about this just yet—I will explain it in detail later on.

Anyway, DirectDraw is a pretty cool tool to use when making 3D games. How many games do you know that don't have some sort of 2D status bars on the screen?

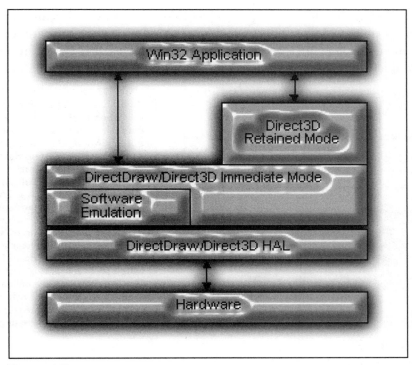

Figure 1.5
Direct3D architecture

COM with Me

OK, here's the deal: you may know—and I do know—that COM is the most boring subject on the planet, but it must be covered peripherally in order for you to use Direct3D efficiently. When I was learning DirectX all those years ago, my eyes used to glaze over at the sight of the word *COM*. But try to stay awake for the next few paragraphs. You will thank yourself later.

First things first. COM stands for *Component Object Model*. The really great thing about DirectX is that although it was written to COM specifications, the COM part is almost transparent to us. If you have any experience programming OLE, then don't worry; it's not even nearly as bad as that. Here is Microsoft's definition of COM: "COM is the foundation of an object-based system that focuses on reuse of interfaces. It is also an interface specification from which any number of interfaces can be built." What?

And now my explanation: COM is an object-based system that is quite similar to the C++ system of objects. In fact, a COM object is binary compatible with a C++ object. What this means is that in C++ you can use COM objects as if they were normal C++ objects. Well almost, but bear with me and you'll see what I'm talking about.

So to put all this nonsense together, let's look at a small example:

Say you have a Direct3D *object*. From this object you can get an `IDirect3D8` *interface*. With this interface you can call the *method* `SetDisplayMode()`. Simple? Simple.

> **NOTE**
>
> The "I" at the beginning of `IDirectDraw7` stands for "interface."

If you have not had experience with C++ then these terms may be confusing, so let's run over them quickly. An *object* is basically a collection of code and data. The code of the object operates on, or uses, the data of the object to perform some task. A *COM object* is like a black box that represents data or hardware. You access whatever it is that the object represents through interfaces. An *interface* is a group of functions called *methods*. The object's code that you can call are called *methods*. You may be familiar with methods under the title *member functions*, but this term is not really used with COM.

The IUnknown Interface

One of the rules for a COM object is that it absolutely must support the `IUnknown` interface. This isn't a big deal because the `IUnknown` interface only has three methods. Have a look at these beauties:

- `AddRef()`
- `QueryInterface()`
- `Release()`

Hmmm. Interesting. The reason that a COM object must support these methods is because a COM object is in control of its own life span. You may think that is just a little too much power to give a computer program, but it turns out that it is a rather useful feature. What it means is that the object must know to destroy itself when it is no longer needed. This is done using what is called a *reference counter*. When the object is created, its reference count is set to 1. Every time another object is created that references the first object, its reference count is incremented. Similarly, when an object no longer needs to reference the first object, its reference count is decremented. When the first object is no longer needed, its reference count will be zero. When the reference count is zero the object is required to deal-locate any resources it has and remove itself from memory. Self-termination. Pretty slick, huh? If Windows can do it, you think they would have put that feature into the T1000, wouldn't you?

Let's look at `AddRef()` and `Release()` first, because they are related. Neither of these functions takes any parameters. They are used to implement the concepts I just discussed. When an object needs to reference another object it calls `AddRef()` to increment the reference count. And `Release()` is used to tell the object that it is no longer being referenced and that it should therefore decrement its reference count.

Here are some steps that you might follow in the code in some hypothetical application.

1. Create a new Direct3D interface.
2. Do some work with the new interface.
3. Create a copy of the interface pointer.
4. Increment the reference count of the Direct3D pointer.
5. Do work with the newly copied pointer.
6. Delete the new pointer.
7. Decrement the reference count of the object.
8. Do some work with the original pointer.
9. Release the original pointer.
10. The reference count is now 0, so the object will remove itself from memory.

Now let's look at an example in pseudocode, because too much theory and not enough practice makes me want to play my Dreamcast. The code below will not compile so don't use it as an example. I am showing you this just to demonstrate interactions with COM.

```
// Pointer to hold address of Interface
LPDIRECT3D8 pD3D = 0;

// Create the new Interface
Direct3D8Create( &pD3D );

// Do some work with the pointer
```

```
// Pointer to hold a copy of the other Interface pointer
LPDIRECT3D8 pCopyOfPointer = 0;

// Copy the pointer
pCopyOfPointer = pD3D;

//Increment the reference count
pCopyOfPointer->AddRef();

// Do some work with the new pointer

// Finished with original pointer decrement the ref count and then reset It
pCopyOfPointer->Release()1
pCopyOfPointer = 0;

// Do more work with the original pointer

// Done with the original pointer to decrement the reference count and reset It
// The ref count Is now 0 so the object will self destruct
pD3D->Release();
pD3D = 0;
```

That's pretty easy, isn't it? When the object is created its reference count will be 1. If you create new references, then you should tell the object about them so that it knows when to kill itself. And when you no longer need the references you should tell the object also. After you call Release() on a pointer, you should treat that pointer as if it is invalid and reset it to NULL.

You don't actually *have* to tell the object when you have more than one pointer looking after it, but you should. Imagine if you didn't: say you have one pointer and you copy it but don't tell the object. Then you release the first pointer, but the second copy is still stored away somewhere. If you then go to use the copy, it will point to a random memory location and your program will most likely be killed until it dies. Not a pretty sight, trust me.

TIP

Use AddRef() and Release() whenever you are messing with pointers for COM objects.

`QueryInterface()` requires a little bit more discussion. Another requirement of COM is that once an interface is defined it *cannot* be changed. For example, you'll soon find that you'll be using interfaces with names like `IDirect3D8` and `IDirectInput8`. That "8" at the end does not necessarily mean it is part of DirectX 8.0. It actually means that it is the eighth revision of the interface for that object. That is, back in the mid-1990s when `IDirect3D` was around, Microsoft was not allowed to change that interface. Instead, when it wanted to add new features, it had to create an entirely new interface and call it `IDirect3D2` .

You may think this unnecessary, but actually it is incredibly good programming practice. In effect, what this means is that if someone tries to run your game in 85 years on Windows 2086 when the latest interface is `IDirect3D163`, your code will still run as well as it did the day you wrote it. Right, so how does `QueryInterface()` fit into the COM picture?

Well, suppose your code is designed so that it will run with the interface `IDirect3D8`, but it can fall back to `IDirect3D2` with more limited features if revision 8 is not available. How do you check what interfaces are obtainable? That, ladies and gentlemen, is where `QueryInterface()` comes into its own. All you have to do is call the `QueryInterface()` method of the object to see what functionality it supports. You just have to say, "Excuse me, Mr. Direct3D object, I have a query for you. Do you support the `IDirect3D8` interface, and if so can you provide me with a pointer to that interface? Thank you." And that's it. You will then be given a pointer to the interface you requested if it is supported. Let's see this puppy in action with some pseudocode:

```
// Create a pointer to hold the interface pointers
LPDIRECT3D pD3D = 0;           // Pointer for revision 1
LPDIRECT3D6 pD3D6 = 0; // Pointer for revision 6

// Get a pointer for revision 1
pD3D = CreateD3DObject();

// Check if revision 6 of the interface is supported
pD3D->QueryInterface( IID_IDirect3D6, (void**)&pD3D6 );

if( pD3D6 != NULL )
        // SUCCESS!
else
        // Revision 6 is not supported
```

If you're a little confused, don't worry. I know it's kind of abstract and all over the place right now, but you'll nail it down when you look at code throughout the book.

COM in Action

Now for a little discussion about the intricacies of using COM in practice. The thing about COM is that with all this talking about "objects," you might think that you actually get a tangible object that you can shoot around memory or down a network pipe or something. Nope. All your interactions with COM objects take place through pointers. There are three steps that you must perform before you can use any of the methods belonging to an object, and they go a little like those below. Don't worry about the specifics of the code—it's just there to help you visualize what is going on. I will cover the creation of Direct3D objects in detail in later chapters.

1. Create a variable to hold a pointer to the object, and initialize it to NULL like this:

   ```
   LPDIRECT3D8 pDirect3D = 0;
   ```

2. Create the object that you want to use. You don't do this directly; instead, you call a function to do it for you. When you create the object, you pass the address of the variable created in step 1, which will subsequently be filled with the address of the object if the call was successful. On the other hand, if the call fails, the variable will be set to NULL.

   ```
   pDirect3D = Direct3DCreate8( D3D_SDK_VERSION );
   ```

3. You can now use the pointer any way you want. You call your methods through the pointer that you received just as if you had a pointer to a normal C++ object like this:

   ```
   pDirect3D->GetDeviceCaps( 0, D3DEVTYPE_HAL, &Caps )
   ```

That's how COM works. Before moving on, I want to show you some of the differences between C and C++ when you are using COM.

Accessing COM with C

Although I will be using the C++ syntax in this book when dealing with DirectX, it is always useful to see how you would do it with C. Remember, total understanding is the goal here. Let's look at the C++ way first because it is the easiest:

```
pDirect3D->GetDeviceCaps( 0, D3DEVTYPE_HAL, &Caps )
```

Here `pDirectDraw` is a pointer to a DirectDraw object, and the method being called is `SetDisplayMode()`. That's pretty easy, isn't it? It's just like calling a normal C++ member function. The C way is different because obviously it has no support for objects. I'll show you the code and then explain it:

```
pDirect3D->lpVtbl->GetDeviceCaps( pDirect3D, 0, D3DEVTYPE_HAL, &Caps )
```

If you are using C notation, all you do is stick in an extra pointer named `lpVtbl` between the object pointer and the method name. Then you set the first function parameter to the name of the pointer to the interface that contains the method. In other words, stick in the pointer variable at the start of the line as the first parameter. This variable has the same effect as the `this` pointer in C++. Use this technique for every single COM method call that you make and you won't go wrong.

Since this book uses C++, this calling convention is inconsequential. But if you ever work on a project using straight C, you will know what to do.

Conclusion

This is great—you've covered the foundations for all the ideas that your brain will be filled with. You also saw all the components that make up DirectX and what they do, as well as a more detailed insight into Direct3D, our friend for the next several hundred pages. And then you saw—I can hardly bring myself to say it—COM! So now that you have the groundwork covered, I can move on and discuss the tools that you'll be using to fully grasp the power of Direct3D and DirectDraw.

CHAPTER 2

90 Percent Preparation, 10 Percent Initialization

To learn DirectX well, you need to take it one step at a time. Now I will donate an entire chapter, albeit a short one, to the subject of preparation, in order to avoid something that I have been warned about 10 million times. André LaMothe, author of I-don't-know-how-many best-selling game development books, and also the series editor for this book, told me that he receives about 50 e-mails a day because some of his readers can't get his programs to compile. So here, with screen shots and diagrams, are the steps to set up your development environment to use DirectX.

This chapter will cover

- installing the DirectX SDK.
- setting up Visual Studio to use DirectX.
- setting up your project to use DirectX.
- some tips and tricks that you can use when you are developing for DirectX.

For all of the code in this book I'm going to be using Visual C++ 6.0. I will be doing so for a number of reasons, including the fact that almost everybody has it already. If you don't have a copy, then you can pick it up for next to nothing, especially if you are a high school or university student. Visual C++ is very intuitive and easy to learn, so you shouldn't have any problems mastering it. Anyway, Microsoft pretty much rules the world, proven by the fact that you are learning to develop games using Microsoft DirectX to run on Microsoft Windows. So why break with tradition and go with another company's products? It would only introduce "issues." And I hate "issues."

If that last paragraph wasn't enough justification for the Borland diehards, then I guess I'm just going to have to say, "Resistance is futile!"

Installing the DirectX SDK

The DirectX Software Development Kit (SDK) is located in the \DirectX SDK directory on the CD-ROM that accompanies this book. The installation is pretty simple—just click the setup icon—but there are a few things to look out for during the installation.

When the dialog box comes up asking you whether you want the Debug or Retail version of DirectX, choose the Debug version. The Debug version is slightly slower, but this disadvantage is easily outweighed by the advantages. A big plus is that it can output detailed debug messages during debugging. For instance, instead of just getting an error return value like `D3DERR_UNSUPPORTED` you could get a message like "Direct3D does not support bump mapping in software."

You can change the amount of information that you want DirectX to output by changing the DirectX settings in Control Panel. You should see a new DirectX icon appear in Control Panel after you install the SDK.

You will find all sorts of interesting stuff in the SDK directory. I won't give paths because they seem to change with every release, and I want this book to be applicable to future releases. There are hundreds of demo applications that demonstrate a lot of DirectX features. There are also the SDK Help files, which are extremely helpful, as well as some sample materials like 3D models, textures, sound effects, music, and so on. Look through the SDK directory and get familiar with its layout, because you will be using it a lot.

> **CAUTION**
>
> Although they demonstrate a wide variety of skills, a lot of sample applications are written pretty poorly. Their standard is improving with each release, and almost all of them are good quality now, but many people have serious issues trying to get them to compile. If you can't get them to compile, don't fret. Just look at the code and learn from it. The code that demonstrates the skill works—it's just the application's base that makes all sorts of links to scattered files.

Setting Up Visual Studio to Use DirectX

If you haven't used Visual C++ before, then it would be a pretty good idea for you to pull the—gulp—manuals out and have a glance through them. Even though I'm going to show you a number of steps that you can use to get going with Visual C++, you can increase your efficiency by reading about the keyboard shortcuts and stuff like that. Or you can do what I do and never read the manuals and figure things out by trial, error, and pounding your fists against the table!

Even if you have used Visual C++ before, you should still have a look through the next few pages because they discuss how to get Visual C++ to work with DirectX. If I receive one e-mail asking me about this material from someone who skipped this section, it's going be time to open up a can of whoopass! Follow these steps and they *will* compile; please, please, for the love of money, trust me.

Okay, let's get on to what there is to learn. Figure 2.1 shows Visual C++ in action without any open projects. Visual C++ actually ships with DirectX, but it is usually an older version, so what you want to do is to tell it that you have installed a newer version of the DirectX SDK and that it should use the newer files instead.

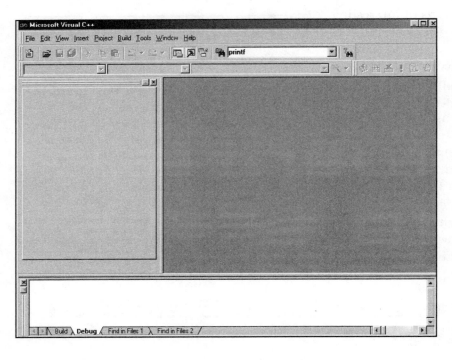

Figure 2.1

Visual C++ with no open projects

The first thing you want to do is let Visual C++ know where in the DirectX SDK you installed the files that it needs. Go to the Tools menu and select Options. Figure 2.2 shows this menu.

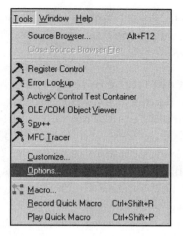

Figure 2.2

Setting the options

The Options dialog box, with the Directories tab activated (shown in Figure 2.3) will appear.

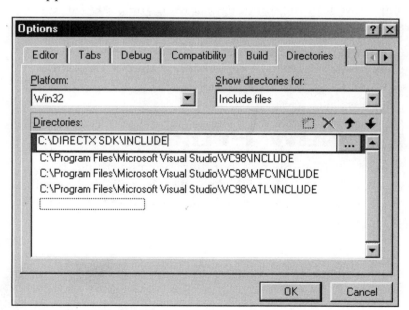

Figure 2.3

The Options dialog box

Select the Directories tab. Select Include files from the right drop-down combo box. The Options dialog box should now resemble that shown in Figure 2.3. Click in the empty area beneath the current directories and enter the directory name where the new DirectX include files are located. This is usually \SDK Install Path\include. Now use the arrow icons to move your new directory entry to the very top of the list, as shown in the screen shot. The reason for doing so is because that list is the search order for include files. When you type something like

```
#include <d3d8.h>
```

Visual C++ searches directories on your hard disk in the order they are listed in the dialog box. So if you forget to enter the include directory, or if you leave it at the bottom of the list, Visual C++ either will be unable to find the correct file or will include the wrong file. It will probably be the latter case with DirectX, because Visual C++ ships with the include files for previous versions of DirectX. This leads to all kinds of annoying errors that are very hard to track down. So if you get link errors like "LNK2001: Unresolved External. . . blah blah," check to see whether you have your paths set up properly.

Next, enter the paths for the library files. This is almost exactly the same process as for the include files. The only difference is to select Library files from the right drop-down combo box. Then enter the path for the library files. This is usually \SDK Install Path\lib. Again move it to the top of the list using the arrow buttons. Click on OK and you're done.

And that's all there is to setting up Visual Studio to use DirectX. You will never have to do this again unless you (a) install a newer version of the SDK in a different directory or (b) reinstall Visual C++. Simple? Of course it is!

Creating a New Project

Creating a new project is a relatively simple task, but there are a few things to note as you go through the process. To start, select File, New. The New dialog box will appear, as shown in Figure 2.4. If it is not already selected, select the Projects tab at the top of the dialog box.

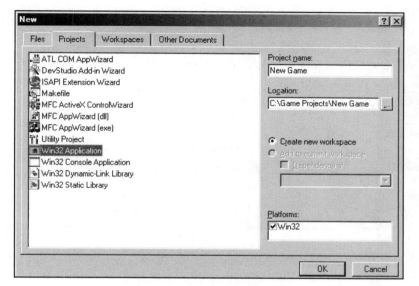

Figure 2.4

The New project dialog box

In the list box, select Win32 Application. Type a name for your project into the Project name text box. If you don't like the default location for your project, change it by typing a new path into the Location text box.

Now click on the OK button, and yet another dialog box will appear, as shown in Figure 2.5. Make sure that an empty project is selected, and then click on OK.

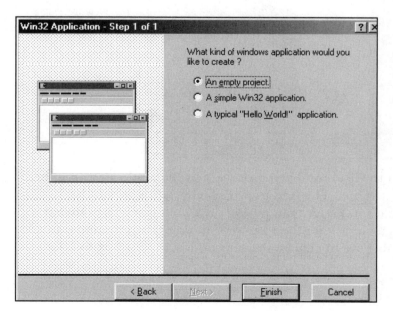

Figure 2.5

The New Win32 project dialog box

Adding a File to Your Project

Of course now that you have your project created, you would probably like somewhere to enter your code, so let's figure out how to do that. Follow these steps whenever you want to add a new source file (.cpp) or header file (.h). First, select Project, Add To Project, New, as shown in Figure 2.6.

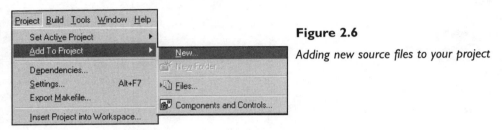

Figure 2.6

Adding new source files to your project

This will bring up the New file dialog box, as shown in Figure 2.7. You may recognize this dialog box. It is very similar to the New project dialog box. In fact, if you press the Projects tab, you will see that it is the very same dialog box.

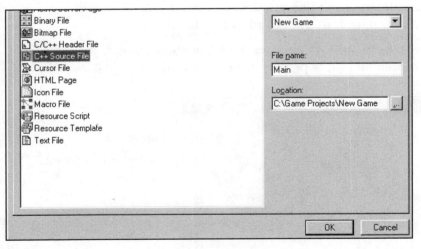

Figure 2.7

The New file dialog box

Select C++ Source Files in the list box. Then give the new file a title by typing the name into the File name text box. The Add to project check box should be checked. Click OK and that's it. Easier than paying off a politician? Of course it is. You follow the same steps to add other file types. For instance, if you wanted to add a header file, then you only have to change the selection in the list box to C\C++ Header File.

Setting Up Your Project to Use DirectX

If you're about to flip back a few pages because you think I already explained this, look closely at the heading above. Before, I was showing you how to set up Visual Studio to use DirectX. You only had to follow those steps once. This time I'm explaining how to let your project know that you will be using DirectX. You'll have to repeat the following procedures every time you create a new DirectX project, so keep those ears perked!

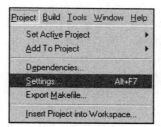

Figure 2.8

Setting up your project for DirectX

First select Project, Settings, as shown in Figure 2.8. This will bring up—you guessed it—the Project Settings dialog box, with the Link tab showing (see Figure 2.9). If the Link tab is not showing, select it, and the dialog box will magically transform into what you see in Figure 2.9.

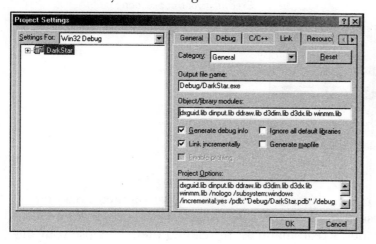

Figure 2.9

The Project Settings dialog box

See where the Object/library modules text box is? In that box, type the following before any other link files that may be there:

```
dxguid.lib d3d8.lib d3dx8.lib winmm.lib
```

These files are the *library files*. Without them, your DirectX applications will not be able to compile or run properly, so if you get unresolved external link errors, this could be another source of the problem.

Compiling and Executing

It's very simple to execute your application in Visual C++. Just select Build, Execute, as shown in Figure 2.10 (the shortcut for this procedure is Ctrl+F5). This will compile, then link, and finally execute your program. Any errors will be displayed in the output bar along the bottom of the screen. Alternatively, if you just want to build (compile and link without executing) your program, just select Build from the menu or press F7. You can double-click on the errors and you will be taken to the line of code in which the error occurred. If you want to debug-execute your application, then select Build, Start Debug, Go, or press F5. Of course you don't have any code to compile yet, but that will be remedied very soon!

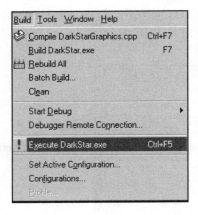

Figure 2.10

Executing your application

That's about all you need to get going with Visual Studio. I recommend reading through the manuals for Visual Studio if you have not used it before. If you're anything like me, you probably never read manuals. In reading them you lose your dignity, right? So go sneak off to a fast-food restaurant and sit in the corner where no one will see you and spend 20 minutes reading those Visual Studio manuals. If one of your friends shows up, you can hide them in magazines with pictures of big stereos or something and save face. Watch out for the security cameras, though!

Some Rules to Live By

Before moving on, I'd like to cover a few rules that you should strive to follow while using DirectX. DirectX applications and games, even if they are just demos, become very large very quickly, so you'll save yourself endless headaches by taking these guidelines to heart.

Adding a Little Structure to Your Life

The first thing you should do before rushing into any programming project, not just DirectX-related ones, is to create a good directory structure on your hard disk to hold your project. I usually create a root directory, say for instance called "Zen Game." Then inside the root directory, I create directories like "Graphics" for graphics, "SoundFX" for sound effects and music, and so on. The only files in the root directory are text files such as a rolling list of features and a to-do list.

You should create a directory structure even if you are just testing out a new idea. You'll no doubt have times when you'll suddenly discover something new and then think, "Holy digits, Batman, what would happen if I added this? Oh, that kicks grass. Let's add this. That's cool as muck. Oh, look at this. . . . " and so on. Before you know it, you've got a whole new project on your hands, one that ends up an unfathomable mess because there is no structure.

The next thing to remember is to—please, for the love of money—use good file-naming conventions. Do not call the sound file on level 8 for the green lizard dying grlizl8d.wav. Instead, use the power of post-1995 technology and call it Green Lizard—Level 8—Dying.wav. The same goes for all the other files types that you accumulate.

Remember federal government health warnings: Every time you use the following tip, you add another five minutes to your life.

> **TIP**
>
> **Create good directory structures for your projects, and use proper naming conventions.**

Did You Back Up?

I have a cartoon taped to the wall behind my desk. The first panel shows a disgruntled employee screaming down a phone line at an IT person, "My computer doesn't work! The hard drive crashed!! What do I do?!" The IT person coolly responds, "Did you back up?" The next frame shows the employee flattening himself against the wall, quivering in fear, as far from the computer as he can get. He responds, "WHY? Is it gonna blow?!"

If only I had taken that cartoon to heart. A few months before I started writing this book, I had a directory on my hard disk labeled "Game Programming Stuff." Inside this one directory was every article I had ever written, every bit of code I had ever done having to do with games, every project—in fact everything to do with anything even remotely related to games. You can probably predict where this story is going. I meant to copy the directory to my desktop but wasn't paying attention. I depressed over the Recycle Bin. And as I was smart enough to turn off confirmations in Windows, all I saw was an animated file moving as I left to get some junk food. When I came back I assumed the directory was somewhere on my cluttered desktop and quickly went, "Hmmm, what the heck is in my Recycle Bin? Think I'll free up some space and empty that puppy." Windows went to work. You'd be amazed how fast a 40, gig, Ultra DMA 66, 7200 RPM hard disk with 2 megabytes of cache can wipe away your life's work. I know I was amazed because you can still see the hole in my desk where my jaw dropped.

But I had been preaching to people for years about the importance of backing up. So I had a backup, didn't I? Of course I did. It just so happens that I had made one the week before onto a bunch of CD-ROMs. But by some curious twist of fate I managed to leave them in a clear jewel case, upside down, on the windowsill, in the summer. You'd also be amazed what the sun can do to the data on a CD-ROM. My CD-ROM drive is still in therapy!

Luckily, I had a backup from two weeks before that, so I managed to save almost everything—but I did lose those two weeks worth of stuff.

TIP

Back up regularly, and don't be a complete idiot like me.

Care to Comment?

Commenting code is so important in game programming. Much more so than in other forms of software engineering. This is because games cross over so many disciplines and schools of thought that you will *not* remember how everything works, even a few weeks down the line, especially if you are working in a team moving at a fast pace.

It is a fact that game programmers have a reputation among standard programmers for sloppy code and improper commenting. I don't agree with the sloppy bit—I think that just comes from the fact that game programmers' code is so cutting edge and incredibly advanced that it is just naturally harder to follow. But this just underlines the necessity for proper commenting.

Games are becoming so big—with budgets soon to be approaching Hollywood standards—that it has become virtually impossible for someone to create a complete game on their own. Thus, making a serious game means working in a team. Teams must be able to communicate, and that means being able to follow one another's progress. Commenting only takes a few seconds, and doing so makes it easier for others to follow your code. Other people will respect and look up to you if they can see that your code is well presented and easy to follow. It is good to have people associate you with an air of professionalism. So, do like Jackie Chan and make the double slash your best friend.

By the way if you're a little rusty on your code commenting techniques, have a look in the programming section of http://www.gamedev.net and search for the article on code documentation.

TIP

Always comment your code clearly.

Conclusion

You now know how to install the SDK, how to set up Visual Studio to use DirectX, and also how to incorporate DirectX into your individual projects. You also learned some useful tips that I think will really help you to get the most out of DirectX.

CHAPTER 3

The Structure of a Direct3D Application

Several years ago there was an archaeologist digging in the fridgit heights of Tibet, searching for some scriptures written by a man named Yang in times of yore. This archaeologist found a smallm tattered piece, of paper with some barely legible handwritten text in a language long lost to the ravages of time. The archaeologist spent four years studying and deciphering the text. I can now bring you what he found. The scripture revealed the following: "Learn the structure of the game loop, learn it well, and thou shall live in eternal riches." By the way, the archaeologist's name was Bob, and I modified the translation slightly. Bob thought it had something to do with a potent rice-wine recipe. Why would anybody write about that?

In this chapter you're going to learn about a whole bunch of stuff, including

- the game loop and why it is important.
- the structure of a DirectX application.
- some current and older titles on the market.

The Game Loop

I want to move on now to show you how a real-life game looks under the hood. When you have a good idea about the overall structure of a game, then it is easier to focus in on the details of each area.

I've used the term *game loop* a few times now, but I haven't really given its definition yet. If you've programmed simple DOS applications you know that they execute in a sequence. This type of application has the technical term *sequential logic* applied to it. As you can probably guess, these are very basic and generally only print things like "Hi Mom," or the dreaded "Hello World" to the screen. The next type of programming is a step up from a sequential logic program and is called an *extended logic* application. It starts execution and then goes off into procedures and loops and so on. You may also be aware of another type of programming that is called *event-driven* programming. Event-driven programs execute according to the actions of the user and the operating system, not in any identifiable or predictable way (fitting to Windows, huh?). Later chapters dealing with programming Windows will cover this style in detail.

When writing games, you will use a combination of all the programming styles above, but they will also all be encapsulated by, or work in conjunction with, a massive loop that continuously executes from the start of the game to the end. This loop is called the *game loop,* and it controls every detail of the execution of the game. In fact, this loop *is* the game. The speed of execution for this loop ultimately determines the speed at which the game can execute. In other words, if the loop is being processed 85 times a second, then the frame rate will also be 85 frames per second. Conceptually the game loop operates in a cyclical manner but it does have tangents that it can go off into.

Let's examine a typical, albeit simplified, game loop and the tasks that it looks after. Have a look at Figure 3.1. Here you can see graphically the game loop under discussion.

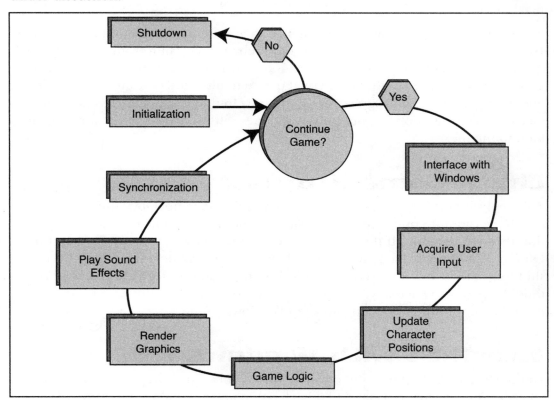

Figure 3.1

The game loop

Initialization

Initialization occurs as soon as you start the game. This is the point at which all resources that the game will need to run properly are acquired. For example, memory will be allocated to hold textures and sound files, and the graphics adapter will be initialized and the display mode set. Any other hardware, such as the sound card or input devices, may also be initialized at this point.

The longest stage in this process is loading all the game data off the storage device—such as the hard disk or CD-ROM—into main memory. Generally, game data is stored in compressed form on the disk so that space requirements can be kept to a minimum. It is best to decompress the data once during initialization, rather than during the actual playing of the game, in order to keep performance maximized.

While all this is happening it is a good idea to give the user something to look at (such as a storyboard or company logo), thereby keeping him from getting bored. Also, if any stage of the initialization takes longer than about three seconds, it is a good idea to provide some sort of visual queue to illustrate how much time is left. Something akin to the progress bars commonly found in the Windows user interface is perfectly acceptable, but polished games will probably have a more artistic look to them.

Check Game Status

The next step is to check if the user wants to quit the game. Obviously, the user will hardly ever want to quit directly after starting, but this must be checked every iteration through the loop. If the user indicates that he does want to quit by selecting Quit or something from a menu somewhere, then the game initially goes into a shutdown mode and then returns control of the computer to Windows. Most of the time the player will actually be playing and not exiting, so in this case it's time to move forward to the next step and keep Windows happy.

Interface with Windows

To interface with Windows, put on some thick rubber gloves, spray some antibacterial agent into the air, and stand well back—Windows is a moody beast! Interfacing is necessary to keep Windows from kicking your game to death or kicking itself to death. If you're running Windows 2000 or one of its successors, it is your game that will be kicked to death. On the other hand, if you're running Windows 98 or Me, or one of its successors, then Windows will be quite happy to kick itself to death!

Windows is a shared environment, which means that it, and not your game, is in control. (Well, Windows *tries* to be in control, but I won't say anything if you don't.) Windows may be juggling the resources of hundreds of other applications at the same time as yours, so when Windows tells you to do something, you do it, otherwise the whole house of cards comes falling down. Or, on the Windows 2000 front, your program will be beat out of memory for being such an arrogant little son-of-a-gun. Such tasks include handling exit messages, repainting the application's window, dealing with display mode changes, and so on. I'll cover this stuff in so much detail it will make you sick in the next few chapters.

Acquire User Input

Your game may not be the most exciting interactive entertainment experience in the galaxy if your players have no control over it. So this is the stage at which you figure out what the player is trying to get your game to do. You do so by polling the joystick, receiving keyboard input, reading what the mouse is doing, and examining the VR bodysuit. Then you combine all these contributions into a single combined input. You can then do what you want with it—usually you'll move the player, modify the target, scroll through the menu, or change whatever zillion other things that a game can do.

Update Character Positions

This stage is a direct result of the previous stage. Using the input gathered, you update the positions of all the objects in the game affected by the input. Aside from the things I already mentioned, this also includes setting flags for further processing in later stages. For instance, if the character just walked over a position that is supposed to cause his life to increase, then his life had better increase or your game will be likened to something very smelly.

Game Logic

This is an extremely important part of any game. It is at this stage that the artificial intelligence (AI), physics modeling, and all other updates are completed. It is also a very complex stage, and you have to have your Zen wits about you to do it properly.

The artificial intelligence moves all the characters around and lets them play out their roles in killing you, beating you in a race, or bouncing a ball back to you with a beeping paddle. It is the physics modeling that allows them to act out this behavior in a way that is realistic and believable to us humans.

Render Graphics

Rasterization is undoubtedly the most complex stage of the entire process. If you don't believe me, pick up the book you are now reading. Heavy, isn't it? All that for this one stage in the process. The first thing that happens is all the mathematical calculations are performed on the 3D objects so that they are moved into position and can then be drawn easily. This part is called the *transformation pipeline*. After that, the scene background, 3D models, and foreground bitmaps are rendered, in that order. However, they are not rendered directly to the screen. First they are drawn into off-screen memory on the graphics card or in main memory. When the rendering is complete, the entire rendered picture is blasted at the speed of light into the graphics card's visual memory, and only then are the results updated onto the screen.

Although I mentioned that this is a very time-consuming stage in the process, it may not stay that way forever. For instance, in a computer with an AGP 4X bus and a very fast 3D accelerator with transform and lighting support, most of the graphics work is done in parallel with the CPU by dedicated processors. This leaves more CPU time to work on things like advanced artificial intelligence, physics modeling, realistic sound, and all the other bits and pieces that fell by the wayside in the past.

Playing Sound FX

This section is sort of self-explanatory, but let's look at a few technical things that go on behind the scenes. Until recently, sound processing was very processor-intensive. This was because the sound card had a limited number of output audio channels that it could play simultaneously. If a game wanted to play more sounds than there were spare channels— which was almost always—then a monstrously complex queuing and mixing system had to be put in place. The problems arose when the game had background music playing, and then a higher priority sound like an explosion, came along, and interrupted the music until it was finished, and then the music would start jiggin' again. This led to popping and clicking and a loss of the immersion that the game was trying to provide. But these days, with DirectSound, such problems don't exist. DirectSound does the entire complex mixing process, using hardware acceleration if it is available. You know, Microsoft doesn't deserve half the criticism it gets—it should be redirected at nonupgradable computers with transparent, colored cases.

Synchronization

I used to have an old game; I think it was called *Stunt Driver* or *Stunt Racer*. I've spent hours looking for the thing. I'm sure it'll turn up the night I'm having the party to celebrate this book being published. It was made back in the late '80s or early '90s, and it was one of the first 3D racing games. You even got to design your tracks with roller-coaster-loop-style roads. It was great. But last year when I loaded that puppy up on my Pentium II 400MHz, I realized that if you so much as sent a hint of an electron down the keyboard cable, the car would shoot to the far side of Tokyo (if you're in Tokyo, then Dublin) faster than you can say *sushi* (or Guinness). It was pretty funny until I realized I couldn't fix it. I took the case off and remembered that they don't connect the Turbo button to anything these days. Oh well.

The problem was that the game was not programmed with proper synchronization. It must have been made for an old IBM XT or AT machine without much foresight into the future processing power of PCs.

> **NOTE**
>
> *Synchronization* allows your game to progress at a constant playable rate across computers with differing speeds.

Most books don't spend much time on synchronization, and only show you how to lock your frame rate to 30 frames per second. This has all sorts of disadvantages, like if the computer is too slow to run at 30 fps, then all the timing will be screwed up. And if the computer is faster, you're just wasting the available power. I'm going to explain a great way to let your frame rate fluctuate to take advantage of the host computer, while keeping the volatile objects in the game moving at a stable rate. That's the way the professionals do it, so why shouldn't you do it too?

Shutdown

This stage is the exact opposite of the initialization stage. You'll probably want to start by checking to see if the player wants to save his game progress. Then simply save any settings such as the current screen resolution and stuff like that. Finally, reset any hardware you changed, release *all* memory allocated, and finally pull out the Colt .44 and end the game's misery. Control is then returned to Windows (gulp), and your player is free to do what he wishes. Your job is done, and you can go munch on junk food. Mmmm.

Remember, except for the initialization and shutdown steps, these steps happen tens, if not hundreds of times per second. I am going to cover each of the steps in the game loop in an awful lot of detail, with a few exceptions. I'm not going to cover any sound programming because it is also a big subject, and I would prefer if my book did not break the shelves that will support it. Also, I'm not going to cover too much AI or physics modeling mainly because there are people out there who have already written great books on the subject. Have a look at *Tricks of the Windows Game Programming Gurus* by André LaMothe. That book makes an excellent companion to this one and covers all the topics that I just mentioned.

Real-Life Games

Now that you have seen what the game loop looks like, you will be able to turn a more educated eye on actual games on the market. Let's check out some real games and see how the game loop relates to them. Have a look at Figures 3.2 through 3.7 and see how many things you can spot that are happening.

In Figure 3.2 and 3.3, you can see shots of the first level of *Alien vs. Predator*. Although it may be hard to tell from these static pictures, the player is in fact walking forward. So what exactly is the game doing? Well, roughly 65 times a second, on my PC, the computer is performing a million different calculations to move the 3D view into place and render it realistically. While all that is happening, the AI is scanning your position and updating the location of your enemy aliens. The physics modeling is making sure you don't fall through the floor and that the camera sways slightly as you walk. And of course the background ambient music is playing along with the foreground sound effects. You might have thought previously that all of these steps happened at the same time, although now you know that they are performed serially. That is, one step is worked on, then the next, and so on. When everything is done, the game moves on and repeats these steps all over again.

Figure 3.2

Alien vs. Predator

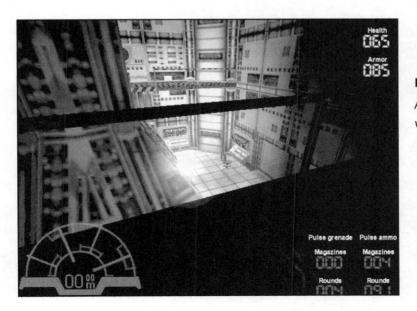

Figure 3.3

Another one from Alien vs. Predator.

Figures 3.4 through 3.6 show scenes from *Incoming*. Take a moment to look at each of them and think about all of the processes that are going on. It will help you to gain a better understanding of both the scale and the structure of the task that you are about to begin. Think about all the items that you can spot on the screen. For example, study the 3D rendering, physics modeling, sound effects (imagine them), user interface, and ambience that the game tries to convey.

Figure 3.4

Incoming

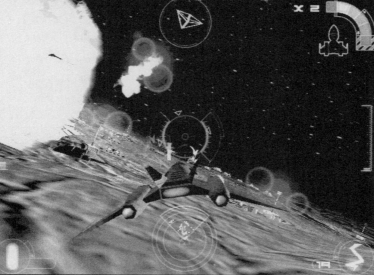

Figure 3.5

Another scene from Incoming

Figure 3.6

Yet another scene from Incoming

Conclusion

This is not just the end of the third chapter, but also Part I of the book. It's also the time to write your will, double-check your parachute, and make sure the pilot isn't taking any psychotropic substances (I'm not), because things are going to get really creepy. You are about to enter (this is classified) the world of Windows game programming. If you are not really ready to test your wits and try to make it to the next stage of Zen, then turn back now while you still have a chance. The natives will guide you no further; they are too fearful. But you can make it, if you stick with me. Let's move out...

Part Two

Windows Programming

CHAPTER 4

1 Did Not Have a Relationship with MS Windows

When I was learning to program Windows a long time ago, I taught myself from a book, just like you are doing now. The problem was that the book I was learning from was lousy, and I became lost and confused and just got prejudiced against Windows programming in general. So I put it off for a long time and continued with DOS game programming. While the world was moving on, I was stuck with DOS and probably missed some of the opportunities that Windows would have afforded me. So if you have had an experience like mine learning Windows, this chapter should be a pleasant surprise. As I taught myself Windows programming, I know what it is like to learn this way. So this section of the book should be a refreshing look at Windows for you. I am going to take everything at a nice pace, explaining everything along the way.

Alternatively, if you are straight from the DOS world, or these days the "Windows console programming world," then I hope this chapter will be the best possible introduction to Windows programming that you can find. Obviously, I'm not going to teach you everything about Windows; that would take an entire book. However, I will show you a plethora of Windows programming techniques that are useful for game development. If this whole Windows programming world makes a few synapses fire and you would like to extend your knowledge and become a complete Windows guru, then have a look at *Programming Windows* by Charles Petzold. That book is the definitive guide to Windows programming, which, I believe, is now on its fifth edition. I will be teaching you everything you need to know to program games.

This chapter will cover

- the architecture of Windows, including the sharing model and an overview of the multitasking kernel with which you will interact when programming for the Windows platform.
- Microsoft programming guidelines.
- messages and the event-driven model of programming.

I think the problem most people have with Windows is that it's not what they expect it to be when they look under the hood. On the outside, Windows looks like it was designed by the Apple marketing department. In fact, it seems almost intuitive. But when you see how it works underneath, you may become slightly nauseous. I think that's the reason the so-called DOS diehards dismissed Windows as a joke and could not in their wildest dreams imagine Windows would become a suitable target platform for game development. My, oh my, were they wrong or what! But if you have any experience programming advanced DOS, then you know that calling a function named 0x13h to set the display mode falls just slightly short of intuitive.

If you know anything about Windows programming, then erase that sector of your memory and rewrite it with the information that I am going to give you in this section of the book. You will thank yourself later. On the other hand, if you happen to think that this section of the book is awful and has done you irreparable damage, then you have my permission to send me sickening amounts of hate mail. My address is ceo@apple.com.

The Importance of Windows

So why exactly is Windows important? Why did history dictate that Windows would take over the world and that every developer worth two grains of salt would move to Microsoft products, and why is the sky blue? Well, the answers are complicated, but I think they lie somewhere in the word "competition." If a good product comes out and it does not have any proper competition, then it will obviously succeed. Don't get me wrong; I know that Apple computers have been around for a long time, but when a company adopts the attitude "If we build it, they will buy it," what kind of respect is that giving to the consumer? None. So when Microsoft spends billions on market research and user interface research, then you can see that the company at least has an interest in keeping its consumers happy. I don't want you to think that I'm a Microsoft missionary or anything; I'm just pointing out a few of my extremely subjective, probably misguided, views. (Bill, just put the money in my Swiss sub-account #88888).

Despite its shortcomings, Windows is now *the* king, so if you want to get stinking rich you had better lose any anti-Windows feelings that you have and just accept that this is the way of the world. If you are developing a game, then you may as well look at the market like this: 100 percent of PC-based game players are running Microsoft products on their PCs (it's not really 100 percent, but the rest don't really count). And that is why Windows is important; it is the *status quo*.

Now normally this is the section where most authors would put in a history of Windows. But that's not going to help you write great games is it? So instead, I'll give you a short summary. Windows 1.0: stunk. Windows 2.0: stunk. Windows 3.0: buggy as a flea circus. Windows 3.1: not bad. Windows 3.11: better. Windows 95:

I think I may like this Windows stuff. Windows 98: now we're getting somewhere. Windows Me: it's just 98, nothing is going to change that. Windows 2000: we are starting to kick some serious grass. So, to summarize the summary: Windows 98, Me, and 2000 are great products to develop games for. They have an extremely high market penetration, they are stable (just smile and nod), and most of all, they are user-friendly.

With that extremely mental look at why Windows succeeded on the end-user front out of the way, let's now have a look at what advantages Windows has over DOS in a programming view. I think you'll probably agree that aside from the UI (user interface) stuff, the most important development that Windows has over DOS is the ability to run more than one program at the same time. For instance, you could be writing a book in Microsoft Word while having Creative Labs PlayCenter play Britney Spears's "Baby One More Time" (how the heck did that get in there? Damn MP3s!) and have *Quake III Arena* minimized and ready to play at the click of a mouse. And if I want to include a screen shot of *Quake III* in the book, as in the last chapter, all I have to do is hop over to *Quake III* and press the Print Screen button, then come back to Word and press Paste. How cool *is* that? I mean can you imagine that kind of interfunctionality between programs even six years ago? Not even nearly.

Nice Programs Share Their Toys

This extra functionality is not down to the individual programs. It is down to the man in charge: Windows. How does Windows manage this feat of pure brilliance? After all, there is only one processor, one chunk of memory, one video card, and so on. How do the applications share all this stuff between them? They can't talk to each other because there is no real standard language to allow this to happen.

Well, it's down to what is called the *sharing model* of programming. Windows allows each program to run as if it is the only program running on the PC at that time. Each application doesn't have to even put two bytes worth of a thought into whether or not there are other applications running at the same time.

> You may be wondering what a *kernel* is. Well I'll tell you. A kernel is the very low-level core part of the operating system that is used to manage the basic operations of the operating system, such as program management, disk i/o, memory access, and other assorted mundane tasks. The kernel is where all the multitasking technology that I talk about in this section is located within Windows.

Windows handles the hard part of pushing the processor and other hardware around between different applications. This is the so-called multitasking word that we heard so much about from the Microsoft marketing people during the run-up to the release of Windows 95.

NOTE

By the way, in case you hadn't noticed, I'm assuming for this discussion that you are using a post-Windows 3.11 operating system.

So what exactly is *multitasking*? Well, if you think about it, you can probably guess the answer. Let's look at what is happening on a typical Windows system. Say there are three programs running at the same time. Are they really running at the same time, and if not, what exactly is going on? It turns out they are not. Under the covers Windows is messing around with the processor so fast that you cannot tell what it's doing. So what exactly *is* it doing? Well, it is giving each program a little bit of time with the processor to compute whatever it needs to compute. Then when its allotted time is up, Windows rips the rug out from under its feet and hands control over to another application. This occurs in a cyclical manner, and as I mentioned it happens so fast that it looks as if all the different applications are running at the same time. The technical term for this juggling process is *time slicing*, so now you will know that it means if it pops up in a conversation.

Of course the deeper you start to look at the issue of multitasking, the more complicated it gets. I don't want to get too bogged down in details, but let's look at some of the issues that govern how Windows chooses to divide up processor time. Say you've got a Windows machine running a nuclear power plant and a game of solitaire. In this simplistic look at multitasking you might assume that the game of solitaire should get half of the processor time, and the power plant should get the other half. But the solitaire game is sitting idle most of the time waiting for user input, while the power plant needs constant monitoring. So this 50/50 sharing doesn't seem to make sense. Some smart people came to this very conclusion, so they implemented a very elegant multitasking system in Windows called a *priority-based preemptive multithreaded multitasking system*. That will probably give you a cramp in your tongue if you try to say it out loud (see Figure 4.1).

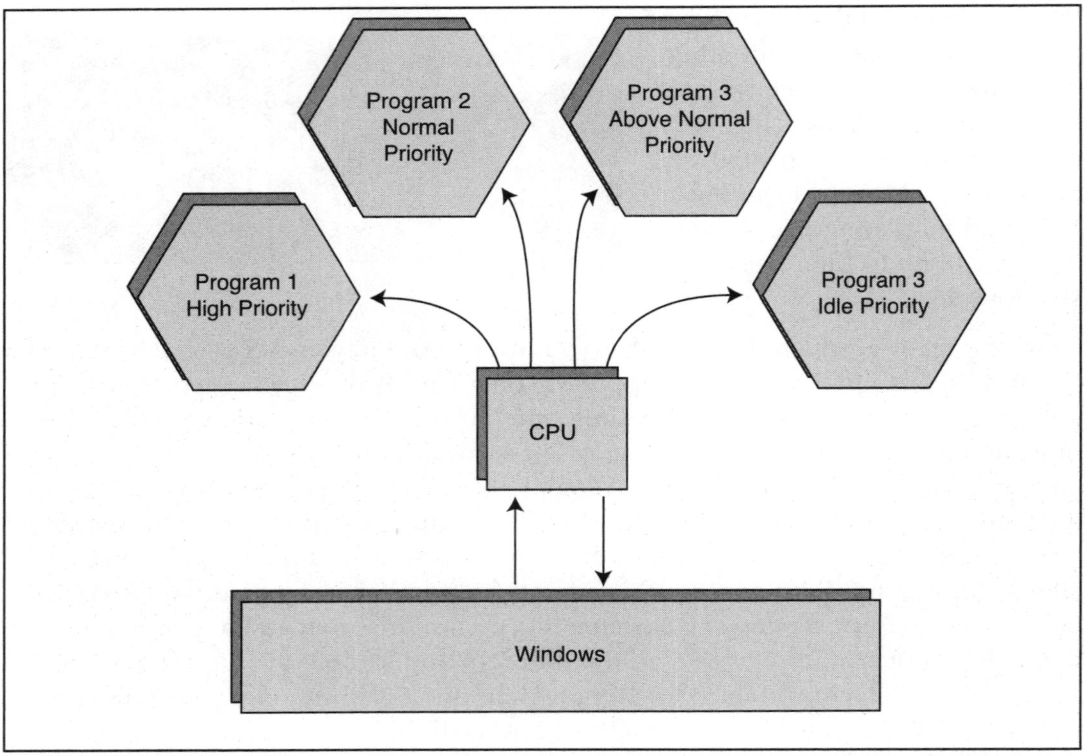

Figure 4.1

The Windows multitasking model

The *priority-based* part means that applications that are more important should get more processor time. For example, the power plant could have a priority of *real-time,* which means that it should get as much of the processor as it can, even at the expense of other applications. And the solitaire application could request a status of *normal,* and Windows would give it some processor time whenever it came around to getting some free time. Windows is not particularly anxious to give solitaire the processor because it knows it can survive just fine for a few moments on its own.

The *preemptive* bit means that Windows is not going to wait around for your application to say that it is done with the processor. It will just rip control away from your application when it feels like it. This is useful because if a high-priority application needs processor time it should not have to wait for the card game to free up the computer, should it? The power plant would blow up. And that can't be a good thing.

The *multithreaded multitasking* part is kind of interesting. *Multitasking* obviously means doing more than one thing at the same time. *Multithreading* means is that an executable, called a *process* in technobabble, can be broken up into smaller chunks that can also execute in parallel. These smaller chunks are called *threads,* and they are extremely useful. For instance, say you are looking at Visual C++. There are a whole bunch of threads executing in parallel. Some of them are checking for file updates on the disk, some are redrawing the window, some are watching your input and checking for mistakes, etc. To do all of this serially would cause problems. For instance, what would happen if the screen needed updating while a compile was in progress? Well, the screen would not get updated, that's what. You may have noticed issues like this showing up in pre-95 versions of Windows, which only supported cooperative multitasking.

A *cooperative multitasking* system is pretty much poor man's multitasking. It was implemented in 16-bit versions of Windows, and it was really bad compared to current implementations. Basically, it works in a round-robin fashion. One program would process a message, then the next program would get a chance, etc., etc. However, this created kind of a sluggish feel to the operating system.

At this point you may be starting to sweat and thinking, "I don't want to hear all this multitasking jargon, I just want to make games." Well, the good news is that when you're programming Windows, you don't need to go near multitasking unless you want to. And usually you won't. "Peter, why are you telling me this then? I don't have time to waste, dude." Well, because as I mentioned earlier, I am hoping to provide you with a complete understanding of the development environment. And Windows makes up a large proportion of that environment. Trust me, every bit of extra knowledge you can get about Windows, the better you will be able to make great games.

Hungarian Notation

As you will be programming Windows for the rest of this book, it may become useful to learn some of the guidelines for programming Windows. "Oh great, guidelines. Like come on dude, rules are meant to be broken. Guidelines are, like, so nineties." Windows is freakin' massive. It's got around 15 million lines of code, and thousands of the greatest minds in the world put it together. Its development spans decades. So how do you keep up standards between all those people? I'm afraid code commenting alone just isn't going to cut it. The solution: programming guidelines. The great thing about the guidelines for Windows is that they have such an incredibly intuitive name: Hungarian notation. Not many people know this but I found out from my technical editor in Oklahoma that the inventor was, in fact, from Hungary. His name is Charles Simonyi, and he is an apparently brilliant programmer at Microsoft.

Anyway, Hungarian notation has to do with the naming conventions that are applied to pretty much all the names that you come up with when you are programming. The standard allows different programmers to look at your code and immediately tell what type your variables are without looking at the definitions. For instance, say you've got a variable called "Width." Is that a number, a character string, or what? Well, if it was labeled in the Hungarian style it would look like this: `cxString`. From that I can tell it is an integer containing the width of a string. Don't worry if you can't tell yet—I'm about show you the definitions for the standard in a minute.

Basically, the Hungarian notation style defines a number of prefixes that are put on class names, variables, pointers, and so on, allowing instant recognition of the underlying type. Now this is just like a voluntary code of practice when programming Windows, but I suggest that you try to stick to it. I won't always use it, but you should really get in the habit of using it when you can. You remember what I was saying a couple chapters back about group communication and the air of professionalism, right?

So with that in mind, Table 4.1 showsof the major prefixes involved in the standard. Don't worry if you don't know what words like *handle* mean just yet. I'll be explaining them shortly in this and the next chapter. The thing to remember is that every single snippet of Microsoft code, from Windows to Office to technical libraries, follows this standard. So learning it will make it immensely easier for you to enter this crazy world of Windows.

Table 4.1   Hungarian Notations Prefixes

Prefix	Meaning
p	Pointer
x	Handle
3z	Null terminated string
s	String
fn	Function
dw	DWORD (unsigned long)
l	Long (long)
w	WORD (unsigned short)
b or f	BOOL (int); "f" means "flag"
cx or cy	int used for length; "c" means "count"
I	int
by	BYTE (unsigned char)
c	char or WCHAR or TCHAR
C	Class

All of those prefixes should appear in lowercase at the start of your variable name except for the class prefix, which should be uppercase. Now besides those prefixes, there are some other rules that have to be adhered to as well. They tend to be type-specific, so I'll go through each form of declaration and explain the points as I go. I will also give some examples so that you can clearly see these rules in use.

Variables

The thing with variables is that you will probably always (I hope so anyway) want to give them descriptive names. For instance, say you've got a variable that's going to count the number of times a loop has executed. Naturally, you'll choose the words like *Loop* and *Counter* to describe this variable. There are 10 million permutations of how these words can be put together, like "loopcount" and so on. However, the convention of putting underscores (_) in your variable names is now a big no-no.

You can't call the variable `loop_counter` anymore. I don't care how much you want to, you just can't. Well, you can, but everyone will shun you from the elite group of Zen gurus.

The Hungarian way is to separate subwords in a variable by uppercase letters. That is, the first letter of every subword is uppercase, like this: `LoopCounter`. Global variables should be prefixed with either a "g" or "g_". Like `g_NumPlayers`, although the "g" with the underscore suffixed is used much more often. Prefixes are the only place where underscores can be used in variable names.

Constants

The constants include typedefs, `#define`s, and variables that you want to be constants. These are always written entirely in uppercase, like this: `MAX_PLAYERS`. I know, I know. There's an underscore in there. It's okay to separate words with underscores if the type is a constant and the name is in all uppercase letters.

Classes

Classes are just like variables except you prefix the class name with an uppercase "C" and then the first letter of the name should also be uppercase. Like this: `CEnemy` or `CBox`. Member variables of a class should be prefixed with "m_". For example, `m_Width`.

Functions

Functions have no particular prefixes attached to them. They follow the same rules as variables. Here is an example: `void CountScore()`. However, if you happen to have a function pointer, then that should be prefixed with "pfn".

And that's all there really is to Hungarian notation. It's not something that you need to study; it will come naturally as you program Windows. I haven't covered every detail of the standard, partly because I think it is boring, and partly because it *is* boring. If you spot any prefixes that you don't recognize, try to figure them out by looking at how they are used in context. If that doesn't work, then look at the definition. You'll have this notation stuff cracked in no time. Now let's move on to something a little more interesting: events!

Events: A New Style of Programming

First they make you learn how to program a new operating system. Then they tell you what you can call your variables. What next? Only learning how to think and program in a completely new way; nothing too big!

Have you ever looked at a Windows program and thought about exactly how it works under the surface? Like how does it manage to know when its screen is hidden by another application, and how does it know where the mouse is? And how does it know to save its work and exit when Windows wants to shut down? Is Windows somehow *talking* to your program? It seems that way, doesn't it. But two programs talking to each other? How messed up does that sound?

Well, it's not messed up at all, and yes, Windows is talking to the applications and the applications are talking back. Not talking in the form that we know as humans, but they send messages back and forth between themselves, keeping each other happy with information about what's happening in the world and how they are going to respond to those events. So what do they talk about? Generally, most of the talking is coming from Windows, and it contains all sorts of information for your application. Let's look at some of the information that Windows might want to send.

Start up Notepad now and do the following: Type **I am going to be rich** into Notepad. Here is what will happen. Windows will first sense if you move the mouse out of the way and tell your application that the mouse is currently moving across its application window, or *client area*. Windows will then send Notepad a series of messages in this order:

1. The i key has been pressed and the Shift key is active.
2. The letter I has been activated.
3. The i key has been released and the Shift key is active.

This series will be repeated for the rest of the letters in that sentence. Now go to the File menu and click on Exit.

Windows will then send the following messages to Notepad:

1.   The mouse is moving across your client area.

2.   The mouse is now moving across your *nonclient area* (i.e., menu space).

3.   There has been a mouse click in the nonclient area.

4.   The File menu has been activated.

5.   The user has selected Exit.

6.   You should now close.

Obviously, the information that Windows sends will not be quite as linguistic as that, but that will give you the general essence of what is going on. Windows communicates with applications about absolutely everything that is going on in the system. This has a possible downside though, doesn't it? Like you don't want to be programming functions to handle all sorts of superfluous Windows stuff, you want to be programming your game. Ahh, but that, my friend, is the great thing about Windows. You don't have to deal with anything that you don't want to.

For instance, if you don't want anything special to happen when the user starts to resize your window, then you can safely ignore the message. All you do is tell Windows that you would like it to perform the default action, and it will go on its merry way. In this case that default action is repainting the window getting larger or smaller until the user is happy.

Don't Shoot the Messenger

So how does Windows actually get down to the business of communication? Does it use string variables, smoke signals, or what? Well, none of the above, actually. All of this is done using one integer that identifies the message and two 32-bit variables, which are the parameters to that message. For example, if the message was "Resize," then the variables might contain the new width and height of the window.

The communication is achieved like this. When your program starts, it gives to Windows a pointer to a function called the *window procedure* (otherwise known as WndProc). This window procedure is set up specifically to handle the messages and parameters that Windows will pass to it. Inside this function there is generally some logic, usually a switch statement, which figures out what the message is and what it means. Then one of two things happens. If your program wants to deal with the message, it will call code somewhere to deal with the message and then return success or failure to Windows. On the other hand, if your application can't be bothered to deal with the Windows gossip, then it just passes the message back and tells

Windows to go deal with its own problems and stop being a pain. The unwanted message is sent back to Windows through what is called the *default window procedure*.

Messages will arrive in your program in one of two ways. If the message is particularly important, then Windows will actually *send* the message directly to your WndProc and expect immediate processing. On the other hand, if the message is just your average run-of-the-mill message, such as a mouse movement message, then Windows will *post* the message to a *message queue*. It is then up to your application to go and fetch this message from the queue and process it at its own leisure (see Figure 4.2). There is, in fact, a separate message queue for each application that is running. These separate queues get their data from a master system message queue.

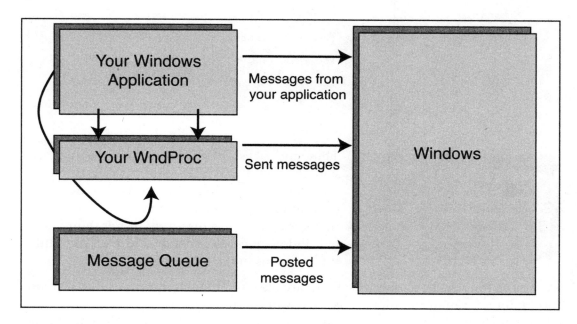

Figure 4.2

The message architecture of Windows

This get-the-message-from-the-queue action is performed by a tight loop, not too dissimilar from the game loop, which executes throughout the life of your program. The loop just sits there and checks if a message is available, and if so, it gets the message and passes it to WndProc for further processing. Again, the WndProc, either decides that it wants to process the message, does so, and then returns success or failure to Windows, *or* it just sends the message straight back so that Windows can perform its default behavior.

I don't want to get too bogged down in theory right now, so I'll wait until the code in the next couple of chapters before getting really jiggy. But let's take a look at what a message looks like to *you,* the human (or cyborg), when you are programming. I'll give you a few examples because I'm feeling particularly generous.

Table 4.2   Windows Messages

Message	Meaning
WM_SIZE	The window is being resized.
WM_PAINT	The window needs to be redrawn.
WM_MOUSEMOVE	The mouse is moving.

NOTE

If you're curious, the WM_ prefix stands for "Windows message."

These messages will be sent to your program, as I said, through the WndProc or message queue, and along with each message will come two integers with parameters for the message. More on that later. There are hundreds, if not thousands, of Windows messages that deal with all the stuff that happens in the Windows world.

As well as the standard messages, there are also user-defined messages that you, the programmer, can make up. For instance, you could have a message that means "Battle Stations: Non-Microsoft computer detected on the network. Move in for the kill." Of course, that message would only make sense to your program. This type of message is generally called a *user message,* or more technically, WM_USER.

I've mentioned those parameter thingies a few times already, but let's have an applied look at them now. The parameters to messages are usually referred to as the LPARAM and WPARAM. Hmmm. I like those names. Not! I suppose an explanation is in order. If you refer back to Table 4.1, you'll see that "L" stands for "long," or 32-bit integer, and "W" stands for "word," or unsigned 16-bit integer. Obviously, the PARAM stands for "parameter." So that's where the "W" and "L" come from. But these days, both LPARAM and WPARAM are 32-bit, so they should really be called LPARAM1 and LPARAM2. The "W" bit is just left over from the 16-bit days of Windows 3.1.

Now you can start to build up a picture in your mind of how your application or game "lives" in a PC running Microsoft Windows. It no longer *owns* the computer as it would if it were a DOS application. Your application now *cohabits* the PC, and it doesn't just do stuff—it either asks permission to do stuff, or it gets Windows to do it. For instance, in Direct3D, you don't change the screen resolution. First you ask for Windows to cooperate with you because you may wish to change the screen resolution. Then you ask Direct3D to change the resolution to one that Windows has deemed appropriate for you. If you ask for the resolution to be set to something that would damage the monitor, or that the graphics card does not support, Windows will simply tell you *no*. So keep this concept of your application being a slave that has to ask for permission from the honorable Windows for just about everything.

You may think that this business of handing control over to a higher power is a pain and will lead to more hassle. In fact, it is very helpful; it means you don't have to deal with all the nonsense like figuring out what graphics cards are installed and what speed the user would like the mouse to move at and so on. You can let Windows deal with the details while you do what you're supposed to be doing: making great software.

Conclusion

You now have all the information that you need to program Windows. This would be a good time to go write some Windows applications and mess around with the code. Then come back and look at Direct3D in the next chapter.

Only kidding! I wouldn't rush you like that. In the next chapter you're going to start programming your first Windows application in a nice step-by-step manner. How cool is that? After only a chapter you'll have all the knowledge that you require to program Windows.

CHAPTER 5

GOODBYE WORLD

There comes a time in every Web site's life when it must be hacked. My Web site had that experience the other day. It was set up so that I could amuse my editors with a compressed 380 MB download for the CD layout for this book, since I was finding it hard to get a courier company to figure out where I live. When I finished setting up the site, I went to check that it could be accessed from another computer easily. That's when I noticed something interesting on the front page. The background had changed to black, and in big red letters was written "(Expletive) the U.S. government." I won't say where the hackers were located, although their country is well known for its Kung Pao chicken. Can't we all just get along? Or at least won't they increase their imports of our goods?

How does my story relate to this chapter? Well, you are about to have your mind hijacked by the knowledge of how to program Windows! Yeah, that's it. Trust me, some people are totally damaged by this stuff!

In this chapter you are going to learn some seriously cool stuff—like what it's like to write your first Windows application. In this chapter I'll

- give you a brief overview of the structure for the most straightforward, uncomplicated, easy Windows application that you're ever likely to see. It won't be an easy ride though; you'll have to keep your Zen intellect with you.

- show you in detail things like the message box function.

- teach you how to play mean jokes on your friends!

Your First Windows Program

I woke up this morning to the soft melodic tune of a small rose-colored robin. It was perched on the bow of a sturdy tree, whose leaves spiraled into colors of wine red, golden brown, and soft yellow. The wind whispered through the branches, telling all the creatures of the forest to wake to the warming of the sun. The sun's rays darted playfully among the trees, creating a glistening reflection against the fresh dew that lingered on the foliage and across the moist earth.

"Another day is upon us!" the bird called cheerfully. "Hello world!"

"Shut up!" I shouted back.

I hate the morning. I hate the autumn. And I hate stupid birds interrupting my peaceful slumber! But as much as I hate it, the morning should be the *only* time that one should be forced to hear (or utter) those evil words: "Hello World." That's why I am going to break from tradition and flatly refuse to include them in your first Windows program.

Your first Windows program will have the apt title "Resistance Is Futile!" I thought this would be a good way to open the chapter to Windows programming.

OK, get ready to actually type some code. For this section, load up Visual Studio and type out and run this code as you go. Or load the code off of the companion CD. Try to balance this book against something on your desk so that it is standing upright beside your monitor. That way you can look at the monitor and book easily and you won't strain yourself. Put some blue-tack underneath if the book keeps sliding off.

While teaching you Windows programming, I am going to use the format of showing each line of code and then explaining it. At the end, I will show the complete listing so that you can see how it looks in one piece.

Now, so that you have it fresh in your mind, here is one of those original console-style applications that I'm sure is very similar to the first application that you programmed:

```c
// Typical console Hello World style application
/////////////////////////////////////////////
// Resistance Is Futile!, DOS style

#include <stdio.h>

int main()
{
        // Output the text

        printf( " Resistance Is Futile!" );

        // Return  control to the operating system
        return 0;
}
```

And the output is:

```
Resistance Is Futile!
```

Pretty simple, I'm sure you'll agree. Let's see what a Windows version would look like. The following program will create a message box that displays the same text as the DOS example.

The New Include Files

The first bit of code you type out is obviously the #include files, so let's take a look at them now. In fact, you only need to include one file to allow your program to run in Windows. That file has the fitting name windows.h. This file includes a whole bunch of other files that make up the operating system's API, or application programming interface. Every single function call that you will ever make to Windows is included in this file or one of the files that it includes.

And here are the first few lines of code:

```
/////////////////////////////////////////////////////////////////////////////////
///////////////
// Goodbye world

#define WIN32_LEAN_AND_MEAN

// The main windows include file
#include <windows.h>
```

You may be wondering what exactly WIN32_LEAN_AND_MEAN do. Well, it has to do with the current split in the methods that you can use to develop applications for the Windows platform. The first way is our way. That is, you program all the Windows logic yourself and then customize it to be what you want your program to be. The other, dirty, way is to use MFC, or the Microsoft Foundation Classes. MFC is good for standard Windows applications, and I have used it extensively for that purpose, but you want to avoid that puppy for games. MFC adds 10 million layers of software between Windows and your code so that everything works in a seamless, object-oriented fashion. However, the more layers you have, the slower things get done. And in games we want things to move faster than a drunken cow on ice skates.

The problem with MFC is that its looks can be deceiving. On the outside it looks pretty slick; you push a button and moments later you can witness the result. But inside: yuck! There are pulleys everywhere, thousands of gears running around, fan belts puffing away under the strain, and bits of electric wire held together with sticky tape. Basically, it looks like the internals of a Russian commercial airliner.

And because of all this extra "functionality," a few million extra lines had to be added to the Windows.h files to support it. But if you're not dealing with MFC, why should your build times be slowed down by it? You're right, they shouldn't. So when you define WIN32_LEAN_AND_MEAN, all the extra garbage that you don't need is excluded by preprocessor #ifdefs, thereby decreasing your build times.

The New Entry Point

The entry-point is the first piece of code that will be executed when your program starts. In DOS, and some other operating systems, this entry point was always called main(). So as you can see in the DOS "Hello World" example, all the code is contained within the main() function. You can also see that the main() function has no parameters. Actually, it does have parameters that are used to tell you what was written at the command prompt when your program was launched, but you can safely act as if they were not there.

In Windows programming the entry point completely changes. It has a slick new name and new parameters that you cannot ignore. It is called WinMain(). Let's look at its prototype now.

```
int WINAPI WinMain( HINSTANCE hInstance,
HINSTANCE hPrevInstance,
PSTR pstrCmdLine,
int iCmdShow );
```

Don't worry, it's much easier than it appears. Let's start at the top. You can see that the function returns type int. But what is that WINAPI thing all about? Well, WINAPI is a preprocessor cover for a C call that looks like the following:

```
__stdcall
```

What WINAPI is a cover for is pretty much inconsequential; what it means is kind of important. WINAPI tells the compiler that the parameters for the function are to be passed in left-to-right order, as opposed to the normal right-to-left. You may see WINAPI written as PASCAL, CDECL, or APIENTRY. These all mean the same thing, but the standard is to use WINAPI. Just remember that WINAPI is always the second word in the WinMain() declaration.

The next part of WinMain() is obviously the name of the function. You absolutely must put a function called WinMain() somewhere or your Windows application won't even compile. Can you imagine trying to write a DOS or console app without the main() function?

The parameters of the `WinMain()` function cause some people to go into convulsions, so we'll tackle them one at a time.

- **hInstance**. Remember the discussion on Hungarian notation in the last chapter, where you saw that "h" stands for "handle," which I said I would explain later? Well, now is that time. Internally, Windows is looking after 10 zillion different objects, from applications' windows to applications, to colors, to hardware, to everything you can imagine. There has to be some sort of way to maintain a list of these items so that they can be managed efficiently. What Windows does is give each item that it looks after a unique number, like a bar code. It can then refer to these objects simply by using that number. This number is called a *handle*.

  An *instance* is how Windows refers to your application. When you load your application into memory, you create an instance of it. If you start up Notepad twice, then there are two instances of it in memory. Each instance is referred to with a unique number, or handle. So *hinstance* is "the handle to this instance of the application." `hInstance` is useful because it is how Windows tracks your applications' requests. For example, if you ask Windows to create a window, then Windows is going to want to know with which application to associate the new window, so you pass it the `hInstance` when you make your request.

- **hPrevInstance**. This item is obsolete and you can safely ignore it. Back in the old days of 16-bit Windows, each application could save a bit of memory if it knew that an instance of itself was already in memory. It could refer to its previous incarnation using this variable. However, in 32-bit Windows there is a protected memory model, which means that this variable can no longer be used. It will always be set to `NULL`.

- **pstrCmdLine**. This is similar to the parameters that get passed to the DOS main function. It is a pointer to a string that describes what was placed on the command line after the name of your executable. For instance, say someone opened up a command prompt and typed

  ```
  WinWord.exe  999 Windows crashes left on the wall, 999 crashes
  ```

  then Microsoft Word will start, and the pstrCmdLine variable in that application will contain the data:

  ```
  999 Windows crashes left on the wall, 999 crashes
  ```

  Unless you want to retrieve any information from the command prompt, which is unlikely in games, you can pretty much ignore the `pstrCmdLine` variable. The only reason you might want to study this variable is if you wanted to pass some sort of debugging information to your program.

- **iCmdShow**. Last but not least is the iCmdShow variable. You can tell from the Hungarian notation that this variable is an integer. If you expand it out it says, kind of backwards, "integer containing the show command." The *show command* is the way that Windows wants your application to initially display its application window. For instance, if the user specified that all new applications are to be started minimized, then this variable would contain information that would say "minimized." Table 5.1 lists the possible values for iCmdShow.

Table 5.1   iCmdShow Values

Value	Meaning
SW_FORCEMINIMIZE	Forces a window to be minimized even if the thread that owns the window is not responding
SW_HIDE	Hides this window because another one is about to be activated
SW_MAXIMIZE	Causes the specified window to be maximized
SW_MINIMIZE	Causes the specified window to be minimized, and then minimizes the next window in the Z-Order
SW_RESTORE	Activates the specified window, and then resets the window to its previous size and position
SW_SHOW	Activates and displays the specified window
SW_SHOWMAXIMIZED	Activates and displays the specified window as maximized
SW_SHOWMINIMIZED	Activates and displays the specified window as minimized
SW_SHOWMINNOACTIVE	Minimizes the window without affecting the activation status of the currently active window
SW_SHOWNA	Displays the window in its current state without affecting the activation status of the currently active window
SW_SHOWNOACTIVATE	Displays the window in its most recent size and position without affecting the activation status of the currently active window
SW_SHOWNORMAL	Activates, restores, and displays the specified window. Use this flag when displaying a window for the first time.

For now you can pretty much ignore this variable. In the next chapter I will point out where it becomes useful when you learn how to create a real Windows application. The SW_ prefix means "Show Window," the same as the function ShowWindow().

And that's all there is to the WinMain() entry point. I bet that's the longest introduction to a single function that you have ever read. Don't worry—it just gets worse! And now that there is a declared entry point, you can write some code. In this case you are going to call a standard Windows-based message box function.

The MessageBox() Function

The great thing about the message box function is how easy it is. If that little beauty wasn't premade for use, you would have to write your own, and that could be over 100 lines of code. Here is the code to call it:

```
// Display the message box
MessageBox( NULL,
            " Resistance Is Futile!",
            "Lower your shields",
            MB_OK | MB_ICONEXCLAMATION);
```

That seems simple enough, but again I'm going to go through it one step at a time so that you're on even footing because some of those parameters may look a little confusing. First things first—let's look at the prototype for MessageBox():

```
int MessageBox( HWND hWnd,              // The owner window handle
                PCSTR pstrMessage,      // The message text
                PCSTR pstrCaption       // The text in message box caption
                UINT uType );           // The message box style
```

- **hWnd.** Again, you can tell by the prefixed "h" that this is a handle. However, in this case it is a handle to a window. Window handles are very similar to the instance handles that I was talking about earlier. Windows applies a bar code to each window that it manages. In this case the hWnd variable refers to the window that spawned the message box. It is not important to specify a value here, so I just set it as NULL. I'll cover window handles throughout this chapter.

- **pstrMessage.** I'll start by explaining what PCSTR means. It means "pointer to a constant string." You may see this also written as LPCTSTR. In the past the "LP" bit meant "long pointer," or in other words, "32-bit pointer." However, these days all pointers are 32-bit, so the "1" bit is superfluous. This variable is a pointer to a string containing the text that you want to display to the user in the message box.

- **pstrCaption**. This is similar to the `pstrMessage` parameter except the text to which this variable points is used in the caption of the message box.

Table 5.2 Message Box Styles

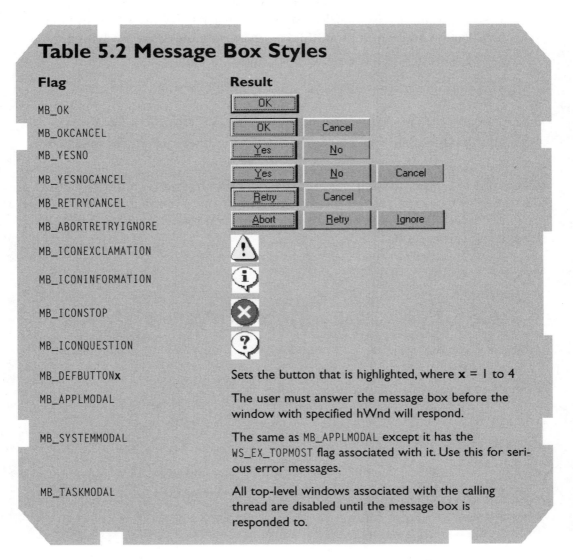

Flag	Result
MB_OK	OK
MB_OKCANCEL	OK Cancel
MB_YESNO	Yes No
MB_YESNOCANCEL	Yes No Cancel
MB_RETRYCANCEL	Retry Cancel
MB_ABORTRETRYIGNORE	Abort Retry Ignore
MB_ICONEXCLAMATION	
MB_ICONINFORMATION	
MB_ICONSTOP	
MB_ICONQUESTION	
MB_DEFBUTTONx	Sets the button that is highlighted, where **x** = 1 to 4
MB_APPLMODAL	The user must answer the message box before the window with specified hWnd will respond.
MB_SYSTEMMODAL	The same as MB_APPLMODAL except it has the WS_EX_TOPMOST flag associated with it. Use this for serious error messages.
MB_TASKMODAL	All top-level windows associated with the calling thread are disabled until the message box is responded to.

- **uType**. uType requires a little bit more explanation. This variable defines the style of the message box. Refer to Table 5.2 for the full list of styles that you can set for your message box. You may be wondering what that "|" thingy is if you haven't come across it used in this fashion before. It is called the *bitwise OR operator*, and you can use it to combine two values into a single value. It works like this: You give the operator two values. It then proceeds to compare them in binary form. If either bit is equal to 1, then the resulting bit is set to 1. So for example, say MB_OK = 0001 and MB_ICONINFORMATION = 0100 in binary form (they don't, by the way, this is just an example). Watch what happens:

```
MB_ICONINFORMATION | MB_OK  ==  0100 | 0001 == 0101
```

The flags for both variables are now held within a single value! How cool is that?

Now let's look at what kind of styles the message box supports. Table 5.3 shows just about all the values that you can pass in the last parameter to the MessageBox function.

If you want to figure out what the user pressed on one of those multiple button message boxes, you can look at the return value. It turns out that the return value for the MessageBox() function contains the button that the user pressed. Table 5.3 shows the possible return values.

Table 5.3 MessageBox() Return Values

Return Value	Meaning
IDABORT	The user selected the Abort button
IDCANCEL	The user selected the Cancel button
IDIGNORE	The user selected the Ignore button
IDNO	The user selected the No button
IDYES	The user selected the Yes button
IDRETRY	The user selected the Retry button
IDOK	The user selected the OK button

And that's all there is to message boxes. I know I've spent ages describing MessageBox(), but that's just so you can come back later if you need to. Remember, all the information in last couple of pages follows from a single function call. So it's not that complicated, it just has a bunch of options. The trick to learning Windows—I should have mentioned this before—is to learn to block out all the extra stuff and focus on the core. Keep that in mind and everything will be fine.

The Return Value

The return value is just like in DOS or console applications. Following is the code:

```
return 0;
```

Pretty simple, huh? The only reason that I include it is to tell you about the general format that Windows return values take. If the return value is less than zero, then that generally means failure or some sort of error. On the other hand, if the return value is greater than or equal to zero, then it can mean anything. You can test for failure or success with two extremely useful macros that come standard with Windows. They are called FAILED() and SUCCEEDED() and they take an HRESULT value, which between you and me is just a 32-bit integer. You would use them like this:

```
if( FAILED( x ) )
      // Error handling code      .
      .
      .


if( SUCCEEDED( y ) )
      // Success code
      .
      .
```

Get used to those macros because you will be using them extensively when you get to start programming Direct3D.

By the way, when you are debug-executing in Visual C++, the return value from your application is displayed in the output bar along the bottom of your screen when the application exits. If you stick to some standards about the values you return, then this can turn into an invaluable tool in helping you debug. I'll talk more about this later.

The Results

OK, are you ready for this? Check out Figure 5.1 for a look at your first Windows application.

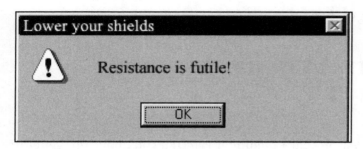

Figure 5.1

Behold the fruits of your labor.

That is so cool! The thing to do now is call in your friends, relatives, parents, kids, pets, and enemies and show them what you have achieved. They will worry. Such progress so quickly—surely you are a threat to world dominance!

By the way, if you have not done it yet, I would recommend that you get the manuals out and figure out how to get the Visual C++ debugger working because it is very important in more advanced Windows programming, which you are about to learn.

But before that, it would be really great if you could look at the entire code listing. So here it is, in all its glory.

```
///////////////////////////////////////////////////////////////////////////////
//////////////
// Resistance Is futile, Win32 Message Box style

#define WIN32_LEAN_AND_MEAN

// The main windows include file
#include <Windows.h>

// The windows entry point
int WINAPI WinMain( HINSTANCE hInstance,
 HINSTANCE hPrevInstance, PSTR pstrCmdLine, int iCmdShow )
{
        // Display the message box
        MessageBox(     NULL,
```

```
        "Resistance Is futile!",
        "Lower your shields",
        MB_OK | MB_ICONEXCLAMATION );

    // Return to windows
    return 0;
}
```

It's not so bad when you look at it that way. Try messing around with it and running it a few times. For instance, put in different messages, change what icons are being displayed, and so on. Here's one really great use for this, which provides me with endless hours of amusement. Say you've got a friend called Mike. Change the message to "Hi, I'm Mike and I really like [insert name]." Then get to Mike's computer and put it in his StartUp folder in the Start menu. This causes the program to run automatically every time he starts his PC. Then sit back and laugh. It's best if the person doesn't know a great deal about computers. It'll take him ages to get rid of the program, especially if you call it SysMon.exe or something similar. It's good to see my inner child is alive and well!

Conclusion

I think you'll agree that you haven't seen anything too taxing just yet with Windows programming. The thing to do, as I mentioned before, is to learn to keep your head above the mud. That is, every single Windows function call has got billions of options to go along with it. So just remember the core and you'll be fine. If you need to use one of the extras, you can open up my book sometime in the future or look it up in the Help files and get the required information. Just remember the basics. The rest will sink in with use over time.

I'm restating those points because I want you to keep a cool head when you get to the next chapter, because you are going to have to absorb a lot of new information there. You are going to write your first *real* Windows application. Cool or what? After the next chapter you will have the capability to write any Windows program you want. Well almost; you will by the end of this section anyway.

Remember in the last chapter I said to turn on the fan because something was about to hit it? Well, now might be the time to put on some goggles and run for cover...

CHAPTER 6

SELLING YOUR SOUL

A week and a half ago I was lying peacefully beside a pool at a villa in the south of Portugal. Oh, you can't get much more relaxed than that. I was there for a whole two weeks, and I did absolutely nothing. It was great. But it couldn't last—I was jerked back into reality by an Airbus A300, which carried me back to cold, dreary Ireland where I am now, typing away. Sometimes I hate the space-time continuum. In five days I'll be driving 500 miles to my new home for a few years, Dundee, Scotland. A week after that I'm flying 15,000 miles to attend a game developers' conference in San Jose, California. Then I've got to come back again. Then a month after that I'm flying a thousand miles between Edinburgh and Dublin and back again. That adds up to about 20,000 miles too many.

The reason I'm telling you this is not because I think you're particularly interested in my travel arrangements, but because it is somewhat akin to the distance your brain will have to travel to work itself around Windows. Windows started out a small, tight operating system-type thingy that could fit on a 350K floppy. Now it barely fits on a 650MB CD. Between its humble beginnings and the present, it has gained countless tangents and bits and pieces that it didn't have before. Luckily enough, all these extras are packaged into nice little groups that you can focus on one at a time. But the one overriding factor is that the way you start programming a Windows application has been the same since the 1980s and it will remain pretty much the same for the foreseeable future. And that is what you are going to focus on in this chapter: how to start programming a *real* Windows application. Doesn't it just make the hairs on your neck stand on end?

In this chapter covers

- all the steps necessary to create a real Windows application, including a detailed look at WinMain() and WndProc(), the message handler.
- an introduction to the Graphical Device Interface(GDI for short).
- how to turn a Windows application into a Windows game.

100 Lines of Code

You can think of the little Windows group I'm going to discuss as the *core*. Everything you are about to learn is directly applicable to every single Windows application that you will ever write, so take the headphones out of your ears, spit out your gum, sit up straight, and pay attention! A completely generic, basic Windows application that does nothing takes about 100 lines of code.

"What!? 100 lines! Ahhhh!" You are pessimistic, aren't you? Most people think that the 100 lines gives them nothing, but in fact you get a heck of a lot of functionality. Specifically you get a window that will

- automatically clip its contents to its boundary.
- automatically repaint its client area.
- handle movement and resizing, including the complex redrawing that this involves.
- have Minimize, Maximize, and Restore buttons, along with a working system menu.

Believe me, trying to program that kind of functionality yourself would take tens of thousands of lines of code. Remember: behind the Windows API that you will be using there are *15 million* lines of code.

Relax—It's Only Nine Function Calls

Let's take a look at the technical requirements for this little endeavor. It will comprise two functions: WinMain(), which is the entry point, and WndProc(), which is the message handler for Windows. You have to make nine function calls to get it running, and then a further two for use at run time. You also have to fill in a couple of structures. So remember it like that and you'll have an easy ride. You can generally condense the creation of a Windows program into a few simple steps, and here they are in all their glory:

1. Fill in a *Windows class.* This describes how your window will function.
2. Register the class. This lets Windows know about the class.
3. Create the window, referring to the class as a description.
4. Make the window visible and initialize it.
5. Check for messages in the message queue.
6. Process any messages in the message queue.
7. Repeat steps 5 and 6 for the remainder of the application.

Again, I'll use the procedure of walking through the code, line by line, before showing you the complete code listing at the end. You may find it helpful to briefly run through the code listing now, so that you can visualize both the length of it and where each line fits into the bigger picture. Let's now look at the code.

First, as always, is the include file. It's just the typical windows.h that you included before.

```
//////////////////////////////////////////////////////////////////////////////////
///////////////
// Title: First Windows Application
// Author: Peter Walsh
// Notes: This code can be used as a base for any windows program

#define WIN32_LEAN_AND_MEAN

// The main windows include file
#include <windows.h>
```

Now you need to move on to WinMain(). This is just like the last chapter except that, as you'll see, the contents of this function have completely changed from what you saw in the MessageBox() example in the last chapter.

A Walk through WinMain()

As a reminder, here is the WinMain() header, so you don't have to go flipping back pages to the last chapter.

```
// The windows entry point. The application will start executing here
int WINAPI WinMain( HINSTANCE hInstance,
        HINSTANCE hPrevInstance, PSTR pstrCmdLine, int iCmdShow )
{
```

This function header will always look the same, and it will always have these same variables in it. If you need a refresher, take a look back to Chapter 5, where I describe this function header in detail. Now, the next thing you need to do is declare a few variables that you will be using in this function.

Your Variables: A Handle, a Message, and a Touch of Class

Luckily, there are only three of them, so they shouldn't be too hard for you to remember. Have a look at these beauties:

```
HWND hWnd;              // The handle to the main window
MSG msg;                // The message windows is sending
WNDCLASSEX wc; // The window class used to create the window

// This is the name of the class and also the window title
static char pstrAppName[] = "First Windows App, Zen Style";
```

Getting a Handle on Handles

The hWnd variable is the handle for the window that you are going to create. As I mentioned before, a handle is a unique number, or bar code, that Windows applies to each window that it looks after for easy identification and management. A lot of people who are new to Windows have a tough time getting their minds around handles, so that's why I keep talking about them so much. The more you hear about handles, the easier it will be to understand them. I'll point them out whenever they show up.

The MSG Structure

Every time you check for a message in the queue, you need somewhere to store it before you pass it on to WndProc. The msg structure performs this task beautifully. Here is the definition for this structure:

```
typedef struct tagMSG
{
        HWND    hwnd;           // The window handle that is the message target
        UINT    message;// The message.  eg WM_COMMAND
        WPARAM wParam;  // The first parameter for the message
        LPARAM  lParam;// The second parameter for the message
        DWORD   time;           // The time the message occurred
        POINT   pt;             // The mouse position when the message occurred

} MSG, *PMSG;
```

You will rarely, if ever, have to deal with the internals of this structure yourself, but it's always a good idea to have an idea of what things look like on the inside. This variable is generally just used as a holder during the communication process. You'll see it in action shortly.

Actually, on saying that, you will probably deal with the wParam member, but I'll talk about that toward the end of this chapter.

The WNDCLASSEX Structure

In the past I might have described a WNDCLASSEX as a pretty large structure. That was before I encountered DirectX. Now I would call it fairly modest. So when I give you the definition of this structure, don't panic. The members WND-CLASSEX are just a bunch of complicatedly-named variables for relatively simple ideas. By the way, don't confuse this window class with anything to do with a C++ class. It's just a structure to hold information about the window that you want to create, nothing else.

NOTE

If you're interested, the EX on the end of WNDCLASSEX stands for "extended." Once upon a time, not too long ago, the class structure was called WNDCLASS. However, that is now obsolete, and you should only use WNDCLASSEX.

```
typedef struct tagWNDCLASSEX
{
        UINT          cbSize;          // The size of this structure
        UINT          style;           // The style for the window
        WNDPROC       lpfnWndProc;     // A pointer to WndProc
        int           cbClsExtra;      // Extra stuff.  Just ignore it.
        int           cbWndExtra;      // Extra stuff.  Just ignore it.
        HINSTANCE     hInstance;       // The application's instance handle
        HICON         hIcon;           // A handle to the application's icon
        HCURSOR       hCursor;         // A handle to the application's cursor
        HBRUSH        hbrBackground;   // A handle for the background brush
        LPCSTR        lpszMenuName;    // A string with the name of the menu
        LPCSTR        lpszClassName;   // String with the name of the class
        HICON         hIconSm;         // A handle to small application icon

} WNDCLASSEX, *PWNDCLASSEX;
```

I'll go through line by line how to fill that puppy out in two ticks of a clock crystal. However, there is one more variable declaration to look at first:

```
static char strAppName[] = "First Windows App, Zen Style";
```

This is a simple character array that holds the name of the application. You'll see that this variable will be used a number of times as you progress through the code. It is used for the window caption and also the class name.

Now, let's get back to that window class structure. First up you need to tell the structure how big it is:

```
// Fill in the window class with the attributes for our main window

// The size of this structure in bytes
wc.cbSize       = sizeof( WNDCLASSEX );
```

So, what's the point of telling a structure how big it is? It sounds unnecessary and a waste of time at the outset, but if you think about it, doing so is quite useful. Say you pass Windows the pointer of a structure that Windows passes to a piece of hardware that controls the cooling of a plutonium reactor. Windows would really like it if that pointer you passed it were valid. But how can it tell? Well, all Windows has to do is check the first four bytes of the pointer that you sent it. If that number matches the size of a known structure, then Windows knows that it has a valid pointer to a structure. Cool, huh? Otherwise it would have to assume that the programmer is always right. Ha! That would almost be as stupid as putting Windows in charge of a plutonium reactor!

Now specify how you want the window to behave:

```
wc.style        = CS_HREDRAW | CS_VREDRAW | CS_OWNDC;
```

The style member specifies the way that your new window will react to certain events. Table 6.1 lists the flags to which the style member can be set. I have bolded the most common flags; you can pretty much ignore the others.

Table 6.1   WNDCLASSEX Style Flags

Flag	Meaning
CS_BYTEALIGNCLIENT	Causes the client area of the window to be aligned horizontally to the byte boundary
CS_BYTEALIGNWINDOW	Causes the window to be aligned horizontally to the byte boundary
CS_CLASSDC	Ensures that every window created with this class shares the same device context
CS_DBLCLKS	**Ensures that the window receives double click messages instead of multiple mouse up and mouse down messages**
CS_HREDRAW	**Causes the client area to be redrawn if the windows size changes horizontally**
CS_VREDRAW	**Causes the client area to be redrawn if the windows size changes horizontally**
CS_NOCLOSE	Disables the close box on the window
CS_OWNDC	**Every window that uses this class will gets its own device context.**
CS_PARENTDC	The clipping region for this window will be set to be the same as for the parent window.
CS_SAVEBITS	Windows will save the image for client area of the window to speed up redrawing.

NOTE

The CS_ prefix stands for "class style." I've set the most common flags; your window will be redrawn if it is moved or sized (CS_VREDRAW and CS_HREDRAW), and it will have its own device context (CS_OWNDC) so that its drawing is super fast. I'll explain device contexts (or DCs, as they are commonly known) in the next chapter.

```
// Useless information.  Just set to zero.
wc.cbClsExtra           = 0;
```

```
// Useless information.  Just set to zero.
wc.cbWndExtra          = 0;
```

These two entries, `cbClsExtra` and `cbWndExtra`, can be used to allocate extra memory in the Windows class for some advanced features, but I can't see us needing them at all. You can pretty much pretend they don't exist. However, in Windows it is always a good idea to initialize every entry to 0, even if you are not interested in them. Alternatively, just `memset()` the structure to 0 before you use it, and then you only have to fill in the fields you want to.

```
// The name of our event handler
wc.lpfnWndProc          = WndProc;
```

Now this entry might be a little confusing because you haven't created your `WndProc()` function yet, but just pretend that you have, and put its name into the `lpfnWndProc` entry. As you can see, this entry requires a pointer to a window procedure. Remember in the last chapter when I said that you give Windows a pointer to your `WndProc()` so that it can send messages to your application? Well, this is the place you give Windows that pointer. By filling in this field with the pointer to your window procedure, Windows will be able to send messages to your application.

```
// A handle to the applications instance
wc.hInstance          = hInstance;
```

Do you also remember when I told you that when you ask for a window, Windows needs to associate it with your application by using an instance handle? Well, this is the place for that. Simply fill in the `hInstance` variable that you got from the formal parameter in the `WinMain()` function header.

```
// The handle for the brush to use for the window background
wc.hbrBackground       = (HBRUSH)GetStockObject( DKGRAY_BRUSH );
```

The next thing to do is to tell Windows how you would like the background of your window to be painted. This is done using what is called a *brush,* which I will be discussing in detail in Chapter 7, "Getting Jiggy with Windows." For now just know that a brush describes a color, pattern, or both and that it is used in Windows to fill regions such as the background of a window. Now you don't know how to create brushes yet, so let's use one that I created earlier. Actually, it wasn't me—it was a programmer somewhere in the depths of the Microsoft OS programming building, near Seattle, on the seventh ring of hell.

Windows comes with a number of ready-made objects such as Pens (which are for drawing lines), Brushes (for filling areas), and Fonts (for displaying text). You can access these *stock objects* through the function `GetStockObject()`. Here is its prototype:

```
HGDIOBJ GetStockObject( int fnObject );
```

That `HGDIOBJ` means "Handle to a Graphical Device Interface OBJect." The Graphical Device Interface, or GDI, as it is commonly known, is a section of Windows that is used to output text and graphics to devices like the monitor and the printer. However, I'll leave that whole can of worms for the next chapter. What you can do now is have a look at how this function works.

It works a little like this: You give it the name of the stock object that you want, and it gives a handle for that object to you. Sound simple? Good. So I want my window to be drawn with a dark gray background. As you can see, I specified `DKGRAY_BRUSH` as the parameter. The function then gives me a handle, which I subsequently pass back to Windows in the class structure. Windows can be like that sometimes; you have to do stuff in kind of a roundabout manner. For completeness let's take a look at what other stock objects Windows supports (see Table 6.2). I'll only include the brushes and pens for now because the fonts are of no consequence just yet.

Table 6.2   Stock Objects

Flag	Meaning
`BLACK_BRUSH`	Black Brush
`WHITE_BRUSH`	White Brush
`GRAY_BRUSH`	Gray Brush
`LTGRAY_BRUSH`	Light Gray Brush
`DKGRAY_BRUSH`	Dark Gray Brush
`HOLLOW_BRUSH	NULL_BRUSH`	The brush is invisible (doesn't draw anything).
`DC_BRUSH`	Win98 and Win2000 and later only. This is the solid color brush. You can set the color using SetDCBrushColor().
`BLACK_PEN`	Black Pen
`WHITE_PEN`	White Pen
`DC_PEN`	Win98 and Win2000 and later only. This is the solid pen color. You can set the color using SetDCPenColor().

Next, you need to tell Windows what icon you want to use for your application. This is the little picture that shows up on the upper-left corner of your window. For example, if you're looking at Visual C++, the icon is that groovy-looking colored infinity symbol.

```
// A handle to the icon to use for the window
wc.hIcon                        = LoadIcon( NULL, IDI_APPLICATION );
```

Tell Windows about your icon with the LoadIcon() function. Here is its prototype:

```
WINUSERAPI HICON WINAPI LoadIconA( HINSTANCE hInstance, LPCSTR lpIconName);
```

That WINUSERAPI thing is simply there to help the compiler produce better code. It tells the compiler that the function is located away in a DLL somewhere. You can ignore it. You can see that the function returns an icon handle. The first parameter, hInstance, is used to tell Windows that you want to load the icon from an application that is in memory somewhere. I don't want to do that, so I just set that parameter to NULL. The second parameter is a string describing what the icon is called. I just want the standard icon, which looks somewhat like a little window, so I specify IDI_APPLICATION.

If you're thinking, "Hey, wait a minute. IDI_APPLICATION doesn't look like any string I've ever seen," then you're kind of right. If you hunt through the file windows.h like I have just done, you'll find it's a macro that converts a resource number into a string. Just smile and nod; it's a Windows thing. I told you this place was crazy!

Now you can load some other slightly more interesting stock icons with this function as well. Table 6.3 shows these other premade icons.

Table 6.3   Standard Icons

Flag	Example	Meaning
IDI_APPLICATION		Default application icon—usually a small window
IDI_ASTERISK | IDI_INFORMATION		Asterisk icon
IDI_ERROR | IDI_HAND		Error icon
IDI_EXCLAMATION | IDI_WARNING		Exclamation point icon
IDI_QUESTION		Question mark icon
IDI_WINLOGO		Windows logo icon

```
// A handle to a smaller version of the apps icon
wc.hIconSm                    = LoadIcon( NULL, IDI_APPLICATION );
```

This is very similar to the last entry except that it is used to specify a smaller version of the icon that is to be associated with this window class. This is not particularly bothersome, so just set it to the default IDI_APPLICATION again. Windows will automatically find the smaller version in the icon chain.

```
// A handle to the cursor to use while the mouse is over our window
wc.hCursor                    = LoadCursor( NULL, IDC_ARROW );
```

This field sets the mouse cursor. When you set the cursor, you tell Windows what you would like the mouse cursor to look like while the mouse cursor is over your window. As with most Windows applications, you will just want the regular white arrow cursor; this is specified by the IDC_ARROW value.

You can of course pick from any of the other arrows that Windows supports. If you pick an alternate cursor Windows will automatically change the picture to the one that you specified as soon as you move the mouse over your application window. It will also automatically restore the cursor to whatever it was as soon as the mouse leaves the client area of your application. The rest of the cursors are shown in Table 6.4.

Table 6.4 Standard Windows Cursors

Flag	Example	Description
IDC_APPSTARTING	▨	Standard arrow and small hourglass
IDC_ARROW\	▨	Standard arrow
IDC_CROSS	+	Crosshair
IDC_HELP	▨?	Arrow and question mark
IDC_IBEAM	I	I-beam
IDC_NO	⊘	Slashed circle
IDC_SIZEALL	✛	Four-pointed arrow pointing north, south, east, and west
IDC_SIZENESW	↗	Double-pointed arrow pointing northeast and southwest

Table 6.4   Standard Windows Cursors (continued)

Flag	Example	Description
IDC_SIZENS	↕	Double-pointed arrow pointing north and south
IDC_SIZENWSE	↖	Double-pointed arrow pointing northwest and southeast
IDC_SIZEWE	↔	Double-pointed arrow pointing west and east
IDC_UPARROW	↑	Vertical arrow
IDC_WAIT	⧗	Hourglass

Now you need to tell Windows if you have a menu or not.

```
// A handle to the resource to use as our menu
wc.lpszMenuName      = NULL;
```

In this case I do not have a menu, so I just set the lpszMenuName entry to NULL. I'll show you how menus work in Chapter 7.

Remember the character array that I created to hold the name of the application? This is where it comes into use. We are now going to give Windows a name for the class. You can call it anything you want, but in this case I am calling it "First Windows App, Zen Style," the very same title as the window caption. In fact, you could call the class something different if you wanted to. I'm just too lazy to make two string variables.

```
// The human readable name for this class
wc.lpszClassName      = strAppName;
```

The reason you want to give the class a name is so that you can refer to it later and possibly change it if you want to. For instance, you could tell Windows that you no longer wanted the window to redraw when the horizontal size changes. The class name also allows you to create more than one window based on the same class. An example of this would be if you wanted to create a window that was exactly the same as the current window. You would not have to create a new class structure and fill it in again. Instead, you simply create a window and give it the name of the class that you created previously. Anyway, all this is kind of complex for now, but I'll run through any pertinent stuff again as it comes up.

Registering the Window Class

OK, excellent—you've filled out the window class structure. That's most of the battle over. The thing is that although I've been using the phrase "You need to tell Windows" a bunch of times, Windows doesn't even know that class structure exists yet. So how do you tell Windows about the structure? Well, the process is called *registering* the class, and the function to do it has the fitting name RegisterClassEx(). Here is its prototype:

```
WINUSERAPI ATOM WINAPI RegisterClassEx(CONST WNDCLASSEX *);
```

As you can see, it takes a pointer to a WNDCLASSEX structure as its only parameter. So all you have to do is give it the address of your wc structure and you're all set. That prototype looks kind of complex, but you know everything that's there except for ATOM, which is simply a cover for type unsigned short. What it means is that if the function fails, you can usually look up the error by calling the function GetLastError(). Generally, this function will never fail unless the host computer is exceptionally low on memory, in which case Windows would be about to crash anyway, so you don't need to worry about it. Here is the code that I used:

```
RegisterClass( &wc );
```

Creating the Window

Now that you have registered with Windows the class that describes how the window is going to look and feel, you can actually get down to the business of creating the window itself. This requires a single function call to CreateWindowEx(), which has a number of complicated-looking parameters. They are not *actually* complicated, but Microsoft thought it would be a good idea to make them look that way.

I now present to you the honorable CreateWindowEx() prototype in all its splendor:

```
HWND CreateWindowEx(
  DWORD dwExStyle,        // extended window style
  LPCTSTR lpClassName,    // pointer to registered class name
  LPCTSTR lpWindowName,   // pointer to window name
  DWORD dwStyle,          // window style
  int x,                  // horizontal position of window
  int y,                  // vertical position of window
```

```
    int nWidth,           // window width
    int nHeight,          // window height
    HWND hWndParent,      // handle to parent or owner window
    HMENU hMenu,          // handle to menu, or child-window identifier
    HINSTANCE hInstance,  // handle to application instance
    LPVOID lpParam        // pointer to window-creation data
);
```

Isn't it a beauty? I don't think so either. But I suppose that now might be a good time to explain what all those parameters mean. First let's look at how I filled in the function call in the application:

```
hWnd = CreateWindowEx( NULL,
                       strAppName,
                       strAppName,
                       WS_OVERLAPPEDWINDOW,
                       CW_USEDEFAULT, CW_USEDEFAULT,
                       512, 512,
                       NULL,
                       NULL,
                       hInstance,
                       NULL );
```

Now this is very important: Notice how this function returns a handle to a window. This is the handle to the new window that you are creating. You must keep this window handle around somewhere, usually in a global variable, because every time you want to modify the window, you need to use this variable. If the call fails, because the computer is out of memory or if the parameters are incorrect, then hWnd will be set to NULL. You may want to test for this eventuality in your own programs. I usually don't, simply because I have never in my life seen this function fail, but if you are having issues trying to get your window to display, then you may want to check this out.

- **dwExStyle**. You can use this parameter to specify any of the extended styles that Windows supports. The application doesn't have any extended styles, so I just set it to NULL, but Table 6.5 lists most of the values that you can set this to. You don't need to worry about them for now; this is for when you get more advanced and you want a good reference to come back to. I left out some of the flags because they are for dealing with foreign-language versions of Windows, like Arabic, which reads text right to left, and so they are obviously inconsequential to us. The WS_ stands for "Windows style," and the EX_ stands for "extended."

Table 6.5   Extended Window Styles

Flag	Meaning
WS_EX_ACCEPTFILES	The window will accept files that are dragged onto it.
WS_EX_APPWINDOW	Causes the top-level window to be forced onto the task bar when it is visible
WS_EX_CLIENTEDGE	The window will have a border with a sunken edge.
WS_EX_CONTEXTHELP	Causes a help button to appear in the title bar of the window
WS_EX_CONTROLPARENT	Allows the user to switch focus between child windows using the tab key
WS_EX_DLGMODALFRAME	The window will have a double border.
WS_EX_MDICHILD	Causes the window to have MDI (multiple document interface) properties
WS_EX_NOPARENTNOTIFY	The child window will not notify its parent about when it is created or destroyed with WM_PARENTNOTIFY messages.
WS_EX_OVERLAPPEDWINDOW	This flag is the same as combining WS_EX_CLIENTEDGE and WS_EX_WINDOWEDGE styles.
WS_EX_PALETTEWINDOW	Combines the WS_EX_WINDOWEDGE, WS_EX_TOOLWINDOW, and WS_EX_TOPMOST styles
WS_EX_STATICEDGE	Creates a 3D border
WS_EX_TOOLWINDOW	Creates a tool window that is usually used as a toolbar. The title bar is thinner and uses a smaller font.
WS_EX_TOPMOST	Causes the window to remain on top of other non-topmost windows even if the window is inactive
WS_EX_WINDOWEDGE	Causes the window to have a raised edge

- **lpClassName**. This parameter is again the string that holds the name of the class. I set it to the variable strAppName. It has got to be the same as the name you gave to the class, otherwise Windows won't know what to do with your window.

- **lpWindowName**. This parameter is also a pointer to a string, although in this case the string defines what the caption for the window will be. I set it to be the same as the class name, that is "First Windows App, Zen Style." You can set this to anything you want; it doesn't have to be same as the class.

- **dwStyle**. This parameter specifies the standard style settings for the window. I set it to WS_OVERLAPPEDWINDOW, which means that the window will have a thick border, a caption, and a system menu, along with minimize, maximize, and restore control boxes. You can also specify other styles using the entries in Table 6.6. Again, Table 6.6 is just for reference; you'll almost always want to use WS_OVERLAPPEDWINDOW.

Table 6.6   Standard Styles

Flag	Meaning
WS_BORDER	The window will have a thin, single line border.
WS_CAPTION	The window will have a title bar. This automatically includes the WS_BORDER style.
WS_CHILD	The window will be a child of another window. This cannot be used with WS_POPUP.
WS_CLIPCHILDREN	When creating the parent window, this flag causes areas occupied by the child windows to be excluded during drawing.
WS_DISABLED	The window is initially disabled when it is created.
WS_DLGFRAME	The window will have a border that is the same as for a dialog box. This style prevents you from having a title bar.
WS_GROUP	Specifies the first control in a group of controls, which continues until the next WS_GROUP flag is encountered.

Table 6.6 Standard Styles (continued)

Flag	Meaning
WS_HSCROLL	The window will have a horizontal scroll bar
WS_MAXIMIZE	The window will be maximized when it is initially created.
WS_MAXIMIZEBOX	The window will have a maximize button. This cannot be combined with WS_EX_CONTEXTHELP. WS_SYSMENU must also be specified
WS_MINIMIZE	The window will be minimized when it is initially created.
WS_MINIMIZEBOX	The window will have a minimize button. This cannot be combined with WS_EX_CONTEXTHELP. WS_SYSMENU must also be specified
WS_OVERLAPPED	The window will have a title bar and a border.
WS_OVERLAPPEDWINDOW	Creates an overlapped window with a title bar, a system menu, and minimize and maximize boxes
WS_POPUP	Causes the window to be a pop-up window. Use this for full screen Direct3D applications.
WS_POPUPWINDOW	Creates a pop-up window with a border and system menu
WS_SYSMENU	The window will have a window menu on its title bar.
WS_TABSTOP	Specifies that a control can be accessed via the user pressing the tab key.
WS_THICKFRAME	The window has a border that can be sized.
WS_VISIBLE	The window will be visible when it is changed
WS_VSCROLL	The window will have a vertical scroll bar.

- **x, y.** You can enter the position where you want the window's initial position to be, specified in screen coordinates, in this parameter. More on screen coordinates in Chapter 7. If you can't really be bothered to specify coordinates, or if you don't particularly care where the window initially appears on the screen, then you can just put in CW_USEDEFAULT. Actually, CW_USEDEFAULT isn't really a cop-out; it's generally a good idea to specify it. If you specify you want your window to start at coordinates (650, 450), what happens if the user's resolution is only 640 x 480? While your application would start near the center of a 1280 x 1024 screen, it would not even be visible with a resolution of 640 x 480. So I usually just let Windows figure out the screen coordinates and move on to the fun stuff.

- **nWidth, nHeight.** Whereas the x, y coordinates specify where your window begins, these coordinates specify where you want your window to end. Again, you can either specify a fixed value or let Windows do it for you with CW_USEDEFAULT. In the example I entered both a width and a height of 512.

- **hWndParent.** CreateWindowEx() is used for the creation of all types of windows, including child windows and control windows such as push buttons and check boxes. So if you were creating a child window, you would put in the parent window's handle here. I'm just making a normal window, so I entered NULL.

- **hMenu.** I haven't covered menus just yet—that will be in Chapter 7. However, were you to have a menu, you would enter its handle here. I don't, so I again just entered NULL. Darn, there are so many handles here you'd think Microsoft would be moving into the production of doors!

- **hInstance.** There is that instance handle rearing its ugly head again. This is where you tell Windows which application to associate with the new Window. I specified the instance handle that I got through the formal parameter, hInstance, from WinMain(). In other words, I am telling Windows that the new window belongs to *me*.

- **lpParam.** This entry is labeled "Advanced—just ignore" in just about every single book I have ever read about Windows programming. It used to annoy the heck out of me because I never knew what it did. Well, now that I am a Windows guru I can tell you, but work with me here because it involves some stuff that you haven't covered yet. And there is a reason that other authors label it "advanced." Because it is. You'll probably never even use it. I'm just telling you so your curious conscience will be able to sleep at night!

I'll just give you an overview of happens. When you call CreateWindowEx(), it first creates the window and then immediately sends the message WM_CREATE to the WndProc() function. When WndProc() returns, CreateWindowEx() returns and WinMain() continues. But the interesting thing is that you can pass information along with the WM_CREATE message as a parameter. All you have to do is include a pointer to any information you want in this lpParam parameter. Then, in WndProc() you can access that information by looking at the lpCreateParams member of the CREATESTRUCT passed as a pointer through the LPARAM.

Your eyes glazing over. Stick with me; you *will* get through this stuff. When you have completed the Windows section of this book, come back and read the paragraph above again. It will make much more sense. You just have to give the Microsoft nanobots time to work their way through your system. *Resistance is futile!*

And that is all there is to CreateWindowEx(). Simple, huh? What do you mean *no*? Well, give it time to sink in. You know, the great thing about Windows is that as soon as you get to the point when you think, "Ahh. Finally that part is over. Now everything will be much easier," you suddenly fall one ring further into the pit. It just gets deeper and deeper. And deeper. Until finally one glorious day you look up and go, "Ahh. I have finally mastered Windows." And as you're clawing your way out of the pit, gripping onto the edge, ready for that final lunge for the top, DirectX comes up and stomps on your fingers with an evil grin.

However, luckily for you, the rest of this chapter will be a breeze.

Displaying the Window

Now that the window has been created it just needs to be made visible and painted. So let's start with making it visible. There is a function called ShowWindow(), which does this. Here is its prototype:

```
BOOL ShowWindow(
  HWND hWnd,       // handle to window
  int nCmdShow     // show command for the window
);
```

The first parameter, hWnd, is the handle to the window of which you want to change the visibility status. In this case I want to make the window that I just created visible, so I need to enter the window handle that I received from the CreateWindowEx() call. Remember the one that I said should be saved in a global somewhere? Well this is where it comes into use.

Remember the iCmdShow formal parameter in the WinMain() header? Well, this is where it becomes useful. You can just pass the iCmdShow variable to this function, and the window will automatically display as Windows wanted it to. On the other hand, if you feel like retaining a bit of control and making your window always display *your* way, then you can enter any of the values in Table 5.1. For instance, if you wanted the program to start maximized, then you would enter SW_SHOWMAXIMIZED for the second parameter.

Here's the code:

```
// Display the window we just created
ShowWindow( hWnd, iCmdShow );
```

Now draw the window for the first time. This ensures that the window shows the information that we want it to display, rather than just a blank screen. Unfortunately in this case there is only a blank screen, but it is still useful to put forward the initial call. The function to do this is called UpdateWindow(). It has the following prototype:

```
BOOL UpdateWindow(
  HWND hWnd    // handle of window
);
```

As you can see, it just takes a single parameter: a handle to a window to update. This function works by sending a WM_PAINT message to WndProc(), which I will discuss shortly. Following is the code:

```
// Draw the window contents for the first time
UpdateWindow( hWnd );
```

The Message Loop

You're making excellent progress, and you'll be glad to hear that you have come to the last section of WinMain(): the message loop. I have already discussed how the message architecture of Windows works, but I'll just restate the main points. Now that you have come to implementation, it is important that you understand what you are doing. So, following are the conclusions reached in the previous chapter about messages:

- Windows communicates, or talks to, applications to tell them about updates to the system as well as notifications, like the mouse has moved or the window needs repainting.

- If a message is important, Windows will send it directly to your window procedure.
- Alternatively, if the message is not particularly important, the message is *posted* to the local message queue for your application. It is up to your application to retrieve that message and pass it on to the window procedure manually.
- There is a master system message queue and there is a local message queue that is unique to each application. The movement of messages between the master queue and the local queue is transparent, and you don't need to worry about it.

At this point you are going to program the logic that gets the messages from the queue that were posted. The messages then need to be massaged a little before you pass them on to WndProc() for further processing. Here is the code:

```
// Start the message loop
while( GetMessage( &msg, NULL, 0, 0 ) )
{
        // Convert virtual key messages into character messages
        TranslateMessage( &msg );

        // Send the message to WndProc(), the event handler
        DispatchMessage( &msg );
}
```

That's pretty simple, isn't it? The details follow.

GetMessage()

As discussed before, this is a loop. The first function is the Boolean test case for the while loop; it is called GetMessage(). Here is the prototype:

```
BOOL GetMessage(
  LPMSG lpMsg,              // address of structure with message
  HWND hWnd,               // handle of window
  UINT wMsgFilterMin,      // first message
  UINT wMsgFilterMax       // last message
);
```

This function deserves a bit of explanation. First off, how does it sustain the loop? Well, when the loop starts, GetMessage() is called. GetMessage() sits and waits until a message has arrived before it returns. That is, it is a *blocking function*. While it is waiting for a message, your application is just sitting there doing nothing, because GetMessage() has stalled it. This is not a problem, by the way; it is architectural. As soon as GetMessage() receives a message, it returns TRUE, which allows the loop to continue another iteration.

However, there is one message that GetMessage() will not return TRUE for. If the message is WM_QUIT, GetMessage() will return FALSE, which will cause the loop to fail, which in turn means that your application can safely exit.

So to summarize the last two paragraphs: When GetMessage() retrieves a message the loop iterates, the message is modified slightly and then forwarded to WndProc() for processing. Then the loop completes and GetMessage() is called again. If the message happens to be WM_QUIT, then the loop cancels and you can exit your application. That's fairly intuitive, isn't it? Just smile and nod—it will sink in over time; trust me.

Now for a quick look at the parameters. The first parameter is lpMsg, which accepts a pointer to a message structure. So what you do is pass it a pointer to a message structure, and GetMessage() will fill that structure with the message information that is waiting in the queue. As you can see, I passed the address of the message structure msg that I defined at the start of WinMain(). After the message has been copied into your container structure, it is removed from the queue, unless it is a WM_PAINT message, in which case it stays in the queue until it is processed by WndProc().

The second parameter is hWnd. If you specify NULL, then messages will be retrieved for every window associated with the calling thread. On the other hand, if you only want to retrieve messages for a particular window, then you can specify its handle here. I only have one window so I just set the handle to NULL.

The next two parameters, wMsgFilterMin and wMsgFilterMax, are for very advanced purposes that I'm not going to go into detail on. You can use these parameters to specify integers that define certain regions of messages that you want to exclude from being received. For instance, you could specify that you only wanted to receive mouse or keyboard messages.

TranslateMessage()

TranslateMessage() is kind of an uninteresting function. It is used to massage certain messages into a more appropriate form. It is basically used for keyboard messages—in particular, keyboard accelerator messages—and provides an easier way for your application to access keyboard data. You can pretty much just use the smile-and-nod routine with TranslateMessage(). In other words, you can ask anybody what it means and they'll say something like "Uhhmmm, something to do with virtual key messages and accelerators, uhhmmm, can I get you some coffee?" In fact until recently even the MSDN (Microsoft Developer Network) documentation was just a 20-page repetition of the word "Uhhh." These days it says, "The TranslateMessage() function translates virtual-key messages into character messages"; in other words, it is says what I said with the "Uhhmmms" removed!

Anyway, here is its prototype:

```
BOOL TranslateMessage( CONST MSG *lpMsg );
```

As you can see, it takes one parameter, a pointer to a MSG structure. For this application I entered the address of the MSG structure that contains the message retrieved with the GetMessage() call earlier on.

DispatchMessage()

DispatchMessage() is the business. This is the function that passes the message retrieved from the local message queue and then passes it on so that it can finally be processed by WndProc(). Here is the prototype:

```
LONG DispatchMessage( CONST MSG *lpmsg );
```

As you can see, it is pretty similar to TranslateMessage(). Again, it takes a single parameter: a pointer to a MSG structure. I specified the structure that I have been using all along, that is, the msg variable.

And that is the message loop. There is only one more line! You just need to see how to exit the application.

The Return Value Returns!

I know, what a cheesy heading. The only reason I used it was because I discussed the return value a little bit in the last chapter, but here I can give you a few more details on it.

I'll show you the code and then give some explanation:

```
// Return control to windows with the exit code
return msg.wParam;
```

This is the code that gets executed if a WM_QUIT message is received from the local message queue. When a WM_QUIT message is received, the WPARAM parameter is set to the exit code that was requested. Hang on a second: I see a circular explanation developing. Let me digress for a minute.

To exit your application, a WM_QUIT message must be transmitted to your application from Windows; but how does it get there in the first place? To exit your application you must call the function PostQuitMessage(). This function takes a single integer parameter, which is the exit code. This can be any number, but you can use it to specify all sorts of stuff. For instance, you could exit with code 100 if there was a fatal error, or 20 if everything was all right. The selection is completely arbitrary and up to you, but by keeping to some sort of system, the exit code can help you figure out how the application is doing during debugging.

Now the next thing that needs a little more explanation is the little output window in Visual C++. When you debug-execute and then exit your program, the value with which the program returns is displayed, like this:

```
The thread 0xFF045B61 has exited with code 35.
```

That "code 35" bit is the return code from your Windows application.

So now you just need to figure out how to return the exit code. It's pretty simple— just return the WPARAM of the WM_QUIT message that is held in the msg variable, as I did in the code above. Cool, huh?

And that is WinMain() in its entirety. The only thing I need to discuss now is the message handler, commonly known as WndProc(). Let's take a look at that now.

A Stroll through WndProc()

WndProc() is the function that really sets the architecture of your applications as different as compared to regular DOS or console applications. It is the guts of the event-driven model that I talked about earlier. To get it fresh in your mind, I'll just cover the points reached before about the WndProc() function:

- WndProc() is responsible for processing the messages that come from Windows.
- The messages may be either sent directly from Windows or posted to a message queue, in which case the message loop retrieves them and then passes them on to WndProc() using the DispatchMessage() function.
- If your application does not want to process the message that it receives from Windows, it can pass the message back, using the DefWindowProc() function, and Windows will perform the default behavior for that message.
- On the other hand, if WndProc() does want to process the message, it does so and then returns 0 back to Windows to indicate success.

- In the case that you want to halt Windows from doing other processing with the message you can return TRUE from the function. This is kind of complex but I talk about it more in later chapters.

OK, enough theory; let's look at the code. First off is the function prototype, which again looks like it fell off the top of the ugly tree and hit every branch on the way down!

```
long CALLBACK WndProc( HWND hWnd,                    // Window handle
                       UINT uMessage, // The Message
                       WPARAM wParam, // The first parameter
                       LPARAM lParam );     // The second parameter
```

I'll run through those parameters so you know what they are.

- hWnd. You have probably spotted that this is a window handle. The reason the window procedure needs a window handle is because most of the messages that you receive will be associated with a window. For instance, you will only receive mouse movement messages if the mouse is over the client area of your application's window.

  Every time WndProc is called this parameter will be filled with the handle for the window that is responsible for the message. This is good because of the possibility that you may have a window procedure looking after more than one window. By looking at the hWnd you can differentiate between multiple windows.

- uMessage. This parameter actually holds the message that Windows is sending. It can be equal to any of the hundreds of predefined messages that Windows supports. Examples include WM_MOUSEMOVE for mouse movement or WM_KEYDOWN if a key has been pressed.

- wParam and lParam. These are the two variables that hold the parameters for the message. Their contents can be different for each message. For instance, for the WM_SIZE message, which indicates a window is changing its size, the parameters would contain the new size information. Because there are millions of messages and the parameters can change for each one, it would be impossible for me to tell you what they mean ahead of time. I will show you many examples, but if you find yourself in a situation where you are dealing with a message that you haven't come across before, then it would be a good idea to look it up in the MSDN Help files. If you have a question—trust me— MSDN will answer it.

So what exactly do you do in WndProc()? Well, I'll start by defining two variables that you are going to need:

```
PAINTSTRUCT PaintStruct;        // Structure used during windows painting
HDC hDC;                        // Handle to device context for painting
```

These two variables are used when you are repainting your window. The PAINTSTRUCT is a structure that contains information about the client area of your applications window. Let's take a look at this puppy so that you know what it does. Here is its definition:

```
typedef struct tagPAINTSTRUCT {
    HDC    hdc;                 // Handle to the device context
    BOOL fErase;                    // Flag for background erasure
    RECT rcPaint;               // Update rectangle
    BOOL fRestore;              // Internal stuff. Just ignore
    BOOL fIncUpdate;            // Internal stuff.  Ignore
    BYTE rgbReserved[32];       // Internal stuff.  Ignore
} PAINTSTRUCT;
```

The parameters are as follows:

- **hdc.** This is a handle to a device context. As I said previously, I'm not going to cover Windows graphics until the next chapter, but for now you can know that a device context is used for drawing, like a painter's palette.

- **fErase.** This flag toggles on or off the erasure of the background. If this flag is set to TRUE, then whenever an area is marked as invalid Windows will erase it with the background color for the window *before* calling your drawing code. Alternatively, if the flag is set to FALSE, then the background will not be erased and it is up to your code to keep the window looking presentable.

- **rcPaint.** This variable contains the rectangle that bounds the area of your window that needs to be repainted. If you have not seen the RECT type before, then now would be a good time to look at it.

```
typedef struct _RECT {
    LONG left;          // The left coordinate for the rectangle ( x1 )
    LONG top; // The top coordinate for the rectangle ( y1 )
    LONG right;         // The right coordinate for the rectangle ( x2 )
    LONG bottom;        // The bottom coordinate for the rectangle ( y2 )
} RECT;
```

As you can see, it is a fairly simple structure with four elements to hold the dimensions for a rectangle. I have put the equivalents in parentheses for those of you who are used to using rectangle structures with x, y coodinates.

The Switch

Now you come to the part of figuring out what message Windows is sending. It is not as complicated as it sounds; all you do is switch the uMessage formal parameter. Here's the code:

```
// Switch the windows message to figure out what it is
switch( uMessage )
{
```

Then all you have to do is case through all the messages that you want to process. In this case you just want to do the minimum amount. Actually, the minimum is to process just one message, but you are going to do three so that you have a better idea of what's going on. Here's the code:

```
case WM_CREATE: // The CreateWindow() function was just called in WinMain()
        {
                // One Time Initialization
                return 0;
        }

        case WM_PAINT:          // The window needs to be redrawn
        {
                // Tell windows we want to start updating the window
                hDC = BeginPaint( hWnd, &PaintStruct );

                // Do any drawing with the GDI here

                // Tell windows we have finished updating the window
                EndPaint( hWnd, &PaintStruct );
                return 0;
        }

        case WM_DESTROY:        // The window is about to be closed
        {
                // Our main window is closing.
                // This means we want our app to exit.
                // Tell windows to put a WM_QUIT message in our message queue
                PostQuitMessage( 0 );
                return 0;
        }
```

```
        default:                         // Some other message
        {
                // Let windows handle this message
                return DefWindowProc( hWnd, uMessage, wParam, lParam );
        }
}
}
```

Let's take each message one at a time and see what is going on.

WM_CREATE

This message is called immediately after you call the `CreateWindow()` function in `WinMain()`. Remember, this is where you got the handle to your new window. This message allows you to do any one-time initialization that you may want to do. For instance, you could allocate memory or load a file into memory. You don't really have anything to do, so I just returned 0 so that Windows knows that the message has been processed successfully.

WM_PAINT

This message is sent whenever a section of the window needs to be repainted. To *repaint* a window means to redraw an area that is no longer valid. A window can become invalid for a number of reasons, for example, if the user drags another application on top of your window and then drags it back again. Windows does not save what your window looked like, it just tells you the area that needs redrawing. Other examples include a screen resolution change or your own application sending itself a message to redraw an area.

So what is going on inside the `WM_PAINT` message? The first thing to do is to get a handle to a device context. As I've mentioned before, the device context (DC) allows you to draw to your window. Without a DC you can't do very much at all. Now there are 10 million ways to get a DC, but in this case you are going to acquire it by calling a function named `BeginPaint()`. Here is its prototype:

```
HDC BeginPaint( HWND hwnd, LPPAINTSTRUCT lpPaint );
```

As you can see, it returns a handle to a device context. The first parameter, `hwnd`, is a handle to the window for which you want to retrieve a device context. The second parameter, `lpPaint`, is a pointer to a `PAINTSTRUCT` structure. For my code I passed the handle to the window that was given in the `WndProc()` formal parameter, and the address of the `PaintStruct` variable that I declared at the start of the function. `lpPaint` does not need to be filled with anything; instead, this function will fill in the structure itself.

After calling `BeginPaint()`, you can do any drawing that you want. You will find out shortly that every drawing function requires a handle to a device context. You are not doing any drawing yet, so the next thing to do is to tell Windows that you have finished updating the window by calling the function EndPaint().

```
BOOL EndPaint( HWND hWnd, CONST PAINTSTRUCT *lpPaint );
```

As you can see, EndPaint() takes the same parameters as the BeginPaint() function. The first parameter takes a handle for a window that is finished drawing. The second parameter takes a pointer to the `PaintStruct` variable that you passed to `BeginPaint()`. After you call `EndPaint()`, the handle to the device context is no longer valid and any drawing functions you call will fail.

Now that you have finished with the message, it is important that you return 0 to Windows so that it knows you have successfully processed the message. This is particularly important for the `WM_PAINT` message because it will not be removed from the queue until it has been processed. So if you never process it, the message queue can become overrun with `WM_PAINT`, and processing will pretty much grind to a halt. So do like van Gogh and paint until your ears bleed! Or something like that. In other words, process the `WM_PAINT` message and call `BeginPaint()`, `EndPaint()`, and then return 0.

WM_DESTROY

This message is sent to your application whenever Windows or the user specifies that it would like your window to close—for example, if the user pressed the little close button or selected Close from the system menu. If Windows is shutting down, it will also ask your window to close.

Normally when the window is closing, you want your application to exit. Look at that last sentence carefully. Your application is *not* the window. The window is just a construct that your application requested Windows to create. Your application can survive quite happily without a window.

`WM_DESTROY` simply means that the window is about to be closed and you should do any processing that you need to do, such as deallocating any resources that were associated with the window. However, in this case, since this is the main window, you want to actually exit your application when the main window is closed. So what you do is this: Whenever you detect a `WM_DESTROY` message, you then tell Windows to generate a `WM_QUIT` message, which your message loop will subsequently detect and therefore you can safely quit. But how do you generate a `WM_QUIT` message? Well, there is a function to do it, called `PostQuitMessage()`.

```
VOID PostQuitMessage( int nExitCode );
```

`PostQuitMessage()` takes a single parameter, an exit code. Remember when I kept nattering on about the return code? This is where you can specify an exit code. Call this function with any code you want, and your application will exit with the return code set to the exit code. Cool, huh?

Don't forget that you are merely telling Windows to *post* a WM_QUIT message to the queue. Your application will not exit immediately after calling `PostQuitMessage()`. That means that you still need to return 0 to Windows so that it knows the message was processed successfully.

Letting Windows Take Care of It

I've mentioned this a bunch of times already, but here it goes again: you only have to process the messages that you want. The rest you can pass back to Windows, and it will process them itself using the default behavior. You pass messages back by sticking the `default` keyword into your `switch` statement to catch any messages that were not caught by `case` statements. Then you take these messages and send them to Windows using the `DefWindowProc()` function, which incidentally stands for *default window procedure*.

```
LRESULT DefWindowProc(
    HWND hWnd,        // handle to window
    UINT Msg,         // message identifier
    WPARAM wParam,    // first message parameter
    LPARAM lParam     // second message parameter
);
```

As you can see, it takes the exact same parameters as your `WndProc()` function, and you can pass the parameters straight on verbatim. Notice in the code that I am returning from `WndProc()` with the return value from `DefWindowProc()`. This allows Windows to know that it processed the messages itself correctly. Don't ask me; I only work here!

And that, ladies and jellybeans, is the `WndProc()` function. If you want to process any other messages, then you just have to stick in extra `case` statements into the `switch` statement.

So what do you think? Would you like to see the whole shebang? I thought so.
Here goes:

```cpp
///////////////////////////////////////////////////////////////////////////////
//////////////
// Title: First Windows Application
// Author: Peter Walsh
// Notes: This code can be used as a base for any windows program

#define WIN32_LEAN_AND_MEAN

// The main windows include file
#include <windows.h>

// The window procedure to handle events
long CALLBACK WndProc( HWND hWnd, UINT uMessage,
                                        WPARAM wParam, LPARAM lParam )
{
        PAINTSTRUCT PaintStruct;        // Structure used during windows painting
        HDC hDC;                        // Handle to device context for painting

        // Switch the windows message to figure out what it is
        switch( uMessage )
        {
                case WM_CREATE:// The CreateWindow() function was just called
                {
                        // One Time Initialization
                        return 0;
                }

                case WM_PAINT: // The window needs to be redrawn
                {
                        // Tell windows we want to start updating the window
                        hDC = BeginPaint( hWnd, &PaintStruct );

                        // Do any drawing with the GDI here

                        // Tell windows we have finished updating the window
                        EndPaint( hWnd, &PaintStruct );
                        return 0;
                }
```

```cpp
        case WM_DESTROY:        // The window is about to be closed
        {
                // Our main window is closing.
                // This means we want our app to exit.

                // Tell windows to put a
                // WM_QUIT message in our message queue
                PostQuitMessage( 0 );
                return 0;
        }

        default:                            // Some other message
        {
                // Let windows handle this message
                return DefWindowProc( hWnd, uMessage, wParam, lParam );
        }
    }
}

// The windows entry point. The application will start executing here
int WINAPI WinMain( HINSTANCE hInstance, HINSTANCE hPrevInstance,
                                        PSTR pstrCmdLine, int iCmdShow )
{
    HWND hWnd;              // The handle to our main window
    MSG msg;               // The message windows is sending us
    WNDCLASSEX wc; // The window class used to create our window

    // The name of our class and also the title to our window
    static char strAppName[] = "First Windows App, Zen Style";

    // Fill in the window class with the attributes for our main window

    // The size of this structure in bytes
    wc.cbSize                   = sizeof( WNDCLASSEX );

    //   The style of the window.
    wc.style                    = CS_HREDRAW | CS_VREDRAW | CS_OWNDC;
    // Useless information.  Just set to zero.
    wc.cbClsExtra               = 0;
    // Useless information.  Just set to zero.
    wc.cbWndExtra               = 0;
```

```c
// The name of our event handler
wc.lpfnWndProc          = WndProc;
// A handle to the applications instance
wc.hInstance            = hInstance;
// The handle to the brush to use for the window background
wc.hbrBackground        = (HBRUSH)GetStockObject( DKGRAY_BRUSH );
// A handle to the icon to use for the window
wc.hIcon                = LoadIcon( NULL, IDI_APPLICATION );
// A handle to a smaller version of the apps icon
wc.hIconSm              = LoadIcon( NULL, IDI_HAND );
// A handle to the cursor to use while the mouse is over our window
wc.hCursor              = LoadCursor( NULL, IDC_CROSS );
// A handle to the resource to use as our menu
wc.lpszMenuName         = NULL;
// The human readable name for this class
wc.lpszClassName        = strAppName;

// Register the class with windows
RegisterClassEx( &wc );

// Create the window based on the previous class
hWnd = CreateWindowEx( NULL,                // Advanced style settings
                    strAppName,             // The name of the class
                    strAppName,             // The window caption
                    WS_OVERLAPPEDWINDOW,    // The window style
                    CW_USEDEFAULT,          // The initial x position
                    CW_USEDEFAULT,          // The initial y position
                    512, 512,               // The initial width / height
                    NULL,                   // Handle to parent window
                    NULL,                   // Handle to the menu
                    hInstance,              // Handle to the apps instance
                    NULL );         // Advanced context

// Display the window we just created
ShowWindow( hWnd, iCmdShow );
// Draw the window contents for the first time
UpdateWindow( hWnd );
```

```
// Start the message loop
    while( GetMessage( &msg, NULL, 0, 0 ) )
    {
        // Modify key messages
        TranslateMessage( &msg );
        // Send the message to WndProc() the event handler
        DispatchMessage( &msg );
    }

    // Return control to windows with the exit code
    return msg.wParam;
}
```

And the results? Have a look at Figure 6.1.

Figure 6.1

Your first Windows application

Pretty cool, huh? Go ahead—take her out for a spin! Check out the resizing and redrawing capabilities, the working Minimize, Maximize, and Restore buttons. And that system menu! What a beauty!

Turning an Application into a Game

Now, there is one teensy-weensy problem that I neglected to mention before. The code I just showed you is no good for a game. Well, it's not actually that bad, but let's run over a few structural issues. Remember when I was talking about the message loop, and GetMessage() in particular? I was saying that GetMessage() was a blocking function and that if no messages were available, then your program sat there doing nothing. Well, this is fine for normal Windows applications. If there are no messages, then the operating system isn't doing anything and neither is the user, so there is no reason to do anything else except loaf.

The issue here is that in games you need every single available processor cycle; you can't afford to sit around waiting for the user to do something. Even if the user is doing nothing, you still need to be able to render the screen, play sounds, and so on.

So how do you get around this issue? Well, it will require some slight modification to the message loop. What I'll do is show you the new code and then run through it:

```
// Start the message loop
while( TRUE )
{
        // Check if a message is waiting for processing
        if( PeekMessage( &msg, NULL, 0, 0, PM_REMOVE ) )
        {
                // Check if the message is to quit the application
                if( msg.message == WM_QUIT )
                        // Exit the message loop
                        break;

                // Change the format of certain messages
                TranslateMessage( &msg );
                // Pass the message to WndProc() for processing
                DispatchMessage( &msg );
        }
        else
        {
                // Put any idle code here

        }
}
```

Interesting, huh? Overall it still looks similar, but there are some important changes. You'll notice that instead of putting GetMessage() as the test case for the while loop, I have created an infinite loop. The reasons will become clear in a second. Now as soon as the loop starts, call the function PeekMessage().

```
BOOL PeekMessage(
    LPMSG lpMsg,         // pointer to structure for message
    HWND hWnd,           // handle to window
    UINT wMsgFilterMin,  // first message
    UINT wMsgFilterMax,  // last message
    UINT wRemoveMsg      // removal flags
);
```

Basically it takes the same parameters as GetMessage() except for the last parameter, wRemoveMsg. Let's look at the architectural differences first. PeekMessage() does not stall the machine while getting a message. Instead, it looks in the queue and returns immediately with TRUE if there is a message and FALSE otherwise. wRemoveMsg can be set to PM_REMOVE if you want PeekMessage() to remove the message from the queue if it finds one. This is generally what you will want to do.

You can see that if a message is not found the code moves into the else block of code. This is the place where most of your game code will be originally executed, but I'll cover that later. On the other hand, if a message is found, the message is first tested to see if it is WM_QUIT, in which case the application will exit. If it is a normal message, it is processed as before by TranslateMessage() before being transported to WndProc() by DispatchMessage().

So the thing to look out for is that the loop no longer stalls if a message is not available; instead, the normal game loop is executed. This is exactly what I was trying to achieve, so the game loop is now 100 percent game compatible. Phew! I was worried there for a minute!

Conclusion

Pretty cool, huh? Well, not really. You can't quite do much with the window yet except for the standard stuff that I talked about earlier. Don't fret though. In the next chapter I'm going to cover all sorts of fun stuff, like how to draw to your window, how to implement menus, implementing advanced features for mouse and keyboard input, as well as a bunch of other stuff that will help you make really great (read: *profitable*) software.

If you're feeling a bit shaky about Windows, then don't worry—as I said it will take a while for all these new concepts to make sense. Now would be a really good time to try to write your own Windows application from scratch. Try changing the window background color, the window caption text, and any other stuff. By messing around you will see how everything fits together. Don't worry about the details like trying to remember formal parameters and stuff like that. Just get an understanding of the overall structure and how everything relates to everything else.

Now for the fun stuff...

CHAPTER 7

GETTING
JIGGY WITH
WINDOWS

This is really groovy—you now know how to create a Windows application that has all the basic functionality you could wish for. Now you need to journey deeper into the Windows labyrinth. In this chapter I am going to cover a whole bunch of cool stuff that will allow you to create your first graphical Windows application.

Remember I was talking about Windows being grouped into sections? Now that you have mastered the basics you can move on to the next part of Windows: graphical output! Graphics in Windows are handled by what is called the *Graphical Device Interface*, or GDI. By the end of this chapter you will have a solid understanding of the crazy world of the GDI. In particular, this chapter will cover

- using the GDI to output cool stuff to the screen like points, lines, rectangles, ellipses, text, and detailed bitmaps.
- the architecture of the Windows GDI including pens, brushes, raster operations, and default color selection.
- using internal and external resources like bitmaps and menus.
- accessing the keyboard and mouse using Windows *and* how to write your own asynchronous input handler.

Let's start by looking at our soon-to-be very good friend: the device context.

The Device Context

I touched on the device context, or DC, a little bit in the last chapter, but I kind of skimmed over it so you wouldn't get too distracted from the main focus. The DC is a big topic so let's start with a metaphor. The DC is similar to the canvas an artist would use when painting a picture. For instance, you can use pens to draw lines and brushes to fill larger areas with a color or pattern. The DC also has hundreds of functions—such as line and square functions, for example—to help you draw to the screen.

Although the DC is like a canvas, there are some differences. The biggest is that you don't always have the DC. Generally, Windows has a finite number of DCs that it shuffles around between each application whenever it wants to draw. So if you want to draw a line, you first tell Windows what you want to do, then it gives you a handle to a device context, and finally you draw whatever you want. When you are finished drawing you tell Windows that you are finished and hand the DC back to it. After you return the DC the handle is no longer valid and you cannot use it anymore.

I want to discuss a few little gotchas about the GDI in general before I move on. The biggest issue with the GDI is that it is very slow. When you want to do proper graphics, use DirectDraw. So why am I even teaching the GDI? Well, because it is also really useful. For instance, in DirectDraw there is absolutely no support for drawing shapes like circles or squares. You have to write all that nasty complex code yourself. So when you are in development you don't want to spend ages developing circle-drawing code; you just want a circle to be drawn. Luckily for us, the GDI works with DirectDraw almost exactly like it works with the rest of Windows. What this means is that the GDI is really useful, pretty easy, and slower than an Apple.

Let's get back to business. Now the thing to discuss is exactly *when* you want to draw to the screen. You will almost always only want to draw after you receive a WM_PAINT message from Windows. WM_PAINT will tell you what part of the screen needs to be updated so that you don't waste time redrawing the entire screen. There are other times that you may want to redraw portions of screen, such as during mouse movement code; however, WM_PAINT is where everything else goes.

All this theory is making my brain turn to jelly, so let's look at some code.

Obtaining the Device Context

I covered this in the last chapter, but let's just run over it again quickly. You used the function BeginPaint() to return a handle to a device context. Some background information for you: BeginPaint() works by first sending a WM_ERASEBKGND to WndProc(), which erases the area that needs updating with the background color specified in the window class. After that it returns with the DC's handle. Here's the code:

```
case WM_PAINT:
{
        // Tell Windows we want to start updating the window
        hDC = BeginPaint( hWnd, &PaintStruct );

// Do any drawing with the GDI here
```

```
                // Tell Windows we have finished updating the window
                EndPaint( hWnd, &PaintStruct );

        return 0;
        }
```

So BeginPaint() takes a handle to the window that you want to draw to and also the
address of a PAINTSTRUCT structure to hold information about the window as parameters. The PAINTSTRUCT parameter structure does not have to be initialized with anything. After that, move in to update the window using the GDI. I'll cover that in a
minute. And then when you are finished, tell Windows with a call to EndPaint().
EndPaint() again takes the same parameters as BeginPaint(). Finally, return 0 to tell
Windows that you have successfully processed the message.

The Color of Light

Direct light is made up of differing intensities of three colors: red, green, and blue.
No, the primary colors are not red, blue, and yellow. You can tell your art teacher
to go take a hike. Those colors are for reflected light, and have to do with the
amount of light that is absorbed by the reflecting surface. Anyway, by varying the
intensities of red, green, and blue, you can make any color you want.

The more colors you want to define, the more detail you need to put into the
descriptions for the intensities of the red, green, and blue (RGB) components of
the original color. Let's look at some common ways of describing the RGB components.

Originally, there was almost no RGB at all. The monitor was black and white, or
more usually black and green (don't ask me). The individual pixels on the monitor
could only be on or off, so only one bit of information was needed per pixel. This
was great because it really was really low on memory overhead. The only problem
was that it was designed for humans, and most of us humans like color.

The next step up was 2-bit color, which gave an impressive four different colors or
four shades of the same color that could be used. Again, not very good unless you
happened to be a sea slug. The next progression was 4-bit color. With four bits you
can define 16 colors. That's kind of in the right direction—simple games could be
designed—but still not even nearly good enough for displaying images like photo-
graphs.

The real breakthrough was with 8-bit color. If you do the mathematics you'll see
that this should allow 256 colors. However, using a bit of wizardry you could

actually display a few hundred thousand colors. It works like this: instead of each of the 256 entries being assigned a specific color, it would be set to an index. In other words, although you could only have 256 different colors at a time on the screen, you could choose from a much larger palette. This led to much more realistic renderings for games, as well as other applications. However, all this meddling with color palettes and indexes got to be a pain after a while, and game designers and players wanted more.

TIP

You can work out the possible colors from a bit value very easily. The equation is

$$2^{\text{Number Of Bits}}$$

In other words, pick up a calculator, press 2, then press the y^x button, then type in the number of bits, and finally press the equals button. Cool, huh? For example:

$2^8 = 256$ $2^4 = 16$ $2^{24} = 16,777,216$

16-bit color was the answer to the problem. This allows up to around 65,536 possible colors to be displayed simultaneously. 16-bit color has a few problems. Sure, 16 divides by 8 evenly, but by 3? Nope. You think 3 colors, maybe 15 bits, or 5 bits for each color. Nah. That would make sense. Instead, we have 16 bits: 5 for red, 5 for blue, and usually 6 for green. Why the extra green bit? Well, because it turns out that humans can see green more clearly than any other color. Must be because our ancestors used to wander around in the forest too much instead of doing what they should have: picking up chicks in bars.

By the time people came around to realizing that there was more to the world than a mere 16 bits, 24-bit color was starting to make an impact. 24-bit color provides a full 8 bits per color component. In other words, it adds up to total of 16,777,216 possible color combinations, which is approaching the limits of the human eye's ability to perceive the differences in color. Now you may have heard about 32-bit color. This is basically the same as 24-bit color except that the extra 8 bits are wasted. In games the extra 8 bits can be used for extra information such as transparency, in which case it is known as the alpha channel. If all 32 bits were used, then they would add up to 4,294,967,296 possible colors, which is way more than any human eye could perceive.

8-bit (8 bits per pixel) format is used most often. So if you were drawing a line and you set red, green, and blue to 255, the color would be white. If all were set to zero, then the color would be black. If red were set to 255 and the rest zero, then the color would be red. If red and blue were set to 255 and green was zero, then the color would be purple. If all were set to 125, the color would be a medium gray.

I'll return to all this stuff a little later on. For now it's just theory, so keep it in mind but don't worry about it too much.

Windows Coordinates

Windows uses a slightly inverted Cartesian system as default. In English that means that horizontal, or x-coordinate, measurements are as you would expect. That is, they start at the origin, which is the left side of the screen, and increase to the right to infinity. Vertical, or y-coordinate, measurements, on the other hand, start at the top of your screen and increase downward to infinity.

Have a look at Figure 7.1. On the left you can see a normal Cartesian coordinate system. X increases to the right of the origin and decreases to the left. And the y-coordinate increases above the origin and decreases if you move below the origin. Look at the other graph in the figure. It shows how the coordinate systems work in Windows. As you can see, the y-axis is inverted. The reason for this is because it is more in tune with what the actual electron gun is doing in the monitor.

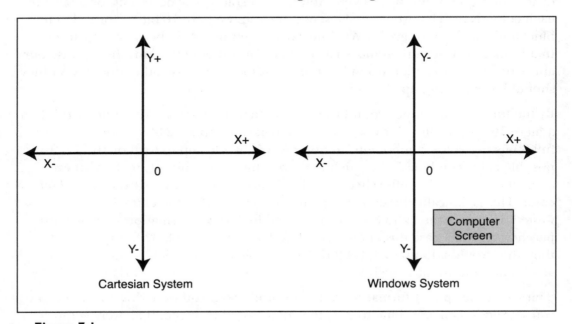

Figure 7.1

Coordinate systems

Code Blue! Calling Dr. da Vinci

Now the good stuff. Let's look at the guts of the GDI that allow you to draw to the screen. You can tell theory to go take a flying leap because this is war! Anyway, let's start with the simplest type of graphical object: the point. A *point* is made up of two coordinates: an x-coordinate, which specifies how far horizontally it is from the origin, and a y-coordinate, which specifies how far away it is from the origin in the vertical direction. I will be specifying points like everybody else does: two numbers separated by a comma, within parentheses. The x-coordinate is *always* written before the y-coordinate. For example, a point that is 10 units up and 15 units across looks like this: (15, 10). Check out Figure 7.2 for some more examples.

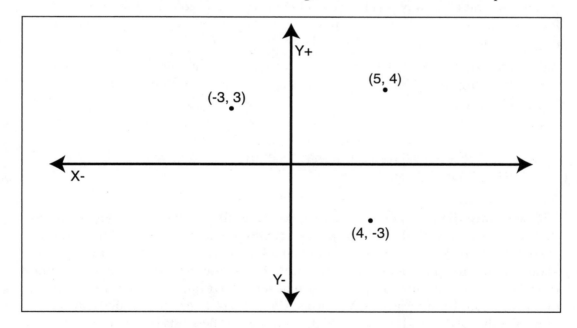

Figure 7.2

Points on a Cartesian system

By the way, Windows comes with a groovy premade structure for holding points that you should probably be aware of. It looks like this:

```
typedef struct tagPOINT {
    LONG x;               // The x-coordinate
    LONG y;               // The y-coordinate
}POINT;
```

This structure is needed for a lot of drawing functions, so stick it in an active-synapse quadrant of your brain.

Points

OK, now let's look at how Windows does it. There is a function called SetPixel() that allows you to set any pixel in your client area to any color you want. By the way, for this discussion I'm going to assume that you are within the WM_PAINT handler of WndProc() and BeginPaint() has already been called. Cool? Cool.

Aaiight. So you have called BeginPaint() and you have a handle to the device context. Next thing you need to do is call SetPixel(). It looks a little like this:

```
COLORREF SetPixel(
   HDC hdc,             // handle to device context
   int X,               // x-coordinate of pixel
   int Y,               // y-coordinate of pixel
   COLORREF crColor     // pixel color
);
```

Let's start with the parameters. The first, hdc, takes the handle to the device context that you retrieved with the call to BeginPaint(). Remember when I said that almost every call you make to the GDI would need a handle to the DC? Well, it will almost always be the first parameter to the function. By the way, when I say, "make a call to the GDI," there is nothing in particular that sets a GDI function apart from any other function. In other words, Windows API calls are logically grouped into sections like the GDI, etc., but in reality they are just endless lists of functions contained somewhere in Windows.h.

The next couple of parameters take the coordinates of the pixel that you want to change. It's very intuitive: if you want to change the pixel at the location (10, 43), then you pass 10 for the x parameter and 43 for the y parameter.

The last parameter takes the color that you want to set the color to. For this and all other color parameters in Windows, you pass a color that is specified as a 32-bit value. They are grouped together into a COLORREF value, which between you and me means "color reference" and is a 32-bit integer. However, you luckily don't have to do any crazy bit-alignment vectors or anything to get your color into the COLORREF format. Instead, all you do is call the macro RGB(). I'll cover this macro in a second.

The return value from SetPixel() is kind of interesting. Because you set the color using a 32-bit color value, you never know if the color you requested is available. If the case arises that the color you request is not available, then Windows will set the color to the closest color available. The return value contains the color that Windows used to set the color of the pixel.

The RGB() macro is used to change three 8-bit color specifiers into a single 32-bit COLORREF value. It takes three parameters: a red, green, and blue value, in that order. Color values are *always* written with red first, green second, and then blue last. Anyway, here is an entire call to SetPixel() that will set the pixel that is 10 pixels away from the left of the window, and 43 pixels down from the top of the window, to a bright red color.

```
SetPixel( hDC, 10, 43, RGB( 255, 0, 0 ) );
```

Pretty cool, huh? If you want to change the location, just change the coordinate values. And to change the color, just change the values in the RGB() macro. Have a look at Figure 7.3. That's a zoomed-in version.

Figure 7.3

Pixel plotting

By the way, there is another companion function to SetPixel(), called GetPixel(). This function allows you to figure out the color of any pixel at coordinates that you specify. It looks like this:

```
COLORREF GetPixel( HDC hdc, int XPos, int nYPos );
```

The first parameter is a handle to the device context that contains the pixel that you want to test. The second and third parameters take the coordinates of the pixel that you want to test. You probably won't use this too often, but it's always good to know about it.

Lines

Lines are very similar to points. In fact, they are really just two points with a line between them. To specify a line you need two points: the origin of the line and of course the destination. Think of drawing lines in Windows the same as you would think of drawing lines with a pen in real life. That is, you *move* the pen somewhere, then you engage the pen and draw a line to a destination point. Unless you pick up and *move* the pen's position, the next line you draw will start where the last one ended. Hence there are two functions that you need to use when you draw a line. They are MoveToEx() and LineTo(). That Ex stuck on the end of MoveToEx() stands for "extended." It is there because the previous version, called MoveTo(), was designed for 16-bit Windows and cannot function very well in a 32-bit environment. So just remember to stick on the 'Ex' at the end and everything will be cool.

Let's take a look at their prototypes:

```
BOOL MoveToEx(
   HDC hdc,            // handle to device context
   int X,              // x-coordinate of new current position
   int Y,              // y-coordinate of new current position
   LPPOINT lpPoint     // pointer to old current position
);
```

Again the first parameter is a handle to the device context, and the next two take the first points for the line. The fourth parameter is kind of interesting. It takes a pointer to a POINT structure, and it returns the previous position of the pen. You don't need to specify anything here if you don't want to; I almost always just pass NULL for this parameter. By the way, this is an example of why the new extended version was needed. In the past, the previous point was returned as a single 32-bit integer—in other words, two 16-bit values combined into a single 32-bit value. So when Win32 came along you couldn't fit two 32-bit values into a single 32-bit value. And at the time there was no 64-bit data type; hence the extended version. Enough history—let's move on.

```
BOOL LineTo(
    HDC hdc,      // device context handle
    int nXEnd,    // x-coordinate of line's ending point
    int nYEnd     // y-coordinate of line's ending point
);
```

LineTo is a little bit simpler. It takes an hDC and the coordinates to which you want to draw the line. This is the function that actually draws the line. MoveToEx() only updates the starting position for the line. By the way, when you call LineTo() it updates the current position of the pen to the end point of the line. So if you call LineTo() again it will draw another line from the end of the previous line without the need to call MoveToEx(). Cool, huh?

Anyway, let's look at a small example and see what it will achieve:

```
// Move the starting position to (10,10)
MoveToEx( hDC, 10, 10, NULL );

// Draw a line to (100,100)
LineTo( hDC, 100, 100 );
```

And the result will be Figure 7.4.

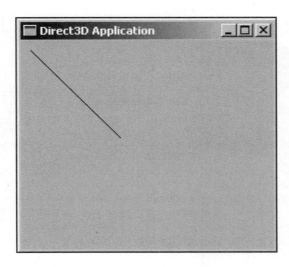

Figure 7.4

You've drawn a line!

Rectangles

The thing with rectangles is that their appearance is controlled using a bunch of functions, so bear with me on this one. Rectangles are drawn in two parts: the outer border is drawn using the current pen, which I haven't discussed yet, and the inside is drawn using the current brush, which I also haven't discussed yet. So in the meantime I'll just draw it using the defaults—that is, the inside will be white and the border will be black. The function to draw these puppies is called...wait for it...wait for it...Rectangle()!

```
BOOL Rectangle(
   HDC hdc,             // handle to device context
   int nLeftRect,       // x-coord of rectangle's upper-left corner
   int nTopRect,        // y-coord of rectangle's upper-left corner
   int nRightRect,      // x-coord of rectangle's lower-right corner
   int nBottomRect      // y-coord of rectangle's lower-right corner
);
```

It's pretty self-explanatory. It needs, as usual, a DC handle and then the four coordinates for the sides of the rectangles. The colors and all that stuff get done elsewhere, and I will discuss those settings shortly. Here is an example call to the Rectangle() function:

```
Rectangle( hDC, 10, 10, 100, 100 );
```

This will draw a simple black-and-white rectangle from (10, 10) to (100, 100), as shown in Figure 7.5. Is that just the slickest or what?

Figure 7.5

Drawing a rectangle

Ellipses and Circles

This section has kind of a misleading heading because there is no function to draw circles—you just draw symmetric ellipses instead! Ellipses are really similar to rectangles. In fact, the only difference is the name of the function. Have a look at the prototype:

```
BOOL Ellipse(
  HDC hdc,           // handle to device context
  int nLeftRect,     // x-coord of ellipse's upper-left corner
  int nTopRect,      // y-coord of ellipse's upper-left corner
  int nRightRect,    // x-coord of ellipse's lower-right corner
  int nBottomRect    // y-coord of ellipse's lower-right corner
);
```

As you can see, you don't specify an ellipse with anything as complex as a radius and center. No way. Just put in the bounds like you would with a rectangle, and all will be cool. Here is what a sample call would look like:

```
Ellipse( hDC, 10, 10, 200, 150 );
```

And that will create an ellipse like the one in Figure 7.6.

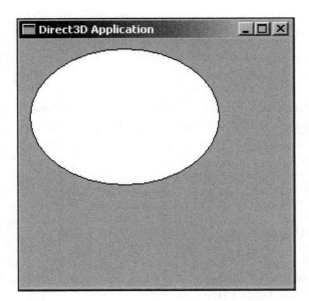

Figure 7.6

Rendering an ellipse

Text

Text output in Windows is achieved using the aptly-named function TextOut(). It's quite easy to use and only requires a few simple parameters.

```
BOOL TextOut(
  HDC hdc,              // handle to device context
  int nXStart,          // x-coordinate of starting position
  int nYStart,          // y-coordinate of starting position
  LPCTSTR lpString,     // pointer to string
  int cbString          // number of characters in string
);
```

First off, as always, is the handle to the device context. Then come the x, y coordinates for where you want the text to appear in the window. And the fourth parameter is simply the string that you want to display. This can be something as simple as "Make it so, Mr. Data," or whatever you want. And finally, the last variable, cbString, takes the length of the string (the number of characters) that you are displaying. Get this correct, please, because you could cause memory errors if Windows reads too far into the string. Anyway, just follow the method that I use below and everything will be fine.

```
// Create a string to hold the output text.
char OutputString[] = "Make it so, Mr. Data";

// Output the Text
TextOut( hDC, 10, 10, OutputString, strlen( OutputString ) );
```

See the way I first created a character string to hold the data and then passed it to OutputText()? Well, the reason for this is so that changes in the length of the string can be detected by strlen() on the fly and you don't need to sit there counting characters. Pretty cool, huh?

> **TIP**
>
> strlen() is a simple function that takes a string and returns the number of characters in the string. It's really useful for situations like the one above where you have to specify the number of characters for the function to work. You don't want to count them yourself, do you? Nah, I didn't think so.

Check out Figure 7.7 for the results.

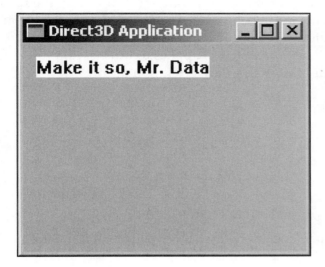

Figure 7.7

Outputting text

Text Transparency

Now the really annoying thing about that text in Figure 7.7 is the white border around the outside. That white is the current background color. You could change the background color to match the actual background color of the window, but that would require all sorts of testing. And what would you do if you were rendering the text over an image? Wouldn't it be great if, instead of messing with colors, you could make the text transparent so that only the actual characters were drawn and the rest of the original background was left in place? I thought so, too, and so did the Microsoft people, and as a result they put in a really handy function called SetBkMode(), which means "set background mode."

```
int SetBkMode(
    HDC hdc,        // handle of device context
    int iBkMode     // flag specifying background mode
);
```

It just takes a handle to a DC for the first parameter. Actually, to prevent myself from getting repetitive strain injuries, I'm not going to mention the first parameter anymore. I know that you know that hdc means "handle to device context" and that it is almost always the first parameter when dealing with GDI functions.

The second parameter, iBkMode, means "background mode." There are only two possibilities for this puppy, and they are OPAQUE and TRANSPARENT. If you set the mode to OPAQUE, then the background color will be rendered. On the other hand, if you set the mode to TRANSPARENT, then you will only get the foreground object rendered. By the way, this function is not just for text; it also applies to brushes and funky nonsolid lines, which I will be discussing shortly. Here it is in action:

```
// Set the background mode to transparent
SetBkMode( hDC, TRANSPARENT );

// Create a string to hold the output text.
char OutputString[] = "Make it so, Mr. Data";

// Output the Text
TextOut( hDC, 10, 10, OutputString, strlen( OutputString ) );
```

As you can see, it is the exact same code as before, except it has the SetBkMode() added to it.

And Figure 7.8 shows the results.

Figure 7.8

Transparent text

Cool, huh? By the way, if you actually do want to change the background color for the text, then there is a function to do that. This function is not just for text; it can be used for brushes, pens, etc., as well. It is called SetBkColor() and looks like this:

```
COLORREF SetBkColor( HDC hdc, COLORREF crColor );
```

You can see it takes a handle to a DC and also a color that you want to change the color to. The return value is the color that Windows picked if the color you requested was unavailable.

Colored Text

Text just isn't that good in black, is it? No, I don't think so either. Let's see if you can't spice it up a little bit. There is a function buried deep in the bowels of the GDI known to the wise ones as SetTextColor(). And guess what: it allows you to set the color of the text. It looks like this:

```
COLORREF SetTextColor(
  HDC hdc,            // handle to device context
  COLORREF crColor   // text color
);
```

As you can see, it returns a COLORREF. This is the same situation as with SetPixel(). If you request a color that is not available, then Windows will set it to the closest match and return the final color. After the hdc, the second parameter takes the color that you want to set the text to. If you were to call this function, then it would probably look something like this:

```
SetTextColor( hDC, RGB( 0, 255, 0 ) );
```

This is called before you output the text of which you want to change the color. Anyway, the results are shown in Figure 7.9.

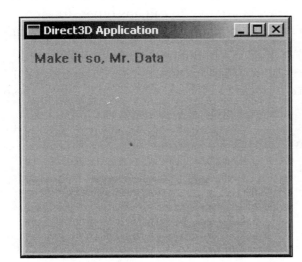

Figure 7.9

Colored text

I guess it doesn't look as cool printed in black and white, but what can I do? I just work here.

Oh, That Is So Picasso!

Now that you know how to draw the basic shapes, lines, and points, I'm going to show you how to modify them so that you can render them in any color you want with all sorts of style settings. The GDI is kind of what is called a *state machine*. What that means is that you set properties for things like color and style, and this affects the output of all the other functions. For instance, if you set the current line style to dashed, the result will be that all lines drawn will be dashed. That includes the lines that border other objects such as rectangles and ellipses. So what I'm going to do now is run through each of the settings that you can change and the functions that control them.

By the way, a lot of the things that control settings are metaphors for real-world objects. For instance, the pen is used for lines, etc. However, in Windows-speak these are referred to as *objects,* or more specifically *GDI objects.* These objects have nothing to do with C++ objects or anything like that. It's just Windows lingo.

Pens

As I mentioned above, the pen object is for drawing lines. A pen can have many parameters to define its style. For instance, a line has a color, a width, and also a pattern, such as dashed. You set these parameters when you create the pen. You can create pens on the fly and keep them around for a while or get rid of them as soon as you are finished with them.

After you have created a pen, you need to select it into the device context before you can use it. After it has been selected, you are free to call any other drawing functions and the line style will automatically be updated. Then, when you are finished with the pen, you deselect it and finally destroy it.

It is important to follow the last few steps, because pens take up memory and GDI resources, and you are just hogging resources if you don't release and destroy them when you are finished. Also, note the importance of releasing an object *before* you destroy it. If you attempt to delete an object that is currently selected, then you can get some interesting results, generally involving the Reset button.

Let's start with creating a pen. You do this with the function CreatePen(). Not a very creative name for the function, but it does the job and it looks like this:

```
HPEN CreatePen(
  int fnPenStyle,    // pen style
  int nWidth,        // pen width
```

```
COLORREF crColor    // pen color
);
```

The function returns a handle to a pen; keep this in mind because all of your interactions with GDI objects occur with handles. They come in various flavors, and in this case it is HPEN. The parameters are easy as soon as you know what they are, so let's look at them now.

- **fnPenStyle.** This parameter takes the style for the pen that you want to create. There are many different styles, such as solid, dashed, dotted, dashed and dotted, and so on. Check out Table 7.1 for the full rundown.

- **nWidth.** This is the width for the line. As you can see, it takes an integer value. If the width is set to less than zero, then the width is changed to 1, which is the minimal width. Don't forget that if the width is set to anything other than 1, the only style available is PS_SOLID.

- **crColor.** This is of course the color to which you want to set the line. Again, you can set any color using the RGB() macro, and Windows will automatically pick the closest matching color for you.

Table 7.1   Pen Styles

Value	Example	Meaning
PS_SOLID	————	The pen is solid.
PS_DASH	– – – –	The pen is dashed. This is only available if the pen width is set to 1.
PS_DOT	··············	The pen is dotted. This is only available if the pen width is set to 1.
PS_DASHDOT	– · – · – ·	The pen alternates between dashes and dots. This is only available if the pen width is set to 1.
PS_DASHDOTDOT	— · · — · · —	The pen alternates between a dash and two dots. This is only available if the pen width is set to 1.
PS_NULL	NA	The pen is not visible.
PS_INSIDEFRAME	NA	The pen is solid. In drawing functions, the pen coordinates are shrunk to fit entirely inside the bounding coordinates.

So to pull it all together, here is a snippet of code that will show you what an actual call to CreatePen() looks like:

```
HPEN Pen = CreatePen( PS_DASHDOT, 1, RGB( 255, 0, 0 ) );
```

Here I am creating a new pen that has the PS_DASHDOT style, has a width of 1 pixel, and is bright red. See the way I created an HPEN variable called Pen and then immediately filled it with the handle of the new pen? That's the shorthand way of doing it.

There is an alternate way to create pens which may come in useful to you at some time, although I can say I have never used it. But some people swear by it. I'll leave my bias out and let you decide. This other way requires you to fill in a structure called LOGPEN, which means "logical pen," and then pass it to the function CreatePenIndirect(). The structure looks like this:

```
typedef struct tagLOGPEN {
    UINT     lopnStyle;
    POINT    lopnWidth;
    COLORREF lopnColor;
} LOGPEN;
```

It basically just contains values that are the same as the parameters for the CreatePen() function: lopnStyle holds the style, lopnWidth holds the width, and lopnColor holds the color. One thing to look out for in this version is the lopnWidth variable, which holds the width of the pen. In the structure it is a POINT structure, and the width goes into the x-coordinate of it. The y-coordinate is unused.

The CreatePenIndirect() function looks like this:

```
HPEN CreatePenIndirect( CONST LOGPEN *lplgpn );
```

As you can see, it just takes the address of a LOGPEN structure. Here's a quick example to show you how this method of pen creation would be put into practice:

```
// Create the LOGPEN structure
LOGPEN lPen;

// Initialize a point structure with the pen's width in the X variable
POINT ptWidth;

ptWidth.x = 1; // The width
ptWidth.y = 0; // Not used
```

```
// Fill in the structure
lPen.lopnStyle = PS_DASHDOT;
lPen.lopnWidth = ptWidth;
lPen.lopnColor = RGB( 255, 0, 0 );

// Create the pen, passing the address of the LOGPEN structure
HPEN Pen = CreatePenIndirect( &lPen );
```

OK, so now that you know two ways to create a pen, let's look at how to actually select one into the device context. The function to do this is called `SelectObject()`, and it is used to select any GDI object like pens, brushes, etc., into use.

```
HGDIOBJ SelectObject(
    HDC hdc,            // handle to device context
    HGDIOBJ hgdiobj     // handle to object
);
```

After the handle to the DC, the only parameter is a handle to a GDI object. In this case your handle is to a pen. So what you want to do is pass the handle that you received from the `CreatePen()` or `CreatePenIndirect()` function, like this:

```
SelectObject( hDC, Pen );
```

Pretty easy, huh? Now that you have done that, you can draw any lines or objects that you want to and their style will automatically change to the current pen that has been selected. For instance, if I draw a line now that I have selected the new pen, the line style automatically reflects the change in pen. The pen, as shown in Figure 7.10, is now red. (You'll have to trust me on this—when it came to print the book my editors and I couldn't find a shade of gray that looked like red.) Also notice that it has gaps to reflect the PS_DASHDOT style. Figure 7.11 shows a line with a thickness of 5 pixels.

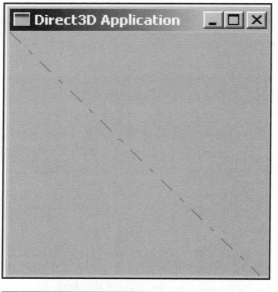

Figure 7.10

Dash-dot line style

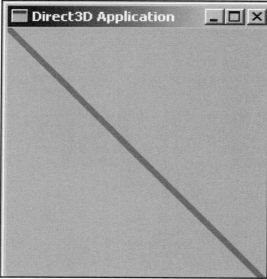

Figure 7.11

Five-pixel-width line

OK, let's say that all you wanted to draw was a line. You are now finished drawing and want to destroy the pen that you created earlier. This is a seriously stupid way of doing things, so pay attention. Trust me, if there was a better way, I would show you, but there isn't. The problem is, before you can delete an object, you have to

deselect it. So you would think there would be a function named
`DeleteSelectedObject()`, wouldn't you? Nope. Instead, you perform this utter madness: Select something else, such as a stock object, into the device context. When you select a new object, the handle to the previous selected object is returned. You can then call DeleteObject() on the handle you received from SelectObject(). I'll show you the quick way of writing this first and then break it down so you can see each step.

```
DeleteObject( SelectObject( hDC, GetStockObject( BLACK_PEN ) ) );
```

Nice, huh? Not! OK, let's see what's going on. First I'm getting a handle to a stock pen with the GetStockObject() function. Then I pass the handle to SelectObject(), which returns the handle to the previous pen that I want to delete. That handle is then passed to DeleteObject(), which finally completes the job. It is the same as the multiline example that follows:

```
// Get a stock pen
HPEN hStockPen = GetStockObject( BLACK_PEN );

// Get the handle to the previously selected pen object by selecting in a new //
pen.
HPEN hOldPen = SelectObject( hDC, hStockPen );

// Delete the previously selected pen object
Delete Object( hOldPen );
```

You can do it the second way if you want to; it is more intuitive, but then again it requires that you make two temporary variables. All these snippets of code are starting to add up, so I'm just going to take a minute to show you an entire WM_PAINT message handler. This code will draw a blue horizontal line and a red vertical line.

```
case WM_PAINT:
{
// Tell windows we want to start updating the window
        hDC = BeginPaint( hWnd, &PaintStruct );

        // Set the background more to transparent
        SetBkMode( hDC, TRANSPARENT );

        // Create a red pen, with 1 pixel width, and a dotted style
        HPEN RedPen = CreatePen( PS_DOT, 1, RGB( 255, 0, 0 ) );
```

```c
// Create a solid blue pen, with a 4 pixel width
HPEN BluePen = CreatePen( PS_SOLID, 4, RGB( 0, 0, 255 ) );

// Select the red pen into the device context
SelectObject( hDC, RedPen );

// Move the current position to (10,10)
MoveToEx( hDC, 10, 10, NULL );
// Draw a vertical line down to (10,400)
LineTo( hDC, 10, 400 );

// Now select the blue pen into the device context
SelectObject( hDC, BluePen );

// Move the current position back to (10,10)
MoveToEx( hDC, 10, 10, NULL );
// Draw the horizontal line over to (400, 10)
LineTo( hDC, 400, 10 );

// Delete the red pen normally because it is not currently selected
DeleteObject( RedPen );
// Delete the blue pen the stupid way because it is selected
DeleteObject( SelectObject( hDC, GetStockObject( BLACK_PEN ) ) );

// Tell windows we have finished updating the window
EndPaint( hWnd, &PaintStruct );
return 0;
}
```

You can see the results of this code in Figure 7.12.

Figure 7.12

Using the GDI to draw lines with pen objects

It's not that visually exciting I know, but just wait until you get the rest of the GDI stuff out of the way. Then you'll really get to see how great the GDI can get.

Brushes

In the previous section I covered a lot of ground on pens that is directly applicable to brushes, so don't worry—this will be a much shorter section. So what exactly are brushes? Well, as I mentioned before, they are used to fill areas with a color, pattern, or both. When I say "areas" I mean anything from the inside of a rectangle or ellipse to the contents of the entire window. Remember when we specified a brush in the window class in the last chapter? Well, you can specify patterns in that brush as well, so that the background of your application window looks cool. You can use predefined brushes, or you can make your own. Before you can use a brush, you of course have to create it, so let's look at that process now. A brush is created with the function CreateBrushIndirect().

```
HBRUSH CreateBrushIndirect( CONST LOGBRUSH *lplb );
```

Unfortunately, there is no CreateBrush() function as there is for pens, so you have to fill in a LOGBRUSH structure to define the brush, which I will cover in a second. As you can see, the function returns a handle to a brush. This handle works in the same way as the handle for the pen. When you create the brush, you get a handle. When you want to use it, you select it into the device context using the handle, and when you destroy it the handle is no longer valid. Let's have a look at this structure:

```
typedef struct tagLOGBRUSH {
    UINT      lbStyle;
    COLORREF  lbColor;
    LONG      lbHatch;
} LOGBRUSH;
```

Again, it is very similar to the LOGPEN structure that you looked at earlier. Let's look at the variables in detail.

- **lbStyle**. This value holds the style for the brush. There are a bunch of different styles. Table 7.2 shows the possible values.

Table 7.2   Brush Styles

Value	Meaning
BS_SOLID	The area will be filled with a solid color.
BS_PATTERN	The brush is defined using a DDB bitmap in memory. Set lbHatch to a handle for the bitmap.
BS_NULL or BS_HOLLOW	The brush is empty. In other words, nothing is drawn. For example, a rectangle would have a border with a transparent internal region.
BS_HATCHED	The pattern is defined by a premade stock pattern. Set lbHatch to the desired pattern.
BS_DIBPATTERN	The brush is defined using a DIB bitmap in memory. Set lbHatch to a handle to the bitmap created with CreateDIBSection().
BS_DIBPATTERNPT	The brush is defined using a DIB bitmap in memory. Set lbHatch to a pointer that points to the bitmap created with CreateDIBSection().

To summarize Table 7.2: If you want a transparent brush, use BS_HOLLOW. If you want to fill an area with a color, use BS_SOLID. Or, if you want to fill an area with a pattern, use BS_HATCHED, and then set the lbHatch variable to the brush style that you want.

- **lbColor.** This, obviously, is the variable that holds the color for the brush, although its meaning can change depending on the other flags. If lbStyle is set to BS_HOLLOW or BS_NULL, then the color is ignored, because it is transparent. If the style is set to BS_HATCHED, then lbColor is the color that is used for the foreground pattern. And if the style is set to BS_SOLID, then the color is just what the area is filled with.

- **lbHatch.** This is kind of an interesting member of the structure. It is pretty much ignored unless you are using a hatch style or one of the more exotic styles. It can be set to any of six premade brushes that Windows supports. Have a look at Table 7.3 for the possible values.

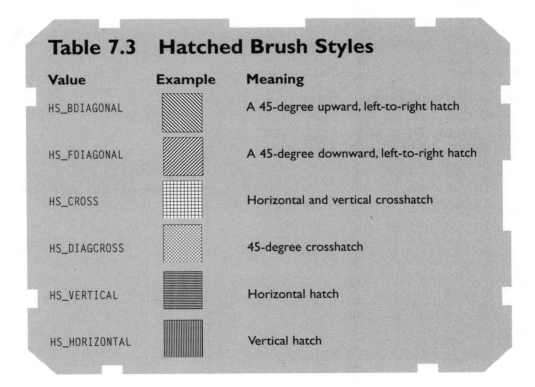

Table 7.3   Hatched Brush Styles

Value	Example	Meaning
HS_BDIAGONAL		A 45-degree upward, left-to-right hatch
HS_FDIAGONAL		A 45-degree downward, left-to-right hatch
HS_CROSS		Horizontal and vertical crosshatch
HS_DIAGCROSS		45-degree crosshatch
HS_VERTICAL		Horizontal hatch
HS_HORIZONTAL		Vertical hatch

Let's look at a full rundown of what you would do to create a brush. Here's the code:

```
LOGBRUSH CrossHatchBrush;

CrossHatchBrush.lbStyle = BS_HATCHED;
CrossHatchBrush.lbColor = RGB( 255, 0, 0 );
CrossHatchBrush.lbHatch = HS_DIAGCROSS;

HBRUSH hCrossBrush = CreateBrushIndirect( &CrossHatchBrush );
```

When you want to use a brush, follow the same pattern as you would for pens. That is, after you have created the brush, select it into the device context for it to be used. The function to do this is exactly the same as the one used for pens.

Following is a small example of a brush being selected into the device context:

```
SelectObject( hDC, hCrossBrush );
```

Simple or what? Now you can draw a rectangle, and it will be drawn to the specifications of the currently selected brush. For instance, the following code:

```
Rectangle( hDC, 0, 0, 250, 250 );
```

now has the effect shown in Figure 7.13.

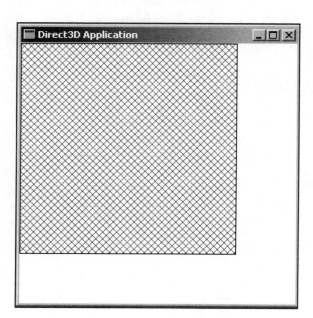

Figure 7.13

Rendering rectangles with brushes

As with pens, destroying brushes follows the same pattern. (Get it, *pattern?*) Just make a call to DeleteObject() to get rid of it. Don't forget all the extra bits if the brush is currently selected. For example:

```
DeleteObject( SelectObject( hDC, GetStockObject( BLACK_BRUSH ) ) );
```

Notice that I selected a stock *brush* this time and not a pen. This gives me the handle to the previously selected brush. If I had specified BLACK_PEN, the handle to the previous pen would be returned, which is not what I want in this situation.

Let me just cover one last snippet to do with brushes. And that is how to set the background of your window to a brush. All you do is create the brush before you create the window class, specify the brush in the window class, and then destroy the brush just before you exit. Check out the code that follows. I have bolded the important bits.

```
int WINAPI WinMain( HINSTANCE hInstance,
             HINSTANCE hPrevInstance,
                 PSTR pstrCmdLine, int iCmdShow )
{
        HWND hWnd;              // The handle to our main window
        MSG msg;               // The message windows is sending us
        WNDCLASSEX wc; // The window class used to create our window

        // The name of our class and also the title to our window
        static char pstrAppName[] = "Direct3D Application";

        LOGBRUSH CrossHatchBrush;

        CrossHatchBrush.lbStyle = BS_HATCHED;
        CrossHatchBrush.lbColor = RGB( 0, 0, 0 );
        CrossHatchBrush.lbHatch = HS_CROSS;

        HBRUSH hCrossBrush = CreateBrushIndirect( &CrossHatchBrush );

    // Fill in the window class with the attributes for our main window

        // The size of this structure in bytes
        wc.cbSize                   = sizeof( WNDCLASSEX );
        //  The style of the window.
        wc.style                    = CS_HREDRAW | CS_VREDRAW | CS_OWNDC;
        // Useless information.  Just set to zero.
```

```c
        wc.cbClsExtra           = 0;
        // Useless information.  Just set to zero.
        wc.cbWndExtra           = 0;
        // The name of our event handler
        wc.lpfnWndProc          = WndProc;
        // A handle to the applications instance
        wc.hInstance            = hInstance;
        // The handle to the brush to use for the window background
        wc.hbrBackground        = hCrossBrush;
        // A handle to the icon to use for the window
        wc.hIcon                = LoadIcon( NULL, IDI_APPLICATION );
        // A handle to a smaller version of the apps icon
        wc.hIconSm              = LoadIcon( NULL, IDI_APPLICATION );
        // A handle to the cursor to use while the mouse is over our window
        wc.hCursor              = LoadCursor( NULL, IDC_ARROW );
        // A handle to the resource to use as our window
        wc.lpszMenuName = NULL;
        // The human readable name for this class
        wc.lpszClassName        = pstrAppName;

        // Register the class with windows
        RegisterClassEx( &wc );
        // Create the window based on the previous class
        hWnd = CreateWindowEx( NULL,                    // Advanced style settings
                    pstrAppName,                        // The name of the class
                    pstrAppName,                        // The window caption
                WS_OVERLAPPEDWINDOW,                    // The window style
                    CW_USEDEFAULT, CW_USEDEFAULT,   // The initial x, y position
                    512, 512,                                       // The initial
width / height

                    NULL,                                                   // Handle to
parent window                                 NULL,
// Handle to the menu
                    hInstance,                                      // Handle to the
apps instance
                    NULL );                                 // context pointer.Just
ignore

        // Keep the window handle in a global
        g_hWndMain = hWnd;
```

```c
        // Display the window we just created
        ShowWindow( hWnd, iCmdShow );
        // Draw the window contents for the first time
        UpdateWindow( hWnd );

        // Start the message loop
        while( TRUE )
        {
                // Check if a message is waiting for processing
                if( PeekMessage( &msg, NULL, 0, 0, PM_REMOVE ) )
                {
                        // Check if the message is to quit the application
                        if( msg.message == WM_QUIT )
                                // Exit the message loop
                                break;

                        // Change the format of certain messages
                        TranslateMessage( &msg );
                        // Pass the message to WndProc() for processing
                        DispatchMessage( &msg );
                }
                else
                {
                        // Run the game loop

                }
        }


        DeleteObject( hCrossBrush );

        // Return control to windows with the exit code
        return msg.wParam;
}
```

Figure 7.14 shows the results. You probably won't use this feature very much, but it's always good to know what's going on. Windows will automatically draw the brush to the background of your window for you.

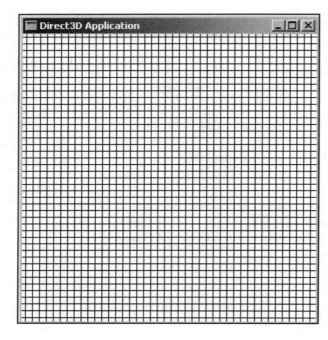

Figure 7.14

Using a background brush

Getting Advanced with the Device Context

Remember when I was talking about when you wanted to draw? I said that you should pretty much stick to the WM_PAINT handler because that is where you are meant to draw. However, game programmers are inclined to break a whole bunch of rules. The WM_PAINT handler is great for normal applications because it provides a great way to asynchronously draw to the screen. But it just does not have the performance that game developers need. Also, game developers generally want to keep interactions with Windows to a minimum because it is slower than a legless mule. So I'm going to show you a new way that is really great and will fit into the structure of your game much better.

Now for this discussion I'm going to move our drawing code to a function called within the message loop. Following is the message loop, and you can see where the new function, named GameLoop(), is called from.

```
while( TRUE )
{
        // Check if a message is waiting for processing
        if( PeekMessage( &msg, NULL, 0, 0, PM_REMOVE ) )
        {
                // Check if the message is to quit the application
                if( msg.message == WM_QUIT )
                        // Exit the message loop
                        break;

                // Change the format of certain messages
                TranslateMessage( &msg );
                // Pass the message to WndProc() for processing
                DispatchMessage( &msg );
        }
        else
        {
                // Run the game loop
                GameLoop();
        }
}
```

As you can see, the GameLoop() function is called whenever there are no messages in
the queue to be processed, which is almost always. Right now the game loop is
empty, but from now on the code will be added in this function.

```
int GameLoop()
{
        // This is where the main game loop code goes
        return 0;
}
```

By the way, when I say move the drawing to GameLoop(), the WM_PAINT handler
should stay intact so that it can get rid of the paint messages in queue. Even if you
are not drawing anything it is always a good idea to keep the WM_PAINT handle looking like it does in the following:

```
case WM_PAINT:
{
        // Tell windows we want to start updating the window
        hDC = BeginPaint( hWnd, &PaintStruct );
```

```
        // Do any GDI drawing here

        // Tell windows we have finished updating the window
        EndPaint( hWnd, &PaintStruct );
        return 0;
}
```

Anyway, getting back to using the DC outside of WM_PAINT. To do this you need two functions: one to acquire the DC and the second to give it back. The first is called GetDC() and it looks like this:

```
HDC GetDC( HWND hWnd );
```

As you can see, it just takes a handle for the window for which you want to retrieve the DC. The return value is the DC for the window. After calling this function, you can use the DC just as you would with a call to BeginPaint().

When you are finished with the DC, you need to release it; this is achieved with the ReleaseDC() function, which has this prototype:

```
int ReleaseDC( HWND hWnd, HDC hDC );
```

This function again takes the handle to the window that owns the DC, and the handle to the actual DC itself. I cannot stress enough the importance of releasing the DC after you have finished with it. As I said before, Windows usually only has a finite number of DCs, and if your code keeps acquiring them without releasing them, the drawing system will ultimately fail (actually these days, in 32-bit Windows, there are *a lot* of DC's around, but pretend I never told you that).

OK, so now that you know about the functions for the DC, you can take a look at an example. I'll start with a simple one that draws a single rectangle and then move on to a groovy random shape drawing thing that draws at the speed of light!

```
int GameLoop()
{
        // Create a handle to the DC
        HDC hDC;

        // Get a DC for this window
        hDC = GetDC( g_hWndMain );

        // Draw the rectangle
        Rectangle( hDC, 10, 10, 100, 100 );
```

```
        // Release the DC back to Windows
        ReleaseDC( g_hWndMain, hDC );

        return 0;
}
```

Pretty simple, huh? It's basically the same as for the WM_PAINT handler, except for swapping the calls to BeginPaint() and EndPaint() with GetDC() and ReleaseDC(). The results of this code are pretty much the same as for Figure 7.4, so you can flip back a few pages if you want to see it.

Now let's look at a slightly cooler example. This uses a few functions that I have not explained yet, but don't worry—I'll cover them in a second.

```
int GameLoop()
{
        // Create a handle to the DC
        HDC hDC;

        // Get a DC for this window
        hDC = GetDC( g_hWndMain );

        // RECT structure to hold the dimensions of the client area
        RECT ClientRect;

        // Get the client area size
        GetClientRect( g_hWndMain, &ClientRect );

        // Make sure the window is not minimized
        if( ClientRect.bottom == 0 || ClientRect.right == 0 )
        {
                // Return if the window is minimized
                ReleaseDC( g_hWndMain, hDC );
                return 0;
        }

        // Create a solid pen for the rectangle border
        // with a random width and random color
        HPEN hPen = CreatePen( PS_SOLID, rand()%5,
                                        RGB(    rand()%255,
                                    rand()%255,
                                        rand()%255 ) );
```

```cpp
// Brush structure to describe the brush
LOGBRUSH logBrush;

// The color will be random
logBrush.lbColor = RGB( rand()%255,
                        rand()%255,
                        rand()%255 );
// We are not using a hatch
logBrush.lbHatch = 0;
// The fill should be solid
logBrush.lbStyle = BS_SOLID;

// Create the brush
HBRUSH hBrush = CreateBrushIndirect( &logBrush );

// Select the brush into the device context
SelectObject( hDC, hBrush );
// Select the pen into device context
SelectObject( hDC, hPen );

// Draw the rectangle using random dimensions
Rectangle( hDC, rand()%ClientRect.right,
                rand()%ClientRect.bottom,
                rand()%ClientRect.right,
                rand()%ClientRect.bottom );

// Get rid of the brush
DeleteObject( SelectObject( hDC, GetStockObject( BLACK_BRUSH ) ) );
// Get rid of the pen
DeleteObject( SelectObject( hDC, GetStockObject( BLACK_PEN ) ) );

// Release the DC back to Windows
ReleaseDC( g_hWndMain, hDC );

return 0;
}
```

You can see the results of this code in Figure 7.15, but I suggest you actually run the code from the CD, because you won't get the full effect looking at a static image.

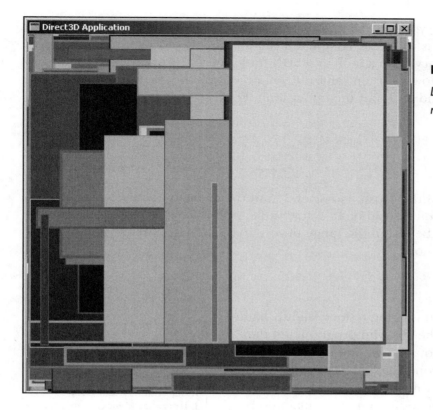

Figure 7.15

Drawing multiple rectangles

The code may look long, but you have seen everything in there before except for two possibilities. First off is the function GetClientRect(), which looks like this:

```
BOOL GetClientRect( HWND hWnd, LPRECT lpRect );
```

This function is pretty cool. You pass it the handle to a window, and a pointer to a RECT structure, and it will give you the dimensions of the client area for the window. By the way, check out the little snippet of code after I call GetClientRect(), where I make sure the dimensions of the window do not equal zero. If they are zero, then the window must either be minimized or sized so small that nothing is visible. The reason for this check is that if we pass a value of zero to the modulus sign, we get a "divide by zero" error, which stinks, but the check alleviates us of this issue so it's fine.

Now for the second issue I'm pretty sure you know about, but I'll just run through it anyway. It is the rand() function, and here is its prototype:

```
int rand( void );
```

rand() is very simple; you just call it and it will return a random number. rand() is found in stdlib.h. It is not really completely random, but if you want to know more about that discrepancy, have a look in MSDN under rand(). Anyway, if you want a random number below a certain value, all you do is stick the modulus sign (%) after the function and then put the upper limit. For instance, in the code above I wrote:

```
logBrush.lbColor = RGB(          rand()%255,
                                 rand()%255,
                                 rand()%255 );
```

This sets the color of the brush. However, I want the color to be random, so I stuck in the rand() function instead of an actual value. And of course, as it is a color, I wanted the value to be within the range of zero to 255. That is the purpose of the "%255" after the function.

Bitmaps

OK, this little section is going to look slightly hallucinogenic because the guy who programmed the GDI's bitmap functionality was not quite over his recent alien abduction. That's the conclusion I came to, anyway. Some of this stuff is really weird, but stick with me because I'm going to try to explain everything in a nice, step-by-step fashion.

Windows has to work on so many different computers that some interesting ideas had to be adopted. For instance, every graphics card will handle the display of visual memory differently. So for bitmaps to work independent of the host system, the way they are supposed to, the GDI bitmap model has been

> A *bitmap* is a chunk of digital information used to represent images in your computer in a fairly device-independent manner. A bitmap has a width and a height defined by the number of pixels horizontally and vertically, respectively. A bitmap also has a bit depth, which is the number of bits that are used to define the color of a pixel, such as 24, 8, 16, etc.

abstracted to just left of the delta quadrant. You'd think that to make a bitmap display in a window you might follow steps like: (1) loading the image off of the storage device and (2) copying the image into currently visible memory. That process is still vaguely in practice, but there are a bunch of other steps in the way, so let's look at the architectural stuff first.

Bitmaps are heavily involved with device contexts. As I was talking about earlier, a DC is like a canvas, and as such, it is used to represent images. That is abstraction number 1. Now, there is the main DC, which is used to represent the client area for your window. But when you load a bitmap, you need another DC to hold the bitmap. However, after you create the DC and before you fill the DC with the bitmap, you need to make the DC compatible with the main DC, otherwise you won't be able to interchange images between them. To make the DC compatible means to make the bit depth and other factors the same. Then the image can be copied to the target DC, at which point the image is finally displayed. Then, when you are finished, you *delete* the DC that you *created* and *release* the main DC that you *acquired*. Try figuring that out on your own!

Now before you start, I want to make a few additions to the Win32 application, to make it into even more of a game. They have to do with the GameLoop() function that was added before. The first addition is another function that is called GameInit(). This new function will be called directly *before* the call to ShowWindow() in WinMain(). The second addition is called GameShutdown(), and this will be called directly before exiting. The code that follows shows their positions in the code for clarity.

GameInit() is empty for now, but it provides a good place to do any initialization that is needed. The same is true for GameShutdown(), although it is obviously for when the game has finished and you want to release any resources that you acquired.

```
int WINAPI WinMain( HINSTANCE hInstance, HINSTANCE hPrevInstance,
                                             PSTR pstrCmdLine, int
iCmdShow )
{
.
.
.
// WinMain Stuff, e.g. registering the window class
.
        // Initialize the game
        GameInit();

// Display the window we just created
ShowWindow( hWnd, iCmdShow );
.
// More stuff, e.g. Message Loop, etc
.
// Shutdown the game
        GameShutdown();

        return msg.wParam;
}
```

With that out of the way, let's move back to bitmaps. As this is kind of complex, I'm going to show you the whole shebang and then do the line-by-line thing.

```c
// Global handle to the image
HANDLE hImage;

// Game Initialization can be done here
int GameInit()
{
    // Create a string to hold the path to the bitmap
    char Path[] = "ZEN PIC.BMP";

    // Load the image from disk into memory
    hImage = LoadImage( NULL, Path, IMAGE_BITMAP,
                                    0, 0, LR_LOADFROMFILE );

    return 0;
}

int GameLoop()
{
    // Get a handle to the DC for the client area
    HDC hDC = GetDC( g_hWndMain );
    // Create a DC that is compatible with the main DC
    HDC hImageDC = CreateCompatibleDC( hDC );

    // Structure to hold information about the bitmap
    BITMAP Bitmap;

    // Holds the dimensions of the bitmap
    SIZE ImageSize;

    // Get information about the bitmap we loaded in GameInit()
    GetObject( hImage, sizeof( BITMAP ), &Bitmap );

    // Get the dimensions for the bitmap
    ImageSize.cx = Bitmap.bmWidth;
    ImageSize.cy = Bitmap.bmHeight;

    // Select the image into the device context
    SelectObject( hImageDC, hImage );
```

```
        // Copy the image to the main device context
        BitBlt( hDC, 0, 0, ImageSize.cx, ImageSize.cy, hImageDC, 0, 0, SRCCOPY );

        // Delete the DC for the bitmap
        DeleteDC( hImageDC );
        // Release the main DC
        ReleaseDC( g_hWndMain, hDC );

    return 0;
}

int GameShutdown()
{
        // Delete the bitmap from memory
        DeleteObject( hImage );

        return 0;
}
```

First off is the GameInit() function. As I said before, this is called just before the message loop is entered. This is the point at which I load the image off of the disk and into memory using the LoadImage() function. Before I do that, I create a character string to hold the path of the image. You don't really need to do this; it's just for clarity. If you wanted to, you could put the string directly into the function call. By the way, if you are specifying a path with the slash (\) in it, don't forget to double it. This is because the slash is an escape sequence normally. So "C:\Zen\Great Game" would be "C:\\Zen\\Great Game."

Here is the prototype for LoadImage():

```
HANDLE LoadImage(
  HINSTANCE hinst,     // handle of the instance containing the image
  LPCTSTR lpszName,    // name or identifier of image
  UINT uType,          // type of image
  int cxDesired,       // desired width
  int cyDesired,       // desired height
  UINT fuLoad          // load flags
);
```

This has got to be the most abstracted function call I have ever seen. Let's wade through it and see what there is to find.

- **hinst.** Used if you are loading the image as a resource. Since I'm just loading a bitmap image from disk, I set this parameter to NULL.
- **lpszName.** The location of the image. This is the place where I entered the path of the image.
- **uType.** Takes the type of image that you want to load. It can be used to load cursors and icons as well, so if you were doing this you would specify the appropriate flag. I am loading an image so I specified IMAGE_BITMAP.
- **cxDesired** and **cyDesired.** Take the desired dimensions for the image. If you specify a size, the image will be scaled to fit your requirements. Normally you will want to maintain the original size of the image as I do in this situation. To maintain the original size just enter 0.
- **uLoad.** Takes a flag to describe how the file is being loaded. I am loading the file from a disk, so I specified LR_LOADFROMFILE.

  LoadImage() is a very complicated function, with a zillion options. If you want to know more about this function, check out the MSDN documentation. Don't worry though—the way I've shown you will be fine for your game development needs. The only thing you need to do is change the path to the file. The rest of the options are for more exotic needs like loading cursor resources, which does not come into practice in game development; you will normally write your own cursor handling routines. I'll show you how to do that bit of wizardry in chapter 15.

See the way the function returns a HANDLE? It is a generic HANDLE because this function can be used in so many ways. Just think of it like an HBITMAP, or in other words a handle to a bitmap. Note that I am saving this handle in the global variable hImage. This is so that I can easily access it from other functions throughout the life of the program. After this the GameInit() function exits and the program will shortly enter the message loop, which repeatedly calls the GameLoop() function. And I mean repeatedly—it is called about 145 times a second on my PC.

Let's now move on to what happens in the GameLoop() function. The first thing I do is get the device contexts set up. I get the main device context in the standard way using GetDC(). However, the DC for image is created in kind of an interesting way, using the function CreateCompatibleDC(). Keep in mind that the main DC is *acquired*, while the DC for the new bitmap is *created*. Remember this because at the end you need to *release* the main DC and *destroy* the image DC. Now, back to the DC creation. The function to do it looks like this:

```
HDC CreateCompatibleDC( HDC hdc );
```

As you can see, it returns a handle to a device context. This is the handle to the device context that you are creating. But the function also *takes* an HDC as a parameter. What's that all about? Well, you are creating a DC that is compatible with another DC. So what you do is pass a DC that you want the new one to be compatible with. In this case I want the bitmap that I created to be compatible with DC of my window, so I specified the DC that I acquired with GetDC(). My eyes are blurring with all this DC stuff. Yours probably are too, but really, don't worry—it is just going to get worse!

Now that I have loaded the bitmap, it is in memory and has its own DC. However, I know nothing about it. This is a bit of a problem because if you want to copy the image, you kind of need to know how big it is. So, to find out about the bitmap object, use a function called GetObject(). This function is designed specifically for the purpose of retrieving information about an object. Here it is:

```
int GetObject( HGDIOBJ hgdiobj, int cbBuffer, LPVOID lpvObject );
```

As you can see, it is designed for any object, not just bitmaps, so again it has been abstracted to the delta quadrant. Luckily, it is not complicated. The first parameter, hgdiobj, takes the handle of the object that I want to find out about. In this case I obviously want to find out about the bitmap so I specified the hImage global variable that contains the handle to image I retrieved in the GameInit() function.

The second parameter, cbBuffer, takes the size of the structure that I want to fill with information about the object, in bytes. This may seem strange, but it is because the function can return information on more than one object type. In this case I am finding out about a bitmap, so I used the structure that has been designed specifically for this purpose: BITMAP. I specified the size using the sizeof() operator. And finally, lpvObject takes the address of the structure that I want to fill with information. If the function fails, the return value is 0. Otherwise it is the number of bytes written to the structure.

By the way, this is what the BITMAP structure looks like:

```
typedef struct tagBITMAP {
    LONG    bmType;       // The type of bitmap.  Must be zero
    LONG    bmWidth;      // The width in pixels
    LONG    bmHeight;     // The height in pixels
    LONG    bmWidthBytes; // The width in bytes. (Width*Depth)
    WORD    bmPlanes;     // Number of color planes
    WORD    bmBitsPixel;     // The number of bits per pixel
    LPVOID  bmBits;       // Pointer to the actual bitmap data
} BITMAP;
```

Using the information contained in this structure, I extracted the width and height of the image and saved it in a SIZE structure. Following is the SIZE structure:

```
typedef struct tagSIZE {
    LONG cx;
    LONG cy;
} SIZE;
```

It is very similar to the POINT structure except it is for holding the size of something as the name implies.

OK, so the next thing I did was select the actual image data into its DC. This is done with the SelectObject() function that you saw in use previously with pens and brushes. It works just as before; I specified the bitmap's DC for the first parameter and the handle to the bitmap as the second. Now that the image is selected and compatible with the main DC, I can copy it over with the BitBlt() function. Between you and me, "BitBlt" means "bit block transfer." Oh my; It is now almost 1:00AM and I just looked over at MSDN on my other monitor and saw the number of parameters I have to explain for this function. Sigh.

The BitBlt() function has this prototype:

```
BOOL BitBlt(
    HDC hdcDest,  // handle to destination device context
    int nXDest,   // x-coordinate of destination rectangle's upper-left
                  // corner
    int nYDest,   // y-coordinate of destination rectangle's upper-left
                  // corner
    int nWidth,   // width of destination rectangle
    int nHeight,  // height of destination rectangle
    HDC hdcSrc,   // handle to source device context
    int nXSrc,    // x-coordinate of source rectangle's upper-left
                  // corner
    int nYSrc,    // y-coordinate of source rectangle's upper-left
                  // corner
    DWORD dwRop   // raster operation code
);
```

It's not actually as bad as I let on earlier; in fact it is quite intuitive.

- **hdcDest**. Takes a handle to the destination device context. In this case I want to copy to the client area of my window, so I specified the handle I received from the call to GetDC().

- **nXDest** and **nYDest**. Take the coordinates at which you want the image to start at. So if you specify (10, 10), then the upper-left corner of the image after it has been copied will be at (10, 10). I specified (0, 0) in the example.

- **nWidth** and **nHeight**. Take the width and height that you want the image to occupy on the destination DC. If you specify a size smaller than the actual size of the source image, then the source image will be *cropped* to fit rather than *scaled*. If you want to scale an image, use the StretchBlt() function, which I will be discussing shortly. I specified the actual size of image, which you recall I received from the GetObject() function call.

- **hdcSrc**. Takes a handle to the device context that contains the source image. I specified the DC that I created with the call to CreateCompatibleDC().

- **nXSrc** and **nYSrc**. Take the coordinates within the source image that specify where you want to *begin* copying. If you specify anything other than (0, 0), then the parts of the image before the coordinates you specified will be cropped.

- **dwRop**. Stands for *raster operation*. The raster operation is the Boolean operation that Windows can apply to the image as it is copied. I specified SRCCOPY, which means that I want to copy the image exactly as it is in the source DC. You can specify many other ROP codes that modify the image depending on the situation. Table 7.4 lists these ROP codes.

Table 7.4   Raster Operation Codes for BitBlt()

Value	Meaning
BLACKNESS	Fills the destination rectangle using the color associated with index 0 in the physical palette
WHITENESS	Fills the destination rectangle using the color associated with index1 in the physical palette
DSTINVERT	Inverts the destination rectangle
MERGECOPY	Merges the colors of the source rectangle with the specified pattern by using the Boolean AND operator
MERGEPAINT	Merges the colors of the inverted source rectangle with the colors of the destination rectangle by using the Boolean OR operator
NOTSRCCOPY	Copies the inverted source rectangle to the destination
NOTSRCERASE	Combines the colors of the source and destination rectangles by using the Boolean OR operator and then inverts the resultant color
PATCOPY	Copies the specified pattern into the destination bitmap
PATINVERT	Combines the colors of the specified pattern with the colors of the destination rectangle by using the Boolean XOR operator.
PATPAINT	Combines the colors of the pattern with the colors of the inverted source rectangle by using the Boolean OR operator. The result of this operation is combined with the colors of the destination rectangle by using the Boolean OR operator.
SRCAND	Combines the colors of the source and destination rectangles by using the Boolean AND operator
SRCCOPY	Copies the source rectangle directly to the destination rectangle
SRCERASE	Combines the inverted colors of the destination rectangle with the colors of the source rectangle by using the Boolean AND operator
SRCINVERT	Combines the colors of the source and destination rectangles by using the Boolean XOR operator
SRCPAINT	Combines the colors of the source and destination rectangles by using the Boolean OR operator

Now you are getting somewhere. When `BitBlt()` completes, the image has been copied to the destination window and the job is finished. Well, almost. I still need to release the DC resources that I acquired. I got rid of the DC I created for the bitmap first using the function `DeleteDC()`.

```
BOOL DeleteDC( HDC hdc );
```

This function simply takes a handle to the DC that you want to delete. I'm going to admit right now that I screwed up on my first pass making the code in the last example. I called `ReleaseDC()` on the DC that I created. Bad move. `ReleaseDC()` is used *only* for

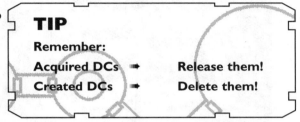

TIP

Remember:

Acquired DCs ➡ Release them!

Created DCs ➡ Delete them!

DCs acquired with `GetDC()`. If you create a DC, then you must use the function `DeleteDC()`. Otherwise you cause some sort of GDI reset and your screen goes to LaLa land. That's what happens in Windows 2000; in Windows 98 I just got the blue screen of a long, tortuous death.

The last thing I did in `GameLoop()` was release the main DC with the standard `ReleaseDC()` function that you saw before. And that is all there is to displaying a bitmap. Ten million pages of jargon and confusing explanations. Man, I love the GDI!

Now before I exit the application I put some cleanup code into the `GameShutdown()` function. This is because I want to get rid of the bitmap that is in memory so that it doesn't hog resources and cause a memory leak. Technically, you don't really need to do this because Windows will automatically release any resources your application acquired when it quits, but you know how reliable Windows can be. I released the bitmap using the function DeleteObject():

```
BOOL DeleteObject( HGDIOBJ hObject );
```

As you can see, it just takes a handle to an object that you want to delete. I want to delete the image, so I specified the global handle to the image that I acquired in the `GameInit()` function with `LoadImage()`.

The results of the code are shown in Figure 7.16. I created that image in about five minutes from scratch in Adobe Photoshop 5.5, which is just the best image editor in the galaxy.

Figure 7.16

Displaying bitmaps in a window using BitBlt()

That's pretty much it for normal bitmap copying. Although it took several pages to explain, it really is only about 20 lines of code, so remember it like that and all will be cool.

Advanced Bitmaps

The thing with bitmaps is that you almost always want to scale them to fit into a particular area or shape. For instance, say I wanted the bitmap image in the last example to appear in the upper-left corner of the window, but only with a 200 x 200 pixel dimension. Well, to solve this problem there is another function called StretchBlt(). This works in a very similar way to BitBlt(), with a few exceptions. First off, it is quite a bit slower. Secondly, if you specify a size that does not match the source image, then it will be scaled to fit the dimensions that you asked for. It looks like this:

```
BOOL StretchBlt(
   HDC hdcDest,        // handle to destination device context
   int nXOriginDest, // x-coordinate of upper-left corner
   int nYOriginDest, // y-coordinate of upper-left corner
   int nWidthDest,    // width of destination rectangle
```

```
    int nHeightDest,    // height of destination rectangle
    HDC hdcSrc,          // handle to source device context
    int nXOriginSrc,    // x-coordinate of upper-left corner in source
    int nYOriginSrc,    // y-coordinate of upper-left corner in source
    int nWidthSrc,      // width of source rectangle
    int nHeightSrc,     // height of source rectangle
    DWORD dwRop          // raster operation code
);
```

As you can see, the parameters are very similar to the original BitBlt() function, but I'll run through them just to be sure. The first parameter takes a handle to the destination device context. The second and third parameters take the coordinates for the upper-left corner for where you want the image to be copied. The next two parameters take the new width and height for the bitmap. The sixth parameter takes a handle to the source device context. The next two parameters take the position where you want to start copying the source image from. If you specify anything other than (0, 0), then the image before the position you specify will be cropped. Then the ninth and tenth parameters specify how much of the source image you want to copy. And finally, the last parameter takes the raster operation, which is the same as the ROP codes for BitBlt().

So let's see what this function does in practice. If I replaced the call to BitBlt() in the last example with a call to StretchBlt() like this:

```
StretchBlt(  hDC,                             // Destination device context
             10, 10, 300, 300,      // Destination dimensions
             hImageDC,                        // Source device context
               0, 0,
               ImageSize.cx, ImageSize.cy, // Source   dimensions
             SRCCOPY );                       // Raster operation
```

then the result will look like that shown in Figure 7.17.

Figure 7.17.bmp

Using `StretchBlt()` *to copy and scalebitmap images*

The quality is not perfect, but hey, it does the job. One really useful application for this function is for background art on menu screens. For instance, if you have an Intro screen with a background image that covers the entire screen, you can run into some problems. Perhaps you may not know what resolution the computer is currently set to. You could create a number of versions of the same picture, all at different resolutions, but this can be a waste of memory. Instead, just create a single medium resolution image, and then scale it using `StretchBlt()` to match the current resolution.

What's on the Menu?

Menus come under the term *resources*. Resources are generally a messy subject; I am going to pretty much ignore most of them, because they are for normal Windows programming rather than games. Using resources is a way to include data that would normally be external to the program, inside the actual executable image. For instance, you could include short sound files, bitmaps, icons, cursors, and, of course, menus, as well as any other data. You generally won't use too many resources in games because there are better ways to achieve results without them, and you'll also want to keep our interactions with Windows to a minimum anyway. Using resources will just complicate things. However, a menu is the one thing that you pretty much cannot improve upon easily, so I am going to show you how to do them now.

A Natural at Resources

There are two ways to create resources: the easy way and the hard way. The easy way is to use Visual C++'s built-in resource-editing tools; the hard way is to write a resource script in semi-C and do a lot of praying. Personally, I enjoy when things are done for me, so I'm going to go for the easy option. Don't worry, though, there are no catches to the easy way.

The thing is that the resource editor is more designed for MFC style applications; so the resource editor is not enabled by default for normal Win32 applications, which is what you are creating. To start with, the editor needs to be enabled. This is a two-step process, the first of which is to add what is called a *resource script* to your project. A resource script is the file that contains all the data about your resources, such as the locations of external files, etc. The resource script is plain text, so you can open it up and look at it if you want, although there is generally no reason to do so.

Adding the resource script is simple—just go to the select Project, Add To Project, New, as shown in Figure 7.18.

Figure 7.18

Adding a resource script

This will bring up the New dialog box, as shown in Figure 7.19. Select Resource Script from the list box, and enter a name for it in the File name text box. You can use any name you want, but for simplicity I usually just call it "resource." Press the OK button and two files will be created. The first will be resource.rc; this is the resource script. The second will be resource.h; this will contain definitions that are critical for the compiler to understand the resource script. Now, the resource script has automatically been added to your project, and a new Resource tab should have appeared at the bottom of the Visual C++ sidebar, as shown in Figure 7.20. By the way, if a big white box shows up on your screen with a single folder, called resource.rc, in it, just close the window.

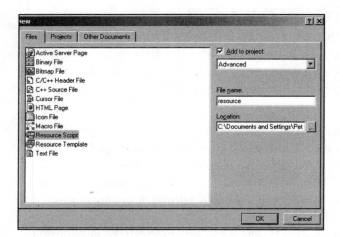

Figure 7.19

The New resource dialog box

Although the resource script has been added to your project, if you try to reference any of the material in it you will have compiler errors. To avoid errors, return to your main file that contains WinMain() and #include the resource.h file, and everything will work like it's supposed to.

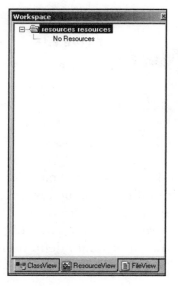

Figure 7.20

The sidebar with the new resource tab

OK, so now that that's done, let's take a quick look at how to add a new resource. In this case, I am going to add a new menu to the project. To do so, right-click on the resources folder in the sidebar and click Insert. This will bring up the Insert Resource dialog box, as shown in Figure 7.21.

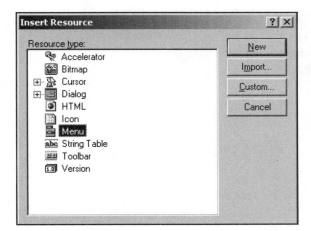

Figure 7.21

Inserting a menu resource

Select Menu from the list box and press New. This has the effect of adding a blank menu to the project. The menu is normally given a name like IDR_MENU1 or something along those lines. To give a more descriptive name, just right-click on the menu and click Properties, which brings up the Menu Properties dialog box, as shown in Figure 7.22. I have called the menu IDR_MAINMENU.

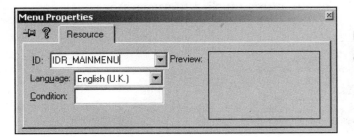

Figure 7.22

Changing the name of the menu

A Menu Fit for a King

OK, you've got a blank menu; let's do something with it. Figure 7.23 shows the menu editor in Visual C++. It works just like a normal menu except that you can type the entries yourself. To type the main menu bar headers, just click in the shaded box. When you type one entry, a new blank entry appears automatically.

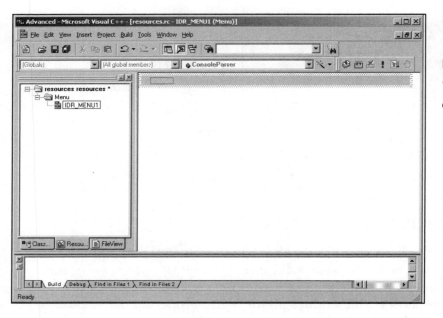

Figure 7.23

Visual C++'s menu editor

Now take a look at Figure 7.24. Here I have created a small menu with basic entries like New, Exit, etc. Also notice the separator bar above the Exit entry. To create a separator bar, just double-click on an entry and click the separator check box.

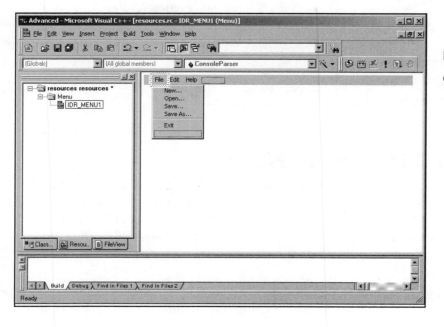

Figure 7.24

Creating a menu

Pay particular attention to the fact that after you name your menu entry, Visual C++ automatically creates an ID for the entry. The names are normally quite good. For instance, when I created an entry called Exit on the File menu, the name created will be ID_FILE_EXIT. You can look at the name created for you by double-clicking on any of the entries and looking at the ID combo box of the Properties dialog box.

The next part, making the menu display in your window, is slightly more complex. Well, it's not that bad; it's only a single line of code!

Gluing the Menu to the Window

The elusive single line of code is in fact one of the members of the window class structure that you filled out way back in prehistory. Here is the new version with the change bolded for visibility:

```
// The size of this structure in bytes
wc.cbSize                 = sizeof( WNDCLASSEX );
// The style of the window.
wc.style                  = CS_HREDRAW | CS_VREDRAW | CS_OWNDC;
// Useless information.  Just set to zero.
wc.cbClsExtra      = 0;
// Useless information.  Just set to zero.
wc.cbWndExtra      = 0;
// The name of our event handler
wc.lpfnWndProc     = WndProc;
// A handle to the applications instance
wc.hInstance       = hInstance;
// The handle to the brush to use for the window background
wc.hbrBackground      = (HBRUSH)GetStockObject( WHITE_BRUSH );
// A handle to the icon to use for the window
wc.hIcon              = LoadIcon( NULL, IDI_APPLICATION );
// A handle to a smaller version of the apps icon
wc.hIconSm               = LoadIcon( NULL, IDI_APPLICATION );
// A handle to the cursor to use while the mouse is over our window
wc.hCursor               = LoadCursor( NULL, IDC_ARROW );
// A handle to the resource to use as our window
wc.lpszMenuName       = MAKEINTRESOURCE(IDR_MAINMENU);
// The human readable name for this class
wc.lpszClassName      = pstrAppName;
```

Previously the lpszMenuName entry for the WNDCLASSEX structure was set to NULL because there was no menu. This time, the change is quite easy. The MAKEINTRESOURCE() macro converts an integer value into a value that is compatible with the Windows resource management internals. I specified IDR_MAINMENU, which must be the same as the name specified in the resource editor. By the way, if you happen to be getting compile errors, don't forget to #include the file resource.h or whatever you called it. IDR_MAINMENU is in fact a preprocessor cover for a unique number defined in resource.h. If you run the application now, it will look like Figure 7.25.

Figure 7.25

The application with a cool menu attached

You are really getting places now. There is only one problem with the menu: it doesn't work. You can click the items all you want, and they just won't do anything. So let's get to work on fixing that.

I think I should cover the architecture first, and t goes a little like this: When you select an item from the menu, Windows sends your application a WM_COMMAND message. The low-order word of the WPARAM contains the ID of the menu item that was selected. You can access the low-order word easily using the LOWORD() macro. It takes a 32-bit integer and returns the lower 16 bits. After you figure out which menu item was selected, you can execute the appropriate code. Have a look at my WM_COMMAND handler that follows. This handler handles messages *only* for the Help, About and the File, Exit menu items.

```
case WM_COMMAND:
{
```

```
switch( LOWORD( wParam ) )
{
        case ID_HELP_ABOUT:
        {
                MessageBox( NULL, "I Love Menus!",
                        "Menu Induced Message Box", MB_OK );
                break;
        }

        case ID_FILE_EXIT:
        {
        PostQuitMessage(2);
                break;
        }

        default:
        {
                break;
        }

}
return 0;
}
```

It's pretty simple. After I detect the WM_COMMAND message, I immediately test the state of the WPARAM to figure out which menu item was selected. If it was the Help, About item, then I display an incredibly informational MessageBox(). On the other hand, if the user selects File, Exit, I tell Windows to post a WM_QUIT message using the PostQuitMessage() function. Notice that after I handle each menu item I immediately break and return 0; this lets Windows know that I handled the message successfully.

Handling Keyboard Input: Windows Way

Input is not too hard, but it is so abstracted that it can reduce some people to tears. I'm going to start with the keyboard because it is the main input device that people use with computers, particularly in a lot of games. Mouse input will follow shortly!

I'm going to give you some insider information about how the keyboard works. When you press a key, a number of things occur. The first is that a signal is sent to a small processor within the keyboard. This processor generates a *scan code* that is sent to another smaller processor inside the PC. The scan code is an OEM code that is specific to the key that was pressed. It has nothing to do with an ASCII code. So after it leaves the keyboard it arrives at what is called the PIC, or *programmable interrupt controller*. This chip interrupts the main processor and tells it to stop doing whatever it was doing and deal with the keyboard event. The processor then grabs the scan code and forwards it to some software, usually provided by the operating system, to further process the data. In the old days, when DOS was around, the scan code was turned into an appropriate ASCII code and put into a buffer. These days it gets a little more complicated. The code is forwarded to Windows, where things get really discombobulated. Windows turns the scan code into a message, which winds its way through a zillion queues and processing places before it finally gets plopped into your code, in your WndProc(), in the form of either a WM_CHAR, WM_KEYDOWN, or WM_KEYUP message. Phew!

Let's look at the differences between these messages. A WM_KEYDOWN message is used to inform you about a change in the state of a key. For instance, if a key was up and is now down you get a WM_KEYDOWN message. And then when it returns to normal your WndProc() gets a WM_KEYUP message. The problem with the WM_KEY*x* messages is that they don't tell you much about the character that the user is trying to input into the computer. That is the purpose of the WM_CHAR message. This message contains the actual ASCII code for the character that has been pressed. If you get a WM_CHAR message, then you will also get the WM_KEY*x* messages, but they are not mutually exclusive in any way. That is, you can process one without the other. You will get them in this order:

1. WM_KEYDOWN; e.g., the "K" key has been pressed.
2. WM_CHAR; e.g., the letter "k" has been input.
3. WM_KEYUP; e.g., the "K" key has been released.

You can also use the WM_KEYDOWN message to detect keys that don't have any associated ASCII codes—for instance, if the user pressed the F1 key. For WM_KEY*x* messages, Windows describes the keys using what are called *virtual key codes*. They are constants that look like VK_*x*, where "x" is the name of the key. For instance, VK_RETURN is for the Enter key, VK_SPACE is for the Spacebar, and VK_A is for the "A" key, amd so on. You can find a full list of the codes in */Platform SDK / User Interface Services / User Input / Virtual Key Codes* in the MSDN library.

Now with all the theory out of the way, let's look at some code. In this code I'm going to use WM_KEY*x* codes to detect if the user presses F1, in which case I will display a small message box to the user telling him to go take a long walk off a short pier. I will also use the WM_CHAR message to detect if the user presses an uppercase "X," in which case the program will exit.

```
case WM_KEYDOWN:
{
        switch( wParam )
        {
                case VK_F1:
                {
                        MessageBox( NULL,
                          "Take a long walk off a short pier, I'm sleeping!",
                                "ZZZZZzzzzzzzz....", MB_OK );
                        break;
                }
                default:
                        break;

        }

        return 0;
}

case WM_CHAR:
{
        switch( wParam )
        {
                case 'X':
                {
                        PostQuitMessage(0);
                        break;
                }
                default:
                        break;
        }

        return 0;
}
```

That's not too bad, is it? Let's look at what is going on here. First off is the WM_KEY-DOWN message handler. All I did was switch through the WPARAM of the message, which contains the virtual key-code for the key that was pressed. I am only testing for the F1 key, so that is the only case test. If the F1 key is pressed, then the message box is displayed. Notice the break statement that drops back to the return 0 statement. It is very important to always return 0 from the messages that you process in the WndProc()

The WM_CHAR handler works in a very similar fashion. If an uppercase "X" is pressed, then the program will exit. The WM_CHAR message automatically takes into account the current state of the Caps Lock key as well as the Shift key, and anything else that would otherwise change the form of the character. By the way, most of this wizardry is in fact done by the TranslateMessage() function that I talked about in previous chapters. Getting back to the example, the case statement checks to see if the wParam contains the 'X' and if so exits the program. Note the drop out using break statements and the final return statement. If you seem to be unable to compile your code after writing what looks like a correct WM_CHAR handler, then I have the solution for you. It is a common mistake to forget to put in the single quotes around the letter that you are testing for. So now you know!

The WM_KEYUP works exactly the same as the WM_KEYDOWN message except that the message is sent when the key is released.

Don't Get Asynchronous on Me

This is the point at which I tell you that everything I just told you is not really applicable to games. You're probably getting used to it by now. The way I have been talking about is perfectly acceptable for normal Windows applications and even parts of your game. However, there is so much interaction with Windows that I personally would rather get a root canal than force my game to bow down to the likes of Windows' keyboard input structure. Anyway, the real reason is that the message loop does not really fit into the structure for our game. Remember, we want to keep as much as we can inside the game loop.

There is also a serious issue with the standard method for input handling: it is serial. That is, it cannot tell you about more than a single key press at the same point in time. For instance, say you are running forward in a game, holding the Forward key down. Then you spot an enemy and decide to shoot him while running. You press the Control key simultaneously with the Forward button. Windows can't deal with that at all. It will simply stop the message from the Forward key and tell you the Control key has been pressed. The end result is that the character stops moving and fires, which is not what you asked for, and you along with your game company will be killed until you die from it by an angry mob of game players.

So how do you get around this? Well, the best possibility would be if there was some sort of function that you could call whenever you wanted to get more information about any key. The function could take a request and look up the state of the key in some sort of table and then return and tell you if the key is pressed or not. Would you be surprised if I told you that Microsoft, had created a function with that exact functionality, and it has the beautiful name of GetAsyncKeyState() bestowed upon it? The *asynchronous* bit means that it is not synced to any particular event. In other words, you can call it whenever the heck you want. It looks like this:

```
SHORT GetAsyncKeyState( int vKey );
```

It's quite simple, as you can see; it only takes a single parameter, which is the virtual key code of the key that you want to check on. The return value can be kind of complex if you look at it one way, and kind of easy if you look at it another way. There are all sorts of bit vectors set that tell exactly when the key was pressed in relation to the last time you called the function. However, you are going to ignore all that wackiness and concentrate on getting the state of the key. The good news is that you can pretty much treat the return value as a Boolean value. That is, it will return TRUE if the specified key was down and FALSE otherwise. Cool, huh?

I have just spent quite a while on jelly theory, so let's solidify this stuff by looking at some code. I'm going to write a few simple lines that draw a rectangle if the Spacebar is pressed. Have a look at this:

```
int GameLoop()
{
        HDC hDC = GetDC( g_hWndMain );

        if( GetAsyncKeyState( VK_SPACE ) )
                Rectangle( hDC, 20, 20, 300, 400 );
        else
                InvalidateRect( g_hWndMain, 0, TRUE );

        ReleaseDC( g_hWndMain, hDC );

        return 0;
}
```

Much easier than messing with key messages, don't you think? Let's just run over what is going on. First the DC is acquired with `GetDC()` so that I can draw to the screen. Then I check to see if the Spacebar has been pressed using the `GetAsyncKeyState()` function. Notice that all I have to do is a simple Boolean test with the function within the `if` statement. If the key has been pressed, then I draw a simple rectangle using the `Rectangle()` function. Alternatively, if the key is depressed, then I just wipe the screen using the `InvalidateRect()` function. Finally, I release the DC and return from the loop. Figure 7.26 shows the results.

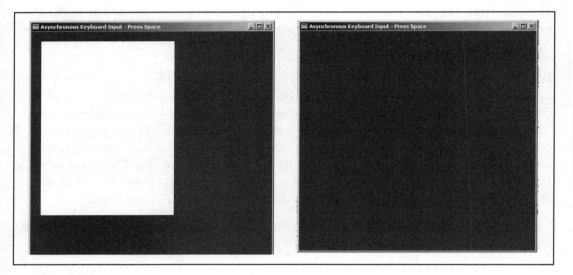

Figure 7.26

Using asynchronous keyboard input to display a rectangle

I haven't covered the `InvalidateRect()` function yet, so here it is:

```
BOOL InvalidateRect( HWND hWnd, CONST RECT *lpRect, BOOL bErase );
```

This function takes a handle to the window that you want to invalidate as the first parameter. The second takes the address of a rectangle that contains the coordinates of the area that you want to invalidate. If you pass `NULL`, then the entire window is cleared. And finally, the last parameter is a flag that specifies whether you want to erase the background.

> **TIP**
>
> To *invalidate* a window means that you want Windows to send a `WM_PAINT` message to your `WndProc()` telling it that part, or all, of the window needs to be cleared.

Now with all that keyboard stuff under the belt, I'm all keyed up to start talking about mice. *Keyed*, get it?

The Mice Are Coming!

I feel quite stupid right now, but I'm not going to tell you why until you get to asynchronous mouse input—but don't skip forward to find out.

The mouse works kind of like the keyboard. When you press a button, a little processor in the mouse generates a signal that is sent to the PIC on the motherboard, which subsequently interrupts the processor, which allows Windows to process the mouse event and turn it into a message. There are quite a number of mouse messages, but they all work in pretty much the same way.

The messages dealing with the mouse buttons are listed in Table 7.5

Table 7.5   Mouse Messages

Message	Meaning
WM_LBUTTONUP	The left mouse button has been released
WM_LBUTTONDOWN	The left mouse button has been pressed
WM_RBUTTONUP	The right mouse button has been released
WM_RBUTTONDOWN	The right mouse button has been pressed
WM_MBUTTONUP	The middle mouse button has been released
WM_MBUTTONDOWN	The middle mouse button has been pressed

Those names are kind of misleading in some circumstances. The reason is that when the code was written there was not a single left-handed person on the face of the planet. They all appeared in the last 12 years—a Microsoft marketing manager told me so. Okay, I'm only joking; it's just that the Windows mouse code was written without much foresight.

The thing is that in these politically correct days, people refer to the mouse buttons as the *primary* button, the *secondary* button, and the, uhhmmm, *middle* button. The reason for this is because left-handed people like to have their mice on the other side of the keyboard because it is more comfy. However, they also like the buttons to be reversed, so in effect, the left mouse button becomes the right mouse button and vice versa. There is an option in Control Panel to reverse the buttons so that they work this way. Anyway, to draw a conclusion: Naming variables with left and right prefixes was a bad idea. Instead, they should have had the prefixes WM_Px, WM_Sx, and WM_Mx for primary, secondary, and middle, respectively.

The reason that I'm doing all this complaining is because as soon as you leave the cozy world of Windows and move into DirectInput, all this reversible button stuff is lost, so you may make every left-handed person who uses your software very annoyed. Watch out for this little issue.

Anyway, there is one other mouse message that kind of keeps to itself and doesn't really fit in with the other messages. It is called WM_MOUSEMOVE, and it is sent to your WndProc() whenever the mouse changes its position. Again, you can deal with all of these messages, some of them, or none of them. It's totally up to you, dude.

Too much theory and not enough fun makes Johnny a dull boy, so let's look at some totally cool examples. This first example uses the mouse to implement a relatively simple drawing application. You can draw lines by holding down the left mouse button and moving the mouse. Figure 7.27 shows one that I created earlier.

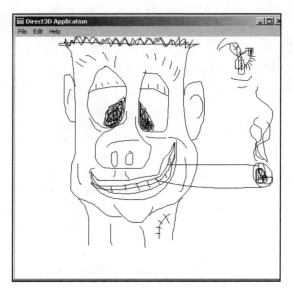

Figure 7.27

What an artist!

Here is the code for this example:

```
case WM_LBUTTONDOWN:
{
        // Turn drawing on
bDraw = TRUE;
        return 0;
}


case WM_LBUTTONUP:
{
// Turn drawing off
        bDraw = FALSE;
        return 0;
}


case WM_MOUSEMOVE:
{
        // Acquire a DC for drawing
        HDC hDC = GetDC( g_hWndMain );

        // Initialize the variables.  Because they are static variables this code
        // is only executed once
     static int xPos = LOWORD( lParam );
     static int yPos = HIWORD( lParam );

        // Check if drawing mode is turned on
if( bDraw )
{
                // Move to the last mouse position
                        MoveToEx( hDC, xPos, yPos, NULL );
                // Draw the line to the current mouse position
                LineTo( hDC, LOWORD( lParam ), HIWORD( lParam ) );
        }

        // Save the mouse's last position
xPos = LOWORD( lParam );
        yPos = HIWORD( lParam );
```

```
        // Release the DC
        ReleaseDC( g_hWndMain, hDC );

        return 0;
}
```

Not much code for all that functionality, huh? Anyway, let's quickly run through it. When the user presses the primary mouse button, a WM_LBUTTONDOWN message is sent to the WndProc(). In this handler I set a Boolean variable that controls drawing to TRUE. In effect, I am hitting a switch that turns the pen on. The next handler is for WM_LBUTTONUP and occurs when the user depresses the primary mouse button. This code does the exact opposite of WM_LBUTTONDOWN. The bDraw variable is set to FALSE so that drawing is turned off; after all, I only want the line to be drawn when the primary mouse button is down.

Now comes the code for WM_MOUSEMOVE. This code is executed whenever the mouse changes position. The first thing I did was to acquire a DC. Next up I declare two static variables and initialize them with the current position of the mouse. Don't forget that these variables are *static,* so they remember their values throughout the life of the program and their initialization code only executes once. Next up I check if drawing mode is on; if it is then I move the current drawing position to the previous position of the mouse. Then I draw a line to the current position of the mouse. When that completes, all that is left for me to do is to store the value of the current position so that it can be used next time the mouse moves. And finally, I release the DC so that Windows stays happy.

By the way, there is a small problem with the code in the previous example. If you resize the window or if the window needs repainting for any reason, you will lose all of your drawing. This could be easily fixed with some code that records the mouse positions into a linked list and redraws the list whenever the screen needs to be updated. In fact, this is how all vector drawing programs work.

Don't Sync Out on Me, Man

Aaiiight, it's time to get jiggy. This is another one of those points where I tell you that everything I just showed is substandard to another, nicer, faster, and all around shinier method of doing the same thing. I already discussed a lot about asynchronous input with the keyboard, but let's look at how it's done with the mouse.

Oh yeah, before beginning I better tell you why I feel like an idiot. Well, here's the thing: With asynchronous keyboard input you get a nice intuitive name like GetAsyncKeyState(). You might think there would be another nice function called GetAsyncMouseState(), wouldn't you? Well, there's not. So a few years back when I could not find any prebuilt asynchronous mouse input handlers, I decided I would write one myself. And I did. It took me about 20 minutes to modify the message system into a nice stable asynchronous state table system. And I have been using that code for a very long time in I don't know how many applications. I was even going to give it to you, my loyal reader, and explain it in my book. It was in the table of contents and everything. But then earlier today as I was researching the GetAsyncKeyState() function, I was struck by a blinding shot of knowledge. The asynchronous mouse input handler for the mouse is *also* GetAsyncKeyState(). I had no reason to write that code manually!

So the moral of the story is that if you think something should be there, then it probably is—you just have to look really hard for it in MSDN.

Let's reexamine that GetAsyncKeyState() function. There are, in fact, three virtual key codes that have to do with the mouse. They are listed in Table 7.6.

Table 7.6   Virtual Key Codes for the Mouse

Key Code	Meaning
VK_LBUTTON	The primary mouse button
VK_RBUTTON	The secondary mouse button
VK_MBUTTON	The middle mouse button

If you specify any of those values as a parameter to the function, then it will return the status of the mouse buttons. For instance, if you wrote the following code:

```
if( GetAsyncKeyState( VK_RBUTTON ) )
            PostQuitMessage( 0 );
```

within the GameLoop() function then the application would exit as soon as you pressed the secondary mouse button. Pretty cool, huh? So now you know how asynchronous input works.

Actually, you have covered so much stuff so far, in so many areas, that you can probably consider yourself a total Windows guru by now. In fact, if you remember even 30 percent of the stuff in this chapter, then you are well on the way to getting rich!

Asynchronous Graphics

I better point out something about the GDI before moving on. It likes to work in what are called *batches*. That is, when you call a GDI function, such as LineTo(), you are *not* drawing a line. You are just asking the GDI to draw one at some point in the future. That point will be when a buffer of drawing commands becomes full. The other big *caveat* is that your requests are generally not even processed in the order you wrote them in. So if you draw something, then draw a rectangle over it, you will still see flickers of the original because from time to time it gets out of order.

There are so many times when this becomes a total pain. The way around it is a function called GdiFlush(). It takes no parameters and simply tells the GDI to process and dump everything in its buffer to the display adapter. That way you can be sure that certain drawing effects have actually completed if another one is going to rely on it.

Synchronization

I want to discuss a little bit about controlling the flow of the space-time continuum. For example, at some point you may want to display an image for a few seconds before moving on to do something else. Well, this is where a function that pauses execution comes in very useful. And I have that very function for you now; it has the name Pause(); And this is what it looks like:

```
void Pause( int MilliSecs )
{
        // Get the current time
        int Time = GetTickCount();

        // Wait until the specified time has elapsed.
        while( (UINT)GetTickCount() - (UINT)Time < (UINT)MilliSecs ){}
}
```

All you do is call it, passing the number of milliseconds that you want to pause for. Just in case you didn't know, there are 1,000 milliseconds in a second. So if you want to pause for five seconds, then you would pass the value 5,000 to the function.

By the way, as this relies on some Win32 functions, it obviously has some limitations. One of them is that it is not accurate below about 55 milliseconds on Windows-95-and-later-based operating systems, and 10 milliseconds on Windows NT-4.0-and-later-based operating systems.

Let's take a look at how this puppy works. First off I call the Win32 function GetTickCount(), which returns the number of milliseconds that have passed since the current Windows session started. Then I sit in a tight loop until the correct amount of time has elapsed. I do this by subtracting the start time from the current time and then seeing if this value is less than the requested delay. If it is, then I continue, waiting, otherwise I return.

Advanced Rendering Using Raster Operations

There comes a time in every programmer's life where he just wants to draw a moving object on the screen and a moving object appears on the screen. You don't want a mirror effect of endless copies of the object being drawn and staying there. Well, this is a total pain and it will haunt you forever in 2D graphics programming. The problem is this: When you draw an object, you destroy the image that was underneath the new object. So when you move the object to its new position, you want the old area to be restored, right? Well, this entails doing a whole bunch of things like saving the underlying image, copying the new image, and then redrawing the saved portion again to erase the image. I am going to cover this effect in detail when we come to talk about 2D graphics with Direct3D, but for now I'm going to show you an interesting way of drawing simple objects without bothering with all that copying stuff. Also, the GDI is so darn slow that even simple programs grind to a halt when a lot of blitting (image copying) starts.

The method works like this: What if instead of drawing a normal rectangle, the lines just inverted the image underneath? Hmmm...What does this achieve? Well, it means that the rectangle is perfectly visible on just about every surface (except medium gray). But most importantly, it means that if you draw the rectangle twice, it will be erased! See, you draw it once, inverting the original, then you draw it again, inverting the inverted colors. In other words, returning it to normal. This is the effect that I use in this chapter's sample application, called *Zong,* to draw the bat and the ball. Flip ahead to Figure 7.29 to see what I'm talking about. This may be a slightly confusing topic, so following are the steps I used to draw the ball in *Zong:*

1. Set the brush to transparent so that the inside of the ball is hollow.
2. Select a standard solid pen into the device context.
3. Set the drawing to inverted.
4. Draw the ellipse at its new position. This creates an inverted ellipse on the screen.

   — Wait for Next Screen Update —

5. Now draw the ellipse *again*. This inverts the inverted colors, thereby returning them to normal. The ellipse is now erased.
6. Repeat steps 3 and 4 every time you want to move the ball.

So how do you set the drawing mode to inverted? Well, it all has to do with what is called the *binary raster operation,* or in Windows lingo, the ROP2. The ROP part stands for *raster operation,* as mentioned earlier, and the 2 stands for *binary.* The function is called SetROP2() and it looks like this:

```
int SetROP2( HDC hdc, int fnDrawMode );
```

The fnDrawMode parameter takes the new raster operation that you want to use. It can be any of the 16 parameters listed in Table 7.7. The important entries are bolded.

Table 7.7 Raster Operations

Parameter	Meaning
R2_BLACK	**The pixel is set to black.**
R2_COPYPEN	**The pixel is set to the color of the pen.**
R2_MASKNOTPEN	The pixel is a combination of the colors common to both the screen and the inverse of the pen.
R2_MASKPEN	The pixel is a combination of the colors common to both the pen and the screen.
R2_MASKPENNOT	The pixel is a combination of the colors common to both the pen and the inverse of the screen.
R2_MERGENOTPEN	The pixel is a combination of the screen color and the inverse of the pen color.
R2_MERGEPEN	The pixel is a combination of the pen color and the screen color.

Table 7.7 Raster Operations (continued)

Parameter	Meaning
R2_MERGEPENNOT	The pixel is a combination of the pen color and the inverse of the screen color.
R2_NOP	The pixel remains unchanged.
R2_NOT	**The pixel is inverted.**
R2_NOTCOPYPEN	The pixel is the inverse of the pen color.
R2_NOTMASKPEN	The pixel is the inverse of the R2_MASKPEN color.
R2_NOTMERGEPEN	The pixel is the inverse of the R2_MERGEPEN color.
R2_NOTXORPEN	The pixel is the inverse of the R2_XORPEN color.
R2_WHITE	**The pixel is set to white.**
R2_XORPEN	The pixel is a combination of the colors in the pen and in the screen, but not in both.

When you want to do some animation, you set the raster operation to R2_NOT. Then if you want to get back to normal, set the raster operation to R2_COPYPEN.

Zong!

I believe you have reached the next stage of your Zen learning. It is now time for *Zong*—the game of the great ones! This game turned out much cooler than I was originally planning. At the start, I wanted a simple Win32 game that brought together all the points that I talked about in the last few chapters. I messed around for a while and came up with a one-player *Pong*-type game called... *Zong*. When you say *Zong*, you need to say it like Dr. Evil says "one million dollars" in Austin Powers.

As I was saying, I wanted it to be a simple example. Not necessarily entertaining, but more educational. Unfortunately, I couldn't help myself! My friends won't stop asking me for copies. They keep playing it all the time. See what you can achieve with the power of Zen? I spent three hours putting this puppy together and then another two debugging. And look at the results: An entertaining game that people like to play. You don't have to have a Hollywood budget to make fun software. By the way, *Zong* bores the heck out of me, but then again I designed it, so I'll leave the decision up to you. Figure 7.28 shows the Intro screen, 7.29 the game in action, and 7.30 the Help screen.

Figure 7.28.bmp

Zong's Intro screen

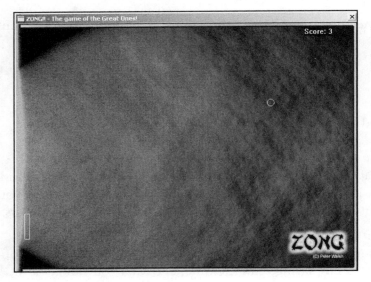

Figure 7.29.bmp

Zong in action

Figure 7.30

Zong's Help screen

You may have noticed from Figure 7.29 that *Zong* is completely single player. That is, there is no computer opponent or anything like that. The point of the game is to achieve 10 points. Every time you hit the ball you get a point, and every time you miss the ball and it falls into the lake of fire you lose a point. Every two points you get increases the speed of the ball, and vice versa. It is not particularly hard to win, and it is next to impossible to lose.

Have a look at the full code listing that follows. It is fairly long, but most of it is dealing with the interface and Windows.

```
//////////////////////////////////////////
// Chapter 7
// ZONG!!!!!!!!! The game of the great ones
// Author: Peter Walsh
// Stardate 14.11.2000

#define WIN32_LEAN_AND_MEAN

// The main windows include file
#include <windows.h>
#include <stdlib.h>
```

```cpp
void DrawBat();                         // Draws the bat
void DrawBall( HDC hDC );               // Draws the ball
void MoveBall();                        // Moves the ball
void DrawScore();                       // Draws the score
void Pause( int MilliSecs );    // Pause function

int GameInit();                         // Initialization
int GameLoop();                         // The game loop
int GameShutdown();                     // Shutdown

const int BAT_WIDTH = 10;               // The width of the bat (pixels)
const int BAT_HEIGHT = 50;              // The height of the bat (pixels)
const int BAT_INITIAL_X = 15; // The distance from the left (pixels)
const int BAT_SPEED = 6;        // The bat speed of movement (pixels per keypress)
const int BALL_SPEED = 3;       // Ball speed (pixels per movement event)
const int BALL_RADIUS = 7;      // The size of the ball (pixels)

// Variable holding the speed of the ball
int g_BallSpeed = BALL_SPEED;

// Used for redrawing code
BOOL g_bRedrawBat = TRUE;
BOOL g_bRedrawBall = TRUE;

// The score holder, initialized to three
int g_Score = 3;

// A global device context because
// we are drawing a lot
HDC g_hDC;

// A global handle to the main window
HWND g_hWndMain;

// A structure to hold info about the ball
typedef struct
{
        int x, y;       // Position
        int Radius;     // Size
```

```c
}BALL, *PBALL;

// A structure to hold info about the bat
typedef struct
{
        int x, y;        // Position
        int Width, Height;// Size

}BAT, *PBAT;

// The global bat structure
BAT g_Bat;
// The global ball structure
BALL g_Ball;


// The window procedure to handle events
long CALLBACK WndProc( HWND hWnd, UINT uMessage,
                                    WPARAM wParam, LPARAM lParam )
{
        PAINTSTRUCT PaintStruct;        // Structure used during windows painting
        HDC hDC;                  // Handle to device context for painting

        // Handle to the background bitmap
        static HBITMAP hBitmap = 0;

        // Switch the windows message to figure out what it is
        switch( uMessage )
        {
                case WM_CREATE:// The CreateWindow() function was just called
                {
                        // Load the background bitmap
                        hBitmap = (HBITMAP)LoadImage( 0, "ZONGBG.BMP",
                                                            IMAGE_BITMAP, 0, 0,
                    LR_LOADFROMFILE );
                        return 0;
                }
```

```
case WM_KEYDOWN:
{
        switch( wParam )
        {
                // Exit if the escape key is pressed
                case VK_ESCAPE:
                {
                        if( MessageBox( g_hWndMain,
                                "Do you really want to quit the \
                                game of the great ones?",
                                        "Bye Bye", MB_YESNO ) == IDYES

                        PostMessage( g_hWndMain, WM_DESTROY, 0, 0 );

                        break;
                }

        }

        return 0;
}

case WM_PAINT: // Redraw the background bitmap
{
        // Tell windows we want to start updating the window
        hDC = BeginPaint( hWnd, &PaintStruct );

        // Structure to hold info about the bitmap
        BITMAP Bitmap;

        // Get information about the bitmap
        GetObject( hBitmap, sizeof( BITMAP ), &Bitmap );

        // Create a compatible DC for the bitmap
        HDC hBitmapDC = CreateCompatibleDC( hDC );

        // Select the bitmap into the new DC
        SelectObject( hBitmapDC, hBitmap );
```

```cpp
                    // Copy the bitmap to the main DC
                    BitBlt( hDC, 0, 0, Bitmap.bmWidth,
                    Bitmap.bmHeight, hBitmapDC, 0, 0, SRCCOPY );

                    // Get rid of the new DC
                    DeleteDC( hBitmapDC );

                    // Tell windows we have finished updating the window
                    EndPaint( hWnd, &PaintStruct );

                    // The window has just been redrawn so we should not
                    // redraw the ball and bat to erase the previous ones.
                    // They are already erased!  Otherwise you get artifacts
                    g_bRedrawBat = FALSE;
                    g_bRedrawBall = FALSE;

                    return 0;
            }

        case WM_DESTROY:        // The window is about to be closed
        {
                    // Delete the background bitmap
                    DeleteObject( hBitmap );

                    // Our main window is closing.
              // This means we want our app to exit.
                    // Tell windows to put a WM_QUIT message in our message queue
                    PostQuitMessage( 0 );
                    return 0;
        }

        default:
        {
                    // Let windows handle this message
                    return DefWindowProc( hWnd, uMessage, wParam, lParam );
        }
        }
    }
}
```

```c
// The windows entry point. The application will start executing here
int WINAPI WinMain( HINSTANCE hInstance, HINSTANCE hPrevInstance,
                                    PSTR pstrCmdLine, int iCmdShow )
{
        HWND hWnd;              // The handle to our main window
        MSG msg;                        // The message windows is sending us
        WNDCLASSEX wc;         // The window class used to create our window

        // The name of our class and also the title to our window
        static char strAppName[] = "ZONG!! - The game of the Great Ones!";

        // Fill in the window class with the attributes for our main window

        // The size of this structure in bytes
        wc.cbSize                       = sizeof( WNDCLASSEX );

        //   The style of the window.
        wc.style                        = CS_HREDRAW | CS_VREDRAW | CS_OWNDC;
        // Useless information.  Just set to zero.
        wc.cbClsExtra         = 0;
        // Useless information.  Just set to zero.
        wc.cbWndExtra         = 0;
        // The name of our event handler
        wc.lpfnWndProc        = WndProc;
        // A handle to the applications instance
        wc.hInstance          = hInstance;
        // The handle to the brush to use for the window background
        wc.hbrBackground      = (HBRUSH)GetStockObject( BLACK_BRUSH );
        // A handle to the icon to use for the window
        wc.hIcon                        = LoadIcon( NULL, IDI_APPLICATION );
        // A handle to a smaller version of the apps icon
        wc.hIconSm                      = LoadIcon( NULL, IDI_APPLICATION );
        // A handle to the cursor to use while the mouse is over our window
        wc.hCursor                      = LoadCursor( NULL, IDC_ARROW );
        // A handle to the resource to use as our menu
        wc.lpszMenuName       = NULL;
        // The human readable name for this class
        wc.lpszClassName      = strAppName;

        // Register the class with windows
        RegisterClassEx( &wc );
```

```cpp
// Create the window based on the previous class
hWnd = CreateWindowEx( NULL,                // Advanced style settings
                       strAppName,          // The name of the class
                       strAppName,          // The window caption
                       WS_OVERLAPPED |
                       WS_CAPTION |
                       WS_SYSMENU,          // The window style
                       CW_USEDEFAULT,       // The initial x position
                       CW_USEDEFAULT,       // The initial y position
                       647, 505,            // The initial width / height
                       NULL,                // Handle to parent window

                       NULL,                // Handle to the menu
                       hInstance,           // Handle to the apps instance
                       NULL );              // Advanced context

// Keep a global copy of the window handle
g_hWndMain = hWnd;

// Display the window we just created
ShowWindow( hWnd, iCmdShow );
// Draw the window contents for the first time
UpdateWindow( hWnd );


// Initialize the game
GameInit();


// Start the message loop
while( TRUE )
{
        // Check if a message is waiting for processing
        if( PeekMessage( &msg, NULL, 0, 0, PM_REMOVE ) )
        {
                // Check if the message is to quit the application
                if( msg.message == WM_QUIT )
                        // Exit the message loop
```

```
                                break;

                        // Change the format of certain messages
                        TranslateMessage( &msg );
                        // Pass the message to WndProc() for processing
                        DispatchMessage( &msg );
                }
                else
                {
                        // Run the game loop
                        GameLoop();
                }
        }

        // Run shutdown code
        GameShutdown();

        // Return control to windows with the exit code
        return msg.wParam;
}

int GameInit()
{
        // Game Initialization
        g_hDC = GetDC( g_hWndMain );

        // Load up the starting logo
        HBITMAP hBitmap = (HBITMAP)LoadImage( 0, "ZONG.BMP",
                                IMAGE_BITMAP, 0, 0, LR_LOADFROMFILE );

        // Structure to hold information about the image
        BITMAP Bitmap;

        // Get info about the image
        GetObject( hBitmap, sizeof( BITMAP ), &Bitmap );

        // Create a compatible DC for the image
        HDC hBitmapDC = CreateCompatibleDC( g_hDC );

        // Select the image into the new DC
        SelectObject( hBitmapDC, hBitmap );
```

```
        // Copy the image to the main DC
        BitBlt( g_hDC, 0, 0, Bitmap.bmWidth, Bitmap.bmHeight,
                                        hBitmapDC, 0, 0, SRCCOPY );

        // Delete the new DC
        DeleteDC( hBitmapDC );

        // Delete the bitmap
        DeleteObject( hBitmap );

        // Display the bitmap for 2 seconds
        Pause( 2000 );

        // Invalidate the window, so the normal background is drawn
        InvalidateRect( g_hWndMain, 0, TRUE );

        // Initialize the bat and ball structures to 0
        ZeroMemory( &g_Ball, sizeof( BALL ) );
        ZeroMemory( &g_Bat, sizeof( BAT ) );

        // Initialize the bat
        g_Bat.Height = BAT_HEIGHT;
        g_Bat.Width = BAT_WIDTH;
        g_Bat.x = BAT_INITIAL_X;
        g_Bat.y = 0;

        // Initialize the ball
        g_Ball.Radius = BALL_RADIUS;
        g_Ball.x = g_Ball.y = 100;

        return 0;
}

int GameLoop()
{

        // Used to synchronize the speed the bat moves at
        static BatTime = 0;
        // Used to synchronize the speed of the ball
        static BallTime = 0;
```

```
HRESULT Res;

RECT ClientRect;
GetClientRect( g_hWndMain, &ClientRect );

// Check if all the points are used up. ie a lose
if( g_Score == 0 )
{
        // Ask the user if they want to restart
        Res = MessageBox( NULL, "You totally suck! Wanna try again?",
                                                "Results", MB_YESNO );

        if( Res == IDYES )
        {
                // He does, so reset the score and ball speed and pos
                g_Score = 3;
                g_BallSpeed = BALL_SPEED;
                g_Ball.x = rand()%ClientRect.right;
                g_Ball.y = rand()%ClientRect.bottom;
        }
        else
                // He does not, so quit
                PostMessage( g_hWndMain, WM_DESTROY, 0, 0 );

        return 0;

}

// Check for a winner
else if( g_Score == 10 )
{
        // Give congrats and ask if restart
        Res = MessageBox( NULL,
                "You are now a Zong Guru!!!  \
                Do you want to play again?", "Results", MB_YESNO );

        if( Res == IDYES )
        {
                // He does so reset the score and ball speed, and pos
                g_Score = 3;
```

```
                    g_BallSpeed = BALL_SPEED;
                    g_Ball.x = rand()%ClientRect.right;
                    g_Ball.y = rand()%ClientRect.bottom;
            }
            else
                    // He does not so quit
                    PostMessage( g_hWndMain, WM_DESTROY, 0, 0 );

            return 0;
    }


    // Check if this is the first time the game loop is run
    if( BatTime == 0 )
    {
            // Draw the bat, ball, and score for the first time
            DrawBat();
            DrawBall( g_hDC );
            DrawScore();

            BatTime = 1;
    }


    // Check if the user wants to move the bat up
    if( GetAsyncKeyState( VK_UP ) )
    {
            // Make sure at least a millisecond has passed
            // since the last move
            if( (GetTickCount() - BatTime) > 1 )
            {
                    // Update the time
                    BatTime = GetTickCount();

                    // Update the position of the bat
                    g_Bat.y -= BAT_SPEED;
                    // Draw the bat
                    DrawBat();
            }
    }
```

```
// Check if the user wants to move the bat down
if( GetAsyncKeyState( VK_DOWN ) )
{
        // Make sure at least a millisecond has passed
        // since the last move
        if( (GetTickCount() - BatTime) > 1 )
        {
                // Update the time
                BatTime = GetTickCount();

                // Update the position of the bat
                g_Bat.y += BAT_SPEED;
                // Draw the bat
                DrawBat();
        }
}

// Check if 10 milliseconds have passed since
// the last move.
if( (GetTickCount() - BallTime) > 10 )
{
        // Update the time keeper
        BallTime = GetTickCount();
        // Move the ball
        MoveBall();
        // Draw the ball
        DrawBall( g_hDC );
}

// Holds the previous score
static int OldScore = g_Score;

// Redraw if the score has changed
if( g_Score != OldScore )
{
        // Draw the score
        DrawScore();
        // Update the score holder
        OldScore = g_Score;
}
```

```
// Check if the user wants to pause the game
if( GetAsyncKeyState( VK_PAUSE ) )
{
        // Start an infinite loop until the user presses pause again
        while( 1 )
        {
                // This function prevents unwanted multiple key presses
                Pause( 250 );
                if( GetAsyncKeyState( VK_PAUSE ) )
                        break;
        }
}

// Check if the user wants help
if( GetAsyncKeyState( VK_F1 ) )
{
        // Game Initialization
        g_hDC = GetDC( g_hWndMain );

        // Load up the help image
        HBITMAP hBitmap = (HBITMAP)LoadImage( 0, "ZONGHELP.BMP",
                                IMAGE_BITMAP, 0, 0, LR_LOADFROMFILE );

        // Structure to hold information about the image
        BITMAP Bitmap;

        // Get info about the image
        GetObject( hBitmap, sizeof( BITMAP ), &Bitmap );

        // Create a compatible DC for the image
        HDC hBitmapDC = CreateCompatibleDC( g_hDC );

        // Select the image into the new DC
        SelectObject( hBitmapDC, hBitmap );

        // Copy the image to the main DC
        BitBlt( g_hDC, 0, 0, Bitmap.bmWidth,
                        Bitmap.bmHeight, hBitmapDC, 0, 0, SRCCOPY );

        // Delete the new DC
        DeleteDC( hBitmapDC );
```

```c
                // Delete the bitmap
                DeleteObject( hBitmap );

                // Prevent multiple keypresses
                Pause( 250 );

                // Start infinite loop until F1 is pressed again
                while( 1 )
                {
                        // Check for the keypress
                        if( GetAsyncKeyState( VK_F1 ) )
                        {
                                // Redraw the normal screen
                                InvalidateRect( g_hWndMain, 0, TRUE );
                                // Prevent multiple keypresses
                                Pause( 250 );
                                break;
                        }
                }
        }

        return 0;
}


int GameShutdown()
{
        // Shutdown Code
        ReleaseDC( g_hWndMain, g_hDC );

        return 0;
}


void DrawScore()
{
        // Holds the dimensions of the client area
        RECT ClientRect;
        // Get the dimensions for the client area
        GetClientRect( g_hWndMain, &ClientRect );

        // String variable to hold the score
        char TextScore[5];
```

```cpp
        // Convert the score from an integer to a string
        itoa( g_Score, TextScore, 10 );

        // Create a string to hold description text
        char OutputText[30] = "Score: ";

        // Join the strings
        strcat( OutputText, TextScore );

        // Set the score color to yellow
        SetTextColor( g_hDC, RGB( 255, 255, 0 ) );

        // Set the background color to black
        SetBkColor( g_hDC, 0 );

        // Output the string to the window
        TextOut( g_hDC, ClientRect.right - 100, 10,
                        OutputText, strlen( OutputText ) );
}


void DrawBat()
{
        // The previous location of the bat
        static RECT OldRect;

        // Initialize a RECT with the current position of the bat
        RECT Rect = { g_Bat.x, g_Bat.y,
            g_Bat.Width + g_Bat.x, g_Bat.Height + g_Bat.y };

        // Holds the dimensions of the client area
        RECT ClientRect;
        // Get the dimensions for the client area
        GetClientRect( g_hWndMain, &ClientRect );

        // Make sure the bat isn't outside the client area
        if( g_Bat.y < 0 )
                g_Bat.y = 0;

        if( (g_Bat.y + g_Bat.Height) > ClientRect.bottom )
                g_Bat.y = ClientRect.bottom - g_Bat.Height;
```

```
            // Select a hollow brush
            SelectObject( g_hDC, GetStockObject( NULL_BRUSH ) );
            // Set the draw mode to Inverse
            SetROP2( g_hDC, R2_NOT );

            // Draw the last rectangle again to erase it.
            if( g_bRedrawBat )
                    Rectangle( g_hDC, OldRect.left,
                        OldRect.top, OldRect.right, OldRect.bottom );
            else
                    g_bRedrawBat = TRUE;

            // Draw the new rectangle
            Rectangle( g_hDC, Rect.left,   Rect.top,
                                            Rect.right,  Rect.bottom );

            // Save the dimensions of this rectangle
            OldRect = Rect;
}

void MoveBall()
{
            // Holds the dimensions of the client area
            RECT ClientRect;

            // Controls the direction the ball moves
            static int MultiplierX = 1;
            static int MultiplierY = 1;

            // Get the dimensions of the client area
            GetClientRect( g_hWndMain, &ClientRect );

            // Check if the user missed the ball
            if( g_Ball.x < ClientRect.left )
            {

                    // Reset the ball position to the center of the window
                    g_Ball.x = rand()%ClientRect.right;
                    g_Ball.y = rand()%ClientRect.bottom;
```

```c
        if( g_Ball.x < BAT_INITIAL_X * 4 )
            g_Ball.x = BAT_INITIAL_X;

        // Flash the screen with a white flash
        BitBlt( g_hDC, 0, 0, ClientRect.right,
                ClientRect.bottom, 0, 0, 0, DSTINVERT );

        // Make sure the invert is completed
        GdiFlush();

        // Pause so the user sees the flash for 1/4 second
        Pause( 250 );

        // Reinvert the screen to bring it back to Normal
        BitBlt( g_hDC, 0, 0, ClientRect.right,
                ClientRect.bottom, 0, 0, 0, DSTINVERT );

        // Make sure the invert completes.
        GdiFlush();

        // Set the ball moving away from the bat
        MultiplierX = 1;

        // Decrement the score
        g_Score--;

        // Decrease the ball speed if the score is even
        if( g_Score%2 )
            g_BallSpeed--;
    }

// If the ball is beyond the right of the window
// then reverse its direction
if( g_Ball.x > ClientRect.right )
    MultiplierX = -1;

// If the ball is beyond the top of the window
// then reverse its direction
if( g_Ball.y < ClientRect.top )
    MultiplierY = 1;
```

```
        // If the ball is beyond the bottom of the window
        // then reverse its direction
        if( g_Ball.y > ClientRect.bottom )
                MultiplierY = -1;


        // Fill a RECT structure with the current position
        // of the bat
        RECT BatRect = {          g_Bat.x + g_Ball.Radius / 2,
                                  g_Bat.y,
                                  (g_Bat.Width + g_Bat.x) + g_Ball.Radius / 2,
                                  g_Bat.Height + g_Bat.y };

        // Fill a POINT structure with the position of the ball
        POINT BallPoint = { g_Ball.x, g_Ball.y };

        // Check if the ball is touching the bat
        if( PtInRect( &BatRect, BallPoint ) )
        {
                // Change the direction of movement away from the paddle
                MultiplierX *= -1;

                // Move the ball 5 pixels right.  This prevents it
                // getting stuck in the paddle
                g_Ball.x += 5;

                // Increase the score
                g_Score++;

                // If the score is even then increase the score
                if( g_Score%2 )
                        g_BallSpeed++;
        }

        // Update the position of the ball
        g_Ball.x += ( MultiplierX * g_BallSpeed );
        g_Ball.y += ( MultiplierY * g_BallSpeed );



}
```

```c
void Pause( int MilliSecs )
{
        // Get the current time
        int Time = GetTickCount();

        // Wait until the specified time has elapsed.
        while( (UINT)GetTickCount() - (UINT)Time < (UINT)MilliSecs ){}
}

void DrawBall( HDC hDC )
{
        // Holds the previous dimensions of the ball
        static RECT OldRect;
        // Holds the current dimensions of the ball
        RECT BallRect;

        // Fill in a RECT structure to describe the ball
        BallRect.left   = g_Ball.x - g_Ball.Radius;
        BallRect.top    = g_Ball.y - g_Ball.Radius;
        BallRect.right  = g_Ball.x + g_Ball.Radius;
        BallRect.bottom = g_Ball.y + g_Ball.Radius;

        // Select a hollow brush
        SelectObject( hDC, GetStockObject( NULL_BRUSH ) );
        // Set the drawing mode to inverted
        SetROP2( hDC, R2_NOT );

        // Draw the last ball again to invert it.
        if( g_bRedrawBall )
                Ellipse( hDC, OldRect.left,
                    OldRect.top, OldRect.right, OldRect.bottom );
        else
                g_bRedrawBall = TRUE;
        // Draw the new ball
        Ellipse( hDC, BallRect.left,  BallRect.top,
                                BallRect.right, BallRect.bottom );

        // Save the position of the current ball.
        OldRect = BallRect;
}
```

Initialization

Although the *Zong* code is long, it isn't that hard. Let's see what's going on. First off I do all the usual stuff like creating the window, registering the classes, and so on. Just after the CreateWindowEx() call, the WM_CREATE message is sent to the window procedure. In this message I load the main background image for the game off of the disk and save it in memory. This is so that it can be accessed easily later on when the window needs to be redrawn. The redrawing of the background is in fact achieved in the WM_PAINT message handler. I could have put it in the game loop, but I want to show you how you can mix where you draw. In WM_PAINT I just do all the usual stuff that you do to display an image, such as creating a DC, selecting the bitmap into it, and then copying it to the main DC. Finally, in the WM_DESTROY handler, I remove the image from memory, as all good programmers should do.

After the usual WinMain() stuff, GameInit() gets called. A couple of interesting things happen here. First off I get a DC and save it in a global variable, g_hDC. Normally you want to be careful about acquiring a DC for the entire duration of a program, but in this case it is okay. Remember I requested that the application has its own DC in the class definition with the CS_OWNDC flag? Well, this allows me to keep the DC around. But don't forget to release it at the end! Anyway, then I load the Intro screen into memory and display it in the standard way, except that afterwards I pause execution with my Pause() function so that it is displayed for two seconds. Then I invalidate the window so that the normal background is drawn from the WM_PAINT handler. Then I initialize the size of the bat and ball structures.

Zong's Game Loop

The game loop in *Zong* looks after a whole bunch of stuff, as you would expect. The first thing I do is get the size of the client area. This is so that if I reset the position of ball, I know that it will be within the bounds of the window.

Then I move on to check the score. This is where I decide if the game loop should continue. If the score is zero, then the game gives a real polite message (not!) and asks the user to either quit or continue playing. Also, if the score is 10, then the user gets a congratulations message and is asked if he wants to continue. If the user continues, the score, ball speed, and ball position are reset; otherwise, I just post a WM_DESTROY message. This is the same as calling PostQuitMessage(), except that it ensures that the WM_DESTROY handler is called, which is where I release the background image from memory.

Then I check for input by looking at the state of the keys with the `GetAsyncKeyState()` message and update the position of the bat appropriately. I also check for the Pause button, which pauses the game, and the F1 button, which causes the Help screen to be displayed. Next I execute the game logic that updates the position of the ball. The ball is only updated if a certain period of time has passed. This allows the game to progress evenly across different computers. Finally I draw the score. The score is only redrawn if it has changed since the previous draw.

Shutdown

Shutdown is very simple, since there are hardly any resources in the game. In the `GameShutdown()` function, I release the global DC for the main window. Then in the `WM_DESTROY` handler, I release the main background image.

Some Meandering Thoughts on *Zong*

Overall I think *Zong* is pretty cool. I would have liked to make it a bit cooler with all sorts of neat fire effects, but the GDI is just not fast enough. I got it to a reasonable speed on my computer, but I can't expect everybody to have the same specs. Don't worry! When we get to super-fast graphics using Direct3D, you are going to see some seriously funky stuff.

Anyway, have fun with *Zong*. While away a few nights becoming engrossed in it. Okay, don't—do something useful like looking through the code. Mess with variables. See if you can find some bugs. I left a couple in there that will make you think for a bit if you try to fix them. For instance, go to the Help menu by pressing F1 and then come back. Notice how the bat isn't visible until you move it? See if you can figure out why and fix the problem.

By the way, you won't be using the GDI very much at all while you are making games. As I mentioned previously, the only reason I am teaching it to you is because you can use it with Direct3D and it is quite useful for that purpose. If not this, I would have left it out. But at least you now have the skills to create normal Windows applications as well as games. About the only piece of knowledge that you are missing for regular Windows is how to use custom controls like push buttons and stuff like that. I would highly recommend the book *Programming Windows* by Charles Petzold if you want to look into this area.

Conclusion

I am impressed. Check over the last 100 or so pages and just look at all the cool stuff you now know how to do: drawing points, circles, rectangles, and ellipses, creating menus, using asynchronous mouse and keyboard input, etc. And who could forget *Zong?* You now have like everything you need to program Windows. In fact, you now know so much that it is time to move on to the main focus of this book: Direct3D!

It may have taken a while to get to this stage, but I think it was worth it. You are going to be amazed at what you will achieve in the rest of the book using Direct3D to create amazing 2D and 3D worlds. May the Zen be with you—there is some seriously ugly code about to show up. But I have faith that you will make it; just try to harness the power of the Zen!

Part Three

2D DirectX Graphics

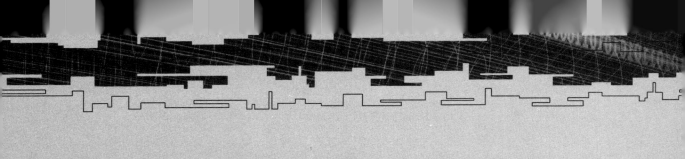

CHAPTER 8

How Many Lines of Code?

This is the point at which you can breathe a sigh of relief and thank the Great Ones because you have now reached a level of knowledge that will allow you to begin the next stage of your great journey: the exploration of Direct3D. This chapter will cover

- the theory behind 2D graphics when using low-level APIs like DirectX.
- all the terms that will make up the language that you will be speaking.
- a technical look at the stages that you need to go through to set up Direct3D.
- how to interact with Direct3D surfaces and how to draw.

Microsoft And The Infinite Wisdom

In the past, graphics in DirectX were split into two sections: DirectDraw handled 2D graphics and Direct3D handled 3D graphics. Direct3D was further split into Retained Mode, which was easy to use but bloated and slow, and Immediate Mode, which was *very* fast but quite complex and hard to use. So because of all the bad press, as I mentioned briefly before, Retained Mode was slowly erased from history. And Immediate Mode was standardized and refined into a much easier-to-use form without sacrificing speed. That was the general run of things up to DirectX 7.0.

However, now with DirectX 8.0 there have been some major modifications to the entire structure of DirectDraw and Direct3D. In fact, Microsoft has said that DirectX 8.0 is the most significant upgrade and structural change since the initial release of DirectX all those years ago. So what have they done? Well, they decided that DirectDraw and Direct3D should be joined into a single entity, called DirectX Graphics. In reality, everything that was previously DirectDraw is now accessed through Direct3D. Have a look at Figure 8.1 to see how the new structure of DirectX 8.0 compares with the previous layout. As you can see, it has been quite simplified.

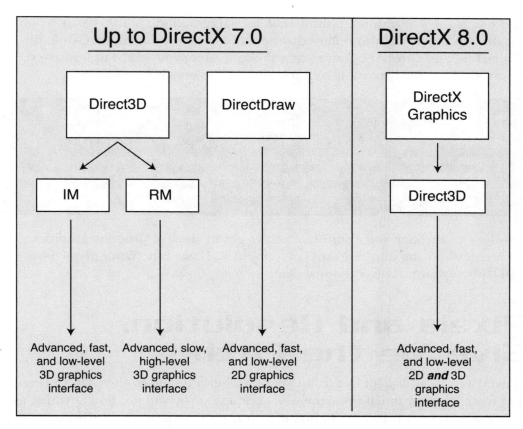

Figure 8.1

The new structure of graphical interfaces in DirectX 8.0

So why bother with all this restructuring? Well, it turns out that the development of DirectDraw had all but come to an end by DirectX 5.0. DirectDraw was a well-specified, well-implemented, and accepted interface. There was just nothing else to do with it. The real developments have been with 3D graphics technology. The release of 2D games has also all but come to an end. This modularization of 2D and 3D was becoming a bottleneck to the further development of 3D technologies. The solution? Join them.

However, with all the advantages of uniting the two technologies comes a big disadvantage to good-natured writers like myself. Previously, if you wanted to set up Direct3D, you were looking at writing a good 800 lines of code before even a single polygon was drawn. Now, after the restructuring, it takes about 200. Just what the heck am I supposed to write about?

And just as I was beginning to think that last paragraph was a little harsh, I found out that Microsoft has also removed almost all linkages between the GDI and DirectDraw and Direct3D. Don't worry though, after some studying I discovered that it is still perfectly possible to integrate them manually (read: *hack*).

> **NOTE**
>
> One thing to keep in mind is that although I am referring to Direct3D a lot in this chapter, I am not necessarily talking about 3D techniques. In fact for most the next few chapters I will be talking *only* about 2D graphics. Don't forget that as of version 8, Direct3D looks after both the 2D and 3D aspects of graphical output.

Now let's go through some stuff that you've got to know to program graphics. We are now moving into *real* hard-core graphics. There is no fancy dressed-up GDI stuff anymore. This is the real deal.

Pixels and Resolution: Give Me the Pitch

I talked about pixels a lot in the last chapter when I discussed the GDI. In Direct3D they work in pretty much the same way, except that you will not find anything as nice as a SetPixel() function. So how exactly do you set a pixel with DirectDraw? Well, it requires that you go through a number of steps, and these steps require that you know a bunch of theory.

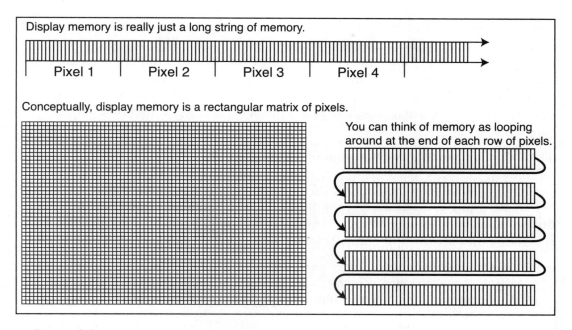

Display memory is really just a long string of memory.

Pixel 1   Pixel 2   Pixel 3   Pixel 4

Conceptually, display memory is a rectangular matrix of pixels.

You can think of memory as looping around at the end of each row of pixels.

Figure 8.2

Display memory

The 2D Rendering Process

I want to take a moment to look at the steps for getting a visual update to the screen using Direct3D. The process will almost always follow this pattern.

First, the application locks the memory associated with currently visible memory that it wants to update. The locking process is necessary because of the inherent multitasking nature of Windows. When you update the memory you don't want any other applications to be messing with the same memory that you are updating at the same time. When you *lock* the memory you tell Windows that you are doing some important work and that no other application can touch the memory until you signal that you are finished with it. When you are finished you *unlock* the memory. Locking also prevents windows from processing any screen resolution requests, or any other potentially damaging code, for the duration of the lock.

When you lock the memory you receive a pointer to the area of memory to which you requested exclusive access. This is just a pointer. But isn't the screen a rectangular matrix of pixels? How do you access a pixel, say (10, 42), using just a pointer to the beginning of a section of memory? Well, in fact it is quite easy, but the method differs depending on the bit depth of the screen. Have a look at Figure 8.2 to help you visualize the difference between the conceptual impression of the display and the logical layout in reality. I'll start with an example that uses an 8-bit display. This is the easiest because each byte is equal to a specific pixel. That is, the second byte is equal to the second pixel and so on. So if you want to set the pixel that is 10 pixels across and 42 pixels down, which byte is that offset from the pointer?

The following formula allows you to figure it out easily:

Offset in Display = (Screen Width * y) + x

See what's going on? You take the width of the screen and multiply it by the y-coordinate. Then you simply add the x-coordinate to the product. The result? The correct index into memory, of course! Have a look at Figure 8.3 to see this visually.

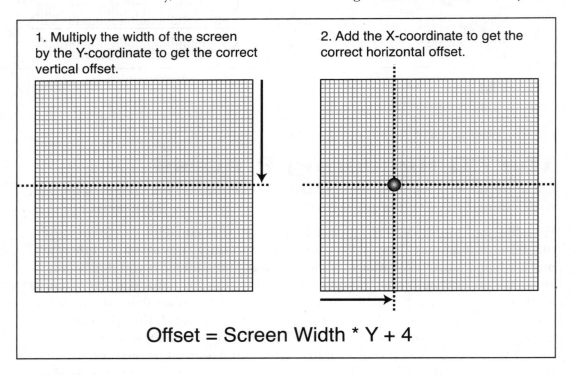

Figure 8.3

Obtaining the correct offset into display memory

To get the offset you treat the pointer as if it is a single dimension array and use the offset as the index like this:

```
PointerToDisplayMemory[ Offset ] = Color;
```

Or in pseudocode it might look like this:

```
// Screen dimensions
#define SCREEN_WIDTH 640
#define SCREEN_HEIGHT 480


.
. // Other game code
.

// Get a pointer to display memory
BYTE* pDisplayMemory = Lock( DisplayMemory );

// Set the pixel at (10, 42) to color index 15
pDisplayMemory[ SCREEN_WIDTH * 42 + 10 ] = 15;

// Unlock the display memory
Unlock( DisplayMemory );
```

However, if you are using a 32-bit display mode, then the method differs slightly. This is because instead of 1 byte there are now 4 bytes of memory for each pixel. So a better formula would be the following:

Offset in Display(Bytes) = ((Screen Width * y) + x) * (Number of bytes per pixel)

However, if you set your pointer to be a 32-bit pointer like a DWORD, you don't have to multiply by the bit depth because the pointer is already the correct length (see Figure 8.4). More on this later.

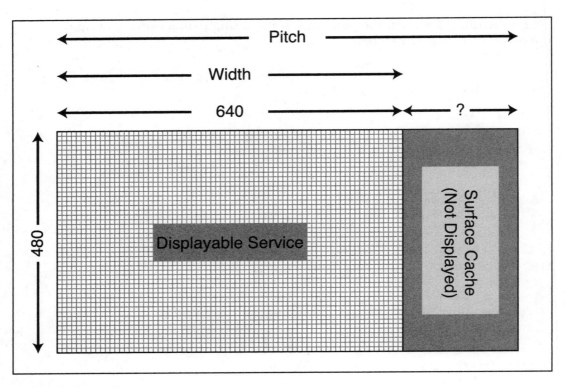

Figure 8.4

The differences between width and pitch

But wait, there's more! Since the memory that you are dealing with is typically located on the graphics card itself, there may be some little discrepancies between it and normal memory. Since graphics cards are highly complex and optimized pieces of technology, you may be forced to take into account a few requirements. Actually, you usually do not; Direct3D takes care of them for you except when you are accessing memory directly. Most graphics cards require that the image be aligned to some bit vector, usually 32 bits. That sounds much more complex than it actually is. In essence it means that the width of the display memory on the graphics card may be greater than the width that you requested. This extra space is not actually displayed. It is normally used as a cache or for some other purpose, and it is called the *pitch*.

Keep the following straight in your head: The *width* is the actual width of the display memory that you requested in pixels. For instance, if the resolution is 640 x 480, then the width is 640 pixels. The pitch is the extra memory that may be included with the display memory so that the card can optimize memory access *plus* the width of the screen, and it is in bytes. Figure 8.4 shows the relationship between the width and pitch of a surface. So how do you get around this pitch issue? Well, it is a simple addition. The following formula for indexing into display memory with Direct3D is final and you should use it:

$$\text{Display Offset (Bytes)} = ((\text{Pitch} * y) + x) * \text{Num Bytes per pixel}$$

See? Instead of multiplying by the *width* of the surface, you multiply by the *pitch* of the surface. Don't forget that the pitch is in bytes, so if you are using a 32-bit pointer you must divide the pitch by 4.

The pitch is easily accessible from Direct3D when you lock the surface. All this may seem like a pain just to set a pixel, but think of it like this: it's only a couple of lines of code, so all you have to so is code it once into a SetPixel() function and you will never have to do it again.

Just to ensure that you understand it, here is a small bit of pseudocode showing how to set a pixel using all the topics I just talked about:

```
#define SCREEN_WIDTH 640
#define SCREEN_HEIGHT 480
#define SCREEN_BYTEDEPTH 4 //bytes per pixel


.
. // Other game code
.


// Get a pointer to display memory
DWORD* pDisplayMemory = Lock( DisplayMemory );

int pitch = GetPitchOfLockedSurface();
// Set the pixel at (10, 42) to red
pDisplayMemory[ (((Pitch * 42) + 10)) ] = D3DCOLOR_XRGB(255,0,0);
// Unlock the display memory
Unlock( DisplayMemory );
```

Keep in mind that this is pseudocode. Those function names are *not* real. I'll show you how to do it properly soon. Right now I just want to make sure that you get all the theory straight in your head. One of the biggest complaints about a lot of game books is that they jump straight into the code without covering the theory properly. How nice am I?

A Bit about Display Modes

Now display modes are kind of an interesting subject. A *display mode* is another name for resolution, and as such it means the number of horizontal pixels multiplied by the number of vertical pixels. Windows supports a number of display modes—in fact, pretty much any mode higher than 640 x 480 x 8. Your display adapter also supports a number of display modes. And finally, your monitor supports another set of display modes. The display modes that are available for you to use are those that are supported by Windows *and* the display adapter *and* the monitor. You don't have to worry about this too much—Windows figures it all out for you. Typical display modes are 640 x 480, 800 x 600, 1280 x 1024, and 1600 x 1200. Higher resolutions offer better visual quality but require more memory and more processing time.

Keep this in mind when you are requesting a display mode change from DirectDraw. It may simply tell you "no" because the display mode failed to pass one of the tests mentioned in the previous paragraph. Direct3D may also reject your request because the system does not have the capabilities to support the mode. For instance, the display adapter may have run out of memory. Figure 8.5 shows the process of putting together a list of supported display modes that your game can use.

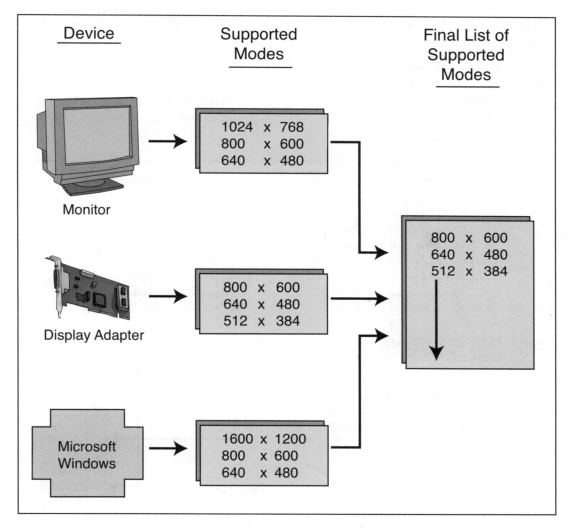

Figure 8.5

Computing the supported display mode list

Palettes

Big business up until about 1997, palettes are used for display modes that use 8 or fewer bits per pixel. As I mentioned briefly in the last chapter, in 8-bit mode each pixel is not a color as such; instead it is an index into a color table. This means that a much larger number of colors can be used. Although only 256 colors can be displayed at a time, the palette can be changed on the fly, allowing better quality images to be displayed.

I said palettes were big business until 1997, because after this time the majority of computers had enough processing power to use the higher bit-depth display modes efficiently. These days it is hard to find any games that use, or even support, such low color display modes. Figure 8.6 shows the contrasts between palettized and normal higher bit-depth surfaces.

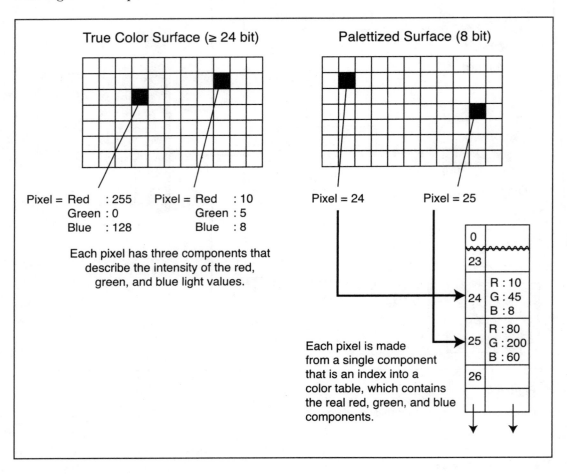

Figure 8.6

Contrast between palettized and normal surfaces

Error Handling

Looking out for errors in DirectX is a big issue because they pop up every two seconds, and can sometimes be erratic and hard to accurately track down. So to help in your endeavor to create good programs, I am going to show you a great way to keep track of what's going on.

When you debug-execute your program it is possible to output text to the debug output window. This is very useful for tracking down annoying errors that cause your application to quit for no reason. This tip will save you hours of debugging time.

The function to output text is called OutputDebugString(), and it looks like this:

```
void OutputDebugString( LPCTSTR lpOutputString );
```

It is a simple function that just takes the string you want to output. As I can be quite lazy, I used to get tired of calling this function because it is so long. So I created a cover that looks like this:

```
void SetError( char* String )
{
        OutputDebugString( String );
        OutputDebugString( "\n" );
}
```

That brings the character count down from 17 to 8, and you don't have to remember to always put in the new-line character. So now all you have to do is make a call to this function whenever an error pops up. And don't worry about extra function calls slowing down your application; as soon as the DEBUG indicator is removed when you do a RELEASE build, the OutputDebugString() function is eliminated and the optimizing compiler realizes this and removes the call to the function altogether.

So if you write

```
SetError( "Wow, I'm outputting text to the debug window" );
```

then the debug output window will look like Figure 8.7. Cool, huh?

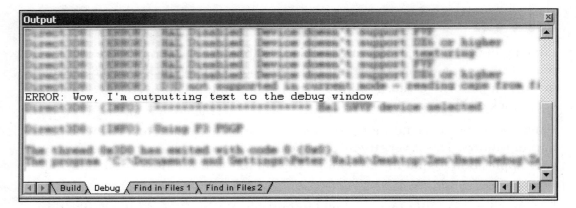

Figure 8.7

Outputting text to the debug window

One other thing to cover is return values. In Direct3D, since it follows COM specifications, it is good to stick to some standard return values. If a function fails, then you should return the value E_FAIL. On the other hand, if a function succeeds and you need to indicate this, then return the value S_OK. The E_ stands for "error," and the S_ stands for "success."

And finally a note about error testing: In the beginning, when DirectX was new, the sample applications that shipped with the product were not exactly written to a very high standard. They used awful programming practice, and a lot of people took these poor examples to heart. And of course a lot of the early authors who wrote about DirectX also passed on these bad practices, thus allowing even more people to fall into the trap. I'll show you the main one just so that you know.

DirectX function calls usually have return values that represent something. The values are almost always of the type HRESULT, which between you and me is just a 32-bit integer. For instance, if you called a function and it succeeded, the return might be D3D_OK. Or in another case, if a certain function failed, then the return value might be D3DERR_INVALIDDEVICE, or D3DERR_NOTAVAILABLE, etc. There are hundreds of them. The *bad* way to test for the success or failure of an operation was like this (pseudocode):

```
HRESULT r = 0;
r = Direct3DdoSomethingImportant();
if( r != D3D_OK )
        return E_FAIL;
```

Can you see what's wrong? Well, maybe it's not so clear. The thing is that there is no guarantee from Microsoft that in the future success will be indicated by D3D_OK. What if all of a sudden the function returned D3D_THAT_WENT_SWELL? It went OK, but yet the application would still indicate failure for no reason.

To get around this problem you should use the two macros that I mentioned before: FAILED() and SUCCEEDED(). Using these macros, the code would look like this:

```
HRESULT r = 0;
r = Direct3DdoSomething();
if( FAILED( r ) )
        return E_FAIL;
```

or

```
HRESULT r = 0;
r = Direct3DdoSomething();
if( ! SUCCEEDED( r ) )
        return E_FAIL;
```

That is much better code, and it will avoid all of the problems that the other method had the potential to throw up. The macros automatically figure out the error code for you and let you know if the function succeeded or failed.

Getting Your Hands Dirty

OK, let's break from the theory for a bit. Originally I was going to go through all the theory and then dive into the cool stuff, but why wait? Let's just jump in now and see what you can achieve. Besides, all the other topics will be easier to understand if you get how to set up DirectX.

First things first: Let's cover exactly where we are going with the following code. I am going to start by assuming that you have the generic Windows setup code already in place. That is, all the usual stuff like filling in the class structure and registering it, setting up a basic event handler called WndProc(), and the three functions that I talked about in the last chapter—GameInit(), GameLoop(), and GameShutdown()— are in place. (If you need a review of what these functions do, then refer back to Chapter 7.). I am using a WM_OVERLAPPEDWINDOW style and have set the initial size to the dimensions (512, 512).

The Direct3D Include Files

When using Direct3D you need to include two new header files with your project, d3d8.h and d3dx8.h. The former file contains all the usual Direct3D information, and the latter includes thousands of useful extra functions.

CAUTION

At this point make sure that you have set up your project properly following the guidelines laid out in **Chapter 2**. Have you set up the directory paths in **Visual C++**, and have you included the right library files in the **Project Settings** dialog box? If not, then run back to **Chapter 2** and see how to do so. I don't want any e-mails about compiling problems.

The include files look like this:

```
#include <d3d8.h>
#include <d3dx8.h>
```

Getting Ready to Rock—Initializing Direct3D

Now, unfortunately, you need to deal a little bit with the dreaded COM. Don't worry though, you probably won't even notice it's there! The big daddy of Direct3D is of course the IDirect3D8 interface. This is a COM interface. As I mentioned in Chapter 1, you do not create COM objects yourself; instead, you call a function to do it for you. In this case that function is called Direct3DCreate8(), and its prototype looks like this:

```
IDirect3D8* Direct3DCreate8( UINT SDKVersion );
```

The parameter to this function is always D3D_SDK_VERSION. There are no other valid parameters that this can be set to. This identifier allows Direct3D to know that it is being compiled with the correct header files, because the differences between DirectX 7.0 and 8.0 are so large. The identifier D3D_SDK_VERSION is updated for you with each new release of DirectX.

My opinion is that you should make the call to Direct3DCreate8() from the GameInit() function. Don't ever call this function from the WM_CREATE handler in WndProc(), just because Microsoft says so. Notice that the function returns a pointer to an IDirect3D8 interface. As you will be using this interface quite a bit, it's a good idea to keep it in a global variable.

I created a global variable called g_pD3D, like this:

```
LPDIRECT3D8 g_pD3D = 0;
```

Now here is a little useful information for you. Variable descriptor names and types can be very long in Direct3D; however, they follow rules. If the interface to which you want to acquire a pointer is called IDirectSound, then the name of the variable type will be LPDIRECTSOUND. Notice how the "I," which stands for *interface*, has turned into an "LP," which stands for *long pointer*. And the entire name is now uppercase.

So the variable g_pD3D is an LPDIRECT3D8, which means that it is a *32-bit pointer to the eighth revision of the IDirect3D interface*. It's much simpler than it sounds, really. And of course the g_ part just indicates that it is a global. Also notice that I have initialized the variable to zero. Always, *always* do this in DirectX. This is necessary because so much of your interactions with DirectX are through pointers that you need a good way to determine whether your pointers are valid. If you make a point of always initializing pointers to NULL, and then resetting them to NULL when they are no longer in use, then you have an easy way to test for valid pointers.

Let's get on and make that function call to get a pointer to the IDirect3D8 interface. Don't forget that the following code is being placed in the GameInit() function.

```
g_pD3D = Direct3DCreate8( D3D_SDK_VERSION );
if( g_pD3D == NULL )
{
        SetError( "Could not create IDirect3D8 object" );
        return E_FAIL;
}
```

Pretty simple so far. Just call the function and it will return the requested pointer to the interface. Of course, because nothing happens perfectly all the time, you need to check for failure. In this case if the function call fails, it will set the pointer to NULL, and that is what the if statement tests for. If you're wondering why I didn't use the FAILED() macro, it is because that macro is *only* used to test HRESULT values, not pointers. Pointers will be set to NULL if the call fails. Notice how I immediately return E_FAIL at this point. If this call fails, there is simply nothing else to do; all of Direct3D relies on the creation of the IDirect3D8 object, so if you get a failure here, the computer is either extremely low on memory or Direct3D is not installed properly on the host machine.

Setting Up the Surfaces

Remember when I was talking about the GDI and all that business about device contexts? Well, in Direct3D a *surface* is quite similar to a device context except that you are now dealing with the bare metal. There are hardly any abstractions when dealing with surfaces compared to the GDI. A surface represents a rectangular matrix of memory that is used to represent an image. If you want to mess with the image, you lock it, get a pointer to the memory, modify the image, and finally unlock the surface. There is no business about compatibility like with the GDI. In fact, there are hardly any functions provided by Direct3D to help you deal with surfaces! If you want anything done, you do it yourself!

Now this section would have been really long, but of course all that changed with the unification of Direct3D and DirectDraw. There are only a few simple steps to cover because Direct3D now does a lot of the setup code for you. The first thing that it does is to set up the *flipping surfaces*. But what exactly is a flipping surface?

The Display Process

Hmmm…Let's look into this puppy and some of the issues that come into play when designing graphical applications. There are, in fact, a number of devices that participate. You don't have to interact with most of them because it is done for you, but it's still important to know what is going on.

The code that creates the image and the original graphics are held in system memory. The processor takes these two items and uses them to create the image that you want to display. This image is still in system memory, and before it can be displayed it must be passed over the system bus to the display adapter. The display adapter then moves the image into memory that is currently visible. When it is ready to be displayed, the image is passed through a DAC, or Digital to Analog Converter, which converts the digital image into analog form so that it can be passed to the monitor. The monitor then amplifies the signal to control electro-magnets and electron guns, which control the paths of electrons that eventually end up illuminating the phosphor coating on your monitor, and displays the image. Notice how many components there are in this process! Check out Figure 8.8 for a visual representation.

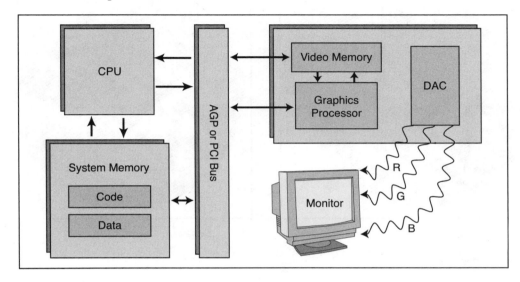

Figure 8.8

The hardware components involved in the display process

However, the important factors are on the graphics card. You may know that the graphics card, main processor, and monitor all operate in parallel. This has many advantages in speed, but it does lead to a whole bunch of issues. The problem is that the system can update the display memory whenever it wants, and the graphics card can also read from this memory to update the monitor whenever it wants. The graphics card will update the monitor at the current *refresh rate* of the monitor. This is the number of times per second (*hertz*) that the electron gun scans through and updates every pixel on the screen. Common refresh rates range from 60Hz, which is quite flickery and annoying, up to 130Hz, which creates a nice rock-solid image.

But what happens when the system starts to update an image on the graphics card that has already been 50 percent converted to analog for use by the monitor? Since the system is faster than the monitor, the entire image will be updated within the card before the monitor displays it. However, the first half of the image has already been displayed! When the monitor finishes drawing this cycle half the screen will show the old image, and the rest will show the new image. This is very common and creates an effect called *tearing;* you can see an example of this in Figure 8.9.

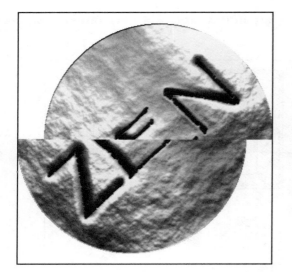 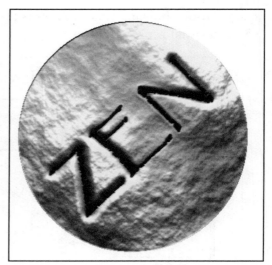

Figure 8.9

The tearing effect

Double Buffering and the Vsync

So how do you get around all the issues that lead to tearing? Well, it just so happens that every time the electron gun finishes a scan through the monitor it sends out a signal to the graphics card to let it know. This is due to the fact that after the scan has completed, it takes a long time for the gun to realign itself back to the upper-left corner of the monitor. When I say a long time, I mean like 1/60th of a second. That may seem short to you, but in computer time it is an eternity. Anyway, the monitor signals the graphics card so that it knows to stop sending information for a little bit while the monitor fixes itself. This signal is called the *vertical sync,* or *vsync* for short. You can see when the vsync occurs in Figure 8.10.

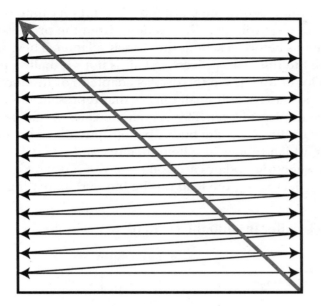

Figure 8.10

The vertical retrace occurs when the monitor completes the final horizontal trace at the bottom of the screen. At this point it has to reset itself to the upper-left corner of the screen so that it canstart the next frame.

This is good because it means that you can achieve all sorts of useful stuff during this period. For instance, how cool would it be if you knew when the vsync was occurring, and then you copied the information to the display adapter during this period? Well, it would be very cool because it would mean the entire copy process would complete before the monitor even knew what was happening, and the tearing process would no longer be an issue!

But if you wait for the vsync every frame, then you're wasting enormous amounts of processing time, and the game would become almost unplayable. A better option would be if you could somehow build up the image at normal speed and then copy the image to the display adapter whenever an optimal vsync popped up. This means that you require a chunk of memory in main system memory that *pretends* to be the display adapter. Then, when the time is right, you blast the entire chunk of memory to the display adapter during the vsync. This chunk of memory is known as a *back buffer*. Its name comes from the fact that it is always in the background— that is, it's never displayed. It just holds the image temporarily before it gets on its way to the display adapter.

Back buffers are not just useful for avoiding the tearing problem. Every time you access the display adapter, the request you make has to move from the processor all the way across the PCI or AGP bus before reaching the display adapter. These buses are incredibly slow as compared to the main processor. This is not normally a problem, unless you are sending a lot of updates to the display adapter. For instance, suppose you are updating the position of 500 small images that represent mosquitoes every frame directly to the display adapter. This is going to cause a real performance drain because of all the traffic across the bus. A better option is to do all the updates to the back buffer, which resides in system memory and is very fast, compared with the bus. Then when the updates are complete you just have to copy the final image once, thus decreasing the load on the bus and increasing overall performance.

Figure 8.11 shows how the back buffer fits into the chain of events in the graphics pipeline.

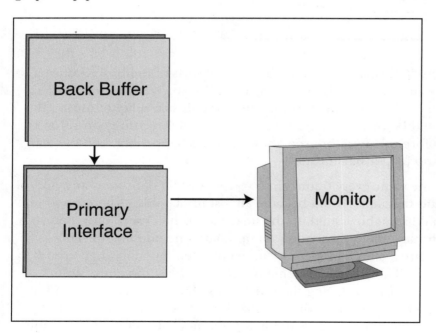

Figure 8.11

You draw to the back buffer, which is not visible, while the primary surface is being displayed. Then the back buffer is copied to the primary surface in a single operation.

Now to bring some Direct3D terminology into all of this theory. Each buffer is a Direct3D surface. Remember what this means? They are both rectangular matrices of pixels that are used to represent an image. The front buffer is referred to in Direct3D as the *primary surface* because it is always on the display adapter and it is always the one displayed by the adapter. And the back buffer is, uhhmmm, still referred to as the *back buffer*, although if you had more than two buffers, which is entirely possible, they would be called the *secondary surface, tertiary surface*, and so on. The technical term for the copying of information between the surfaces, which you came across when you were looking at the GDI, is *blitting*.

Page Flipping

A further development on back buffering is *page flipping*. Generally, this process is faster than back buffering and offers the same benefits. The two are quite easy to confuse, so make sure you get them straight. Think about what would happen if you created the back buffer somewhere on the display adapter itself rather than in system memory. Although the buffer is on the adapter, it is still not visible; rather, it is contained in extra memory that is not currently in use.

In this case there is no need to *copy* the information to visible memory. Instead, you could just tell the adapter that it should start displaying data from the back buffer itself. So the process works like this: While the display adapter is updating the screen, you update the back buffer. Then when you're finished you swap pointers so the back buffer becomes the primary surface, which is now displayed, and vice versa. And the process continues. In this case it is more useful to think of the two areas of memory on the display adapter as *pages*, rather than buffers.

Again, like the buffer situation, both the pages are surfaces. There is the *primary surface* and the *back buffer*. And the technical term for this process of changing the location of memory being displayed is *flipping*. Check out Figure 8.12, which shows page flipping in action.

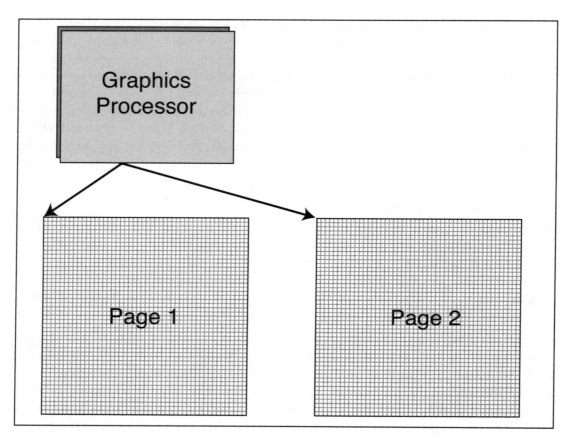

Figure 8.12

In page flipping the graphics card alternates between the different graphics pages. This avoids the copy operation that is necessary in the back buffer process.

Back to Setting Up

OK, now that you are a graphical guru you can get back to the setup. This first example is going to be windowed, as opposed to full screen. What this means is that you must create a back buffer that is compatible with the primary surface. To do this you need to retrieve information about the current display settings of the monitor, such as the bit depth, resolution, and so on. The function to do this is called `IDirect3D8::GetAdapterDisplayMode()`. Here it is:

```
HRESULT GetAdapterDisplayMode( UINT Adapter, D3DDISPLAYMODE* pMode );
```

Actually, just before I explain this, I want to explain how I presented this function. Notice how I wrote the interface name followed by a :: (double colon) followed by the function name. This is standard practice for C++ object-oriented and COM programming. If you have not come across this before you can think of the double colon as the same as the possessive 's (apostrophe followed by "s") in English. That is, it indicates ownership. So in English it means *IDirect3D8's function called GetAdapterDisplayMode()*, or more simply *GetAdapterDisplayMode() is a member of the IDirect3D8 interface.*

This function takes two parameters: the first, Adapter, takes the identifier of the adapter that you want to retrieve information about. For now you just want information about the default primary display adapter. There is an identifier that always represents the default adapter, and it is D3DADAPTER_DEFAULT. The second parameter, pMode, takes a pointer to a D3DDISPLAYMODE structure that you want to be filled with information about the device.

D3DDISPLAYMODE is a simple structure that holds the resolution, bit depth, refresh rate, and format of the current device's present display mode. The structure has this definition:

```
typedef struct _D3DDISPLAYMODE {
    UINT            Width;          // The width in pixels
    UINT            Height;         // The height in pixels
    UINT            RefreshRate;    // The refresh rate in hertz
    D3DFORMAT       Format;         // The format of the display mode
} D3DDISPLAYMODE;
```

All of these members are self-explanatory, except for Format. This takes a member of the D3DFORMAT enumerated type. Have a look at the Table 8.1 for the possible values of this member variable. I have bolded the values that you are most likely to come into contact with. Some of these are very complex and won't make sense just yet, but don't worry—all the important ones will be covered throughout the book.

Table 8.1   D3DFORMAT Enumerated Type

Value	Meaning
D3DFMT_UNKNOWN	The format is not known
D3DFMT_R8G8B8	24-bit RGB pixel format with 8 bits per pixel
D3DFMT_A8R8G8B8	32-bit ARGB pixel format with alpha
D3DFMT_X8R8G8B8	32-bit RGB pixel format with 8 bits per pixel color (8 bits wasted.)
D3DFMT_R5G6B5	16-bit RGB pixel format
D3DFMT_X1R5G5B5	16-bit pixel format with 5 bits per pixel (1 bit wasted.)
D3DFMT_A1R5G5B5	16-bit pixel format with 5 bits per pixel and 1 bit for alpha
D3DFMT_A4R4G4B4	16-bit ARGB pixel format
D3DFMT_R3G3B2	8-bit RGB pixel format
D3DFMT_A8	8-bit alpha only
D3DFMT_A8P8	8 bits for alpha, 8 bits are an index into a color palette
D3DFMT_P8	8-bit color index
D3DFMT_L8	8-bit luminance only
D3DFMT_A8L8	16-bit alpha and luminance
D3DFMT_A4L4	8-bit alpha and luminance
D3DFMT_V8U8	8-bit bump map format
D3DFMT_L6V5U5	16-bit bump map with luminance
D3DFMT_X8L8V8U8	32-bit bump map with luminance. 8 bits per element.
D3DFMT_Q8W8V8U8	32-bit bump map format
D3DFMT_V16U16	32-bit bump map format
D3DFMT_W11V11U10	32-bit bump map format
D3DFMT_UYUV	UYUV format
D3DFMT_YUY2	YUY2 format

Table 8.1   D3DFORMAT Enumerated Type (continued)

D3DFMT_DXT1	DXT1 texture compression format
D3DFMT_DXT2	DXT2 texture compression format
D3DFMT_DXT3	DXT3 texture compression format
D3DFMT_DXT4	DXT4 texture compression format
D3DFMT_DXT5	DXT5 texture compression format
D3DFMT_D16_LOCKABLE	16-bit z-buffer. The application can lock this surface.
D3DFMT_D32	32-bit z-buffer
D3DFMT_D15S1	16-bit z-buffer with 1 bit for the stencil buffer
D3DFMT_D24S8	32-bit z buffer with 8 bits for the stencil buffer
D3DFMT_D16	16-bit z-buffer
D3DFMT_D24X8	32-bit z-buffer with 24 bits for the depth buffer (8 bits wasted.)
D3DFMT_D24X4S4	32-bit z-buffer with 24 bits for the depth buffer, 4 bits for the stencil buffer, and 4 bits wasted
D3DFMT_VERTEXDATA	Vertex buffer surface
D3DFMT_INDEX16	16-bit index buffer
D3DFMT_INDEX32	32-bit index buffer

Now with all of that information out of the way, here is how I actually made the call:

```
HRESULT r = 0;
D3DDISPLAYMODE d3ddm;


    .
    .
    .


r = g_pD3D->GetAdapterDisplayMode( D3DADAPTER_DEFAULT, &d3ddm );
if( FAILED( r ) )
{
```

```
    SetError( "Could not get display adapter information" );
    return E_FAIL;
}
```

Creating the Device

The *device* is an object that is used to represent the capabilities of the graphical hardware in the system. A device can represent only one piece of graphical hardware. If you have two display adapters, for instance, then you need two devices. All of your rendering, particularly in 3D, will take place using the device. In COM-speak the device functions are accessed through the IDirect3DDevice8 interface.

Again, like the IDirect3D8 interface, you will be using the IDirect3DDevice8 interface a lot, so it is a good idea to keep it in a global variable for easy access. For this sample I used the following code to define the global pointer to the device:

```
LPDIRECT3DDEVICE8 g_pDevice = 0;
```

Again, note the initialization of the pointer to NULL. To create the actual device requires quite a lot of information. Acquire an interface to IDirect3DDevice8 through the function IDirect3D8::CreateDevice(). Here is the prototype:

```
HRESULT CreateDevice(
    UINT Adapter,                            // The adapter to base the device on
    D3DDEVTYPE DeviceType,                   // The type of device
    HWND  hFocusWindow,                      // Target render window for this device
    DWORD BehaviorFlags,                     // Defines the behavior of the device
    D3DPRESENT_PARAMETERS* pPresentationParameters,    // Presentation params
    IDirect3DDevice8** ppReturnedDeviceInterface       // Holds pointer to device
);
```

That is quite a hefty function but is not as bad as it looks. Don't get too freaked out about it because a lot of this has to do with 3D stuff because of the unification of DirectDraw and Direct3D. For now you are just going to focus on the 2D stuff. Let's look at how I called it before I describe the parameters:

```
r = g_pD3D->CreateDevice( D3DADAPTER_DEFAULT,

                                                  D3DDEVTYPE_HAL,
                                                  g_hWndMain,
                                                  D3DCREATE_SOFTWARE_VERT
EXPROCESSING,
```

```
                                                   &d3dpp,
                                                   &g_pDevice );
```

- **Adapter.** Takes an integer that identifies which display adapter you wish the new device to represent. For now I just want the default adapter, so I specified D3DADAPTER_DEFAULT.

- **DeviceType.** Takes a member of the D3DDEVTYPE enumerated type. Table 8.2 shows the possible values for this parameter.

Table 8.2 D3DDEVTYPE Enumerated Type

Value	Meaning
D3DDEVTYPE_HAL	The device uses hardware acceleration if it is available.
D3DDEVTYPE_SW	The device is forced to do all operations in software.
D3DDEVTYPE_REF	The device has all possible hardware functionality implemented in software. However, it is very slow and should only be used for debugging.

At the moment there are three possible types of device: hardware, software, and reference. If you specify that you would like a hardware device using the D3DDEVTYPE_HAL flag, then the device will use hardware-accelerated rasterization, shading, and transform and lighting depending on the capabilities of the adapter. Alternatively, if you request a software device using D3DDEVTYPE_SW, then the device will perform all calculations in software. The reference device, specified by D3DDEVTYPE_REF, is kind of interesting. This type of device supports all of the functionality normally implemented by hardware, in software. This means it is extremely useful during debugging. Microsoft recommends that you *never* even think about using this type of device for general use in a shipping game because it is so slow. It is only for testing. In general, your best bet is to do what I have done, and that is to request a hardware device.

- **hFocusWindow.** This parameter takes the handle to the window that you want to be used as the default target-rendering window. That is, later on when I discuss how to present the back buffer to the primary surface, this variable will become useful. Just specify the handle to the window that you received from the `CreateWindowEx()` call in `WinMain()`. I specified `g_hWndMain`, which is a global

> Back in the old days, device types were not as simple as they are now. For starters, there were other devices, such as the MMX device. However, the distinction between hardware and software devices was still there. Hardware devices were referred to as HAL, or *hardware abstraction layer*, devices. The name comes from the fact that Direct3D is essentially a layer that allows many different cards that work in different ways to work under the same interface. In essence, it abstracts the hardware interface into a Direct3D interface. The software devices used to be known as HEL, or *hardware emulation layer*, devices. This name originates from the software layer that was implemented if no hardware acceleration features were available.

variable that I use to store the handle to the main window. Something to note is that if your application is going to be running full screen, you must set the `WS_EX_TOPMOST` style flag in your call to `CreateWindowEx()`. I'll return to this point when I get to the discussion on full-screen applications.

- **BehaviorFlags.** This parameter takes flags that describe how you want your device to behave. Table 8.3 shows the possible values for this parameter, with the important values bolded.

Table 8.3   Behavior Flags for Devices

Value	Meaning
D3DCREATE_FPU_PRESERVE	Indicates the application needs double FPU precision or FPU exceptions enabled. This causes DirectX to constantly reset the state of the FPU, thus reducing performance.
D3DCREATE_HARDWARE_VERTEXPROCESSING	**Vertices will be processed in hardware**
D3DCREATE_SOFTWARE_VERTEXPROCESSING	*Vertices will be processed in software*
D3DCREATE_MIXED_VERTEXPROCESSING	**Vertices will be processed in both hardware and software**
D3DCREATE_MULTITHREADED	The application needs Direct3D to be multithread safe. Reduces performance.
D3DCREATE_PUREDEVICE	Direct3D will not support any Get*() function calls for anything stored in state blocks. No emulation is provided.

The flags specified in bold type are mutually exclusive and cannot be used together. The flag in bold italic type, D3DCREATE_SOFTWARE_VERTEXPROCESSING, is the one that I specified and is the flag you will probably want to use most often until you get much more advanced.

- **pPresentationParameters.** Takes a pointer to a D3DPRESENT_PARAMETERS structure. This structure is quite complex, so I am not going to describe it in detail just yet. Before the call to CreateDevice() I used this code to initialize the structure:

```
D3DPRESENT_PARAMETERS d3dpp;

.
.// Other code
.

ZeroMemory( &d3dpp, sizeof( D3DPRESENT_PARAMETERS ) );
d3dpp.Windowed = TRUE;
```

```
d3dpp.SwapEffect = D3DSWAPEFFECT_DISCARD;
d3dpp.BackBufferFormat = d3ddm.Format;
```

The code starts by initializing the structure to 0. This is always a good idea, particularly with DirectX. Next I set the
Windowed member of the structure to
TRUE, which tells DirectX that I will not
be running the application in full-
screen mode.

TIP

If you want more information on
the D3DPRESENT_PARAMETERS struc-
ture, check out DirectX 8.0 C++
Documentation / Direct3D C++
Reference / Enumerated Types /
D3DPRESENT_PARAMETERS.

Then the SwapEffect member is set to D3DSWAPEFFECT_DISCARD. This is a complex
topic for now, but I will give you an overview. When you present the back
buffer to the primary surface, Direct3D will normally make sure that the
back buffer is left untouched. However, this guarantee can cause a slight
drain on performance in some situations. If you set the SwapEffect to
D3DSWAPEFFECT_DISCARD, you are telling Direct3D that it is free to mess around
with the back buffer in whatever way it wants. What this means is that you
must redraw the back buffer every frame. In debug mode Direct3D lets you
know that you are redrawing successfully by filling the back buffer with
garbage, effectively forcing you to program properly. How nice.

Actually, I have found that with some display adapters that the discard flag
seems to cause some problems. If you find that you get an erratic flicker on
your screen like once every seven seconds, even though you know you're
correctly writing to the back buffer, then you may want to change this flag to
D3DSWAPEFFECT_COPY.

Finally, I set the format of the back buffer by setting the BackBufferFormat to
be the same as the primary surface. Remember we acquired this information
earlier with the call to GetAdapterDisplayMode()?

- **ppReturnedDeviceInterface.** I think Microsoft may be trying to force RSI onto
  programmers by creating variable names this long! This parameter takes the
  address of a pointer that will hold the address of the new interface. I specified the address of the global device pointer that I created earlier, g_pDevice.

Hey hey! Direct3D is now initialized! That was a breeze compared to what you used
to have to do. Trust me—when I said it used to take 800 lines, I really meant it.

Shutting Down DirectX

The only thing you need to do now is look at the shutdown code. Shutting down correctly is very important in DirectX. Because games are such resource hogs, it is imperative to return the system to the state that it was in before the application started. If you don't, the user will be very annoyed, which is usually a bad thing.

For now all you need to do is release the interfaces that you acquired pointers to. This is where that bit of COM comes back. Remember the Release() functions from COM in Chapter 1? This code is implemented in the GameShutdown() function:

```
if( g_pDevice )
{
        g_pDevice->Release();
        g_pDevice = 0;
}



if( g_pD3D )
{
        g_pD3D->Release();
        g_pD3D = 0;
}
```

Notice how I check if the pointer is valid before I call the Release() function on it. I cannot stress enough the significance of doing this. If the acquisition of the pointer to the device fails and you try to call Release() on a dud pointer, then you will cause a memory exception and your program will be terminated by Windows. And this is really important: See how I release the device before I release the Direct3D pointer? That is because the Direct3D object creates the device. You should in general release pointers in the order opposite to how you create them. And again notice the resetting of the pointer to NULL after the release. Always do this—it will help you create much more stable code.

And that's all the code you need to create the foundation of a Direct3D application that so far does about as much as a politician—that is, not much at all. Don't worry though—the good stuff is about to happen! First let's look at the complete code listing because I have covered a lot of new information. It's always good to see how this stuff fits into the bigger picture.

```
/////////////////////////////////////////////

// Name: Direct3D Initialization

//

#define WIN32_LEAN_AND_MEAN
// The main windows include file
#include <windows.h>
#include <mmsystem.h>

#include <d3d8.h>
#include <d3dx8.h>

int GameInit();
int GameLoop();
int GameShutdown();

void SetError( char* String );
LPDIRECT3D8 g_pD3D = 0;
LPDIRECT3DDEVICE8 g_pDevice = 0;

HWND g_hWndMain;
void SetError( char* String )
{
        OutputDebugString( String );
        OutputDebugString( "\n" );
}



// The window procedure to handle events
long CALLBACK WndProc( HWND hWnd, UINT uMessage,
                                   WPARAM wParam, LPARAM lParam )

{

        // Switch the windows message to figure out what it is
        switch( uMessage )
        {
                case WM_CREATE:// The CreateWindow() function was just called
                {
```

```
                    // One Time Initialization
                    return 0;
            }
            case WM_PAINT: // The window needs to be redrawn
            {
                    ValidateRect( hWnd, NULL );

                    return 0;
            }

            case WM_DESTROY:        // The window is about to be closed
            {
            // Our main window is closing.  This means we want our app to exit.
            // Tell windows to put a WM_QUIT message in our message queue
            PostQuitMessage( 0 );
            return 0;
            }

            default:                        // Some other message
            {
                    // Let windows handle this message
                    return DefWindowProc( hWnd, uMessage, wParam, lParam );
            }
        }
    }

// The windows entry point. The application will start executing here
int WINAPI WinMain( HINSTANCE hInstance, HINSTANCE hPrevInstance,
                                    PSTR pstrCmdLine, int iCmdShow )
{
        HWND hWnd;              // The handle to our main window
        MSG msg;               // The message windows is sending us
        WNDCLASSEX wc; // The window class used to create our window

        // The name of our class and also the title to our window
        static char strAppName[] = "First Windows App, Zen Style";
        // Fill in the window class with the attributes for our main window
        // The size of this structure in bytes
        wc.cbSize                       = sizeof( WNDCLASSEX );
```

```cpp
// The style of the window
wc.style                      = CS_HREDRAW | CS_VREDRAW | CS_OWNDC;
// Useless information.  Just set to zero.
wc.cbClsExtra        = 0;
// Useless information.  Just set to zero.
wc.cbWndExtra        = 0;
// The name of our event handler
wc.lpfnWndProc       = WndProc;
// A handle to the applications instance
wc.hInstance         = hInstance;
// The handle to the brush to use for the window background
wc.hbrBackground     = (HBRUSH)GetStockObject( DKGRAY_BRUSH );
// A handle to the icon to use for the window
wc.hIcon             = LoadIcon( NULL, IDI_APPLICATION );
// A handle to a smaller version of the apps icon
wc.hIconSm           = LoadIcon( NULL, IDI_APPLICATION );
// A handle to the cursor to use while the mouse is over our window
wc.hCursor           = LoadCursor( NULL, IDC_CROSS );
// A handle to the resource to use as our menu
wc.lpszMenuName      = NULL;
// The human readable name for this class
wc.lpszClassName     = strAppName;

// Register the class with windows
RegisterClassEx( &wc );

// Create the window based on the previous class
hWnd = CreateWindowEx( NULL,          // Advanced style settings
            strAppName,                      // The name of the class
                       strAppName,           // The window caption
                       WS_OVERLAPPEDWINDOW,  // The window style
                       CW_USEDEFAULT,        // The initial x position
                  CW_USEDEFAULT,             // The initial y position
                       512, 512,             // The initial width / height
                       NULL,                 // Handle to parent window
            NULL,                            // Handle to the menu
```

```
                                        hInstance,                              // Handle
to the apps instance
                                        NULL );                                 //
Advanced context

        g_hWndMain = hWnd;
        // Display the window we just created
        ShowWindow( hWnd, iCmdShow );
        // Draw the window contents for the first time
        UpdateWindow( hWnd );

        if( FAILED( GameInit() ) )
        {
                SetError( "Initialization Failed" );
                GameShutdown();
                return E_FAIL;
        }

        // Start the message loop
        while( TRUE )
        {
                // Check if a message is waiting for processing
                if( PeekMessage( &msg, NULL, 0, 0, PM_REMOVE ) )
                {
                        // Check if the message is to quit the application
                        if( msg.message == WM_QUIT )
                                // Exit the message loop
                                break;

                        // Change the format of certain messages
                        TranslateMessage( &msg );
                        // Pass the message to WndProc() for processing
                        DispatchMessage( &msg );
                }
                else
                {
                        GameLoop();
                }
        }
```

```
                    GameShutdown();
                    // Return control to windows with the exit code
                    return msg.wParam;


        }



int GameInit()
{
                    HRESULT r = 0;              // Holds return values
                    // Structure to hold information about the current display mode
                    D3DDISPLAYMODE d3ddm;
                    // Structure to hold information about the rendering method
                    D3DPRESENT_PARAMETERS d3dpp;
                    // Acquire a pointer to IDirect3D8
                    g_pD3D = Direct3DCreate8( D3D_SDK_VERSION );
                    if( g_pD3D == NULL )
                    {
                            SetError( "Could not create IDirect3D8 object" );
                            return E_FAIL;

                    }

                    // Get the current settings for the default display adapter
                    r = g_pD3D->GetAdapterDisplayMode( D3DADAPTER_DEFAULT,

                    &d3ddm );
                    if( FAILED( r ) )
                    {
                            SetError( "Could not get display adapter information" );
                            return E_FAIL;

                    }


                    // Initialize the structure to 0
                    ZeroMemory( &d3dpp, sizeof( D3DPRESENT_PARAMETERS ) );
                    // Tell Direct3D that we will not be running full screen
                    d3dpp.Windowed = TRUE;
                    // Tell Direct3D that it is free to mess with the back buffer
                    d3dpp.SwapEffect = D3DSWAPEFFECT_DISCARD;
                    // Set the back buffer format to be the same as the primary surface
                    d3dpp.BackBufferFormat = d3ddm.Format;
                    // Acquire a pointer to IDirect3DDevice8
```

```
        r = g_pD3D->CreateDevice( D3DADAPTER_DEFAULT,
                                                    D3DDEVTYPE_HAL,
                                      g_hWndMain,
D3DCREATE_SOFTWARE_VERTEXPROCESSING,
                             &d3dpp,
                                  &g_pDevice );
        if( FAILED( r ) )
        {
                SetError( "Could not create the render device" );
                return E_FAIL;
        }


        return S_OK;
}


int GameLoop()
{
        return S_OK;
}


int GameShutdown()
{

        // Release the pointer to IDirect3DDevice8
        if( g_pDevice )
        {
                g_pDevice->Release();
        }


        // Release the pointer to IDirect3D8
        if( g_pD3D )
        {
                g_pD3D->Release();
        }


        return S_OK;
}
```

That is the layout of the code. One thing to note is that I changed the `WM_PAINT` handler slightly. For now, I am not using the DC at all, so instead of calling `BeginPaint()` and `EndPaint()`, I replaced both calls with a call to `ValidateRect()`. This tells Windows that it should assume that I have updated whatever part of the window that it thought needed updating.

Then the only new code is in `GameInit()`. Just remember the following steps for when you want to initialize Direct3D in windowed mode:

1. Acquire an interface pointer to IDirect3D8 using `Direct3DCreate8()`.
2. Get the current settings of the default adapter using `GetAdapterDisplayMode()`.
3. Set the format for the back buffer using the `D3DPRESENT_PARAMETERS` structure.
4. Create the device using the `CreateDevice()` function.

And that's it!

Moving to Full Screen

Windowed mode is all very well and good, but it has many drawbacks. The biggest issue is that most 3D accelerators do not work in a windowed environment. This has to do with the complex nature of maintaining all the relationships between the different subsystems of Windows, like the GDI and Direct3D. Windowed mode also imposes constraints on the programmer and makes simple programming quite complex. This is because when programming in a window, you do not know what the current display mode is set to. You must write your code to use whatever is already set. What this all boils down to is that the majority of the code discussed for the rest of the book, both 2D and 3D, will operate in a full screen environment because it is faster, easier, and reflects how real games run.

So what do you do differently? Well, here is the code used before to create the device:

```
// Tell Direct3D that we will not be running full screen
d3dpp.Windowed = TRUE;
// Tell Direct3D that it is free to mess with the back buffer
d3dpp.SwapEffect = D3DSWAPEFFECT_DISCARD;
// Set the back buffer format to be the same as the primary surface
d3dpp.BackBufferFormat = d3ddm.Format;
// Acquire a pointer to IDirect3DDevice8
r = g_pD3D->CreateDevice( D3DADAPTER_DEFAULT,
```

```
                                              D3DDEVTYPE_HAL,
                                              g_hWndMain,

                                                                    D3DCRE-

                                                                    &d3dpp,
                                          &g_pDevice );
```

ATE_SOFTWARE_VERTEXPROCESSING,

The only difference to go full screen is that you now have to fill in the D3DPRESENT_PARAMETERS structure differently. Let's take a moment now to put together a function that you can call that will do all this.

Let's start off the file with a function to initialize Direct3D, called InitDirect3DDevice(). Here is the code:

NOTE

From this chapter onward, I am starting to build up a library of functions that you will be using in the rest of the book. It is called Engine.h, and you can locate it on the companion CD. If you include this file with your applications, you will have access to all the functions that I will be discussing.

```
int InitDirect3DDevice( HWND hWndTarget, int Width, int Height, BOOL bWindowed,
                        D3DFORMAT FullScreenFormat, LPDIRECT3D8 pD3D,
                        LPDIRECT3DDEVICE8* ppDevice )
{
        // Structure to hold information about the rendering method
        D3DPRESENT_PARAMETERS d3dpp;
        // Structure to hold information about the current display mode
        D3DDISPLAYMODE d3ddm;
        HRESULT r = 0;
        if( *ppDevice )
                (*ppDevice)->Release();
        // Initialize the structure to 0
        ZeroMemory( &d3dpp, sizeof( D3DPRESENT_PARAMETERS ) );
        // Get the settings for the current display mode
        r = pD3D->GetAdapterDisplayMode( D3DADAPTER_DEFAULT, &d3ddm );
        if( FAILED( r ) )
        {
                SetError( "Could not get display adapter information" );
                return E_FAIL;
        }
```

```cpp
        // The width of the back buffer in pixels
        d3dpp.BackBufferWidth = Width;
        // The height of the back buffer in pixels
        d3dpp.BackBufferHeight = Height;
        // The format of the back buffer
        d3dpp.BackBufferFormat = bWindowed ? d3ddm.Format : FullScreenFormat;

        // The number of back buffers
        d3dpp.BackBufferCount = 1;
        // The type of multisampling
        d3dpp.MultiSampleType = D3DMULTISAMPLE_NONE;
        // The swap effect
        d3dpp.SwapEffect = D3DSWAPEFFECT_DISCARD;

        // The handle to the window that we want to render to
        d3dpp.hDeviceWindow = hWndTarget;
        // Windowed or full screen
        d3dpp.Windowed = bWindowed;

        // Let Direct3D manage the depth buffer
        d3dpp.EnableAutoDepthStencil = TRUE;
        // Set the depth buffer format to 16 bits
        d3dpp.AutoDepthStencilFormat = D3DFMT_D16;

        // Use the default refresh rate available
        d3dpp.FullScreen_RefreshRateInHz = 0;

        // Present the information as fast as possible
        d3dpp.FullScreen_PresentationInterval =
                                bWindowed ? 0 : D3DPRESENT_INTERVAL_IMMEDIATE;
        // Allow the back buffer to be accessed for 2D work
        d3dpp.Flags = D3DPRESENTFLAG_LOCKABLE_BACKBUFFER;
        // Acquire a pointer to IDirect3DDevice8
        r = pD3D->CreateDevice( D3DADAPTER_DEFAULT,
                        D3DDEVTYPE_HAL, hWndTarget,
                                        D3DCREATE_SOFTWARE_VERTEXPRO-
CESSING,
                                        &d3dpp, ppDevice );

        if( FAILED( r ) )
        {
```

```
            SetError( "Could not create the render device" );
            return E_FAIL;
    }

    g_DeviceHeight = Height;
    g_DeviceWidth = Width;

g_SavedPresParams = d3dpp;
    return S_OK;
}
```

Call this function from `GameInit()` directly after you acquire an interface to
`IDirect3D8`.

So what is all that extra junk? Fortunately, most of it is just setting up standard
Direct3D stuff—it looks much more complex than it actually is. You can use these
settings for just about anything and they will remain the same. Just smile and nod if
you get a little confused. The function takes seven parameters, in this order: a handle to the target window, the width of the back buffer, the height of the back
buffer, a flag specifying whether you want full screen or windowed mode, a back
buffer format flag (which should be zero for windowed mode), a pointer to an
`IDirect3D8` interface, and finally a pointer to a pointer that will receive the address
of the newly-created device.

Anyway, for starters, here is an overview of what is going on. The first thing is to
declare two structures, `d3ddm` and `d3dpp`, which are `D3DDISPLAYMODE` and
`D3DPRESENT_PARAMETERS` structures, respectively. You saw these a little bit before when
you were setting up for windowed use. Next, get the current display settings just as
before, in case the Windowed mode was specified. The `d3dpp` structure is quite complex, so have a look at the following steps for filling it in:

1. The first two members, BackBufferWidth and BackBufferHeight, obviously
   take the width of the back buffer in pixels.

2. Then set the BackBufferFormat member to the format of either the current
   display if the request was for windowed mode, or to the format specified in
   the FullScreenFormat formal parameter.

3. Next, `BackBufferCount` takes the number of back buffers that you want to create; for now you only want one.

4. Then set `MultiSampleType` to `D3DMULTISAMPLE_NONE`. I will cover what this is when I
   come to the 3D chapters.

5. Next, set the `SwapEffect` member to `D3DSWAPEFFECT_DISCARD`. As I explained previously, this causes Direct3D to increase performance slightly because it does not have to spend time guaranteeing the state of the back buffer.

6. `hDeviceWindow` takes a handle to the window that you want to use as the rendering target.

7. The `Windowed` member specifies to Direct3D whether you want to run in full screen or not, and it is set using the `bFullScreen` formal parameter.

8. Set `EnableAutoDepthStencil` to `TRUE`. This causes Direct3D to look after the depth buffer. Again, I will cover this in more detail in later chapters.

9. Next up is `AutoDepthStencilFormat`, which you set to `D3DFMT_D16`, which means "16-bit depth buffer."

10. Set the `Flags` member to `D3DPRESENTFLAG_LOCKABLE_BACKBUFFER`, which means that you can access the back buffer manually to do 2D work. Unfortunately, this causes a slight performance drain on some display adapters.

11. Set `FullScreen_RefreshRateInHz` to 0. This causes Direct3D to set the refresh rate to the default rate. You can specify a specific rate here if you want, but it may not be supported and device creation may fail.

12. Finally, set `FullScreen_PresentationInterval` to `D3DPRESENT_INTERVAL_IMMEDIATE` if full-screen mode is requested. On the other hand, if you want to set the display mode to windowed, then this parameter *must* be set to zero.

Note that at the end of `InitDirect3DDevice()` you save a copy of the presentation parameters in a global variable. This is for an advanced topic, *device validation,* which I will talk about toward the end of the chapter, but just keep it in mind for now.

After all of that, the device is created exactly as before with a call to `IDirect3D8::CreateDevice()`. Here is the newly laid-out `GameInit()` function with the call to `InitDirect3DDevice()`. Not much has changed.

```
int GameInit()
{
        HRESULT r = 0; // Holds return values
        // Acquire a pointer to IDirect3D8
        g_pD3D = Direct3DCreate8( D3D_SDK_VERSION );
        if( g_pD3D == NULL )
        {
                SetError( "Could not create IDirect3D8 object" );
                return E_FAIL;
        }
```

```
// Create the device
r = InitDirect3DDevice( g_hWndMain, 640, 480,
                            FALSE, D3DFMT_X8R8G8B8, g_pD3D, &g_pDevice );
if( FAILED( r ) )
{
        SetError( "Initialization of the device failed" );
        return E_FAIL;
}

    return S_OK;
}
```

Rendering with Direct3D

Now you must figure out what you need to do to actually draw using Direct3D. First things first: Let's create a new function, which will be called from the GameLoop() function, entitled Render(). This function will be called every iteration of the game loop and will contain all the code that has to do with rendering and rasterization. It is good to modularize your games by having clearly defined functions with a clear purpose; doing so allows you to keep everything under control.

CAUTION

One really important thing to make sure you get correct is the extents of your surfaces. If you ask for a surface of size 640 x 480, then the last addressable pixel is in fact (639, 479). This is because the memory is zero based. That is, the first pixel is at (0, 0) not (1, 1). If you attempt to write to a pixel at (640, 480), then you will cause a memory overwrite error, which is a total bummer, dude.

Now there is an incredible array of ways in which you can render with Direct3D, but the thing that changes the process the most is the bit depth. I am going to show you code that is compatible with 32-bit display modes. Just about every graphics card released in the last four years can handle this. If yours does not, see if you can pick up a better one. Why not other bit depths? Well, 24-bit color is not supported by all cards, and sometimes there are issues with the ordering of the red, green, and blue components of the color. Sixteen-bit color again has problems. The main one is that there is not a standard about the number of bits per color; sometimes there are 5 bits for green, sometimes there are 6. It is all very annoying. And 8-bit color obviously only supports 256 colors, which is not enough for your purposes.

Getting in the Back Door

If you want to render with Direct3D, you'd better figure out how to get access to the back buffer, because that is what gets transferred to the primary surface to be displayed. Let me just recap what I talked about earlier.

To get an image to the screen using Direct3D you must do the following:

1. Clear the back buffer because you can't be sure of what was there previously.
2. Acquire a pointer to the back buffer surface.
3. Lock the back buffer so that you have access to it.
4. Draw into the back buffer memory.
5. Unlock the memory so that Direct3D can proceed with the rendering process.
6. Release the pointer to the back buffer.
7. Present the back buffer to the primary surface.

And those seven steps contain, in a nutshell, the 2D rendering process with Direct3D. The previous steps have to be done every time you iterate through the game loop. They are all placed within the Render() function, which is called from GameLoop() every pass. Figure 8.13 shows how to implement it.

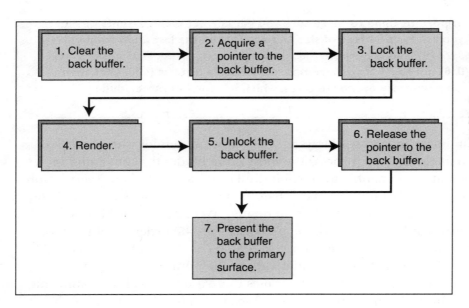

Figure 8.13

The 2D rendering process with Direct3D

Step 1: Clear the Back Buffer

This is easy to do and only requires a single function call to—you guessed it—
IDirect3DDevice8::Clear()! Though it has such a simple purpose, it has a
surprisingly large number of parameters:

```
HRESULT Clear(  DWORD Count, CONST D3DRECT* pRects, DWORD Flags,
                            D3DCOLOR Color, float Z, DWORD Stencil );
```

Here is how I made the call:

```
g_pDevice->Clear( 0, 0, D3DCLEAR_TARGET, D3DCOLOR_XRGB( 0, 0, 0 ), 0.0f, 0 );
```

The way this function works is kind of interesting. You pass it a list of rectangles
that you want to clear, and it will fill that list of rectangles with the color that you
request. But wait, there's more! This function can also be used to clear other esoteric surfaces that I have not covered yet, like z-buffers and stencil buffers.
However, for now I'm not interested in all that extra functionality. I just want to
clear the back buffer, right? Cool, let's see how to do that. The first parameter,
Count, takes the number of rectangles that are in the list. Since I don't have a list of
rectangles I set this parameter to 0. The second parameter, pRects, takes a pointer
to the start of the list of rectangles. Again, since I don't have a list I set this to NULL.
The effect of setting the first two parameters to 0 causes Direct3D to clear the
entire surface. The Flags parameter takes a flag that specifies what you want to
clear; the possible values for this are listed in Table 8.4.

Table 8.4   Clearing Flags

Flag	Meaning
D3DCLEAR_STENCIL	Clears the stencil buffer with the value specified in the Stencil parameter
D3DCLEAR_ZBUFFER	Clears the z-buffer with the value specified in the Z parameter
D3DCLEAR_TARGET	Clears the main surface with the color specified in the Color parameter

D3DCLEAR_TARGET is the flag that you're after to clear the surface. The fourth parameter is Color, and it takes the color that you want to use to clear the surface with. I used the incredibly useful macro D3DCOLOR_XRGB() to help me fill in this value. This macro works in the exact same way as the RGB() macro that you encountered before when dealing with the Windows GDI. The fifth parameter, Z, takes a value to fill the z-buffer with. You only specify a value here if you are actually filling the z-buffer with something and if you have specified the appropriate clear flag. The final parameter, Stencil, is the same; specify a value if you want to, but otherwise don't bother. I'll talk more on these buffers later.

Step 2: Get a Pointer to the Back Buffer

This step is pretty easy. It requires that you create a pointer to IDirect3DSurface8. I defined this variable at the top of the Render() function:

```
LPDIRECT3DSURFACE8 pBackSurf = 0;
```

A surface object simply represents a surface in memory. Remember when I briefly discussed surfaces? I said that they are very similar to device contexts except that they are much lower-level. You are really dealing with the metal when you mess with surfaces. To get a pointer to the back buffer surface you have to request it from the device, which manages the back buffer. This is done using the function IDirect3DDevice8::GetBackBuffer(), which has this prototype:

```
HRESULT GetBackBuffer( UINT BackBuffer,
                       D3DBACKBUFFER_TYPE Type, IDirect3DSurface8** ppBackBuffer );
```

I called the function like this:

```
r = g_pDevice->GetBackBuffer( 0, D3DBACKBUFFER_TYPE_MONO, &pBackSurf );
if( FAILED( r ) )
{
        SetError( "Couldnt get backbuffer" );
}
```

The first parameter takes an integer that defines which back buffer you want access to. The thing is that the first back buffer has index 0, the second is 1, and so on. Since I only have one back buffer, I set this parameter to zero. The second parameter is completely superfluous and shouldn't even be there. You can only specify D3DBACKBUFFER_TYPE_MONO. In the future, when stereovision displays become widespread, there will be other applicable flags. The final parameter takes a pointer to a pointer that will hold the address of the surface that you are requesting access to.

Step 3: Lock the Back Buffer

OK, you're almost there. To lock the buffer requires another variable to be declared, which is of the D3DLOCKED_RECT type.

I declared it like this at the top of the Render() function:

```
D3DLOCKED_RECT LockedRect;
```

D3DLOCKED_RECT looks like this:

```
typedef struct _D3DLOCKED_RECT {
    INT              Pitch;
    void*            pBits;
} D3DLOCKED_RECT;
```

When you lock the surface, this structure is filled with the required information for you. Pitch contains the pitch of the surface in bytes. Remember that pitch is the extra information at the right edge of the surface that you want to skip over when you are indexing into the memory plus the total width of the surface. pBits contains a pointer to the start of the memory that you have locked.

Now I need to actually make the call to IDirect3DSurface8::LockRect(), which has this prototype:

```
HRESULT LockRect( D3DLOCKED_RECT* pLockedRect,
                                  CONST RECT* pRect,  DWORD Flags );
```

I called the function a little like this:

```
r = pBackSurf->LockRect( &LockedRect, NULL, 0 );
if( FAILED( r ) )
{
        SetError( "Could not lock the back buffer" );
}
```

The first parameter takes the address of the D3DLOCKED_RECT structure I was talking about a minute ago. The second parameter takes the address of a RECT structure that defines the area of the surface that I want to lock. Since I want access to the entire surface I set this parameter to NULL. And the third parameter takes flags that can be used in advanced circumstances. I can't see needing them at all, so they are safe to ignore; so I set this parameter to 0.

By the way, you should know that locking a surface takes a very long time, so you should strive to only do it once per frame. For instance, you would definitely not call LockRect() every time you call a pixel-plotting or line-drawing function. Instead, you lock the surface once and send the pointer that you receive to the various drawing functions. I'll talk more about this soon.

Step 4: Rendering into the Back Buffer

Actually, I'm going to leave showing you how to draw because that's what the rest of the book is for. Don't worry though—it is only for a moment. I want to get the shut-down code out of the way so that you can move full steam into the good stuff. What I *will* show you a line of code that allows you to access the memory that is locked, and it looks like this:

```
DWORD* pData = (DWORD*)(LockedRect.pBits);
```

What's going on here? Remember I said that this code is for 32-bit display modes? Well, since each pixel has 32 bits describing it, it is a good idea to massage that pointer you received from the LockRect() function into something a little more useful: a 32-bit pointer! And that is exactly what that line of code does. I'll return to this in a second.

Step 5: Unlock the Back Buffer

When you are done using the memory it is very important that you unlock it. When you lock a surface you cause a Win16 global critical section lock (in Windows 98, Windows Me, and successors). What this means is that if you don't unlock the memory, your machine will have a long and tortuous death. In Windows 2000 and later your computer will not die, but it will get very slow until you exit from your application. So remember: always unlock your surfaces!

It is very simple to do this—just call IDirect3DSurface8::UnlockRect() like this:

```
pBackSurf->UnlockRect();
```

As you can see, it does not take any parameters. Simple, huh?

> **CAUTION**
>
> I'm writing this twice because it is so important. Unlock your surfaces when you are done using them!

Step 6: Release the Surface

This is almost as important as unlocking the surface. When you call
`IDirect3DDevice8::GetBackBuffer()` it increases the internal reference count of the
object, just like the `AddRef()` function does. If you forget to call `Release()` each time
you acquire a pointer, you have the potential to cause a memory leak. Releasing the
surface is just as simple as unlocking it. It only takes a single call to `Release()`, as
shown here:

```
pBackSurf->Release();
pBackSurf = 0;
```

Notice how I set the pointer to zero after calling `Release()`. This is because after
you call `Release()` on an object the pointer is no longer valid. You want to avoid any
accidental references to invalid memory.

Step 7: Copy the Back Buffer to the Primary Surface

Again, this step is very simple, requiring only a single function call to
`IDirect3DDevice8::Present()`. This function works in the same way as `Blt()` did for the
GDI. It copies a surface to another surface, or just a portion of a surface. In this
case I want to copy the back buffer surface to the primary surface. The function
looks like this:

```
HRESULT Present(  CONST RECT* pSourceRect,  CONST RECT* pDestRect,
                        HWND hDestWindowOverride,  CONST RGNDATA* pDirtyRegion );
```

The first parameter must be set to `NULL` unless you are using swap chains (more
than one back buffer), which I won't be spending too much time on. This is the
same for the second parameter. Just set it to `NULL` and all will be well. The third
parameter takes a window handle that can be used as an override of the default target window if you want to render somewhere else. Just set it to `NULL`. And the final
parameter is one of Microsoft's peculiarities; it is completely useless and must be
set to `NULL`. So, you may find it amusing that your average call to `Present()` will look
like this:

```
g_pDevice->Present( NULL, NULL, NULL, NULL );
```

Nice, isn't it?

Putting It All Together

Here is the entire Render() function in one place. It's not that bad, is it?

```
int Render()
{
        HRESULT r;
        D3DLOCKED_RECT LockedRect;
        LPDIRECT3DSURFACE8 pBackSurf = 0;
        if( !g_pDevice )
        {
                SetError( "Cannot render because there is no device" );
                return E_FAIL;
        }

        g_pDevice->Clear( 0, 0, D3DCLEAR_TARGET,
                                        D3DCOLOR_XRGB( 0, 0, 0 ), 1.0f, 0 );
        r = g_pDevice->GetBackBuffer( 0, D3DBACKBUFFER_TYPE_MONO, &pBackSurf );
        if( FAILED( r ) )
        {
                SetError( "Couldnt get backbuffer" );
        }

        r = pBackSurf->LockRect( &LockedRect, NULL, 0 );
        if( FAILED( r ) )
        {
                SetError( "Could not lock the back buffer" );
        }

        DWORD* pData = (DWORD*)(LockedRect.pBits);
        // -------------- Draw here --------------------
        pBackSurf->UnlockRect();
        pData = 0;

        pBackSurf->Release();
        pBackSurf = 0;

        g_pDevice->Present( NULL, NULL, NULL, NULL );
        return S_OK;
}
```

Drawing

You're finally here. This is what you have been waiting for. You finally get to start drawing using Direct3D! I feel the power of the Great Ones approaching.

I think the best place to start is at the beginning: learning how to plot pixels. You are about to experience, in graphics programming, the equivalent of what "Hello World" is to standard programming. Don't worry though—you are a Great One, and as such you will progress much faster than you did when you learned how to program!

Plotting Pixels

You already know the theory behind plotting pixels. The thing with drawing to display memory is that in reality it is just that: memory. It is just a long strand of bits. So what do you think happens if you have a screen that has a resolution of 640 x 480 and you write to the pixel at (640, 481)? Well, you will be writing to other memory that could contain anything from critical Windows code, to hard disk access code, to who knows what. So you have to make sure that when you write to display memory you keep your coordinates inside the dimensions of the screen. This process is called *clipping*, and it simply means to draw within the lines.

Let's look at the goals here. You want to write a function that will set a pixel at an x, y coordinate to a specific color. Seems simple enough. What will the function need in order to accomplish this task? I think x, y coordinates would be nice, and the color. But it will also need the pitch of the surface so that it can locate the correct position. And of course it will need a pointer to the start of the image data. This function is going to be 32-bit-dependent. That is, it will only work for surfaces that have a 32-bit depth. I think a really cool name would be SetPixel32(). Rockin' baby! Let's see how it works:

```
void SetPixel32( int x, int y, DWORD Color, int Pitch, DWORD* pData )
{

if( (x > g_DeviceWidth) || (x < 0) )
            return;
        if( (y > g_DeviceHeight) || (y < 0) )
            return;
        pData[ (((Pitch/4) * y) + x) ] = Color;
}
```

It is pretty simple. First I make sure that the coordinates are within the bounds of the screen. Then I index into the back buffer surface pointer using the formulas I talked about before. If you look back now you may be wondering why I am not multiplying by the number of bytes. Well, this is because the pointer is already 32 bits, so if I increase the array indexer by one, I in fact progress the pointer by 4 bytes. This is also the reason that I divided the pitch by 4, because it is defined in bytes. The divide-by-4 operation converts it into a DWORD value. Look out for this in your own code.

Now just to bring all this together I'm going to give you a little example that draws thousands of pixels to the screen really fast. If you look back to the last code listing that shows the Render() function, you will see a line of code that says Draw here. If you put the following code in that position and then execute it, you will get some groovy results, like what you see in Figure 8.14:

```
for( int i = 0 ; i < 10000 ; i++ )
{
SetPixel32( rand()%(g_DeviceWidth-1), rand()%(g_DeviceHeight-1),
                  D3DCOLOR_XRGB( 255, 0, 0 ), LockedRect.Pitch, pData );
}
```

Figure 8.14

Pixel plotting in action

You've got to see it in action; it is just so much cooler than a static image. This causes the program to draw 10,000 random red pixels each frame.

Drawing Rectangles

Rectangles are the next step up in graphics. So how exactly is a rectangle drawn? Well, your average low-budget rectangle that has no border is really just rows of lines drawn one after the other. And this is exactly how you are going to draw your rectangles. It is pretty simple if you think about it; all you have to do is draw a horizontal line of pixels for each vertical line. Surprisingly, drawing a line is actually quite a complex process, so instead you are going to do simple memory fills. This is OK since you only need horizontal lines anyway.

Like the pixel-plotting function, your Rectangle32() function needs a pointer to the display memory, and the pitch of the destination surface. And, of course, it also needs the actual coordinates of the rectangle that you want to draw. For this I am using the D3DRECT structure, which is binary compatible with the standard Windows RECT structure. Here is the prototype for this new structure:

```
typedef struct _D3DRECT {
    LONG x1;
    LONG y1;
    LONG x2;
    LONG y2;
} D3DRECT;
```

Okay, let's have a look at how to draw rectangles:

```
void Rectangle32( D3DRECT* pRect, DWORD Color, int Pitch, DWORD* pData )
{
        int y1 = pRect->y1;
        int y2 = pRect->y2;
        int x1 = pRect->x1;
        int x2 = pRect->x2;

        int Pitch4 = Pitch / 4;
        DWORD Offset = y1 * Pitch4 + x1;
        for( int y = y1 ; y < y2 ; y++ )
        {
                for( int x = x1 ; x < x2 ; x++ )
                {
                        pData[ Offset + x ] = Color;
```

```
        }

                Offset += Pitch4;

        }

}
```

This function works by looping through each y-coordinate, then each x-coordinate, and setting the appropriate pixel. After each horizontal line is drawn, the offset is incremented by the pitch of the surface to bring the pointer around to the next line. The only problem with it is that it is *so* slow. In fact, this is about the slowest way that you can possibly draw rectangles. There is so much pointer dereferencing, multiplications, divisions, looping, and on and on, that this function takes an eternity to run. It also sets each pixel individually rather than filling an area of memory. And you know what? It doesn't even take advantage of hardware acceleration.

So let's fix all these issues with a new function: Rectangle32Fast(). This function will only, you may be surprised to hear, have a single line of code. The thing is that these days there is no need to draw rectangles manually since just about every graphics card on the planet supports hardware-accelerated drawing of rectangles. So how do you do it? Well, I am going to use a function that you have seen before: the IDirect3DDevice8::Clear() function. Of course this means that I must pass a pointer to the device to the function as well. But it will no longer need access to the pitch of the surface or the pointer to the data. Anyway, here it is:

```
void Rectangle32Fast( D3DRECT* pRect, DWORD Color, LPDIRECT3DDEVICE8 pDevice )
{
        pDevice->Clear( 1, pRect, D3DCLEAR_TARGET, Color, 0.0f, 0 );
}
```

The first parameter to Clear() takes the number of rectangles in the list, which is just one for this function. The second parameter takes the address of the D3DRECT structure and the rest of the parameters you already know about. Pretty simple, isn't it? And this is 500 percent faster than the previous function. Not bad, if I do say so myself. The only *caveat* for this rectangle function is that it will *only* work with the back buffer, so try to use it on other surfaces. The normal Rectangle32() function will work anywhere.

You can see a groovy example of rectangles by putting the following code in place of the pixel-plotting code I was talking about before:

```
for( int i = 0 ; i < 100 ; i++ )
{
        D3DRECT Rect = { rand()%(g_DeviceWidth-1), rand()%(g_DeviceHeight-1),
```

```
rand()%(g_DeviceWidth-1), rand()%(g_DeviceHeight-1) };
       Rectangle32Fast( &Rect,
           D3DCOLOR_XRGB( rand()%255, rand()%255, rand()%255 ),
           g_pDevice );
}
```

The results look like those in Figure 8.15.

Figure 8.15

Accelerated rectangles with Direct3D

Bitmaps: The Direct3D Way

Bitmaps work in Direct3D in a very similar way to how they worked with the GDI. Of course, with DirectDraw they are not as abstracted. Like the back buffer, an `IDirect3DSurface8` object represents a bitmap. Unfortunately, when DirectDraw and Direct3D were joined, most of the functions that made it easy to move bitmaps between the GDI and DirectDraw were lost. So now when you load bitmaps you have to follow some interesting steps. Figure 8.16 shows the process graphically.

1. Use the GDI to load the image into memory using the `LoadImage()` function.
2. Get information about the size of the bitmap using the GDI `GetObject()` function.
3. Remove the image from memory.
4. Create a surface based on the information retrieved in step 2.
5. Use Direct3D to load the bitmap directly onto the surface.

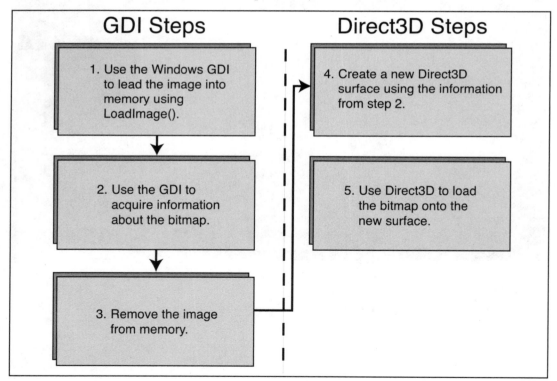

Figure 8.16

Rendering with Direct3D

It seems silly to load it twice, but in fact this way is easier than trying to convert GDI device contexts into Direct3D surfaces. Here is the code:

```c
int LoadBitmapToSurface( char* PathName,
LPDIRECT3DSURFACE8* ppSurface, LPDIRECT3DDEVICE8 pDevice )
{
        HRESULT r;
        HBITMAP hBitmap;
        BITMAP Bitmap;

        // Load the bitmap first using the GDI to get info about it
        hBitmap = (HBITMAP)LoadImage( NULL, PathName,
                        IMAGE_BITMAP, 0, 0, LR_LOADFROMFILE | LR_CREATEDIBSECTION );
    if( hBitmap == NULL )
        {
                // The file probably does not exist
                SetError( "Unable to load bitmap" );
                return E_FAIL;
        }

        // Get information about the object
        GetObject( hBitmap, sizeof( BITMAP ), &Bitmap );
        // Unload the bitmap from memory
        DeleteObject( hBitmap );

        // Now create a surface using the information gained from
        // the previous load
        r = pDevice->CreateImageSurface( Bitmap.bmWidth,
                                                Bitmap.bmHeight,
                        D3DFMT_X8R8G8B8, ppSurface );
        if( FAILED( r ) )
        {
                SetError( "Unable to create surface for bitmap load" );
                return E_FAIL;
        }

        // Load the image again, this time using Direct3D to load
        // it directly to the new surface
        r = D3DXLoadSurfaceFromFile( *ppSurface, NULL, NULL, PathName,
                                                                NULL,
D3DX_FILTER_NONE, 0, NULL );
```

```
if( FAILED( r ) )
        {
                SetError( "Unable to load file to surface" );
                return E_FAIL;
        }


        return S_OK;
}
```

You saw a lot of the code before when I talked about the GDI. After I load the file, get information about it, and then close, I create a new surface using the `IDirect3DDevice8::CreateImageSurface()` function.

```
HRESULT CreateImageSurface(  UINT Width,  UINT Height,
                                     D3DFORMAT Format,  IDirect3DSurface8** ppSurface );
```

This function takes parameters that define the width, height, and format of the surface, as well as a pointer to a pointer that will be filled with the address of the new surface.

Next up I use the DirectX utility function `D3DXLoadSurfaceFromFile()` to load the image from the disk directly onto the newly created image. This is an extremely useful function because it will automatically convert the format of the image on disk to match the format of the destination surface. Doing this on your own takes a long time.

```
HRESULT D3DXLoadSurfaceFromFileA(
        LPDIRECT3DSURFACE8 pDestSurface,              // The destination surface
                CONST PALETTEENTRY* pDestPalette,     // The associated palette
        CONST RECT* pDestRect,                        // The destination rectangle
                LPCSTR pSrcFile,                                   // Path
of the source file
        CONST RECT* pSrcRect,                         // The source rectangle
        DWORD Filter,                                            // The filter to
    use
        D3DCOLOR ColorKey,                                  // The color key
        D3DXIMAGE_INFO* pSrcInfo );                   // Information about the image
```

It is not as bad as it looks. I say that about nearly every single function that I explain, don't I? I think that Microsoft thought it would be a good idea to make simple stuff look hard. The first parameter takes a pointer to the destination surface. This surface must have already been created. The second parameter takes a pointer to a palette to use if the surface is palettized. This one is not, so it is safe to set this to NULL. The third parameter is pDestRect, and it takes a pointer to a RECT structure that defines the dimensions of the destination image to which you want to copy. The fourth parameter, pSrcRect, takes the path of the file that you want to load. The pSrcRect parameter again takes a pointer to a rectangle that defines an area in the source image from which you want to copy. Filter takes an identifier that defines which filters you want to use during the load process. Table 8.5 shows the values that you can specify for the Filter parameter.

Table 8.5   Filters for D3DXLoadSurfaceFromFile()

Value	Meaning
D3DX_FILTER_BOX	Each pixel is computed by averaging a 2_2(_2) box of pixels from the source image. This filter works only when the dimensions of the destination are half those of the source, like with mipmaps.
D3DX_FILTER_LINEAR	Each destination pixel is computed by sampling the four nearest pixels from the source image. This filter works best when the scale on both axes is less than two.
D3DX_FILTER_NONE	No scaling or filtering will take place. Pixels outside the bounds of the source image are assumed to be transparent black.
D3DX_FILTER_POINT	Each destination pixel is computed by sampling the nearest pixel from the source image.
D3DX_FILTER_TRIANGLE	Every pixel in the source image contributes equally to the destination image. This is the slowest of the filters.
D3DX_FILTER_MIRROR	Specifying this flag is the same as specifying the D3DX_FILTER_MIRROR_U, D3DX_FILTER_MIRROR_V, and D3DX_FILTER_MIRROR_W flags.
D3DX_FILTER_MIRROR_U	Pixels off the edge of the texture on the u-axis should be mirrored, not wrapped.
D3DX_FILTER_MIRROR_V	Pixels off the edge of the texture on the v-axis should be mirrored, not wrapped.
D3DX_FILTER_MIRROR_W	Pixels off the edge of the texture on the w-axis should be mirrored, not wrapped.
D3DX_FILTER_DITHER	The resulting image must be dithered using a 4x4 ordered dither algorithm.

I set the Filter parameter to D3DX_FILTER_NONE. There is no need to filter the image, because it is not being scaled as I set the size of the surface using the actual size of the bitmap. ColorKey takes a color to use as a color key if you want to use one. A color key is a specific color that is set as transparent and will not be copied. For instance, if you set black (RGB(0,0,0)) as the color key, then all of the image would be copied *except* the black pixels (I'll talk more about this later). The final parameter is pSrcInfo, and it takes the address of a structure to be filled with information about the image. This is not necessary unless you actually want to get information about the loaded image, so I set it to NULL.

And that's how to load an image. This function creates a surface for you and loads the image from the disk into it, automatically converting the format of the source image to match the surface. The next thing to do is figure out how to copy it to the back buffer.

Copying Surfaces to the Back Buffer

After your surface has been filled with an image from the disk, you can display the image by copying it to the back buffer, which is subsequently presented to the primary surface. (See Figure 8.7.) There are in fact two ways to copy your image to the back buffer. The first way is to do a direct copy. This means that the image is copied *exactly* as it is on the original surface. This only works if the source surface's size is less than or equal to the destination surface, and the format of the two surfaces match. No scaling, color conversion, alpha effects, color keying, or anything else advanced is possible. You would use this method if you were sure that the source surface was already in the same format as the destination.

Alternatively, if you want to copy a surface that does not pass the requirements laid out in the previous paragraph, then you will want to use the second method, which takes slightly longer to perform. This method can scale the image using very advanced filtering techniques as well as doing format conversions and color keying on the fly.

> **NOTE**
>
> One very important thing to remember is that you must not try to perform copy operations while the surfaces are locked. If you try, the operations will fail.

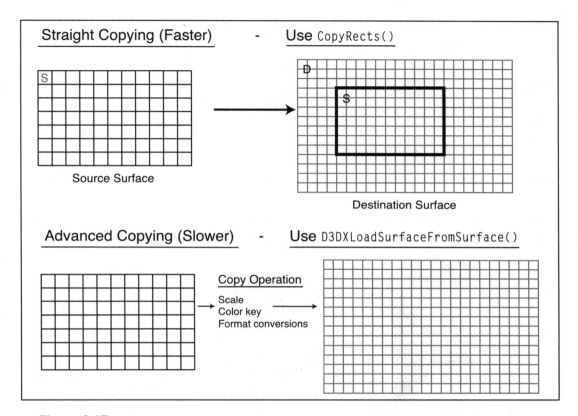

Figure 8.17

2D copying methods with Direct3D

Straight Copying

Let's look at straight copying first, because it's easier. The objective is to copy one surface to a coordinate on the second surface. To do this you need six coordinates: two for the upper-left corner of the source image, two for the lower-right corner of the source image, and finally two for the destination point on the target surface. You can group the first four coordinates into a RECT structure and the second two coordinates into a POINT structure. This is handy because it is exactly what the function requires! And the name of this function is IDirect3DDevice8::CopyRects(). In the past it was called Blt(), but when you have a chance to fix something that isn't broken, why waste the opportunity?

Good old Microsoft. Anyway, it looks like this:

```
HRESULT CopyRects(

    IDirect3DSurface8* pSourceSurface,        // Pointer to source surface
    CONST RECT* pSourceRectsArray,            // Pointer to source rectangle
    UINT cRects,                              // Number of rectangles
    IDirect3DSurface8* pDestinationSurface,   // Pointer to destination surface
    CONST POINT* pDestPointsArray             // Pointer to destination POINT
);
```

Have a look at Figure 8.18, which shows how the rectangles and points relate to the surfaces.

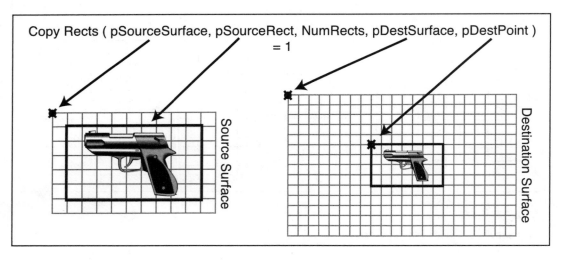

Figure 8.18

The CopyRects() function

This is a simple function, although it has the capability to do advanced batch copying. For now you will just use it to copy single surfaces. The first parameter, pSourceSurface, takes a pointer to the source surface, which must be a valid surface. Next is pSourceRectsArray, which takes a pointer to an array of rectangles that defines the regions that you want to copy. If you only want to copy one section of the image, then you only have to pass the address of a single RECT or D3DRECT structure. cRects takes the number of rectangles in the list specified in pSourceSurface. Again, you are only using one rectangle, so you can just enter 1. The fourth parameter, pDestinationSurface, takes a pointer to the destination surface, which of course must also be valid. The final parameter is pDestPointsArray, which takes a pointer to a list of `POINT` structures. For every rectangle in the list, you can specify a point of destination using this parameter. Since you are only specifying a single rectangle, you only have to use a single point.

The following code shows how to load a file from the disk into a surface, then copy it to the back buffer, and finally present it to the primary surface:

```
// Create a surface pointer
LPDIRECT3DSURFACE8 pSurface = 0;
// Create the surface and then load the file off the disk onto the surface
LoadBitmapToSurface( "Zen.bmp", &pSurface, g_pDevice );

// Structure to hold information about the surface
D3DSURFACE_DESC d3dsd;
// Get information about the newly created surface
pSurface->GetDesc( &d3dsd );

// Destination point
POINT DestPoint = { 100, 100 };
// Source dimensions
RECT rect = { 0, 0, d3dsd.Width, d3dsd.Height };

// Copy the surface
g_pDevice->CopyRects( pSurface, &rect, 1, pBackSurf, &DestPoint );
// Release the surface
pSurface->Release();
pSurface = 0;

// Release the back surface
pBackSurf->Release();
pBackSurf = 0;

// Present the back buffer to the primary surface
g_pDevice->Present( NULL, NULL, NULL, NULL );
```

This code is located in the main `Render()` function, which is called from `GameLoop()`. Obviously it is not particularly optimized, because the file is being loaded and unloaded for every frame of the game. A better option would be to load the file at startup in the `GameInit()` function, then access it regularly during the life of the game, before removing it in the `GameShutdown()` function. Figure 8.19 shows the original image, and Figure 8.20 shows a screen shot from the program with the image shown on the primary surface.

Figure 8.19

The original file on disk

Figure 8.20

The file loaded to a new surface, copied to the back buffer, and finally presented to the primary surface

Advanced Copying

From time to time you may find that the CopyRects() function does not have the functionality that you are looking for. For instance, you may have two surfaces that have different formats between which you want to copy images. In such a situation the CopyRects() function would fail, because it only supports copying between surfaces of the same format. Well, there just happens to be a function that will copy a surface for you, and that provides advanced functionality like filtered scaling and color keying. The new lingo for this term is *loading* a surface rather than *copying*.

The Direct3D function that does this advanced stuff for us is called D3DXLoadSurfaceFromSurface(), and it looks like this:

```
HRESULT D3DXLoadSurfaceFromSurface(
    LPDIRECT3DSURFACE8 pDestSurface,        // Pointer to the destination surface
    CONST PALETTEENTRY* pDestPalette,       // Pointer to destination palette
CONST RECT* pDestRect,               // Pointer to destination rectangle
LPDIRECT3DSURFACE8 pSrcSurface,          // Pointer to source surface
    CONST PALETTEENTRY* pSrcPalette,        // Pointer to source palette
    CONST RECT* pSrcRect,                   // Pointer to source rectangle
```

```
  DWORD Filter,                          // Filter to use during scaling
  D3DCOLOR ColorKey                      // Color key value
);
```

The parameters for this function are almost identical to the
D3DXLoadSurfaceFromFile() function that you looked at before. They are listed in
Table 8.5.

Table 8.6 D3DXLoadSurfaceFromSurface() Parameters

Parameter	Definition
pDestSurface	A pointer to the destination surface
pDestPalette	Takes a pointer to the destination palette, or zero if there is no palette
pDestRect	Takes a pointer to a rectangle that defines the dimensions for the destination. If this is smaller than the image and a filter is specified, then the image will be scaled. Otherwise the image will be cropped. *NULL* indicates the entire surface is the destination.
pSrcSurface	A pointer to the source surface.
pSrcPalette	A pointer to the source palette, which again can be 0 if there is no palette. Palettes are only used for surfaces with a bit depth less than or equal to 8 bits.
pSrcRect	Takes a pointer to the rectangle to use as the source image. Anything outside these boundaries will be clipped.
Filter	The filter to use during scaling operations is defined in this parameter. This can be set to any of the values contained in Table 8.5. More on this soon.
ColorKey	Takes a D3DCOLOR value to use as the color key. Any pixels that match this color will be set to 32-bit black (0xFF000000). Specifying zero for this parameter disables color keying during the copy process.

Filtered Scaling

When you scale an image larger or smaller you distort the number of pixels that were originally used to represent the colors of the image. This can lead to *pixelization,* where the image becomes blockish when enlarged, or *speckling,* when the image is shrunk. There are some advanced mathematical formulas that can be used to combat these artifacts, and luckily for you, DirectX supports them. So before I go on to explain how to use the function, I am going to show the differing results of using the three main filters that Direct3D supports.

Point Filtering

In this case, the pixel that is chosen for the final scaled image will be the pixel that is closest to the original pixel. If the image is being enlarged, then the same color will be replicated to fill the new areas, leading to pixelization. Figure 8.21 shows the original image and Figure 8.22 shows a section of an image that was originally 300 x 300 and then scaled to 640 x 480. Figure 8.22 shows part of the image zoomed in so that the artifacts are more obvious.

Here is an example call for a point-filtered scaled load:

```
D3DXLoadSurfaceFromSurface( pBackSurf, NULL, &rect2, pSurface, NULL,
                                                        &rect,
D3DX_FILTER_POINT, 0 );
```

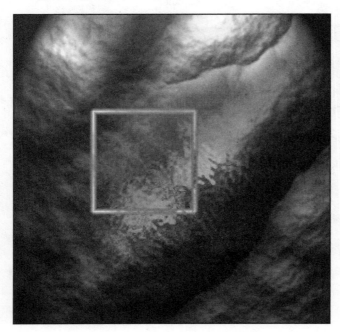

Figure 8.21

The original image with the zoomed section highlighted

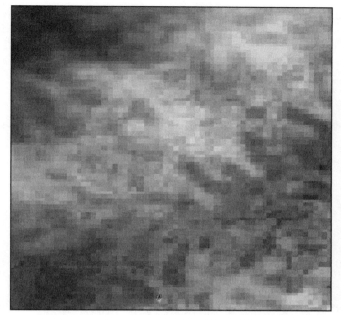

Figure 8.22

Scaling using point filtering

Linear Filtering

This method produces a much better quality of image, although it is slower than point filtering. The final pixel is computed by averaging the four nearest pixels in the source image. Figure 8.23 shows the results.

Here is an example call for a linear-filtered scaled load:

```
D3DXLoadSurfaceFromSurface(
pBackSurf, NULL, &rect2,
pSurface, NULL,
&rect, D3DX_FILTER_LINEAR, 0 );
```

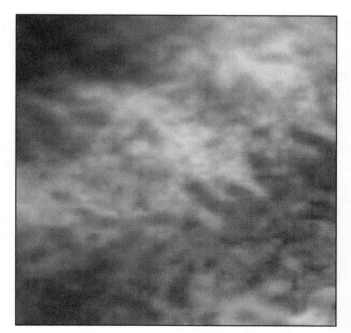

Figure 8.23

Scaling using linear filtering

Triangular Filtering

This filter offers the best quality results, although it is also the slowest. The final pixel is found by using the values of a much larger array of the original pixel and its surrounding pixels. Figure 8.24 shows the effect of this filter, although in printed form it may be hard to tell the difference between triangular and linear mode. This method of filtering is sometimes referred to as *bicubic* filtering.

Here is an example call for a triangular-filtered scaled load:

```
D3DXLoadSurfaceFromSurface( pBackSurf, NULL, &rect2, pSurface, NULL,
&rect, D3DX_FILTER_TRIANGLE, 0 );
```

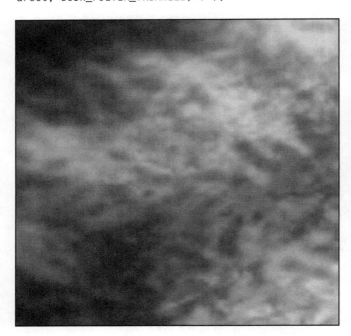

Figure 8.24

Scaling using triangular filtering

Using the GDI with Direct3D Surfaces

Until version 8 came along, it was very easy to use the GDI with surfaces. In fact, there was a function included in the `IDirectDrawSurface7` interface called `GetDC()`, which allowed you to use a surface as if it were a device context. This was incredibly useful for development, because you could use the GDI to draw things like lines and circles for you until you developed your own code later in the development cycle. Well, times have changed, and with unification all interoperability between surfaces and the GDI were removed. However, when you know Windows like the back of your hand—and with a bit of luck, a browse through MSDN, and some hacking—it is in fact possible to get them to work together manually.

This did involve me tearing hairs out of my head, but I have put together three functions that allow you to copy a GDI device context to a Direct3D surface, with cropping and source color key support, that actually works. I say that because color key support has also been pretty much removed from DirectX graphics as well.

Anyway, here is how the process works. You create a new DC that is compatible with the current display mode. Then you create what is called a *device-independent bitmap,* or DIB. This is just your average run-of-the-mill bitmap that you can draw to by selecting it into the new device context. When you create the DIB you give it properties like width, height, and a bit depth of 32. When you are finished drawing to the DC, you copy it using the function I created, which I will discuss shortly. And finally, when you are finished you delete the DIB and the DC. Sounds easy, huh? Wait until you see the monstrously ugly code. It may burn your eyes. This stuff is pretty complex so don't feel like you have to memorize it; just use the functions whenever you want to use the GDI with Direct3D.

Creating a Direct3D-Compatible Device Context

I called this function CreateD3DCompatibleDC because that is what it does! I'll show you the code and then explain it:

```
HDC CreateD3DCompatibleDC( int Width, int Height, HBITMAP* phDibSection )
{
        // Create a new DC that is compatible with the current display mode
        HDC hDC = CreateCompatibleDC(0);
        // Temp pointer to the DIB data
        void* pDibSection = 0;

        // Structure to hold information about the bitmap
        BITMAPINFO bi;
        ZeroMemory( &bi, sizeof( BITMAPINFO ) );
        // The size of this structure in bytes
        bi.bmiHeader.biSize = sizeof( BITMAPINFOHEADER );
        // The width of the new bitmap
        bi.bmiHeader.biWidth = Width;
        // The height of the new bitmap( negative for a top down image )
        bi.bmiHeader.biHeight = -Height;
        // Obsolete - just set to one
        bi.bmiHeader.biPlanes = 1;
        // The bit depth of the surface
        bi.bmiHeader.biBitCount = 32;
        // The compression format.  BI_RGB indicates none
        bi.bmiHeader.biCompression = BI_RGB;

        // Create a new DIB
        HBITMAP hDibSection = CreateDIBSection( hDC, &bi,
                    DIB_RGB_COLORS, &pDibSection, NULL, NULL );
```

```
// Select the bitmap into the new DC
        SelectObject( hDC, hDibSection );

        // Update the pointer to the handle to the bitmap
        *phDibSection = hDibSection;
        // Return the handle to the device context
        return hDC;
}
```

Looking at that reminds me of being in the kitchen when someone is peeling onions. And it's going to get worse in just a second. The function's first two parameters take values that define the dimensions for the new surface. The third parameter is a little bit more interesting. It takes a pointer to a handle to an HBITMAP. That's the thing with Direct3D-compatible DCs. You need to keep track of the DIB as well as the DC, and that is exactly what this pointer is for. It is filled with the handle to the newly created bitmap. The return value is a handle to the new compatible DC.

So what is going on in the function then? Well, I start out by creating a normal compatible DC with the standard GDI CreateCompatibleDC() function. I specify 0 as the DC handle because this indicates that I want it to be compatible with the current display mode, which in this case is going to be 32 bits deep. Then I create a BITMAPINFO structure, which contains an area for palette information, which I am not using, and another structure called BITMAPINFOHEADER. This second structure is where the business happens. It contains all sorts of entries, but the five that I filled in are the only ones you need to worry about. Don't forget to initialize the structure to 0 like I did, because if you are only filling in some of the entries you don't want the others to contain garbage values.

Then I use that information to create a new DIB using the GDI function CreateDIBSection(). It looks a little like this puppy:

```
HBITMAP CreateDIBSection(  HDC hdc, CONST BITMAPINFO *pbmi,
                UINT iUsage, VOID *ppvBits, HANDLE hSection, DWORD dwOffset );
```

Table 8.7. gives the parameters.

Table 8.7   CreateDIBSection() Parameters

hdc	A handle to a device context that will create the DIB
pbmi	A pointer to a BITMAPINFO structure that contains information about how you want to create the new DIB
iUsage	Takes a value that specifies whether you want RGB or a palettized bitmap. DIB_RGB_COLORS indicates RGB.
ppvBits	Takes a pointer that will be filled with the address of the start of the bitmap data
hSection	A handle to a file if you are using one. This is an advanced feature, so you can just set it to NULL.
dwOffset	Also for file mapping, and you can set it to NULL

After creating the DIB, I selected it into the DC so that any GDI drawing functions are written to the DIB. Then I update the formal parameter pointer to the handle to the DIB section. By the way, *Dib section* just means a part of memory that is currently being used to hold a bitmap. It is just more Windows lingo.

Now before I show you how to actually copy a DC to a surface, let's take a short look at how to remove these Direct3D-compatible DCs from memory.

Deleting the Compatible DC from Memory

It is very important to remember that, when you create a DC using the CreateD3DCompatibleDC() function, you are also creating a bitmap, which uses quite a lot of memory. So when you delete the DC you also have to delete the bitmap. I have created a function called DeleteD3DCompatibleDC() for this very purpose, and here it is:

```
void DeleteD3DCompatibleDC( HDC hDC, HBITMAP hDibSection )
{
        // Delete the bitmap
        DeleteObject( hDibSection );
        // Delete the DC
DeleteDC( hDC );
}
```

Copying a DC to a Direct3D Surface

Be careful—the wrath of the evil ones is close. The following code is nasty on a scale I don't want to think about. Again, I'll show you the code and then run through what is going on.

```
HRESULT CopyDCToSurface( LPDIRECT3DSURFACE8 pDestSurf, POINT* pDestPoint,

            HDC hDCSource, HBITMAP hDibSection, RECT* pSrcRect, COLORREF ColorKey
)
{
        HRESULT r = 0;
        // The source rectangle
        RECT SourceRect;
        // The destination origin point
        POINT DestPoint;

        // Holds information about the bitmap
        DIBSECTION DibSection;

        // Holds information about the surface when locked
        D3DLOCKED_RECT LockedRect;
        // Get information about the bitmap in the DC
        GetObject( hDibSection, sizeof( DIBSECTION ), &DibSection );
        int SrcTotalWidth = DibSection.dsBm.bmWidth;
        int SrcTotalHeight = DibSection.dsBm.bmHeight;

        // If no source rectangle was specified then this indicates
        // that the entire bitmap in the DC is to be copied
        if( !pSrcRect )
                SetRect( &SourceRect, 0, 0, SrcTotalWidth, SrcTotalHeight);
        else
                SourceRect = *(pSrcRect);
        // If no destination point was specified then the origin // is set to (0,0)
if( !pDestPoint )
                DestPoint.x = DestPoint.y = 0;
        else
```

```
DestPoint = *(pDestPoint);
        // Return failure if a valid destination surface was not specified
        if( !pDestSurf )
                return E_FAIL;
        // Return failure if a valid source DC was not specified
        if( !hDCSource )
                return E_FAIL;
        // Lock the source surface
        r = pDestSurf->LockRect( &LockedRect, 0, 0 );
        if( FAILED( r ) )
        {
SetError( "Unable to lock the surface for GDI transfer" );
                return E_FAIL;
        }


        // Convert the source and destination data pointers
        // to DWORD( 32 bit) values
        DWORD* pSrcData = (DWORD*)(DibSection.dsBm.bmBits);
        DWORD* pDestData = (DWORD*)(LockedRect.pBits);
        // Convert the pitch to a 32-bit value
        int Pitch32 = LockedRect.Pitch/4;


        // Compute the dimensions for the copy
        int SrcHeight = SourceRect.bottom - SourceRect.top;
        int SrcWidth = SourceRect.right - SourceRect.left;
        // Compute the index into memory
        DWORD SrcOffset = SourceRect.top * SrcTotalWidth + SourceRect.left;
        DWORD DestOffset = DestPoint.y * Pitch32 + DestPoint.x;
        // If not using a color key then a faster copy can be done
        if( ColorKey == -1 )
        {
                // Loop for each row in the image
                for( int y = 0 ; y < SrcHeight ; y++ )
                {
                        // Copy this line of the image
                        memcpy(       (void*)&(pDestData[ DestOffset ]),
                                              (void*)&(pSrcData  [ SrcOffset   ]),
                                       SrcWidth*4);
                        // Increase the destination pointer by the pitch
                        DestOffset+=Pitch32;
                        // Increase the source pointer by the total width
```

```
                    SrcOffset +=SrcTotalWidth;
            }
        }
        else    // a color key was specified
        {
            // Loop for each row in the image
            for( int y = 0 ; y < SrcHeight ; y++ )
            {
                // Loop for each column
                for( int x = 0 ; x < SrcWidth ; x++ )
                {
// If the source pixel is not the same as the color key
                    if( pSrcData[ SrcOffset ] != ColorKey )
                            // Then copy the pixel to the destination
                            pDestData[ DestOffset ] = pSrcData[ SrcOffset
];
                    // Move to the next pixel in the source
                    SrcOffset++;
                    // Move to the next pixel in the destination
                    DestOffset++;
                }
            }
        }

        // Unlock the surface
        pDestSurf->UnlockRect();

        // Return success
        return S_OK;
}
```

As I said, that is a very nasty function, so let's see what is going on so that you don't get left behind. Most of it is pretty simple; it just looks hard.

First off, how about those formal parameters? I designed this function to be fairly similar to the Direct3D functions.

- **pDestSurf.** A pointer to the destination surface, which must be valid.
- **pDestPoint.** Takes the address of a structure that contains the point at which you want to begin drawing on the destination surface. For instance, if you specified (30, 30), then the origin of the copy would start at that point. Alternatively, if you specify NULL for this parameter, rather than giving the

address of a POINT structure, then it is assumed that drawing will start at (0, 0). hDCSource takes a handle to the source DC. This also must be valid and have been created with the CreateD3DCompatibleDC() function.

- **hDibSection**. Takes a handle to the bitmap that was created with the device context.

- **pSrcRect**. Takes the address of a RECT structure that contains the portion of the source DC that you want to copy. Areas outside of the bounds will be cropped. If you specify NULL, then the entire DC is copied.

- **ColorKey**. Allows you to specify a color key value. Note that it is in the GDI COLORREF format rather than the Direct3D D3DCOLOR format. You can set the color using the RGB() macro. If you don't want to use color keying, then just specify –1. Any colors in the source image that match the color key will not be copied, allowing you to take advantage of transparency. I'll show you some examples of this when I show you what you can achieve with the code.

Now let's look at an overview of the code. It is pretty long so I won't spend too much time on the details. The first thing I did was to use the GetObject() function to get information about the bitmap within the DC. Then I checked that all the values passed to the function are valid. If either an invalid source DC or destination surface is specified, then the function returns failure because this is a fatal error. If no source rectangle is specified, then it is assumed the request is for the entire source DC to be copied, so the rectangle structure is updated to reflect this. It is a similar case for the destination point; if none is specified, then it is assumed to be (0, 0). After all that checking is done, I locked the destination surface so that it is possible to get at the data. Then I got a pointer to the source DC memory, which is contained in the BITMAPINFOHEADER structure within the BITMAP structure.

The actual copying is an interesting process. The first step is to figure out exactly where to start copying from and to. The source DC offset is figured out using the usual format of multiplying the width by the y-coordinate, and then adding x. The destination point is also computed this way. Then the code branches because there are two ways to copy; if no color key is specified, then the copying can be done faster. The program loops for each vertical line of the image and copies it a line at a time using the memcpy() function. After each line is copied the destination pointer is incremented by the pitch of the surface, and the source pointer is incremented by the total width of the DC. The effect is that both pointers wrap around to the right place on the next line.

On the other hand, if a color key is specified, then each pixel has to be compared one by one, which is considerably slower. In this case, the program loops for each row of the image and then loops again for each column, effectively looping through each pixel in the image. Each pixel is tested against the color key; if it matches then it is skipped, otherwise it is just copied as normal.

Now I want you to see the kind of functionality that I have been talking about in the previous pages. Following is a small example program that shows the different ways to load and display images. Half of the display code is for displaying an image using the GDI, and the other half uses Direct3D to do the same thing. You can alternate between which system you want to use by pressing the Spacebar.

Here is the code, with the relevant parts bolded:

```
//
/////////////////////////////////////////////
// Direct3D vs GDI sample
// Author: Peter Walsh
// 9th Dec 2000
//


#define WIN32_LEAN_AND_MEAN
// The main windows include file
#include <windows.h>
#include <mmsystem.h>

#include <d3d8.h>
#include <d3dx8.h>

#include "Engine.h"
int GameInit();
int GameLoop();
int GameShutdown();
int Render();

#define RENDER_GDI 2   // Render with the GDI
#define RENDER_D3D 1   // Render with Direct3D
#define RENDER_BOTH 0  // Render with both

int g_RenderMode = 0;
LPDIRECT3D8 g_pD3D = 0;
LPDIRECT3DDEVICE8 g_pDevice = 0;
```

```cpp
LPDIRECT3DSURFACE8 g_pBackSurface = 0;
LPDIRECT3DSURFACE8 g_pD3DBitmapSurf = 0;
HBITMAP g_hGDIBitmap = 0;
HDC g_hGDIBitmapDC = 0;
HWND g_hWndMain;
// The window procedure to handle events
long CALLBACK WndProc( HWND hWnd, UINT uMessage,
                                 WPARAM wParam, LPARAM lParam )
{
      // Switch the windows message to figure out what it is
      switch( uMessage )
      {
            .
            . // Generic WndProc() code
            .
      case WM_KEYDOWN:
            {
                  switch( wParam )
                  {
                        case VK_SPACE:
                        {
                              g_RenderMode++;
                              if( g_RenderMode > 2 )
                                    g_RenderMode = 0;
                              break;
                        }

                        default:
                              break;
                  }

                  return 0;
            }

            .
            . // More generic WndProc() code
            .

      }
}
```

```c
// The windows entry point. The application will start executing here
int WINAPI WinMain( HINSTANCE hInstance, HINSTANCE hPrevInstance,
                                    PSTR pstrCmdLine, int iCmdShow )
{
        .
        .         // Generic WinMain() code
        .
        if( FAILED( GameInit() ) )
        {
                SetError( "Initialization Failed" );
                GameShutdown();
                return E_FAIL;
        }

        // Start the message loop
        while( TRUE )
{
                // Check if a message is waiting for processing
                if( PeekMessage( &msg, NULL, 0, 0, PM_REMOVE ) )
                {
                        // Check if the message is to quit the application
                        if( msg.message == WM_QUIT )
                                // Exit the message loop
                                break;

                        // Change the format of certain messages
                        TranslateMessage( &msg );
                        // Pass the message to WndProc() for processing
                        DispatchMessage( &msg );
                }
                else
                {
                        GameLoop();
                }
        }

        GameShutdown();

        // Return control to windows with the exit code
        return msg.wParam;
}
```

```
int GameInit()
{

        HRESULT r = 0;
        // Acquire a pointer to IDirect3D8
        g_pD3D = Direct3DCreate8( D3D_SDK_VERSION );
        if( g_pD3D == NULL )
        {
                SetError( "Could not create IDirect3D8 object" );
                return E_FAIL;
        }

        // Create the device
        r = InitDirect3DDevice( g_hWndMain, 640, 480, FALSE,
                                        D3DFMT_X8R8G8B8, g_pD3D, &g_pDevice );
if( FAILED( r ) )
        {
                SetError( "Initialization of the device failed" );
                return E_FAIL;
        }

        // Clear the back buffer
        g_pDevice->Clear( 0, 0, D3DCLEAR_TARGET, D3DCOLOR_XRGB( 0,0,0 ), 1.0f, 0 );
// ---------- GDI Code
        // Create a Direct3D-compatible DC to hold the GDI
    // bitmap
        g_hGDIBitmapDC - CreateD3DCompatibleDC( 128, 128, &g_hGDIBitmap );
        // Create a temporary DC to hold the bitmap as it is loaded off disk
        HDC hTempDC - CreateCompatibleDC(0);
        // Load the image from the disk
        HBITMAP hTempBitmap - (HBITMAP)LoadImage( 0, "ZenGDI.bmp",
                                                        IMAGE_BITMAP, 0, 0,
LR_LOADFROMFILE );
        // Select the image into the temp DC
        SelectObject( hTempDC, hTempBitmap );
        // Copy the image to the Direct3D-compatible DC
        BitBlt( g_hGDIBitmapDC, 0, 0, 128, 128, hTempDC, 0, 0, SRCCOPY );
        // Delete the temporary bitmap
        DeleteObject( hTempBitmap );
        // Delete the temporary device context
```

```
            DeleteDC( hTempDC );
// ------------- Direct3D code
        // Get a pointer to the back buffer and save it in a global variable
        r = g_pDevice->GetBackBuffer( 0,
                                D3DBACKBUFFER_TYPE_MONO, &g_pBackSurface );
        if( FAILED( r ) )
        {
                SetError( "Couldnt get backbuffer" );
                return E_FAIL;
        }

        // Create a surface to hold the Direct3D bitmap
        g_pDevice->CreateImageSurface( 128, 128, D3DFMT_X8R8G8B8,

&g_pD3DBitmapSurf );
        // Load the image from disk into the surface
        D3DXLoadSurfaceFromFile( g_pD3DBitmapSurf, NULL,
                        NULL, "ZenD3D.bmp", NULL, D3DX_FILTER_NONE, 0, NULL );

        srand( GetTickCount() );
        return S_OK;
}

int GameLoop()
{
        Render();
        if( GetAsyncKeyState( VK_ESCAPE ) )
                PostQuitMessage(0);
        return S_OK;
}

int GameShutdown()
{
        // Delete the DC and bitmap for the GDI image
        DeleteD3DCompatibleDC( g_hGDIBitmapDC, g_hGDIBitmap );
        // Release the pointer to the back surface
        if( g_pBackSurface )
                g_pBackSurface->Release();
        // Release the surface holding the D3D image
        if( g_pD3DBitmapSurf )
                g_pD3DBitmapSurf->Release();
```

```c
        // Release the pointer to IDirect3DDevice8
        if( g_pDevice )
                g_pDevice->Release();
        // Release the pointer to IDirect3D8
        if( g_pD3D )
                g_pD3D->Release();
        return S_OK;
}


int Render()
{
        // Make sure the device is valid
        if( !g_pDevice )
        {
                SetError( "Cannot render because there is no device" );
                return E_FAIL;}


        // Source size of the D3D image
        RECT D3DSrcRect = { 0, 0, 128, 128 };
        // Destination point for the D3D image
        POINT D3DDestPoint = { rand() % (g_DeviceWidth - 128),
                                        rand() % (g_DeviceHeight - 128) };
        // Destination point for the GDI image
        POINT GDIDestPoint = { rand() % (g_DeviceWidth - 128),
                                        rand() % (g_DeviceHeight - 128) };
        // Copy the GDI device context if that render mode is active
        if( g_RenderMode == RENDER_GDI || g_RenderMode == RENDER_BOTH )
                CopyDCToSurface( g_pBackSurface,
                                &GDIDestPoint, g_hGDIBitmapDC, g_hGDIBitmap, 0, -1 );
        // Copy the D3D surface if that render mode is active
        if( g_RenderMode == RENDER_D3D || g_RenderMode == RENDER_BOTH )
                g_pDevice->CopyRects( g_pD3DBitmapSurf,
                                &SrcRect, 1, g_pBackSurface, &D3DDestPoint );
        // Present the back buffer to the primary surface
        g_pDevice->Present( NULL, NULL, NULL, NULL );
        return S_OK;
}
```

And that's how you do that! The results of this code are shown in Figure 8.25. The image with D3D written across it is being drawn using Direct3D and the GDI image is using the GDI for its display

Figure 8.25

Using the GDI and Direct3D to render 2D images at the same time

And now for a demonstration of the other really cool feature of the GDI copying code: color keying. If I change the GDI source image to look like that in Figure 8.26...

Figure 8.26

Source image modified with black stripes.

...and then modify the code that draws the image using the GDI to look like this:

```
CopyDCToSurface( g_pBackSurface, &GDIDestPoint,
                        g_hGDIBitmapDC, g_hGDIBitmap, 0, RGB( 0, 0, 0 ) );
```

then the results will look like those in Figure 8.27.

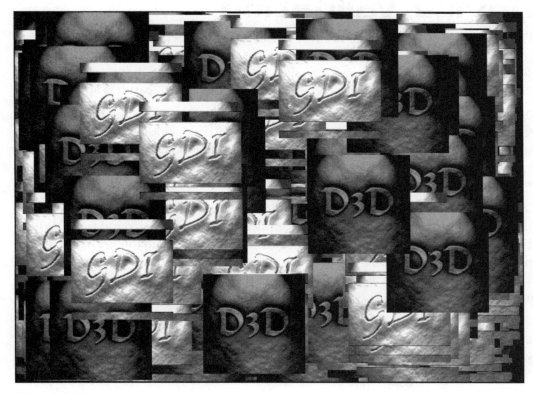

Figure 8.27

Using the GDI with Direct3D to render to surfaces

See? The bits that were black are now transparent! This is a feature that can be very useful for 2D graphics, particularly in 3D situations like when you want to render a dashboard or something similar over the top of a 3D image.

Device Validation

There comes a time in the life of every device when things just go postal. The user is being a pain, the CPU is busy, and the graphics card just won't cooperate. These devices sometimes lose their ability to stay sane. They become what is known technically as *lost*. Well, maybe it's not a very technical name, but at least it is applicable.

Devices can become lost for a number of reasons; however, I love the Microsoft explanation and I have just got to show it to you. The documentation says, "By design, the full set of scenarios that can cause a device to become lost is not specified." What? So it is by design that they are not quite sure what can put their own code into a certain mode? How Microsoft is that?

Let's get back to business. Generally, a device can be lost because the user presses Alt+Tab or some other event causes the application to lose foreground focus. When this happens the Direct3D device loses control of the display adapter. That is, any images such as textures that were stored on the graphics card can be considered lost and overwritten. You can also pretty much assume that the resolution has changed and any other display settings have been reset.

So what does all this mean to you? Well, it pretty much boils down to this: You don't have control and you just have to sit there and wait around until it is given back to you. When a device is lost, the functions that you call may go into what is called *silent failure* mode. This means that the functions fail, but they still return success.

So how do you get the device back in control? At the start of every frame:

1. Test the *cooperative level* of the device. It will be in either "Not Available" mode or "Now Available Again" mode.

2. If the device is not available, then you just sit there and wait. On the other hand, if the device is available again, then you have to move to step 3.

3. Now you need to release any surfaces that Direct3D is managing for you. In this case it is only managing the back buffer, so you need to make sure that you call `IDirect3DSurface8::Release()` on that puppy or you may cause a memory leak.

4. With all that stuff done, you can call `IDirect3DDevice8::Reset()` on the device using a saved copy of the presentation parameters that was saved in the `InitDirect3DDevice()` function.

5. Now that the device is reset, you can reacquire a pointer to the new back buffer. Don't forget that it will be filled with garbage, so it is a good idea to clear it again using the `IDirect3DDevice8::Clear()` function (see Figure 8.28).

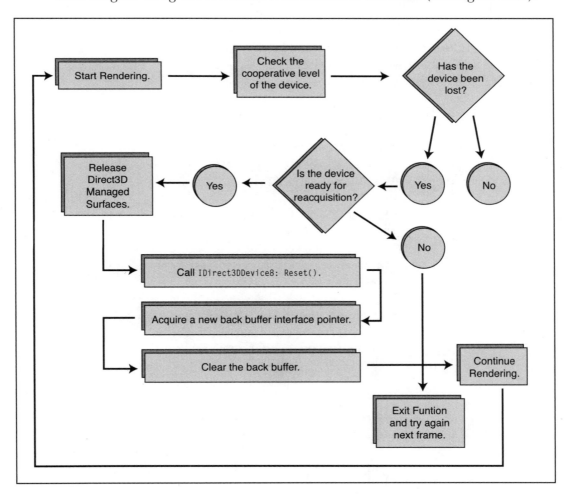

Figure 8.28

The device validation process

That sounds all right doesn't it? So what does the code look like? Well, the first change is to put a call in to ValidateDevice() at the top of the Render() function. ValidateDevice() is a function that will make sure the device is okay for rendering before the Render() procedure continues. The code for ValidateDevice() looks like this:

```
HRESULT ValidateDevice()
{
        HRESULT r = 0;
        // Test the current state of the device
        r = g_pDevice->TestCooperativeLevel();
        if( FAILED( r ) )
        {
                // If the device is lost then return failure
                if( r == D3DERR_DEVICELOST )
                        return E_FAIL;
                // If the device is ready to be reset then attempt to do so
                if( r == D3DERR_DEVICENOTRESET )
                {
                        // Release the back surface so it can be re-created
                        g_pBackSurface->Release();
                        // Reset the device
                        r = g_pDevice->Reset( &g_SavedPresParams );
                        if( FAILED( r ) )
                        {
                                // If the device was not reset then exit
                                SetError( "Could not reset device" );
                                PostQuitMessage( E_FAIL );
                                return E_FAIL;
                        }

                        // Reacquire a pointer to the new back buffer
                        r = g_pDevice->GetBackBuffer( 0,
                                        D3DBACKBUFFER_TYPE_MONO, &g_pBackSurface );
                        if( FAILED( r )
                        {
                                SetError( "Unable to reacquire the back buffer" ):
                                PostQuitMessage( 0 );
                                return E_FAIL;
                        }
```

```
        g_pDevice->Clear( 0, NULL, D3DCLEAR_TARGET,
                                        D3DCOLOR_XRGB( 0, 0, 0 ), 0.0f, 0 );
                        RestoreGraphics();
                }
        }

        return S_OK;
}


HRESULT RestoreGraphics()
{
        return S_OK;
}
```

The call is made in Render() like this:

```
int Render()
{
        HRESULT r = 0;
        // Make sure the device is valid
        if( !g_pDevice )
        {
                SetError( "Cannot render because there is no device" );
                return E_FAIL;
        }

        // Return if the device is not ready;
        r = ValidateDevice();
        if( FAILED( r ) )
        {
                return E_FAIL;
        }


        .
        .       // Other Render() code
        .


}
```

There are some new functions in there that you have not seen before. `IDirect3DDevice8::TestCooperativeLevel()` is a remnant of functionality in previous versions of DirectDraw, so its name doesn't quite match its purpose of figuring out if a device is lost. This function will only return `D3D_OK` if the device is in a normal state, `D3DERR_DEVICELOST` if the device is unavailable, or `D3DERR_DEVICENOTRESET` if the device is ready for reacquisition.

The `IDirect3DDevice8::Reset()` function takes a single parameter, a pointer to a `D3DPRESENT_PARAMETERS` structure, which contains information about how you want the device to be re-created. I used the copy of the structure that I saved in the `InitDirect3DDevice()` function that I discussed earlier.

I almost forgot. See that extra call to the empty function `RestoreGraphics()`? If you have Direct3D managing more than just the back buffer for you, then this is where you could add code to restore those objects. But other than that, the function should look familiar. So just take a step back to look at the bigger picture for a second.

- `Render()` is called every frame by `GameLoop()`.
- The device is validated by `ValidateDevice()` every frame inside `Render()`.
- If the device is lost, then `Render()` exits.
- If the device is available again, then it is recaptured and rendering continues.

So now you can go ahead and take her out for a spin. Go on, load up the example off the CD and look at those lovely bitmaps. Now press Alt+Tab, which would have previously killed the application. And now go back to the application. How cool is that? It automatically resets itself. Man, I love great code!

Conclusion

Wow, I bet this chapter was a bit of an eye opener into the murky world of Direct3D for you. You covered an awful lot of new territory. In fact, I want to keep going, but before I'd know it this introduction chapter would get far too advanced. So I'll leave that for the next chapter.

Now would be a good time to flip back over the pages in this chapter and reread through the functions that I showed you that make it easier to work with Direct3D. In the next chapter you will be bringing all this foundation knowledge together to start creating a 2D engine with an, a Direct3D font engine, and a *Quake*-style console! How cool does that sound?

CHAPTER 9

PUTTING DIRECT3D TO WORK

I had a near-death experience the other day. I was flying back to Scotland after a Christmas break in Ireland, and the plane had a bit of an accident on landing. A gust of wind blew it sideways just before touchdown, causing it to land on one wheel at a 35-degree angle, causing the wing to just miss smashing into the ground and turning the plane into a giant fireball. It made me look at life in a completely different way. And I realize something now: I am truly invincible!

Anyway, in this chapter you're going to extend your Zen skills into new realms. In previous chapters you have looked at an awful lot of theory, and a good bit of code too. Now that you understand the foundation code, you can start to move up to the next level and create code that is much more impressive. This chapter will cover

- how to copy Direct3D surfaces using cool color-keyed transparency.
- how to develop your own bitmap-based font engine.
- the development of an advanced class-based sprite engine.
- advanced animation effects using dynamic layers.

Sound interesting? I thought it might. Right, let's get down to business.

Color-Keyed Surface Copying

I've come to the conclusion that there are a lot of quirks in this new unified Direct3D thingy. A lot of functionality that I used to take for granted has been removed. One of the most annoying is color-keyed transparent copying of surfaces.

> **NOTE**
>
> I talked about color keying in the preceding chapter. You specify a color that you want to be treated as transparent, such as purple. Then when you go to copy the surface, any pixels that match the color key are not copied, which results in an image with transparent sections.

In version 8 the transparency code seems a little bit screwy. If you specify a color key these days, the pixels that match the color key are simply set to black, which isn't very useful unless you happen to have a plain black background. I've messed around with it a lot and come to the conclusion that it is more productive to just write your own surface copying routine that performs color keying manually. Of course, the downside to this is that you lose out on hardware acceleration, but it's not that much slower.

So what's involved in this operation? Well, let's see. . . . To copy between surfaces on a per pixel basis means that both surfaces will have to be locked. It would also be nice if you could specify a rectangle in the source image that you could copy, rather than the entire source surface. And of course you need to specify a point on the destination surface where you want to copy the image. And the function will need a color key. Then all that's required is to loop through each pixel in the source and see if it matches the color key. As long as it does not match it is safe to copy to the destination. Let's look at the code:

```
HRESULT CopySurfaceToSurface( RECT* pSourceRect,
    LPDIRECT3DSURFACE8 pSourceSurf, POINT* pDestPoint,
    LPDIRECT3DSURFACE8 pDestSurf, BOOL bTransparent, D3DCOLOR ColorKey )
{
    // Holds error return values
    HRESULT r = 0;

    // Holds information about the surfaces when they are locked
    D3DLOCKED_RECT LockedSource;
    D3DLOCKED_RECT LockedDest;

    // Make sure the source surface is valid
    if( !pSourceSurf )
            return E_FAIL;

    // Make sure the destination surface is valid
    if( !pDestSurf )
            return E_FAIL;

    // The source rectangle
    RECT SourceRect;
    // The destination point
    POINT DestPoint;

    // Holds information about the source surface
    D3DSURFACE_DESC d3dsdSource;
    // Get information about the source surface
    pSourceSurf->GetDesc( &d3dsdSource );

    // Holds information about the destination surface
    D3DSURFACE_DESC d3dsdDest;
    // Get information about the destination surface
```

```
pDestSurf->GetDesc( &d3dsdDest );

        // If a source rectangle was specified then copy it
        // into the local RECT structure
        if( pSourceRect )
                SourceRect = *pSourceRect;
        else
                // Otherwise set the rectangle to encompass the
                // entire source surface
                SetRect( &SourceRect, 0, 0,
                        d3dsdSource.Width, d3dsdSource.Height );

        // If a destination point was specified then copy it
        // to the local POINT structure
        if( pDestPoint )
                DestPoint = *pDestPoint;
        else
        {
                // Otherwise set the point to (0,0)
                DestPoint.x = DestPoint.y = 0;
        }

        // Lock the source surface
        r = pSourceSurf->LockRect( &LockedSource, 0, D3DLOCK_READONLY  );
        if( FAILED( r ) )
                // Fatal Error
                return E_FAIL;

        // Lock the destination surface
        r = pDestSurf->LockRect( &LockedDest, 0, 0 );
        if( FAILED( r ) )
        {
                // Fatal error, so unlock the source
                // surface before exiting
                pSourceSurf->UnlockRect();
                return E_FAIL;
        }

        // Modify the pitch to be DWORD compatible
        LockedSource.Pitch /= 4;
        LockedDest.Pitch /= 4;
```

```cpp
// Get 32-bit pointers to the surface data
DWORD* pSourceData = (DWORD*)LockedSource.pBits;
DWORD* pDestData = (DWORD*)LockedDest.pBits;

// Get the offset into the source surface
int SourceOffset =
        SourceRect.top * LockedSource.Pitch + SourceRect.left;
// Get the offset into the destination surface
int DestOffset = DestPoint.y * LockedDest.Pitch + DestPoint.x;

// Loop for each row of the source image
for( int y = 0 ; y < SourceRect.bottom ; y++ )
{
        // Loop for each column of the source image
        for( int x = 0 ; x < SourceRect.right ; x++ )
        {
                // If transparency was requested
                if( bTransparent )
                {
                        // Then check to see if the current source pixel
                        // matches the color key.  If it does then do
                        // not copy it.
                        if( pSourceData[ SourceOffset ] != ColorKey )
                        {
                                // The current pixel does not match the color
                                // key so it is ok to copy it to
                                // the destination
                                pDestData[ DestOffset ] =
                                        pSourceData[ SourceOffset ];

                        }
                }
                else // Transparency was not requested
                {
                        // Copy the source pixel to the destination
                        // without any comparison
                        pDestData[ DestOffset ] =
                                pSourceData[ SourceOffset ];

                }

                // Increment to the next pixel in the destination
```

```
DestOffset++;
                                // Increment to the next pixel in the source
                                SourceOffset++;
                }

                // Move the source offset to the next row of the image
                // by adding the pitch minus the width of the source image
                SourceOffset += LockedSource.Pitch - SourceRect.right;
                // Move the destination offset to the next row of the image
                DestOffset += LockedDest.Pitch - SourceRect.right;
        }

        // Copying is complete so unlock the surfaces
        pSourceSurf->UnlockRect();
        pDestSurf->UnlockRect();

        // Return success
        return S_OK;
}
```

The function takes six parameters. The first takes the address of the RECT structure that contains the area within the source image that you want to copy. If you specify NULL for this, then the entire source image is used. This "specify one if you want" idea is common to DirectX and Windows functions, so when I write my own I try to make them operate in a similar way. The second parameter takes the address of the source surface. The third parameter takes the address of a POINT structure that contains the coordinates for where you want the image to be copied to on the destination surface. Again, you can specify a point if you want; if you do not, then copying will start at (0, 0). The fourth parameter takes the address of the destination surface. The fifth parameter is a flag that specifies whether you want to do transparent copying. If you do, then you must include a color key in the sixth parameter.

When calling this function you have to specify the color key using the D3DCOLOR_ARGB() macro. Notice this is not the D3DCOLOR_XRGB() macro that you used before. The D3DCOLOR_XRGB() macro fills the alpha channel of the 32-bit color value with 0xFF(255), which is not what will be in your images normally. What you need to do instead is use the D3DCOLOR_ARGB() macro, which looks like this:

```
D3DCOLOR D3DCOLOR_ARGB( Alpha, Red, Green, Blue )
```

If you were using bright pink for your transparent color, then you would call it like this:

```
D3DCOLOR_ARGB( 0, 255, 0, 255 );
```

Back to the function. The function starts by verifying that the supplied information is correct. Then informa-

tion is collected about the source and destination surfaces. This is so that I am able to verify that the source image does not go outside the bounds of the destination image. Since I am locking the surface and doing pointer arithmetic, I do not want to go outside the bounds of the locked surface, otherwise a nasty overwrite error will occur. After that I check if a source rectangle or a destination point was supplied. If they were, then they are used, otherwise the defaults (entire source image and a destination point of (0,0)) are used. Then I lock the surfaces so that I can read and write to them. You may have noticed that I specified the D3DLOCK_READONLY flag for the lock of the source surface. In some situations this can lead to a slight improvement in performance. Obviously, you would only use this flag if you were not going to write to the surface, as is the case with the source image.

Next up I modify the pointer to be 32 bits, and also divide the pitch by 4, since it is a BYTE value and it needs to be a DWORD. Then I computed the offset into the source and destination images using the usual (y * pitch/4 + x) formula. Then it is a case of looping through each pixel and comparing it to the color key, and then copying it if it does not match. When the copying is complete, unlock both surfaces.

So if I loaded an image in GameInit() and then copied it to the back buffer every frame in GameLoop() using this code...

```
CopySurfaceToSurface( 0, pTransSurf, 0, g_pBackSurface,
                      TRUE, D3DCOLOR_ARGB( 0, 255, 0, 255 ) );
```

...and the source image looked like Figure 9.1, then the output to the screen would look like Figure 9.2.

Figure 9.1

The source image with transparent areas

Figure 9.2

The source image copied onto another surface using transparency

Keeping Track of Time

One other thing that is about to become very important is *synchronization,* so you should look at some foundation functions that look after time before you get to more advanced code. If you have ever done any programming for DOS, you may have written some synchronization functions yourself at some stage. If you haven't, then you may be happy to learn that there are 10 million ways to do it, but the way I'm going to show you is going to kick the pants off any other code you may have seen in the past.

Timing Back in the Old Days

OK, let's look at the foundations of timekeeping first. Inside your computer there is a chip that produces a signal every so often that keeps track of time. In fact, there are three timers, but two are for other purposes like memory refreshing, speaker tone generation, and other interesting topics like that and you can't use them. The one timer that you *can* use isn't very good for a lot of purposes, because it isn't very accurate. That isn't to say that it is like a cheap digital watch; the problem is that the clock signal only occurs a few hundred times a second, which isn't very often. What this means in general is that the most accurate signal you can get is about every 54 milliseconds for Windows 95 and later, or every 10 milliseconds for Windows NT 3.1 and later. For now I'll stick to the Windows 95 version.

NOTE

Just in case you didn't know it, there are 1,000 milliseconds in a second.

As I said, with Windows 95 the two smallest units of time that you can differentiate between are 54 milliseconds apart. This may seem like a small amount of time, but in fact it is an eternity. What if you wanted to keep track of playing a MIDI sound file that had to be checked up on once every 10 milliseconds? It just wouldn't work. Well, it turns out that the chip in the computer is in fact programmable. You are able to set it to much higher frequencies. Of course the downside to this is that the actual clock in the computer will get out of sync. For instance, if you doubled the frequency of the clock, then the computer would think that a minute had passed every 30 seconds. Bummer, dude. You can get past this by just remembering to reset the clock at the end of your program. Another problem is that Windows NT/2000 doesn't very much like programs that mess with the hardware directly, so you should try to find a better way to get the time.

Windows Timing

So what other options are there? Well, Windows does have a message-based timing system. You tell Windows to set up a timer for you and give it an interval for the timer. Programs can have as many timers as they want, but each one is going to slow the system slightly. Windows will then send a WM_TIMER message to your program at each interval that you requested. For instance, if you specify 1,000 milliseconds, then you will get a WM_TIMER message roughly every second. With the message, in the WPARAM, will be the ID for the timer. You can use this to distinguish between different timers if you had more than one.

To set up a timer you call the function SetTimer(), and it looks like this:

```
UINT SetTimer(
  HWND hWnd,
  UINT nIDEvent,
  UINT uElapse,
  TIMERPROC lpTimerFunc
);
```

A good place to call this function is in the handler for WM_CREATE or your GameInit() function. Table 9.1 lists the parameters for this function.

Table 9.1   SetTimer Parameters

Parameter	Definition
hWnd	Takes the handle for the window that will receive the time messages.
nIDEvent	Takes an identifier for the timer. This can be anything you want, but it is a good idea to keep #defined identifiers for the timer. For instance, you could have BLINKING_LIGHT_TIMER set to 1, COUNTDOWN_TIMER set to 2, etc. That way it is easier to spot bugs.
uElapse	The interval that you want to use for this new timer, specified in milliseconds.
lpTimerFunc	Takes the pointer to a timer callback function if you don't want to use the WndProc() to handle the messages. Specify NULL if you don't have one.

So if you were creating a new two-second interval clock that made lights blink, then you would do this:

```
int GameInit()
{
        SetTimer( g_hWndMain, BLINKING_LIGHT_TIMER, 2000, NULL );
}
```

Then to handle the WM_TIMER messages you would put the following code in the message handling code located in WndProc():

```
case WM_TIMER:
{
```

```
switch( wParam )
      {
              case BLINKING_LIGHT_TIMER:
              {
                      MakeTheLightBlink();
                      break;
              }
      }
}
return 0;
}
```

When you are finished with a timer you need to destroy it using the `KillTimer()` function, which looks like this puppy:

```
BOOL KillTimer( HWND hWnd, UINT uIDEvent );
```

It just takes the handle for the window that the timer is associated with and the ID that you gave for the timer. `KillTimer()` should be called in `GameShutdown()`, the `WM_DESTROY` handler, or whenever you are finished using it.

```
KillTimer( g_hWndMain, BLINKING_LIGHT_TIMER );
```

Now here's the deal. Windows timers are great for things that don't really need to be that accurate, but for anything other than that they totally stink. They are way worse than the hardware timers that I was talking about before. What you want is an extremely high performance timer for your code. What you are about to see has not, as far as I'm aware, been published in any game programming.

64-Bit High Precision Timers

This stuff is so new that it may not be supported on some computers, although I have yet to find one that doesn't. Windows calls these "High Performance Counters." So what exactly are they?

Well, as far as I can tell, high performance timers are based on the actual clock that is used to drive the processor, or some other crystal that is very fast. There isn't much documentation around on this subject so just smile and nod and be happy that it works. Just to give you an idea of the precision for these timers, I get 1,193,182 ticks per second on my computer, or more precisely one tick every 0.0000838095 millisecond. How slick is that? By the way, the rate that the timer goes at will vary between computers, but don't worry—this is not a problem.

With the kind of resolution that these timers look after, you need a very large variable to hold the times. A 32-bit variable can only hold numbers up to 4,294,967,296, which means that after almost exactly 60 minutes the variable would overflow. People obviously use their computers for much longer than that, so the only solution is to go with a 64-bit variable, which can hold numbers up to 18,446,744,073,709,551,616, which means that the timer will not overflow for 490,237 years. I don't think I'll wait around to see that event!

So how do you set up a high performance timer? Well, it all begins with a function called QueryPerformanceCounter(), and it looks like this:

```
BOOL QueryPerformanceCounter( LARGE_INTEGER *lpPerformanceCount );
```

What this does is tell you the frequency that the timer runs at in ticks per second. If the host computer does not support high performance counters, then the function will return FALSE. The parameter for the function takes a LARGE_INTEGER, which between you and me is two 32-bit variables packed into a structure like this:

```
typedef union _LARGE_INTEGER {
        DWORD   LowPart;
        DWORD   HighPart;
} LARGE_INTEGER;
```

The reason for this silliness is that until recently there was no ANSI standard for how to deal with 64-bit integers in C++. ANSI, or the American National Standards Institute, are the people who manage the development of the C and C++ languages. So without a standard, the only way to deal with 64-bit numbers using a 32-bit processor like the Pentium is to stick two 32-bit variables together in a structure.

That's all very nice, but do game programmers look like the kind of people who drop standards just because some standards agency can't get its act together? I didn't think so either, so let's do like Microsoft did and cheat! It turns out that those forward-thinking guys at MS slipped in a 64-bit variable type, and it is called __int64. (That is two underscores side by side, by the way.) It has been covered by the more aesthetically pleasing INT64 definition. The compiler will automatically modify your code to work with 32-bit processors for you during the compile process when you use this variable.

Now just in case you are a little confused, __int64 is exactly like other type specifiers like char, or regular 32-bit int. It will even turn royal blue when you type it in! How nice. Following is how you might declare and use a 64-bit integer:

```
int64 BigInteger = 0;        // Declare a 64-bit integer
int RegularInteger = 0;              // Declare a regular 32-bit integer
```

```
RegularInteger++;              // Increment the regular integer
BigInteger++;                  // Increment the 64-bit integer

// Cast the 32-bit integer to 64 bits and then compare it to the 32-bit variable
if( BigInteger == (_int64)RegularInteger )
{
        DoSomething();
}


// Using INT64 is exactly the same as using __int64
INT64 Another64BitInteger = 0;
```

See? It works just like any other variable. You don't want to use 64-bit integers for any high performance code because on a 32-bit processor they will take twice as long to process. That won't be a problem with the new Itanium processor though, which is fully 64-bit.

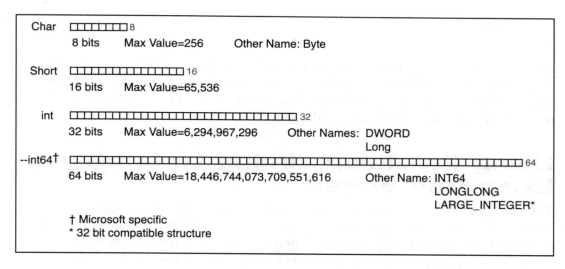

Figure 9.3

Integer types in Microsoft C++

Anyway, the point of all this is that if you see any of those LARGE_INTEGER thingies around, then just cast them to INT64, and then they will be much easier to deal with. With that in mind let's look at a new function that I have added to the engine file that initializes timing and figures all the frequency stuff out.

It's called InitTiming().

```
// Global variable that holds the number of ticks per second
INT64 g_Frequency = 0;

HRESULT InitTiming()
{
        // Get the number of counts per second
        QueryPerformanceFrequency( (LARGE_INTEGER*)&g_Frequency );

        // If the frequency is 0 then this system does not have
        // high performance timers
        if( g_Frequency == 0 )
        {
                SetError( "The system does not support high resolution timing" );
                return E_FAIL;
        }

        return S_OK;
}
```

As you can see it just gets the frequency and double-checks that the system actually supports this form of timing. You should call this from your GameInit() function. Now I can show you some really useful functions that build on all this timing technology that I have been talking about.

Using Precision Timing to Control Execution Speed

There are times when you need to control the speed at which your application executes. For instance, if you wanted to make sure that no more than 30 frames elapsed per second during debugging, then you could get the execution rate and pause for a certain amount of time between each frame. I have created a function for this exact purpose, and it has the fantastically original name Pause().

```
void Pause( int Milliseconds )
{
        // Convert the milliseconds to seconds
        INT64 SecondsDelay = (INT64)Milliseconds * 1000;

        INT64 StartTime;
```

```
INT64 CurrentTime;

        // Get the start time
        QueryPerformanceCounter( (LARGE_INTEGER*)&StartTime );

        while(TRUE)
        {
                // Get the Current Time
                QueryPerformanceCounter( (LARGE_INTEGER*)&CurrentTime );

                // If enough time has passed then break from the loop
                if( (CurrentTime - StartTime) > (INT64)SecondsDelay )
                        break;

        }
}
```

Again, it is pretty simple. First off I convert the millisecond delay into a second delay so that it's easier to compare to the times further down in the function, which are specified relative to seconds. Then I get the current time using the `QueryPerformanceCounter()`, which looks like this:

```
BOOL QueryPerformanceCounter( LARGE_INTEGER *lpPerformanceCount  );
```

This function is very similar to `QueryPerformanceFrequency()` in that it will return `FALSE` if the host system does not support high resolution timing. Otherwise it fills the variable pointed to by `lpPerformanceCount` with the current tick count.

Next up I go into an infinite loop that continually checks the time. The elapsed time is computed by subtracting the current time from the start time. As soon as the correct amount of time has passed I break from the loop, the function returns back to its calling point, and execution resumes. In other words the code waits until the desired time has elapsed. Cool, huh?

Before I move on I just want to show you another little function that I wrote. Because the frequency of the clock is variable depending on the computer being used, I found myself quite often checking what the frequency actually was. This little function gets the number of ticks that elapse for every millisecond of time. Again, like all the code for the book, you can find it in the engine.h file on the companion CD.

```
float GetNumTicksPerMs()
{
        return ((float)g_Frequency / 1000.0f);
}
```

Tracking the Frame Rate

Now that you are an old hand at performance counters, you can build a frame rate counter. These little devices are useful for performance testing your code, and they are very simple to make. Figure 9.4 shows the process.

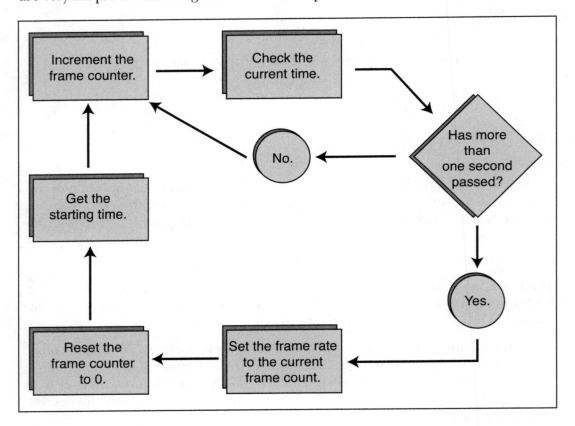

Figure 9.4

Frame rate tracking process

All you have to do is call a function every frame that increments a frame counter. Then, after a second has elapsed, transfer the value of the frame counter into a global frame rate variable and reset the counter to 0, as in the code that follows:

```
void FrameCount()
{
        INT64 NewCount = 0;              // The current count
        static INT64 LastCount = 0;      // The last count
        INT64 Difference = 0;            // The difference since the last count

        // Get the current count
        QueryPerformanceCounter( (LARGE_INTEGER*)&NewCount );

        // If the count is 0 then this system does not have
        // high performance timers
        if( NewCount == 0 )
                SetError( "The system does not support high resolution timing" );

        // Increase the frame count
        g_FrameCount++;

        // Compute the difference since the last count
        Difference = NewCount - LastCount;

        // If more than a second has passed
        if( Difference >= g_Frequency )
        {
                // Record the number of elapsed frames
                g_FrameRate = g_FrameCount;
                // Reset the counter
                g_FrameCount = 0;

                // Update the last count
                LastCount = NewCount;
        }

}
```

So now that you have the frame rate, how great would it be if you could actually print it on the screen? Well, that would certainly be cool, and you could do it using the GDI copying code that I talked about in the last chapter, but then again that would be too slow for a proper game engine. So what would be better? Well, how about writing your own bitmap-based font engine?

Developing a 2D Font Engine

Writing a font engine is such an important task during the development of a game that it surprises me how little it is written about. As far as I can tell, there is only one book about DOS development from the mid-1990s that covers this stuff. Let's see how to do it with DirectX.

You may be wondering exactly why you would even want to write a new font engine. Didn't Microsoft spend millions developing the TrueType specification for the Windows font engine? Well yes, they did, but it has a bunch of drawbacks if you want to use it in your game. First off it does not work well with Direct3D, which means that a GDI to surface conversion is necessary and inherently slow. Secondly, TrueType is boring, since all of the fonts have to be a plain color. Developers and users want games to be really visually exciting, and single-color fonts just aren't going to cut it. And finally, it's just fun figuring out how to do this yourself. (I already have a life, thank you. I bet the first letter that pops up on your screen in a few pages will make you happy, too.)

So how hard can it be to get a letter from the keyboard to appear on the screen? Well, it's harder than you might think. You would start by getting the letter that was pressed in the WM_CHAR message handler. But then what next?

There are a few options. You could set up about 50 if statements that check to see which letter was pressed, and then copy an appropriate bitmap image that represents that key. However that would be a total waste of time and it wouldn't be modular, extendable, or reusable. What if you could create a single large bitmap to hold all the bitmaps for the letters, and you could somehow map the ASCII code for each key into the correct x, y coordinates within the source alphabet bitmap? You're right, it would be slick.

ASCII Codes and Your Source Alphabet

NOTE

You probably already know this, but **ASCII** stands for the *American Standard Code for Information Interchange*, a standard developed many years ago to allow the interchange of information between computers from different manufacturers. However it has a big drawback in that it does not support any foreign languages properly, so it is slowly but surely being replaced by Unicode, which is another story altogether.

Let's start with a little bit of theory about life, the universe, and everything. In other words, ASCII codes. Once you get the ASCII code, you need to somehow transform it into an x-coordinate and a y-coordinate that are indexes into a bitmap. Two coordinates from a single number? How do you do that? Well, the ASCII code that you are interested in starts at 32, which is for space. It then continues in the following order:

```
!"#$%&'()*+,-./0123456789:;<=>?@ABCDEFGHIJKLMNOPQRSTUVWXYZ
[\]^_'abcdefghijklmnopqrstuvwxyz{|}~
```

. . . which isn't very interesting. Now before I continue, let's talk about your source alphabet for a minute. You can either make your own or use one of the bitmaps that I have included on the CD. You need to make each letter very small. For instance, your average small font will be roughly 8 x 16 pixels, and a large font could be up to 64 x 64 for each letter. After that you need to put them together into a grid in an alphabet bitmap. It doesn't matter how many letters you have in each row of the alphabet image, and it doesn't matter how many columns you have either; the code I will show you soon will figure it all out. However, what is very important is that you make sure that each letter is exactly the same size as all the other letters. That is, if you decide that your letters are going to be 8 x 16, then make sure that there are no 7 x 15 letters around, and that your letters are lined up to the proper grid boundaries! Otherwise, the code will break.

Figure 9.5 shows a sample bitmap for the alphabet. The letters in that picture are 64 x 64 pixels in dimensions. Figure 9.6 shows the alphabet that I made with letters that are 16 x 32 and 8 x 16. Notice they are in the same order as the ASCII standard.

Figure 9.5

A large 64 x 64 sample font with black as the transparent color

Figure 9.6

Smaller fonts: 16 x 32 on the left, and 8 x 16 on the right.

Notice that for my alphabets I chose to use 10 characters per row. Let's get back to working out coordinates. While talking about this, let's use the uppercase letter "A," which has an ASCII code of 65. In my alphabet image, "A" is in the fourth column and the fourth row. Now let's get to how you convert 65 into (4, 4).

Start by subtracting 32 from the ASCII code so that the letters start from zero. This makes the calculations much easier. So the new code is now 33. Then divide this code by the number of letters that are in a row of your alphabet image. So, for me, that would be 33 divided by 10. The resulting quotient of this operation will contain the correct row that contains the letter, and the resulting remainder will contain the correct column. For the letter "A" you get a quotient of 3 and a remainder of 3. Which is correct, because the rows and columns are zero based (0, 1, 2, 3,…), so 3 is, in fact, the fourth index.

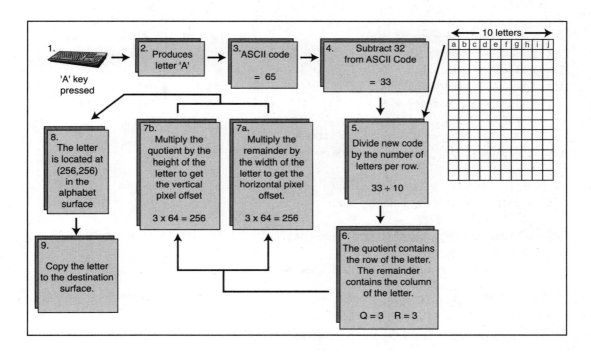

Figure 9.7

Calculating the coordinates of letters within a font bitmap

Then, to get the pixel offset, you just need to multiply the width of your letter by the column and the height by the row. In the 64 x 64 image, that means the letter "A" starts at (256, 256) and extends to (320, 320).

What I have done is put together four functions that help you to easily use your own font engine. The way the engine is currently constructed, you can only have one font loaded at a time, but it would be easy to extend its functionality. However, I'll leave that little task up to you.

Anyway, the first function is used to load the alphabet image into memory and figure out the dimensions to use. The alphabet is stored in a global surface. LoadAlphabet() looks like this:

```
// Globals

int g_AlphabetWidth = 0;                    // The width of the Alphabet bitmap
int g_AlphabetHeight = 0;                   // The height of the Alphabet bitmap
int g_AlphabetLetterWidth = 0;        // The width of a letter
int g_AlphabetLetterHeight = 0;             // The height of a letter
int g_AlphabetLettersPerRow = 0;            // The number of letters per row


// The surface holding the alphabet bitmap
LPDIRECT3DSURFACE8 g_pAlphabetSurface = 0;


// Has the alphabet bitmap been loaded yet?
BOOL g_bAlphabetLoaded = FALSE;

HRESULT LoadAlphabet( char* strPathName, int LetterWidth, int LetterHeight )
{
        // Make sure a valid path was specified
        if( !strPathName )
                return E_FAIL;

        // Make sure the size of the letters is greater than 0
        if( !LetterWidth || !LetterHeight )
                return E_FAIL;

        HRESULT r = 0;

        // Load the bitmap into the global surface
        r = LoadBitmapToSurface( strPathName, &g_pAlphabetSurface, g_pDevice );
        if( FAILED( r ) )
        {
                SetError( "Unable to load alphabet bitmap" );
                return E_FAIL;
        }

        // Holds information about the alphabet surface
        D3DSURFACE_DESC d3dsd;
```

```
        // Get information about the alphabet surface
        g_pAlphabetSurface->GetDesc( &d3dsd );

        // Update globals with the letter dimensions
        g_AlphabetWidth = d3dsd.Width;
        g_AlphabetHeight = d3dsd.Height;
        g_AlphabetLetterWidth = LetterWidth;
        g_AlphabetLetterHeight = LetterHeight;

        // Compute the number of letters in a row
        g_AlphabetLettersPerRow = g_AlphabetWidth / g_AlphabetLetterWidth;

        // Set the loaded flag to TRUE
        g_bAlphabetLoaded = TRUE;

        return S_OK;
}
```

It looks kind of complex, but you've seen all this stuff before. The function takes as parameters the path to the source bitmap, and the dimensions of the letters within the bitmap. It then uses the LoadBitmapToSurface() function that I showed you in the last chapter. After that, it's just a matter of filling in the global variables with information about the alphabet.

If you want to use another alphabet, then you need to unload the previous alphabet from memory first. The code that follows does exactly that:

```
// Unloads the alphabet from memory
HRESULT UnloadAlphabet()
{
        // Check if the alphabet exists
        if( g_pAlphabetSurface )
        {
                // Release the surface
                g_pAlphabetSurface->Release();
                // NULL the pointer
                g_pAlphabetSurface = 0;
                // Set the loaded flag to FALSE
                g_bAlphabetLoaded = FALSE;
        }
        return S_OK;
}
```

Again, you have seen this before. The alphabet surface is just released and the pointer reset to zero. The next function is the one that actually prints a character to the screen.

```
// Print a character to a surface using the loaded alphabet
void PrintChar( int x, int y, char Character, BOOL bTransparent,
                    D3DCOLOR ColorKey, DWORD* pDestData, int DestPitch )
{
        HRESULT r = 0;

        div_t Result;   // Holds the result of divisions

        // The offset into the alphabet image
        int OffsetX = 0, OffsetY = 0;

        POINT LetterDestPoint = { 0, 0 };      // The destination point for the letter
        RECT LetterRect = { 0, 0, 0, 0 };      // The source rectangle for the letter

        // If the alphabet has not been loaded yet then exit
        if( !g_bAlphabetLoaded )
                return;

        // The characters are specified in ASCII code, which begins at 32 so
        // we want to decrement this value by 32 to make it zero based
        Character -= 32;

        // Divide the character code by the number of letters per row.
        // The quotient will help get the vertical offset and the
        // remainder will help get the horizontal offset
        Result = div( Character, g_AlphabetLettersPerRow );

        // Get the horizontal offset by multiplying the remainder
        // by the width of the letter
        OffsetX = Result.rem * g_AlphabetLetterWidth;
        // Get the vertical offset by multiplying the quotient
        // by the height of the letter
        OffsetY = Result.quot * g_AlphabetLetterHeight;
// Fill in the source rectangle with the computed offsets
        SetRect( &LetterRect, OffsetX, OffsetY,
        OffsetX + g_AlphabetLetterWidth, OffsetY + g_AlphabetLetterHeight );

        // Fill in the destination point
```

```
LetterDestPoint.x = x;
LetterDestPoint.y = y;

// Holds info about the alphabet surface
D3DLOCKED_RECT LockedAlphabet;
// Lock the source surface
r = g_pAlphabetSurface->LockRect( &LockedAlphabet, 0,
                                                    D3DLOCK_READONLY  );

if( FAILED( r ) )
{
        SetError( "Couldnt lock alphabet surface for PrintChar()" );
        return;
}


// Get a DWORD pointer to each surface
DWORD* pAlphaData = (DWORD*)LockedAlphabet.pBits;

// Convert the BYTE pitch to a DWORD pitch
LockedAlphabet.Pitch /=4;
DestPitch /= 4;

// Compute the offset into the alphabet
int AlphaOffset = OffsetY * LockedAlphabet.Pitch + OffsetX;
// Compute the offset into the destination surface
int DestOffset = y * DestPitch + x;

// Loop for each row in the letter
for( int cy = 0 ; cy < g_AlphabetLetterHeight ; cy++ )
{
        // Loop for each column in the letter
        for( int cx = 0 ; cx < g_AlphabetLetterWidth ; cx++ )
        {
                if( bTransparent )
                {
                        // If this alphabet pixel is not transparent
                        if( pAlphaData[ AlphaOffset ] != ColorKey )
{
                                // Then copy the pixel to the destination
                                pDestData[DestOffset] =
                                        pAlphaData[AlphaOffset];
                        }
```

```
                            // Increment the offsets to the next pixel
                }
                else
                {
                            pDestData[ DestOffset ] = pAlphaData[ AlphaOffset ];
                }

                AlphaOffset++;
                DestOffset++;
        }

        // Move the offsets to the start of the next row
        DestOffset += DestPitch - g_AlphabetLetterWidth;
        AlphaOffset += LockedAlphabet.Pitch - g_AlphabetLetterWidth;
    }

    // Unlock the surface
    g_pAlphabetSurface->UnlockRect();

}
```

This function is just the business. It takes a lot of parameters, which are listed in Table 9.2

Table 9.2   Printchar Parameters

Parameter	Definition
x	Takes the x-coordinate for where you want the letter to end up
y	Takes the y-coordinate for where you want the letter to end up
Character	The character that you want to display
bTransparent	Takes the flag indicating whether you want to use color keying during the copy operation
ColorKey	The color key that you want to use if you specified that you want transparency
pDestData	A pointer to destination picture data in a locked surface
DestPitch	Takes the pitch of the destination surface in bytes

Now let's take a brief look at the code. When you divide using the div() function, which is contained in stdlib.h, you need to use the div_t structure. The structure looks like this:

```
typedef struct _div_t {
        int quot;
        int rem;
} div_t;
```

It is a simple structure, returned from div(), that contains the quotient and remainder of the divide operation. So now you know what the second line of PrintChar() does!

After that, the program continues through the process that I was talking about before. The ASCII code is decremented by 32 and then divided into the number of characters in the source image. The remainder and quotient are then used to work out correct offsets into the image. Next up the source alphabet is locked so that I can get access to the data. Then I get the actual pixel offsets into the alphabet using the usual OffsetY*Pitch/4+OffsetX routine. Then it is just a case of looping through each pixel and comparing it to the color key and copying it over. Finally, the alphabet is unlocked and the function returns, one letter richer.

Printing Multiple Characters to the Screen

There comes a time in every Zen game programmer's life when he wants to push the envelope, reach for new heights, expand his horizons, and most importantly, print more than one character to the screen. In fact, some go so far as to print an entire string of characters! This is very easy (see Figure 9.8). All you have to do is get a function to accept a string and then loop through each character and call the PrintChar() function for each one, just like this:

```
void PrintString( int x, int y, char* String, BOOL bTransparent,
                    D3DCOLOR ColorKey, DWORD* pDestData, int DestPitch )
{
    // Loop for each character in the string
    for( UINT i = 0 ; i < strlen( String ) ; i++ )
    {
        // Print the current character
        PrintChar( x + (g_AlphabetLetterWidth * i), y, String[i],
                    bTransparent, ColorKey, pDestData, DestPitch );
    }
}
```

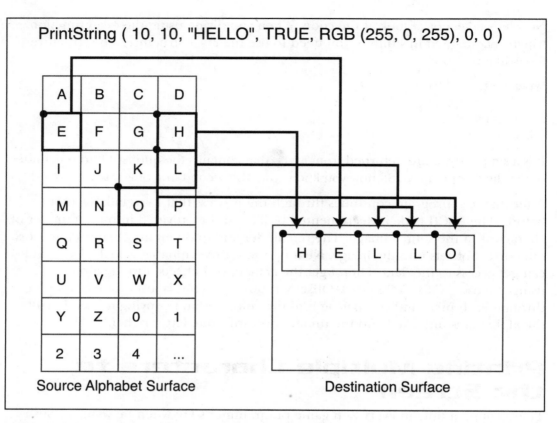

Figure 9.8

Printing multiple characters with PrintString()

Start Up that Engine!

And that, ladies and gentlemen, is one slick font engine. You could expand it if you want, by using a structure or class to hold information about the alphabet instead of the globals, and then using an array or list to add functionality to hold more than one font in memory at the same time. You could then modify the `PrintChar()` routine to also take a parameter that specifies which font you want to use. But the way it is now is good enough for the purposes of this book.

So let's see this puppy in action. If you put the following code in your `GameInit()` function...

```
LoadAlphabet( "Alphabet Small.bmp", 16, 32 );
```

...and this code in `GameShutdown()`...

```
UnloadAlphabet();
```

...and this code in `Render()`, which is called from `GameLoop()`...

```
PrintString( 10, 400, "The Alphabet begins with Z!!", TRUE,
        D3DCOLOR_ARGB( 0, 255, 0, 255 ), (DWORD*)Locked.pBits, Locked.Pitch );
```

then you will see the output shown in Figure 9.9. Pretty cool, huh? The background is just a normal bitmap that I cooked up in Photoshop to make the screenshot more interesting.

Figure 9.9

The output from the font engine

OK, I started off this section on fonts talking about printing the frame rate to the screen. I have put together a function that will do this, and it is shown in the listing that follows:

```
// Prints the frame rate to the screen
void PrintFrameRate( int x, int y, BOOL bTransparent,
        D3DCOLOR ColorKey,
DWORD* pDestData, int DestPitch )
{
    char string[4]; // String to hold the frame rate

    // Zero out the string
    ZeroMemory( &string, sizeof( string ) );

    // Convert the frame rate to a string
    itoa( g_FrameRate, string, 10 );
```

```
        // Output the string to the back surface
        PrintString( x, y, string, bTransparent, ColorKey, pDestData, DestPitch );
}
```

You can now display the frame rate by calling the function from Render like this:

```
PrintFrameRate( 550, 400, TRUE,
        D3DCOLOR_ARGB( 0, 255, 0, 255 ), (DWORD*)Locked.pBits, Locked.Pitch );
```

The result is what you see in Figure 9.10.

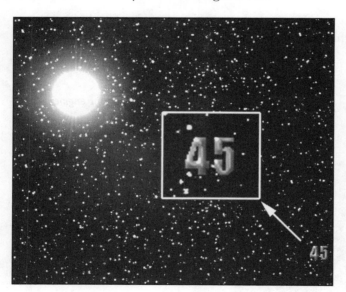

Figure 9.10

Displaying the frame rate on the screen

I have enlarged the frame rate section for clarity. So that's another addition to your engine. What you really need now is some game-specific functionality that can be built on top of your current knowledge. Something like a sprite engine, for instance.

Developing a 2D Sprite Engine

You have the capability to load bitmaps and copy them to the back surface, print text, and so on. But what you don't have is an easy way to display multiple moving objects, or *sprites*, as they are known in technobabble.

You may be interested in knowing where the name *sprite* comes from. I'm not going to tell you because I don't have a clue, but there is a man who does. His name is Alfred, and he is the janitor who cleans the nuclear reactor underneath the Pentagon. He looks just like the guy in *Die Hard 2*, except for his fishnet stockings.

Sprites are generally small bitmaps, usually with transparent areas, that are used to represent objects in a game, such as characters, scenery like plants and rocks, and other entities like bullets or explosions (see Figure 9.11). In fact, just about everything graphical can be represented by a sprite. So what does a sprite need? It will need a bitmap to display, or a chain of bitmaps if you want to do animation. It will also need a position, a velocity, and self-state information.

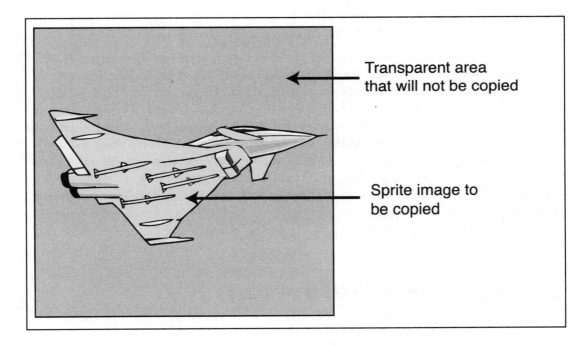

Figure 9.11

A sample sprite

A sprite has a position based on screen pixels that define where it will be displayed on the screen. But you don't want to compute a new position manually for a sprite every frame. A better method is to give the sprite a velocity and have it update its own position every frame. The best way to facilitate this is by calling an update function for the sprite each frame, which will automatically modify the position for you, based on the velocity of the sprite.

The self-state information is required because a sprite generally has more than one state that it can be in. For instance, if the sprite represents a character that is walking, then you will want to animate through walking images. However, later if the character is dying, you will want to change the state to dying, which will display the fall-over-in-a-violent-bloody-savage-death animation.

I have set up the sprite like this: There is a source surface that contains all the images for the sprite. There is also an active surface that contains the sprite that is currently being displayed. If you want to change the currently-displayed sprite, then you tell the sprite to select a new image, which is subsequently copied from the source surface to the active surface. The next time you tell the sprite to render itself it will draw the new active sprite.

That's most of the theory that goes into the development of a sprite engine. Now let me talk a little bit about the implementation that I am going to use. Since sprites represent objects, and since this stuff can start to get very complex, it makes a lot of sense to encapsulate all this functionality into C++ objects. Previously, I have been using straight C everywhere, but it is time to move up a level. If you need help moving from C to C++, check out the tutorial in Appendix A. Don't worry—I am not going to go class crazy, there is no inheritance (yet!) or anything like that. One downside is that C++ is slightly harder to explain, because you have to show the class definition, which is really ugly and puts everybody off. So here's a tip: When I show you the definitions, just smile and nod and pretend it's a list of prototypes. I will still go through the member functions line by line just like before. Back to the drawing board!

Sprite Class Definition

Now don't panic—here is the class definition for the sprite structure:

```
class CSprite
{
public:
        CSprite();
        ~CSprite();

// Functions:
public:

        HRESULT Initialize( char* strPathName,
                        int SpriteWidth, int SpriteHeight, int NumSprites );
        HRESULT Initialize( LPDIRECT3DSURFACE8 pSourceSurface,
                        int SpriteWidth, int SpriteHeight, int NumSprites );
        void Shutdown();
```

```cpp
        HRESULT SelectActiveSprite( int SpriteNum );
        HRESULT Render( LPDIRECT3DSURFACE8 pDestSurface );

        void SetColorKey( D3DCOLOR ColorKey );
        D3DCOLOR GetColorKey(){ return m_ColorKey; }

        void SetPosition( int x, int y ){ m_x = x; m_y = y; }
        void GetPosition( int* px, int* py){ *px = m_x, *py = m_y; }

        void GetBounds( RECT* pRect );
        BOOL CheckForCollisionWith( CSprite* pOtherSprite );

        void SetVelocity( int vx, int vy )
        {
                m_VelocityX = vx;
                m_VelocityY = vy;
        }
        void GetVelocity( int* pvx, int* pvy )
        {
                *pvx = m_VelocityX;
                *pvy = m_VelocityY;
        }

        void SetNext( CSprite* pNext ){ m_pNext = pNext; }
        CSprite* GetNext(){ return m_pNext; }

        void Update();

// Variables
public:
        int m_SurfaceWidth;           // The width of the sprite surface
        int m_SurfaceHeight;   // The height of the sprite surface
        int m_SpriteWidth;            // The width of a sprite
        int m_SpriteHeight;           // The height of a sprite
        int m_NumSprites;             // The number of sprites in the sprite surface

        BOOL m_bTransparent;   // Is this sprite transparent?

        int m_State;           // The current state of this sprite
```

```
protected:
        LPDIRECT3DSURFACE8 m_pSpriteSurface; // The sprite surface
        LPDIRECT3DSURFACE8 m_pActiveSurface; // The current active sprite

        BOOL m_bInitialized;    // Has the sprite been initialized?

        D3DCOLOR m_ColorKey;    // The color key for this sprite

        int m_x, m_y;                       // The position of the sprite
        int m_VelocityX;                    // The x-velocity of the sprite
        int m_VelocityY;                    // The y-velocity of the sprite

        CSprite* m_pNext;                   // Used for linked list of sprites
};
```

What did I just say? Don't panic! Keep your Zen wits about you!

Before getting to the interesting stuff, I'll give you the constructor that simply initializes all the member variables to zero. By the way, I am using the Microsoft naming convention of prefixing member variables with m_. You should do this also; it helps to get rid of confusion between local, global, and member scope.

```
CSprite::CSprite()
{
        m_SurfaceWidth = 0;
        m_SurfaceHeight = 0;
        m_SpriteWidth = 0;
        m_SpriteHeight = 0;
        m_NumSprites = 0;

        m_pSpriteSurface = 0;
        m_pActiveSurface = 0;

        m_bInitialized = FALSE;

        m_ColorKey = D3DCOLOR_ARGB( 0, 255, 0, 255 );

        m_bTransparent = TRUE;

        m_x = m_y = 0;
```

```
            m_VelocityX = 0;
            m_VelocityY = 0;

            m_State = 0;
            m_pNext = 0;
}
```

As you can see, the sprite uses bright pink as the default color key. You can change this using the SetColorKey() and GetColorKey() functions implemented in the class definition.

Sprite Initialization

I have included two ways to initialize a sprite. This is for optimization; sometimes you will display lots of sprites based on the same source image. For instance, you might have 10 enemy ships that all look the same. Instead of loading the source image 10 times, you would just load it once and let each of the 10 sprite objects reference the same image. Of course you may also just have a single sprite, in which case it is quicker to initialize it from a file. And that is what the two ways to initialize a sprite are:

- **Method 1.** Initialize the sprite from a file.
- **Method 2.** Initialize the sprite from a surface already in memory.

Following is the code for initializing the sprite from a file on the disk. I have bolded the part that is different from the other initialization method, which I will show you shortly.

```
HRESULT CSprite::Initialize( char* strPathName, int SpriteWidth,
                                      int SpriteHeight, int NumSprites )
{
        if( m_pSpriteSurface )
        {
                m_pSpriteSurface->Release();
                m_pSpriteSurface = 0;
        }

        if( m_pActiveSurface )
        {
                m_pActiveSurface->Release();
                m_pActiveSurface = 0;
```

```
}

        HRESULT r = 0;

        NumSprites--;

        r = LoadBitmapToSurface( strPathName, &m_pSpriteSurface, g_pDevice );
        if( FAILED( r ) )
        {
                return E_FAIL;
        }

        m_SpriteWidth = SpriteWidth;
        m_SpriteHeight = SpriteHeight;
        m_NumSprites = NumSprites;

        D3DSURFACE_DESC d3dsd;
        m_pSpriteSurface->GetDesc( &d3dsd );

        m_SurfaceWidth = d3dsd.Width;
        m_SurfaceHeight = d3dsd.Height;

        r = g_pDevice->CreateImageSurface( m_SpriteWidth,
                        m_SpriteHeight, D3DFMT_X8R8G8B8, &m_pActiveSurface );
        if( FAILED( r ) )
        {
                Shutdown();
                return E_FAIL;
        }

        RECT SpriteRect = { 0, 0, SpriteWidth, SpriteHeight };
        POINT SpritePoint = { 0, 0 };

        g_pDevice->CopyRects( m_pSpriteSurface, &SpriteRect, 1,
                                        m_pActiveSurface, &SpritePoint );

        m_bInitialized = TRUE;

        return S_OK;
}
```

Table 9.3 gives the parameters.

Table 9.3   CSprite: Initialize Parameters

Parameter	Definition
strPathName	Takes the path of the image that you want to use a source for the sprite
SpriteWidth	The width of a sprite
SpriteHeight	The height of a sprite
NumSprites	Takes the number of sprites that are in the source image

The function starts by checking if it has already been initialized, and if it has been, it releases the resources that it previously acquired. This ensures that resources don't cause memory leaks. Then I decrement the number of sprites, since they are zero based in the image file. Next the source bitmap is loaded from the disk and the member variables are updated to reflect the dimensions of the new image. Then I create a new image surface that is the same size as the sprite for the active surface. Finally, the first sprite in the source image is copied to the active surface by default.

The other Initialize() function looks like this:

```
HRESULT CSprite::Initialize( LPDIRECT3DSURFACE8 pSourceSurface,
                             int SpriteWidth, int SpriteHeight, int NumSprites )
{
        if( m_pSpriteSurface )
        {
                m_pSpriteSurface->Release();
                m_pSpriteSurface = 0;
        }

        if( m_pActiveSurface )
        {
                m_pActiveSurface->Release();
                m_pActiveSurface = 0;
        }

        HRESULT r = 0;
```

```
            NumSprites--;

            if( !pSourceSurface )
            {
                    SetError( "Invalid source sprite surface" );
                    return E_FAIL;
            }

            m_pSpriteSurface = pSourceSurface;
            pSourceSurface->AddRef();

            m_SpriteWidth = SpriteWidth;
            m_SpriteHeight = SpriteHeight;
            m_NumSprites = NumSprites;

            D3DSURFACE_DESC d3dsd;
            m_pSpriteSurface->GetDesc( &d3dsd );

            m_SurfaceWidth = d3dsd.Width;
            m_SurfaceHeight = d3dsd.Height;

            r = g_pDevice->CreateImageSurface( m_SpriteWidth, m_SpriteHeight,
                                D3DFMT_X8R8G8B8, &m_pActiveSurface );
            if( FAILED( r ) )
            {
                    Shutdown();
                    return E_FAIL;
            }

            RECT SpriteRect = { 0, 0, SpriteWidth, SpriteHeight };
            POINT SpritePoint = { 0, 0 };

            g_pDevice->CopyRects( m_pSpriteSurface, &SpriteRect, 1,
                                        m_pActiveSurface, &SpritePoint );

            m_bInitialized = TRUE;

            return S_OK;
    }
```

It does exactly the same thing as the first function except that the first parameter is now a pointer to a surface. Also, instead of loading a file, the pointer to the source surface is copied and the source surface's reference count is incremented. It is very important to increment the reference count; if you don't, you could find that the sprite's source surface suddenly disappears from memory and you get memory faults. You could combine these two functions into one with a little bit of logic, but I wanted you to be clear on the two methods.

I have also included a Shutdown() function with the sprite so that you can release the sprites resources on the fly, if you want. It looks just like the destructor.

```
void CSprite::Shutdown()
{
        if( m_pSpriteSurface )
        {
                m_pSpriteSurface->Release();
                m_pSpriteSurface = 0;
        }

        if( m_pActiveSurface )
        {
                m_pActiveSurface->Release();
                m_pActiveSurface = 0;
        }


        m_SurfaceWidth = 0;
        m_SurfaceHeight = 0;
        m_SpriteWidth = 0;
        m_SpriteHeight = 0;
        m_NumSprites = 0;

        m_pSpriteSurface = 0;

        m_bInitialized = FALSE;
}
```

This function just releases the surfaces and resets the member variables to zero.

Sprite Rendering

So now that you have your sprite initialized, it would be nice if you could render it. The Render() function is shown in the code that follows:

```
HRESULT CSprite::Render( LPDIRECT3DSURFACE8 pDestSurface )
{
        if( !pDestSurface )
                return E_FAIL;

        HRESULT r = 0;

        RECT SourceRect = { 0, 0, m_SpriteWidth, m_SpriteHeight };
        POINT DestPoint = { m_x, m_y };

        if( m_bTransparent )
                r = CopySurfaceToSurface( &SourceRect,
                                m_pActiveSurface, &DestPoint,
                                pDestSurface, TRUE, m_ColorKey );
        else
                r = g_pDevice->CopyRects( m_pActiveSurface,
                        &SourceRect, 1, pDestSurface, &DestPoint );

        return r;
}
```

As you can see, it is very simple. The function takes a pointer to the surface onto which you want to render. You would usually specify the back surface for this. The function starts by making sure that you specified a valid destination surface. Then the source and destination coordinates are worked out, based on the member variables that were set during the Initialize() function. Then the active surface is copied to the destination surface pixel by pixel if transparency was requested, or using hardware acceleration otherwise.

Sprite Animation

Let me show you a sample sprite that I put together. It includes rings at different stages of an oscillating motion, as shown in Figure 9.12.

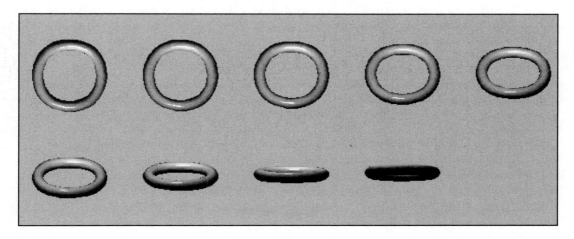

Figure 9.12

Multiple sprite images for animation

If I call `CSprite::Render()` every iteration through the game loop, then the first full ring will be rendered. However, if I oscillate (go forward then backward repeatedly) through the different rings, then the result will be an impressive animation effect. The code to select different sprites is shown in the following listing; it looks very similar to the code that I showed you before to select a letter out of the alphabet bitmap.

```
HRESULT CSprite::SelectActiveSprite( int SpriteNum )
{
        HRESULT r = 0;

        div_t Result;

        int OffsetX = 0;
        int OffsetY = 0;
        int SpritesPerRow = m_SurfaceWidth / m_SpriteWidth;

        if( SpriteNum > m_NumSprites )
                return E_FAIL;
```

```
        Result = div( SpriteNum, SpritesPerRow );

        OffsetX = Result.rem * m_SpriteWidth;
        OffsetY = Result.quot* m_SpriteHeight;

        if( OffsetX > m_SurfaceWidth )
                return E_FAIL;

        if( OffsetY > m_SurfaceHeight )
                return E_FAIL;

        RECT SpriteRect = { OffsetX,
                OffsetY, OffsetX + m_SpriteWidth, OffsetY + m_SpriteHeight };
        POINT DestPoint = { 0, 0 };

        g_pDevice->CopyRects( m_pSpriteSurface, &SpriteRect,
                                    1, m_pActiveSurface, &DestPoint );

        return S_OK;
}
```

Just like in the alphabet code, I get the offset into the source image by dividing the requested sprite number by the number of sprites in a row. The remainder then contains the column, and quotient is equal to the row. After the offsets are computed, the sprite is copied using hardware acceleration to the active surface.

Before I show you an example, I want to show you the position and velocity code. You can modify the velocity of the sprite using the functions GetVelocity() and SetVelocity(), which are implemented in the class definition. By default, the velocity for the sprite is 0 in both directions. You may have noticed in the class definition that there is a velocity for the x-axis and for the y-axis.

The velocity modifies the position of the sprite like this: Every frame you call the function CSprite::Update(). This function updates the position of the sprite based on the velocity. Basically, all it does is add the x-velocity to the x-position and the y-velocity to the y-position. If the velocity is positive, the sprite will appear to move forward along the axis, and backward if the velocity is negative.

Here is the code:

```
void CSprite::Update()
{
        m_x += m_VelocityX;
        m_y += m_VelocityY;
}
```

Don't forget that it is important to make sure that the sprite stays within the bounds of the screen. If you try to draw to somewhere off the screen, the copy operation will either fail and/or you will cause a memory fault. Before I move on, let's see an example of sprites in action.

Sprites in Action

I'll start with a simple example and then increase the complexity so that you can see the process. Let's start by just rendering the sprite to (0, 0) on the back surface without any animation. The first thing to do is declare a global sprite variable:

```
CSprite g_RingSprite;
```

Then somewhere in the GameInit() function you could put this code to initialize the sprite:

```
g_RingSprite.Initialize( "Rings.Bmp", 128, 128, 9 );
```

And to render the sprite you would put this code in Render():

```
g_RingSprite.Render(
g_pBackSurface );
```

This produces what you see in Figure 9.13.

Figure 9.13

Rendering sprites to the back buffer

Which is really great for all of five seconds until you think about how much cooler it would be if it were animating through the rings. To do this you could add the following code to Render():

```
static BOOL bIncrease = TRUE;
static int CurrentSprite = 0;

if( CurrentSprite > 9 )
        bIncrease = FALSE;

if( CurrentSprite < 0 )
        bIncrease = TRUE;

if( bIncrease )
        CurrentSprite++;
else
        CurrentSprite--;

g_RingSprite.SelectActiveSprite( CurrentSprite );

g_RingSprite.Render( g_pBackSurface );
```

Static variables retain their values throughout the life of the program and are only initialized the first time that the function is executed. So basically the preceding code causes the CurrentSprite integer to oscillate between zero and nine.

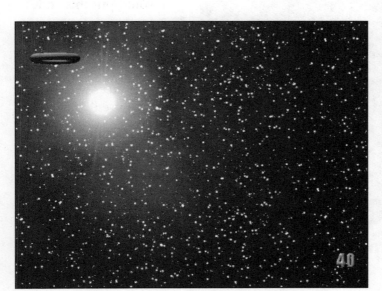

Figure 9.14 shows a frame of the rings animating, although to get the full effect you should run the executable from the companion CD.

Figure 9.14

Animating sprites

Pretty cool, huh? Well, it's about to get better. Let's see if you can't get this baby to bounce around the screen. To make the ring move you need to give it a velocity, so change the GameInit() code to the following:

```
g_RingSprite.Initialize( "Rings.Bmp", 128, 128, 9 );
g_RingSprite.SetVelocity( 5, 5 );
```

And change the Render() code to::

```
static BOOL bIncrease = TRUE;
static int  CurrentSprite = 0;

if( CurrentSprite > 9 )
        bIncrease = FALSE;

if( CurrentSprite < 0 )
        bIncrease = TRUE;

if( bIncrease )
        CurrentSprite++;
else
        CurrentSprite--;

g_RingSprite.SelectActiveSprite( CurrentSprite );

int VelX, VelY, PosX, PosY;

g_RingSprite.GetPosition( &PosX, &PosY );
g_RingSprite.GetVelocity( &VelX, &VelY );

if( PosX > 639 - 128 )
        VelX = -VelX;

if( PosY > 479 - 128 )
        VelY = -VelY;

if( PosX < 0 )
        VelX = -VelX;

if( PosY < 0 )
        VelY = -VelY;
```

```
g_RingSprite.SetVelocity( VelX, VelY );

g_RingSprite.Update();

g_RingSprite.Render( g_pBackSurface );
```

This new code moves the ring around until it comes close to hitting the edges of the screen. If it's about to go out of bounds, then the velocity is reversed. Take a look at Figure 9.15, which shows a frame of the moving, animated ring.

Figure 9.15

Moving, animated sprites using member velocities

Now let me go one step further and show you the capabilities of the sprite class when dealing with multiple sprites referencing a single source image. This is totally slick. For this I am going to create an array of CSprites and modify them in loops.

To start with, I define an identifier to hold the number of sprites that I want to display:

```
#define MAX_SPRITES 8
```

Then I modify the global sprite variable into an array:

```
CSprite g_RingSprites[MAX_SPRITES];
```

Now I also need a global surface to hold the rings that will be referenced by all the sprites:

```
LPDIRECT3DSURFACE8 g_pRingSurface = 0;
```

Then, down in GameInit(), the rings bitmap is loaded to the global surface and the initialization code to work in a loop with the arrays is modified. I also ensure that each sprite gets its own random velocity. Each sprite then has its position set to a random location on the screen:

```
LoadBitmapToSurface( "Rings.bmp", &g_pRingSurface, g_pDevice );

for( int SpriteCount = 0 ; SpriteCount < MAX_SPRITES ; SpriteCount++ )
{
        g_RingSprites[SpriteCount].Initialize( g_pRingSurface, 128, 128, 9 );
        g_RingSprites[SpriteCount].SetVelocity( rand()%8, rand()%8 );

        g_RingSprites[ SpriteCount ].SetPosition( rand()%(g_DeviceWidth - 128),
                                                  rand()%(g_DeviceHeight - 128));
}
```

The modified Render() code now looks like this:

```
static BOOL bIncrease = TRUE;
static int CurrentSprite[MAX_SPRITES];

for( int SpriteCount = 0 ; SpriteCount < MAX_SPRITES ; SpriteCount++ )
{

        if( CurrentSprite[ SpriteCount ] > 9 )
                bIncrease = FALSE;

        if( CurrentSprite[ SpriteCount ] < 0 )
                bIncrease = TRUE;

        if( bIncrease )
                CurrentSprite[ SpriteCount ]++;
        else
                CurrentSprite[ SpriteCount ]--;

        g_RingSprites[ SpriteCount ].SelectActiveSprite(
                                        CurrentSprite[ SpriteCount ] );

        int VelX, VelY, PosX, PosY;

        g_RingSprites[ SpriteCount ].GetPosition( &PosX, &PosY );
        g_RingSprites[ SpriteCount ].GetVelocity( &VelX, &VelY );
```

```
        if( PosX > 639 - 128 )
              VelX = -VelX;

        if( PosY > 479 - 128 )
              VelY = -VelY;

        if( PosX < 0 )
              VelX = -VelX;

        if( PosY < 0 )
              VelY = -VelY;

        g_RingSprites[ SpriteCount ].SetVelocity( VelX, VelY );

        g_RingSprites[ SpriteCount ].Update();

        g_RingSprites[ SpriteCount ].Render( g_pBackSurface );
}
```

And finally, it is important to release the ring surface at the end of the program. Since the surface is not part of the CSprite class it is not automatically released when the program exits. To do this, all you have to do is add the following code to game shutdown:

```
if( g_pRingSurface )
{
        g_pRingSurface->Release();
        g_pRingSurface = 0;
}
```

The preceding code will produce what you see in Figure 9.16.

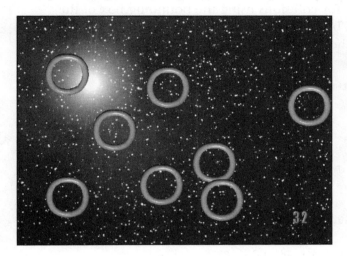

Figure 9.16

Multiple moving, animated sprites

Advanced Sprite Topics

I want to take a minute to give you an overview about some other sprite topics. The 2D coverage in this book is aimed at eventually bringing you up to being a competent Direct3D programmer, and so with that in mind I am skipping over some topics that are generally restricted to straight 2D games. For instance, automatic background recovery, in which the sprite automatically restores the back surface to the state it was in before the sprite was drawn, will not be covered. This is fine though, because in 3D the entire back surface is redrawn every frame anyway. If you want some more coverage of this particular topic, then check out *Tricks of the Windows Game Programming Gurus* by André LaMothe, which is a good source of information for 2D graphics

2D Collision Detection

2D collision detection is another topic that is generally restricted to straight 2D games, although I can think of a few 3D situations in which it might come in useful. So with that in mind, I have included some *really* basic collision detection code in the CSprite class. There are two functions that look after collision detection, GetBounds() and CheckForCollisionWith(). GetBounds() is shown here:

```
void CSprite::GetBounds( RECT* pRect )
{
        SetRect( pRect, m_x, m_y, m_SpriteWidth + m_x, m_SpriteHeight + m_y );
}
```

The code simply fills in a rectangle structure with the bounding box of the sprite. You generally only want to check for collisions using the bounding box of the sprite, rather than pixel-by-pixel, because doing otherwise would be way too slow. The function that actually does the collision detection, CheckForCollisionWith(), is shown in the code that follows:

```
BOOL CSprite::CheckForCollisionWith( CSprite* pOtherSprite )
{
        if( !pOtherSprite )
                return 0;

        RECT ThisRect, OtherRect, TempRect;

        GetBounds( &ThisRect );
        pOtherSprite->GetBounds( &OtherRect );

        if( IntersectRect( &TempRect, &ThisRect, &OtherRect ) )
                return TRUE;
        else
                return FALSE;
}
```

The function takes a pointer to another sprite as a parameter, which is to be compared with this sprite. The bounding rectangles of the two sprites are acquired, and then I used the Win32 IntersectRect() function, which takes the three parameters, to determine if a collision has taken place. The first is a rectangle to be filled with the overlap of the two rectangles, and the other two take the two rectangles that you actually want to compare. If the rectangles do overlap, then IntersectRect() will return TRUE, or FALSE otherwise. The result of the IntersectRect() function is returned to the calling point.

Advanced Inherited Sprites

When you develop your engine further you may start to develop advanced sprites with detailed behavioral patterns. Your best bet to implement this is to inherit new classes from the generic CSprite class. Then you can put in your specialized movement and reaction code into an overridden Update() function, for example. However, like I was saying before, the main thrust of the book is 3D, so I will go into more detail on topics like advanced object movement when we get to the 3D chapters.

Getting Down with Layers

You now have just about enough of a code base to create a really slick 2D game. Well, as long as the game fits within the monitor like *Zong*. But don't really cool games give you the feeling that you are exploring new worlds, and that you are immersed (I hate that word) in something much bigger than a 640 x 480 screen? Of course they do. Think of quality 2D games like *Red Alert* from the Command and Conquer series. You can scroll the map around for what seems like miles.

And what about old favorites like *Mario 3* or *Sonic*? Isn't it great how sometimes the character seems to be behind foreground scenery—like bushes—that scrolls by? Well, all of this functionality can be encapsulated into what you can think of as a layer. A *layer* is simply a bitmap that scrolls and wraps across the screen. *Scrolling* means that the destination render start point of the bitmap moves around the screen. For instance, in one frame it could be at (10, 0), and the next frame it would move across to (10, 1). *Wrapping* means that if the bitmap scrolls so that part of it goes past the extents of the screen, the portion of the bitmap that is not visible is automatically copied to the other side of the screen so that it becomes visible. So if you use a wrap and scroll bitmap that has no visible joints between the boundaries of the image, then you get a really cool effect that you can use to create amazing star fields, snowstorms, foreground scenery—the list goes on and on.

For this code I am placing a few restrictions on the bitmaps that you can use as layers.

- If the layer is moving horizontally, then it has to be the same width as the back buffer, which is 640 for this code.
- If the layer is moving vertically, then it has to be the same height as the back buffer, which is 480 for this code.
- If the layer is moving both horizontally and vertically, also known as diagonally, then it must be the same size as the back buffer (i.e., 640 x 480).
- The source bitmap cannot be larger than the back buffer. So the maximum size is 640 x 480.

Not too bad. Now before you take a look at the code, let me show you a couple of examples of layers, to get you excited. Check out Figures 9.17 and 9.18. Actually, since the examples are animated and the publisher wouldn't pay for an LCD screen on every page, you should run the examples off the CD to see the full effect.

Figure 9.17

Using layers to emulate a star field

That may not look totally cool now, but run it and you will see the effect! Please run it, pleeeeease. It just looks rad, dude.

Figure 9.18

Layering a mountain scene (over space? It really is that late!)

Implementing Layers

Layers are very similar to sprites in that they have a source bitmap to render as the layer, a position, and a velocity. In fact, the main difference is that a layer has no collision detection because it rarely interacts with the characters; layers are just eye candy. The rendering code for layers is much more complex. So let's look at the code.

All of the layer functionality will be encapsulated by the CLayer class. You can have as many layers as you want, but don't forget that each 32-bit 640 x 480 layer takes up 1.2MB, so they do put a big drain on performance. At 30 frames per second that means 36MB per second must be transferred across the bus.

Here is the CLayer class definition:

```
class CLayer
{
public:
        CLayer();
        ~CLayer();

// Functions
public:
        void SetColorKey( D3DCOLOR ColorKey );
        D3DCOLOR GetColorKey(){ return m_ColorKey; }

        void SetVelocity( int vx, int vy )
                        { m_VelocityX = vx; m_VelocityY = vy; }
        void GetVelocity( int* pvx, int* pvy )
                        { *pvx = m_VelocityX; *pvx = m_VelocityY; }

        void SetPosition( int x, int y ){ m_x = x; m_y = y; }
        void GetPosition( int* px, int* py){ *px = m_x, *py = m_y; }

        void Update();

        HRESULT Initialize( char* strPathName, BOOL bTransparent );

        HRESULT Render( LPDIRECT3DSURFACE8 pTargetSurface );

        void Shutdown();
```

```
// Variables
protected:
        LPDIRECT3DSURFACE8 m_pLayerSurface;    // The layer source surface

        BOOL m_bTransparent;            // Is the layer transparent
        D3DCOLOR m_ColorKey;            // The color key

        int m_x, m_y;                           // The position
        int m_VelocityX;                        // The x-velocity
        int m_VelocityY;                        // The y-velocity

        int m_SurfaceWidth;                     // The width of the surface
        int m_SurfaceHeight;            // The height of the surface

        // The movement direction for the layer
        enum MOVEMENT{ None, Horizontal, Vertical, Both }m_MoveDirection;

};
```

The class is pretty much the same as the CSprite definition, so I won't spend too long explaining everything. I will explain all the member variables as I go through the functions.

First up is the constructor, which as usual just sets all the member variables to 0:

```
CLayer::CLayer()
{
        m_pLayerSurface = 0;
        m_bTransparent = TRUE;
        m_ColorKey = D3DCOLOR_ARGB( 0, 255, 0, 255 );

        m_x = m_y = 0;
        m_VelocityX = 0;
        m_VelocityY = 0;

        m_SurfaceWidth = 0;
        m_SurfaceHeight = 0;

        m_MoveDirection = None;
}
```

And the destructor simply releases the associated surface:

```
CLayer::~CLayer()
{
        if( m_pLayerSurface )
        {
                m_pLayerSurface->Release();
                m_pLayerSurface = 0;
        }
}
```

Layer Initialization

Straight after you create a CLayer object you will want to call Initialize(), just like with the CSprite class.

```
HRESULT CLayer::Initialize( char* strPathName, BOOL bTransparent )
{
        if( m_pLayerSurface )
        {
                m_pLayerSurface->Release();
                m_pLayerSurface = 0;
        }

        HRESULT r = 0;

        r = LoadBitmapToSurface( strPathName, &m_pLayerSurface, g_pDevice );
        if( FAILED( r ) )
                return E_FAIL;

        m_bTransparent = bTransparent;

        D3DSURFACE_DESC d3dsd;

        m_pLayerSurface->GetDesc( &d3dsd );

        m_SurfaceWidth = d3dsd.Width;
        m_SurfaceHeight = d3dsd.Height;

        return S_OK;
}
```

Initialize() takes a path to a surface that you want to use for the layer, and a flag specifying whether you want transparency. Rendering uses hardware acceleration if you do not ask for transparency, and as a result can be faster, depending on the setup of your system. You may have noticed in the constructor that the default color key is set to bright pink, or ARGB(0, 255, 0, 255).

The function starts by checking if a bitmap has already been loaded, and if so, it releases it. Then the LoadBitmapToSurface() function that I showed you in the last chapter is used to load the bitmap from the disk into memory. Finally, I update the member variables that look after the transparency and surface dimensions. And that's all there is to initializing a layer!

Layer Rendering

Next I need to show you the actual code to render the layer, which is pretty long, but not nearly as complicated as it looks if you know the theory. I have put comments in to break the code into sections, which correspond to sections of the explanation after the code.

```
HRESULT CLayer::Render( LPDIRECT3DSURFACE8 pTargetSurface )
{

// --------- SECTION 1

// If there is no target surface then return failure
    if( !pTargetSurface )
        return E_FAIL;

    // Holds information about the target surface
    D3DSURFACE_DESC d3dsd;

    // Get information about the target surface
    pTargetSurface->GetDesc( &d3dsd );

    // Create local copies of the layer position for modification
    int OffsetX = m_x;
    int OffsetY = m_y;

    // If the layer's position is less than 0 then rendering
    // will fail.  It turns out that moving the layer forward
    // by the surface width + the negative offset creates
```

```
// the same effect.  So (-10,-10) changes to (630,470)
        if( OffsetX < 0 )
        {
                OffsetX = d3dsd.Width + m_x;
        }
        if( OffsetY < 0 )
        {
                OffsetY = m_SurfaceHeight + OffsetY;
        }


        // Figure out which way the layer is moving
        switch( m_MoveDirection )
        {

// --------- SECTION 2

                case None:
                {
                        // The layer is not moving so just straight copy it
                        CopySurfaceToSurface( 0, m_pLayerSurface, 0,
                                        pTargetSurface, m_bTransparent, m_ColorKey );
                        return S_OK;

                }

// --------- SECTION 3

                case Horizontal:
                {
                        // The layer is moving horizontally so it needs to
                        // be split into two different regions;
                        // left and right
                        RECT RectL, RectR;

                        // The right rectangle starts at the offset
                        POINT DestPointR = { OffsetX, OffsetY };
                        // The left rectangle starts at the origin
                        POINT DestPointL = { 0, OffsetY };

                        // Fill in the source dimensions for the right
                        // rectangle
                        SetRect( &RectR, 0, 0,
```

```
                m_SurfaceWidth - OffsetX, m_SurfaceHeight );

                        // Fill in the source dimensions for the left
                        // rectangle
                        SetRect( &RectL, m_SurfaceWidth - OffsetX, 0,
                                OffsetX, m_SurfaceHeight );

                        // Copy the left rectangle to the destination surface
                        CopySurfaceToSurface( &RectL, m_pLayerSurface, &DestPointL,
                                        pTargetSurface, m_bTransparent, m_ColorKey );
                        // Copy the right rectangle to the destination surface
                        CopySurfaceToSurface( &RectR, m_pLayerSurface, &DestPointR,
                                        pTargetSurface, m_bTransparent, m_ColorKey );

                return S_OK;
                }

// --------- SECTION 4

                case Vertical:
                {
                        // The layer is moving vertically so it
                        // needs to be split into 2 regions; top and bottom
                        RECT RectT, RectB;

                        // Fill in the destination for the top rectangle
                        POINT DestPointT = { OffsetX, 0 };
                        // Fill in the destination for the bottom rectangle
                        POINT DestPointB = { OffsetX, OffsetY };

                        // Fill in the source dimensions for the top rectangle
                        SetRect( &RectT, 0, m_SurfaceHeight - OffsetY,
                                        m_SurfaceWidth, OffsetY );

                        // Fill in the source dimensions for the bottom rectangle
                        SetRect( &RectB, 0, 0,
                                        m_SurfaceWidth, m_SurfaceHeight - OffsetY);

                        // Copy the top rectangle to the destination surface
                        CopySurfaceToSurface( &RectT, m_pLayerSurface, &DestPointT,
                                        pTargetSurface, m_bTransparent, m_ColorKey );
```

```
                // Copy the bottom rectangle to the destination surface
                          CopySurfaceToSurface( &RectB, m_pLayerSurface, &DestPointB,
                                    pTargetSurface, m_bTransparent, m_ColorKey );


                          return S_OK;
                }

// --------- SECTION 5

                case Both:
                {
                          // The layer is moving diagonally so
                          // it needs to be split into four regions
                          RECT Rect0, Rect1, Rect2, Rect3;

                          // Fill in the destination points for the four rectangles
                          POINT   DestPoint0 = { OffsetX, OffsetY },
                                  DestPoint1 = { OffsetX, 0 },
                                  DestPoint2 = { 0, OffsetY },
                                  DestPoint3 = { 0, 0 };

                          // Fill in the dimensions for the source rectangles
                          SetRect( &Rect0, 0, 0, m_SurfaceWidth - OffsetX,
                                                    m_SurfaceHeight - OffsetY );
                          SetRect( &Rect1, 0, m_SurfaceHeight - OffsetY,
                                                    m_SurfaceWidth - OffsetX, OffsetY );
                SetRect( &Rect2, m_SurfaceWidth - OffsetX, 0,
                                                    OffsetX, m_SurfaceHeight - OffsetY );
                          SetRect( &Rect3, m_SurfaceWidth - OffsetX,
                                         m_SurfaceHeight - OffsetY, OffsetX, OffsetY );

                          // Copy the rectangles to the destination surface
                          CopySurfaceToSurface( &Rect0, m_pLayerSurface, &DestPoint0,
                                         pTargetSurface, m_bTransparent, m_ColorKey );
                          CopySurfaceToSurface( &Rect1, m_pLayerSurface, &DestPoint1,
                                         pTargetSurface, m_bTransparent, m_ColorKey );
                          CopySurfaceToSurface( &Rect2, m_pLayerSurface, &DestPoint2,
                                         pTargetSurface, m_bTransparent, m_ColorKey );
                          CopySurfaceToSurface( &Rect3, m_pLayerSurface, &DestPoint3,
                                         pTargetSurface, m_bTransparent, m_ColorKey );
```

```
        return S_OK;

                }
        }

        return S_OK;
}
```

Section 1

`CLayer::Render()` starts off in the standard way with some error checking. If a target render surface, such as the back buffer, is not specified appropriately, then the function returns failure. Then the code moves on to get information such as the width and height of the target surface.

Then I make sure that the member variables that hold the position of the layer are not negative. If they are negative, then that means that drawing should start before (0, 0), which obviously just isn't physically possible, although I hear those crazy Russians are working on a machine to do this right now! But you can't just yank the coordinates back to (0, 0) because that would prevent you from creating a cool animation effect. So what do you do? As always, you cheat! With a bit of thought you may notice that a picture that is wrapped starting at (−10, −10) will look exactly the same as if it were starting at (630, 470). See the pattern? Exactly, Watson, just add the negative coordinate to the dimensions of the screen and you get the correct coordinate. Aha!

So if the starting coordinate happened to be (−12, −12), then

Negative X Coordinate + ScreenWidth = New X Coordinate

-12 + 640 = 628

Negative Y Coordinate + ScreenHeight = New Y Coordinate

-12 + 480 = 468

(628, 468) which is correct!

After that, the code moves on to decide which way the layer is moving. The movement variable is, in fact, figured out in the `Update()` function, which I will show you shortly.

Section 2—No Movement

This is the simplest and fastest case. If the layer is not moving, then you only need to copy it straight to the destination surface starting at (0, 0). After the copy operation, the function returns.

Section 3—Horizontal Movement

If the layer is moving horizontally, then you need to split the source surface into two rectangles, since if it starts at an x-coordinate greater than 0 there will be some of the image hanging off the end that needs to be wrapped around. (The coordinates may get a little confusing, so try and keep your head above the mud for the next few minutes.) So you split the source surface into two rectangles, left and right. When I say *left* and *right*, I mean in terms of the destination surface.

So the left rectangle needs to start at (0, OffsetY), or more simply, at the very left side of the screen. The y-offset is there in case the layer is smaller than the height of the surface and it was being drawn lower than the top of the screen. So that's the destination point covered. Now the left rectangle in fact takes its data from the *right* side of the source image, because of the wrapping idea. See Figure 9.19. Get it?

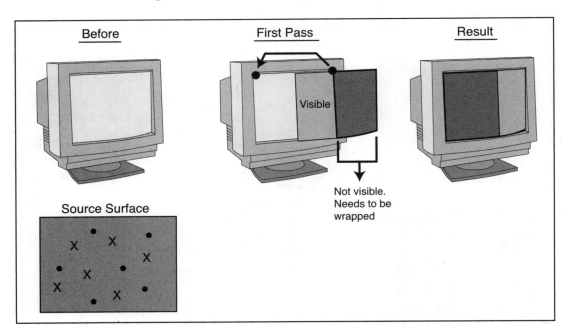

Figure 9.19

Rendering horizontal layer movement

The right side of the source is wrapped to the left side of the destination. Cool. So within the source image the rectangle needs to start at (Surface Width—x-offset) and extend down to (x-offset, Surface Height).

The right rectangle needs to start at (OffsetX, OffsetY) on the destination surface, which means that the left side starts at the left offset. Again, the y-offset is there in the case of a surface that is smaller than the height of the surface. Don't forget that the data for the right rectangle comes from the left side of the source surface. So it needs to start at (0, 0) and extend down to (Surface Width—x-offset, Surface Height).

Cool? Cool. So then the two rectangles are copied using the `CopySurfaceToSurface()` function that I showed you at the start of this chapter.

Section 4—Vertical Movement

Vertical movement is very similar to horizontal movement except that it is, uh...vertical. The process is the same. See Figure 9.20. You need to split the surface into two: a top rectangle, which takes its data from the bottom of the source surface, and a bottom rectangle, which takes its data from the top of the source surface.

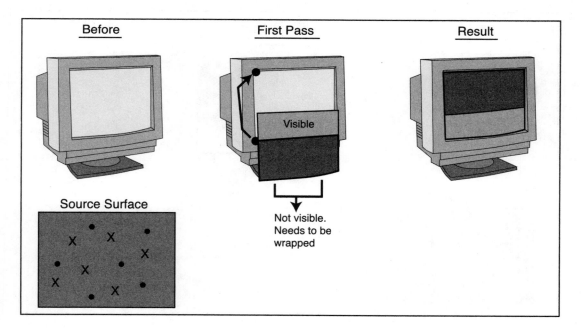

Figure 9.20

Rendering layers with vertical offsets

The top rectangle starts at (OffsetX, 0) on the destination, which is usually equal to (0, 0) unless the surface is thinner than the destination surface and it has a horizontal offset attached. In the source surface the top rectangle starts at (0, Surface Height—Y Offset) and extends down to (Surface Width, OffsetY).

The bottom rectangle has a destination point of (OffsetX, OffsetY). In the source image the rectangle starts at (0, 0) and extends to (Surface Width, Surface Height—Offset Y).

Again, after the rectangles are computed, you copy them from the layer surface to the destination surface using the CopySurfaceToSurface() function.

Section 5—Diagonal Movement

Diagonal movement is the most complex, because it actually requires four copy operations to fill the destination surface completely with the source layer. Hence, as you can see in the code, there are four rectangles to hold the source coordinates and four POINT structures to hold the destination coordinates.

Like the previous cases, the source rectangles are pretty much opposite their destination counterparts. For instance, looking at Figure 9.21, you can see that Rectangle 3 goes to Rectangle 1, and so on. As soon as all the rectangles and points are filled in, the layer sections are copied one by one to the destination surface.

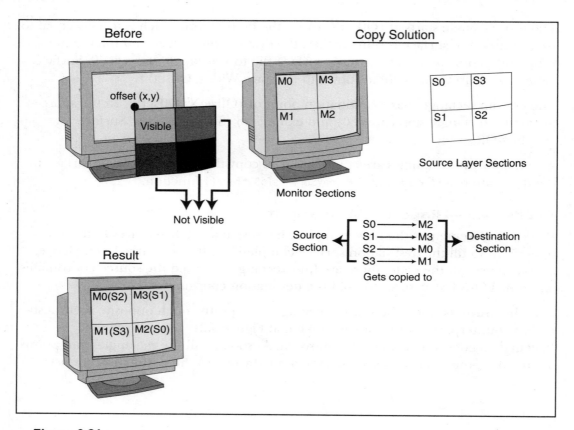

Figure 9.21

Rendering layers with horizontal and diagonal offsets

Layer Velocity and Position Updates

Cool, man. You are like totally almost through this layer stuff, so don't keel over and die just yet; the results are worth all the code! Okay, so just like sprites, layers can have a velocity too, which you can change using the GetVelocity() and SetVelocity() functions implemented in the class definition. You update the position of the layer by calling the Update() function on the layer every frame, which is shown in the code that follows:

```
void CLayer::Update()
{
        // Figure out the movement direction
        if( m_VelocityX != 0 && m_VelocityY == 0 )
```

```
m_MoveDirection = Horizontal;

        else if( m_VelocityY != 0 && m_VelocityX == 0 )
                m_MoveDirection = Vertical;

        else if( m_VelocityY != 0 && m_VelocityX != 0 )
                m_MoveDirection = Both;

        else if( m_VelocityY == 0 && m_VelocityX == 0 )
        {
                m_MoveDirection = None;
                return;
        }

        // Update the member variable that holds the position
        m_x += m_VelocityX;
        m_y += m_VelocityY;

        // Ensure overflows are dealt with
        if( m_x >= g_DeviceWidth )
                m_x = m_x - g_DeviceWidth;

        if( m_x <= -g_DeviceWidth )
                m_x = m_x + g_DeviceWidth;

        if( m_y >= g_DeviceHeight )
                m_y = m_y - g_DeviceHeight;

        if( m_y <= -g_DeviceHeight )
                m_y = m_y + g_DeviceHeight;
}
```

This is your standard function that figures out directions and ensures that coordinates are within acceptable bounds. One interesting thing to look out for in this function is the last block of code that checks for overflows. If the velocity causes the destination point to be positioned past the edge of the screen, then it needs to be reset back to the start of the frame. You could achieve this by setting the coordinates to (0, 0), but this could lead to jumping. For instance, if you have a velocity of 13 that is moving the position of the layer by 13 pixels each frame, it will eventually get to (637, 0). Now the next movement would cause the position to overflow 10 units to (650, 0). If you set the position back to zero, then the movements will go like this: 13->13->13->3->13->13, etc. See, the movement is only 3 as it resets to zero near the boundary.

So, to get by this, just add the difference that should be moved to the new offset. Instead of resetting the x-coordinate to zero, it would now be set to 10; in other words, the scrolling remains smooth. Slick or what, my friend? Slick or what?

And that is all there is to layers. They are a really effective way to add impressive effects to your game without requiring too much extra processing power. By the way, all the code for layers and other techniques I've shown you is located in the engine.h file on the CD. If you want to use any code in your own projects just include the engine.h file.

Conclusion

I want to break this chapter here because you have covered a lot of new concepts. I think you'll definitely agree that your code is starting to get advanced. Your synaptic matrix has had a lot of work absorbing theory, and getting a grip on foundation code. It was nice to able to use all that knowledge and build on it to create some of the advanced features you have looked at in this chapter, like advanced surface copying, sprites, layers, and a font engine.

In the next chapter I am going to show you how to develop a *Quake*-style console. Sounds cool, huh? It's harder than you think you know, and I bet you will never look at *Quake* in the same way again. With that thought causing synaptic lightning overflows, let's move further. . . further into the depths of creation.

CHAPTER 10

CALIFORNIA-
STYLE
CONSOLES

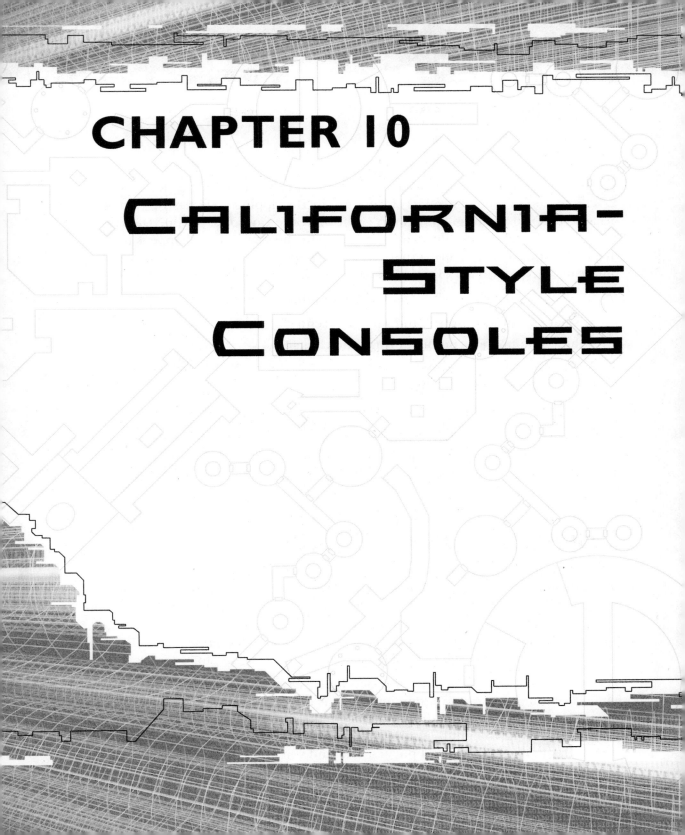

My first thought when I was about to write this chapter was, "Just what the heck am I going to call it?" I can't call it "Developing a *Quake*-style Console" because that's just boring. So I chose "California-Style Consoles." Get it? *Quake* the game...earthquakes...California? So sue me! (By the way, if there happens to be a major earthquake in California that turns this chapter opening into a sick, insulting, bad joke rather than a witty connection, then please accept my apologies.)

In this chapter you are going to get filled with information on

- what exactly a console is and why it is useful
- how to animate a console during state changes
- managing a list of console entries and rendering them at realistic offsets
- outputting text to the console
- parsing command input
- writing an external pluggable command parser

Don't worry about what all that means just yet—it is all implementation-dependent. So before going any further, let's talk about what a console exactly is and why it is useful.

Console Overview

For the purposes of this discussion, a *console* is a command window that you can access during the game. The command window can be used to report data and errors to the user as well as being a place where they can enter more complex commands to the game, such as changing game variables and so on. This kind of functionality could be included in a game that ships with a built-in editor that allows you to build your own levels or "mods" like *Quake* and *Half Life,* for example.

The console also offers you, the game developer, several advantages. While the game is running, you can program in functions that you can call from the console. These functions can be used during debugging or for more advanced development. One example might be during advanced development, when you want to mess with variables that control physics, etc., and you don't want to recompile after each modification to the system. Instead, you could just type something like "SET GRAVITY 100" into the console and immediately see the results.

Debugging full-screen games can be a complete nightmare, unless like me you happen to have two 19-inch monitors. So instead, you can get your console to output the value of particular problem variables and so on. You get the idea. They are just all-around cool. And most of the ideas that you learn from the development of a console can be used in other areas as well. I have designed this console to be pretty much 100 percent portable to your own code projects. As a result, some of the code is a little more involved than a straight implementation, but I hope that this may help seed a few ideas in your head as well.

What's so hard about creating a console, then? Well, nothing really—just the coordination of a bunch of stuff at the same time. A console usually has the following features:

- It is accessible from the game with a single key press, such as the F11 key.
- It is able to render itself on top of any graphics already rendered.
- It looks cool if it animates down when activated and scrolls back up when deactivated.
- It manages a list of previously-typed commands and other text output, scrolling them up when a new entry is placed in the console, and re-rendering the text when the console changes. It also needs to discard entries that no longer fit on the screen.
- It hijacks key commands from the game into its own key processing routines while it is active.
- If the user types something into the console, it is generally because he wants something to happen. As a result, each string needs to be parsed and compiled into a list of commands and associated parameters. These commands then need to be passed to an external command parsing and execution unit that is supplied by the game.

Implementing the Console

For the console I am going to be encapsulating the code into a C++ class again, because it is much easier to transfer C++ code between projects than straight C code. In fact, there are three classes. The first is the CCommand class, which holds commands and parameters that have been entered by the user and partly parsed by the console. The second class is CEntry, which basically holds and renders text from the user or computer. And finally, the CConsole class manages everything.

CConsole works by maintaining a list of CEntrys. The number of CEntrys is dependent on the number of text rows that can fit in the screen, which is dependent on the height of the currently selected alphabet font. The CEntry at the very bottom of the console is known as the *active entry* (see Figure 10.1). This is the entry that takes input from the keyboard if the console is active. Each character that the user presses is added to the entry until the user presses Enter. When the user hits the Return key, the currently-typed text is passed to a preparsing function that organizes the raw string into a command and a list of parameters, which are subsequently packaged into a CCommand object and sent to the external command parser, if one exists.

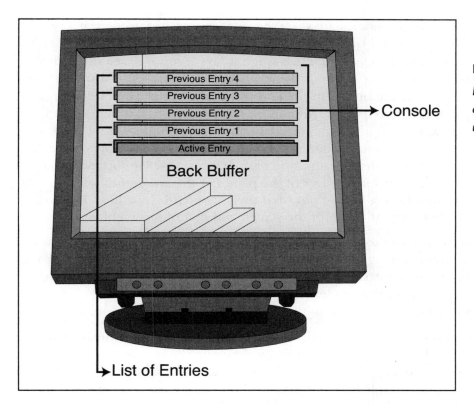

Figure 10.1

How the console uses entries

The commands that the user can type are in the form COMMAND PARAM1, PARAM2, PARAM*X*, and so on. Spaces or commas can separate the parameters. An example command would be as follows:

```
SetDisplayMode 640, 480
```

In this case, SetDisplayMode is the command, 640 is the first parameter, and 480 is the second parameter. It is then up to the external parser to decide what it wants to do with the command and parameters. If the command does not exist, then the parser returns failure and the text "— Unknown Command —" is output to the console.

Visibility of the console can be determined by any key, but in this case I have chosen the F11 key. I could have chosen the Tilde (~) key like in *Quake,* but this is a really bad choice. In the United States the Tilde key is generally in the upper-left corner of the keyboard, underneath the Esc key. However, in Europe this key is generally located just above the Right Shift key, cohabiting with the number, or pound, sign (#). So in the *Quake* manuals when it says "Press ~ to see the console," most people on the west side of the Atlantic get kind of confused (Europeans can be like that; trust me, I am one). On the keyboards, where the Tilde key is on U.S. keyboards, in Europe there is a key with a ` on it and an ¬ on it, which seems to be for those other Europeans who don't speak English yet. (You just wait, France— your day will come!) So be nice when you eventually release your first commercial game and make sure that the keys that you choose to use are supported in your major target sales regions *and* the rest of the planet, if the amount of sales can justify your effort in bothering to find out what their keyboards look like! The console's size is set by using the width of the screen and half of its height.

Rendering of the console to the back buffer is fairly easy. The console has its own surface that is independent of the back buffer. First, the console renders the background bitmap to the console surface. Then each text row renders itself to the surface. Finally, when the entire rendering is complete, the console surface is copied to the back surface and presented to the primary surface and the monitor.

If the console was previously disabled, and is just becoming active, then it is set to animate downward. This is achieved easily by changing the source rectangle during the copying of the console surface to the back surface. The same is true for when the console becomes disabled; the y-coordinate for the source rectangle is decremented each frame until it becomes invisible, at which point rendering stops.

The CEntry Class

So now that you know the theory, let's look at some code. Unfortunately, as always when showing you a class, I have to blast the entire definition at you first before talking about the code. I'm gonna show you the CEntry class first since the console relies heavily on its functionality. Here is the definition:

```
class CEntry
{
public:
        CEntry();       // The constructor
        ~CEntry();  // The destructor

// Variables:
protected:
```

```
        char* m_pstrText;        // The text buffer for this entry
        CEntry* m_pNext;         // Pointer to next entry( row )

        int m_VerticalPos;       // The y-position to render

// Functions:
public:
        // Returns the next entry(row)
        CEntry* GetNext(){ return m_pNext; }
        // Sets the next entry(row)
        void SetNext( CEntry* pNext ){ m_pNext = pNext; }
        // Draws the text using the GDI to the console surface
        int RenderText( int NumHorzChars, DWORD* pData, int DestPitch );
        // Adds a character to the text buffer
        int OnChar( char Key );
        // Returns the text in the buffer
        int GetText( char* pstrText, int Length );
        // Clears and then sets the text in the buffer
        int SetText( char* pstrText );
        // Returns the number of characters in the buffer
        int GetTextLength(){ return strlen( m_pstrText ); }
        // Sets the vertical position of this entry
        void SetVerticalPos( int Pos ){ m_VerticalPos = Pos; }
        // Returns the vertical position for this entry
        int  GetVerticalPos(){ return m_VerticalPos; }
};
```

The class contains only three member variables. The first is m_pstrText, which is a pointer to a string that contains the text for this entry to display. m_pNext is a pointer to another CEntry, and it is used to create a linked list of CEntrys for management by the CConsole object. And finally, m_VerticalPos contains the y-coordinate at which this entry should be rendered.

The y-coordinate is important since each entry, or row of text, needs to be moved up each time the console displays new data. In DOS—you know how when you type something and press Enter, all the rows of text move up a row? Well, that's how the entry works. When a new row of text is ready to be displayed, the console loops through each of the existing entries and increases its y-coordinate by the height of the current font (see Figure 10.2). Actually, to get technical, the y-coordinate is *decremented* since the text is moving *up* toward the top of the screen, so in other words, the y-coordinate of the row goes *down* to move the text *up*. Confusing, ain't it?

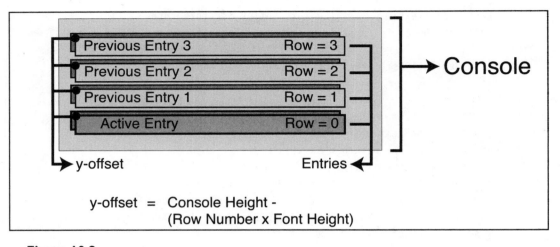

Figure 10.2
Computing the vertical offsets for the list of entries

Anyway, there are a few one-line functions implemented right in the definition, which I will run over for you. GetNext() and SetNext() are used for the implementation of the linked list. It is pretty standard stuff: SetNext() lets you set the pointer to the next CEntry in the list, and GetNext() retrieves the same pointer. SetVerticalPos() is used to set the y-coordinate at which the entry should be rendered, as I mentioned in the previous paragraph. GetVerticalPos() simply returns the position of the entry. GetTextLength() returns the length of the text in the string contained in the entry, in characters.

And that leaves four other functions to talk about, well, six if you include the constructor and destructor. The constructor is shown in the code that follows:

```
CEntry::CEntry()
{
        // Allocate memory for the buffer
        m_pstrText = new char[MAX_CHARSPERLINE];
        if( m_pstrText )
                ZeroMemory( m_pstrText, sizeof( char[MAX_CHARSPERLINE] ) );
        else
                m_pstrText = 0;

        // Zero out member variables
        m_pNext = 0;
        m_VerticalPos = 0;
}
```

This code does the usual zeroing out of the member variables. However, it also allocates space for the string in the member variable. Right now each row is set using the MAX_CHARSPERLINE identifier, which is equal to 256. In other words, each row takes up 256 bytes of memory. This could be considered a little excessive, and you could introduce a much more elegant dynamic memory allocation routine if you wanted to, but why complicate things? So with a 640 x 480 screen, about 14 rows are visible, which means the console takes up about 3.5KB of memory for strings, which is almost the same amount as a 32 x 32 pixel texture—in other words, not much at all.

Notice that I don't use the usual malloc() function to allocate memory for the strings. Instead, I use the more elegant C++ implementation of the new operator. To get rid of memory allocated with new, you use the delete operator rather than the usual free() function that you might use with C.

The destructor for CEntry is shown in the code that follows:

```
CEntry::~CEntry()
{
        // Delete the text buffer if it exists
        if( m_pstrText )
        {
                delete m_pstrText;
                m_pstrText = 0;
        }
}
```

The destructor uses the delete operator that I mentioned before to release any memory allocated by the string.

Adding Text to the Entry

Text is added to the console by hooking it up to the keyboard handlers in the WndProc() function. I'll show you how that works when I talk about the CConsole class. After the console takes the keyboard input, it passes it to the OnChar() function of the active entry. OnChar() has two options: it can either add the current character to the string buffer or it can remove the previous character if the new character is the Backspace key. Simple? Good. The code to do this is shown in the following:

```
int CEntry::OnChar( char Key )
{
        // Check if the backspace key was pressed
```

```
if( Key == '\b' )
        {
                // Make a temporary string holder
                char pstrTemp[MAX_CHARSPERLINE];
                // Get the length of the buffer
                int Length = strlen( m_pstrText );

                // If the buffer is empty then return
                if( Length == 0 )
                        return S_OK;

                // Reduce the length of the string by one
                Length--;

                // Copy the string(-1) to the temp string
                CopyMemory( pstrTemp, m_pstrText, Length );
                // Zero out the buffer
                ZeroMemory( m_pstrText, sizeof( char[MAX_CHARSPERLINE] ) );
                // Copy the text back into the buffer
                CopyMemory( m_pstrText, pstrTemp, Length );
        }
        else // A normal key was pressed
        {
                // Make sure the buffer has not overflowed
                if( strlen( m_pstrText ) > MAX_CHARSPERLINE )
                        return E_FAIL;

                // Append the text buffer with the character
                strncat( m_pstrText, &Key, 1 );
        }

        return S_OK;
}
```

A lot of the functions involved in the creation of a console are string manipulation functions. These were programmed way back in the last era of programmingm when people believed that itsy-bitsy, confusing function names increased productivity. I will run over these in case you have not seen them before.

This function starts by checking if the key is the Backspace key. If it is, then a new temporary string is created to hold the current string. The original string is zeroed out, and the temporary string is copied back to the original string, minus one character. This is not the optimal way to do this, but it is quite clear.

The `strlen()` function is used to get the length of a string. It stands for "string length" and could have been called StringLength(), but that would just be silly, wouldn't it? All you do is call it, passing a string as the parameter, and it returns the length of the string to you in bytes. It is very useful, so keep it in mind (if you forget about it, turn back to this page and read this sentence).

If the key pressed is just a normal alphanumeric character, then it is just added to the string buffer using the `strncat()` function. This stands for "strangle cat." Uhhmmm...I mean, I'm not actually sure what it stands for. It might be "string concatenate." Anyway, just smile and nod and be happy in the knowledge that `strncat()` will add a character to the end of a string for you. Notice that I make sure that the buffer actually has room for more text before I add it. You don't want to be overflowing into Windows critical code, that's for sure.

Replacing and Editing Text

Sometimes you will want to actually just set the entire contents of the text buffer using a string. For instance, if you were using the console to output debug messages and a function wants to output "Hello? Creator? Are you out there? I don't feel very well," you don't want your poor function to have to type that letter by letter—it could be dead by the time it reaches the screen. So in the `CConsole` class there just happens to be a function called `CConsole::OutputString()`. This function is really just a cover function that calls `CEntry::SetText()` within the active entry. `SetText()` is shown in the code that follows:

```
int CEntry::SetText( char* pstrText )
{
        // Clear out any text that is already there
        ZeroMemory( m_pstrText, sizeof( char[MAX_CHARSPERLINE] ) );

        // Make sure the supplied text doesn't overrun our buffer
        int Length = strlen( pstrText );
        if( Length > MAX_CHARSPERLINE )
                Length = MAX_CHARSPERLINE;

        // Copy the supplied text into our buffer
        CopyMemory( m_pstrText, pstrText, strlen( pstrText ) );
```

```
        return S_OK;
}
```

It is quite a simple function; its only parameter is a pointer to the string that you want to set the text to. The function starts by wiping out any other data that may be in the buffer already. Then the code checks to make sure the new string is short enough to fit in the buffer. Finally, the text is copied over and the function returns.

I have also coded a short function called GetText(). This is called whenever the user presses Enter and the string in the entry needs to be moved for parsing into commands and parameters. GetText() is shown in the code that follows:

```
int CEntry::GetText( char* pstrText, int Length )
{
        // Make sure the length doesn't overrun our buffer
        if( Length > MAX_CHARSPERLINE )
                Length = MAX_CHARSPERLINE;

        // Copy the string
        CopyMemory( pstrText, m_pstrText, Length );

        return S_OK;
}
```

That's so simple it makes me want to talk about something more complex. GetText() takes a pointer to a string that you want to copy the string into, and also the length of the destination string so that you can be sure that the string is capable of receiving the source string. If it's not big enough, then only as much data as will fit is copied.

Rendering Text

Remember when I was talking in general terms about how the console rendering works? First the background for the console is drawn, which erases the previous version of the console, and then each of the rows of text is rendered in a loop. Well, the code to render the row of text in an entry is this:

```
int CEntry::RenderText( int NumHorzChars, DWORD* pData, int DestPitch )
{
        // Only draw the number of characters that fit on the screen
        int Length = strlen( m_pstrText );
        if( Length > NumHorzChars )
```

```
        Length = NumHorzChars;

    PrintString( 10, m_VerticalPos, m_pstrText, TRUE,
                    D3DCOLOR_ARGB( 0, 255, 0, 255 ), pData, DestPitch );

    return S_OK;
}
```

This function takes as parameters the maximum number of characters that can fit in a line, a pointer to the start of the destination surface (which must be locked), and also the pitch of the destination surface. The code starts by limiting the number of characters displayed to the amount that was specified would fit on the screen in the NumHorzChars formal parameter. Then the string is rendered using the PrintString() function developed in Chapter 9. I'm pretty sure that is the only dependency of the console code. Remember when I said that it was almost 100 percent portable code? Well, it uses my PrintString() function here, so if you decide to use this code in one of your own projects, then just stick in your own text rendering function there instead.

You now know how CEntry, the workhorse of the console, works, so let's move things up a gear and check out CConsole, the management function.

Getting Down with CConsole

I have talked a lot about CConsole in general, but let's get down and dirty and look at the internals of this beast. You know that CConsole looks after CEntrys, but what else does it have to do? Well, it is also required to manage the visibility of the console, massage keyboard input into appropriate forms, preparse strings into CCommand objects (which I'll show you soon), and pass CCommand objects to the external parser. Before I go on let's look at the class definition. It may be ugly, but it is stable, intuitive, and a really great conversationalist!

```
class CConsole
{
public:
        CConsole();
        ~CConsole();

// Functions:
public:
```

```cpp
        void Shutdown();
        HRESULT Initialize( LPDIRECT3DDEVICE8 pDevice, LPDIRECT3DSURFACE8
pTargetSurface );
        void Render();

        BOOL GetVisibility(){ return m_bVisible; }
        void SetVisibility( BOOL bVisible )
        {
                // The render code will figure out when the console
                // is not visible.
                m_bVisible = TRUE;

                // If bVisible is true then the console must be invisible
                // and about to animate down.  Otherwise it will be
                // animating up.
                m_Animation = bVisible ? Down : Up;

        }

        void OutputString( char* pString );
        void Clear();
        int OnChar( char Key );
        int OnKeyDown( WPARAM wParam );

        void SetParserCallback( CONSOLE_PARSER_CALLBACK pfnCallback );
        void PreParse( char* pstrText, CCommand* pCommand );

protected:
        void RotateEntries();


        // Variables:
protected:
        BOOL m_bInitialized;    // Has the console been initialized?

        int m_Width;    // The width of the console surface
        int m_Height;   // The height of the console surface

        LPDIRECT3DSURFACE8 m_pConsoleSurface; // Pointer to the console surface
        // Pointer to the background bitmap surface
        LPDIRECT3DSURFACE8 m_pConsoleBackgroundSurf;
```

```
// Pointer to the target render surface( eg back buffer )
        LPDIRECT3DSURFACE8 m_pTargetSurface;
        LPDIRECT3DDEVICE8 m_pDevice;    // Pointer to the device

        BOOL m_bVisible;            // Is the console visible?

        // The current state of the console
        enum ANIM{ Up, Down, None }m_Animation;

        CEntry* m_pActiveEntry;          // The active entry (accepts key input)
        CEntry* m_pEntryList;  // The list of old entries

        // Pointer to an external console parser
        CONSOLE_PARSER_CALLBACK m_pfnCallback;
        // Is there an external parser?
        BOOL m_bParserCallback;

};
```

Stop cringing! It will all make sense in two ticks of an iMac processor. (On second thought, you could be here for a long time!)

Let's look at the member variables first. The console looks after three surfaces. m_pConsoleSurface is the surface that the console renders to before it is copied to the back buffer. This surface is equal to the width of the destination surface and half of its height. m_pConsoleBackgroundSurface is the surface that holds the background bitmap for the console. I have created a simple 640 x 240 bitmap for my console, and you can see it in Figure 10.4. Kinda slick looking, isn't it? I love Photoshop! You should see it in color.

Figure 10.4

The background for the console

The final surface isn't really a new surface, but a local copy of a pointer to the destination surface, which is usually the back buffer. Since the target surface for the console is unlikely to ever change, I keep a local copy of it. I'll discuss this more when I show you the CConsole::Initialize() function. You may also notice that I keep a local copy of the device in m_pDevice. This is to increase portability; I could just refer to g_pDevice in every function, but that would mean that you would have to have a global g_pDevice sitting around in your code somewhere, which may not be the case.

The m_bInitialized variable is a simple Boolean value that indicates whether the CConsole::Initialize() function has been called yet. It can be used in functions where it is critical that the console has been initialized before they are called—rendering, for example. m_bVisible is another Boolean value that flags whether the console is visible. If it is not, then the Render() function exits as soon as it is called.

m_Width and m_Height hold the dimensions of the console surface. For a 640 x 480 screen, the console would be 640 x 240 in size. m_Animation is kind of interesting; it holds the current animation state of the console. You can see that the possible states for this enumeration are Up, Down, or None.

NOTE

If you have not come across enumerations before, then they may seem kind of confusing. An *enumeration* is a data type that will accept values that are not really strings or numbers but allow you to have more readable code. An enumerated variable is basically a variable where you set the values to which it can be equal.

For instance, you may have an enumeration called Week that can be set to Monday, Tuesday, and so on. If you try to set the value to anything except a weekday, you get a compile error. You declare enumerations like this:

```
enum Tag{ Value1, Value2, ValueX... } Variable Name;
```

To declare the Week enumeration that I was talking about before, you would write:

```
enum WEEK{ Mon, Tues, Wed, Thurs, Fri, Sat, Sun } WeekDay;

WeekDay = Monday;

if( SomeTestCase )
        WeekDay = Tuesday;
```

If WeekDay were set to Monday and you wrote:

```
WeekDay++;
```

then WeekDay would now be set to Tuesday. This is because internally, the compiler represents each value as a number, so Monday = 0, Tuesday = 1, and so on.

If you wrote:

```
WeekDay = PetersDayOff;
```

then the compiler would generate an error because (1) PetersDayOff was not specified as a possible value for WeekDay in the declaration of the enumeration and (2) I never get a day off!

Back to the drawing board. m_pEntryList and m_pActiveEntry are pretty interesting variables, and they will turn up a bunch of times throughout the chapter. m_pEntryList contains the address of the first CEntry in the list of entries. m_pActiveEntry contains a pointer to the currently active entry. As I mentioned before, this is the entry that will be given keyboard input.

The final two members are m_pfnCallback, which holds a pointer to the external command parsing function, and m_bParserCallback, which flags whether a parsing function has been specified. More on this later.

The constructor for the console is your standard one that just sets all the member variables to zero.

```
CConsole::CConsole()
{
        m_pConsoleSurface = 0;
        m_pConsoleBackgroundSurf = 0;
        m_pTargetSurface = 0;

        m_Width = 0;
        m_Height = 0;

        m_bInitialized = FALSE;
        m_bVisible = FALSE;

        m_Animation = None;

        m_pActiveEntry = 0;
        m_pEntryList = 0;

        m_pfnCallback = 0;
        m_bParserCallback = FALSE;
}
```

Nothing too complex there. The destructor also does the usual resource deallocation:

```
CConsole::~CConsole()
{
        // Release the console surface
        if( m_pConsoleSurface )
        {
                m_pConsoleSurface->Release();
                m_pConsoleSurface = 0;
        }

        // Release the background bitmap surface
        if( m_pConsoleBackgroundSurf )
```

```
        {
                m_pConsoleBackgroundSurf->Release();
                m_pConsoleBackgroundSurf = 0;
        }

        // Release the target surface
        if( m_pTargetSurface )
        {
                m_pTargetSurface->Release();
                m_pTargetSurface = 0;
        }

        // Destroy all of the entries
        CEntry* pEntry = m_pEntryList;
        CEntry* pTemp = 0;

        if( !pEntry )
                return;

        // Loop for each entry
        while( pEntry->GetNext() )
        {
                // Copy the next entry into a temp pointer
                pTemp = pEntry->GetNext();
                // Delete the current pointer
                delete pEntry;
                // Set the current pointer to the next pointer
                pEntry = pTemp;
        }
}
```

Notice the loop to destroy all the CEntrys in the list. I get a temporary pointer to the
first entry and then loop through each subsequent entry in the list, destroying
them as I go. It is really important to always deallocate any resources so that you
avoid memory leaks, which in some situations can be a total pain to track down.
Remember what Zip Wong, a famous 18th-century Direct3D Zen guru, once said:
"Prevention is better than cure." Although there are those who say he was talking
about something I can't mention in such a family-friendly book.

Console Initialization

This is the third major grouping of code I have shown you that has been encapsulated by a class (after sprites and layers), and you may be starting to notice a pattern to how I develop them. I try to develop my classes so that they will integrate well into the rest of the game structure. For instance, I always include an Initialize() function that can be called from GameInit(), a Shutdown() function that can be called from GameShutdown(), and if applicable, some sort of Update() and Render() function that can be called from the GameLoop().

And that is where I will start showing the main implementation code for the console. CConsole::Initialize() is shown in the code that follows:

```
HRESULT CConsole::Initialize( LPDIRECT3DDEVICE8 pDevice,
                              LPDIRECT3DSURFACE8 pTargetSurface )
{
        // Make sure a valid device was specified
        if( !pDevice )
                return E_FAIL;

        // Make sure a valid target surface was specified
        if( !pTargetSurface )
                return E_FAIL;

        HRESULT r = 0;

        // Keep a local pointer of the device
        m_pDevice = pDevice;

        // Keep a local copy of the target surface
        m_pTargetSurface = pTargetSurface;
        m_pTargetSurface->AddRef();

        // Holds information about the target surface
        D3DSURFACE_DESC d3dsd;
        // Get information about the target surface
        m_pTargetSurface->GetDesc( &d3dsd );

        // Set the dimensions of the console the width and 1/2 the height of the target
        m_Width = d3dsd.Width;
```

```cpp
m_Height = d3dsd.Height / 2;

// Create a surface for the console
r = m_pDevice->CreateImageSurface( m_Width, m_Height,
                        D3DFMT_X8R8G8B8, &m_pConsoleSurface );
if( FAILED( r ) )
{
        SetError( "Unable to create image surface for console" );
        Shutdown();
        return E_FAIL;
}


// Load the background bitmap for the console
r = LoadBitmapToSurface( "Console Background.bmp",
                        &m_pConsoleBackgroundSurf, m_pDevice );
if( FAILED( r ) )
{
        SetError( "Unable to load console background image" );
        Shutdown();
        return E_FAIL;
}


m_pEntryList = new CEntry;              // Start the list with a new entry
CEntry* pEntry = m_pEntryList;          // Get a temp pointer to the new entry
m_pActiveEntry = m_pEntryList;          // Set the active entry to start of list

// Compute the number of visible rows of text
int VisibleRows = m_Height / g_AlphabetLetterHeight;

// Loop for each possible visible row of text
for( int i = 1 ; i < VisibleRows ; i++ )
{
        // Create a new entry
        pEntry->SetNext( new CEntry );
        // Set its vertical position to above the previous row
        pEntry->SetVerticalPos( (m_Height-5) -
                                (i * g_AlphabetLetterHeight) );
        // Get a pointer to the new entry
        pEntry = pEntry->GetNext();
}
```

```
        // Set the initialized flag to TRUE
        m_bInitialized = TRUE;

        return S_OK;
}
```

There is a lot going on in there, but if you look at it line by line, you'll realize that you have seen all this code a bunch of times before, except for the last part that deals with the creation of the entries. One thing to note is that this function, as it is currently implemented, will use as a backdrop a bitmap file that has a file name of Console Background.bmp, which is located in the root directory of the game.

Now notice how the list of entries is created. First, a new entry is dynamically created, using the new operator, for the start of the list. This pointer is then copied to be the same for the first active entry. Then the number of visible rows is worked out by dividing the height of the console surface by the height of a character in the alphabet font. Once that is computed, it is simply a case of looping for each row of visible text and creating a new entry for it. During the creation of the entries I set the height of each row by multiplying the height of the font by the number of times the loop has been executed, which luckily enough for you and me is the correct height. I subtract the height of the console surface (– 5) so that the text doesn't go right to the bottom of the console—instead, a 5-pixel gap is left; this is more aesthetically pleasing. (I can't believe I just used that phrase.)

I almost forgot! Check out the line of code that is bolded near the top. Here it is again:

```
m_pTargetSurface = pTargetSurface;
m_pTargetSurface->AddRef();
```

Notice how I increase the reference count of the target surface after I create a new copy of the pointer to it. This way there is no chance that the surface will accidentally disappear from memory if it is released from elsewhere. However, this also makes it very important that you call Release() in the destructor, as I have done. Otherwise there is the potential that you'll cause a memory leak.

Entry Management

Now I need to show you how to manage all the CEntrys that the console is looking after. I talked about what needs to happen in theory before, but let's just nail down what you will want to achieve.

1. When you add a new line of text to the console, you need to move the previous rows further up in the console, hence you need to modify all the y-coordinates for the entries.

2. The console that was previously at the top will no longer be visible, so you need to release it from memory.

3. You need to move the previous active entry up; it will cease to be the active entry.

4. You need to create a new active entry for the bottom of the console to retrieve new text input.

That may sound kind of complicated, but it can all be programmed into a single, fairly short function, which I have entitled CConsole::RotateEntries() and which is shown in the code that follows:

```
void CConsole::RotateEntries()
{
        // Get a pointer to the first entry
        CEntry* pEntry = m_pEntryList;
        // A temporary entry pointer
        CEntry* pTempEntry = 0;
        // A pointer to the new entry
        CEntry* pNewEntry = 0;

        // Loop for each entry to increase the y-coordinates
        while( pEntry->GetNext() )
        {
                // Set the temp entry to the current entry
                pTempEntry = pEntry;
                // Increase the vertical position of the current entry
                pEntry->SetVerticalPos( pEntry->GetVerticalPos() -
                                                g_AlphabetLetterHeight );
                // Set the current entry to the next entry
                pEntry = pEntry->GetNext();
        }
```

```
        // The pEntry variable now points to the last
        // entry in the list and pTempEntry to the 2nd last.

        // Delete the last entry in the list
        delete pEntry;
        // Get a pointer to the new last entry
        pEntry = pTempEntry;
        // Set the new last entry's pNext pointer to zero
        pEntry->SetNext( NULL );

        // Create a new entry for the top of the list
        pNewEntry = new CEntry;

        // Set new entry's pNext variable to previous first entry
        pNewEntry->SetNext( m_pEntryList );
        // Set the start of the Entry list to the new entry
        m_pEntryList = pNewEntry;

        // Set the active entry to the new entry
        m_pActiveEntry = pNewEntry;
        // Set the vertical position of the new entry to the bottom
        // of the console
        m_pActiveEntry->SetVerticalPos( (m_Height-5) - g_AlphabetLetterHeight );

}
```

The function takes no parameters and has protected access because there is no
need for it to be accessed externally. The first loop in the function contains the
code to modify the vertical coordinates for each entry. As you can see, all it does is
decrement the previous position by the height of a letter. Don't forget that to move
a row up, you decrease the y-coordinate. It may seem confusing at first, but you'll
get the hang of it after a few nanoseconds.

After that loop is complete, the variable pEntry points to the last entry in the list,
which is no longer visible, and as such it is sent to that little place in the sky for
dead CEntrys. Finally, a new CEntry is created and added to the bottom of the list,
which is also set to be the new active entry. Is that slick, slick? Damn straight
it is, Homes.

Outputting Strings to the Console

Because of the design of this console, it is really simple to output a string. It only requires a single call to CConsole::OutputString(). Remember I mentioned this briefly before when I was showing you the CEntry::SetText() function? Anyway, here is the code:

```
void CConsole::OutputString( char* pString )
{
        // Move the entries up
        RotateEntries();

        // Set the new active entry to the specified string
        m_pActiveEntry->SetText( pString );
}
```

You just can't get simpler than that now, can you? To output a string you just rotate the entries up, and then set the text of the new active entry to the specified string.

Clearing the Console

I haven't really come up with a reason to do this yet, but sometime you may need to clear the console of all the text that it is displaying. To do so, all you really need to do is loop through each entry and clear the contents using the OutputString() function that I showed you previously.

```
void CConsole::Clear()
{
        // Create a pointer to the first entry
        CEntry* pEntry = m_pEntryList;

        // Loop for every entry
        while( pEntry->GetNext() )
        {
                // Set the entry's text to nothing
                pEntry->SetText( "" );
                // Get the next entry
                pEntry = pEntry->GetNext();
        }
}
```

After calling this, the console will be cleared the next time the Render() function is called, which you will shortly see.

Class CCommand

I have included code in CConsole that allows you to plug in your own external parsing function for the commands that may be typed into the console. This is so that you don't have to bother subclassing CConsole if you don't want to. The procedure for dealing with commands works like this: First the user types a string in the active entry and presses Enter. At this point, the text from the active entry is retrieved and passed to a preparsing function, which converts the raw string into a command and parameter object. When this stage is complete, the command object is passed to the external parser, where you can process it as you see fit, or reject the command as invalid.

I'll start by showing you the CCommand class, which holds the command and parameter list after preparsing.

```
class CCommand
{
public:

        // Holds the main command.  eg 'SetScreenRes'
        char* pstrCommand;
        // Holds the number of parameters. eg 2
        int NumParams;
        // Holds the parameters.  eg 640 and 480
        char* pstrParams[MAX_PARAMS];

        // Constructor
        CCommand()
        {
                // Initialize all the variables to zero
                pstrCommand = 0;
                NumParams = 0;

                ZeroMemory( &pstrParams, sizeof( pstrParams ) );
        }
        // Destructor
        ~CCommand()
        {
```

```
                // Destroy the command string
                // if it exists
                if( pstrCommand )
                        delete pstrCommand;

                // Destroy any parameter strings
                // if they exist
                for( int i = 0 ; i < MAX_PARAMS ; i++ )
                {
                        if( pstrParams[i] )
                                delete pstrParams[i];
                }
        }

};
```

Take a close look at this code because it gets used heavily quite soon. There are three member variables, all of which are very important. pstrCommand is a string of dynamic length that holds the command. This could hold SetDisplayMode, for example. NumParams holds the number of parameters associated with the command. pstrParams could be confusing so look at it carefully. This is how it is declared:

```
char* pstrParams[MAX_PARAMS];
```

That is not a character string; it is an *array* of strings. The number of parameters is limited by the MAX_PARAMS identifier, which for now I have set to 25. I can't see any function needing more than 25 parameters. Memory for the command strings is allocated on a dynamic basis; that is, the memory is only allocated for each parameter if one exists. So if you typed the following:

```
SetPhysicsVariable 100, 300
```

then only space for the two parameters would be allocated. Cool? Excellent.

Setting Up the External Parsing Callback

Setting up the external parsing function is really easy. You do it with the following code:

```
void CConsole::SetParserCallback( CONSOLE_PARSER_CALLBACK pfnCallback )
{
        // Set the function pointer
```

```
        m_pfnCallback = pfnCallback;
        // Set the flag to show that a parser has been specified
        m_bParserCallback = TRUE;
}
```

You can see that the function just updates the member variable with the new address of the specified function and sets the flag for indicating the presence of a valid callback function to TRUE.

CONSOLE_PARSER_CALLBACK is defined as the following:

```
typedef int (*CONSOLE_PARSER_CALLBACK)( CCommand* pCommand );
```

What that means is that you must supply a function that returns an int and takes a pointer to a CCommand class as its only parameter. Function pointers are seriously ugly pieces of work.

So your callback function would look like this:

```
int ConsoleParser( CCommand* pCommand )
{
        return S_OK;
}
```

You'll look at how to write the parsing function soon. To set up the class to recognize this as the callback to use, you would type the following:

```
Console.SetParserCallback( ConsoleParser );
```

See, it really is easy. Just smile and nod!

Preparsing Raw Strings into Command Parameters

This is where things get really jiggy, so stick some matches under your eyelids to keep them open! The function CConsole::PreParse() is responsible for modifying the raw text into commands and parameters. The code is shown in the following:

```
void CConsole::PreParse( char* pstrText, CCommand* pCommand )
{
        // The parameter separators are
        // the comma and space characters
        char Separators[] = " ,";
        // String to hold the current parameter
        char* Token;
```

```cpp
    // The number of parameters
    int TokenCount = 0;

    // Convert the string to lowercase
    strlwr( pstrText );

    // Get the command string
    Token = strtok( pstrText, Separators );

    // If the line was not blank...
    if( Token )
    {
            // ...Set the command string to the token.
            // Create a string in the command to hold the command string
            pCommand->pstrCommand = new char[ strlen( Token ) + 1 ];
            // Copy the string into the command string
            strcpy( pCommand->pstrCommand, Token );
    }
    else // The line was blank
    {
            // Create a single character to hold a blank character.
            // This will notify the keypress event that the line
            // was empty
            pCommand->pstrCommand = new char;
            // Copy a blank character into a new
            strcpy( pCommand->pstrCommand, " " );
            // Set the number of parameters to zero
            pCommand->NumParams = 0;
            // Return; there is nothing left to do
            return;
    }

    // Get the next token in the string
    Token = strtok( NULL, Separators );

    // Loop for the rest of the tokens
    while( Token != NULL )
    {
            // Allocate memory in the command for this parameter
            pCommand->pstrParams[TokenCount] = new char[ strlen( Token ) + 1 ];
            // Copy the parameter into the allocated memory
```

```
            strcpy( pCommand->pstrParams[TokenCount], Token );
            // Get the next token in the string
            Token = strtok( NULL, Separators );
            // Increase the parameter count
            TokenCount++;
            // Make sure there are not too many parameters
            if( TokenCount > MAX_PARAMS )
                    break;
    }

        // Set the number of parameters in command
        pCommand->NumParams = TokenCount;
}
```

As far as I know, not many people deal with these annoying C-style string manipulation routines anymore. There are much better ways to deal with strings, such as the incredibly cool CString class that is part of the MFC library. However, including MFC in a game is like building a Grand Prix car with a diesel truck engine. So stick with me—you will get through this stuff. And think, you'll only have to write this stuff once (or do the smart thing and copy it off the companion CD), and it will be part of your programming library forever.

Let's get back to the code. PreParse() takes two parameters: a pointer to a string that contains the raw text, and a pointer to a CCommand object that will hold the results of the parsing operations.

The function starts with the definition of a character array called Separators, which contains the characters for space and comma. These are the two ways that you can separate commands (e.g., 45, 48, 29 or 45 48 29).

Let me just run over in theory how this whole process works. I define some characters that I want to use as separation commands. Then I convert the entire string to lowercase using the strlwr() function, so that it is easier to pick out commands. Next I use the strtok() function, which in many parts of the galaxy can be considered complex. strtok() works by searching a string for *tokens,* or words in between delimiters (which is a parameter or command in this case), in a string. I set the delimiters as comma and space. strtok() needs to be called more than once. The first time you call it, you set up the string that needs to be searched and the delimiters that you want to use. If a token exists, then it is returned in the Token string, which is then added to the CCommand command list.

Next strtok() is called again in a loop that repeatedly checks for more parameters until there are none left. You may notice in the code that after the first call to strtok(), I do not specify a string to search again. This is because internally strtok() uses a static variable to remember which string I am processing. This can lead to issues if you are trying to process more than one string at the same time. For more information on this topic, have a look at *MSDN Library 6.0 / Visual C++ Documentation / Using C++ / Visual C++ Programmers Guide / Run-Time Library Reference / Alphabetic Function Reference / S / strtok. General Text Routine Mappings.Warnings.*

Plugging the Console into the Game Engine

I discussed before how the console needs to hijack text from the keyboard during the execution of the game without interrupting any existing keyboard code that the game engine may be using. This is so that it can catch key presses that change its visibility when not active, such as the F11 key, or actual character messages while it is active, so that it can display them. To do this I have programmed two message handlers into the console. The first is OnChar(), and it deals with character messages from WM_CHAR messages, and the second is OnKeyDown(), which traps WM_KEYDOWN messages.

OnChar()

Let's look at OnChar() first:

```
int CConsole::OnChar( char Key )
{
        // This holds the last key pressed
        static char LastKey = 0;

        // If the console is not visible
        // then ignore the keypress
        if( !m_bVisible )
                return 0;

        // Ignore the enter key
        if( Key == '\r' )
                return 0;
```

```
        // Change the tab key to a space key
        if( Key == '\t' )
                Key = ' ';

        // Only allow one space
        if( (Key == ' ') && (LastKey == ' ') )
                return 0;

        // Make sure the first character in a line
        // is not a space
        if( (Key == ' ') && (LastKey == 0 ) )
                return 0;

        // Only send the message to the active
        // entry if the Last Key is not being
        // reset
        if( Key != 0 )
                m_pActiveEntry->OnChar( Key );

        // Update the last key pressed variable
        LastKey = Key;

        return 0;
}
```

The function is pretty involved, but basically it just massages certain character messages to keep the command parser happy later on. First up is a static variable that holds the last key that was pressed; you will see the reasoning behind this shortly. Then the first if statement checks if the console is visible; if it is not, then there is no point in wasting time on checking keys, so the function exits. Next up \r, which is the escape code for the Enter key, is rejected because the OnKeyDown() function looks after command keys. Then the Tab key is modified into a space because you have no reason to support the Tab key. The next test is to make sure that only one space is allowed, because if there are more, the command parser can get confused. By the way, this is why the static variable is there to remember what the last key was. And finally, the character, if it passes all the tests, is passed on to the active entry's OnChar() command, which you'll recall simply adds the character to the end of its string buffer.

You attach `OnChar()` to the `WndProc()` `WM_CHAR` handler like so:

```
case WM_CHAR:
{
        Console.OnChar( wParam );

        return 0;
}
```

OnKeyDown()

Whereas `OnChar()` looks after character input, the purpose of `OnKeyDown()` is more to do with control. This function tracks buttons that don't have proper ASCII codes, such as F11, which controls the console's visibility. It also looks out for the Enter key, which signals that the current string of text in the active entry should be parsed. Here's the code:

```
int CConsole::OnKeyDown( WPARAM wParam )
{
        int Result = 0; // Holds result of parse operation

        // Figure out which key was pressed
        switch( wParam )
        {
                // The F11 key was pressed
                case VK_F11:
                {
                        SetVisibility( !GetVisibility() );

                        break;
                }
                // The enter key.
                case VK_RETURN:
                {
                        // Ignore if the console is not visible
                        if( !m_bVisible )
                                return 0;

                        // Reset the last key pressed
                        OnChar( 0 );
```

```cpp
                // Check if a parser has been set
                if( m_bParserCallback )
                {
                        // Create a temporary string
                        char* String = new char[MAX_CHARSPERLINE];
                        // Get the string from the active entry
                        m_pActiveEntry->GetText( String, MAX_CHARSPERLINE );

                        // If nothing was typed just ignore it
                        if( !MATCH( String, "" ) && !MATCH( String, " " ) )
                        {
                                // Create a new command class
                                CCommand Command;
                                // Convert the string into a command
                                PreParse( String, &Command );
                                // Send the command to the parser
                                Result = m_pfnCallback( &Command );
                                if( FAILED( Result ) )
                                        OutputString( "-- Unknown Command --" );
                        }

                        // Destroy the temporary string
                        delete String;
                }

                // Move all the entries up
                RotateEntries();
                break;
        }

        // The left arrow key was pressed
        case VK_LEFT:
        {
                // Treat this like a backspace press
                OnChar( '\b' );
                break;
        }

}

return 0;
```

```
}
```

To connect it to the game engine you just have to call this function from the
`WM_KEYDOWN` handler of `WndProc()` like this:

```
case WM_KEYDOWN:
{
        Console.OnKeyDown( wParam );

        return 0;
}
```

Rendering. . . Finally!

It's finally time to see how to draw this bad boy console to the screen. Rendering is
done with the `CConsole::Render()` function, which is shown in the following code:

```
void CConsole::Render()
{
        // Make sure the console has been initialized
        if( !m_bInitialized )
                return;

        // Holds the current vertical position of the
        // console during scrolling operations
        static int CurrentY = m_Height;

        // If the console is animating down then
        // subtract from the current Y coord
        if( m_Animation == Down )
                CurrentY-=10;
        // Else if the console is going up
        // then add to the current Y coord
        else if( m_Animation == Up )
                CurrentY+=10;

        // Stop the animation if the console has completely expanded
        if( m_Animation == Down && CurrentY == 0 )
                m_Animation = None;

        // Stop the animation if the console has completely retracted
        if( m_Animation == Up && CurrentY == m_Height )
```

```
                {
                        m_bVisible = FALSE;
                        m_Animation = None;
                }

                // Set the source rectangle
                RECT SourceRect = { 0, CurrentY, m_Width, m_Height };
                // Set the destination point
                POINT DestPoint = { 0, 0 };

                // If the console is not visible then return
                if( !m_bVisible )
                        return;

                // Copy the background surface to the console surface
                D3DXLoadSurfaceFromSurface( m_pConsoleSurface, NULL, NULL,
                        m_pConsoleBackgroundSurf, NULL, NULL, D3DX_FILTER_LINEAR, 0 );

                // Get a pointer to the start of the entry list
                CEntry* pEntry = m_pEntryList;

                D3DLOCKED_RECT LockedRect;

                m_pConsoleSurface->LockRect( &LockedRect, 0, 0 );

                // Loop for each entry in the list
                while( pEntry->GetNext() )
                {
                        // Render this entry
                        pEntry->RenderText( MAX_CHARSPERLINE,
                                (DWORD*)LockedRect.pBits,LockedRect.Pitch );
                        // Move to the next entry
                        pEntry = pEntry->GetNext();
                }

                m_pConsoleSurface->UnlockRect();

                // Copy the console to the target surface
                m_pDevice->CopyRects( m_pConsoleSurface, &SourceRect, 1,
                                                        m_pTargetSurface, &DestPoint );


        }
```

This function is the business. The first half of the code is for the animation in between state changes. If the console is animating, then its vertical position is modified by + or –10 until it is either completely extended or retracted, respectively. Then the code copies the background surface to the console surface. Finally, each entry is rendered to the console in a loop. Figure 10.4 shows the rendered console.

Figure 10.4

The console, rendered over the background

And when all of that is finished, the entire console is blasted onto the back buffer, and what do you know? You have a *Quake*-style console. Phew—that took more code than I would have liked. But hey, now you understand it, so that's cool. And check out the animation in action in Figure 10.5.

Figure 10.5

Animation effects from the console

It is probably pretty hard to see it moving, but just think: it's not the console that must move...the console does not exist...it is your *mind* that must be moved. (Man, I should write movies!)

There is just one last thing to discuss....

Programming the Command Parser

Right, first off you need to know exactly what a *command parser* actually is. It is basically just a function that compares a received string to a bunch of known strings, and if it finds a match, it executes some code. So it looks like you need an easy way to compare some strings. You could do this with the strcmp() function, which stands for *string compare*. This function takes two strings and returns zero if they are the same. So you could write this:

```
if( !strcmp( StringA, StringB ) )
        DoSomething();
```

But that is damn ugly, so I wrote a macro to cover it called MATCH():

```
#define MATCH(a, b) (!strcmp( a, b ))
```

Now you can write the following:

```
if( MATCH( StringA, StringB ) )
        DoSomething();
```

So, to start with, you have your plain parser that does nothing:

```
int ConsoleParser( CCommand* pCommand )
{
        return S_OK;
}
```

Let's begin by creating some local copies of the information contained within the CCommand object by adding this code:

```
int ConsoleParser( CCommand* pCommand )
{
        char* pstrCmd = pCommand->pstrCommand;
        char* pstrParams[MAX_PARAMS];
        memcpy( &pstrParams, &(pCommand->pstrParams),
                                                sizeof( pstrParams ) );
        int NumParams = pCommand->NumParams;

        return S_OK;
}
```

Commands with No Parameters

This is one of the most simple pieces of code to write. Check it out:

```
if( MATCH( pstrCmd, "exit" ) || MATCH( pstrCmd, "quit" ) )
{
        // Quit the game
        PostQuitMessage(0);
        return 0;
}
```

Easy or what? How about a console command to clear the console itself?

```
if( MATCH( pstrCmd, "cls" ) )
{
        Console.Clear();
        return 0;
}
```

Commands with Parameters

Most of the time the parameters to your commands will be numbers, rather than strings, so it makes sense to make a helper function to convert strings to numbers. Here is one that I wrote:

```
int ParseStringForNumber( char* pString )
{
        // Some boolean tests
        if( MATCH( pString, "on"  ) )
                return 1;
        if( MATCH( pString, "off" ) )
                return 0;
        if( MATCH( pString, "true" ) )
                return 1;
        if( MATCH( pString, "false" ) )
                return 0;
        if( MATCH( pString, "yes" ) )
                return 1;
        if( MATCH( pString, "no" ) )
                return 0;

        // Some spelled number tests
        if( MATCH( pString, "zero" ) )
```

```
            return 0;
    if( MATCH( pString, "one" ) )
            return 1;
    if( MATCH( pString, "two" ) )
            return 2;
    if( MATCH( pString, "three" ) )
            return 3;
    if( MATCH( pString, "four" ) )
            return 4;
    if( MATCH( pString, "five" ) )
            return 5;
    if( MATCH( pString, "six" ) )
            return 6;
    if( MATCH( pString, "seven" ) )
            return 7;
    if( MATCH( pString, "eight" ) )
            return 8;
    if( MATCH( pString, "nine" ) )
            return 9;
    if( MATCH( pString, "ten" ) )
            return 10;

    // Try converting to string
    return atoi( pString );
}
```

Using this code, I could now program the following command handler into
ConsoleParser():

```
if( MATCH( pstrCmd, "add" ) )
{
    // Make sure at least two parameters were specified
    if( NumParams < 2 )
            return E_FAIL;

    // Convert the two parameters to integers
    int a = ParseStringForNumber( pstrParams[0] );
    int b = ParseStringForNumber( pstrParams );

    // Add the two parameters
    int Result = a + b;
```

```
// Holds the output string
char OutputString[20];

// Convert the result back into a string
itoa( Result, OutputString, 10 );

// Output the results
Console.OutputString( OutputString );

return S_OK;
}
```

Can you see what it does? Well, duh, of course it adds two numbers. Check out the pictorial version in Figure 10.6. Slick or what? I output the "Goodbye World" bit with a call to CConsole::OutputString().

Figure 10.6

Typing commands into the console

You can also add numbers specified in words! Check out Figure 10.7.

Figure 10.7

Using string detection in the console

Conclusion

And that is truly everything there is to creating a console. I will leave the programming of the console functions up to your own implementation. You should have enough knowledge from the base parser that I showed you to be able to advance your own functions.

I hope this journey into the depths of consoles opened your eyes a little bit more to the kind of forethought and planning that must go into every aspect of game development. I designed the code to be easily extendable, so take her out for a spin and mess with the code. See just how advanced you can get.

Well, I have to say that all this 2D stuff has definitely been fun, but dude, it is like totally time to move up a dimension. When moving to 3D, I am always reminded of an old saying, coined by Robin Hood (I think), which is close to my heart. It goes: "Some ponder the question of what it is to be—or not to be, for that matter. However, the true Zen Direct3D gurus ponder the question, 'Where the heck has the daylight gone? How long have I been sitting here coding, man?'"

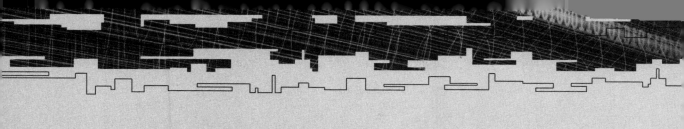

Part Four

3D
Mathematics

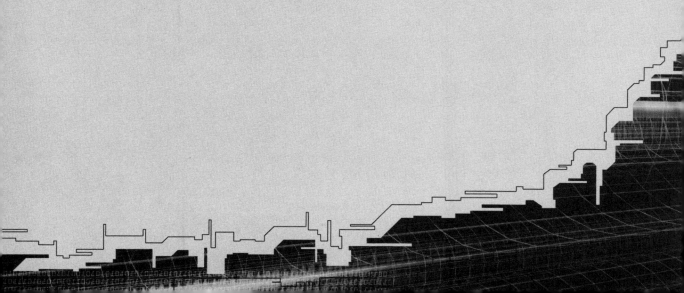

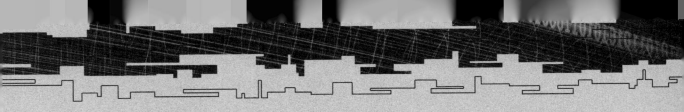

CHAPTER 11

GETTING FAT WITH 3D

I think I've typed one too many pages. Just this morning I was looking for my wallet, and all the while my background mind was formulating a plan for how I could get out of looking, and get someone else to look for me. And what was the plan? *Press Start, Find, Lost Personal Possessions.* I had to explain to the rest of my brain that I actually live in the real world. And a few nights ago I was telling a girl something along the lines of "Of course I can hold my drink," when fate came and kicked me where it hurts, and I dropped my pint of beer to the ground. I immediately looked for the nearest Edit, Undo menu item. Sad, isn't it?

Now the link between that little story and this chapter is exceptionally thin. However, as Zen gurus know, to smile and nod is a powerful way of showing the capability of grasping a concept, even if you don't quite know what it is yet. The point is that this stuff can get very intense at times, so you need to be paying attention all the time. If you find yourself getting stuck, just take a deep breath, eat some junk food, and then come back. In the end, all this new knowledge will come together and you will at last understand what Plato would call "the truth."

In this chapter you will confront

- 3D Cartesian theory.
- the construction of 3D geometry.
- the types of objects in a 3D world.
- triangle setups for efficient rendering.
- all the new vocabulary and lingo that you will need to mingle with the Zen gurus of this world.

Basically, this chapter will introduce all the theory, terms, conditions, and lingo that you will need to communicate effectively with me in the following chapters, as well as with any other Zen gurus that you talk to in the future.

What Is a Dimension?

The best way to start talking about 3D is by comparing it to what you are already familiar with, and that is dimensions. Everybody I know seems to have some messed-up version of what they think a dimension is, based on some mental picture they have of a 3D cube drawn on a piece of paper. So let's get this whole dimension thing nailed down. By the way, the definitions I'm giving you are applicable to related mathematics for games only, so don't go running to your physics teacher and moan about me!

Getting Jiggy with Philosophy

Let's start with a discussion about the space-time continuum. It all has to do with dilithium crystals. In the real world in which we live, all distances, directions, and movements are relative. What that means is that there is no real start and finish to any movement; you start relative to something and you end relative to something.

If that seems a little up in the air, let me give you a few eye-opening examples. Say you get on a plane at London Heathrow Airport on your way to San Francisco International Airport. After you take off, you may think that you are traveling at almost 1,000 kilometers per hour (km/h) toward your destination. In fact you are not. Well, then again you are, but it depends how you look at it. What you are doing is traveling 1,000 km/h relative to London and the ground beneath you. But zoom out a bit. Now you are looking at planet earth, and it is traveling at something like 64,000 km/h around the sun. So which way are you going now? Depending on the rotation of the earth, you may be traveling 65,000 km/h parallel with the earth's orbit trajectory, or 63,000 km/h in the same direction, or somewhere in between.

Then say you get in a spaceship and accelerate away from the earth at 65,000 km/h. Are you actually traveling at 65,000 km/h, or are you now stopped? See? There is just no way to tell. You are only moving when you compare yourself to something else. All stars are moving relative to each other, so there is just nothing static upon which to compare yourself. That is, there is no origin. There is no beginning and no end to space. Some people may say that there is, but I'd love for them to show me how far down the interstate outside New York I have to go to find it! If you find this hard to imagine this, then try to think of it in terms of time, which happens to be the fourth dimension. When did time start? What happened before that? Now try that with physical space. Where does the universe start, and where does it end? (I hear that there is a really good restaurant there.) Nowhere. Either it curves back on itself, so that if you keep going in one direction you eventually get back in the same place, like if you walked around the world, or else it just never ends. Either way, there is no way to tell where you are, how fast you are going, or what direction you are going in. Which way is up, for instance? What *is* up?

Now, I don't want to get too carried away with this junk. Personally, the pursuit of material wealth keeps me occupied enough, without having to worry about where I am all the time. But the point of all this is so that you can compare it to dimensions in games, where all movements are absolute. *Absolute* means that all positions, movements, and directions are stated relative to a known point, called the *origin*. Get it? In the real world all movement is relative to something else, of which you don't know the position. In games, all positions and movements are relative to a known point, the origin.

Representing the Universe with Numbers

The whole point of mathematics is that you want to be able to look at or do something without *actually* having to do it. Take flying around space and killing aliens, for instance. It's common knowledge that most aliens are peace-loving creatures, interested only in the pleasures of life itself. So actually killing aliens would be out of the question. You can use mathematics to create constructs that represent aliens and kill them instead.

1D Universes

But in mathematics you can't just represent the universe in terms of relative distances and points that are "somewhere near something else." You need to nail down some place that is where it is, and everything else can be defined relative to it. Like I said before, this is called the *origin*. So say you have a one-dimensional universe with the origin at zero. Actually, the origin is always at zero; anything else is just silly. Anyway, what this means is that you can now move in two directions. You can move away from the origin in the positive direction, or you could move in the negative direction.

For the discussions here, the positive direction is always to the right of the origin, and the negative is always to the left. When talking about a singly-dimensioned space, you usually describe it using a horizontal axis, like the one shown above in Figure 11.1. The amount that you move away from the origin can be held in a variable, which is usually called x, for the horizontal axis. So if you move one to the right of the origin, then x is now equal to 1, and if you move one to the left, then x is equal to -1. This is all very basic stuff, and I'm sure you know it, but let's cover everything just to be sure you don't miss anything. Notice that only a single variable is needed to define any position on the axis.

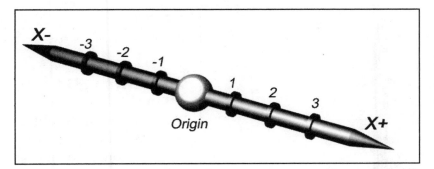

Figure 11.1

A one-dimensional universe

Moving to Two Dimensions

Moving in one direction gets really boring after a while, so eventually two rebel atoms without a cause got together and decided they were sick of moving left and right, and wanted to move up and down

> So let's recap the vocabulary so far. A *dimension* is a direction extending in both directions to infinity. An *axis* is a mathematical term used to represent a dimension in mathematical space. It has units to measure distances moved from the *origin*, which is the point at the center of the axis.

as well. Unfortunately, they died in a car accident before they were able to try. However, the Council of Relativity got together and came to the same conclusion the next day and decided to introduce the *second dimension*.

With a second dimension, you are able to define movements in the vertical and horizontal plane. Of course you know all this because you have been doing 2D graphics for the last 300 or so pages, but don't worry—you will get to new stuff soon! I promise. Anyway, like I was saying, the second dimension, always called the *Y-axis,* is always in the vertical direction. Positive y increases up, and negative decreases down from the origin. Have a look at Figure 11.2, and get this graph in your head and base all future thoughts on it, because this is now what controls your life as an interactive entertainment engineer!

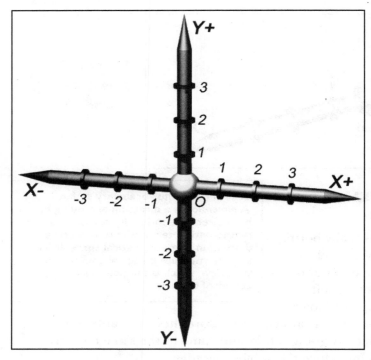

Figure 11.2

A two-dimensional universe

Defining 2D Points

To define points in a 2D world you now need two variables: one to define the distance from the origin horizontally called *x*, and one to define the distance from the origin vertically called *y*. When defining points, you always specify the x-coordinate and then the y-coordinate, just like in the alphabet; x *always* comes before y. For instance, if x is five units from the horizontal origin and y is three in the negative direction from the vertical origin, then you would write it as (5, −3). Simple? Of course it is. Have a look at Figure 11.3 for some examples of defining points.

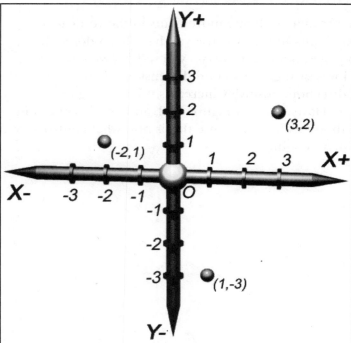

Figure 11.3

Defining points in a 2D universe

2D Lines

I discussed lines way back when I was covering the GDI. As you probably recall, a line is nothing more than two points. The first point defines the start of the line, and the second point defines the finish. Figure 11.4 shows two lines.

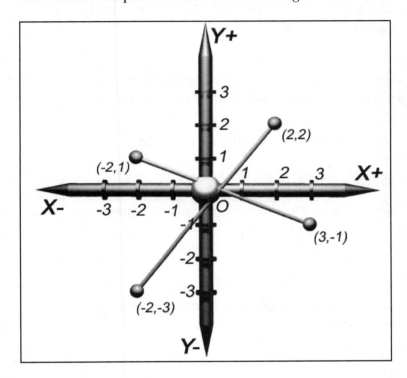

Figure 11.4

Representing lines in a 2D universe

Zen Mathematics

In case you're a little rusty on the mathematics behind the line, I'll show you some of the stuff that you may need from time to time. The line can be represented by this formula:

$y = mx + c$

where y is the vertical coordinate at which the line intercepts the y-axis, x is the horizontal coordinate at which line intercepts the x-axis, and m is the slope.

You can find the length of a line that travels from (x_1, y_1) to (x_2, y_2) using this formula:

$\text{Length} = \sqrt{(x2 - x1)^2 + (y2 - y1)^2}$

To find the midpoint of a line that goes from (x_1, y_1) to (x_2, y_2), you can use this formula:

Middle x-coordinate $= (x_1 + x_2) / 2$

Middle y-coordinate $= (y_1 + y_2) / 2$

The slope of a line that passes through the points (x_1, y_1) and (x_2, y_2) can be found using this formula:

$m = (y_2 - y_1) / (x_2 - x_1)$

where m is the slope.

Triangles

Just as lines are a collection of points, triangles are a collection of three lines. You can define a triangle using three points, surprisingly enough (see Figure 11.5). Keep triangles in mind, because if code is the spear of a Zen guru, then triangles are the buffalo. Triangles are the most important shape in 3D because they are very easy to mess with mathematically. In triangles you don't call the points that make up the corners *points;* instead, they are called *vertices.* Keep the dictionary of your mind open because it is going to be filled new Zen words over the next few chapters.

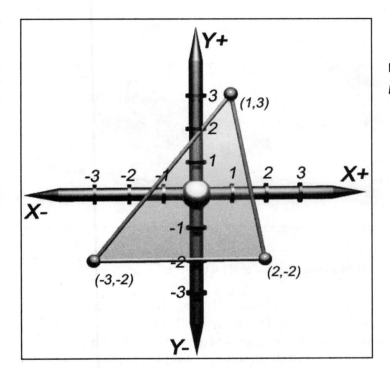

Figure 11.5

Defining triangles in 2D

Triangles can be combined to create much more advanced objects, such as buildings, cars, and junk food. Mmmmm, junk food. (Sorry, I haven't stopped writing for 234 hours.) When you combine triangles to create more advanced objects, you are said to be creating a *mesh*. Have a look at Figures 11.6 to see a mesh of triangles that represents a fighter craft.

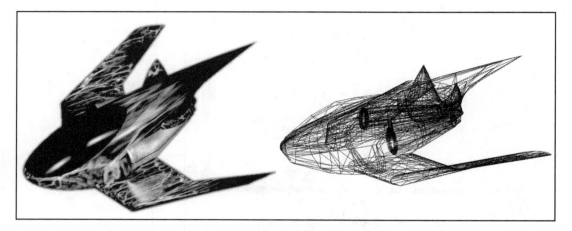

Figure 11.6

A 3D-rendered model, and the same model, rendered to show the faces

When you combine triangles to create a mesh, each triangle has a name, called a *face*. Another name for a mesh is a *model*. The *model* in 11.6 is made from *faces,* each of which is defined by a number of *vertices* (singular *vertex*). A vertex is another name for a point that describes a position on a more complex primitive. Don't worry if you are a little confused by all this new terminology; I will explain everything that is important shortly.

Triangle Mesh Types

You can define an object using a separate triangle for each face, but this can be an unoptimized method of model creation. Take Figure 11.7 as an example.

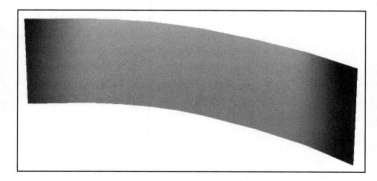

Figure 11.7

The rendered model as it would appear on-screen

Say you have a mesh that renders to look like Figure 11.7. How would that look if it were defined by faces? Well, it might look something like Figure 11.8.

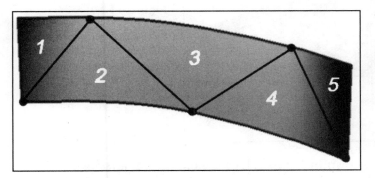

Figure 11.8

The model with component faces highlighted

If you split those faces up so that they were clearer, you would see that they looked like Figure 11.9.

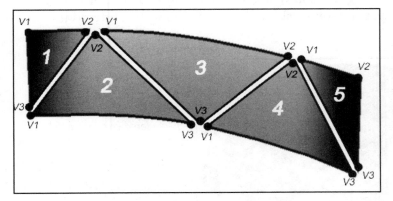

Figure 11.9

The model with the component faces split to highlight the overuse of vertices

By the way, this method of defining a model is called using a *triangle list,* because you have a list of triangles that defines the mesh. Looking at that, you can see there are five faces, each with three vertices, bringing the total to 15 vertices. That may not seem like much, but if you defined an entire model using this method, then there could be a huge amount of unneeded processing going on. So how else might you define this mesh? Well, what if you could share the vertices between the faces? That would definitely lead to an increase in performance. Take a look at Figure 11.10.

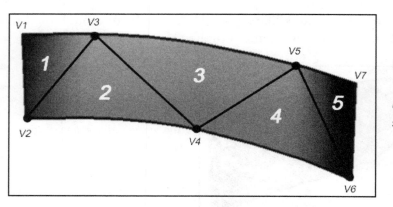

Figure 11.10

The same model, this time using triangle strip vertex sharing to optimize processing

The method of face sharing shown in Figure 11.10 is called using a *triangle strip*. Using this method has brought the number of vertices down to seven, which is over a 50 percent drop in processing for this mesh alone.

Another method for optimizing the construction of models is the use of *triangle fans*. Fans are useful for circular-type meshes. Consider the mesh rendered in Figure 11.11.

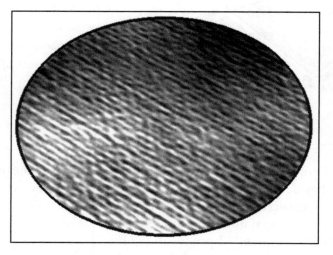

Figure 11.11

A rendered circular model

You could use the standard method, which could result in the triangle formation shown in Figure 11.12. As you can see, there are 12 faces, resulting in 36 vertices. For a simple circle this is awful. Using a little lateral thinking, you could use vertex sharing to define the triangle like that shown in Figure 11.13.

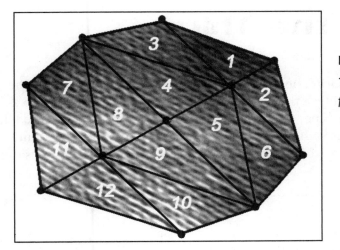

Figure 11.12

The circular model with component faces highlighted

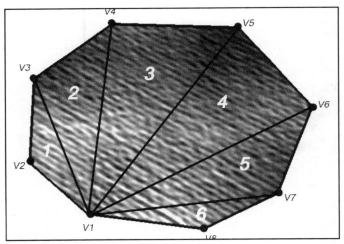

Figure 11.13

The circular model now optimized for vertex sharing with triangle fans

As you can see, the face count has now dropped to six and the vertex count to eight. That is a 50 percent reduction in faces and 77 percent drop in vertices. Slick, huh? It may not seem too important now, but just keep this stuff in mind for when you get to the programming part.

The term for all this stuff that I have talked about, like points, lines, and triangles, is a *primitive*. A primitive is a smaller unit that is used to build something larger, such as a mesh.

Moving to the Third Dimension

The third dimension is my favorite, because it is nice, cozy, and oh so roomy! The third dimension is represented by a third axis, which runs perpendicular to the x- and y-axes. If that sounds confusing, then think of it like this: If the y-axis is the left side of this page, and the x-axis is the bottom of this page, then the z-axis extends into the page. Get it? Cool. Have a look at Figure 11.14 to see the third dimensions graphically.

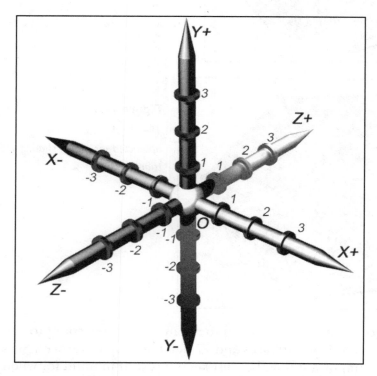

Figure 11.14

A three-dimensional universe

There is a slight problem with the third dimension, and that is that it can work differently depending on whom you talk to. Zen game programmers (who are always right and infallible, by the way) use what is called the *left-handed coordinate system.* Some say the name has something to do with rotating your hand or something. I think that it comes from the fact that the guy who invented it couldn't write with the correct hand!

In the left-handed system the z-axis extends in the positive direction into the page; this is useful for programming. The right-handed system was developed for those mathematical and publishing types. Oh, you know the type—they always have to be different, don't they? Well, it turns out that the right-handed system is better for displaying images, such as scientific graphs, on a page. Figure 11.15 shows the differences between the methods of thinking.

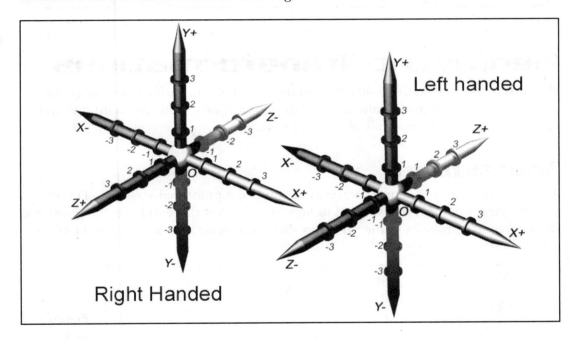

Figure 11.15

Comparison of the left- and right-handed coordinate systems

See the differences in the signs? Most of the time I will be using the left-handed system used in programming unless a graph or something requires, and would look better in, right-handed. I'll point out anything important if it comes up.

When you want to describe a point in 3D, you need a third variable, called Z, which describes the distance of a point from the origin in the depth direction, which like the other axes can be either positive or negative. So when you describe a point in 3D, you do it like this: (x, y, z). So if x = 6, y = 7, and z = 5, then the point would be written as (6, 7, 5).

Geometric Transformations

I've talked about primitives—like how to define them and stuff—but most of the time you don't want just a static triangle sitting on your screen. You want it moved around the screen, so let's talk about that now.

Translation

The word *translation* means to move. So if you had a point that was at (1, 1) and you moved it to (4, 5), you are said to have translated it three units in the positive x direction and four units in the positive y direction. Have a look at Figure 11.16 to see this visually.

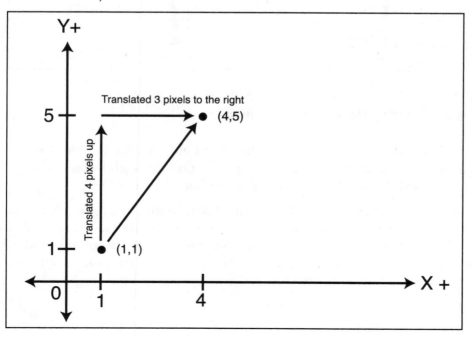

Figure 11.16

Translating a point

The mathematics behind translation are oh-so-simple. All you do is add or subtract the amount by which you want to move the point by to the x- or y-coordinate. That is, if you want to move the point five units to the right, then you would simply add 5 to the x-coordinate. Similarly, if you want to move the point down and to the left by one unit, then you would subtract 1 from the x- and y-coordinates.

In other words:

$$x' = x + \text{TranslationFactor}$$

$$y' = y + \text{TranslationFactor}$$

> **TIP**
>
> In case you're a little rusty on mathematical notation, that "x'" is pronounced "x dash" or "x prime" and it essentially means the new value for x. So if you had the code
>
> ```
> x = x * 5;
> ```
>
> then the mathematical notation would be
>
> ```
> x' = x * 5
> ```
>
> **Cool? Cool.**

Scaling

Scaling is a fairly normal English word, but let me just nail it down for you. To *scale* something means to change its dimensions. In other words, you make it bigger or smaller. However, when you are scaling in the land of Zen, you are not technically changing the size of something; you are actually just changing the position of the points that make up the object relative to the origin. This will become clear in a second. Let's start with a simple example, scaling a triangle that is centered on the origin. Take a look at Figure 11.17.

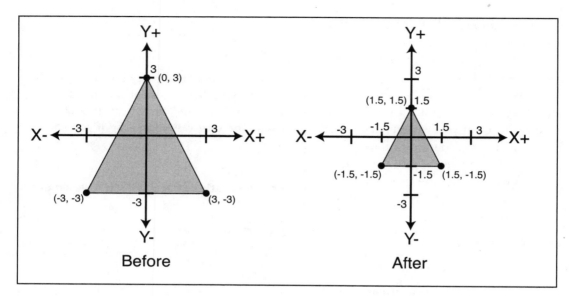

Figure 11.17

Scaling a triangle centered on the origin

To scale a point is very simple; it is merely a matter of multiplying the scaling factor by the coordinates of the point. The scaling factor is a *scalar value,* which means that it is just a normal number, and can range from 0.0 to infinity, with 1.0 as the midpoint. What this means is that if you multiply a point by 1.0, it will stay in the same place. If you multiply by 0.5, it will be half its original distance from the origin. And if you multiply by 2.0, it will be twice as far from the origin as it used to be. Think of the scalar value as a percentage change. So to make it 1,000 percent bigger, you multiply by 10.0, or to make it 10 percent of its original size, you multiply by 0.1.

Let's look at an example. Say you have a point at (10, 20) and you want to move it 50 percent closer to the origin. So:

SCALING FACTOR * XCOORDINATE = NEW X-COORDINATE

SCALING FACTOR * YCOORDINATE = NEW Y-COORDINATE

0.5 * 10 = 5

0.5 * 20 = 10

New Coordinates = (5, 10). Slick, huh?

Or more mathematically:

$$x' = x * \text{ScaleFactor}$$

$$y' = y * \text{ScaleFactor}$$

But that just scales the distance of a point; what if you want to scale an object such as a triangle? It is just as simple. All you do is loop through each of the points and scale them one by one. The result is a triangle that has been scaled larger or smaller by the specified value. In this example I am scaling the triangle by 0.5, which causes it to decrease in size by half. See the way each of the vertices is half the distance that it used to be from the origin?

That's all cool, but what happens when you scale an object that is not centered about the origin? Check this puppy out in Figure 11.18.

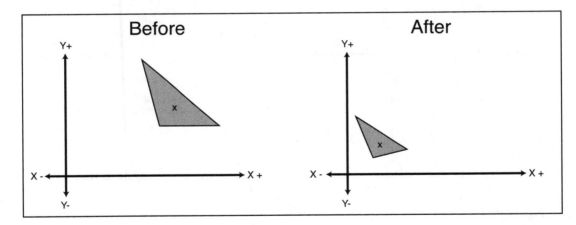

Figure 11.18

Scaling an object not centered about the origin

It has been scaled properly, but look closely. Can you see what's wrong? The triangle has also been translated, or moved, which is not what I wanted at all. The center of the triangle, marked with an x, has moved toward the origin during the scale, which is a total bummer. To fix this is really easy—just translate the triangle so that it is centered about the origin, then scale it, and then finally translate it back to where it is supposed to be.

Aiight, let's get this wagon moving again.

Rollin' with Rotation

Rotation is another one of those easy-to-understand English words that managed to work its way into interactive entertainment engineering. You've probably noticed by now that it is very fashionable to represent simple concepts with complex-sounding words. *Rotation* just means to rotate points about an axis. Check out the graphical examples in Figure 11.19.

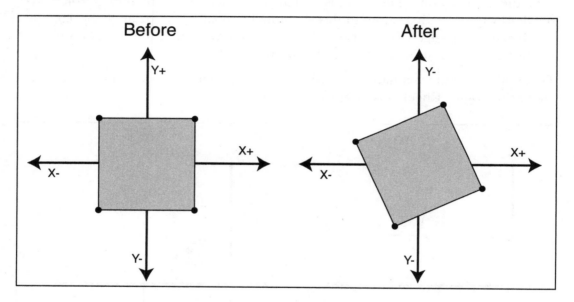

Figure 11.19

Rotating an object centered about the origin

This is pretty easy—until you get to the math! However, like scaling, rotation suffers from annoying problems if the object is not centered about the origin. Check out Figure 11.20.

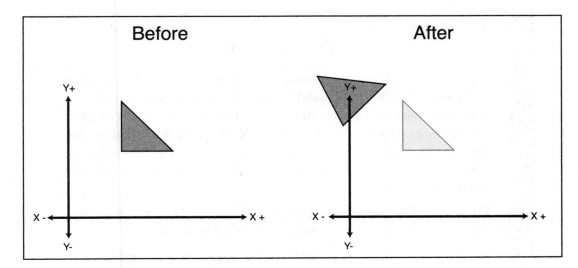

Figure 11.20

Rotating an object not centered about the origin

See? After the rotation, the position of the triangle has also changed. This is because when you are rotating the object, you are in fact rotating the points that make up the face relative to the origin. To get around this, you follow the same procedure as with scaling—you translate the triangle to the origin, perform the rotation, and then finally translate it back to where it should be.

So how do you actually rotate a point around an axis, then? Well, it requires a little bit of—dare I say it?—trigonometry. (Yuck, that word has always made me cringe.) Anyway, let's check it out. There is a bunch of mathematics behind how you arrive at these formulas, but let's leave explanations like that to the math teachers, right? You are only interested in how to get stuff done.

To find the new position of a point, *p*, which is to be rotated about the origin by an angle, Θ (pronounced *theta*, it is a Greek symbol used to represent angles), you do the following:

New X Coordinate = x-coordinate * $\cos(\Theta)$ − y-coordinate * $\sin(\Theta)$

New Y Coordinate = x-coordinate * $\sin(\Theta)$ + y-coordinate * $\cos(\Theta)$

or more mathematically:

$$x' = x * \cos(\Theta) - y * \sin(\Theta)$$
$$y' = x * \sin(\Theta) + y * \cos(\Theta)$$

Sin, Cos, and Tan

If you want a little more information on sin and cos, then this info box is the place for you. sin, cos, and tan are all part of a bunch of functions that make up trigonometry, which has to do with the way angles and distances interact with each other. All of this stuff is based on the humble triangle, like the one shown in Figure 11.21. By the way, in case you didn't know, sin is short for sine, cos is short for cosine, and tan is short for tangent.

Each edge of the triangle has a name, and you can figure out ratios by dividing the lengths of these edges by each other like this:

sin = Length of Opposite ÷ Length of Hypotenuse

cos = Length of Adjacent ÷ Length of Hypotenuse

tan = Length of Opposite ÷ Length of Adjacent

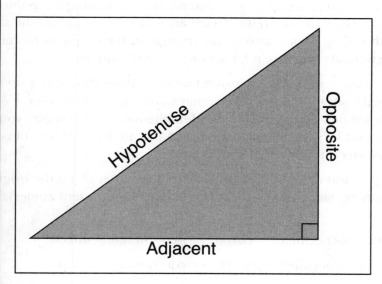

Figure 11.21

Our favorite shape

Using a simple 3, 4, 5 triangle (see Figure 11.22) you can see what sin, cos, and tan compute to:

$$\sin = \quad O \div H \quad = \quad 3 \div 5 = \quad 0.6000$$

$$\cos = \quad A \div H \quad = \quad 4 \div 5 = \quad 0.8000$$

$$\tan = \quad O \div A \quad = \quad 3 \div 4 = \quad 0.7500$$

You can also figure out the lengths of the other side of a triangle, if you only have two sides, using the Pythagorean theorem, which goes like this:

$$H^2 = \sqrt{(O2 + A^2)}$$

So if you only knew the adjacent was 4 and the opposite was 3, then you could do this:

$$H^2 = \sqrt{(3^2 + 4^2)}$$

$$H = 5$$

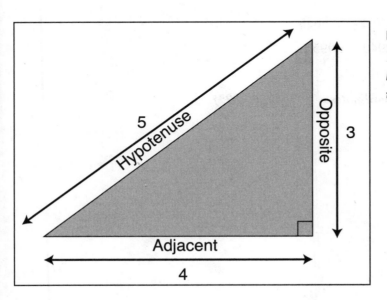

Figure 11.22

Figuring out the ratios

Now let's look at a small example of point rotation. Say you have a point at (4, 5) and you want to rotate it 35° around the origin.

$$x = 4$$

$$y = 5$$

$$\Theta = 35$$

⇓

$$x' = x \times \cos(\Theta) - y \times \sin(\Theta)$$

$$y' = x \times \sin(\Theta) + y \times \cos(\Theta)$$

⇓

$$x' = 4 \times \cos(35) - 5 \times \sin(35)$$

$$y' = 4 \times \sin(35) + 5 \times \sin(35)$$

⇓

$$x' = 4 \times 0.8191 - 5 \times 0.5735$$

$$y' = 4 \times 0.5735 + 5 \times 0.8191$$

⇓

$$x' = 3.2764 - 2.8675$$

$$y' = 2.2940 + 4.0955$$

⇓

New Coordinates = (0.4089, 6.3895)

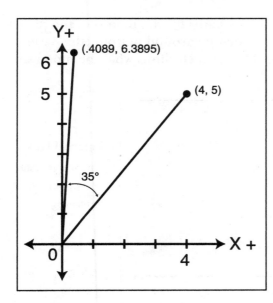

Figure 11.23

Rotating a point 35° around the origin

It's not that hard, really.

Coordinate Systems

The problems that I mentioned above with rotation and scaling can become very annoying and restrictive when you start programming more advanced 3D engines.

Take the following example: Say you have a model of the planets; there is the sun at the origin, then the planets orbiting at varying velocities, and finally the moons rotating around the planets. Have a look at Figure 11.24 to see this.

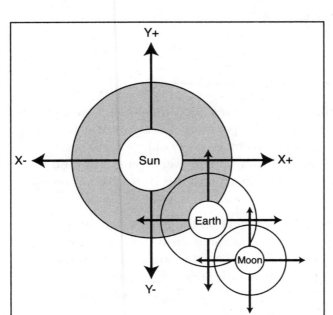

Figure 11.24

Computing positions that are based on parent objects

That's all very nice, but it leads to very complex paths for the moons of the planets, because their trajectory is based upon them rotating around not only the parent planet. but also the sun. Check out Figure 11.25, which shows what the moon's trajectory would look like if you tracked it.

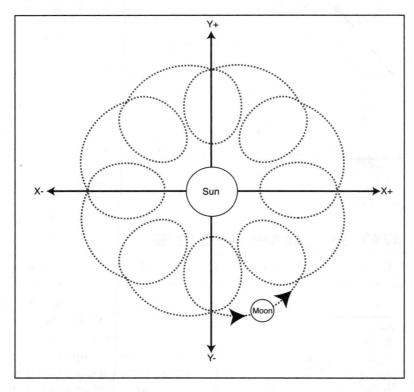

Figure 11.25

Complex rotation paths from reliant positioning

If you extend this whole rotation thing a bit—for instance, imagine if you had a 10-deep object link with each object relying on the position of the parent object to figure out its position—it becomes nonsensical to move every object back to the origin of its parent recursively for every position update every frame. It would get extremely complex and slow. So how do you get around this issue? Well, it requires some lateral thinking.

What if, instead of basing all the points in an object on the main origin of the world, you gave each object its own origin? That way you could easily make positional changes to the object, because it is always centered on the origin. Each object would know the position of its artificial origin relative to the real origin, but would define its points, or vertices, relative to the local artificial origin. Then when it came time to finally render the scene to the back buffer, you could convert the local coordinates into world coordinates with a few simple operations, which I'll cover in depth later.

You can extend the functionality of this to create really advanced frame systems, which make it easy to create the planets model that I was talking about earlier. For instance, you could set up a chain of objects that use the origin of their parents to work out their positions. You could rotate everything around the sun, then you could rotate the earth, which would also move the moon, and finally you could rotate just the moon around itself. The result is the correct path for all the planets and moons. This is just a general overview of the process; I'll show you a much more detailed implementation in the next few chapters.

What's the Vector, Victor?

So, now you know how points, lines, and basic shapes are represented in 3D. But how do you talk about directions and movements? And how do you start talking about paths and figure out how to get from one point to another? Using endless lists of points gets complicated and unproductive after a while, so the solution is to use a mathematical tool that has been designed just for the task.

A *vector* is a mathematical tool that is used to describe directions and distances. In other words, a vector tells you a direction and how far along in that direction you should go. Compare this to a *point,* which only describes a position relative to the origin. The technical name for the distance along a direction is the *magnitude,* which is a scalar value.

As vectors compose a large field of mathematical study, they have their own way of presentation. The usual format is to represent a vector with a lowercase letter in bold. For example, **u** is a vector and so is **v**.

Now for a more technical view. A vector is made up from *components,* or parts just like a point. A 2D vector has two components to describe it, and in 3D there are three. Check out Figure 11.26, which shows a vector from the origin to (2, 2, 2).

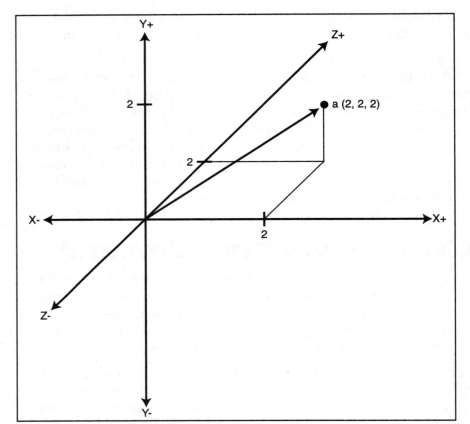

Figure 11.26

A vector from the origin to (2, 2, 2)

Creating Vectors

Well, it is all very nice to have a vector from the origin pointing out somewhere, but what happens when you want to get a vector from one place to another? For instance, say you have a ship at some position, and the evil alien outpost somewhere within sensor range, and you want to figure out the path of a rocket to be fired at the bad guys? Well, it is so simple I might not tell you. Only kidding! All you do is take motifs the source point and subtract it from the destination point. The result is a vector that points from the source to the destination. Try to remember the order of subtraction. To get from the source to the destination, you subtract the source from the destination. If you subtract in the wrong order then the vector will point opposite of the way you intended.

If you have a point at point p1 (10, 8, 7) and you want a vector, **v**, from it to point p2 (7, 3, 4) you would compute the following:

$$\mathbf{v} = p2 - p1$$

$$\Downarrow$$

$$\mathbf{v} = (7, 3, 4) - (10, 8, 7)$$

$$\Downarrow$$

$$\mathbf{v} = (7-10, 3-8, 4-7)$$

$$\Downarrow$$

$$\mathbf{v} = (-3, -5, -3)$$

So the vector from p1 to p2 is $(-3, -5, -3)$.

The Magnitude of a Vector

The *magnitude* of a vector is its length. The length of a vector is represented by putting vertical bars on both sides of the letter representing the vector. So if the vector is **a**, then the magnitude is |**a**|. Now the important question you might be asking yourself is "How do I compute the magnitude of a vector?" Well, it's pretty simple. You just get the square root of the components squared and add them together. Or in notation:

$$|\mathbf{a}| = \sqrt{(x^2 + y^2 + z^2)}$$

So if you had a vector, let's call it **b**, and it had the components $(4, 5, 6)$, then you would compute its magnitude like so:

$$\mathbf{b} = (4, 5, 6)$$

$$|\mathbf{b}| = \sqrt{(4^2 + 5^2 + 6^2)}$$

$$|\mathbf{b}| = \sqrt{(16 + 25 + 36)}$$

$$|\mathbf{b}| = \sqrt{(77)}$$

$$|\mathbf{b}| = 8.7749$$

So the magnitude of **b** is 8.7749.

Adding Vectors

From time to time you will have a path made from a number of vectors, and you will want to find the most efficient path from the start to the end of the path of vectors. Take, for instance, Figure 11.27, which shows two vectors, **a** and **b**. Vector **c** shows the shortest path between **a** and **b**. But how do you work out vector **c**?

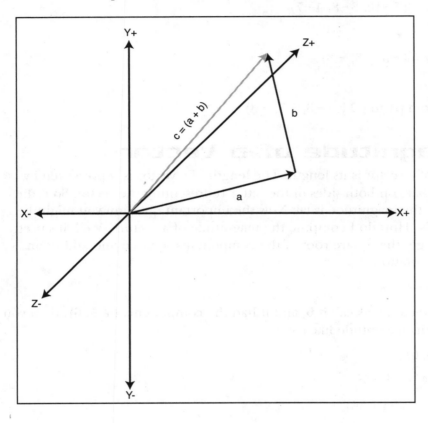

Figure 11.27

Combining vectors by adding them

Well, it's really simple. All you have to do is add the vectors together to combine them into a single vector. Adding **a** and **b** will produce vector **c**. So how do you do it? Simply add the components of the vector together. So if **a** is (5, 2, 3) and **b** is (−2, 4, 2), then you would add the vectors like this:

$$\mathbf{c} = \mathbf{a} + \mathbf{b}$$

$$\Downarrow$$

$$\mathbf{c} = (5, 2, 3) + (−2, 4, 2)$$

$$\mathbf{c} = (5 + (-2), 2 + 4, 3 + 2)$$

$$\mathbf{c} = (3, 6, 5)$$

Subtracting Vectors

If adding two vectors finds the shortest path vector between them, what would happen if you subtracted two vectors?

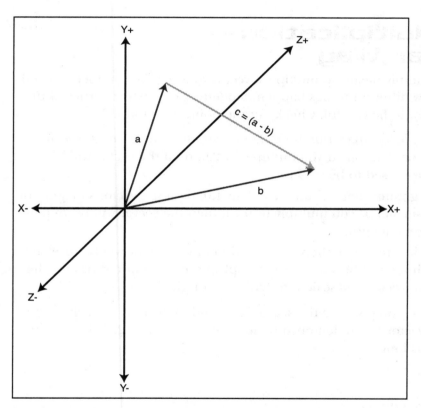

Figure 11.28

Finding a path between two vectors by subtracting them

Vector subtraction retrieves the vector between the end points of the two source vectors. Take a look at Figure 11.28 to see this visually. Subtracting **a** from **b** gets you vector **c**, which is the path from the end of **a** to the end of **b**. Notice the order of subtraction. If you want to get a vector from the end of **a** to **b**, then you subtract **a** from **b**. If you were to subtract **b** from **a**, then the vector would point in the opposite direction. Subtraction is achieved in the same way it was with addition; that is, you simply subtract the components from one another. Let's look at a small example to nail down this puppy. If **a** = (2, 5, 2) and **b** = (7, 2, 1), then check this out:

$$\mathbf{c} = (\mathbf{b} - \mathbf{a})$$

$$\mathbf{c} = (7, 2, 1) - (2, 5, 2)$$

$$\mathbf{c} = (7-2, 2-5, 1-2)$$

$$\mathbf{c} = (5, -3, -1)$$

Vector Multiplication— The Scalar Way

Scalar multiplication simply means to multiply a vector by a regular number with 1.0 as the midpoint. Now different things happen depending on the properties of the scalar you multiply by, so be careful. Check out the points that follow:

- If the scalar is greater than 1.0, then the magnitude (length) of the vector will increase. For example, if you multiply by 2.0, then the vector will be twice as long as it used to be.

- If the scalar is greater than 0.0 and less than 1.0, then the vector's magnitude will be scaled smaller. If you multiply by 0.75, then the vector will be 75 percent of its original length.

- If the scalar is less than 0.0, then the direction of the vector will be reversed and the magnitude will be scaled. So multiplying by −0.5 would reverse the direction of the vector *and* scale it to half of its original size.

To multiply by a scalar you just take the scalar value and multiply it by each of the components of the vector. So to demonstrate let's take a vector **a** (2, 3, 1) that you want to make twice as long.

$$2\mathbf{a} = 2(2, 3, 1)$$

$$2\mathbf{a} = (2\times2, 2\times3, 2\times1)$$

$$2\mathbf{a} = (4, 6, 2)$$

As you can see, you write the scalar as a number followed by the vector. Check out Figure 11.29 for an eye-friendly version.

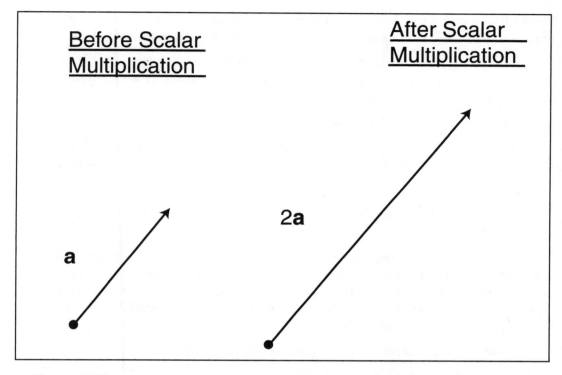

Figure 11.29

Multiplying the vector by the scalar value 2.0 causes the vector to double its magnitude.

Vector Multiplication—
The Dot Way

Since vectors are not normal numbers, you cannot just multiply a vector by another vector like you would a scalar value. You could try but you wouldn't produce anything that useful. However, there are methods classed as multiplication that can be extremely useful when dealing with vectors. The first is called the *dot product,* and it is used to describe the relationship of the angles between two vectors. The dot product can be computed using this equation:

$$\mathbf{a} \cdot \mathbf{b} = |\mathbf{a}| \times |\mathbf{b}| \times \cos(\Theta)$$

In English it means *the dot product of the vectors **a** and **b** is equal to the magnitude of **a** multiplied by the magnitude of **b** multiplied by the cosine of the angle between the two vectors.* Notice that the output from this function is not a vector; instead it is a scalar value.

More on that in a second. Also notice the · symbol used to signify the dot operation. Never use an "x" because that symbol is reserved for the cross product.

Now, most of the time you won't have the angle between the two vectors, and instead you will want to actually find the angle. The dot product is useful for this too, because you can rearrange it into this form:

$$\Theta = \cos^{-1} (\mathbf{a} \cdot \mathbf{b}) / (|\mathbf{a}| \times |\mathbf{b}|)$$

This means *the angle between the two vectors is equal to the inverse cosine of* $\mathbf{a} \cdot \mathbf{b}$ *divided by the magnitude of a multiplied by the magnitude of* $\mathbf{b}$. You can compute $\mathbf{a} \cdot \mathbf{b}$ using this formula:

If $\mathbf{a} = (x_a, y_a, z_a)$ and $\mathbf{b} = (x_b, y_b, z_b)$

then $\mathbf{a} \cdot \mathbf{b} = (x_a \times y_b) + (y_a \times y_b) + (z_a \times z_b)$

Now let's talk a little bit more about the output from $\mathbf{a} \cdot \mathbf{b}$. There are times—like when you are culling back faces, performing lighting calculations, and doing other esoteric jobs—that you don't want the angle between the two vectors, but you do want to know the type of angle between them. You probably recall that there are three types of angles in this world.

- *Acute* angles, which have an angle that is less than 90°
- *Obtuse* angles, which have an angle greater than 90°
- *Perpendicular* angles, which have an angle equal to 90°

Take a look at Figure 11.30 to see the angle types visually.

Anyway, the outcome of $\mathbf{a} \cdot \mathbf{b}$ will be like the following:

- **Acute**. Result will be negative.
- **Obtuse**. Result will be positive.
- **Perpendicular**. Result will be zero.

This may seem unimportant right now, but you will never see the end of it in 3D graphics. It pops up absolutely everywhere. Keep your Zen wits on this topic.

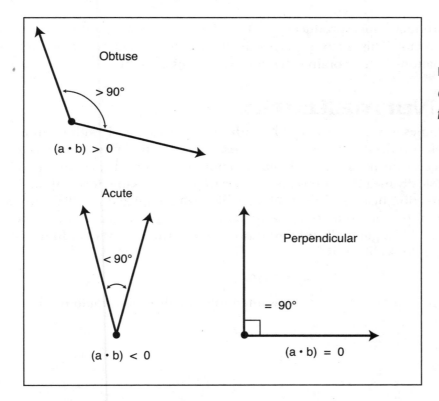

Figure 11.30

Obtuse, acute, and perpendicular angles

Vector Multiplication— The Cross Way

So now that you have seen the first two ways to multiply vectors, let's look at how to do it the third way. I know this is last, but it is definitely not least; it is probably the most complex way. So what does *crossing* two vectors achieve? Well, it gets you a third vector that is a normal to the original two vectors. For a vector to be *normal* to another vector it means that it is perpendicular. That is, the angle between it and the other two vectors is 90°. By the way, another term for the cross product is the *vector product*, so if you see that around, know that it means the same thing as cross product.

If $\mathbf{a} = (x_a, y_a, z_a)$ and $\mathbf{b} = (x_b, y_b, z_b)$

then $\mathbf{a} \times \mathbf{b} = (y_a \times z_b - z_a \times y_b, \; x_a \times z_b - z_a \times x_b, \; x_a \times y_b - y_a \times x_b)$

Unlike the dot product, which produces a scalar value, the output from the cross product is a new vector. This vector is perpendicular to the two source vectors. You will see many situations in the coming chapters where this is useful.

Vector Normalization

There are many times when you are dealing with vectors, particularly with lighting calculations, when you need to have a vector *normalized* or turned into a *unit vector*. To normalize a vector means to maintain its direction but reduce its magnitude to 1.0. What that basically means is you want a vector to point the same way, but only extend in that direction by one unit. This is actually really simple; all you have to do is divide each of the components of the vector by the original magnitude of the vector. The asterisk (*) is generally used to represent a normalized vector. In mathematical notation it looks like this:

$$\mathbf{a}* = \mathbf{a} \ / \ |\mathbf{a}|$$

So if you had a vector **a** (4, 2, 9) that you wanted to normalize, you would do the following:

$$\mathbf{a} = (4, 2, 9)$$

⬇

$$|\mathbf{a}| = \sqrt{(4^2 + 22 + 9^2)}$$

⬇

$$|\mathbf{a}| = \sqrt{(101)}$$

⬇

$$|\mathbf{a}| = 10.04 \quad \text{Got the magnitude.}$$

⬇

$$\mathbf{a}* = (4 \ / \ 10.04, 2 \ / \ 10.04, 9 \ / \ 10.04)$$

⬇

$$\mathbf{a}* = (0.39, 0.19, 0.89) \quad \text{Normalized vector!}$$

Have a look at Figure 11.31 to see a normalized vector.

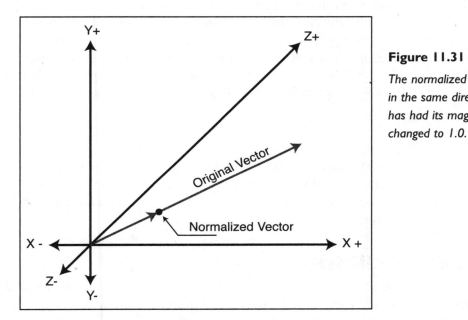

Figure 11.31

The normalized vector points in the same direction but has had its magnitude changed to 1.0.

Now all this mathematical stuff is meant to be just a refresher for you. If you have not come across vectors before, then I suggest that you pull out some mathematics books from your local library, if one still exists near you. That way, you will have a much more efficient learning curve for the rest of the book. Now let's move on to a greener subject....

Matrices—Which Pill to Take?

What is a *matrix*? I cannot tell you what a matrix is. It cannot be explained. In order to understand it you must see it for yourself. So swallow the orange Vitamin C supplement pill, take a deep breath, and then look below at matrix A:

$$A = \begin{bmatrix} a_{11}, a_{12}, a_{13}, a_{14} \\ a_{21}, a_{22}, a_{23}, a_{24} \\ a_{31}, a_{32}, a_{33}, a_{34} \\ a_{41}, a_{42}, a_{43}, a_{44} \end{bmatrix}$$

And that is what a matrix looks like. A matrix is usually written using an uppercase letter, like I used. The different items within the matrix are known as the *components* of the matrix. The subscripted numbers following the lowercase letters signify the position of the component within the matrix. So a^{22} is in the second column and the second row. The matrix above is a 4 x 4 matrix, which means that it has four rows and four columns. This is the most common matrix when you are dealing in 3D coordinates. Below is a 2 x 2 matrix, for comparison.

$$\begin{bmatrix} a_{11}, & a_{12} \\ a_{21}, & a_{22} \end{bmatrix}$$

So now that you know what a matrix looks like, let's discuss what they're for. Matrices were originally developed to aid the study of linear algebra. They can be used to solve simultaneous equations really easily. And they are incredibly useful for 3D calculations, as you will soon see.

Matrix Addition

To add two matrices together is really simple. Just like with vectors, you merely add the components together to get the resulting component. One important thing to remember is that you can only add matrices that have the same dimensions. For instance, you can add a 4 x 4 matrix to another 4 x 4 matrix, but there is just no way to add a 2 x 3 matrix to a 4 x 4 matrix. So, with that in mind, let's take a look at a small example.

Say you have two matrices, A and B, and you want to find C, which contains the result of adding A to B.

$$A = \begin{bmatrix} 3, 6, 5 \\ 4, 5, 2 \\ 1, 9, 4 \end{bmatrix} \qquad B = \begin{bmatrix} 8, 4, 7 \\ 9, 2, 3 \\ 4, 1, 2 \end{bmatrix}$$

$$\Downarrow$$

$$C = A + B$$

$$\Downarrow$$

$$\begin{bmatrix} 3 + 8, 6 + 4, 5 + 7 \\ 4 + 9, 5 + 2, 2 + 3 \\ 1 + 4, 9 + 1, 4 + 2 \end{bmatrix}$$

$$\Downarrow$$

$$C = \begin{bmatrix} 11,\ 10,\ 12 \\ 13,\ 7,\ 5 \\ 5,\ 10,\ 6 \end{bmatrix}$$

You can add matrices any way you like, as long as they are the same dimensions—for example, A + B + C = B + (A + C) etc.

Matrix Subtraction

Matrix subtraction is just like addition, in that all you have to do is subtract the components of the matrix from each other. Again, like addition, the dimensions of both the matrices must be the same. Here is a small example, where the matrix C will be found by subtracting matrix A from matrix B.

$$A = \begin{bmatrix} 4,\ 3,\ 5 \\ 4,\ 5,\ 8 \\ 1,\ 4,\ 4 \end{bmatrix} \qquad B = \begin{bmatrix} 3,\ 1,\ 7 \\ 1,\ 3,\ 3 \\ 4,\ 1,\ 2 \end{bmatrix}$$

C = B − A

$$\begin{bmatrix} 4-3,\ 3-1,\ 5-7 \\ 4-1,\ 5-3,\ 8-3 \\ 1-4,\ 4-1,\ 4-2 \end{bmatrix}$$

$$C = \begin{bmatrix} 1,\ 2,\ -2 \\ 3,\ 2,\ 5 \\ -3,\ 3,\ 2 \end{bmatrix}$$

When subtracting, the order that you subtract is the same as for normal numbers. In other words, A − B − C = A − (B−C) and so on.

Matrix Scalar Multiplication

Sometimes you want to increase each component of a vector by the same amount. For instance, you might want to double the size of each component by multiplying by 2. This is written by putting the scalar by which you want to multiply in front of the matrix. For instance, 2A denotes that you want to multiply the matrix A by 2. The mathematics behind this is really simple. Just multiply each component by the scalar value like this:

$$A = \begin{bmatrix} 4, 5 \\ 3, 2 \end{bmatrix}$$

$$2A = \begin{bmatrix} 2 \times 4, 2 \times 5 \\ 2 \times 3, 2 \times 2 \end{bmatrix}$$

$$A' = \begin{bmatrix} 8, 10 \\ 6, 4 \end{bmatrix}$$

Matrix Multiplication (Real Man's Multiplication)

Although matrix addition and subtraction are pretty easy, multiplication is a total pain when you first see it, but once you get used to it, it gets much easier. First let's talk about the kinds of matrices you are actually able to multiply. They don't have to be the same dimensions like with addition and subtraction. Instead, only the inner dimensions need to be the same. The *inner dimensions* are the two numbers in the middle when you write the dimensions of two matrices beside each other. So look at the descriptions of the matrices that follow:

(a) 3 x $\boxed{3}$ $\boxed{3}$ x 4   (b) 4 x $\boxed{4 \quad 2}$ x 3   (c) 2 x $\boxed{2 \quad 2}$ x 4

The inner dimensions are enclosed in the boxes. So from those examples you can see that the matrices in (a) and (c) can be multiplied together, but the matrices in (b) cannot.

I am now going to unleash some truly nasty mathematics on you—how to multiply a matrix. It works like this. You multiply the rows of the first matrix by the columns of the second matrix, and then add the products together to get the final result for the destination matrix. That probably makes your eyes glaze over if you have not seen this before, so let me show you an example, using two 2 x 2 matrices.

$$A = \begin{bmatrix} 3, 4 \\ 8, 2 \end{bmatrix} \qquad B = \begin{bmatrix} 5, 6 \\ 2, 3 \end{bmatrix}$$

⬇

$$C = A \times B$$

⬇

$$C = \begin{bmatrix} (3 \times 5 + 4 \times 2), (3 \times 6 + 4 \times 3) \\ (8 \times 5 + 2 \times 2), (8 \times 6 + 2 \times 3) \end{bmatrix}$$

⬇

$$C = \begin{bmatrix} 15 + 8, 18 + 12 \\ 40 + 4, 48 + 6 \end{bmatrix}$$

⬇

$$C = \begin{bmatrix} 23, 30 \\ 44, 54 \end{bmatrix}$$

See how it works? Have a look at the matrix below for the mathematical version:

$$\mathbf{C=AB}$$

$$\mathbf{C = \begin{bmatrix} a_{11}, a_{12} \\ a_{21}, a_{22} \end{bmatrix} \quad * \quad \begin{bmatrix} b_{11}, b_{12} \\ b_{21}, b_{22} \end{bmatrix}}$$

$$c_{11} = (a_{11} \times b_{11}) + (a_{12} \times b_{21})$$

$$c_{12} = (a_{11} \times b_{12}) + (a_{12} \times b_{22})$$

$$c_{21} = (a_{21} \times b_{11}) + (a_{22} \times b_{21})$$

$$c_{22} = (a_{21} \times b_{12}) + (a_{22} \times b_{22})$$

Get it? Good. If you need some more help, pull out some high school mathematics books; they normally have a lot of useful information on this stuff.

Now, one really important thing to remember is that the order in which you multiply matrices is really important. For instance, if you have two matrices, A and B, then just about every time $A \times B$ will not equal $B \times A$. Keep this in mind because it is really essential.

Put Down the Gun, Step Away from the Coax Connection, and Identify Yourself

I said that it is almost always true that you must watch out for how you multiply matrices because there are a few exceptions. One of them, which you will come across a lot, is the *identity matrix*. You can think of the identity matrix like the number 1 in normal mathematics. That is, you can multiply anything by it and the result will be same. Like $7 \times 1 = 7$, $238 \times 1 = 238$, and so on.

The identity matrix is represented by the uppercase letter "I," and it looks like this:

A 4 x 4 identity matrix:

$$\begin{bmatrix} 1, 0, 0, 0 \\ 0, 1, 0, 0 \\ 0, 0, 1, 0 \\ 0, 0, 0, 1 \end{bmatrix}$$

A 3 x 3 identity matrix:

$$\begin{bmatrix} 1, 0, 0 \\ 0, 1, 0 \\ 0, 0, 1 \end{bmatrix}$$

A 2 x 2 identity matrix:

$$\begin{bmatrix} 1, 0 \\ 0, 1 \end{bmatrix}$$

As you can see, an identity matrix can be any dimension, as long as it contains all zeros, except along the main diagonal, which must contain ones. Multiplying any matrix by an identity matrix will result in the same matrix. This may seem pointless, but later you will see many areas where this is useful.

So if you have a matrix A, then A × I = A, and I × A = A.

Matrix Concatenation

Now let me discuss why matrices are oh-so-useful in 3D gaming. Basically, you can combine two or more matrices into one matrix that contains all the components of the original matrices. For instance, as I will show you soon, you can use matrices to rotate, scale, and translate points around in 3D space. So if you need to rotate 400 points and then translate them, you can combine the rotation and translation into a single matrix, thus cutting the number of calculations in half!

If you had four matrices that you wanted to combine into one, you just multiply them like so:

$$\text{Result} = \text{Matrix1} \times \text{Matrix2} \times \text{Matrix3} \times \text{Matrix4}$$

Cool or what, my friend? Cool or what.

Invert This Bad Boy

A lot of times when dealing with matrices you will need to find what is known as the *inverse* of a matrix. The inverse of a matrix is kind of complex to nail down because the only way to describe it is in relation to the identity matrix. Basically, if you multiply a matrix by its inverse, the result will be the identity matrix. If that sounds a little up in the air, then you are right—it is! The inversion is one of those things that are very important, although you never want to look too close because each answer you get will generate twice as many questions.

Unfortunately, the mathematics behind trying to find the inverse of any matrix with dimensions larger than 2 x 2 is an unbelievable nightmare. I mean just finding the inverse of a 3 x 3 matrix using a pen and paper would take a few sheets. However, I will show you some code that deals with the inverse later.

Applying Matrices to 3D Transformations

Now you are going to start to get jiggy and make links between the different things you have been learning about in this chapter. Let's take what you know about transformations, 3D coordinate systems, and matrices, and put them together to create something bigger.

Let me start by telling you that for 3D transformations using matrices, all of your calculations will use matrices that have a dimension of 4 x 4 or 1 x 4. The extra row and column are there because there are problems with the matrix theory when dealing with translations. More on this shortly.

So let's see what you want to achieve. What you want is a matrix by which you can multiply a set of points, to transform them to a new position. So you can hold your points in a 1 x 4 matrix like the following:

[x, y, z, 1]

where x, y, and z represent the components of the point and the final 1 is called the *normalization factor*. It is basically there to ensure that translations work properly. You will see this referenced as *reciprocal of homogeneous W* or *rhw* a lot in the DirectX documentation. Don't worry about it too much for now.

Translation

Like I showed you before, you translate a point using this method:

x' = x + XTranslationFactor

y' = y + YTranslationFactor

z' = z + ZTranslationFactor

Now to do this with a matrix all you do is take a 4 x 4 identity matrix and stick in the translation factors in the following locations:

$$\text{Translation Matrix} = \begin{bmatrix} 1, 0, 0, 0 \\ 0, 1, 0, 0 \\ 0, 0, 1, 0 \\ tx, ty, tz, 1 \end{bmatrix}$$

where tx, ty, and tz are the amounts that you want to scale in the x-, y-, and z-axes, respectively.

So what do you do now? Well, let's call the translation matrix T. Then, if you have a matrix containing a point like this:

Point P1 = [x, y, z, 1]

you can multiply it by the translation matrix to get its new position:

P1' = P1 × T

Let's look at a small example. Say P1 = [2, 3, 4, 1] and you wanted to translate this point two units positively in each of the three axes.

$$
P1' = [2, 3, 4, 1] \times
\begin{bmatrix}
1, 0, 0, 0 \\
0, 1, 0, 0 \\
0, 0, 1, 0 \\
2, 2, 2, 1
\end{bmatrix}
$$

Then P1' now equals = [4, 5, 6, 1]

Pretty slick, huh?

Scaling

Remember how to do scaling? You simply multiply each component of the point by the scaling factor, which is a *scale value*. Or, more specifically:

x' = x × XScalingFactor

y' = y × YScalingFactor

z' = z × ZScalingFactor

The matrix for scaling a point looks a little like this:

$$
\text{Scaling Matrix} =
\begin{bmatrix}
sx, 0, 0, 0 \\
0, sy, 0, 0 \\
0, 0, sz, 0 \\
0, 0, 0, 1
\end{bmatrix}
$$

where sx, sy, and sz contain the value describing the amount that you want to scale the point by in each of the axes.

Again, just like translation, all you have to do is multiply a point in matrix form by the scaling matrix to get the new position for the point.

Rotation

Unfortunately, rotation is the black sheep of the matrix transformation family, because there are, in fact, three different ways that you can rotate. You can rotate around the x-axis, the y-axis, or the z-axis. There's a bunch of mathematics behind how you come up with the matrices for rotation, but in the end all you really want is the matrix itself. In this case, I think the background knowledge is too much of a digression, so instead I'm going to show you the completed matrices that you can fill in to rotate a point around an axis.

Rotation in the X-Axis

For rotation around the x-axis the matrix looks like this:

$$X \text{ Rotation} = \begin{bmatrix} 1, 0, 0, 0 \\ 0, \cos(Q), \sin(Q), 0 \\ 0, 2\sin(Q), \cos(Q), 0 \\ 0, 0, 0, 1 \end{bmatrix}$$

In each of the cos or sin entries you just have to put in the angle by which you want to rotate. Be careful not to mix up when to use degrees and radians, by the way. I'll point this out when it becomes pertinent.

Rotation in the Y-Axis

The matrix for y-axis rotation is as follows:

$$Y \text{ Rotation} = \begin{bmatrix} \cos(Q), 0, 2\sin(Q), 0 \\ 0, 1, 0, 0 \\ \sin(Q), 0, \cos(Q), 0 \\ 0, 0, 0, 1 \end{bmatrix}$$

Again, each of the cos and sin entries simply takes the angle by which you want to rotate the point.

Rotation in the Z-Axis

The matrix for z-axis rotation looks like this bad boy:

$$\text{Z Rotation} = \begin{bmatrix} \cos(Q), \sin(Q), 0, 0 \\ 2\sin(Q), \cos(Q), 0, 0 \\ 0, 0, 1, 0 \\ 0, 0, 0, 1 \end{bmatrix}$$

The Transformation Pipeline

Remember when I gave you an introduction to local and world coordinates? I was using the metaphor of the earth and the moon. Well, let's look for a moment at stages an object has to go through before it can be rendered as a proper 3D object. When dealing with objects that rely on the positions of parent objects, it is good to give each object its own set of local coordinates.

The Local to World Transform

In this step you need to convert the positions of all the points that make up the object that you are attempting to render into world coordinates. This is usually a simple step. You will have the main object, which will have a position relative to the main origin. So to convert the local points to world coordinates, all you have to do is add the world offset position to each of the points.

You can do this by setting up a translation matrix, which contains the world origin offset as the translation variables, except you would change the sign of the offset. Then you could multiply this *world matrix* by each point to convert it to a world coordinate. Don't forget that this step is only a temporary change, and that the original points remain the same. You'll see more about this when you start to write the code for the engine.

The World to Camera Transform

The next step is to move the world coordinates of the models into what is called *camera space*. So what the heck is camera space, then? Well, if you think about it you will realize that usually the camera will start at (0, 0, 0) and be looking directly down the z-axis. When the player (camera) starts to move, then the angles of the camera relative to the z-axis start to change. So what you want to do is rotate all the points inversely back to the way they would be, when the camera is still looking down the z-axis. By doing this, you make it much easier to find the correct rendering points on the rendering surface.

The Camera to Projection Transform

The final stage in the transformation pipeline, before rendering, is to make sure that the points are transformed to have the correct perspective. You may know that objects at a distance look smaller than when they are up close. So what you want to do is change the positions of the points in the scene to move toward the center of the screen in proportion to their distance from the position of the camera.

It is quite a complex operation to set up the perspective transform, but luckily for you Direct3D does most of the work, and I'll show you the implementation details in the next chapter. So just to recap, the transformation pipeline will generally look something like this:

Local ➡ World ➡ Camera ➡ Perspective

Clipping

There are two types of clipping that you will come across in 3D applications. The first is *object clipping* and the second is *image clipping*. Direct3D handles image clipping, so you don't need to worry about it too much. It is basically a process of making sure that when you are drawing a polygon that overlaps slightly out of the screen that you make sure it is correctly drawn.

Object clipping, or *mathematical clipping*, is when you mark objects that you want to draw as visible or invisible, depending on whether or not they are located within the *viewing volume*. The viewing volume is bounded by six planes. Take a look at Figure 11.32 to see the viewing volume. You can see the left, right, top, and bottom clipping planes.

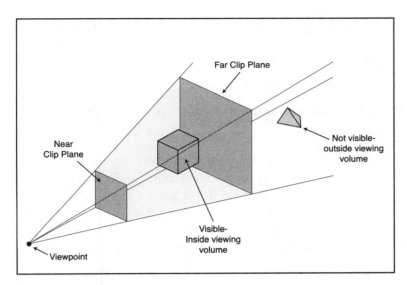

Figure 11.32

Determining object visibility using the viewing volume

In general, Direct3D will look after all of that for you, but what you do need to be concerned with is the near and far clipping planes. These two planes describe the distances from the viewpoint that objects can be before they are considered redundant. For instance, you do not want to waste time drawing objects that are so far in the distance that they do not proportionally increase the quality of the visual experience for the user. Keep in mind that object clipping has to do with sorting out which polygons are to be considered viable for rendering, and the test that determines this is based on the distance in the z direction of the object from the camera. It has nothing to do with determining which faces are visible with relation to their angle to the viewer, which comes under the term *back face culling*.

Back Face Culling

Rendering is a very time-consuming process so a lot of very smart people have come up with a bunch of tricks to help speed up the process. One of them is called *back face culling*, and it is based on the fact that when you look at something you can only see the side that is facing toward you. For instance, if you are looking at a baseball, all you can see is 50 percent of the ball. To see more you have to move it or get a mirror.

The same applies to games. If you cannot see some of the faces in the scene because they are facing away from you, then you shouldn't bother processing them, right? Exactly. Well, it just so happens that there is a really simple test that you can perform to check if any face is facing toward you. All you have to do is get a normal to the face, then get a vector from the current camera position and get a dot product between the two vectors.

Vector **a** = Normal to the face in question

Vector **b** = Vector from camera position to the face in question

Result Scalar r = **a** · **b**

If the resulting scalar, r, is greater than zero, then you know that the angle between the normal of the face and the view vector is obtuse, which in English simply means that the face is not visible to we poor humans who don't have a sixth sense. So using this knowledge, you can remove unneeded faces from the processing pipeline. Have a look at Figure 11.33 to see how the relationship of the between the face normal and the viewpoint help to determine the visibility of the surface.

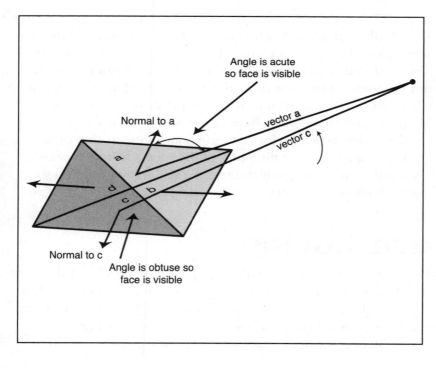

Angle is acute
so face is visible

Normal to a

vector a

vector c

Normal to c

Angle is obtuse so
face is visible

Figure 11.33

Determining face visibility using the dot product

Depth Buffering

Now I want to talk a little bit about the rendering process again, this time more to do with how and when the faces of a scene are drawn. Faces have to be drawn in a certain sequence in order for them to make visual sense. This is very important, so keep those eyes perked. For instance, think about a scene with a small village and snowcapped mountains in the distance. Now think about if you were drawing this scene, layer by layer. If you drew the village first, then the mountains would occlude it when they were drawn. Check out Figure 11.34.

Figure 11.34

Drawing objects in the correct order to prevent occlusion

The Painter's Algorithm

So the moral of the story is that it is important for the rendering code to draw the faces in back-to-front order. That is, the faces furthest from the viewer need to be drawn first. Now the method for doing this is called the *painter's algorithm*, because you are rendering the same way that a painter paints a scene. It seems pretty simple, right? Wrong. It's only simple when you're dealing with faces that happen to exist in agreeable positions. This problem arises because you're checking the distance of the face from the camera. That's fantastic, but a lot of the time you will be coming across faces that are called *special cases,* and there are so many of them that they will make you feel pretty sick.

The problem with the painter's algorithm is that it compares faces based on a single depth value for the entire face. To make it totally foolproof, what you really need is a routine that compares faces on the pixel level.

Z-Buffering

Some other very smart people came up with another idea that works much better, called a *z-buffer.* The "z" comes from the fact that the inventor was a Zen guru, not too much different from what you will soon be, and he wanted the world to know the Zen philosophy. Actually, that is not true at all, but it sounds good!

Anyway, like I was saying, the best way to do a *depth sort* is by comparing each face on a pixel-by-pixel basis (see Figure 11.35). However, computationally, this would take far too long, so a better way is to use what is called *linear interpolation.* That is, you compute the distance from the viewer of the three vertex points that make up the face and then interpolate the rest of the values between them. In other words, you use some educated guesswork to figure out where most of the face is, based on the position of the vertices. This works almost perfectly most of the time, and today it is the standard solution for depth sorting.

Using a z-buffer requires that you allocate a chunk of memory that has the same resolution as the primary surface. For instance, if you were running your game at 800 x 600, then you would set the resolution of the depth buffer to 800 x 600. The depth buffer usually has a depth of 16 bits per pixel, and it basically works by giving each pixel that makes up a face its own depth value, so that when it comes time to draw another face, it is much easier to figure out whether it is supposed to be in front of or behind the other face. All you have to do is compare the depth values for the pixel you are about to render. If the depth value for the pixel in question is less than the current rendered pixel, then the pixel is drawn on top of the old pixel. Otherwise the pixel is not drawn since it is behind the currently drawn face.

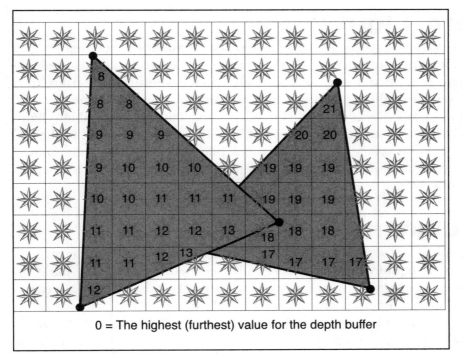

Figure 11.35

Using the z-Buffer to do pixel-by-pixel depth tests

0 = The highest (furthest) value for the depth buffer

Luckily for you, Direct3D handles the management of the depth buffer, so for now all you need is an overview of what it is and how it works. One other thing worth mentioning is the w-buffer. The *w-buffer* is basically a z-buffer, but there are some extra calculations used that make it more visually correct when trying to determine the distances between faces that are very close together, and very near or very far from the viewpoint.

Lighting

A 3D-rendered scene is really great, but it is nothing without lighting and materials. The ambience that you can achieve using lighting and materials can sometimes be truly amazing. Think about the eeriness of some of the *Quake III* levels or how *Alien vs. Predator* can actually scare you if you play it in the dark. Let's talk about lighting first.

There are four types of lights that you can use in Direct3D, and those are point lights, spot lights, directional lights, and, of course, ambient lights. I want to take a minute to show you the differences between these different light types. The following is more of a theory builder; I'll show you implementation details soon.

Ambient Lights

In our world, *ambient light* is the general light level of the room environment around us, and it is the direct light from the sun or other sources that has been reflected so many times that it is no longer possible to tell where it came from. In virtual worlds, ambient light is similar, but it is not computed based on the combined reflections of other light sources. Instead, you explicitly set the ambient light level, and this is basically the minimum level of light that any component in the scene will possess. For instance, if you had a scene that was modeling a desert environment, you would have quite a high ambient light level, as opposed to a creepy cave, which would require a very low ambient light level.

Point Lights

You can think of a *point light* as a normal lightbulb. That is, it has a position in space and it radiates light in all directions equally (see Figure 11.36). One thing that you will discover about the lighting model in Direct3D is that it lacks a certain realism. That is, some properties of light, such as light blocking and shadow casting, are not implemented by the default lighting engine. If you have a point light in front of a wall, then any objects behind the wall, which should be dark, will be lit as if the wall were not there. Don't worry though—this isn't much of an issue.

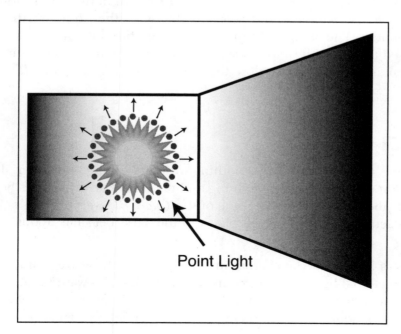

Figure 11.36

Point lights

Point Light

Directional Lights

Directional lights are very similar to point lights, although it is easier to think of them as having a position infinitely far away from the object being lit (see Figure 11.37). Directional lights are good for mimicking objects such as the sun or the moon. Light from a directional light travels in one direction throughout the scene. Inherently, you do not need to set a position for a directional light, only a direction.

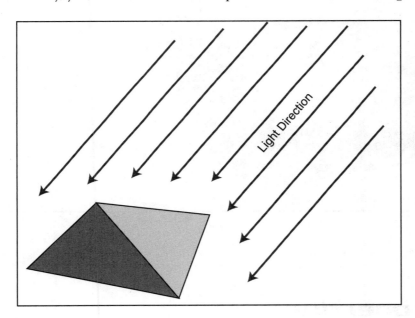

Light Direction

Figure 11.37

Directional lighting

Spot Lights

You probably know what *spot lights* are, since they mimic their real-world counterparts. A spot light has a number of properties, such as its position and the position of its target. To define a spot light you need to define two cones of light. The inner cone, known as the *umbra*, defines the bright circle of light that is at the highest intensity. The outer cone, known as the *penumbra*, surrounds the inner cone and models the falloff from the full intensity light within the umbra, to the light level in the surrounding area (see Figure 11.38). You can change the way the light fades between the umbra and penumbra using the *falloff* property of the light, although the effect is so small, and the computational cost so high, that it is usually better just to stick with a normal falloff curve. There are variables that are used to describe the cones of a spot light in Direct3D. *Theta* specifies the angle for the umbra, and *Phi* is for the penumbra. More on this later.

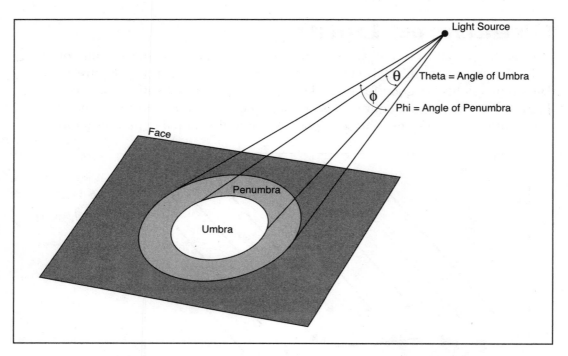

Figure 11.38

Spot lighting

Light Properties

OK, so now that you have seen the different light types, let me take a minute to show you some of the properties that govern how lights work.

First up is the *diffuse color* of the light, which basically governs what color the light is. It is pretty simple, really; if you set the diffuse color of a light to (255, 0, 0), then the light will be red. Next is the *specular color*. This has to do with the *specular highlights* of the object that you want to illuminate. An object with a lot of specular highlights will have a metallic appearance. In other words, it will have a lot of shiny bits. Matte or more plastic objects have few specular highlights.

Lights can also have an *ambient color*. This color basically specifies the darkest possible color that objects within the light's range can be.

A property of light that you will be interested in is, of course, its *range*. The range of a light specifies the distance at which the light no longer has any effect. This is useful for situations like when you have a small candle and you don't want it to light the far side of China like a neutron bomb.

And the final property of light, which drives everyone crazy in its current implementation, is the *attenuation* of the light. I say it drives everyone crazy because as soon as you start messing with the attenuation of lights, you get widely varying results, and it's hard to see the pattern of how it all works (see Figure 11.40). So, while you are learning, I would suggest that you stick with the default values that I will show you when I cover implementation.

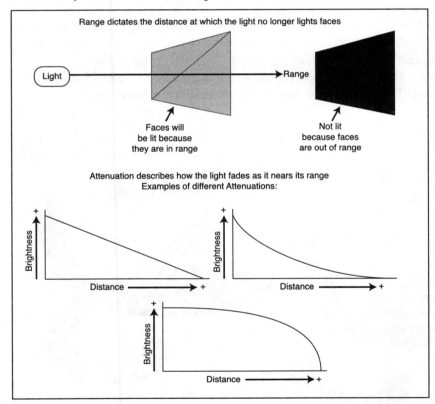

Figure 11.39

How attenuation relates to range

Materials

Whereas the lights define what type of light is emitted onto an object, you can create materials to define how you want your objects to react to the light that falls on it. Materials have many of the same properties as lights, but just keep in mind that materials define how the object reacts to light. The final color that you see on-screen is computed by combining the properties of the source light and the destination material.

Let's start with looking at the diffuse color of a material. Like lights, the *diffuse color* defines the basic color of the object. So setting the diffuse color of the material to green, and then applying that material to an object, will make the object green.

The *ambient color* of the material defines the minimum level of brightness that an object will have once the material has been applied to it. Like I was talking about before, you will set this to reflect on the type of environment that you are attempting to replicate.

The *specular color* defines the color that you want the specular highlights of the object to be. The *specular highlights* are the shiny parts of the object. You can control the amount of highlights that an object has by modifying the *specular power*, which in Direct3D is a scalar value. Setting the specular power to 0.0 will disable specular highlighting. The higher the power, the more highlighting an object will have.

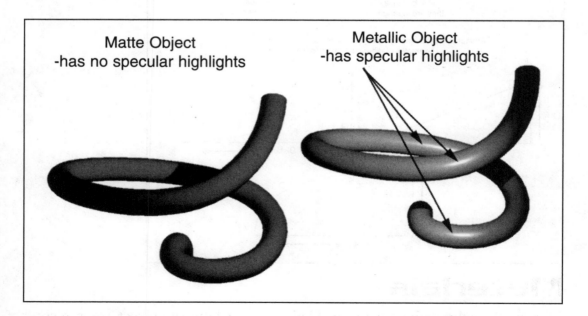

Figure 11.40

Specular highlighting

The final property of materials that you need to know about is the *emissive color*. You can use this member to make an object emit light, or in other words, appear as if it is glowing. Well, that's what all the books say. In fact, the glowing effect is pretty sad, except when you use it with fog. But I'll show you examples later where you can put the emissive material property to good use, such as when modeling the sun.

Conclusion

Well, that's the hard part over. Learning the theory behind all the stuff that you are going to cover in the following chapters is always a pain, but it is important. If you feel like you are a few sandwiches short of a picnic in the rest of the book, feel free to flip back to this chapter, where I am pretty sure you will find the almost implementation independent information on the topics that I will be discussing.

Now I bet you are dying to get to the good stuff and put all this new knowledge into practice. Well, let's not waste time.

CHAPTER 12

GETTING TO KNOW DIRECT3D IN A MORE 3D SORT OF WAY

Y ou now have the knowledge to start really coming to grips with Direct3D. In this chapter I am going to show you all the stuff that you need to get off the ground with Direct3D, like

- the setup code to get 3D rendering going.
- an introduction to Direct3D-specific, concepts such as the flexible vertex format and vertex buffers.
- info on setting up world, view, and projection matrices.

As I've said, I'll be referring to the 3D section of DirectX as *Direct3D*. In the past, what I'll be discussing came under the term *Direct3D Immediate Mode*, which was the low-level layer used to communicate efficiently with graphics hardware. Immediate Mode used to have quite a reputation for being overly complex and too unlike other APIs, such as OpenGL. The only other form of Direct3D that you could use was *Retained Mode*, which as I've said before was a load of <insert expletive here>. With the unification of Direct3D and DirectDraw, Retained Mode was removed, and the immediate mode tag was dropped from the name. So now everything is known as just Direct3D. Cool? Cool. I just wanted to make sure that if you had any previous experience with DirectX you knew where you stood. OK, back to the drawing board...

Getting Back to the Setup Code

Now let's run through all the setup code that I showed you before—except this time I'll show you the 3D stuff, which I glossed over in the 2D chapters, in more detail. You can consider the code I will show you the basis for all the future 3D stuff that I will be developing. I'm going to run through it pretty fast, since you have seen most of it before.

The Include Files

The include files are the same for 3D development as they were for 2D. So like before, somewhere in your project you should have these files included:

```
#include <windows.h>
#include <mmsystem.h>

#include <d3d8.h>
#include <d3dx8.h>

#include "Engine.h"
```

Engine.h is the header file that will be filled with all the 2D code from the previous chapters and the new 3D-related code for the rest of the engine's development.

The Globals

These are basically the same as in the last chapters.

```
CConsole Console;
HWND g_hWndMain;
```

Console is the global console object that I showed you how to create in Chapter 10, and g_hWndMain is just there to make it easy to access the handle to the main window since it is accessed so much.

The Window Procedure

This is just for your reference, so that you know how the WndProc() function looks in my code.

```
long CALLBACK WndProc( HWND hWnd, UINT uMessage,
                                        WPARAM wParam, LPARAM lParam )
{
        // Switch the Windows message to figure out what it is
        switch( uMessage )
        {
                case WM_CREATE: // The CreateWindow() function was just called
                {
                        // One Time Initialization
                        return 0;
                }
```

```
        case WM_PAINT: // The window needs to be redrawn
        {
                // Tell Windows to go away; the window is fine
                ValidateRect( hWnd, NULL );

                return 0;
        }

        case WM_KEYDOWN:
        {
                Console.OnKeyDown( wParam );

                return 0;
        }

        case WM_CHAR:
        {
                Console.OnChar( wParam );

                return 0;
        }

        case WM_DESTROY:        // The window is about to be closed
        {
                // Our main window is closing. This means we want our app to exit.
                // Tell Windows to put a WM_QUIT message in our message queue
                PostQuitMessage( 0 );
                return 0;
        }

        default:                        // Some other message
        {
                // Let Windows handle this message
                return DefWindowProc( hWnd, uMessage, wParam, lParam );
        }
    }
}
```

Pretty simple, I'm sure you'll concur. Notice the links to the console for the keyboard input. If you don't want to attach the console to your project, then you can safely ignore those lines.

Getting Down with `WinMain()`

You probably know the `WinMain()` function like the back of your hand by now, but I want to make sure that you know the positions of the `GameInit()`, `GameLoop()`, and `GameShutdown()` functions.

```
int WINAPI WinMain( HINSTANCE hInstance, HINSTANCE hPrevInstance,
                                PSTR pstrCmdLine, int iCmdShow )
{
        HWND hWnd;              // The handle to our main window
        MSG msg;               // The message Windows is sending us
        WNDCLASSEX wc; // The window class used to create our window

        // The name of our class and also the title to our window
        static char strAppName[] = "First Windows App, Zen Style";

        // Fill in the window class with the attributes for our main window

        // The size of this structure in bytes
        wc.cbSize             = sizeof( WNDCLASSEX );

        //  The style of the window.
        wc.style                    = CS_HREDRAW | CS_VREDRAW | CS_OWNDC;
        // Useless information.  Just set to zero.
        wc.cbClsExtra         = 0;
        // Useless information.  Just set to zero.
        wc.cbWndExtra         = 0;
        // The name of our event handler
        wc.lpfnWndProc        = WndProc;
        // A handle to the applications instance
        wc.hInstance          = hInstance;
        // The handle to the brush to use for the window background
        wc.hbrBackground      = (HBRUSH)GetStockObject( DKGRAY_BRUSH );
        // A handle to the icon to use for the window
        wc.hIcon                    = LoadIcon( NULL, IDI_APPLICATION );
        // A handle to a smaller version of the apps icon
```

```
wc.hIconSm             = LoadIcon( NULL, IDI_APPLICATION );
// A handle to the cursor to use while the mouse is over our window
wc.hCursor             = LoadCursor( NULL, IDC_CROSS );
// A handle to the resource to use as our menu
wc.lpszMenuName = NULL;
// The human readable name for this class
wc.lpszClassName       = strAppName;

// Register the class with Windows
RegisterClassEx( &wc );


// Create the window based on the previous class
hWnd = CreateWindowEx( WS_EX_TOPMOST,        // Advanced style settings
                           strAppName,       // The name of the class
                      strAppName,            // The window caption
                      WS_POPUP |
                      WS_SYSMENU |
                      WS_VISIBLE,            // The window style
                      CW_USEDEFAULT,         // The initial x position
                      CW_USEDEFAULT,         // The initial y position
                      512, 512,              // The initial width/height
                      NULL,                  // Handle to parent window
                      NULL,                  // Handle to the menu
                      hInstance,             // Handle to the apps instance
                      NULL );                // Advanced context

g_hWndMain = hWnd;


// Display the window we just created
ShowWindow( hWnd, iCmdShow );
// Draw the window contents for the first time
UpdateWindow( hWnd );
```

```
if( FAILED( GameInit() ) )
{
        SetError( "Initialization Failed" );
        GameShutdown();
        return E_FAIL;
}

// Start the message loop
while( TRUE )
{
        // Check if a message is waiting for processing
        if( PeekMessage( &msg, NULL, 0, 0, PM_REMOVE ) )
        {
                // Check if the message is to quit the application
                if( msg.message == WM_QUIT )
                        // Exit the message loop
                        break;

                // Change the format of certain messages
                TranslateMessage( &msg );
                // Pass the message to WndProc() for processing
                DispatchMessage( &msg );
        }
        else
        {
                GameLoop();
        }
}

GameShutdown();

// Return control to Windows with the exit code
return msg.wParam;
}
```

There are a few things to point out in WinMain(). First off are the style settings for the window. Make sure that WS_EX_TOPMOST is set for the extended style in the call to CreateWindow(). That will make sure that your game window is always the top-level window and you won't have any problems with other programs. Without this flag you may find that when you click your mouse button, other programs, such as Explorer, end up getting the mouse clicks instead of your program. Secondly, make sure that the standard window styles settings are set to WS_POPUP | WS_SYSMENU | WS_VISIBLE, so that you don't get flickers of an overlapped window showing through your Direct3D surface during periods of high system load.

Finally, note where the top-level game functions are called. GameInit() is called *after* the window is created and displayed for the first time, but *before* the message loop is entered. GameLoop() is called during every iteration of the message loop that a message is not being processed. And lastly, of course, is GameShutdown(), which is called whenever the WM_QUIT message is signaled to the application, which causes the message loop to fail and the application to exit.

GameInit

Now take a minute to look over the GameInit() function, which contains a bunch of code to look after a lot of the developments that you looked at in previous chapters.

```
int GameInit()
{
        HRESULT r = 0;

        // Acquire a pointer to IDirect3D8
        g_pD3D = Direct3DCreate8( D3D_SDK_VERSION );
        if( g_pD3D == NULL )
        {
                SetError( "Could not create IDirect3D8 object" );
                return E_FAIL;
        }

        // Create the device
        r = InitDirect3DDevice( g_hWndMain, 640, 480, FALSE, D3DFMT_A8R8G8B8,
g_pD3D, &g_pDevice );
        if( FAILED( r ) )
        {
                SetError( "Initialization of the device failed" );
                return E_FAIL;
        }

        // Clear the back buffer
        g_pDevice->Clear( 0, 0, D3DCLEAR_TARGET | D3DCLEAR_ZBUFFER,
                                                D3DCOLOR_ARGB(255, 0, 0, 55 ),
                                1.0f, 0 );
```

```
        // Get a pointer to the back buffer and save it in a global variable
        r = g_pDevice->GetBackBuffer( 0, D3DBACKBUFFER_TYPE_MONO, &g_pBackSurface );
        if( FAILED( r ) )
        {
                SetError( "Couldnt get backbuffer" );
                return E_FAIL;
        }

        // Load the alphabet
        LoadAlphabet( "Alphabet vSmall.bmp", 8, 16 );

        // Initialize timing for frame rate counters, etc
        srand( GetTickCount() );
        InitTiming();

        // Initialize the console
        Console.Initialize( g_pDevice, g_pBackSurface );
        Console.SetParserCallback( ConsoleParser );

        return S_OK;
}
```

This is the base GameInit() that will be used for the remainder of the book. There are a few things to look out for to make this 3D-compatible, and I have highlighted them in bold. First off is the creation of the device. Instead of using the previous tag, which was D3DFMT_X8R8G8B8, you are now going to use D3DFMT_A8R8G8B8. This allows the alpha channel to be used, so that later on you can create amazing transparency effects. There are some adapters that have trouble with this mode, but they are old and are not suitable for advanced game development anyway. So if you are an unfortunate soul and you can't get 640 x 480 x 32 with alpha working, then I think it may be time for you to invest in a new card.

By the way, this change of format causes a few problems with the code from before, which can be resolved very quickly. If you have code based on mine, just do a quick find-and-replace of all the D3DFMT_X8R8G8B8 macros and replace them with the D3DFMT_A8R8G8B8 macro. I have the updated engine files in this and subsequent chapters' directories. So if you want to do straight 2D development, use the engine files from before this chapter; otherwise use the ones from after this one. Cool? Cool.

The next thing that you definitely want to look out for is in the call to
IDirect3DDevice8::Clear(). Make sure that you add the flag D3DCLEAR_ZBUFFER to the
clearing flags to ensure that the depth buffer is cleared properly. If you do not,
then you will get strange artifacts on the screen when you start rendering 3D stuff.

Shutting Down with GameShutdown()

In the code following, I have listed the GameShutdown() function.

```
int GameShutdown()
{
        Console.Shutdown();

        UnloadAlphabet();

        // Release the pointer to the back surface
        if( g_pBackSurface )
                g_pBackSurface->Release();

        // Release the pointer to IDirect3DDevice8
        if( g_pDevice )
                g_pDevice->Release();

        // Release the pointer to IDirect3D8
        if( g_pD3D )
                g_pD3D->Release();

        return S_OK;
}
```

Again, it is just the usual shutdown material: shut down the console, unload the
alphabet font, and then release all the Direct3D objects in reverse order to how you
created them.

Getting the GameLoop() Going

Right now the GameLoop() is quite short, because it only does frame counting and rendering, but soon that puppy will be well packed with code, no doubt about it.

```
int GameLoop()
{
        FrameCount();

        Render();

        if( GetAsyncKeyState( VK_ESCAPE ) )
                PostQuitMessage(0);

        return S_OK;
}
```

Rendering with Render()

There are quite a lot of things going on in Render(), so be sure that you take note of all the code that is there now so that later on you don't get lost, because rendering in 3D can get very complex when it wants to be.

```
int Render()
{
        HRESULT r = 0;

        g_pDevice->Clear( 0, 0, D3DCLEAR_TARGET | D3DCLEAR_ZBUFFER,
                                        D3DCOLOR_XRGB( 0, 0, 100 ), 1.0f, 0 );

        // Make sure the device is valid
        if( !g_pDevice )
        {
                SetError( "Cannot render because there is no device" );
                return E_FAIL;
        }

        // Return if the device is not ready;
        r = ValidateDevice();
        if( FAILED( r ) )
        {
```

```
            return E_FAIL;
    }

    D3DLOCKED_RECT Locked;

    g_pBackSurface->LockRect( &Locked, 0, 0 );

    // Render text
    PrintFrameRate( 550, 400, TRUE, D3DCOLOR_ARGB( 255, 255, 0, 255 ),
                                        (DWORD*)Locked.pBits, Locked.Pitch );

    g_pBackSurface->UnlockRect();

    Console.Render();

    r = g_pDevice->Present( NULL, NULL, NULL, NULL );

    return S_OK;
}
```

The only thing to look out for is the addition to the call to
IDirect3DDevice8::Clear(), which must include the D3DCLEAR_ZBUFFER flag or else you
will get a garbled display showing up when you try to render 3D objects.

And that's it. Now you can concentrate on building your 3D graphics engine!

Constructing a 3D Graphics Engine: The Basics

As in 2D graphics, in 3D there are hundreds of steps that you have to go through
before you can develop a proper 3D engine. I am going to take you step by step
through the development of your engine, starting with the simplest step of all: rendering a static triangle. This is going to achieve similar results to those in the SDK
tutorial, except that I will be explaining things better than that joke of a tutorial.

Setting up the Flexible Vertex Format

DirectX is meant to be quite a flexible API, and as such Microsoft had to make sure that it runs as efficiently as possible across as many different game types as possible, even though some may take advantage of every last Direct3D feature and others would only scratch the surface. This leads to all sorts of—for instance, because what if one program wanted to let Direct3D perform all the lighting calculations and another wanted to implement its own high-performance radiosity lighting engine? Well, Microsoft could have gotten over this by providing a massive vertex structure that would accommodate all the needs for every imaginable type of application out there, but this wouldn't be very efficient.

Instead, they came up with what is called the *flexible vertex format,* or FVF for short. FVF allows you to tell Direct3D what information you will be passing to it, and which parts of the 3D-processing pipeline you will be implementing yourself. So if you want to define the color of vertices yourself, then you include members in a vertex structure to hold vertex colors. As a result, you don't have any superfluous information flying around your computer. Which is very cool. Unfortunately, as per usual in programming, an increase in performance generally comes at the expense of usability, so the code you will see can initially look slightly more complex than it needs to be.

So how does the format work? Well, basically all you have to do is set up a structure to hold your vertices in, and tell Direct3D what information is in the structure. The information in the structure must be in a certain order—this is very important, otherwise you will get some really groovy, although not quite productive, effects on the screen. Have a look at Figure 12.1 to see the order that the information must be in. I know that you don't have much of an understanding of what a lot of that means just yet, but it is there for you to come back to soon.

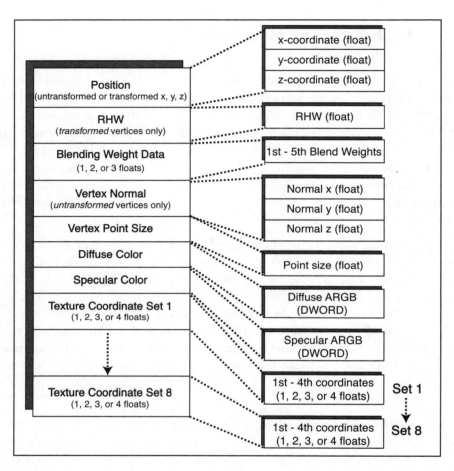

Figure 12.1

The order of information within the flexible vertex format

So with that out of the way let's talk about what you want to achieve, and what information you need to get there. You want to display a single, unlit triangle with an interpolated shade between the different colors of the vertices. So with that in mind, it seems that all you need is a structure to hold each vertex of the triangle. Each vertex should contain a position for the vertex and also a color. Cool? Slick. Check out the code following, which is defined globally:

```
struct ZENVERTEX
{
    int x, y, z, rhw;
    DWORD DiffuseColor;
}
```

The x, y, and z members indicate the transformed position of the vertex, and you'll remember from the last chapter when I talked about matrices that the rhw is there to make sure that 3D matrix operations work out smoothly. And finally, the color component is there to hold the diffuse color of the vertex.

OK, so now that you have our structure, you just need a way to tell Direct3D about what choices you have made. You do this by putting together a bunch of flags into a bit vector. The flags can be any of those listed in Table 12.1.

Table 12.1   Flexible Vertex Format Flags

Flag	Description
D3DFVF_DIFFUSE	The diffuse color component of the vertex
D3DFVF_NORMAL	The normal for the vertex. Cannot be used with D3DFVF_XYZRHW
D3DFVF_PSIZE	The vertex format is specified in point size
D3DFVF_SPECULAR	The specular color component of the vertex
D3DFVF_XYZ	The position for an untransformed vertex. Cannot be used with D3DFVF_XYZRHW.
D3DFVF_XYZRHW	The position for a transformed vertex. Cannot be used with D3DFVF_XYZ or D3DFVF_NORMAL.
D3DFVF_XYZB1 to D3DFVF_XYZB5	Contains position data and a blending weight for multi-matrix vertex blending operations
D3DFVF_TEX0 to D3DFVF_TEX8	Texture coordinate numbers for this vertex
D3DFVF_TEXTUREFORMAT1 to D3DFVF_TEXTUREFORMAT4	Number of values that define a texture coordinate set. The number at the end of the flag indicates how many dimensions are used in the texture coordinates (e.g., D3DFVF_TEXTUREFORMAT2 is two-dimensional).

Again, this table is for your future reference. For now let's keep it simple and define the flags that will be used for the vertex structure that I showed you a second ago:

```
#define CUSTOM_ZENVERTEX (D3DFVF_XYZRHW|D3DFVF_DIFFUSE)
```

See how it works? It is pretty simple; your structure has fields for the position and diffuse color component of the vertex, so you simply have to set the flags for those respective entries.

Getting Jiggy with the Vertex Buffer

Rendering triangles can be a time-consuming process, and dealing with an API such as DirectX make it even longer. The first way you might think about drawing a triangle to the screen is to set up a triangle structure that contains three vertices and then make a call to an API function like `DrawTriangle()`, which would then draw the single triangle. The triangle would be transformed into a form compatible with the current rendering device and then passed across the bus to be drawn by the hardware. And then for the next triangle the whole process would be done again, and so on.

But every time you access the bus, you are taking a performance hit, since the processor has to take time away from your program and spend ages transferring information across the bus, which is much slower than the processor. A better solution would be if you could group a bunch of vertices into a buffer, which could then be spit out in a group to the display hardware.

And this, my friend, is how Direct3D now works as compared to how it used to be. In previous releases, you were not required to use vertex buffers. You start by updating the positions of all the objects in your scene, and next group them into buffers, and then spit them out to Direct3D really fast. This allows for batch processing of the vertices, which is way quicker than doing them one by one. Let's take a minute to look at a vertex buffer in action (see Figure 12.2).

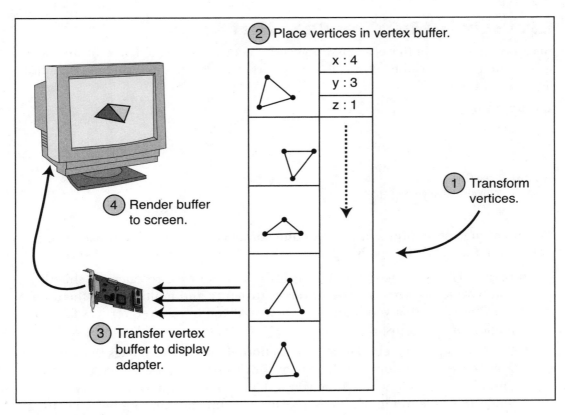

Figure 12.2

Using vertex buffers

Defining the Vertex Buffer

In Direct3D the vertex buffer is encapsulated by the `IDirect3DVertexBuffer8` interface, and you can start by defining a new global vertex buffer at the top of your program code.

```
LPDIRECT3DVERTEXBUFFER8 g_pVB = 0;
```

Pretty simple so far, huh? Good. Notice again, as always when you define a new COM pointer, that you initialize it to `NULL`.

Creating the Vertex Buffer

Because the vertex buffer is a COM object, it needs to be created, and in this case, it is created using a call to `IDirect3DDevice8::CreateVertexBuffer()`, which looks a little like this bad boy:

```
HRESULT CreateVertexBuffer(
  UINT Length,
  DWORD Usage,
  DWORD FVF,
  D3DPOOL Pool,
  IDirect3DVertexBuffer8** ppVertexBuffer
);
```

This is an interesting function but it's quite complex unless you know what you're doing, so let me just take a minute to run through those parameters for you.

- **Length.** This is the length of the vertex buffer in bytes. To calculate this all you have to do is get the size of vertex structure and multiply it by the number of vertices that you want to render. So if you have three vertices for a triangle, you could just do `sizeof( ZENVERTEX ) * 3`.

- **Usage.** This parameter takes a combination of one or more flags that describe how you want it to operate. The flags for this parameter are very advanced and not applicable to anything you will want to do for a while, so I won't cloud the issue too much. Let's get Direct3D up and running before getting stuck down with details. If you want more information on this subject, have a look in *DirectX 8.0 Documentation For C++ / DirectX Graphics / DirectX Graphics C++ Reference / IDirect3DDevice8 / IDirect3DDevice8::CreateVertexBuffer() /*. For now you can just set this parameter to NULL.

- **FVF.** The FVF flag is where you tell Direct3D what format the vertex buffer is going to take by specifying a combination of one or more flags that I showed you before in Table 12.1.

- **Pool.** Use this parameter to specify to Direct3D, using a flag, how you want the vertex buffer to be managed. The best flag is `D3DPOOL_DEFAULT`, which automatically places the vertex buffer into the most appropriate place, whether that is system or video memory.

- **ppVertexBuffer**. Use this parameter to pass the address of a pointer that will be filled with the address of the newly-created vertex buffer, if all goes according to plan. Actually, the creation of a new vertex buffer will probably never fail as long as you get the parameters right. The only reason it might fail, would be because of a lack of memory, in which case your game will probably be grinding to a halt anyway.

So now that you have seen what the function call and parameters look like, let's create some vertices to fill the buffer with. The following code is positioned in the bottom of the GameInit() function.

```
ZENVERTEX ZenVertices[] =
{
        { 150.0f,   50.0f, 0.5f, 1.0f, D3DCOLOR_XRGB( 255, 0, 0 ), }, // x, y, z, ↩
rhw, color
        { 250.0f, 250.0f, 0.5f, 1.0f, D3DCOLOR_XRGB( 255, 255, 0 ), },
        {  50.0f, 250.0f, 0.5f, 1.0f, D3DCOLOR_XRGB( 0, 0, 255 ), },
};
```

Basically, that just creates a list of three vertices, which are colored red, yellow, and blue, respectively. Now let's see how to create a new vertex buffer into which you can copy the new vertices. Again this code is positioned in GameInit(), just after the declaration of the above-mentioned vertices.

```
r = g_pDevice->CreateVertexBuffer( sizeof(ZENVERTEX)*3, 0, CUSTOM_ZENVERTEX,
                                                D3DPOOL_DEFAULT, &g_pVB
                                        );

if( FAILED( r ) )
{
        SetError( "Couldnt create the vertex buffer" );
        return E_FAIL;
}
```

Destroying the Vertex Buffer

Since you are using a global vertex buffer in this example, it is important to free the memory that it occupies before your program exits. Nine times out of 10 Direct3D will do this for you anyway, but it is really good programming practice to release any resources that you have acquired. It is really simple to achieve this; it only takes a single addition to the GameShutDown() function, as follows:

```
if( g_pVB )
        g_pVB->Release();
```

Locking and Filling the Vertex Buffer

Now that the vertex buffer is created, you can copy the new vertices into it. However, since vertex buffers can exist anywhere, from system memory to video memory to shared AGP space, they need some special handling. In fact, as with surfaces, they need to be locked before you are allowed to access the vertex buffer and fill it with a list of vertices. So let's have a look at how to do that with IDirect3DVertexBuffer8::Lock(), which is shown in the following:

```
HRESULT Lock(
  UINT OffsetToLock,
  UINT SizeToLock,
  BYTE** ppbData,
  DWORD Flags
);
```

The parameters to this function are pretty simple. Check them out in table 12.2.

Table 12.2   IDirect3DVertexBuffer8::Lock() Parameters

Parameter	Definition
OffsetToLock	This is the offset from the start of the buffer, in bytes, that you want to lock for modification. You will usually want to lock from the beginning, and as such specify 0.
SizeToLock	This is the offset from the starting offset, specified again in bytes, that you want to lock. To lock the entire buffer from the starting point, specify 0 for this parameter.
ppbData	This parameter takes the address of a BYTE pointer that will be filled with the address of the start of the locked vertex buffer. In other words, after you lock the vertex buffer, you will access the data through this pointer.
Flags	In this parameter, you can specify parameters to control advanced behavior of the vertex buffer if you want; otherwise just specify 0.

Now check out how to actually make the call to `IDirect3DVertexBuffer8::Lock()` and fill the vertex buffer with information, as follows:

```
// Pointer to the vertex buffer
BYTE* pVertices = 0;

// Lock the vertex buffer
r = g_pVB->Lock( 0, sizeof( ZenVertices ), &pVertices, 0 );
if( FAILED( r ) )
{
        SetError( "Could not lock the vertex buffer" );
        return E_FAIL;
}
// Fill the buffer with the vertices
CopyMemory( pVertices, &ZenVertices, sizeof( ZenVertices ) );

// Unlock the buffer
g_pVB->Unlock();
```

See what's going on? First off you just have to create a temporary BYTE pointer that will be used to hold the address of the destination vertex buffer. The next step is to lock the buffer and in the process retrieve a pointer to the start of the buffer. Then it's simply a case of copying the vertex data verbatim from the structures into the buffer. And finally, when you are finished you must unlock the buffer with a call to `IDirect3DVertexBuffer8::Unlock()`, which takes no parameters.

> **CAUTION**
>
> **If you fail to unlock your vertex buffer, then any attempt to render the buffer will fail.**

Rendering the Triangle

There are just a few steps left before you can see the triangle rendered on-screen. The first is to stick some directives into the `Render()` function that will let Direct3D know when you are starting and stopping rendering 3D objects in each frame. This is achieved with two function calls: `IDirect3DDevice8::BeginScene()` and `IDirect3DDevice8::EndScene()`. You should place these two calls *after* any 2D background code you have written and *before* the call to render the console. That way the background gets drawn properly and the console is overlaid on top of the 3D stuff.

3D-Rendering Directives

Following is the code that lets Direct3D know when you will be rendering in 3D.

```
PrintFrameRate( 550, 400, TRUE, D3DCOLOR_ARGB( 255, 255, 0, 255 ),
(DWORD*)Locked.pBits, Locked.Pitch );

g_pBackSurface->UnlockRect();
g_pDevice->BeginScene();

// Do 3D Rendering here

g_pDevice->EndScene();
Console.Render();
```

As you can see, neither function takes any parameters. They may seem fairly superfluous, but without these calls all 3D rendering will fail.

Setting Up Rendering Streams

A *stream* in Direct3D is like a channel of information. A stream can get its information from a few different sources, but it will usually be the vertex buffers. To render a vertex buffer, you need to connect it to a stream. And then when you want to render, you tell Direct3D which stream to use as the source. Get it? The steps in the process are as follows:

1. Create a vertex buffer.
2. Fill the vertex buffer with information.
3. Connect the vertex buffer to a stream.
4. Render the stream.

Check out Figure 12.3 to see what I'm talking about.

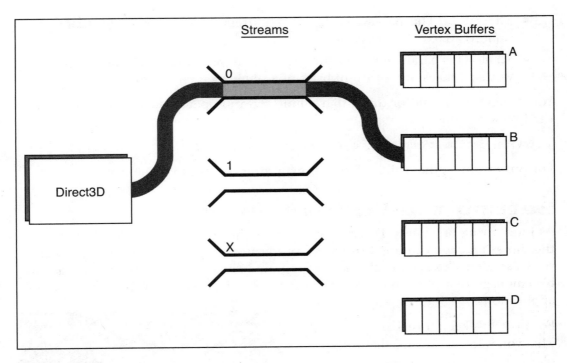

Figure 12.3

Rendering streams attached to vertex buffers

The function to connect a stream to a vertex buffer is called
`IDirect3DDevice8::SetStreamSource()`, and is shown in the following:

```
HRESULT SetStreamSource(
  UINT StreamNumber,
  IDirect3DVertexBuffer8* pStreamData,
  UINT Stride
);
```

This function is really simple; the parameters are as follows:

- **StreamNumber.** This parameter takes the numeric identifier of the stream to
  which you want to connect the vertex buffer. This is just an index value so if,
  like in this case, you only have one vertex buffer, then you can just assign it
  to stream zero. I'll show you some more advanced uses for streams later in
  the book.

- **pStreamData.** This parameter takes the address of the vertex buffer that you want to attach to this stream.

- **Stride** This parameter takes the stride of the vertices in the buffer. In other words, it takes the length in bytes of a single element (vertex).

You can get the result for this with a simple `sizeof()` operation, as I have done with the following code:

```
g_pDevice->SetStreamSource( 0, g_pVB, sizeof(ZENVERTEX) );
```

For this example, that call is placed directly after the call to `BeginScene()`.

Setting the Vertex Shader

As I was saying previously, Direct3D is very versatile and customizable. One of the things that you can do, if you are very advanced, is to write your own custom vertex shader. This is basically a short program written in a kind of complex assembly language that you can use to write extremely advanced and visually impressive applications.

For now let's keep it real and stick with what you want to do, and that is to display a triangle on the screen. Since you are not writing your own shader, you can use Direct3D's built-in shader, which is more than adequate for most needs.

> **NOTE**
>
> Rendering will fail if you don't set a vertex shader. So if you find yourself hunting through endless lines of code because nothing will show up on your screen, make sure that you have set the shader.

So how do you set up Direct3D's shader? Well, it involves a simple function called `IDirect3DDevice8::SetVertexShader()`. This function only takes one parameter and that is the type of FVFs that you are using. In other words, just tell it what information is within your vertex structure as defined a few pages ago. A call to the function would look a little like this:

```
g_pDevice->SetVertexShader( CUSTOM_ZENVERTEX );
```

Drawing Primitives

Now you come to the part where you actually get to draw the triangle to the screen using a function that you may have heard a lot about before. If you have not, well, now is the time to get to know your new friend because you are going to be dealing with each other a lot. The function is called `IDirect3DDevice8::DrawPrimitive()`.

Here it is in all its glory:

```
HRESULT DrawPrimitive(
    D3DPRIMITIVETYPE PrimitiveType,
    UINT StartVertex,
    UINT PrimitiveCount
);
```

This function is pretty simple; as you can see, it only takes three parameters. The first is PrimitiveType, and it is for specifying what type of primitive you are drawing. This can be set to any of the flags shown in Table 12.3.

Table 12.3 DrawPrimitive() Primitive Type Flags

Flag	Description
D3DPT_POINTLIST	The vertices will be rendered as a list of points.
D3DPT_LINELIST	The vertices will be rendered as a list of isolated line segments. This implies that there must be at least two vertices in the list and that the number of vertices cannot be odd.
D3DPT_LINESTRIP	The vertices will be rendered as a single line. There must be at least two vertices in the buffer.
D3DPT_TRIANGLELIST	The vertices will be rendered as a sequence of isolated triangles. Each group of three vertices in the vertex buffer is taken to represent a triangle. There must be at least three vertices in the buffer.
D3DPT_TRIANGLESTRIP	The vertices will be rendered as a triangle strip. Using triangle stripping is a rendering optimization that I discussed in Chapter 11.
D3DPT_TRIANGLEFAN	The vertices will be rendered as a triangle fan. Triangle fanning is a rendering optimization that I discussed in Chapter 11.

The StartVertex parameter takes an index into the vertex buffer for the first vertex that you want to load. Usually you will want to start at the beginning of the buffer and specify 0. The final parameter is PrimitiveCount, which takes the number of primitives that you want to render. A *primitive* can be anything from a point to a line to a triangle, depending on the type of vertex buffer. There's always a maximum number of primitives that you can draw per stream, but the maximum is usually very high and unrestrictive. For instance, on my Matrox Millennium G450 32MB dual-head display adaptor the primitive limit is 65,536.

Now that you have seen the function, let's put this bad boy to work! The following code renders the stream that your vertex buffer is attached to:

```
g_pDevice->DrawPrimitive( D3DPT_TRIANGLELIST, 0, 1 );
```

Simple, huh? You are drawing a single isolated triangle, so the flag of choice is `D3DPT_TRIANGLELIST`, and you want to start at the first vertex so that takes care of the second parameter. And, of course, you only have one primitive to draw so that takes care of the last parameter.

And that's it! If you execute that code, you will get a beautifully shaded triangle that fades colors between blue, yellow, and red—the colors that make up each of the three vertices, respectively. Check out Figure 12.4.

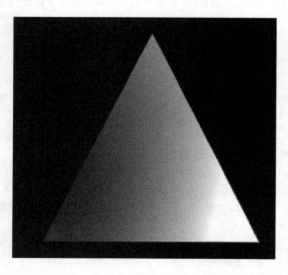

Figure 12.4

Rendering a single triangle to the screen

Now it would be a good idea to show you all the code in one place so that you can see how it fits together. The relevant code is bolded in the following:

```
int GameInit()
{

        HRESULT r = 0;

        // Acquire a pointer to IDirect3D8
        g_pD3D = Direct3DCreate8( D3D_SDK_VERSION );
        if( g_pD3D == NULL )
        {
```

```
                    SetError( "Could not create IDirect3D8 object" );
                    return E_FAIL;
            }

            // Create the device
            r = InitDirect3DDevice( g_hWndMain, 640, 480, FALSE, D3DFMT_A8R8G8B8, 
    g_pD3D, &g_pDevice );
            if( FAILED( r ) )
            {
                    SetError( "Initialization of the device failed" );
                    return E_FAIL;
            }

            // Clear the back buffer
            g_pDevice->Clear( 0, 0, D3DCLEAR_TARGET | D3DCLEAR_ZBUFFER,
                                          D3DCOLOR_XRGB( 0, 0, 55 ), 1.0f, 0 );

            // Get a pointer to the back buffer and save it in a global variable
            r = g_pDevice->GetBackBuffer( 0, D3DBACKBUFFER_TYPE_MONO, &g_pBackSurface );
            if( FAILED( r ) )
            {
                    SetError( "Couldnt get backbuffer" );
                    return E_FAIL;
            }

            // Load the alphabet
            LoadAlphabet( "Alphabet vSmall.bmp", 8, 16 );

            // Initialize timing for frame rate counters, etc
            srand( GetTickCount() );
            InitTiming();

            // Initialize the console
            Console.Initialize( g_pDevice, g_pBackSurface );
            Console.SetParserCallback( ConsoleParser );

            // The vertices for the triangle
            ZENVERTEX ZenVertices[] =
            {
                    { 150.0f,  50.0f, 0.5f, 1.0f, D3DCOLOR_XRGB( 255, 0, 0 ), }, 
    // x, y, z, rhw, color
```

```
                { 250.0f, 250.0f, 0.5f, 1.0f, D3DCOLOR_XRGB( 255, 255, 0 ), },
                {  50.0f, 250.0f, 0.5f, 1.0f, D3DCOLOR_XRGB( 0, 0, 255 ), },
        };

        // Create the vertex buffer
        r = g_pDevice->CreateVertexBuffer( sizeof(ZENVERTEX)*3, 0,
                            CUSTOM_ZENVERTEX, D3DPOOL_DEFAULT, &g_pVB );
        if( FAILED( r ) )
        {
                SetError( "Couldnt create the vertex buffer" );
                return E_FAIL;
        }


        // Pointer to the vertex buffer
        BYTE* pVertices = 0;

        // Lock the vertex buffer
        r = g_pVB->Lock( 0, sizeof( ZenVertices ), &pVertices, 0 );
        if( FAILED( r ) )
        {
                SetError( "Could not lock the vertex buffer" );
                return E_FAIL;
        }

        // Fill the buffer with the vertices
        CopyMemory( pVertices, &ZenVertices, sizeof( ZenVertices ) );

        // Unlock the buffer
        g_pVB->Unlock();


        return S_OK;
}

int Render()
{
        HRESULT r = 0;

        g_pDevice->Clear( 0, 0, D3DCLEAR_TARGET | D3DCLEAR_ZBUFFER,
                                    D3DCOLOR_XRGB( 0, 0, 100 ), 1.0f, 0 );
```

```
// Make sure the device is valid
if( !g_pDevice )
{
        SetError( "Cannot render because there is no device" );
        return E_FAIL;
}

// Return if the device is not ready;
r = ValidateDevice();
if( FAILED( r ) )
{
        return E_FAIL;
}

D3DLOCKED_RECT Locked;

g_pBackSurface->LockRect( &Locked, 0, 0 );

// Render text
PrintFrameRate( 550, 400, TRUE, D3DCOLOR_ARGB( 255, 255, 0, 255 ),
                                            (DWORD*)Locked.pBits,
                                    Locked.Pitch );

// Unlock the back surface
g_pBackSurface->UnlockRect();

// Tell Direct3D we are about to start rendering in 3D
g_pDevice->BeginScene();

// Set the rendering stream
g_pDevice->SetStreamSource( 0, g_pVB, sizeof(ZENVERTEX) );

// Set the vertex shading mode
g_pDevice->SetVertexShader( CUSTOM_ZENVERTEX );

// Draw the triangle
g_pDevice->DrawPrimitive( D3DPT_TRIANGLELIST, 0, 1 );

// Tell Direct3D we have finished drawing in 3D
g_pDevice->EndScene();
```

```
        // Render the console
        Console.Render();

        // Present the back buffer to the primary surface
        r = g_pDevice->Present( NULL, NULL, NULL, NULL );

        return S_OK;
}

int GameShutdown()
{
        Console.Shutdown();

        UnloadAlphabet();

        // Release the vertex buffer
        if( g_pVB )
                g_pVB->Release();

        // Release the pointer to the back surface
        if( g_pBackSurface )
                g_pBackSurface->Release();

        // Release the pointer to IDirect3DDevice8
        if( g_pDevice )
                g_pDevice->Release();

        // Release the pointer to IDirect3D8
        if( g_pD3D )
                g_pD3D->Release();

        return S_OK;
}
```

And that is all it takes to render a static triangle. Pretty easy, huh? Let's get more advanced.

Animation with Matrices

Although the interactive entertainment market was captivated for years by static shaded triangles, there comes a time in every product's life when something better comes along and changes everything. And in this case, that is a new triangle. A better triangle. A triangle that will animate about the x- and y-axes and bring peace and prosperity to us all!

Let's look at what was wrong with the last example. First up was the way that the vertices for the triangle were defined. Remember the way I included that **rhw** component in the vertex definition? Well, that indicates to Direct3D that the vertex coordinates are already transformed. In other words, Direct3D thinks that the mathematics to get the vertices transformed into a position that will appear correctly on the screen has already been done. I did this so that we could look at the most simple way to render a triangle without clouding the main point.

Modifying the Vertex Structure

That's all about to change because you want to start using matrices to let Direct3D perform most of the transformations for you. To do so, you simply need to remove the rhw component from the vertex definition and change the bit vector describing the vertex structure. Then Direct3D will automatically realize that it is now responsible for transforming the vertices. So let's do that now; the new structure for your vertices is as follows:

```
struct ZENVERTEX
{
        float x, y, z;
        DWORD DiffuseColor;
};

#define CUSTOM_ZENVERTEX (D3DFVF_XYZ | D3DFVF_DIFFUSE)
```

Notice how the rhw field has been removed and that it has also been removed from the bit vector flags. Of course, since you are now dealing with untransformed, or raw, vertices you can use more normal numbers for the definitions of the triangle's vertices. I changed the structure definition to this:

```
ZENVERTEX ZenVertices[] =
{
        { -2.0f,-2.0f, 0.0f,-1.0f, 0.0f, 0.0f },
        {  2.0f,-2.0f, 0.0f, 1.0f, 0.0f, 0.0f },
        {  0.0f, 2.0f, 0.0f, 0.0f, 1.0f, 0.0f },
};
```

Notice that in this new definition that the figures for the rhw component are no longer there since it was removed from the structure.

> **NOTE**
>
> Notice that the vertices are defined in clockwise order. This is how Direct3D figures out which faces to back face cull. In this example it is not too important since you are turning off culling, but in other cases it would make the face invisible. Well, not actually invisible, but facing in the wrong direction, with the back face culled. Hence the invisible bit—you wouldn't be able to see it!

Setting Up the Viewport

In Direct3D, a *viewport* is a construct that is partly used to define the viewing volume for your screen. A viewport has at its core an (x, y) position that is used to specify where rendering should start on the screen, a width and height to specify how far that rendering should extend, and two z values that specify the near and far clipping planes in the viewing volume. You probably recall from the last chapter that the clipping planes define the area, in distance from the camera, where objects can be considered for rendering.

Direct3D represents the viewport with the D3DVIEWPORT8 structure, which is shown in the following:

```
typedef struct _D3DVIEWPORT8 {
    DWORD       X;
    DWORD       Y;
    DWORD       Width;
    DWORD       Height;
    float       MinZ;
    float       MaxZ;
} D3DVIEWPORT8;
```

To create a viewport all you have to do is fill in that structure and pass it to Direct3D using the function `IDirect3DDevice8::SetViewport()`, which looks a little like this:

```
HRESULT SetViewport( CONST D3DVIEWPORT8* pViewport );
```

I have created a function called `CreateViewport()`, which I have added to the engine.h file. This function is shown in the following:

```
HRESULT CreateViewport()
{
        HRESULT r = 0;

        if( !g_pDevice )
                return E_FAIL;

        D3DVIEWPORT8 Viewport;

        Viewport.X = 0;
        Viewport.Y = 0;
        Viewport.Width = g_DeviceWidth;
        Viewport.Height = g_DeviceHeight;
        Viewport.MinZ = 0.0f;
        Viewport.MaxZ = 1.0f;

        r = g_pDevice->SetViewport( &Viewport );

        return r;
}
```

As you can see, `CreateViewport()` does not take any parameters. You should always call this function from `GameInit()` from now on, right after creating the device with `InitDirect3DDevice()`. All of the function should be fairly self-explanatory except maybe for the last two entries. Those are where you set the limits for the near and far clip planes. I can't really think of a situation right now why you might want to set these to anything other than the Microsoft recommended defaults, which are 0.0 and 1.0, respectively. Well, I can, but let's stick to the subject.

Setting Up the Projection Matrix

Now it is time to add a little function to the program's code to set up what are called the *transformation matrices*. Recall that I talked about these a little bit in the last chapter. For now I am just going to show you how to set up the projection matrix. This is the most complex matrix to set up, but you only need to do it once at the start of your program. I'll show you the other matrices soon. Just to let you know, the mathematics behind the projection matrix are horrendous. And I mean that, but I'll give you a brief overview because I'm such a nice guy. If you are not a mathematical type, then you can just smile and nod at this explanation because you can use this code as-is, without modification, in just about any project.

The projection matrices that I am about to show you are the Microsoft-recommended versions, and they are compatible with depth buffers called *w-buffers,* which render images with better quality than z-buffers in certain situations. You don't need to worry about w-buffers, really. As far as you are concerned, they are exactly the same as z-buffers; it's a hardware issue. However, what is important is that you set up the projection matrix to be w-buffer compatible, because otherwise, if your display adapter decides to use w-buffering, some effects, such as fog, will not render correctly.

The w-buffer compatible projection matrix looks like this:

$$\begin{bmatrix} w, 0, 0, 0 \\ 0, h, 0, 0 \\ 0, 0, q, 1 \\ 0, 0, -QZ_n, 0 \end{bmatrix}$$

Where...

$$w = \left(\frac{\cos(\text{Field of view} / 2)}{\sin(\text{Field of view} / 2)} \right) * \text{Aspect ratio of the screen}$$

$$h = \left(\frac{\cos(\text{Field of view} / 2)}{\sin(\text{Field of view} / 2)} \right) * 1.0$$

$$Q = \quad \text{Viewport far clip plane}$$

$$\overline{\phantom{\text{(Viewport far clip plane – Viewport near clip plane)}}}$$

(Viewport far clip plane – Viewport near clip plane)

$z^n =$ Near clipping plane; usually 1.0

Field of view = Pi / 4

Aspect ratio of the screen = Viewport width / Viewport height

Viewport far clip plane = Constant (I usually use 1000.0)

Viewport near clip plane = 1.0

Going into the reasoning behind these mathematics is beyond the scope of this book, and is really boring, but if you want more information on the subject, check out *DirectX 8.0 C++ Documentation / DirectX Graphics / Direct3D Rendering Pipeline / Fixed Function Vertex and Pixel Processing / The Projection Transformation / What Is the Projection Transformation?*

Don't worry about the mathematics; the code is simple and I have put together a small function (which follows) that has been added to the engine files:

```
void SetProjectionMatrix()
{
        D3DXMATRIX ProjectionMatrix;
        ZeroMemory( &ProjectionMatrix, sizeof( D3DXMATRIX ) );

        float ScreenAspect = (float)g_DeviceWidth / (float)g_DeviceHeight;
        float FOV = D3DX_PI / 4;

        D3DXMatrixPerspectiveFovLH( &ProjectionMatrix, FOV, ScreenAspect, 1.0f,
1000.0f );

        g_pDevice->SetTransform( D3DTS_PROJECTION, &ProjectionMatrix );
}
```

You should call this function directly after you call the CreateViewport() function that I showed you in the previous section. Actually, the first version of this function that I showed you worked out the mathematics manually. However, there is now a useful function called D3DXMatrixPerspectiveLH(), which works them out for you. All you have to do is pass the address of the matrix you want to be filled, the aspect ratio of the screen (Width/Height), the field of view of the screen (usually Pi / 4 for non-fish-eyed humans), and the distances that you want to use for the near and far clipping planes, which are usually 1.0 and 1000.0, respectively. You can, of course, change the far clipping plane if you want to increase performance at the expense of limiting the distance at which polygons are visible.

> **CAUTION**
>
> Calling `SetProjectionMatrix()` **without first setting up the viewport with** `CreateViewport()` **can cause unpredictable results.**

One thing to note in the `SetProjectionMatrix()` function is how I used the matrices. Notice how they are represented by the `D3DXMATRIX` structure. This is the same as the normal `D3DMATRIX` structure except that it has extensions for users with C++, rather than straight C. `D3DXMATRIX` includes overrides of the () operator, so that you can refer to the elements of the matrix quickly.

Also note the Direct3D function `IDirect3DDevice8::SetTransform()`, which is used to implement the new projection matrix into Direct3D.

> **CAUTION**
>
> When using the C++ () overrides of the `D3DXMATRIX` structure, remember that they are zero-based. So to get at location 1, 1 in the matrix you enter (0, 0). And the last addressable point of a matrix at 4, 4 must be referenced as (3, 3). If you try to access (4, 4), then you will cause a memory fault.

Setting the Camera Position with the View Matrix

For this first example I'll just show you how to set the camera's position to be slightly up and backward from the origin. Later on I'll show you how to develop an advanced camera class that will encapsulate the functionality of the view matrix and make it very simple to make adjustments to the camera. You remember from the last chapter what the view matrix does, right? It rotates and repositions all the vertices in the scene inversely to the camera's position and angle.

The following code will be placed in the `GameInit()` function for now. So let's get started; the first thing to do is to create a new matrix that will hold the new view matrix.

```
D3DXMATRIX ViewMatrix;
```

Fairly simple. Now let's fill it with some positional and directional data. This can be achieved with the function `D3DXMatrixLookAtLH()`, which is shown in the following.

```
D3DXMATRIX* D3DXMatrixLookAtLH(
    D3DXMATRIX* pOut,
    CONST D3DXVECTOR3* pEye,
    CONST D3DXVECTOR3* pAt,
    CONST D3DXVECTOR3* pUp
);
```

This is really not as bad as it looks.

Table 12.4   D3DXMatrixLookAtLH() Parameters

Parameter	Definition
pOut	Takes the address of the view matrix, in, which will be filled when the function completes, and three vectors.
pEye	Takes the position of the camera. So if the camera is located at (0, 0, –5), then you fill a vector with (0, 0, –5) and stick it in this parameter.
pAt	Takes what is called a *look-at point,* which is a vector with the direction that the camera is looking at
pUp	Another vector describing which way is up. It may seem stupid to have to tell a computer which way is up, but hey, some programmers are from Australia, right?! Anyway, the vector for up is of course (0, 1, 0) so you can just pass that as a value for this parameter

Let's see what the function looks like:

```
D3DXMatrixLookAtLH( &ViewMatrix,      &D3DXVECTOR3( 0.0f, 3.0f,-5.0f ),
                                      &D3DXVECTOR3( 0.0f, 0.0f, 0.0f ),
                                      &D3DXVECTOR3( 0.0f, 1.0f, 0.0f ) );
```

See how it works? The first parameter is the address of the view matrix. The second is the position of the camera, the third is where the camera is looking, which in this case is the origin, and finally the fourth parameter is a vector describing which way is up. Simple? Just smile and nod! However, the view matrix is still not set—all you have done is filled in a matrix. To implement your changes you need to tell Direct3D about it with another call to `IDirect3DDevice8::SetTransform()`. This time use the `D3DTS_VIEW` flag to specify that you are talking about the view matrix. The call looks like this puppy:

```
g_pDevice->SetTransform( D3DTS_VIEW, &ViewMatrix );
```

And that is all there is to setting up the view matrix, for now.

Animating the Triangle with the World Matrix

As I'm sure you know, the *world matrix* is there to transform the local coordinates of an object into world coordinates. As such, depending on which object you are rendering, the world matrix will change many times per frame, and that is just how it is going to be in this example. Later I'll show you how to implement some really cool object-based coordinate systems to the engine, but for now let's look at how to set the world matrix.

Start by looking at what you want to achieve. How about getting that boring static triangle to dance? You could try shooting at its feet, but that would be hard since triangles don't have feet. Instead, you could set a slow rotation around the x-axis and a faster rotation around the y-axis using the world matrix.

> **NOTE**
>
> There are hundreds of helper functions that ship with Direct3D that are used to help you program for efficiently by providing you with code that is commonly used. These functions come under the umbrella heading of the "The Direct3D Utility Library," or just the "D3DX Library" for short, and all the functions in this library begin with the D3DX… prefix. You have already seen and used some of these functions, such as D3DXMatrixLookAtLH(). You can see the full list of utility functions, classes, structures, and macros at *DirectX 8 Documentation / DirectX Graphics / Direct3DX C++ Reference*.

To quickly set up a rotation matrix, you can use helper functions from the DirectX utility library. For this example I am using D3DXMatrixRotationY() and D3DXMatrixRotationX(), which allows me to fill in an entire matrix with a single call. Here is how I set the world matrix:

```
D3DXMATRIX RotationX, RotationY, WorldMatrix;

D3DXMatrixRotationY( &RotationY, timeGetTime()/200.0f );
D3DXMatrixRotationX( &RotationX, timeGetTime()/800.0f );
D3DXMatrixMultiply( &WorldMatrix, &RotationX, &RotationY );

g_pDevice->SetTransform( D3DTS_WORLD, &WorldMatrix );
```

See what is going on? First I fill in the Y rotation matrix with a rotation angle based on the current time. I use the same technique to fill in the X rotation, although dividing by a slightly higher number means the rotation will be slower. Then I concatenate both matrices into a single world matrix by multiplying them together. And finally, I implement the world matrix into Direct3D using `IDirect3DDevice8::SetTransform()` with the `D3DTS_WORLD` flag.

Disabling Culling and Lighting

The vertex setup that you have causes Direct3D to assume that you want it to perform lighting calculations on the vertices. Normally this is what you want, except that I haven't shown you how to use lights yet, so the result is a big black triangle. The other problem you currently have is that back face culling is also turned on. Since you are spinning the triangle, this causes it to turn invisible when it is facing away from you, which is a pain. Fixing these two issues is really simple—it just requires a change to the render state.

A *render state* is the current set of values that Direct3D is using to draw to the screen. Direct3D operates like a state machine. What it outputs is dependent on what its current state is. For instance, if one of the states, such as lighting, is turned on, then it will output lit faces, otherwise it will output unlit faces. This can be changed on the fly. That is, you can output a bunch of faces that you want to be lit, then turn off lighting, output some unlit faces, turn it back on, and so on. Almost all of these settings are controlled through a single function, entitled `SetRenderState()`, which is shown here:

```
HRESULT SetRenderState( D3DRENDERSTATETYPE State, DWORD Value );
```

There are probably over a hundred different states that you can change with this function, ranging from enabling the z-buffer to vertex blending operations, so I am not going to throw a massive list at you. I will discuss all the relevant states as they come up. However, if you are feeling particularly curious, you can look up *DirectX 8.0 Documentation / DirectX Graphics / Direct3D C++ Reference / Interfaces / IDirect3DDevice8 / IDirect3DDevice8::SetRenderState* for the full list of render states.

Back to disabling lighting and culling:

```
// Turn off culling so the back of the triangle does not  disappear
g_pDevice->SetRenderState( D3DRS_CULLMODE, D3DCULL_NONE );

// Turn off lighting because we have are own colors for the vertices
g_pDevice->SetRenderState( D3DRS_LIGHTING, FALSE );
```

Put that code in your `GameInit()` function and all will be well. And that's it. Your engine is now way more advanced, so let's see what it can do. Check out Figure 12.5 for the lowdown on the dizzy triangle. By the way, you should really load this one off the CD, because a black-and-white static image just doesn't do it justice.

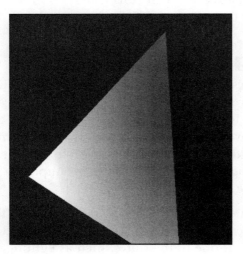

Figure 12.5

The spinning triangle

Turning on the Lights

The last example was definitely better than the first, but how much cooler would it be with real-time lighting? Well, I guess you'll just have to find out! First things first. You need to make some modifications to the structure of the program. You may be noticing that I am making some large structural changes to the programs so far to accommodate the different examples. This is because you don't have the code down yet for a solid engine, but I want to give you a chance to feel out Direct3D and to see how to achieve different effects. After this lighting example, and the next one on textures, you're going to start to put together some code that will be able to support some very advanced graphical implementations. For now, though, let's look at lights.

This example will display a simple triangle that will rotate about the y-axis. As it turns, its corners will come into the range of the light and become lit. For this lighting example you are going to use another vertex format. This one is not going to include any diffuse color information, just data for the position and normal of the vertex.

Here is the structure and its associated tags:

```
struct ZENVERTEX
{
        float x, y, z;
        float nx, ny, nz;
};
#define CUSTOM_ZENVERTEX (D3DFVF_XYZ | D3DFVF_NORMAL)
```

You may be wondering exactly how to fill in those normals, so let me take a minute to talk about them.

Defining Vertex Normals

Normals are very important in lighting calculations because they are used to work out the angle between the source light and the destination, which ultimately determines the brightness of a particular point. Let's start with the basics. There are two types of normals that you need to be concerned with: face normals and vertex normals. Figure 12.6 shows how vertex and face normals relate to the face.

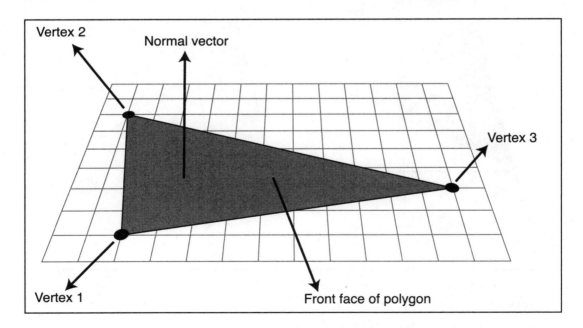

Figure 12.6

The difference between face and vertex normals

A *face normal* is simply a normal to the entire face. In other words, it is a unit vector perpendicular to the face. This is the normal that's compared with the light if you happen to choose flat lighting, which lights a face with a single color, leading to sharp gaps between different faces. The face normal faces away from the face and the other side is the back side, which is usually culled, unless of course you turn culling off.

A *vertex normal* is the normal to the vertex of the face; there is a normal to every vertex in the face. To find out the brightness of a vertex, Direct3D compares the angle of the vector from the light to the vertex to the normal of the vertex. The result of the comparison determines the brightness for the vertex. Then, when the brightness has been figured out for every vertex in the face, the brightness values are interpolated across the face to give a nice smooth gradation. This method of lighting is called *gouraud shading,* although it is pronounced "goorow" or "garrow," depending on whom you are talking to. Figure 12.7 shows visually how the shading is computed, and a comparison of gouraud and flat shading.

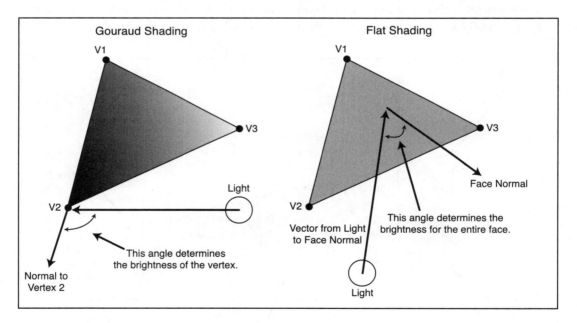

Figure 12.7

Computing brightness for gouraud and flat shading

Let's get back to computing the normals. If you have a single face, which is *planar*, then you just need to set the vertex normals to point in the same direction as the face normal. That is, straight away from the face. On the other hand, if you have a face that is double sided like this one is, then you can achieve better effects by setting the normal to point "out" of the corner, like in Figure 12.8

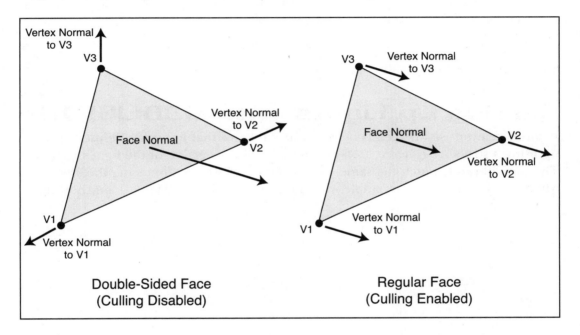

Figure 12.8

The directions for normals for isolated triangular faces

So, looking at the definition for the new vertices below, you can see that I have set the vertices to basically point the same way as the corners of the triangles:

```
// The vertices for the triangle
ZENVERTEX ZenVertices[] =
{
        { -2.0f,-2.0f, 0.0f,-1.0f,-1.0f, 0.0f },
        {  2.0f,-2.0f, 0.0f, 1.0f,-1.0f, 0.0f },
        {  0.0f, 2.0f, 0.0f, 0.0f, 1.0f, 0.0f },
};
```

The normals are highlighted in bold. Later on in the book I'll show you more complex models, which figure out their normals automatically.

Enabling Light Indices

Obviously, if you are using lights, you need to make sure that they are turned on. I showed you earlier how to turn them off, and turning them back on is just as simple. When I say "turn them off" I don't mean in the sense that the scene will be dark. I mean that the lighting component of the rendering engine is disabled. This is the code:

```
g_pDevice->SetRenderState( D3DRS_LIGHTING, TRUE );
```

Simple or what? Next let's look at how to set up the lights.

Setting Up Lights with D3DLIGHT8

If you have ever used Direct3D before, you will know that lights are defined and set up using a structure called D3DLIGHTX, where "X" is the version of the light structure. They are all pretty much the same, but in this case I will be discussing the D3DLIGHT8, which is the one most compatible with the version of Direct3D that I am showing you. The structure looks like this:

```
typedef struct _D3DLIGHT8 {
    D3DLIGHTTYPE    Type;           // The type of light, eg point, directional, etc
    D3DCOLORVALUE   Diffuse;        // The diffuse color
    D3DCOLORVALUE   Specular;       // The specular highlight color
    D3DCOLORVALUE   Ambient;        // The ambient color
    D3DVECTOR       Position;       // The position of the light
    D3DVECTOR       Direction;      // The direction for the light
    float           Range;          // The range of the light
    float           Falloff;        // The falloff model for spotlights
    float           Attenuation0;   // The attenuation of the light as it
                                    //    approaches its range
    float           Attenuation1;
    float           Attenuation2;
    float           Theta;          // The angle of the umbra for spotlights
    float           Phi;            // The angle of the penumbra for spotlights
} D3DLIGHT8;
```

I talked about the different properties of lights a lot in the last chapter, so if you need some more information on any of the components, then flip back and check out the information there. So you want to create a simple point light set back a lit-tle from the face. To set this up I used the following code, placed as usual in the GameInit() function:

```
D3DLIGHT8 Light;
ZeroMemory( &Light, sizeof( D3DLIGHT8 ) );

// Set up the light
Light.Type      = D3DLIGHT_POINT;
Light.Diffuse.r = 1.0f;
Light.Diffuse.g = 1.0f;
Light.Diffuse.b = 1.0f;
Light.Position  = D3DXVECTOR3( 0, 0, -10 );
Light.Range     = 10.0f;
```

As you can see, you only need to fill the fields that you are interested in, as long as you zero out the whole structure after you declare it. For instance, you can see that I did not fill in the Phi or Theta structural entries, since they are used only for spot lights, and this light is a point light source. Notice how I set the position of the light with the D3DXVECTOR structure. I set the range of the light to 10 units.

Now that the light structure is filled in, you need to do a couple of things before it becomes active in the scene. Direct3D has kind of an interesting lighting system, so bear with me for a second while I explain it. Direct3D has an index of lights that you can set the properties for and enable. By default, all lights are off and are not filled with any information. So to enable a light, you have to fill one of the index entries with information and then turn it on. The whole process is below.

1. Create a D3DLIGHT8 structure.
2. Fill in the structure with information about your new light.
3. Register the light in one of the light indices with Direct3D.
4. Enable the light.

Don't forget that although you have enabled the lighting subsystems with the SetRenderState() call, you still need to enable each light that you want to use individ-ually. Let's take a second to see how to do that now:

```
// Attach this light structure to a Direct3D Lighting index
g_pDevice->SetLight( 0, &Light );

// Enable this light
g_pDevice->LightEnable( 0, TRUE );
```

As you can see, it is quite simple. You set the light index using the function `IDirect3DDevice8::SetLight()`. The parameters are the index of the light that you want to set, and the address of a `D3DLIGHT8` structure, which contains information about the light you are creating. The index can range from 1 to the maximum number of lights that the device you are using supports, which will vary from card to card but is normally quite high. Actually, unless you are using one of the newer boards that supports lighting in hardware, then the number of lights is limited only by the `DWORD` value in the structure.

Then, to enable the light, all you have to do is make a call to `IDirect3DDevice8::LightEnable()`, which takes the index of the light whose enabled status you want to change, and a Boolean value specifying the new status for the light, which of course should be true if you are enabling the light. And that is all you have to do to set up a point light. Unfortunately, if you try to run the code so far, you will get nothing except for a spinning black triangle, which is annoying since you are trying to light the thing! The problem is that the face does not have a *material* attached to it yet, and lighting is reliant upon the interaction between both the light and the material, so let's create a material now.

Setting Up Materials

For this example you'll just create a simple material that has a red diffuse color and a yellow ambience. Remember what this means from the last chapter? The *diffuse color* is the main color that defines how the face will look, and the *ambient color* has a more subtle effect and defines how the diffuse color fades out into the ambient color of the scene.

Materials, in Direct3D, are encapsulated by the `D3DMATERIAL8` structure, which as you'll see is quite simple. It just has entries for all the different aspects that affect a material that I talked about in the last chapter, such as diffuse color, specular highlight color, and so on. Here it is:

```
typedef struct _D3DMATERIAL8 {
    D3DCOLORVALUE    Diffuse;
    D3DCOLORVALUE    Ambient;
    D3DCOLORVALUE    Specular;
    D3DCOLORVALUE    Emissive;
    float            Power;
} D3DMATERIAL8;
```

Now materials differ from lights a bit because they are more of a state machine construct. That is, you can only have one active material selected at a time and whichever one is selected is used for all the faces that are output. So if you have a model that has parts that are green and other parts that are red, then you have to render it in two steps. First you would select the green material and render the green parts, and then you would move on to select the red material and render the red parts. It is not as bad as it sounds, so don't worry too much; right now you are just rendering a single face.

To create the material for this face I used the following code:

```
D3DMATERIAL8 Material;
ZeroMemory( &Material, sizeof( D3DMATERIAL8 ) );

// Setup the material
Material.Diffuse.r = 1.0f;
Material.Diffuse.g = 0.0f;
Material.Diffuse.b = 0.0f;
Material.Diffuse.a = 1.0f;

Material.Ambient.r = 1.0f;
Material.Ambient.g = 1.0f;
Material.Ambient.b = 0.0f;
Material.Ambient.a = 1.0f;
```

Basically, all that does is set the colors for the face. Notice that you don't have to fill in all the values for the structure, only the ones you are interested in. Now all you have to do is select it as the active material. This is simple and only requires a single call to IDirect3DDevice8::SetMaterial(), which takes a single parameter, which is the address of a D3DMATERIAL8 structure that you want to use for the new material, like this:

```
g_pDevice->SetMaterial( &Material );
```

And that's it! If you run the code, you should see something like Figure 12.9. You can catch the full listing on the CD in the Chapter 12 code directory.

Figure 12.9

A rotating face, with materials and real-time lighting

Using Textures

Now for a quick introduction to using textures. In the next chapter, you'll start taking the knowledge that you've learned in this chapter to higher levels, and will begin the development of a sophisticated 3D engine. This example is going to be remarkably similar to that last example, except that the face will not be lit. Instead, it will have a groovy texture applied to it using perspective-correct texture mapping.

Let me start with a look at the format of the flexible vertex format that I will be using. Like I mentioned before, don't worry too much right now about how I keep changing the definition for this thing. In the next chapter I will show you a more permanent solution that you will use for the remainder of the code in the book. Here's the format:

```
struct ZENVERTEX
{
        float x, y, z;
        D3DCOLOR DiffuseColor;
        float tu, tv;
};
```

You've seen the position and color entries before. But hang on! What the heck are those tu and tv entries all about? Well, it all has to do with texture coordinates....

Texture Coordinates

Texture coordinates are one of those things that make you go hmmm. That is, until you figure them out, at which point they make perfect sense. So let me start with a definition: *texture coordinates* are kind of locations within a texture. Is that the best I can come up with? Give me a minute, will you? Jeez. Basically, you know and I know what textures are, right? They are simply rectangular bitmap images that can be applied to a face to create a more realistic and immersive atmosphere within the game.

Since textures are just bitmaps, they pretty much follow the same rules as bitmaps, such as having a width, height, and bit depth. However, they also have some other nifty features like alpha channels, which can be used for transparency. For now though let's keep it simple.

The Background

Say you have a face in your game that represents the doors of an elevator opening and closing. As the doors open, the face is scaled smaller, and for some reason or another you decide that you want the texture for the door to squash up as the door closes. This is pretty easy to do—all you have to do is get the width of the texture and scale it as the door is closing. But what happens if later on in the development cycle an artist (you know, the guys who like to think they are more important than programmers) comes up with a better texture for the elevator, but it's a different size? You would have to go all the way back through your code, figure out where the code is that deals with sizing textures, and recompute the variables. Dealing with the actual pixel values of the texture is not productive.

> Remember how I told you that *pixel* comes from the two words *picture element*? Well, when talking about textures you use the term *texel*, from the words *texture element*. This helps you to differentiate between the things you are talking about in technobabble with your associates.

The solution to the problem? How about introducing an intermediate layer that separates the actual texel coordinates from the coordinates that you use in your code? Like you could tell Direct3D that you want the texture to start at the beginning of the face and finish at the end, and Direct3D would automatically figure out the rest for you. Well, it just so happens that this very idea is what has been implemented into Direct3D. Lucky for me, otherwise the last couple of paragraphs would have been completely superfluous. Now, enough background theory—let's look at how it works.

How It All Works

Basically, it goes like this: Texture coordinates are specified in the u- and v-axes. Between you and me, u and v are the same as x and y, respectively, in the Cartesian system. Texture coordinates usually range from 0.0 to 1.0, although values out of this range are used frequently for special effects such as tiling, which I'll show you when you get to the more advanced material. Now keep this in your head: (0.0, 0.0) in texture coordinate space is equal to the coordinate at (0, 0) in the texture. Texture coordinate (1.0, 1.0) refers to the texel at (TextureWidth, TextureHeight). All other values are scaled in between.

Have a look at Figure 12.10. See how it works? If you have a texture with dimensions of (256, 256), then an offset in texture coordinates of (1.0, 0.5) will get you the pixel that is all the way across and halfway down, or in other words, the pixel at (256, 128). Similarly, a texture coordinate of (0.25, 0.0) will get you the pixel in the first row of the texture that is 25 percent across, which is (64, 0). I'll cover more on this soon.

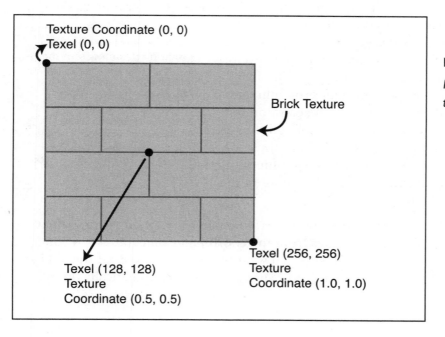

Figure 12.10

Indexing texels with texture coordinates

Texture Coordinate (0, 0)
Texel (0, 0)

Brick Texture

Texel (128, 128)
Texture
Coordinate (0.5, 0.5)

Texel (256, 256)
Texture
Coordinate (1.0, 1.0)

Implementation

Now that you've seen the background and gotten a pretty short introduction to how they work, let me give you some implementation details. Have a look at Figure 12.11 to see what you are trying to achieve in this chapter. You have a triangle, which you're probably getting sick of by now, but bear with me. Recall from the vertex definition that you define how you want the texture to appear on the face by defining the texture coordinates within the vertex itself. So you can see that if you want the first vertex at (–2, –2, 0) to hold the lower-left corner of the texture, then the texture coordinates should be set to (0.0, 1.0). The second vertex at (2, –2, 0) should have the lower-right corner of the texture attached to it, so the correct coordinates are, of course, (1.0, 1.0). And finally, the third vertex is at the top of the triangle. This one is slightly more interesting since it is halfway across the face and at the top, so the correct texture coordinates are (0.5, 0.0).

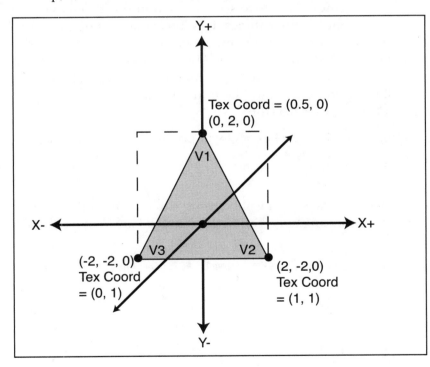

Figure 12.11

Attaching a texture to a face using texture coordinates within the vertex definition.

With all those examples and theory you should now have a pretty good understanding of how texture coordinates work. Don't worry if you are a little confused. I will be talking about them a lot more when you get to advanced texturing effects later.

Check out the code that follows, where I fill in the vertex structures, which sets the vertex positions, colors, and texture coordinates:

```
ZENVERTEX ZenVertices[] =
{
        { -2.0f,-2.0f, 0.0f, D3DCOLOR_XRGB( 255, 255, 255 ), 0.0f, 1.0f},
        {  2.0f,-2.0f, 0.0f, D3DCOLOR_XRGB( 255, 255, 255 ), 1.0f, 1.0f},
        {  0.0f, 2.0f, 0.0f, D3DCOLOR_XRGB( 255, 255, 255 ), 0.5f, 0.0f},
};
```

The texture coordinates are highlighted in bold. Now all that's left to do is everything else!

Creating a Texture from a File

Creating textures is pretty much the same process as you used in the 2D chapters to load bitmaps to surfaces, except for a few things. First up is that you don't really have to worry too much about the format of the texture, such as its bit depth, because Direct3D will handle all that stuff internally. Also, you will not be using the IDirect3DSurface8 interface anymore, because it was created for dealing with 2D implementations. Instead, from now on you will be using the more flexible IDirect3DTexture8, which is built just for 3D stuff.

The first thing I do for this example is declare a global pointer to a texture, just like you used to do for surfaces. Here is the code:

```
LPDIRECT3DTEXTURE8 g_pTexture = 0;
```

Remember that interface name because you will be using it a lot. Now let's move back to GameInit(), where the following code can be used to load any texture from the disk:

```
r = D3DXCreateTextureFromFile( g_pDevice, "Texture.bmp", &g_pTexture );
if( FAILED( r ) )
{
        SetError( "Couldnt load texture" );
        return E_FAIL;
}
```

As you can see, the code uses the Direct3D utility function D3DXCreateTextureFromFile() function to create the texture and it has the following prototype:

```
HRESULT D3DXCreateTextureFromFileA(
  LPDIRECT3DDEVICE8 pDevice,
  LPCSTR pSrcFile,
  LPDIRECT3DTEXTURE8* ppTexture
);
```

The parameters are given in Table 12.5.

Table 12.5   D3DXCreateTextureFromFile() Parameters

Parameter	Definition
pDevice	A pointer to your device
pSrcFile	Takes takes a string identifying the location of the file on disk
ppTexture	Takes a pointer to the address of an IDirect3DTexture8 that will be filled with the address of the newly created texture

I have looked around the documentation and I can't seem to find a list of the file formats that this function supports; however, I can tell you from my tests that it definitely loads the following types:

- Windows device independent bitmaps (*.bmp)
- DirectDraw Surface files (*.dds) (preferred)
- Joint Photograph Experts Group files (*.jpg)
- Targa Files (*.tga)

And it definitely does not load GIFs, PCXs, or TIFFs, which isn't much of a problem, since those formats are hardly ever used for games anyway. What you do get is very good, though, because writing parsers for file types as complicated as Targa or JPEG would be a complete nightmare. By the way, if you need more control over the texture you are loading—for instance, if you wanted to change its dimensions or format—then there is a more advanced function called D3DXCreateTextureFromFileEx(), which takes a whopping 14 parameters. However, you should be able to figure most of them out because they are all very similar to the stuff discussed in previous chapters. You can get more information on that function in *DirectX 8.0 C++ Documentation / DirectX Graphics / Direct3DX C++ Reference / Functions / Texturing Functions / D3DXCreateTextureFromFileEx.*

You may have noticed in the previous bulleted list that I put "preferred" beside the DDS file type. I have done so for a few reasons. First off, the DDS format supports all the proprietary extensions of Direct3D, such as hardware compression and built-in alpha channel support, as well as 100 other features. And secondly, since I don't think there is an image editor in the world that even supports DDS files yet, you are not going to have many problems with people ripping off your artwork through piracy. Now you may be wondering how exactly you create DDS files if no image editor supports them yet. Well, it just so happens that included with the DirectX 8.0 SDK is an editor utility called the DirectX Texture Tool, which allows you to convert other artwork types into the DDS format easily. It supports the creation of really advanced texture types like mipmaps and cubic textures, which I will cover later on in the book.

Slick, let's move on...

Enabling the Texture

Remember when I was talking about lights and I said that you had to enable the light before you could use it with the SetLight() function? Well, textures work in a similar way, except that whatever texture is selected will be applied to whatever primitive is currently being drawn, so in that sense they are similar to materials. If you had an object with more than one texture, then you would draw the first part, change the texture, draw the second, and so on. However, you can select more than one texture at a time, although this is for multitexturing, which I am not going to go into. For now, I'll show you the code to select a single texture into use:

```
g_pDevice->SetTexture( 0, g_pTexture );
```

As you can see, the function that is used to set a texture as active is called IDirect3DDevice8::SetTexture(), and it takes two parameters. The first is the index into which you want to activate the texture into. There can be up to eight selected textures at the same time, so this entry can range from 0 to 7. The second parameter is a pointer to the texture that you want to set active.

And that's it! If you run the example then you will see something like the image in Figure 12.12.

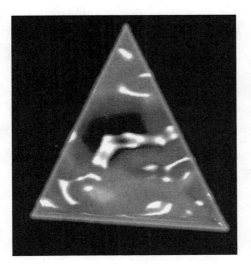

Figure 12.12

Rendering with textures

Conclusion

Check yourself out. You're already starting to look like a regular Zen guru. Well, almost—don't get too carried away just yet! In this chapter I covered a lot of new information from simple rendering, to lighting, texturing, and simple animation.

Don't worry if everything seems a little bit up in the air right now. I covered a lot of different material to give you an introduction to a lot of the different facets that make up Direct3D. In the few chapters I am going to show you how to bring together the knowledge from this chapter with your own intuition to create a reliable, extensible, and, of course aesthetically pleasing 3D engine.

And if you want to know more, you are just going to have to turn the page and read on into the depths of the night....

CHAPTER 13

BUILDING THE ZEN 3D ENGINE

Once upon a time in the not too distant past there was a Zen guru, and his name was... oh wait—it was me. After celebrating my birthday (which is on March 2nd, for those of you who want to send me stuff), I was walking home, not in a very straight line, and I decided that a spicy chicken pizza would be a fantastic idea. Oh my.... That was the night that I discovered what food poisoning is like. So if you ever happen to be walking in a not-too-straight line through the city of Dundee, Scotland, I suggest you stumble clear of that pizza place on the Seagate.

The reason I'm telling you this is because I haven't finished my Chapter Openings 101 course yet. Well, that and also because by the end of this chapter you are going to have a 3D engine that is so cool it will make *you* sick. So then you'll know how I felt!

This chapter will cover

- specifying a standard vertex format for your engine and encapsulating that functionality in a class.
- how to create a base object for the 3D objects that will be used in the game.
- the creation of advanced objects such as points for star fields, lines, faces, cubes, and much, much more.
- rendering techniques such as how to use point lists, line lists, line strips, and also rendering with indexed vertices.
- encapsulating the view matrix into a camera .

Getting a Permanent Vertex Format... Finally!

I hope all that messing with vertex formats in the last chapter didn't annoy you too much.! Although you may want to expand on the functionality of the engine later, I have put together this little list of the stuff that you will want to do for your engine:

- You obviously want the vertex to have a position somewhere in 3D space, so that requires an (x, y, z) coordinate.
- Lighting is a major component of any serious graphical engine, so it's important that each vertex also a normal vector, so that the lighting can be computed.

- You will need to specify the color of the vertex so that any points, lines, faces, and objects have a base color.
- Advanced lighting effects, such as using specular highlight, will require that the vertex has a specular color.
- When you get to using textures later on, it will become important for the vertices to have texture coordinates.

So what does all that mean? Well, it means that every one of your standard vertices should include a position, a normal vector, a diffuse color, a specular color, and of course, texture coordinates. Take a look at Figure 13.1. Now let me show you the implementation. All of this code is included in the Engine.h file.

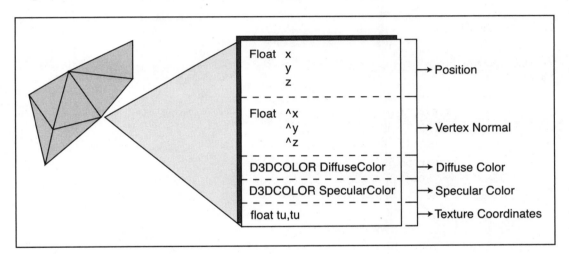

Figure 13.1

The Zen flexible vertex format

The first thing to do is to define the bit vector that describes what is included in the vertex:

```
#define ZENVERTEX_TYPE                          \
(                                               \
                    D3DFVF_XYZ |        \        // Vertex Position
                    D3DFVF_NORMAL |     \        // Vertex Normal Vector
                    D3DFVF_DIFFUSE |    \        // Vertex Diffuse Color
                    D3DFVF_SPECULAR |   \        // Vertex Specular Color
                    D3DFVF_TEX1         \        // Vertex Texture Coords
                                        \
)
```

You probably recognize these flags from the last chapter. Now let's look at the vertex itself. Since most of the code is going to be object based, I encapsulate the vertex into a C++ class to make things easier.

```
class CZenVertex
{
public:
        CZenVertex();
        CZenVertex(      float x, float y, float z,
                         float nx, float ny, float nz,
                         D3DCOLOR DiffuseColor,
                         D3DCOLOR SpecularColor,
                         float tu, float tv);
        ~CZenVertex();

// Functions
public:
        Set(      float x, float y, float z,
                  float nx, float ny, float nz,
                  D3DCOLOR DiffuseColor,
                  D3DCOLOR SpecularColor,
                  float tu, float tv );

protected:

// Variables
public:
        D3DVECTOR m_Position;
        D3DVECTOR m_Normal;
        D3DCOLOR m_DiffuseColor;
        D3DCOLOR m_SpecularColor;
        float m_tu, m_tv;

protected:

};
```

As you can see, it is a pretty simple class. There are two D3DVECTORs that hold the position and normal for the class, and then two D3DCOLORs that hold the diffuse and specular colors of the vertex, respectively. And finally, there are two floats for the texture coordinates.

There are two constructors: the default just initializes all the member variables, while the second provides a simple way to initialize the variables during the declaration of the object. I also include a simple Set() function, which allows you to easily fill in all the variables on the fly. The code for the class is shown here:

```
CZenVertex::CZenVertex()
{
        ZeroMemory( &m_Position, sizeof( D3DVECTOR ) );
        ZeroMemory( &m_Normal, sizeof( D3DVECTOR ) );
        ZeroMemory( &m_SpecularColor, sizeof( D3DCOLOR ) );

        m_DiffuseColor = D3DCOLOR_ARGB( 255, 255, 255, 255 );

        m_tu = m_tv = 0.0f;
}


CZenVertex::CZenVertex( float x, float y, float z,
                        float nx, float ny, float nz,
                        D3DCOLOR DiffuseColor,
                        D3DCOLOR SpecularColor,
                        float tu, float tv)
{
        m_Position.x = x;
        m_Position.y = y;
        m_Position.z = z;

        m_Normal.x = nx;
        m_Normal.y = ny;
        m_Normal.z = nz;

        m_DiffuseColor  = DiffuseColor;
        m_SpecularColor = SpecularColor;
        m_tu = tu;
        m_tv = tv;
}


CZenVertex::~CZenVertex()
{

}
```

```
CZenVertex::Set(  float x, float y, float z,
                  float nx, float ny, float nz,
                  D3DCOLOR DiffuseColor,
                  D3DCOLOR SpecularColor,
                  float tu, float tv )
{
        m_Position.x = x;
        m_Position.y = y;
        m_Position.z = z;

        m_Normal.x = nx;
        m_Normal.y = ny;
        m_Normal.z = nz;

        m_DiffuseColor  = DiffuseColor;
        m_SpecularColor = SpecularColor;
        m_tu = tu;
        m_tv = tv;
}
```

Creating a Base Game Object

When you get more advanced, you're going to have a rendering pipeline that will have to deal with all sorts of objects, from simple points all the way up to complex animating meshes. Obviously, you can't represent items with such differing requirements with a single object, because that would be inefficient. However, it is desirable to be able to deal with all the objects in a similar way, particularly if at some point in the process you are not sure even what type of object you are dealing with. How do you achieve these differing objectives? Well, it's easier than a double rotation death kick. All you have to do is define a generic base class, from which you can then declare child classes, which represent the objects in the game. Then, when you want to refer to the different objects in an independent manner, you only have to deal with pointers from the base class. You can cast the pointers backward and forward as you need to. Have a look at Figure 13.2.

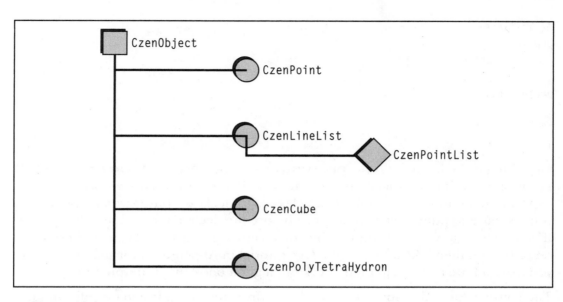

Figure 13.2

Using a base Zen game object as a parent

For now the base class has almost no functionality, because I want to keep it as generic as possible. This is also so that in future derived classes will be easier to derive and control. However, it does contain one member variable that can hold a string identifier for the object. This could be used for human identification in a well-developed editor, or for computer use, if you wanted to use it to differentiate between different object types.

```
class CZenObject
{
public:
        CZenObject();
        ~CZenObject();

// Functions
public:
        virtual HRESULT Render() = 0;

protected:
```

```
// Variables
public:
        char* m_strName;

protected:


};
```

One thing to look out for is the pure virtual Render() function. A *pure virtual function* is one that is not implemented in the class. Rather, it is there because you expect it to be overridden in the child classes. To declare a pure virtual function, you just have to put the virtual keyword before the declaration and initialize it to 0. If you are new to C++ and you haven't come across all this virtual function nonsense before, then take a look at the C++ tutorial in Appendix A for the book, or if you need a little more help then check out a good book that is devoted to C++.

The constructor and destructor don't do anything too complicated, as you can see:

```
CZenObject::CZenObject()
{
        m_strName = 0;
}


CZenObject::~CZenObject()
{
        if( m_strName )
                delete m_strName;
}
```

Encapsulating the View Matrix

Let's face it, messing with a view matrix every time you want to move the viewpoint around your game is not very productive. A better way is to create an object that represents a camera in your code. So if you want to move the camera forward, you simply call a function like Camera.Move() or something similar to that.

That's the theory behind what I am aiming for—let's look now at the implementation. Your camera class is going to need three vectors: one to define its position relative to the origin, one to define where the camera is looking, and finally another to define which way is up. That's it really, for now anyway. Have a look at Figure 13.3 to see how the different vectors relate to the camera.

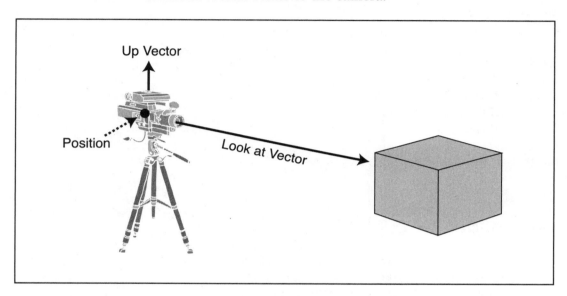

Figure 13.3

How the vectors relate to the camera

Here is the class definition:

```
class CZenCamera : public CZenObject
{
public:
        CZenCamera();
        ~CZenCamera();

// Functions:
public:
        void SetPosition( float x, float y, float z );
        void SetLookPoint( float x, float y, float z );
        void SetUp( float x, float y, float z );

        void Update();
        void Move(float x, float y, float z );
```

```cpp
        void Reset();
        HRESULT Render();
protected:


// Variables
public:
        D3DXVECTOR3 m_Position;
        D3DXVECTOR3 m_LookAt;
        D3DXVECTOR3 m_Up;

protected:

};

CZenCamera::CZenCamera()
{
        ZeroMemory( &m_Position, sizeof( D3DXVECTOR3 ) );
        ZeroMemory( &m_LookAt, sizeof( D3DXVECTOR3 ) );
        ZeroMemory( &m_Up, sizeof( D3DXVECTOR3 ) );

        m_Up.y = 1.0f;

        m_Position.z = -1.0f;

}

CZenCamera::~CZenCamera()
{

}
```

Moving the Camera

As you can see, there are three functions, SetPosition(), SetLookPoint(), and SetUp(),
all of which relate to their corresponding member variables. Move() allows you to
easily update the current position of the camera. Reset() sets all the member variables back to their initial positions, which is centered at the origin, but back one
unit in the z direction, looking at the origin, and the up direction set to (0, 1, 0).

```cpp
void CZenCamera::Reset()
{
        ZeroMemory( &m_Position, sizeof( D3DXVECTOR3 ) );
        ZeroMemory( &m_LookAt, sizeof( D3DXVECTOR3 ) );
        ZeroMemory( &m_Up, sizeof( D3DXVECTOR3 ) );

        m_Up.y = 1.0f;

        m_Position.z = -1.0f;
}

void CZenCamera::Move( float x, float y, float z )
{
        if( x )
                m_Position.x += x;

        if( y )
                m_Position.y += y;

        if( z )
                m_Position.z += z;
}

void CZenCamera::SetPosition( float x, float y, float z )
{
        if( x )
                m_Position.x = x;
        if( y )
                m_Position.y = y;
        if( z )
                m_Position.z = z;
}

void CZenCamera::SetLookPoint( float x, float y, float z )
{
        if( x )
                m_LookAt.x = x;
        if( y )
                m_LookAt.y = y;
        if( z )
                m_LookAt.z = z;
```

```
    }

void CZenCamera::SetUp( float x, float y, float z )
{
        if( x )
                m_Up.x = x;
        if( y )
                m_Up.y = y;
        if( z )
                m_Up.z = z;
}
```

Updating the Camera

Changing the position of the camera is great, but you still need to tell Direct3D what you are doing. To do this, I create a function called Update(), which simply takes the three member vectors and puts them into a view matrix automatically, and then updates Direct3D. This function should be called every frame if you want your changes to take effect.

```
void CZenCamera::Update()
{
        D3DXMATRIX ViewMatrix;
        D3DXMatrixLookAtLH( &ViewMatrix, &m_Position,
                                        &m_LookAt,
                                        &m_Up );

        g_pDevice->SetTransform( D3DTS_VIEW, &ViewMatrix );
}
```

It's not very complicated. The function uses the D3DXMatrixLookAtLH() function, which you saw in the last chapter, to compute the view matrix. When that has been done, the Direct3D internal view matrix is updated with the IDirect3DDevice8::SetTransform() function.

Using the Camera

Using the camera is the simplest part of all. All you have to do is declare a global instance of the camera like this:

```
CZenCamera g_Camera;
```

Then you need to add the call to `CZenCamera::Update()` to the `Render()` function:

```
g_Camera.Update();
```

It doesn't matter where you put it in the function, but make sure you put it after the location of your position update code. What is important is that the camera update code is called every frame. As an example, say you want to set the position of the camera to oscillate forward and backward from the origin. The following code would take care of that:

```
static float z = 0;
static BOOL bForward = FALSE;

if( bForward )
{
        z += 0.1f;
        if( z > 0.0f )
        {
                z = 0.0f;
                bForward = FALSE;
        }
}
else
{
        z -= 0.1f;
        if( z < -5.0f )
        {
                z = -5.0f;
                bForward = TRUE;
        }
}

g_Camera.SetPosition( 0, 0, z );

g_Camera.Update();
```

Getting to the Point

The simplest object that you can render in 3D has got to be the point. It is just a single pixel that has a color and has its position defined by a vertex. I am going to show you two different classes for points. The first is for a single point and is very simple. You could use this for mini-particle effects. The second point class is used to hold an entire list of points for when you want to use a lot of points in the same place, for instance if you were representing the stars.

Creating a Point Object

The code to look after and display a point is pretty easy. Check out the following code, which shows the class definition for CZenObject:

```
class CZenPoint : public CZenObject
{
public:
        CZenPoint();
        CZenPoint( float x, float y, float z, D3DCOLOR Color );

        ~CZenPoint();

// Functions
public:
        HRESULT Render();

        void SetProps( float x, float y, float z, D3DCOLOR Color );
        void GetProps( float& x, float& y, float& z, D3DCOLOR& Color );
protected:

//Variables
public:

protected:
        CZenVertex m_Vertex;

};
```

As you can see, CZenPoint is derived from the CZenObject that I showed you earlier. Like with the CZenVertex class, you can initialize this class easily with the overridden version of the constructor.

```
CZenPoint::CZenPoint()
{

}
```

```
CZenPoint::~CZenPoint()
{

}

CZenPoint::CZenPoint( float x, float y, float z, D3DCOLOR Color )
{
        m_Vertex.m_Position.x = x;
        m_Vertex.m_Position.y = y;
        m_Vertex.m_Position.z = z;

        m_Vertex.m_DiffuseColor = Color;
}
```

I also add two functions, so that it is easy to update the coordinates of the point:

```
void CZenPoint::SetProps( float x, float y, float z, D3DCOLOR Color )
{
        m_Vertex.m_Position.x = x;
        m_Vertex.m_Position.y = y;
        m_Vertex.m_Position.z = z;

        m_Vertex.m_DiffuseColor = Color;
}

void CZenPoint::GetProps( float& x, float& y, float& z, D3DCOLOR& Color )
{
        x = m_Vertex.m_Position.x;
        y = m_Vertex.m_Position.y;
        z = m_Vertex.m_Position.z;

        Color = m_Vertex.m_DiffuseColor;
}
```

So far it's pretty easy. But how the heck do you render a point to the screen in 3D? Well, it's pretty simple, too. You saw a lot of the steps in the last chapter, but let's just go over them quickly.

1. Create a vertex buffer.
2. Lock the vertex buffer.
3. Copy the vertex for the point into the buffer.
4. Unlock the vertex buffer.

5. Attach the vertex buffer to a rendering stream.
6. Call `DrawPrimitive()`.
7. Release the vertex buffer.

This is the process that you follow for just about every simple object that you render. Following is the code:

```
HRESULT CZenPoint::Render()
{
        HRESULT r = 0;

        // New vertex buffer
        LPDIRECT3DVERTEXBUFFER8 pVB = 0;

        // Create the vertex buffer
        r = g_pDevice->CreateVertexBuffer( sizeof( CZenVertex ),
                D3DUSAGE_WRITEONLY, ZENVERTEX_TYPE, D3DPOOL_DEFAULT, &pVB );
        if( FAILED( r ) )
                return E_FAIL;

        // Pointer to vertex buffer data
        void* pData = 0;

        // Lock the vertex buffer
        r = pVB->Lock( 0, 0, (BYTE**)&pData, 0 );
        if( FAILED( r ) )
        {
                pVB->Release();
                return E_FAIL;
        }

        // Copy the vertex for the point into the vertex buffer
        CopyMemory( pData, (void*)&m_Vertex, sizeof( CZenVertex ) );

        // Unlock the vertex buffer
        pVB->Unlock();

        // Attach the vertex buffer to a rendering stream
        g_pDevice->SetStreamSource( 0, pVB, sizeof( CZenVertex ) );

        // Draw the point
```

```
g_pDevice->DrawPrimitive( D3DPT_POINTLIST, 0, 1 );

// Release the vertex buffer
pVB->Release();

return S_OK;
}
```

This code, and variations on it, is going to get used a lot, so I'll run through it step by step to be sure you get it.

Rendering Step 1—Creating the Vertex Buffer

The create the vertex buffer, do the following:

```
// New vertex buffer
LPDIRECT3DVERTEXBUFFER8 pVB = 0;

// Create the vertex buffer
r = g_pDevice->CreateVertexBuffer( sizeof( CZenVertex ),
            D3DUSAGE_WRITEONLY, ZENVERTEX_TYPE, D3DPOOL_DEFAULT, &pVB );
if( FAILED( r ) )
        return E_FAIL;
```

I showed you the CreateVertexBuffer() function in the last chapter, but take note of the first parameter. Since only a single vertex is needed to define a point, the vertex buffer only needs to be large enough to hold one vertex. I define this with a simple sizeof() call.

Rendering Step 2—Locking the Vertex Buffer

Locking the vertex buffer is generally a pretty uneventful process. Here is the code:

```
// Pointer to vertex buffer data
void* pData = 0;

// Lock the vertex buffer
r = pVB->Lock( 0, 0, (BYTE**)&pData, 0 );
if( FAILED( r ) )
{
```

```
        pVB->Release();
        return E_FAIL;
}
```

It is very important that you remember to unlock a vertex buffer before you try to render it, because otherwise the call to DrawPrimitive() will fail. It is possible to lock a vertex buffer more than once, although it is generally not good practice to do so. If you happen to lock the same buffer multiple times, then you must unlock it the same number of times in order for rendering to work properly.

Rendering Step 3—Filling the Vertex Buffer

Like you saw in the last chapter, you fill the vertex buffer with a simple call to CopyMemory(), which is just a cover for memcpy(). Here is the code:

```
// Copy the vertex for the point into the vertex buffer
CopyMemory( pData, (void*)&m_Vertex, sizeof( CZenVertex ) );
```

Rendering Step 4—Unlocking the Vertex Buffer

Like I said before, this is a very important step, because if you don't do it, then you will get a beautifully rendered black screen.

```
// Unlock the vertex buffer
pVB->Unlock();
```

Rendering Step 5—Attaching the Vertex Buffer to a Stream

This is the stage at which you let the hardware know where the next batch of information is going to come from.

```
// Attach the vertex buffer to a rendering stream
g_pDevice->SetStreamSource( 0, pVB, sizeof( CZenVertex ) );
```

Rendering Step 6—Calling DrawPrimitive()

Rendering is almost always done with a call to DrawPrimitive() or one of its friends, which I will introduce you to shortly.

```
// Draw the point
g_pDevice->DrawPrimitive( D3DPT_POINTLIST, 0, 1 );
```

Notice how I use the D3DPT_POINTLIST flag to indicate that I want to render the vertices in the buffer as points.

Rendering Step 7—Releasing the Vertex Buffer

If you don't do this, then every time you make a call to CZenPoint::Render() a new vertex buffer will be created and the old one will turn into a lost soul, or in other words, a *memory leak*. To tell you the truth, the first time I wrote the code for that bad boy I forgot to release the vertex buffer, and you should have seen how fast my computer ground to a halt. In the next sample I draw 300 points every frame, so what that means is that, running at 200 fps, 60,000 new vertex buffers are being created each second. Talk about a memory leak!

```
// Release the vertex buffer
pVB->Release();
```

And that's it! Remember the process, Jedi, because you will be seeing it show up a whole bunch of times throughout this chapter.

Putting Points to Work

And that is all it takes to render a point to the screen. Well, almost. Let me take a minute to show you how to create a swarm of pixels and rotate them around the screen. Keep in mind that this method is quite inefficient compared to the list class I'm going to show you soon. Anyway, first up you need to declare a global array of points like this:

```
const int g_NumPoints = 300;
CZenPoint g_Points[NumPoints];
```

Simple so far? Good, let's move on. Next, all you need to do is to loop through all the points in the array and assign a position and color to them. The following code does exactly that:

```
for( int i = 0 ; i < g_NumPoints ; i++ )
{
```

```
g_Points[i].SetProps(   (float)(rand()%5) - rand()%5,
                        (float)(rand()%5) - rand()%5,
                        (float)(rand()%5) - rand()%5,
                        D3DCOLOR_ARGB( 255, 255, 255, 255 ) );

}
```

To actually draw the points to the screen you need to render them once every frame from the Render() function.

```
D3DXMatrixRotationY( &WorldMatrix, timeGetTime()/1500.0f );
g_pDevice->SetTransform( D3DTS_WORLD, &WorldMatrix );

for( int i = 0 ; i < g_NumPoints ; i++ )
{
        g_Points[i].Render();
}
```

And that's it! If you run this code, you will get a view of stars swirling around the screen. Take a look at Figure 13.4 to see what I'm talking about.

Figure 13.4

Rendering points to create a star field

Just before I go on to show you how to do the point list object, let me talk about lines for a bit, because the point list functionality is somewhat dependent on lines.

Ask No Questions, See No Lines

Lines are really cool in Direct3D, because they are 3D, for one, and because they can be rendered with really cool effects, such as color gradations. What I mean by that is this: you know the way a line is defined by two points, or vertices? Well, if you set the color of the first vertex to yellow and the second vertex to blue, then the color of the line will smoothly and linearly blend from the yellow to blue. You can use this for really cool highlighting in your games.

Getting Classy with Lines

Following is the class definition that I will be using to deal with lines. It is based around two simple member vertices, which define the start and end of the line.

```cpp
class CZenLine : public CZenObject
{

public:
        CZenLine();
        CZenLine(       float x1, float y1, float z1, D3DCOLOR StartColor,
                        float x2, float y2, float z2, D3DCOLOR EndColor );
        ~CZenLine();

// Functions
public:
        void SetProps( float x1, float y1, float z1, D3DCOLOR StartColor,
                        float x2, float y2, float z2, D3DCOLOR EndColor );

        void GetProps( float& x1, float& y1, float& z1, D3DCOLOR& StartColor,
                        float& x2, float& y2, float& z2, D3DCOLOR& EndColor );

        HRESULT Render();

protected:


//Variables
public:
```

```
protected:
        CZenVertex m_StartPoint;
        CZenVertex m_EndPoint;

};
```

I add some simple functions to allow easy updating of the lines, like SetProps() and GetProps().

```cpp
void CZenLine::SetProps( float x1, float y1, float z1, D3DCOLOR StartColor,
                                        float x2, float y2, float z2, D3DCOLOR
EndColor )
{
        m_StartPoint.m_Position.x = x1;
        m_StartPoint.m_Position.y = y1;
        m_StartPoint.m_Position.z = z1;

        m_StartPoint.m_DiffuseColor = StartColor;

        m_EndPoint.m_Position.x = x2;
        m_EndPoint.m_Position.y = y2;
        m_EndPoint.m_Position.z = z2;

        m_EndPoint.m_DiffuseColor = EndColor;
}

void CZenLine::GetProps( float& x1, float& y1, float& z1, D3DCOLOR& StartColor,
                                        float& x2, float& y2, float& z2, D3DCOLOR&
EndColor )
{
        x1 = m_StartPoint.m_Position.x;
        y1 = m_StartPoint.m_Position.y;
        z1 = m_StartPoint.m_Position.z;

        StartColor = m_StartPoint.m_DiffuseColor;

        x2 = m_EndPoint.m_Position.x;
        y2 = m_EndPoint.m_Position.y;
        z2 = m_EndPoint.m_Position.z;

        EndColor = m_EndPoint.m_DiffuseColor;
}
```

Rendering Lines

Now check out the Render() function for lines. I have bold faced the differences between it and the process for rendering points. Notice how about 99 percent of the code remains the same.

```
HRESULT CZenLine::Render()
{
        HRESULT r = 0;

        LPDIRECT3DVERTEXBUFFER8 pVB = 0;

        r = g_pDevice->CreateVertexBuffer( sizeof( CZenVertex )*2,
                D3DUSAGE_WRITEONLY, ZENVERTEX_TYPE, D3DPOOL_DEFAULT, &pVB );
        if( FAILED( r ) )
                return E_FAIL;

        BYTE* pData = 0;

        r = pVB->Lock( 0, 0, &pData, 0 );
        if( FAILED( r ) )
        {
                pVB->Release();
                return E_FAIL;
        }

        CopyMemory( pData, (void*)&m_StartPoint, sizeof( CZenVertex ) );
        CopyMemory( pData + sizeof(CZenVertex), (void*)&m_EndPoint, sizeof(
CZenVertex ) );

        pVB->Unlock();

        g_pDevice->SetStreamSource( 0, pVB, sizeof( CZenVertex ) );

        g_pDevice->DrawPrimitive( D3DPT_LINELIST, 0, 1 );

        pVB->Release();

        return S_OK;
}
```

This time when I create the vertex buffer, I make it large enough to hold two vertices, for the start and end points. Also look at how I did two copy operations to fill the vertex buffer. The first is copied to the start of the buffer, while the second is copied at an offset of one vertex along in the buffer. And the final difference is the use of the D3DPT_LINELIST flag to indicate that the buffer should be rendered as a list of separate lines.

Using Lines

For this sample, I'm going to create a really cool star effect using a bunch of lines that start at the origin and extend out to random points in space. The color of the vertex of the lines at the origin is a random shade of red, which fades out to black at the other vertex.

To start with, I declare a simple array of lines, using a constant to set the array to hold 300 entries. This is a little excessive. So sue me.

```
CZenLine Lines[g_NumLines];
```

Then of course I need to fill in all the lines in the array with start and end points, which I do with code that is almost the same as that I used for setting up the points in the last example. This code is placed in GameInit().

```
for( int i = 0 ; i < g_NumPoints ; i++ )
{
        Lines[i].SetProps(    0,
                              0,
                              0,
                              D3DCOLOR_XRGB( rand()%255, 0, 0 ),
                              (float)(rand()%10) - rand()%10,
                              (float)(rand()%10) - rand()%10,
                              (float)(rand()%10) - rand()%10,
                              D3DCOLOR_XRGB( 0, 0, 0 ));
}
```

That code just sets the start vertex to be at the origin with a color of red, the end vertex to be at a random location between (–10, –10, –10) and (10, 10, 10), and the color to black.

And then to render the line I simply have to call the CZenLine::Render() function, which I just showed you, from the main Render() function.

```
for( int i = 0 ; i < g_NumPoints ; i++ )
{
        Lines[i].Render();
}
```

Simple or what? That's what I thought, too. Check out Figure 13.5 for the results.

Figure 13.5

Rendering with linearly blended lines

Line Lists

The CZenLine class is fine for when you want a single line or a small number of independent lines. However, as soon as you start to render larger numbers of lines it becomes very inefficient to draw them all serially. A better method is to group them all into a list, copy them all into a vertex buffer, and then blast them all to the screen at the same time.

There are two ways to draw lines from a vertex buffer, and your class needs to accommodate both. The first is to treat the vertex buffer as a series of independent lines. So the first line would be v1 to v2, the second would be v3 to v4, and so on. This is called using *line lists* because each line is independent from the others. In other words, the vertex buffer is just a list of different lines. So for a list of lines the end points do not need to touch each other.

The second way to render is to treat the vertex buffer as one big, long line with different points on it. The technical term for this is using a *line strip*. So the line would go from V1 to Vx, where x is number of vertices in the buffer, and intersect at all the other vertices in between. So v1 to v2 would be the first line, v2 to v3 would be the second, and so on. Have a look at Figure 13.6 to see the difference between strips and lists. Notice how in a line strip that the end points of each line segment must touch each other.

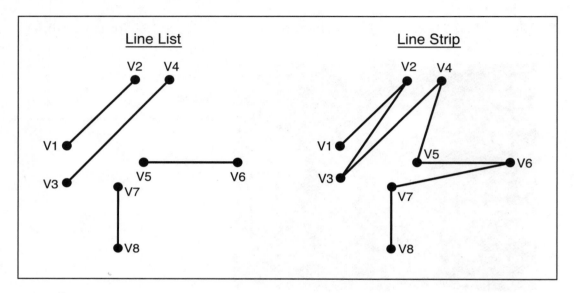

Figure 13.6

Line lists vs. line strips

Before I go on to show you the class that manages the list, let me take a minute to show you the CPointSegment class. This is a small, simple class that has no functions, other than the constructor. It contains a CZenVertex and a pointer for use in the list.

```
class CPointSegment
{
public:
        CPointSegment()
        {
                m_pNext = 0;
        }

public:
        CZenVertex m_Vertex;
        CPointSegment* m_pNext;
};
```

The member variable `m_Vertex` holds the position and color information for the point in the line, and `m_pNext` is for use in the linked list, which I will show you soon.

The CZenLineList Class

The `CZenLineList` class, which I am about to show you, is the most complex class that you have seen so far. It's not really that complicated on the Direct3D side, but it's important that you try and keep your head above the linked list code, which tends to confuse some people. Here is the definition:

```
class CZenLineList : public CZenObject
{
public:
        CZenLineList();
        ~CZenLineList();

// Functions:
public:
        HRESULT AddPoint( float x, float y, float z, D3DCOLOR PointColor );
        void ClearPoints();
        HRESULT Render();

protected:


//Variables
public:
        BOOL m_bConnected;

protected:
        int m_NumPoints;
        CPointSegment* m_pSegmentList;
};
```

Here is a quick overview of the functions before I show them in detail. `AddPoint()` is used to add another point to the line list. `ClearPoints()` empties the list of points and clears any allocated memory. And finally, `Render()` does the usual rendering stuff. The member variable `m_bConnected` is there so that you can specify whether you want to use connected lines, as in a *line strip,* or independent lines, as in a *line list.* Setting this variable to `TRUE` will create a line strip of connected lines. `m_NumPoints` holds the number of points currently in the line. m_pSegment list is kind of interesting; it is used to hold the first of the points in the list.

Initialization and Destruction

The constructor for this class simply initializes all the variables to NULL and sets the m_bConnected flag to TRUE.

```
CZenLineList::CZenLineList()
{
        m_pSegmentList = 0;
        m_NumPoints = 0;

        m_bConnected = TRUE;
}
```

Now have a quick look at the destructor, because this is the first time you will see how some of the linked list machinery works. The following code loops through all the items in the list and deletes them until the entire list is removed from memory.

```
CZenLineList::~CZenLineList()
{
        // Get a pointer to the start of the list
        CPointSegment* pSegment = m_pSegmentList;
        // Create a temporary pointer
        CPointSegment* pTempSeg = 0;

        // Loop while the pointer to the list Is valid
        while( pSegment )
        {
                // Get a pointer to the next Item In the list
                pTempSeg = pSegment->m_pNext;
                // Delete the current segment
                delete pSegment;

                // Iterate the list pointer to the next Item In the list
                pSegment = pTempSeg;
        }
}
```

Looking at code for linked lists can be confusing, so check out the following list of steps to deleting a linked list of segments to see how it works:

1. Create a new pointer and point it to the start of the list.
2. Check to see if the list exists. If it doesn't, then exit.
3. Create a temporary pointer.
4. Set the temporary pointer equal to the next item in the list.
5. Delete the current item in the list.
6. Set the current pointer equal to the temporary pointer, effectively moving to the next item in the list.
7. Loop back to step 3 if the next item exists until the list is empty.

This is pretty much the same code as for the ClearPoints() routine that follows, except that I also reset the list pointer and the variable that tracks the number of points in the list:

```
void CZenLineList::ClearPoints()
{
        // Get a pointer to the start of the list
        CPointSegment* pSegment = m_pSegmentList;
        // Create a temporary pointer
        CPointSegment* pTempSeg = 0;

        // Loop while the list pointer Is valid
        while( pSegment )
        {
                // Get a pointer to the next Item In the list
                pTempSeg = pSegment->m_pNext;
                // Delete the current segment
                delete pSegment;

                // Iterate the pointer to the next Item
                pSegment = pTempSeg;
        }

        // Reset the pointers to 0
        m_pSegmentList = 0;
        m_NumPoints = 0;
}
```

Moving swiftly on, let's take a look at how to add segments to a line list.

Adding Segments

Like I mentioned before, points are added using the AddPoints() function:

```
HRESULT CZenLineList::AddPoint( float x, float y, float z, D3DCOLOR PointColor )
{
        HRESULT r = 0;

        // Check to see if the point list has been created yet...
        if( !m_pSegmentList )
        {
                //...It has not so create a new one
                m_pSegmentList = new CPointSegment;

                // Update the properties for the new segment
                m_pSegmentList->m_Vertex.m_Position.x = x;
                m_pSegmentList->m_Vertex.m_Position.y = y;
                m_pSegmentList->m_Vertex.m_Position.z = z;

                m_pSegmentList->m_Vertex.m_DiffuseColor = PointColor;

        }
        else
        {

                // ...The list already exists so add a new segment to the end of the list
                CPointSegment* pSegment = m_pSegmentList;

                // Find the end of the list
                while( pSegment->m_pNext != NULL )
                        pSegment = pSegment->m_pNext;

                // Add a new segment to the end of the list
                pSegment->m_pNext = new CPointSegment;

                // Update the properties for this new segment
                pSegment = pSegment->m_pNext;

                pSegment->m_Vertex.m_Position.x = x;
                pSegment->m_Vertex.m_Position.y = y;
                pSegment->m_Vertex.m_Position.z = z;
```

```
                pSegment->m_Vertex.m_DiffuseColor = PointColor;

        }

        // Increase the number of points counter
        m_NumPoints++;

        return S_OK;
}
```

The function is divided into two sections to deal with the two different possibilities when it is called. Possibility number one is if no list exists, and a new one has to be created, and number two is if the list already has been created, in which case a new segment needs to be added to the end of the list.

Rendering Line Lists

Rendering line lists is pretty similar to rendering normal lines with the CZenLine class, except it is slightly more complicated. The first difference is that you need to set up a dynamic vertex buffer that changes size according to the number of segments that make up the line list. Secondly, you must tell Direct3D that the lines you are rendering are either a strip or a list.

As I mentioned briefly before, a *line strip* is where all the points in the list contribute to a single line, which passes through each of the points. A *line list* is where every two points in the list are taken to be separate lines.

With that out of the way let's take a look at the rendering code:

```
HRESULT CZenLineList::Render()
{
        HRESULT r = 0;

        // Make sure the line list exists
        if( !m_pSegmentList )
                return E_FAIL;

        // The vertex buffer pointer
        LPDIRECT3DVERTEXBUFFER8 pVB = 0;

        // Create the vertex buffer
        r = g_pDevice->CreateVertexBuffer( sizeof( CZenVertex ) * m_NumPoints,
```

```
                    D3DUSAGE_WRITEONLY, ZENVERTEX_TYPE, D3DPOOL_DEFAULT, &pVB );
        if( FAILED( r ) )
                return E_FAIL;


        // Pointer to vb data
        BYTE* pData = 0;


        // Lock the vertex buffer
        r = pVB->Lock( 0, 0, &pData, 0 );
        if( FAILED( r ) )
        {
                pVB->Release();
                return E_FAIL;
        }


        // Pointer to the segment list
        CPointSegment* pSegment = m_pSegmentList;


        int Offset = 0;


        // Loop to copy the list into the vertex buffer
        while( pSegment )
        {
                // Copy this vertex into the vertex buffer
                CopyMemory( pData + Offset, &(pSegment->m_Vertex), sizeof( CZenVertex
) );


                // Move to the next vertex in the list
                pSegment = pSegment->m_pNext;


                // Increase the offset in the vertex buffer
                Offset += sizeof( CZenVertex );
        }


        // Unlock the vertex buffer
        pVB->Unlock();


        // Connect the vertex buffer to a rendering stream
        g_pDevice->SetStreamSource( 0, pVB, sizeof( CZenVertex ) );


        // m_bConnected = TRUE for a line strip
```

```
        if( m_bConnected )
                g_pDevice->DrawPrimitive( D3DPT_LINESTRIP, 0, m_NumPoints );
        else
                g_pDevice->DrawPrimitive( D3DPT_LINELIST, 0, m_NumPoints/2 );

        // Release the vertex buffer
        pVB->Release();

        return S_OK;
}
```

This code is pretty straightforward, as you can see, but there are a few things that may have caught your eye, so I'll just run through the code quickly. The code starts off by checking to make sure that m_pSegmentList is not NULL, because it is really hard to render a line that doesn't exist! Then I move on to actually creating the vertex buffer. Don't forget that since the line list can be of any length, you need to create the buffer dynamically based on the size of the list. That is why I set the size of the vertex buffer as the size of a single vertex multiplied by the number of vertices in the list.

Another thing to note is how I copy the vertex data into the vertex buffer. I can't just do a straight memcpy(), because each segment is not just a CZenVertex, but also a pointer that is used to manage the list. This pointer would really screw up Direct3D, so the best way to get around it is to just loop through and extract each vertex from the segment object.

Before I call DrawPrimitive(), I check to see whether the object is meant to be drawn as a strip or as independent lines. This decision is based on the m_bConnected member variable. If the object is meant to be drawn as a strip, which is the default, then I set the first flag to D3DPT_LINESTRIP. On the other hand, if the object is a series of independent lines, then I specify the D3DPT_LINELIST flag. When you specify this flag Direct3D requires that there be an even number of vertices in the list, and that the number of vertices must be able to be evenly divided by two. Note how I set the number of elements in the vertex buffer as equal to the number of vertices divided by two. This is because each line requires two vertices.

Rendering Line Strips with CZenLineList

Let me take a minute to show you an example rendering line lists and strips. The first thing to do is to declare a global line object, like so:

```
CZenLineList ZenLineList;
```

Which is pretty easy. Now you need to add points to the list for the lines. The following code, placed in `GameInit()`, does this well:

```
for( int j = 0 ; j < 15 ; j++ )
{
        ZenLineList.AddPoint( (float)(rand()%10 - rand()%10),
                                    (float)(rand()%10 - rand()%10),
                              (float)(rand()%10 - rand()%10),
                              D3DCOLOR_XRGB( rand()%255, rand()%255, rand()%255 ) );

}
```

This code just assigns a random coordinate and color for the segment of the line that is located somewhere between (–10, –10, –10) and (10, 10, 10).

Now you can place the render code into the `Render()` function, which is shown here:

```
ZenLineList.Render();
```

And that's it! That single call will render all the segments of the line strip and give you the results shown in Figure 13.7.

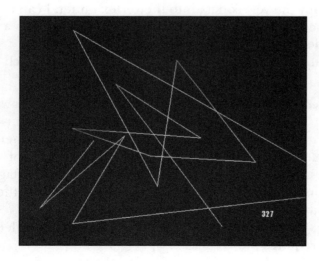

Figure 13.7

The results of using CZenLineList to render line strips

Rendering Line Lists with CZenLineList

But what would you do if you wanted to render a line list instead of a strip? To change the format, you just need to add a single function call. I place this in `GameInit()` just after the loop that sets up the coordinates for the segments:

```
ZenLineList.m_bConnected = FALSE;
```

Everything else can stay exactly the same. The results are shown in Figure 13.8.

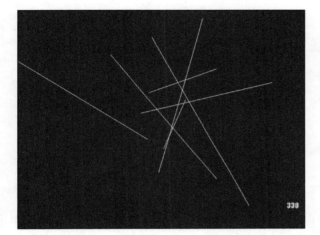

Figure 13.8

The results of using CZenLineList to render line lists

Point Lists

Remember I said that the second way to render single points was from a list, because it was so much faster? Well, this is where you get to see how to do that. I was originally going to create a brand new class for point lists, but since they are almost exactly the same as line lists I figured I'd save myself some trouble and go ahead and just inherit this bad boy from CZenLineList. That way it won't require any new code except for the Render() function. So check out the code that follows, which shows the class definition and the very empty constructor and destructor:

```
class CZenPointList : public CZenLineList
{
public:
        CZenPointList();
        ~CZenPointList();

// Functions
public:
        HRESULT Render();
protected:


// Variables
public:
```

```
protected:

};

CZenPointList::CZenPointList()
{

}

CZenPointList::~CZenPointList()
{

}
```

Nothing new there, so let me now show you the new CPointList::Render() function, which, because I am such a nice guy, I have copied and pasted below for you:

```
HRESULT CZenPointList::Render()
{
        HRESULT r = 0;

        if( !m_pSegmentList )
                return E_FAIL;

        LPDIRECT3DVERTEXBUFFER8 pVB = 0;

        r = g_pDevice->CreateVertexBuffer( sizeof( CZenVertex ) * m_NumPoints,
                D3DUSAGE_WRITEONLY, ZENVERTEX_TYPE, D3DPOOL_DEFAULT, &pVB );
        if( FAILED( r ) )
                return E_FAIL;

        BYTE* pData = 0;

        r = pVB->Lock( 0, 0, &pData, 0 );
        if( FAILED( r ) )
        {
                pVB->Release();
                return E_FAIL;
        }
```

```
        CPointSegment* pSegment = m_pSegmentList;

        int Offset = 0;

        while( pSegment )
        {
                CopyMemory( pData + Offset, &(pSegment->m_Vertex), sizeof( CZenVertex
) ) );

                pSegment = pSegment->m_pNext;

                Offset += sizeof( CZenVertex );
        }

        pVB->Unlock();

        g_pDevice->SetStreamSource( 0, pVB, sizeof( CZenVertex ) );

        g_pDevice->DrawPrimitive( D3DPT_POINTLIST, 0, m_NumPoints-1 );

        pVB->Release();

        return S_OK;
}
```

This code is *exactly* the same as the code used for the rendering of CZenLineList, except for the last line, in which I specify the primitive type as being a D3DPT_POINTLIST, which just tells Direct3D that the primitive list is a list of little points.

You should definitely use this method instead of the single CZenPoint class whenever you want to display more than a few points in the same place, because the more points you use the faster it gets in respect to multiple single point objects. As I said before, this is perfect for displaying realistic star scenes in the sky, or for a space simulation.

Now that you've seen the basics of rendering points and lines, let's take a minute to look at how to create an object to represent something a little more complex: a textured face...

The Face Object

You are slowly but surely getting more complex with the objects you're creating. The next step up from lines and points is, of course, faces, which require three different vertices and possibly a texture if you want one. As a result, the object will require three member variables: one array to look after the vertices, one texture holder, and finally a BOOL value to look after whether the face has a texture assigned to it.

Setting the properties for three different vertices can be a pain if you try to do it in a single function call or as an overridden constructor, since it would need to take like 30 parameters. If you look it up in the Zen guru encyclopedia fifth edition you'll find that having more than 29 parameters can be perceived as being a little excessive in some states.

Let's get back to business. In the following I have listed the code for the CZenFace class definition:

```
class CZenFace : public CZenObject
{
public:
        CZenFace();
        ~CZenFace();

//Functions
public:
        void SetProps( int Vertex, float x, float y, float z,
                       float nx, float ny, float nz,
                       D3DCOLOR DiffuseColor,
                       D3DCOLOR SpecularColor,
                       float tu, float tv );

        HRESULT SetTexture( LPDIRECT3DTEXTURE8 pTexture );
        HRESULT SetTexture( char* strPathName );

        HRESULT Render();
protected:

// Variables
public:
```

```
protected:
        CZenVertex m_Vertices;         // The face vertices
        LPDIRECT3DTEXTURE8 m_pTexture; // The texture for the face

        BOOL m_bTextureSet;            // Flag indicating texture presence

};

CZenFace::CZenFace()
{
        m_pTexture = 0;
        m_bTextureSet = FALSE;
}

CZenFace::~CZenFace()
{
        if( m_pTexture )
                m_pTexture->Release();
}
```

You can see in the code the three member variables that I was talking about for the texture and vertices. Also take note of how I provide two versions of the SetTexture() function-one that loads a texture from the disk, and another that takes the address of a texture that is already in memory. I'll cover these functions in a moment. Also note the SetProps() function, which is used to set the properties for the vertices. The first parameter is the number of the vertex that you want to modify, and can range from zero to two, and the remainder of the parameters deal with the selected vertex.

Setting the Texture

Followig is the code that is used to select a texture for the object from the disk:

```
HRESULT CZenFace::SetTexture( char* strPathName )
{
        // Holds error values
        HRESULT r = 0;

        // Release the previous texture if it existed
        if( m_pTexture )
```

```
            m_pTexture->Release();

    // Load the texture from the disk
    r = D3DXCreateTextureFromFile( g_pDevice, strPathName, &m_pTexture );
    if( SUCCEEDED( r ) )
    {
            // Set the texture flag
            m_bTextureSet = TRUE;
            return S_OK;
    }


    return E_FAIL;
}
```

You have seen all this code before. But this is the first time that I have implemented the SUCCEEDED() macro, so there you can see it in action. I generally prefer using the FAILED() macro to avoid endlessly nesting calls inside code blocks that depend on the success of a previous call. I find that FAILED() leads to more readable code in most circumstances.

The other way to set the texture for an object is to use a texture that you have already created somewhere else in memory. The code for this is as follows:

```
HRESULT CZenFace::SetTexture( LPDIRECT3DTEXTURE8 pTexture )
{
    // Make sure the supplied texture is valid
    if( !pTexture )
    {
            m_bTextureSet = FALSE;
            return E_FAIL;
    }

    // Release the previous texture if it exists
    if( m_pTexture )
            m_pTexture->Release();

    // Set the texture to the new texture
    m_pTexture = pTexture;
    // Increment the reference count of the texture
    m_pTexture->AddRef();

    // Set the texture flag
```

```
        m_bTextureSet = TRUE;

        return S_OK;
}
```

As you can see, this code is very different from its friend that I just showed you. The function starts by making sure the supplied texture is valid. This is important because you never know when a dud pointer might get chucked through this function. Next, the previous texture is released, if it exists. Again, this is important because if you were to simply replace the pointer to the texture, then you would cause a memory leak.

Then it is simply a case of updating the texture pointer to be the same as the supplied texture, which requires that you increment the reference count of the object. Always be sure to manage reference counts carefully when you are juggling pointers with COM objects. Think about what would happen if you didn't: you would update the texture, somewhere else in your code the texture would be released, and then the next time you tried to render with that texture you would cause an invalid memory access, which as always is a total bummer, dude.

Setting Vertex Properties

I mentioned briefly before that I included a short function to help with setting the properties for the object. This function is called SetProps(), and the code for this bad boy is as follows:

```
void CZenFace::SetProps( int Vertex, float x, float y, float z,
                         float nx, float ny, float nz,
                         D3DCOLOR DiffuseColor,
                         D3DCOLOR SpecularColor,
                         float tu, float tv )
{
        // Set the position
        m_Vertices[Vertex].m_Position.x = x;
        m_Vertices[Vertex].m_Position.y = y;
        m_Vertices[Vertex].m_Position.z = z;

        // Set the normal
        m_Vertices[Vertex].m_Normal.x = nx;
        m_Vertices[Vertex].m_Normal.y = ny;
        m_Vertices[Vertex].m_Normal.z = nz;
```

```
        // Set the color
        m_Vertices[Vertex].m_DiffuseColor = DiffuseColor;
        m_Vertices[Vertex].m_SpecularColor = SpecularColor;

        // Set the texture coordinates
        m_Vertices[Vertex].m_tu = tu;
        m_Vertices[Vertex].m_tv = tv;
}
```

What you are looking at here is a function that takes the index for a vertex to update and then updates that vertex with the rest of the parameters. So to fully define a face you must call this function three times, once for each vertex.

Rendering Textured Faces

Rendering the face is done with the usual Render() function. This function differs slightly from previous implementations of Render() in other classes, because it is the first one to use a texture. As such, it has to do some extra work, like checking to see if a texture has been assigned to the face, and if so, telling Direct3D to use it during the rendering process. Here is the code (I have bolded the parts that deal with texturing):

```
HRESULT CZenFace::Render()
{
        HRESULT r = 0;

        // The vertex buffer
        LPDIRECT3DVERTEXBUFFER8 pVB = 0;

        // Create the vertex buffer
        r = g_pDevice->CreateVertexBuffer( sizeof( CZenVertex )*3, D3DUSAGE_WRITEON-
LY,

ZENVERTEX_TYPE, D3DPOOL_DEFAULT, &pVB );
        if( FAILED( r ) )
                return E_FAIL;

        // Pointer to vertex buffer data
        BYTE* pData = 0;

        // Lock the vertex buffer
        r = pVB->Lock( 0, 0, &pData, 0 );
```

```
        if( FAILED( r ) )
        {
                pVB->Release();
                return E_FAIL;
        }

        // Copy the vertices to the vertex buffer
        CopyMemory( pData, (void*)&m_Vertices, sizeof( CZenVertex )*3 );

        // Unlock the vertex buffer
        pVB->Unlock();

        // If a texture exists then inform Direct3D about it
        if( m_pTexture )
                g_pDevice->SetTexture( 0, m_pTexture );

        // Connect the vertex buffer to a rendering stream
        g_pDevice->SetStreamSource( 0, pVB, sizeof( CZenVertex ) );

        // Draw the face
        g_pDevice->DrawPrimitive( D3DPT_TRIANGLELIST, 0, 1 );

        // Remove the texture so it doesn't interfere later
        if( m_pTexture )
                g_pDevice->SetTexture( 0, NULL );

        // Release the vertex buffer
        pVB->Release();

        return S_OK;
}
```

Notice how I reset the texture back to NULL in the Direct3D device. This is so that the code does not interfere with the rendering of any other objects later on. A better solution would be to get and store the previously selected texture, but for now this simple implementation will do fine. Also notice the flag that I use to specify the primitive type. Since I am drawing simple triangles, I use the D3DPT_TRIANGLELIST flag.

And that's it! You can now easily render faces using the CZenFace object. You should be building up a picture in your mind about the similarities in the rendering process between the different objects. But before I move on I'd better show you an example of how to render a face with your newfound functionality. . .

CZenFace in Action

Just like the other classes, rendering with CZenFace takes three simple steps: first you declare the object, then you define its properties, and finally you render it. To start at the beginning for this simple example, I define a global face object:

```
CZenFace ZenFace;
```

Next up, define the properties. The code below is placed in the GameInit() function.

```
ZenFace.SetProps( 0,-2.0f,-2.0f, 0.0f,              // Position
             0.0f, 0.0f,-1.0f,                      // Normal
             D3DCOLOR_XRGB( 255, 255, 255 ),        // Diffuse Color
             D3DCOLOR_XRGB( 255, 255, 255 ),        // Specular Color
             0.0f, 1.0f );                          // Texture Coordinates


ZenFace.SetProps( 1, 2.0f,-2.0f, 0.0f,
             0.0f, 0.0f,-1.0f,
             D3DCOLOR_XRGB( 255, 255, 255 ),
             D3DCOLOR_XRGB( 255, 255, 255 ),
             1.0f, 1.0f );


ZenFace.SetProps( 2, 0.0f, 2.0f, 0.0f,
             0.0f, 0.0f,-1.0f,
             D3DCOLOR_XRGB( 255, 255, 255 ),
             D3DCOLOR_XRGB( 255, 255, 255 ),
             0.5f, 0.0f );


LPDIRECT3DTEXTURE8 pTexture = 0;

// Create the texture
r = D3DXCreateTextureFromFile( g_pDevice, "Texture.jpg", &pTexture );
if( FAILED( r ) )
{
        SetError( "Couldnt load texture" );
        return E_FAIL;
}
```

```
// Copy and attach the texture to the face
ZenFace.SetTexture( pTexture );

// Release the texture
pTexture->Release();
```

Render is the simplest step. This is the code, which is located in the main `Render()` function:

```
ZenFace.Render();
```

What else can I say? Check out Figure 13.9 for the results. It is pretty much the same as the example in the last chapter, but now it is much easier to define multiple faces and put them in arrays, lists, and so on.

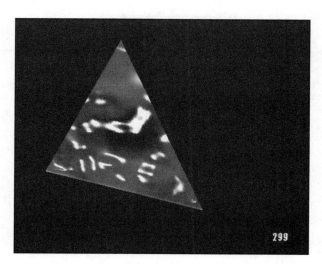

Figure 13.9

Rendering faces with CZenFace

Rendering Cubes with Indexed Vertices

Now that you have seen how to draw simple primitives, the next best object to learn how to draw is the cube. Cubes can be drawn in a number of ways, some very slow, others very fast. I am going to show you the very fast way because it will help to introduce you to a new Direct3D rendering concept: *indexed primitives*. However, before I delve into that too much, let me take a minute to talk about cubes.

You know that the most complex object that Direct3D is capable of rendering is the triangle, and combining multiple triangles creates all other 3D objects.

Anyway, a cube has eight corners and six square sides. Breaking down the squares into triangles is easy—you just use two triangles instead, like in Figure 13.10.

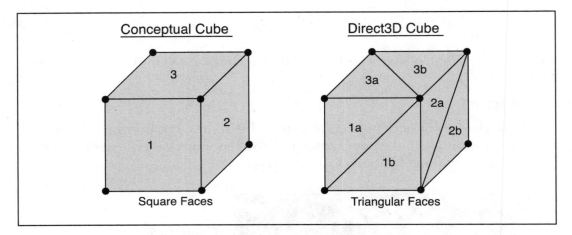

Figure 13.10

Using two triangles to represent a square

That means six sides becomes 12 triangular faces, each with three vertices, meaning that a simple cube has 36 vertices. If you think that sounds a little excessive, then you are right. Why should you need 36 vertices just to represent eight corners? If you look closely you will see that a lot of the vertices have the exact same position as other vertices, and that they are being needlessly copied. Have a look at Figure 13.11.

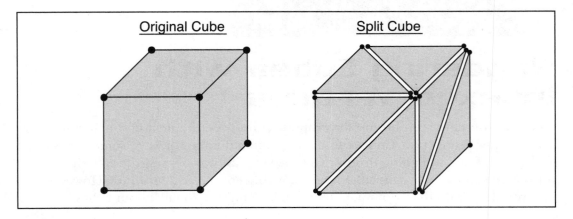

Figure 13.11

Poorly optimized vertex definitions can waste significant processing time.

Wouldn't it be better if you could somehow make a list of the eight corner vertices and then define the faces by saying that they use the previously defined vertices as components? Yes indeedy it would, and those clever guys at Microsoft thought the same thing and created a rendering method called *indexed rendering*. Take a look at Figure 13.12.

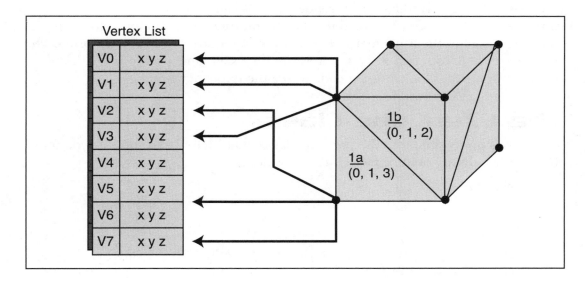

Figure 13.12

Referring to vertices through indices leads to more highly optimized rendering

Indexed Rendering

When you use indexed rendering you need to look after a few new concepts. First is the role of the *vertex buffer*. Before, you used the vertex buffer as a simple list of the primitives that you wanted to draw. For instance, in the point list, the vertex buffer contained a list of points that you wanted Direct3D to render. This time it is slightly different. The vertex buffer will still contain vertices, but they will not be in the order that you want them to be drawn; instead, the vertex buffer will contain a list of every single vertex that is used in the object.

The next thing that's different is the *index buffer*. The index buffer contains a list of integers, which are indices into the vertex buffer. This is a little hard to grasp the first time around, so keep those eyes perked. Say you have a list of vertices in the vertex buffer. And also say that vertices 1, 2, and 3 in the vertex buffer define the first face. To render this face using indexed rendering, all you have to do is set the first three entries in the index buffer to 1, 2, and 3. Get it? Whatever value you set in the index buffer is used to index into the appropriate vertex in the vertex buffer. Using this method you can reuse the same vertex in multiple faces without wasting memory or processing power.

The reason that this is so fast when rendering is because the entire set of vertices can be blasted to the graphics card in a batch and transformed in one easy step. This is opposed to the usual method, which would require you to retransform each vertex every time you used it, even if it was in the exact same position. That's the theory anyway—let's look at some code to see the implementation.

The CZenCube Class

This class is pretty similar to the previous classes that I have been showing you for the other rendering objects. Here is the class definition:

```
class CZenCube : public CZenObject
{
public:
        CZenCube();
        CZenCube( float Width, float Height, float Depth, D3DCOLOR Color );
                { SetVertices( Width, Height, Depth, Color ); }

        SetVertices( float Width, float Height, float Depth, D3DCOLOR Color );

        ~CZenCube();

// Functions
public:
        HRESULT Render();

protected:

// Variables:
public:

protected:
        // Vertices array
        CZenVertex m_Vertices[8];
```

```
        // Direct3D Texture pointer
        LPDIRECT3DTEXTURE8 m_pTexture;

};
```

Remember that although I have defined a texture variable I have not implemented the texture functionality just yet, because you need to get a little more advanced first. So for now you will just have to put up with a plain, colored box.

Construction and Destruction

I have included the code for the constructor and destructor in the following. As you can see, neither of them does very much, but have a quick look at them anyway.

```
CZenCube::CZenCube()
{
        m_pTexture = 0;
}


CZenCube::~CZenCube()
{


}
```

The destructor does absolutely nothing. Stop looking—it really does nothing!

Initialization

SetVertices(), which allows you to set the dimensions for the cube, is really boring and hard to decipher when you look at it, but what it is doing is very important. The code is shown in the following:

```
CZenCube::SetVertices( float Width, float Height, float Depth, D3DCOLOR Color )
{
        // Divide the dimensions so the cube is centered
        Width  /= 2;
        Height /= 2;
        Depth  /= 2;

        m_Vertices[0].m_Position.x = -Width;
        m_Vertices[0].m_Position.y =  Height;
        m_Vertices[0].m_Position.z = -Depth;
```

```cpp
m_Vertices[0].m_Normal.x = -1.0f;
m_Vertices[0].m_Normal.y =  1.0f;
m_Vertices[0].m_Normal.z = -1.0f;

m_Vertices[0].m_DiffuseColor = Color;

m_Vertices.m_Position.x =  Width;
m_Vertices.m_Position.y =  Height;
m_Vertices.m_Position.z = -Depth;

m_Vertices.m_Normal.x =  1.0f;
m_Vertices.m_Normal.y =  1.0f;
m_Vertices.m_Normal.z = -1.0f;

m_Vertices.m_DiffuseColor = Color;

m_Vertices.m_Position.x = -Width;
m_Vertices.m_Position.y = -Height;
m_Vertices.m_Position.z = -Depth;

m_Vertices.m_Normal.x = -1.0f;
m_Vertices.m_Normal.y = -1.0f;
m_Vertices.m_Normal.z = -1.0f;

m_Vertices.m_DiffuseColor = Color;

m_Vertices.m_Position.x =  Width;
m_Vertices.m_Position.y = -Height;
m_Vertices.m_Position.z = -Depth;

m_Vertices.m_Normal.x =  1.0f;
m_Vertices.m_Normal.y = -1.0f;
m_Vertices.m_Normal.z = -1.0f;

m_Vertices.m_DiffuseColor = Color;

m_Vertices[4].m_Position.x = -Width;
m_Vertices[4].m_Position.y =  Height;
m_Vertices[4].m_Position.z =  Depth;
```

```
        m_Vertices[4].m_Normal.x = -1.0f;
        m_Vertices[4].m_Normal.y =  1.0f;
        m_Vertices[4].m_Normal.z =  1.0f;


        m_Vertices[4].m_DiffuseColor = Color;


        m_Vertices[5].m_Position.x =  Width;
        m_Vertices[5].m_Position.y =  Height;
        m_Vertices[5].m_Position.z =  Depth;


        m_Vertices[5].m_Normal.x =  1.0f;
        m_Vertices[5].m_Normal.y =  1.0f;
        m_Vertices[5].m_Normal.z =  1.0f;


        m_Vertices[5].m_DiffuseColor = Color;


        m_Vertices[6].m_Position.x = -Width;
        m_Vertices[6].m_Position.y = -Height;
        m_Vertices[6].m_Position.z =  Depth;


        m_Vertices[6].m_Normal.x =  1.0f;
        m_Vertices[6].m_Normal.y = -1.0f;
        m_Vertices[6].m_Normal.z =  1.0f;


        m_Vertices[6].m_DiffuseColor = Color;


        m_Vertices[7].m_Position.x =  Width;
        m_Vertices[7].m_Position.y = -Height;
        m_Vertices[7].m_Position.z =  Depth;


        m_Vertices[7].m_Normal.x =  1.0f;
        m_Vertices[7].m_Normal.y = -1.0f;
        m_Vertices[7].m_Normal.z =  1.0f;


        m_Vertices[7].m_DiffuseColor = Color;
}
```

The function starts by dividing the supplied width and height by two. This is so that it is centered properly about its local coordinates. Don't worry about this too much just yet; in the next few chapters I will make you sick with local and world coordinates, when I start talking about *frame-based hierarchies*. Anyway, after that the code just runs through each vertex and fills in the appropriate vertex positions for each vertex. Like I was saying, it is very hard to understand what the code is doing just by looking at it. A better way would be to refer back to Figure 13.11, which shows how the cube is broken down.

Rendering the Cube

The render code for the cube is substantially different from the other rendering code that you have already looked at for the reasons I mentioned before. Actually, you are probably happy about this since I'll bet you're getting bored with the similarities between all the render functions. Anyway, check out the code that follows, and then I will explain it:

```
HRESULT CZenCube::Render()
{
        HRESULT r = 0;
        LPDIRECT3DINDEXBUFFER8 pIB = 0;
        // Create the index buffer
        g_pDevice->CreateIndexBuffer( sizeof(short)*36, D3DUSAGE_WRITEONLY,
                                    D3DFMT_INDEX16, D3DPOOL_DEFAULT, &m_pIB );

        // Set the indices for the cube
        short Indices[36] =
        {
                0, 1, 2,        //a
                1, 3, 2,        //b
                1, 5, 3,        //c
                3, 5, 7,        //d
                0, 5, 1,        //e
                0, 4, 5,        //f
                2, 6, 7,        //g
                2, 7, 3,        //h
                2, 0, 4,        //i
                2, 4, 6,        //j
                6, 4, 5,        //k
                6, 5, 7         //l
        };

        // Pointer to the index buffer data
        BYTE* pIndexData;
```

```
        // Lock the index buffer
        m_pIB->Lock( 0, 0, &pIndexData, 0 );

        // Copy the indices into the index buffer
        CopyMemory( pIndexData, (void*)&Indices, sizeof(Indices) );

        // Unlock the index buffer
        m_pIB->Unlock();

        // Pointer to the vertex buffer
        LPDIRECT3DVERTEXBUFFER8 pVB = 0;

        // Create the vertex buffer
        r = g_pDevice->CreateVertexBuffer( sizeof( CZenVertex )*8, ←
D3DUSAGE_WRITEONLY,                     ZENVERTEX_TYPE, D3DPOOL_DEFAULT, &pVB );
        if( FAILED( r ) )
                return E_FAIL;

        // Pointer to the vertex buffer data
        BYTE* pVertexData = 0;

        // Lock the vertex buffer
        r = pVB->Lock( 0, 0, &pVertexData, 0 );
        if( FAILED( r ) )
        {
                pVB->Release();
                return E_FAIL;
        }

        // Copy the vertices into the vertex buffer
        CopyMemory( pVertexData, (void*)&m_Vertices, sizeof( m_Vertices ) );

        // Unlock the vertex buffer
        pVB->Unlock();

        // Connect the vertex buffer to a rendering stream
        g_pDevice->SetStreamSource( 0, pVB, sizeof( CZenVertex ) );
        // Tell Direct3D about the index buffer
        g_pDevice->SetIndices( m_pIB, 0 );
```

```
        // Draw the cube using indices
        g_pDevice->DrawIndexedPrimitive( D3DPT_TRIANGLELIST, 0, 36, 0, 12 );

        // Release the vertex buffer
        pVB->Release();

        return S_OK;
}
```

Can you see what's going on? First I create the index buffer with the
`IDirect3DDevice8::CreateIndexBuffer()` function. This function takes almost the same
parameters as `CreateVertexBuffer()`, but for refreshers here is its prototype:

```
HRESULT CreateIndexBuffer(
    UINT Length,
    DWORD Usage,
    D3DFORMAT Format,
    D3DPOOL Pool,
    IDirect3DIndexBuffer8** ppIndexBuffer
);
```

Table 13.1 gives the parameters.

Table 13.1   IDirect3DDevice8::CreateIndexBuffer() Parameters

Parameters	Definition
Length	Takes the size of the buffer in bytes
Usage	Takes the usage flags, which you can usually just set to `D3DFMT_WRITEONLY`
Format	The format of indices—in other words, whether you are using int's (32 bits) or short's (16 bits) for each index. Some cards don't support more than 16 bits for each index so it is best to stick to just 16.
Pool	Takes the pool type that you want to use. Again, just use the usual `D3DPOOL_DEFAULT` flag.
ppIndexBuffer	Takes the address of a pointer that will be filled with the address of the newly-created index buffer

After that, I create an array with 36 entries with which to fill in the vertices. See how each entry refers to the appropriate vertex in the vertex buffer, *and* note that the vertices are defined in the right order, so that back face culling does not become an issue. To fill in the index buffer the process is the same as for vertex buffers. That is, you lock it, copy the array over, and then unlock it, etc.

The next bit of interesting code is further on in the function, where I call the IDirect3DDevice8::SetIndices() function. This tells Direct3D that you are using an index buffer for rendering. If you don't call this function, then Direct3D won't know what to do later on and the call to IDirect3DDevice8::DrawIndexedPrimitive() will fail. SetIndices() has this prototype:

```
HRESULT SetIndices(
  IDirect3DIndexBuffer8* pIndexData
  UINT BaseVertexIndex
);
```

Table 13.2 gives the parameters.

Table 13.2 IDirect3DDevice8::SetIndices() Parameters

Parameters	Definition
pIndexData	Takes the address of the index buffer that you want to use
BaseVertexIndex	Takes the base vertex in the vertex buffer. You can use this if you want to use a vertex other than the first as the starting vertex. However, this is too advanced for now, so you should just set this parameter to 0.

Finally, I made the call to IDirect3DDevice8::DrawIndexedPrimitive(), which is the call that actually draws the cube. The prototype for this is:

```
HRESULT DrawIndexedPrimitive(
  D3DPRIMITIVETYPE Type,
  UINT MinIndex,
  UINT NumVertices,
  UINT StartIndex,
  UINT PrimitiveCount
);
```

As you can see in 13.3, the parameters are pretty similar to the standard `DrawPrimitive();`.

Table 13.3 IDirect3DDevice8::DrawIndexedPrimitive() Parameters

Parameter	Definition
Type	Takes a flag specifying the type of primitive you want to draw, which in this case is a triangle (D3DPT_TRIANGLELIST).
MinIndex	Takes the minimum vertex to use, which in English means the lowest vertex in the buffer, which will usually be zero.
NumVertices	Used to specify how many vertices are used in this call to DrawIndexedPrimitive() so that Direct3D can optimize processing.
StartIndex	The location in the array at which you want to start reading vertices, which you will usually want to set to 0.
PrimitiveCount	Takes an integer describing how many primitives you want to render.

And that's it!

CZenCube in Action

Despite the amount of code and theory it took to implement the cube class, they are surprisingly simple to work with. First as always, you need to implement the class into an object like this global bad boy:

```
CZenCube ZenCube( 2, 2, 2, D3DCOLOR_XRGB( 255, 0, 255 ) );
```

That simple code creates a new cube that is purple and has a width, height, and depth of two. To render, all you need to do is place this code into the main `Render()` function:

```
ZenCube.Render();
```

Easy or what, my friend? Easy or what. Check out Figure 13.13 to see the cube. I kind of cheated in the figure and added lines to highlight the edges since there are no lights in the scene—it originally just looked like a weird flat polygon.

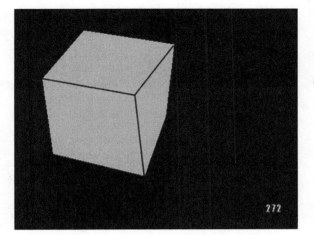

Figure 13.13

Rendering a cube with CZenCube

Conclusion

So you should now be getting a little more confident after your first foray into the creation of more complex objects with Direct3D. Right now what you have is another layer added to the engine. In the next chapter I am going to show you how to build more on top of what you saw in this chapter, and add more complex object classes that can be used to load 3D models from disk, and which have unlimited complexity. You're also going to finally connect the camera to the keyboard and mouse, so that you can start to walk around the land of Zen. And I'm going to introduce you to frame-based hierarchies, which allow you to create cool animation effects.

In terms of completeness you are starting to near the point of what I like to term *easy extensibility*. Which means as more and more of the basic technology is coded, it becomes easier and easier to implement more advanced features. For instance, now that you have coded a simple class to encapsulate the view matrix into a camera object, you can easily add more advanced code to connect the camera to the keyboard and other input devices.

CHAPTER 14

Directing Input with DirectInput

Originally I was planning not to include any information on DirectInput because I wanted to produce a book totally based on DirectX Graphics. To achieve this, I was going to just use the standard Win32 input procedures. This was, of course, until I remembered just how bad those bad boys actually are. So with that in mind, I'm going to show you a little something called DirectInput, which is a really slick section of DirectX that is used to coordinate the input of data for everything from mice and keyboards to 10 million button joysticks and VR body-suits. And it is really easy to use, so you should get the hang of it in no time at all. This chapter will cover

- setting up DirectInput.
- setting up DirectInput devices.
- reading from the keyboard and mouse.
- implementing a slick class-based input system.

In typical Microsoft fashion, they have abstracted the interface so far that you may need to put some pasteurized homogenized dilithium crystals in your cornflakes before you can get your mind around the initial conceptual hurdles. But as soon as that is done the rest is simple.

Johnny 5 Need Input

I hate theory—it always gets in the way of the "doing" part. But as you know well by now you can't program the next *Quake* killer without understanding what a view matrix is, and in DirectInput you can't figure out what a keyboard is doing without knowing what a *keyboard device input constant* is. So let's start at the top—the new header files and libraries...

Read This or Die!

In this little section of this little chapter of this little book is some information that will save you hours and hours of hair tearing. If I receive an e-mail about code not compiling because you haven't read this section, you will be put on my list of people to have capped.

Let's start with the library files. Every section of DirectX has an associated library file. For instance, in Direct3D it is d3d8.lib. For DirectInput the file is called dinput8.lib. That is for version 8.0, by the way; you may have to change yours slightly if you are adapting this code to a later release. You will recall from Chapter 2 that to attach a library file to your project you must go to the Project, Settings menu item, which brings up the Project Settings dialog. From there you progress forward to the Link tab and enter the file name of the libraries you want to include in the Object/Library Module text box. Add the string "dinput8.lib" *after* the dxguid.lib file. Select OK and that's it. If you want more detailed instructions, complete with illustrations, go back to Chapter 2 and take a look around there.

That was simple. Now it's time to kick-start this puppy into action. Remember how you included the files d3d8.h in your source files so that you were able to access Direct3D functionality? Well, it just so happens that to use DirectInput you need to include dinput.h at the top of your source file. So now the code for the include files looks like this:

```
#include <windows.h>
#include <mmsystem.h>

#include <d3d8.h>
#include <d3dx8.h>
#include <dinput.h>
#include "Engine.h"
```

Let's look at how DirectInput is implemented.

DirectInput Overview

First off, why does DirectInput even exist? Well, it all has to do with the nightmare that used to exist in the input world on PCs, which was, in fact, very similar to the nightmare with graphics. Basically, there were just no standards, and trying to program for more advanced devices was completely device-dependent and proprietary.

Earlier I was talking about how hard it was just to figure out if a key was pressed on the keyboard—you had to program an interrupt handler, deal with interrupt chip sets, and all sorts of other nonsense that took away time that could be spent on improving the quality of the content of the game. The mouse was similar—you had to deal with mouse drivers, and hope that the driver conformed to some sort of standardized interface. And joysticks—don't even get me started on those.

Once Windows came along it fixed most of these issues. But, as I mentioned before, dealing with the mouse through events is not exactly productive in a real-time loop environment. So then along came DirectInput to provide standardized access to *all* forms of input through a common interface. If you're wondering how you deal with a 102-key keyboard and a two-axis, two-button mouse in the same way, you are a smart thinker. All will become clear soon, but this will help you to understand why DirectInput has been abstracted so much.

Actually, one other point you may be interested in is that the earlier versions of DirectInput were not even properly implemented—most of them were just covers for standard Win32 API calls. But that has been fixed now, and version 8.0, which I will be showing you, includes performance-enhanced input code.

DirectInput Components

So now you know the history. DirectInput is modeled in a very similar way to Direct3D, but instead it revolves around two objects. First off is the IDirectInput8 COM object, which you can think of as the same as the IDirect3D object. Basically, it does nothing except initialize everything else. And number two is the IDirectInputDevice8 object, which is used to represent an input device. An *input device* is any device that you can receive input from, such as a mouse, keyboard, joystick, VR bodysuit, or VR head-tracking devices (see Figure 14.1).

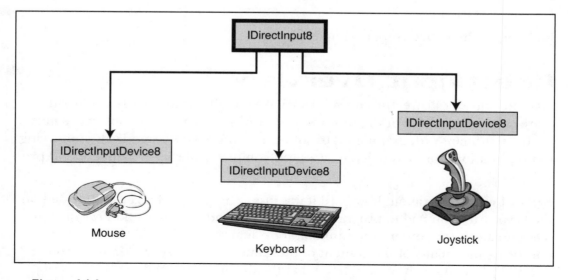

Figure 14.1

The technical structure of DirectInput

Basically, anything and everything that can be plugged into a PC and produces information can be represented with a DirectInput device as long as it has a driver installed. Now let's look at actually using it...

Implementing DirectInput

OK, here is where it starts to get a little weird. I'll begin by showing you an overview of the steps involved, and then work on creating objects to represent the mouse and keyboard.

Setting Up DirectInput

Following are the steps for setting up DirectInput:

1. Create the `IDirectInput8` object with a call to `DirectInput8Create()`.

2. Create an `IDirectInputDevice8` object to represent the device from which you want to receive information with a call to `IDirectInput8::CreateDevice()`.

3. Set the data format for the device that you are getting information from with a call to `IDirectInputDevice8::SetDataFormat()`. This step allows DirectInput to return information to you about the state of the object in an appropriate format.

4. Set the cooperative level for the device with a call to `IDirectInputDevice8::SetCooperativeLevel()`. This is where you set up how you want the device to be shared with other applications that may also want to use it.

5. Acquire the device with `IDirectInputDevice8::Acquire()`. This attaches the physical device to the DirectInput software device so that it can start to receive data from the physical device.

6. Start polling the device with `IDirectInputDevice8::GetDeviceState()`.

7. When you are done, unacquire the device with `IDirectInputDevice8::Unacquire()`.

8. Release the device and DirectInput objects.

I bet that all looks about as clear as the world does to me when I wake up in the morning and realize that I forgot to take out my contact lenses. Don't worry—I'm going to go through it all step by step so that you also can become an Enlightened One. As Socrates would say—you cannot see the truth without taking out your contact lenses before sleeping.

The Code—Initialization and Release

The first thing to do is create a nice little function to initialize everything having to do with input and get it all up and running. I have done just this and named it, funnily enough, InitializeInput(). This code is used to go through all the steps that I was talking about a minute ago. Actually, before that I think it would be kind of useful to declare a global IDirectInput8 object like this:

```
LPDIRECTINPUT8 g_pDI = 0;
```

Kind of an ugly name, but if you rip it apart the g_pDI stands for *global pointer to a DirectInput* object. Again, I'll stress the importance of initializing it to NULL. Okay, now back to initialization. The following function *must* be called from the main GameInit() function:

```
HRESULT InitializeInput()
{
        // Release any previous objects if they exist
        if( g_pDI )
                g_pDI->Release();

        HRESULT r = 0;

        // Create the DirectInput8 object
        r = DirectInput8Create(         g_hInstMain,
                                DIRECTINPUT_VERSION,
                                IID_IDirectInput8,
                                (void**)&g_pDI, NULL );
        if( FAILED( r ) )
        {
                SetError( "Failed to create DirectInput" );
                return E_FAIL;
        }

}
```

This is just the beginning—I'll be expanding it for a while. The first bit of code makes sure that if this function has already been called that the previously created IDirectInput8 object is safely released. Then I move on to actually create the object with the call to DirectInput8Create(). As you can see, it takes a lot of stuff for parameters. Here is its prototype:

```
HRESULT WINAPI DirectInput8Create(
  HINSTANCE hinst,
  DWORD dwVersion,
  REFIID riidltf,
  LPVOID* ppvOut,
  LPUNKNOWN punkOuter
);
```

The first parameter is a handle to the current instance of your application. You can get this from the HINSTANCE passed to you in WinMain() and store it in a global. The next parameter ensures that the correct version of DirectInput is being created. You can specify DIRECTINPUT_VERSION for this parameter, which always contains the latest version of DirectInput. Next up is the interface identifier for the COM object that you want to create. Again, you can use the constant identifier IID_IDirectInput8. The penultimate parameter takes the address of a pointer that will be filled with the address of the newly-created object. In other words, just give it the address of the g_pDI variable. And the final parameter is used for COM aggregation, which you will probably never use so you can set it to NULL.

I have also created a corresponding function, named ShutdownInput(). This function should be called from the main GameShutdown() function. Here is the code:

```
HRESULT ShutdownInput()
{
      if( g_pDI )
      {
            g_pDI->Release();
            g_pDI = 0;
      }

      return E_FAIL;
}
```

As you can see, it just releases the main IDirectInput8 object if it exists.

Coding for the Keyboard

Now I'm going to show you how to create an object that can be used to represent the keyboard in a simple and asynchronous way. All of the following code will be in a class, which I have given the cute and cuddly name of CZenKeyboard.

As I mentioned, this is going to work in a device-independent manner, which means that each key on the keyboard will have a status that is updated independently of your program; whenever you want to check the status of a key you can say, "Tell me the status of key x," and you will get it. It is a very similar process to the GetAsyncKeyState() function that I discussed in previous chapters that dealt with the Windows API. Let me show you the class definition:

```cpp
class CZenKeyboard
{
public:
        CZenKeyboard();
        ~CZenKeyboard();

// Variables
public:

protected:
        LPDIRECTINPUTDEVICE8 m_pKeyDev;
        char m_KeyBuffer[256];

        BOOL m_bInitialized;

// Functions
public:
        HRESULT Initialize();

        BOOL IsKeyDown( int Key );

protected:

};

CZenKeyboard::CZenKeyboard()
{
        ZeroMemory( &m_KeyBuffer, sizeof( m_KeyBuffer ) );
        m_pKeyDev = 0;

        m_bInitialized = FALSE;
}
```

As you can see, it is a pretty simple class. The m_pKeyDev is a pointer to the IDirectInputDevice8 object that is used to represent the keyboard. More on this soon. The m_KeyBuffer array is used to represent the status of the keyboard. Each key has an entry in the array that can be tested. Notice that there are 256 entries in the array and that most keyboards only have 102 keys. This is for future extensibility and foreign languages. m_bInitialized tracks whether the keyboard has been initialized or not. It will not function without initialization, which is done using the Initialize() function. If you look at the constructor you will see that it just zeroes out all the member variables.

Keyboard Initialization

Now it's going to get a little hallucinogenic for a few paragraphs. Don't believe me? Take a look at this bad boy:

```
HRESULT CZenKeyboard::Initialize()
{
        HRESULT r;

        if( !g_pDI )
                return E_FAIL;

        // Release the device if it has already been created
        if( m_pKeyDev )
        {
                m_pKeyDev->Unacquire();
                m_pKeyDev->Release();
        }

        // Create the device for the keyboard
        r = g_pDI->CreateDevice( GUID_SysKeyboard, &m_pKeyDev, NULL );
        if( FAILED( r ) )
        {
                SetError( "Failed to create key device" );
                return E_FAIL;
        }

        // Set the data format for the device
        r = m_pKeyDev->SetDataFormat( &c_dfDIKeyboard );
        if( FAILED( r ) )
        {
```

```
                SetError( "Unable to set the keyboard data format" );
                return E_FAIL;
        }


        // Set the cooperative level
        r = m_pKeyDev->SetCooperativeLevel( g_hWndMain,
                                        DISCL_FOREGROUND |
                                        DISCL_NONEXCLUSIVE );
        if( FAILED( r ) )
        {
                SetError( "Unable to set keyboard cooperative level" );
                return E_FAIL;
        }


        // Acquire the device
        r = m_pKeyDev->Acquire();
        if( FAILED( r ) )
        {
                SetError( "Unable to acquire the keyboard" );
                return E_FAIL;
        }


        // Set the initialization flag to true
        m_bInitialized = TRUE;


        return S_OK;
}
```

Nice, huh? Yeah, I thought so too. I'm going to walk you through it one step at time. First is the code that checks if the device has already been created:

```
// Release the device if it has already been created
if( m_pKeyDev )
{
        m_pKeyDev->Unacquire();
        m_pKeyDev->Release();
}
```

It is important to make sure that the device is not re-created without first releasing the original, otherwise a memory leak may occur. Notice how I call Unacquire() before calling Release()? This is a requirement of DirectInput. It usually won't cause any problems if you don't unacquire the device—but it will cause DirectX to output a debug error string, so it's best to keep it happy.

Creating the Device

Next is the actual creation of the device. This is done with the following code:

```
// Create the device for the keyboard
r = g_pDI->CreateDevice( GUID_SysKeyboard, &m_pKeyDev, NULL );
if( FAILED( r ) )
{
        SetError( "Failed to create key device" );
        return E_FAIL;
}
```

CreateDevice() takes some more interesting parameters. Here is the prototype:

```
HRESULT CreateDevice(
  REFGUID rguid,
  LPDIRECTINPUTDEVICE *lplpDirectInputDevice,
  LPUNKNOWN pUnkOuter
);
```

The first is the GUID (Globally Unique IDentifier) of the device that you want the device to represent. You could either find this out the hard way, documented in the DirectInput 8.0 documentation, or just take the predefined constants, which have been created for normal devices like the keyboard and mouse. In the case of the keyboard, that's GUID_SysKeyboard, which should work on 99.99 percent of all PCs. The second parameter is the address of a pointer that will take the address of the newly-created device. And the final parameter is for advanced COM aggregation, which you don't need to worry about right now, if ever.

Setting the Data Format

You need to set the data format for the device, because you need to know how the device is going to be sending you data. For instance, in the case of the keyboard you are going to want information relating to the status of the buttons, whereas with the mouse you would want information about the coordinates of the x- and y-axes. The following code sets the data format:

```
// Set the data format for the device
r = m_pKeyDev->SetDataFormat( &c_dfDIKeyboard );
if( FAILED( r ) )
{
```

```
        SetError( "Unable to set the keyboard data format" );
        return E_FAIL;
}
```

The function `SetDataFormat()` has this prototype:

```
HRESULT SetDataFormat(
    LPCDIDATAFORMAT lpdf
);
```

The only parameter to this function is a constant specifying the format of the data. As you can see from the preceding code, I specified `c_dfDIKeyboard`. That is one ugly-looking identifier, which if broken down says, *Constant to a data format for a DirectInput-compatible keyboard.* Other possible constants are listed in *DirectX 8.0 Documentation / DirectInput / DirectInput C++ reference / Interfaces / IDirectInputDevice8 / IDirectInputDevice8::SetDataFormat().*

Setting the Cooperative Level

You need to set the cooperative level for the device so that it can be shared properly among different applications. Never forget that you are programming in a shared environment with possibly hundreds of other applications that may want access to the same device. Setting the cooperative level is a very simple process that can be done with the following code:

```
// Set the cooperative level
r = m_pKeyDev->SetCooperativeLevel( g_hWndMain,
                                    DISCL_FOREGROUND |
                                    DISCL_NONEXCLUSIVE );
if( FAILED( r ) )
{
        SetError( "Unable to set keyboard cooperative level" );
        return E_FAIL;
}
```

`SetCooperativeLevel()` looks like this:

```
HRESULT SetCooperativeLevel(
    HWND hwnd,
    DWORD dwFlags
);
```

The first parameter is the handle of the window for which you want to set the cooperative level. In other words, when the window with the specified hwnd is active the input device will be associated with that window with the specified cooperative level. The second parameter takes the cooperative level that you want to use for the device. In this case I have set it to DISCL_FOREGROUND and DISCL_NONEX-CLUSIVE, which should be fine for most of your needs. The possible flags for this parameter are listed in Table 14.1.

Table 14.1 Flags for SetCooperativeLevel()

Flag	Description
DISCL_BACKGROUND	The application wants to get access to the device even when it is not active.
DISCL_EXCLUSIVE	The application wants exclusive access to the device. In other words, no other application can get exclusive access but they can get nonexclusive access.
DISCL_FOREGROUND	The application needs access to the device when the application is in the foreground. The device is automatically unacquired when the application moves to the background.
DISCL_NONEXCLUSIVE	The application wants to get nonexclusive access to the device and will not interfere with other applications accessing the same device.
DISCL_NOWINKEY	Disables the Windows key on the keyboard to prevent accidental focus changes. See the DirectInput documentation for more details.

Acquiring the Device

The input device, which is the keyboard in this case, cannot be used until the DirectInput device acquires it. This code acquires the device:

```
// Acquire the device
r = m_pKeyDev->Acquire();
if( FAILED( r ) )
{
        SetError( "Unable to acquire the keyboard" );
        return E_FAIL;
}
```

`Acquire()` takes no parameters, but it does return whether or not the acquiring of the device was successful. This will get important in just a second. But other than that, that is everything you need to know to set up DirectInput to get data from the keyboard. So let's move on to actually reading data.

Reading Data from the Keyboard

I have put all the code that is used to read from the keyboard into a function called `CZenKeyboard::IsKeyDown()`. That way, all you have to do to figure out if a key—for instance the Spacebar—is pressed is type this code:

```
Keyboard.IsKeyDown( DIK_SPACE );
```

and you would get a TRUE or FALSE return value. The code for this function is shown here.

```
BOOL CZenKeyboard::IsKeyDown( int Key )
{
        HRESULT r = 0;

        // Make sure the keyboard has been initialized
        if( !m_bInitialized )
                return FALSE;

        // Get the state of the keyboard into the key buffer
        r = m_pKeyDev->GetDeviceState( sizeof( m_KeyBuffer ), &m_KeyBuffer );
        if( FAILED( r ) )
        {
                // If the device is not acquired...
                if( r == DIERR_INPUTLOST )
                {
                        // ...then reacquire the device
                        while( r == DIERR_INPUTLOST )
                                r = m_pKeyDev->Acquire();

                        if( SUCCEEDED( r ) )
                                m_pKeyDev->GetDeviceState( sizeof( m_KeyBuffer ),
                                                                &m_KeyBuffer );
                        else
                                return FALSE;
                }
                else
```

```
            // ...Otherwise it was some other error
            return FALSE;
    }

    // Check if the key was set
    if( m_KeyBuffer[Key] & 0x80 )
            return TRUE;
    else
            return FALSE;
}
```

The code starts by making sure that the device has been initialized, because if it has not, it cannot be read from. Then the code updates the buffer that holds the state of the keys with a call to IDirectInputDevice8::GetDeviceState(). This function has the following prototype:

```
HRESULT GetDeviceState(
   DWORD cbData,
   LPVOID lpvData
);
```

What this function does is take the address of a buffer that is used to hold the state of the device. This buffer is then filled with data that reflects the current state of the device. Anyway, the first parameter takes the size of the buffer that you want to put the data in. The second parameter takes the address of the buffer that will be filled with information. In the case of the keyboard, this is just the 256-byte buffer that I created as a member variable for the class.

Notice the code following the call to GetDeviceState() that looks after device validation. Don't forget that, because when you are in a shared environment, access to the input device can be lost at any time. To fix this you just have to check if the call to GetDeviceState() returns DIERR_INPUTLOST. If this is returned, you have to make another call to Acquire(), and then try to get the device state again. If it is another error, then who knows what happened, so you just have to assume the key was not pressed.

The final part of the code checks to see if a key was pressed by comparing if the key specified as the formal parameter to the function has its corresponding high bit set in the buffer. If it has, then the key is down; otherwise, it is not.

Releasing the Keyboard

There is one step that you need to remember to follow before you release the device, and that is to *unacquire* the hardware from DirectInput. The following code, located in the destructor, does this:

```
CZenKeyboard::~CZenKeyboard()
{
        if( m_pKeyDev )
        {
                m_pKeyDev->Unacquire();

                m_pKeyDev->Release();
        }
}
```

Connecting the Keyboard

Now that you have all the code done you probably want to see just how easy it is to use DirectInput. A few steps are necessary.

1. Create a new global CZenKeyboard object like this:
   CZenKeyboard g_Keyboard;
2. Add a call to CZenKeyboard::Initialize() to InitializeInput() like this:
   g_Keyboard.Initialize();
3. Place a call to InitializeInput() into the main GameInit() function.
4. Place a call to ShutdownInput() into the main GameShutdown() function.
5. Check for input anywhere in the game loop by typing this:
   g_Keyboard.IsKeyDown(DIK_SPACE);

And that's it! Notice the use of the DirectInput key codes. You can get a full list of those in *DirectX 8.0 Documentation / DirectInput / DirectInput C++ Reference / Device Constants / Keyboard Device Constants*. They usually follow normal standards like DIK_C for the letter "c" and so on.

Programming the Mouse

The process for programming the mouse is almost identical to that for programming the keyboard. The only difference is that with the mouse you are interested in finding out the status of only two or three buttons instead of 102, and also you want to track the changes in the two axes. With that in mind, let me show you the class definition:

```cpp
class CZenMouse
{
public:
        CZenMouse();
        ~CZenMouse();

// Variables
public:

protected:
        LPDIRECTINPUTDEVICE8 m_pMouseDev;

        BOOL m_bInitialized;

        DIMOUSESTATE m_MouseData;
// Functions
public:
        HRESULT Initialize();
        HRESULT Poll();

        POINT GetMousePos();
        BOOL IsButtonDown( int Button );

protected:

};

CZenMouse::CZenMouse()
{
        m_pMouseDev = 0;

        m_bInitialized = FALSE;
}
```

See? It's pretty much the same as the CZenKeyboard class. m_pMouseDev is the IDirectInputDevice8 object that is used to represent the physical mouse device.

`m_MouseData` is the buffer that holds the data about the mouse. Remember how for the keyboard the buffer was a 256-byte char array? Well, for the mouse it is just a `DIMOUSESTATE` structure.

Like `CZenKeyboard`, `CZenMouse` has a function called `Initialize()` that must be called in order for the object to function correctly. `Poll()` is a function that is used to read data from the mouse into the buffer so that other functions can figure out the status of the buttons and axes.

Initializing the Mouse

This is very similar to the initialization of the keyboard; I've bolded the changes that are pertinent.

```
HRESULT CZenMouse::Initialize()
{
        HRESULT r = 0;

        // Return if the DirectInput object does not exist
        if( !g_pDI )
                return E_FAIL;

        // Release the mouse device if it has already been created
        if( m_pMouseDev )
                m_pMouseDev->Release();

        // Create the mouse device
        r = g_pDI->CreateDevice( GUID_SysMouse, &m_pMouseDev, NULL );
        if( FAILED( r ) )
        {
                SetError( "Unable to create mouse device" );
                return E_FAIL;
        }

        // Set the data format for the mouse
        r = m_pMouseDev->SetDataFormat( &c_dfDIMouse );
        if( FAILED( r ) )
        {
                SetError( "Unable to set the mouse data format" );
                return E_FAIL;
        }
```

```
// Set the cooperative level for the mouse
r = m_pMouseDev->SetCooperativeLevel( g_hWndMain,
                        DISCL_EXCLUSIVE | DISCL_FOREGROUND );
if( FAILED( r ) )
{
        SetError( "Unable to set the cooperative level for the mouse" );
        return E_FAIL;
}

// Acquire the physical mouse into the device
r = m_pMouseDev->Acquire();
if( FAILED( r ) )
{
        SetError( "Unable to acquire mouse" );
        return E_FAIL;
}

// Set the initialization flag to true
m_bInitialized = TRUE;

return S_OK;
}
```

See how similar it is to the setup of the keyboard—it is tantamount to the success of DirectInput in completely abstracting the programming environment from the details of the base hardware. Anyway, enough advertising. Let's look at the differences. First up is that when you make the call to IDirectInput8::CreateDevice(),you need to specify GUID_SysMouse instead of GUID_SysKeyboard. The next difference is the change to the SetDataFormat() call; you need to use the constant c_dfDIMouse identifier, which stands for *constant data format identifier for a DirectInput-compatible mouse.* Phew. And finally, I set the cooperative level for the mouse to DISCL_EXCLUSIVE. The result of this is that standard Win32 mouse procedures become disabled, so you don't have to worry about an annoying mouse pointer on the screen. The DirectInput mouse logic is also faster than the standard Win32 input logic.

Reading Mouse Data

The mouse is slightly different from the keyboard, because you need to poll its state every frame of the game rather than just checking it every time you want to know its status. This is the reason for the CZenMouse::Poll() function; in order to make it function correctly you need to place a call in the main GameLoop() function.

One other thing to discuss is the way in which axis data is returned from the mouse. The axes are read back as *relative coordinates*. This means that every time you poll the mouse you get back the distance that it has moved since the last time you checked it. For instance, you might get something like (5, −1) if you checked the state of the mouse. This means that the mouse moved five units to the right and one unit down since the last poll. Compare this to *absolute coordinates,* which usually report the coordinates of the mouse in units from the upper-left corner of the screen.

Polling

Back to the workshop. Here is the Poll() function.

```
HRESULT CZenMouse::Poll()
{
        HRESULT r = 0;

        // Return if the object has not been initialized
        if( !m_bInitialized )
                return E_FAIL;

        // Get the state of the mouse
        r = m_pMouseDev->GetDeviceState( sizeof( DIMOUSESTATE ), &m_MouseData );
        if( FAILED( r ) )
        {
                // If the mouse has moved focus
                if( r == DIERR_INPUTLOST )
                {
                        // Reacquire the mouse
                        while( r == DIERR_INPUTLOST )
                                r = m_pMouseDev->Acquire();

                        // Try to test the state again
                        if( SUCCEEDED( r ) )
                                r = m_pMouseDev->GetDeviceState( sizeof( DIMOUSESTATE
                                ),
                                                        &m_MouseData );
                else
                        return FALSE;
                }
                else
```

```
                        return E_FAIL;
        }

        return S_OK;
}
```

Basically, it is exactly the same as the code that tests for the keyboard state that I showed you earlier. The only difference is that you need to now specify the size of the DIMOUSESTATE structure for the buffer instead of just a simple array. Notice also the device validation code, which also remains the same.

Reading the Mouse Position

Reading the position of the mouse is really simple. You just have to get the coordinate data out of the data buffer structure and then transfer it into a POINT structure so that it can be returned back to the caller. Here is the code:

```
POINT CZenMouse::GetMousePos()
{
        // Holds mouse data
        POINT MousePos;

        // Get the data from the buffer
        MousePos.x = m_MouseData.lX;
        MousePos.y = m_MouseData.lY;

        // Return the position
        return MousePos;
}
```

Basically, you can just call it and take the POINT structure as the return value that contains the coordinate data. This is the first time that you have come across the DIMOUSESTATE structure actually in use, and you can see it here:

```
typedef struct DIMOUSESTATE {
    LONG lX;    // X Axis coordinate
    LONG lY;    // Y Axis coordinate
    LONG lZ;    // Z Axis coordinate (eg scroll roller)
    BYTE rgbButtons[4];      // Button status(Max4)
} DIMOUSESTATE, *LPDIMOUSESTATE;
```

Reading Button Status

I programmed another function that can be used to easily check the status of the mouse buttons. Don't forget that you must poll the mouse each frame in order to update the button status. Here is the code:

```
BOOL CZenMouse::IsButtonDown( int Button )
{
        // Return the button status from the buffer
        if( m_MouseData.rgbButtons[Button] & 0x80 )
                return TRUE;
        else
                return FALSE;
}
```

You call it with an identifier for the button you want to check, and the function will return either TRUE or FALSE, depending on the status of the button in question. The value you pass will be one the following:

   0 = Primary Mouse Button (left)

   1 = Secondary Mouse Button (right)

   2 = 3rd Mouse Button (usually middle)

   3 = 4th Mouse Button (if applicable)

Shutdown

Shutting down the mouse is exactly the same as shutting down the keyboard. You must unacquire the device first and then release the COM object.

```
CZenMouse::~CZenMouse()
{
        // Unacquire and release the mouse device
        if( m_pMouseDev )
        {
                m_pMouseDev->Unacquire();
                m_pMouseDev->Release();
        }
}
```

Using CZenMouse

There are a couple of final steps to go through to connect CZenMouse to the engine.

1. Create a global instance of CZenMouse.
   ```
   CZenMouse g_Mouse;
   ```
2. Add a call to CZenMouse::Initialize() to InitializeInput().
   ```
   g_Mouse.Initialize();
   ```
3. Add a call to CZenMouse::Poll() to the main GameLoop() function.
   ```
   g_Mouse.Poll();
   ```
4. Access the mouse from wherever you want with CZenMouse::IsButtonDown() and CZenMouse::GetMousePos().

```
// Check the status of the primary mouse button
BOOL bIsDown = g_Mouse.IsButtonDown( 0 )
// Check the position of the mouse
POINT Position = g_Mouse.GetMousePos();
```

And that's it. Shutdown is automatic since the code is located within the destructor. You are now free to use the mouse and keyboard as you see fit.

The State of the Union

Now I'm going to show you the full listing for the InitializeInput(), because there are a few things added to it.

```
HRESULT InitializeInput()
{
        if( g_pDI )
                g_pDI->Release();

        HRESULT r = 0;

        // Create the IDirectInput8 object
        r = DirectInput8Create( g_hInstMain, DIRECTINPUT_VERSION,
                            IID_IDirectInput8, (void**)&g_pDI, NULL );
        if( FAILED( r ) )
        {
                SetError( "Failed to create DirectInput" );
```

```
                return E_FAIL;
        }

        // Initialize the keyboard
        r = g_Keyboard.Initialize();
        if( FAILED( r ) )
        {
                SetError( "Failed to initialize keyboard" );
                return E_FAIL;
        }

        // Initialize the mouse
        r = g_Mouse.Initialize();
        if( FAILED( r ) )
        {
                SetError( "Unable to initialize mouse" );
                return E_FAIL;
        }

        return S_OK;
}
```

Conclusion

Well, there you go! A quicker-than-quick introduction to DirectInput. In the next chapter I'll cover how to advance the camera class and hook it up to the keyboard and mouse so that you can start to move around the worlds that you are creating.

Unfortunately, until then I can't really show you any decent demos with using input, but in the meantime you can check out the companion CD for a pretty boring example. Or you might just want to wait until the next chapter, when things get smokin'.

CHAPTER 15

3D Game Engineering

The other day I got to go on a jet ski for the first time in years. This wasn't your average jet ski though—it was an 800cc Yamaha toy of death. Combining my invincibility (proved by my survival of that near plane crash), a jet ski, and nice weather, I managed to get that bad boy up to 84 km/h. It went so fast that my brain was unable to process the scene coming towards me. The effect is kind of like playing *Quake* on those old PC's that can't manage more than 10 FPS. It was a lot of fun and I would definitely suggest that if you haven't been on one before to go out and get on one. Or... program a jet ski simulator using some of the amazing code that I am going to show you in this chapter!

Anyway, let me get back to programming—in this chapter you are going to learn far too much stuff, such as how to

- load advanced 3D objects from external 3D editors into Direct3D, complete with materials and textures.
- encapsulate the functionality of materials and lights into classes.
- program more advanced timing systems and more on the vsync.
- set Direct3D's font system to render with TrueType fonts.
- extend the functionality of the camera and connect it to the keyboard and mouse.
- start the creation of an advanced frame-based rendering system.

Oh, my fingers are yelling at me after looking at all they have to type. Actually, I wouldn't really call them fingers anymore—they have all worn away. These days I have to type with my nose!

Before beginning, I've got to ask you to bear with me for the lack of examples in this chapter. This chapter and the next were originally one and the same, but it started getting too big so I split it in two. So in this chapter I'm explaining all the technology, while in the next you'll see all the amazing effects that the code can create. Cool? Cool. Let's get started...

Encapsulating Materials into CZenMaterial

Materials are great as structures, but they are even better when encapsulated into a standardized class. You looked at materials briefly before, but I'll run over the implementation details again quickly. A *material* is a structure that defines how light interacts with a face. Only one material can be selected at any one time, and all outputted faces will have their lighting characteristics based on the currently selected material. When you select a new material, the previously selected material is automatically removed. If you need more information on the theory behind how materials work, then have a look back at Chapter 11, where I provided a lot of information on them. I'll also be using materials extensively throughout this chapter.

In Direct3D, materials are encapsulated by the D3DMATERIAL8 structure, which is as follows:

```
typedef struct _D3DMATERIAL8 {
    D3DCOLORVALUE    Diffuse;  // The diffuse color
    D3DCOLORVALUE    Ambient;  // The ambient color
    D3DCOLORVALUE    Specular; // The specular color
    D3DCOLORVALUE    Emissive; // The emissive color
    float            Power;            // The specular power
} D3DMATERIAL8;
```

As you can see, it is a fairly simple structure, made up almost entirely of D3DCOLOR-VALUE structures. The diffuse light defines the general color for the object, the ambient light defines how the light blends with the surrounding ambient light, the specular color specifies the color of the highlighted reflected light from the face, and the emissive color defines the color of light that the object puts out. And finally, the power defines how shiny the surface is. D3DCOLORVALUE contains four floating-point entries: three for the red, green, and blue color components and a fourth for the alpha component.

```
typedef struct _D3DCOLORVALUE {
    float r;
    float g;
    float b;
    float a;
} D3DCOLORVALUE;
```

The reason I'm showing you these structures is so that you can see my justification for even bothering to encapsulate the structure inside another class. I am doing so basically for programming efficiency. If you wanted to set up a material using normal programming methods, then you would have to type all of this:

```
D3DMATERIAL8 Material;
ZeroMemory( &Material, sizeof( D3DMATERIAL8 ) );

Material.Diffuse.r = 1.0f;
Material.Diffuse.g = 1.0f;
Material.Diffuse.b = 1.0f;

Material.Ambient.r = 1.0f;
Material.Ambient.g = 1.0f;
Material.Ambient.b = 1.0f;

Material.Specular.r = 1.0f;
Material.Specular.g = 1.0f;
Material.Specular.b = 1.0f;


Material.Emissive.r = 1.0f;
Material.Emissive.g = 1.0f;
Material.Emissive.b = 1.0f;

Material.Power = 1.0f;
```

That is an awful lot of code just to set up a material. Wouldn't it be better if you could just write something like this:

```
CZenMaterial Material;

Material.SetDiffuse( 1.0f, 1.0f, 1.0f );
Material.SetAmbient( 1.0f, 1.0f, 1.0f );
Material.SetSpecular( 1.0f, 1.0f, 1.0f, 1.0f );
Material.SetEmissive( 1.0f, 1.0f, 1.0f );
```

I thought so too. Anyway, the class is your basic encapsulation routine, and it shouldn't need too much explanation.

```
// ---------------- class CZenMaterial
class CZenMaterial
{
```

```
public:
        CZenMaterial();
        ~CZenMaterial();

// Variables
public:
        D3DMATERIAL8 m_Material;
protected:

// Functions:
public:
        void SetDiffuse( float r, float g, float b );
        void SetAmbient( float r, float g, float b );
        void SetSpecular( float r, float g, float b, float Power );
        void SetEmissive(  float r, float g, float b );

        HRESULT Update();
protected:

};
```

The only member variable is m_Material, which is the D3DMATERIAL8 structure. First, let me show you the code that updates the values within the material structure:

```
CZenMaterial::CZenMaterial()
{
        ZeroMemory( &m_Material, sizeof( D3DMATERIAL8 ) );

        m_Material.Diffuse.r = 1.0f;
        m_Material.Diffuse.g = 1.0f;
        m_Material.Diffuse.b = 1.0f;
}


CZenMaterial::~CZenMaterial()
{

}
// Sets the diffuse color
void CZenMaterial::SetDiffuse( float r, float g, float b )
{
        m_Material.Diffuse.r = r;
        m_Material.Diffuse.g = g;
```

```
                m_Material.Diffuse.b = b;
}
// Sets the ambient color
void CZenMaterial::SetAmbient( float r, float g, float b )
{
                m_Material.Ambient.r = r;
                m_Material.Ambient.g = g;
                m_Material.Ambient.b = b;
}
// Sets the emissive color
void CZenMaterial::SetEmissive( float r, float g, float b )
{
                m_Material.Emissive.r = r;
                m_Material.Emissive.g = g;
                m_Material.Emissive.b = b;
}
// Sets the specular color and power
void CZenMaterial::SetSpecular( float r, float g, float b, float Power )
{
                m_Material.Specular.r = r;
                m_Material.Specular.g = g;
                m_Material.Specular.b = b;
                m_Material.Power = Power;
}
```

And what material class would be complete without a function to implement the
material as the active material within Direct3D?

```
HRESULT CZenMaterial::Update()
{
                return g_pDevice->SetMaterial( &m_Material );
}
```

The SetMaterial() function takes the address of a D3DMATERIAL8 structure that you
want to set as the active material. To use CZenMaterial is a simple three-step
process.

1. Declare a new material:
   ```
   CZenMaterial NewMaterial;
   ```

2. Set the properties for the material:
   ```
   NewMaterial.SetAmbient( 0.0f, 0.5f, 0.3f );
   NewMaterial.SetDiffuse( 1.0f, 0.0f, 0.0f );
   ```

3. Set the material as active to start using it:

```
NewMaterial.Update();
```

And that's it! You'll see materials implemented a lot more in a second when I show you how to load 3D models.

> **NOTE**
>
> You *must* have a material selected into Direct3D, or else objects will not work if you enable lighting. So if one day you are pulling out your hair wondering why objects show up with lighting disabled and suddenly disappear as soon as you enable it, make sure you have selected a material.

Loading External 3D Models

You know all those cool spaceships, asteroids, guns, people, and other interesting stuff that you find in your average 3D game? They are usually all designed in an advanced 3D editor such as 3D Studio MAX from Discreet, or Alias Maya. Then the objects are transferred into tools that are specifically designed for the game's engine. Finally, they are put into a form ready for the game to load them in at run time.

Well, I don't have a multimillion-dollar budget at my disposal, so I can't create tools for the engine. But what I can do is show you how to load very advanced 3D objects from external editors such as 3D Studio MAX directly into your game. Now, there is one little part that I cannot help you with here, and that is how to actually create these objects. You are going to need to learn how to actually use 3D Studio MAX or one of the many other quality-rendering tools available on the market in order to create the content for your games. However, if you don't know yet how to use a modeler, don't worry! There are many quality sites on the Net that give away free models for home use. For instance, check out http://www.3Dcafe.com and go to the section of free stuff to see what I am talking about.

The Zen engine will support DirectX X files as its native model format. X files are kind of like normal model files, except spookier. The format did originate in Redmond, after all! But seriously, the X file format is a very advanced model format that is capable of holding meshes, materials, animations, frames, and just about anything else that can go into a 3D scene. The only problem with the X file format is that nobody supports it! Well, until very recently there was no Save As, X File command in any modelers, which was a total pain because the only other way to convert a 3D model file into the DirectX format was to write a converter yourself or deal with the devil and use the Conv3DS.exe tool. Yuck.

Dealing with the Devil: Conv3DS.exe

In this day and age of GUIs, mice, and 3D-accelerated graphics, you might think that Microsoft would produce a tool to deal with its own file format that worked in a graphical manner. I mean, they're making a tool that is used to manipulate graphical objects that will only execute in Windows, a graphical OS, and what do they do? They make a character mode program. Where do files end up in post Win98 systems? Somewhere like

```
C:\Documents and Settings\Peter Walsh\Desktop\The Zen of Direct3D Programming\Chapter
x\Examples\Example x\
```

How long does that take to type into a console window? A long time. Say you are in your editor program, such as 3D Studio MAX, which is shown in Figure 15.1. You need to create your model or import it from somewhere. Go to File, Export and select the 3D studio *.3ds format. Save your file wherever you want. Next, you want to find the Conv3DS.exe utility, which is located in

```
C:\ DirectX Install Path \ bin \ DXUtils \ XFiles
```

What you want to do is take the file and copy it to wherever your 3DS models are located.

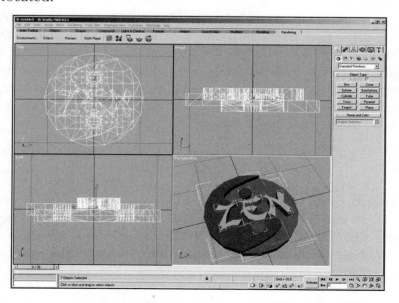

Figure 15.1

3D Studio MAX

Next you need to go to the Start menu and select the Run command. If you are in Windows 95, 98, or Me, then type "command.com" and press Enter. If you are in Windows 2000 or later, then type "cmd" and press Enter. This will bring up the command window. Now use the CD command to change to the directory where your models are located. Got it? Good. Now you just need to type

```
conv3ds ModelName.3ds
```

You can see Conv3DS.exe at work in Figure 15.2. Hopefully this will create a new file called ModelName.x. I say "hopefully" because Conv3DS.exe is notorious for crashing and screwing up if it doesn't like the source file. Check the documentation for clues if your model is not converting properly. Otherwise, now you have an X file! Don't tell Mulder, but I'm about to show you some code to finally decode the X files once and for all!

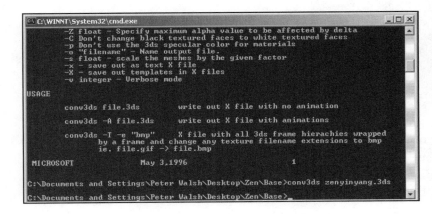

Figure 15.2

Conv3DS.exe in action

The Default Texture

One of the problems that can pop up when loading models is that they may be straight meshes, they may have materials, and they may even have an associated texture. In fact, there may be many textures and materials for the same model. The problem is that you never know ahead of time, from a code perspective, what properties the model you are loading is going to have. This problem manifests itself when you try to render the model and you go to set the texture for the model, or section of the model, and one doesn't exist. The results can range from memory protection errors to other visual artifacts, and it is best to approach the issue with prevention in mind.

So how do you solve the problem? Well, one way is to assume that all models have some sort of texture applied to them from the start. If you are loading a model that doesn't have a texture, then you can assign a default texture to it. A *default texture* is just a small texture that you are sure is always in memory, and which you can assign to problem faces that don't have textures defined. Normally it is a good idea to make the default texture stand out so that beta testers can easily spot places in a game where the texturing has become messed up for one reason or another. Or you can just use a blank white texture if you want your models to blend in and only use their materials. It's up to you. For the Zen engine default texture I have used the texture shown in Figure 15.3.

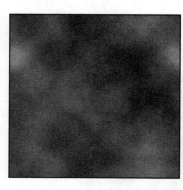

Figure 15.3

The default texture for the Zen engine

As you can see, for now I have chosen a texture that sort of blends in, but it is simple to change because the default texture is always located in the root directory of the game and is named DefaultTexture.bmp. Implementing the default texture is extremely easy—just create a global texture like this:

```
LPDIRECT3DTEXTURE8 g_pDefaultTexture = 0;
```

Then add this code to the main GameInit():

```
r = D3DXCreateTextureFromFile( g_pDevice, "DefaultTexture.bmp", &g_pDefaultTexture );
if( FAILED( r ) )
{
        SetError( "Unable to load default texture" );
        return E_FAIL;
}
```

And finally the shutdown code to GameShutdown():

```
if( g_pDefaultTexture )
        g_pDefaultTexture->Release();
```

And that's it—you now have a global default texture that you can access whenever you want. It is automatically loaded and unloaded when the game starts and quits, respectively.

The Holy Grail: CZenMesh

You will probably use CZenMesh more than any of the other classes in the engine, because a game is basically just a collection of animated meshes.

Before starting I want to talk a little bit more about X files. You'll recall that I said they are very advanced. Well they are also, in typical Microsoft fashion, incredibly complicated to deal with. The documentation is awful—I nearly became ill trying to follow the instructions the first time I tried. For instance, if you want a laugh, check out *DirectX 8 Docs / DirectX Graphics / Advanced Topics in DirectX Graphics / X Files / Using X Files / Loading an X File*. If you manage to follow those instructions without pulling out any hair, e-mail me and I will personally send you a cheesy congratulations e-card.

Luckily for you, during my trials I stumbled across a much easier way to deal with X files. It involves the use of a DirectX utility function entitled D3DXLoadMeshFromFile() and a COM interface called ID3DXMesh. And those are what I am going to base the CZenMesh function around.

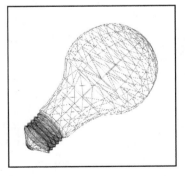

Figure 15.4

A mid/high polygon lightbulb mesh

The Class Definition

Here is the class. Take a quick look, and then I will explain it:

```
class CZenMesh : public CZenObject
{
public:
        CZenMesh();
        ~CZenMesh();
```

```cpp
// Variables:
public:
        int m_NumMats; // Number of materials structures for the object

protected:
        LPD3DXMESH m_pMesh;                        // The mesh

        LPDIRECT3DTEXTURE8* m_pTextures;           // The mesh's textures
        CZenMaterial* m_pMaterials;                // The mesh's materials

// Functions:
public:
        HRESULT LoadXFile( char* pstrPathName );   //Loads a mesh
        HRESULT Render();                          // Renders the mesh

        int GetSize(){ return sizeof( *this ); }

protected:

};

CZenMesh::CZenMesh()
{
        m_pMesh = 0;
        m_NumMats = 0;

        m_pTextures = 0;
        m_pMaterials = 0;
}
```

I'll start with the variables. m_NumMats is used to store the number of materials stored in the mesh. This is important, because each part of the mesh with a separate material or texture needs to be drawn individually. The process follows:

1. Select the current texture and material.
2. Draw the portion of the mesh that uses that material and texture.
3. Move to the next portion of the mesh.
4. Repeat until done.

The m_pMesh member variable is a pointer to an ID3DXMesh interface. This object encapsulates all of the technology needed to deal with meshes and is very useful.

More on this soon. m_pTextures is a pointer that is used to create an array of pointers to all the textures used by the model. And finally, m_pMaterials is used to create an array of pointers to CZenMaterial objects that look after the materials.

The class has three functions. LoadXFile() is pretty self explanatory—it takes the path of a file and loads it into the mesh. Render() is there to—you guessed it—render the mesh to the screen. The third function is GetSize(), which I'm not going to tell you about just yet. Its use will become clear when you learn to develop frames. Just smile and nod at it for now!

Loading X Files

As Phoebe from *Friends* would put it, things are going to get kind of floopy for a minute. I'll show you the whole shebang and then go through it step by step. Careful though, this is way ugly code:

```
HRESULT CZenMesh::LoadXFile( char* pstrPathName )
{
        HRESULT r = 0;

        // The buffer to hold the materials
        LPD3DXBUFFER pMaterialBuffer = 0;

        // Load the x file from disk
        r = D3DXLoadMeshFromX( pstrPathName, D3DXMESH_MANAGED, g_pDevice, 0,
                                        &pMaterialBuffer, (DWORD*)&m_NumMats, &m_pMesh
);
        if( FAILED( r ) )
        {
                SetError( "Failed to load XFile with file name:" );
                SetError( pstrPathName );
                return E_FAIL;
        }


        // Create a new texture array
        m_pTextures = new LPDIRECT3DTEXTURE8[ m_NumMats ];
        // Create a new material array
        m_pMaterials = new CZenMaterial[ m_NumMats ];

        // Get a pointer to the start of the material buffer
        D3DXMATERIAL* pMaterials = (D3DXMATERIAL*)pMaterialBuffer-
>GetBufferPointer();
```

```cpp
          // Loop for each material in the buffer
          for( int i = 0 ; i < m_NumMats ; i++ )
          {
                  // Extract the material from the buffer
                  m_pMaterials[i].m_Material = pMaterials[i].MatD3D;
                  // Brighten the material
                  m_pMaterials[i].m_Material.Ambient =
m_pMaterials[i].m_Material.Diffuse;

                  // If a texture is not set for this material
                  if( !pMaterials[i].pTextureFilename )
                  {
                          // Set the texture to the default texture
                          m_pTextures[i] = g_pDefaultTexture;

                          // Iterate to the next loop because there is no texture
                          continue;
                  }

                  // Create a new texture from the file name supplied
                  r = D3DXCreateTextureFromFile( g_pDevice,
                                  pMaterials[i].pTextureFilename, &m_pTextures[i] );
                  if( FAILED( r ) )
                  {
                          SetError( "Unable to load texture for mesh with file name:"
);

                          SetError( pMaterials[i].pTextureFilename );

                          // If the texture load failed then set
                          // it to the default texture
                          m_pTextures[i] = g_pDefaultTexture;
                  }

          }

          // Release the material buffer
          pMaterialBuffer->Release();

          return S_OK;

}
```

I'll divide the code into sections and walk you through it...

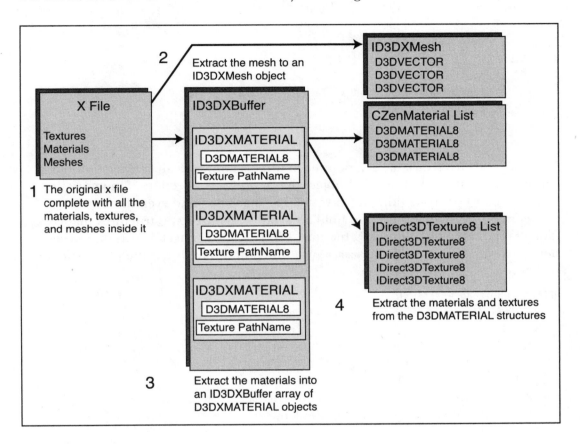

Figure 15.5

Decoding X Files into materials, meshes, and textures

Reading the Files

The function works by taking the path to an X file and then loading it into memory. It performs a number of steps. First it loads an X file—but this involves a number of substeps. The first of these is that all the materials and texture paths associated with the object are loaded into a buffer. The code that performs this is here:

```
// The buffer to hold the materials
LPD3DXBUFFER pMaterialBuffer = 0;
```

```
// Load the x file from disk
r = D3DXLoadMeshFromX( pstrPathName, D3DXMESH_MANAGED, g_pDevice, 0,
                                     &pMaterialBuffer, (DWORD*)&m_NumMats, &m_pMesh
);
if( FAILED( r ) )
{
        SetError( "Failed to load XFile with file name:" );
        SetError( pstrPathName );
        return E_FAIL;
}
```

The pMaterialBuffer variable is a pointer to what is known as an ID3DXBuffer object. An ID3DXBuffer is basically a COM object that represents a section of memory that can be used to store anything from vertices to materials, and everything in between. In this case it is used to hold an array of D3DMATERIAL8 structures that contain all the materials from the X file that will be loaded. This takes us up to the next part, which is the D3DXLoadMeshFromX() function. I have listed the prototype for you here:

```
HRESULT D3DXLoadMeshFromX(
    LPSTR pFilename,                    // The file name
    DWORD Options,                      // Creation options
    LPDIRECT3DDEVICE8 pDevice,          // Pointer to the Direct3D device
    LPD3DXBUFFER* ppAdjacency,          // Adjacency Information
    LPD3DXBUFFER* ppMaterials,          // Materials
    PDWORD pNumMaterials,               // The number of materials
    LPD3DXMESH* ppMesh                  // Pointer to the mesh object
);
```

Table 15.1 gives the parameters for this function.

Table 15.1   D3DXLoadMeshFromX() Parameters

Parameter	Definition
pFilename	Takes the path to the file that you want to load
Options	Takes the creation options that you want to use for the created mesh. You will almost always want to set this to D3DXMESH_MANAGED, which implies that you want Direct3D to look after the memory location for the mesh.
pDevice	Takes a pointer to the device that you are using.
ppAdjacency	Optional—returns adjacency information about the mesh. *Adjacency Information* is a list of indices that describes which faces are connected to each other. In other words, you really don't need them right now.
ppMaterials	Takes a pointer to an ID3DXBuffer that will be filled with all the materials used in the mesh
pNumMaterials	A pointer to a DWORD that will be filled with the number of materials in the buffer.
ppMesh	Takes the address of a pointer that will be filled with a pointer to the newly-created ID3DXMesh object

Decoding the Buffers

So now the X file is in memory. But you need to do some further decoding, such as getting the materials out of the buffer and into a form where they can be easily accessed. Also, all the textures specified in the paths need to be loaded into memory. The next set of steps is to create two arrays to hold the textures and materials from the mesh. Recall from the D3DXLoadMeshFromX() function that the sixth parameter tells how many materials are associated with the mesh. You can use this to set the size of the arrays like so:

```
// Create a new texture array
m_pTextures = new LPDIRECT3DTEXTURE8[ m_NumMats ];
// Create a new material array
m_pMaterials = new CZenMaterial[ m_NumMats ];
```

Recall also that I mentioned that all the material and texture information is held in an `ID3DXBuffer` object. To get at this information you need to get a pointer to the start of the buffer, like this:

```
// Get a pointer to the start of the material buffer
D3DXMATERIAL* pMaterials = (D3DXMATERIAL*)pMaterialBuffer->GetBufferPointer();
```

`ID3DXBuffer::GetBufferPointer()` returns a `void` pointer that is cast to the `D3DXMATERIAL` type. Look carefully at the type cast. It is not your standard `D3DMATERIAL8` structure—it's a `D3DXMATERIAL`. They look very similar so don't get them confused. `D3DXMATERIAL` is listed here:

```
struct D3DXMATERIAL {
    D3DMATERIAL8    MatD3D;
    LPSTR           pTextureFilename;
};
```

See the difference? The `D3DXMATERIAL` includes a standard `D3DMATERIAL8` structure and also the path to the texture, which may or may not exist. If the texture exists, then `pTextureFileName` will include a path to the texture, otherwise it will be set to `NULL`.

The decoding process goes like this pseudocode:

```
for( Each Material In Buffer )
{
        Copy the material into the member material array;
        Make the material brighter by setting the ambient light equal to the ←
diffuse light;

        If( Texture is not specified for the material )
        {
                Set the texture for this face to the default texture;
                Continue to next Iteration.;

        }

        Load the texture for this material into the member texture array;
        If( The Load Fails )
                Set the texture to the default texture;

}

Release the material buffer;
```

That's a fairly clear process, right? Anyway, have a look at the code that follows and see if you can get the hang of it:

```
// Loop for each material in the buffer
for( int i = 0 ; i < m_NumMats ; i++ )
{
        // Extract the material from the buffer
        m_pMaterials[i].m_Material = pMaterials[i].MatD3D;
        // Brighten the material
        m_pMaterials[i].m_Material.Ambient = m_pMaterials[i].m_Material.Diffuse;

        // If a texture is not set for this material
        if( !pMaterials[i].pTextureFilename )
        {
                // Set the texture to the default texture
                m_pTextures[i] = g_pDefaultTexture;

                // Iterate to the next loop because there is no texture
                continue;
        }

        // Create a new texture from the file name supplied
        r = D3DXCreateTextureFromFile( g_pDevice, pMaterials[i].pTextureFilename,
                                                        &m_pTextures[i] );

        if( FAILED( r ) )
        {
                SetError( "Unable to load texture for mesh with file name:" );
                SetError( pMaterials[i].pTextureFilename );

                // If the texture load failed then set
                // it to the default texture
                m_pTextures[i] = g_pDefaultTexture;

        }

}

// Release the material buffer
pMaterialBuffer->Release();
```

One thing you may be wondering is why I am setting the ambient color to be the same as the diffuse color. Well, this is a common technique, and it is used because most of the models that you get out of 3D editors have their ambient colors set to black (0, 0, 0), which causes the models to look very dark in Direct3D. By setting the ambient color to be the same as the diffuse color, you can improve the visual quality of most models. If, however, you find that your models have the ambient light set, then you should remove that line of code from the load function.

And that is everything you need to load the X file into memory and decode those materials and textures. Have a look at the start of this section to see all the code in one place. The next step is to actually render the model to the screen.

Rendering X Files

Rendering is really simple, since you already did all the hard work in the load function. All you have to do now is loop through each material and render the subsets of the mesh that have that material associated with it. For each subset, you have to reset the texture and material with Direct3D. It's not as bad as it sounds. Check this out:

```
HRESULT CZenMesh::Render()
{
        HRESULT r = E_FAIL;

        // Loop for each material
        for( int i = 0 ; i < m_NumMats ; i++ )
        {
                // Set this material as active
                m_pMaterials[i].Update();
                // Set this texture as active
                g_pDevice->SetTexture( 0, m_pTextures[i] );
                // Render this subset of the mesh
                r = m_pMesh->DrawSubset(i);
        }

        // Reset the vertex shader
        g_pDevice->SetVertexShader( ZENVERTEX_TYPE );

        // Return the result of the render operation
        return r;
}
```

Can you see what is happening? First the material and texture for the part of the mesh that is being rendered are activated. Then the subset of the mesh that uses the activated material and texture is rendered. Finally, the code moves on to the next iteration, which loads the next texture and material, and so on.

See the code that I have highlighted in bold? Well, I only just added that after almost going insane trying to get the code to work. The original version didn't have that little snippet added. I discovered, through much heartache, that ID3DXMesh does not reset the vertex shader flexible vertex format when it is done rendering. The result of this is that if you try to render anything, such as a face or a line, after rendering a mesh, you get a thousand internal Direct3D exceptions that output messages like "The FVF format does match the stream" or something equally uninformative. It took me a while to track down that bad boy—so keep this in mind if the problem ever crops up in your own code.

Using CZenMesh

Let's see this puppy in action. For this example I start by creating a little Yin and Yang kind of object with the text "Zen" overlaid on it. I create the object in Rhinoceros 3D and then transfer it to 3D Studio MAX, so that it will export properly and I can convert it with Conv3DS.exe. You can see the model in MAX in Figure 15.6.

Figure 15.6

The Zen model in 3D Studio MAX

When it is complete I run it through the evil Conv3DS.exe utility to convert it into a standard X File. Then, with the model complete, I take a stab at programming the code. For this example I just create a simple global CZenMesh object like this:

```
CZenMesh g_Mesh;
```

Then down in GameInit() I place the following code to load the x file into the mesh:

```
g_Mesh.LoadXFile( "zenyinyang.x" );
```

And then, to render the file, it is a very simple case of placing a call to
`CZenMesh::Render()` in the main `Render()` function, although I want to make sure it
is between the calls to `IDirect3DDevice8::BeginScene` and `IDirect3DDevice8::EndScene()`.
I put the following code into `Render()`:

```
g_Mesh.Render();
```

And the results are spectacular. You can see them in Figure 15.7.

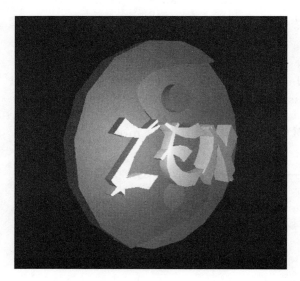

Figure 15.7

The results of rendering with CZenMesh

You may have noticed that I have not given you any code that lets you move the
meshes yet. I'm not being lazy; you will learn all about movement when we get to
frames, which coincidentally is right now. By the way, I kind of cheated on that
screen shot—it comes from the mesh when it is inside a rotating frame. But don't
worry—I am just about to explain those to you.

Introduction to Frames

I talked briefly about frames when I was introducing basic 3D concepts to you. Now
it's time to implement them. Let's run over the basics again. The word "frame"
comes from "frame of reference." Frames are basically used to make it easier to
look after multiple objects in your game, and also to increase the range of motions
with which you can move your objects.

The Right Frame of Mind

Think of a frame as a conceptual anchor for objects. When I say "object" I mean everything from 3D meshes to lights. Basically, anything that can move around in your world should be kept in a frame. Why? Well, think about it this way: Looking after the positional information for hundreds of different objects is a total pain anyway. But it gets really bad when you start to implement interobject dependencies. For instance, say you have a fire mesh on a moving conveyer belt and you want to move a bunch of lights with the fire to make it illuminate its environment. And then you want to have smoke that slowly swirls away from the fire. That means you have a lot of objects (the lights and smoke) that need to have their positions set to reflect on the current position of the parent object (the fire), which is reliant on the position of the conveyer belt.

That chain of updates would be a total pain, involving a million if statements and comparisons, and I don't even want to think about just how bad it could get. The solution is to use frames. Basically, a frame is a conceptual object (you never see it) that looks after its own position, velocity, and orientation. You can add objects to the frame and they will update their positions to reflect the position of the frame. So you could add the lights and fire to the same frame. Then when you want to update them, you only have to make a single update to the frame and the frame will look after setting the properties of its member objects automatically. But the real power of frames is that you can add *child frames* to them as well. So you can create entire chains of frames that are incredibly easy to update.

Take, for example, 100 swarming bats that you want flying fairly randomly but staying within the confines of an ominous-looking dark castle. You could go through a loop 100 times updating each of the bats, but when you add in the updates of all the other objects in your game you start to create an overloaded messy game loop structure. Instead, you could create a frame, which moves slowly in a circle around the tower of the castle. Then you could create 100 child frames and add the bat mesh to each one. The child meshes would then be programmed to fly in some vector that stayed within 50 units of the parent frame. The result? The bats swarm realistically and naturally stay within the confines of the tower. And only a single update call is required for each frame.

So the real power of frames is the way they can take advantage of *additive transformations*. That is, they take into account the positions of their parent frames to set their position. As a final example, let me go back to the planets that I was talking about in the introductory chapters. A frame could be created for the sun, which would be set to rotate slowly. Then a number of child frames could be added to that frame and set to rotate at varying rates and distances from the sun, in order to reproduce the actions of the planets. Further child frames could be added to the planets to emulate the behavior of the moons. The result is that, with only a few calls, you can reproduce incredibly complicated behavior (see Figure 15.8).

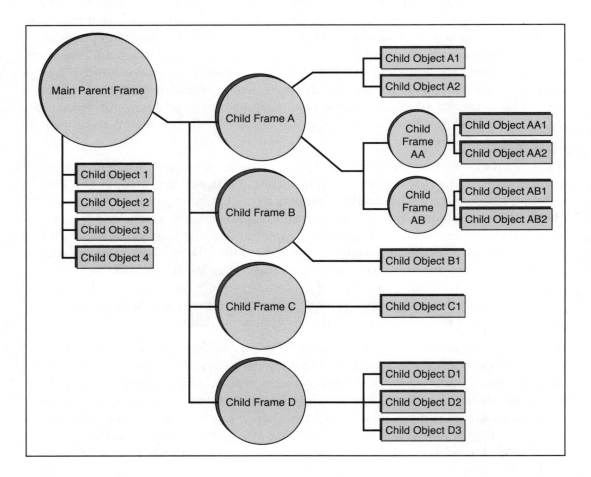

Figure 15.8

Child objects, such as meshes, faces, or lights, rely on the positions of their parent frames to compute their final positions. The parent frames subsequently rely on the positions of their parents, and so on, until the main parent frame is reached.

Modifying the Zen Engine to Use Frames

As you can imagine, frames add significant functionality to any engine. In fact, in one form or another they are implemented in *every* advanced engine on the market. And luckily for you, I'm going to show you all about them. The only problem with frames is that I really don't like the name *frame*. It took me a long time to understand them when I was learning, partly because the book I was leaning from was lousy, and partly because I'm a little slow sometimes. Make sure you don't confuse a frame, as in *frame of reference,* with a frame, as in *frames per second.* They also have nothing to do with frames, as in *HTML frames*, if you are one of those Internet types.

As I mentioned a second ago, frames can hold anything from lights to meshes to points to anything, really. So you may be wondering exactly how a frame knows how to deal with all these different objects if they are all so diverse. Well, you genius you, I'll tell you how. You know how since the beginning I have been declaring every object (like cubes, faces, etc.) as a child to the generic CZenObject? Well, as long as you give each object a fairly standard interface, then the frame doesn't really care about what they are. All it needs to know is that for every call to update the frame it can call Render() on the object. How Render() is implemented is totally object independent. For instance, for the mesh object, it renders the mesh to the screen. But for the light, as you will see shortly, it updates the position and lighting characteristics of the light.

For the first implementation of frames, I am not going to show you how to do the whole child frame thingy. Let's start with the basics and then move up later. So how does it work? Well, it's really easy. All a frame really does is look after a linked list of CZenObjects. A frame also looks after its velocity, position, and orientation. And whenever a call to Render() is made, the frame figures out all the matrices to update the position of the child objects and then proceeds to render them all one by one.

Independent Source Objects

In advanced frame implementations you may hear a phrase like *source object independence* or something similar. What this means is that when you add an object to a frame you are effectively inserting a copy of the object into the frame, which means that as soon as the object is added you can do whatever you want with the original and it won't affect the version within the frame.

I am not going to go down this road for your implementation, firstly because it is a pain to implement, secondly because it gets confusing, and thirdly... nothing, because I can't think of a good third reason. Anyway, what I will do for you is tell you that if you ever advance this code so that it implements this technique, you are going to need a couple of tools. First is a copy constructor added to each object. I have done this for you, and you can peruse the code on the CD if you want to see them all. And second is a little function added to each derivative of CZenObject called GetSize(), which allows you to compute the size of the object in bytes. If you add the following code to every object you will get this functionality for free:

```
int GetSize(){ return sizeof( *this ); }
```

You may also need to read up on RTTI (run-time type information). However, since that is not a concern here, let's move on to more important stuff. Check out the CZenMesh definition, complete with size calculations:

```
// ——————————— class CZenMesh
class CZenMesh : public CZenObject
{
public:
        CZenMesh();
        ~CZenMesh();

// Variables:
public:
        int m_NumMats;

protected:
        LPD3DXMESH m_pMesh;      // The mesh


        LPDIRECT3DTEXTURE8* m_pTextures;            // The mesh's textures
        CZenMaterial* m_pMaterials;                 // The mesh's materials

// Functions:
public:
        HRESULT LoadXFile( char* pstrPathName );            //Loads a mesh
        HRESULT Render();                           // Renders the mesh
```

```
    int GetSize(){ return sizeof( *this ); }

protected:

};
```

Updating the CZenObject Class

There are a number of structural changes that also need to be made to the
CZenObject class. For instance, you now know that the objects are going to be stored
as a list, so the easiest way to achieve this is to build the functionality right into the
CZenObject class. If you need a little update on linked lists, check out a good C++
book. Anyway, I add the following member variable to CZenObject:

```
CZenObject* m_pNext;
```

Basically, this allows the easy creation of a linked list, which I will show you very
soon. For stability, I construct m_pNext as a protected type variable so I also add these
functions:

```
void SetNext( CZenObject* pNext ){ m_pNext = pNext; }
void* GetNext(){ return m_pNext; }
```

A lot of times a descendant will need to know about the properties of its parent
frame. For instance, lights work a little screwily in Direct3D, and they need to get
their position from the parent frame each time they are updated. To achieve this
functionality I add another protected member:

```
void* m_pParentFrame;
```

And its associated access functions:

```
void* GetParentFrame(){ return m_pParentFrame; }
void SetParentFrame( void* pFrame ){ m_pParentFrame = pFrame; }
```

Although I haven't showed you CZenFrame yet, you may be wondering why I implemented the pointers to the parent frame as void pointers instead of as pointers to
CZenFrame's. Well, the reason is because of an annoying factor that often crops up in
programming—*cross dependability*. Basically, the CZenFrame needs pointers to
CZenObjects and CZenObject needs to maintain pointers to CZenFrame. This leads to the
compiler getting a little frazzled. It starts thinking, "So the frame has a pointer
to the object. But the object has a pointer to the frame. But the frame is defined
before the frame, so where is the object? Oh, there's the object. What did I do with
that frame again?" And the compiler refuses to compile. The simple solution is

to just use void pointers in the class that doesn't use them as much, and then just cast them as the need arises. The full definition of CZenObject now looks like this:

```
// ---------------- Class CZenObject
// Used as a base for all other game objects
class CZenObject
{
public:
        CZenObject();
        ~CZenObject();

// Functions
public:
        virtual HRESULT Render();

        void SetNext( CZenObject* pNext ){ m_pNext = pNext; }
        void* GetNext(){ return m_pNext; }

        void* GetParentFrame(){ return m_pParentFrame; }
        void SetParentFrame( void* pFrame ){ m_pParentFrame = pFrame; }

        virtual int GetSize(){ return sizeof( *this ); }
protected:


// Variables
public:
        char* m_strName;
        void* m_pParentFrame;

protected:
        CZenObject* m_pNext;

};
```

Programming Frames

Frames will be completely encapsulated by the CZenFrame class. The class is pretty complicated looking because it has to do a lot of positional and orientation computations. Here is the code for the definition:

```cpp
// -------------- class CZenFrame

class CZenFrame
{
public:
        CZenFrame();
        ~CZenFrame();

// Variables
public:

protected:
        // The local matrix for this frame
        D3DXMATRIX m_mLocal;

        // The position of this frame
        D3DXVECTOR3 m_vPosition;
        // The velocity of this frame
        D3DXVECTOR3 m_vVelocity;

        // The orientation of this frame
        float m_Yaw, m_Pitch, m_Roll;

        // The list of objects in this frame
        CZenObject* m_pObjectList;

// Functions
public:
        void SetVelocity( float x, float y, float z );
        void GetVelocity( float& x, float& y, float& z );

        void SetPosition( float x, float y, float z );
        void GetPosition( float& x, float& y, float& z );

        // Returns the local matrix for this frame
        void GetLocal( D3DXMATRIX& pMatrix );

        void SetYaw( float Yaw ){ m_Yaw = Yaw;  }
        void GetYaw( float& Yaw){ Yaw = m_Yaw;  }

        void SetPitch( float Pitch ){ m_Pitch = Pitch;  }
```

```
void GetPitch( float& Pitch){ Pitch = m_Pitch; }

void SetRoll( float Roll ){ m_Roll = Roll;  }
void GetRoll( float& Roll){ Roll = m_Roll; }

// Update the position of this object
void Update();

// Add an object to the frame
HRESULT AddObject( CZenObject* pNewObject );

// Render the objects
HRESULT Render();


protected:



};
```

Yep, that's quite a class. Let me start with a little more theory about orientation. The *orientation* of an object is defined by three words: the *pitch,* the *roll,* and the *yaw.* To visualize what these words mean, I want you to hold your hand out flat in front of you with your palm toward the ground. Now point the tip of your hand toward the ground a little bit. That is the *pitch,* or more mathematically, the rotation around the x-axis. Now put your hand out flat again and rotate your wrist so the left side of your hand points a little bit more to the ground. This is known as the *roll,* or in other words, the rotations around the z-axis. Now put your hand back flat again and rotate it so it points to the left a little bit. This is known as the *yaw,* or rotation around the y-axis (see Figure 15.9). I'll talk more on this soon, but know that the member variables m_Pitch, m_Roll, and m_Yaw are there to represent their respective counterparts.

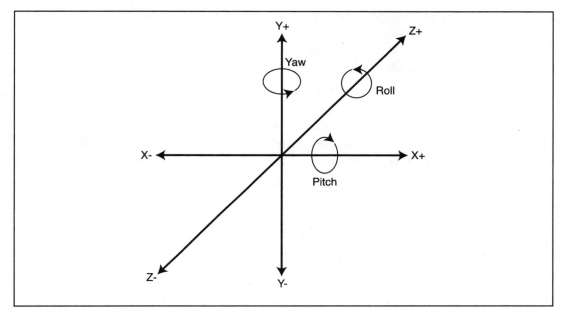

Figure 15.9

How pitch, roll, and yaw relate to orientation

Notice that this class also has a matrix, called m_mLocal, as a member variable. This is the *local matrix* for the frame. This matrix is used to transform all the vertices and other positional data back into world coordinate form. The other two member variables, m_vPosition and m_vVelocity, are vectors for the position and velocity of the frame, respectively. And finally, m_pObjectList is there for the list of objects that I have been talking about.

Now let me take a second to show you the constructor and destructor:

```
CZenFrame::CZenFrame()
{
        // Set the orientation to zero
        m_Yaw = 0.0f;
        m_Pitch = 0.0f;
        m_Roll = 0.0f;

        // Set the position and velocity to zero
        m_vPosition = D3DXVECTOR3( 0.0f, 0.0f, 0.0f );
        m_vVelocity = D3DXVECTOR3( 0.0f, 0.0f, 0.0f );
```

```
        // Initialize the local matrix to an identity
        D3DXMatrixIdentity( &m_mLocal );

        // Zero out the object list
        m_pObjectList = 0;
}
```

Not too much going on here; it just initializes the member variables to 0 and sets the local matrix to be an identity matrix so that calculations are correct. The destructor is slightly more interesting:

```
CZenFrame::~CZenFrame()
{

        // Get a pointer to the object list
        CZenObject* pObject = m_pObjectList;
        // Create a temp pointer
        CZenObject* pTemp = 0;

        // Loop for each object in the list.
        // Note that if there are no objects the loop
        // will not iterate.
        while( pObject )
        {
                // Get a temp pointer to the next object
                pTemp = (CZenObject*)pObject->GetNext();
                // Delete the current object
                free(pObject);
                // Retrieve the pointer to the next object
                pObject = pTemp;
        }


}
```

Frame Position, Velocity, and Orientation

Let me start by showing you the code that you can use to update the position and velocity of the frame. It is very simple and doesn't really need any explanation.

```
// Returns the local transform matrix
void CZenFrame::GetLocal( D3DXMATRIX& Matrix )
{
```

```
        Update();

        Matrix = m_mLocal;
}

// Returns the velocity of the frame
void CZenFrame::GetVelocity( float& x, float& y, float& z )
{
        x = m_vVelocity.x;
        y = m_vVelocity.y;
        z = m_vVelocity.z;
}

// Sets the velocity of the frame
void CZenFrame::SetVelocity( float x, float y, float z )
{
        m_vVelocity.x = x;
        m_vVelocity.y = y;
        m_vVelocity.z = z;
}

// Returns the position of the frame
void CZenFrame::GetPosition( float& x, float& y, float& z )
{
        x = m_vPosition.x;
        y = m_vPosition.y;
        z = m_vPosition.z;
}

// Sets the position of the frame
void CZenFrame::SetPosition( float x, float y, float z )
{
        m_vPosition.x = x;
        m_vPosition.y = y;
        m_vPosition.z = z;
}
```

That may be easy, but wait until you see the code that creates the transformation matrix. Recall that all the objects that belong to a frame have their positions and orientations set based on the properties of the parent frame. Well, this requirement means that the frame must compute a transformation matrix that can be set as the current world matrix during the rendering of the frame, so that the child objects will automatically reflect the attributes of the parent frame. And this process isn't a one-off either—it must happen every frame and involves the following steps:

1. Update the position of the object based on its velocity.
2. Create a translation matrix based on the frame's position.
3. Create an x-axis rotation matrix based on the pitch of the frame.
4. Create a y-axis rotation matrix based on the yaw of the frame.
5. Create a z-axis rotation matrix based on the roll of the frame.
6. Concatenate all those matrices into a single matrix.
7. Keep a copy of the matrix locally in case a child needs it.
8. Finally, set the concatenated matrix as the world matrix.

Here is the code for the CZenFrame::Update() function:

```
void CZenFrame::Update()
{

        // Create some temporary matrices for the
        // rotation and translation transformations
        D3DXMATRIX mRotX, mRotY, mRotZ, mTrans, mRotTemp;

        // Update the position by the velocity
        m_vPosition.x += m_vVelocity.x;
        m_vPosition.y += m_vVelocity.y;
        m_vPosition.z += m_vVelocity.z;

        // Set the translation matrix
        D3DXMatrixTranslation( &mTrans, m_vPosition.x, m_vPosition.y, m_vPosition.z
);

        // Set the rotation around the x-axis
        D3DXMatrixRotationX( &mRotX, m_Pitch );
        // Set the rotation around the y-axis
        D3DXMatrixRotationY( &mRotY, m_Yaw );
        // Set the rotation around the z-axis
        D3DXMatrixRotationZ( &mRotZ, m_Roll );

        // Concatenate the y-axis and x-axis rotation matrices
        D3DXMatrixMultiply( &mRotTemp, &mRotX, &mRotY );
```

```
// Concatenate the x- and y-axes and z-axis rotation matrices
D3DXMatrixMultiply( &mRotTemp, &mRotZ, &mRotTemp );
// Concatenate the x-, y-, and z-axes and translation matrices
D3DXMatrixMultiply( &mTrans, &mRotTemp, &mTrans );

// Update the copy of the local matrix
m_mLocal = mTrans;

// Set the world matrix
g_pDevice->SetTransform( D3DTS_WORLD, &mTrans );

}
```

I know, I know—I hate mathematics too. But now that you have the code you don't need to worry about it anymore. Now let me show you how to add objects to the frame.

Adding Objects to the Frame

Adding objects to a frame involves a number of steps. I could do it the easy way, but because I'm a nice guy I'll show you how the big boys do it. To add an object to the frame you need to do the following:

1. Call the AddFrame() function and pass the address of the object that you want to add.
2. Make sure that the pointer to the object is valid.
3. Inform the object that it has a new parent frame.
4. If the object list has not been created, then create it by setting the object as the first object in the list.
5. On the other hand, if the list does exist, then find the last item in the list and add the new object after that.

Anyway, have a look at the code that follows and see how it connects to the steps just mentioned.

```
HRESULT CZenFrame::AddObject( CZenObject* pNewObject )
{
        // Return if the new object is bogus
        if( !pNewObject )
                return E_FAIL;
```

```
        // Tell the object it has a new parent frame
        pNewObject->SetParentFrame( this );

        // If the object list does not exist yet...
        if( !m_pObjectList )
        {
                // ...Set this object to the start of the list
                m_pObjectList = pNewObject;
        }
        else
        {
                // ...The list has already been created
                // so add this object to the end of the list

                // Get a pointer to the start of the list
                CZenObject* pObject = m_pObjectList;

                // Find the last object in the list
                while( pObject->GetNext() )
                        pObject = (CZenObject*)pObject->GetNext();

                // Add this to the last item in the list
                pObject->SetNext( pNewObject );
        }

        return S_OK;
}
```

You're almost there. The objects can be added and have their properties updated.
All that's left is to render them....

Rendering Frames

Compared to the last few functions I showed you, rendering is remarkably simple.
All you have to do is loop through each of the child objects in the list and call the
`CZenObject::Render()` function. Here is the code:

```
HRESULT CZenFrame::Render()
{
```

```
        // Return if the object list has not been created yet
        if( !m_pObjectList )
                return E_FAIL;

        // Get a pointer to the start of the list
        CZenObject* pObject = m_pObjectList;

        // Update the position and orientation of the frame
        // and set the new world transform matrix
        Update();

        // Loop for each object in the list
        while( pObject )
        {
                // Render the object
                pObject->Render();

                // Increment to the next object in the list
                pObject = (CZenObject*)pObject->GetNext();
        }

        return S_OK;

}
```

What I'm going to do is wait until we get frames fully implemented with hierarchies before showing you some really cool examples of what you can achieve with them. But phew—now that the introduction to frames is out of the way I can elaborate on a million other points. For instance, lights!

The Light of My Life

Lights are another part of Direct3D that take well to encapsulation into a simple class, in fact, way more so than materials. In Direct3D, lights are just structures containing a bunch of colors and property information, and they work on an index basis. That is, you can create a bunch of lights and give each one a unique identifier. To update a light you tell Direct3D the index of the light that you want to modify, and then pass it a new D3DLIGHT8 structure which contains the updated information about the light in question. Think of it as the same way in which Windows uses handles to look after resources. However, the problem is keeping the light structures correlated properly with the index value by which Direct3D references them.

The solution? Just encapsulate everything into an object that looks after itself. So you can think of a light in the game as an actual light. That is, all you have to do is set its position, its color, and whether you want it on or off, and it will look after all the messy details of informing and maintaining its technical status with Direct3D. Another advantage to encapsulating the light is that filling out a massive D3DLIGHT8 structure is every time you want to create a simple light is a total pain.

Defining CZenLight

With all that firing around your brain, let's look at the code. Here is the class definition:

```
// ---------------- class CZenLight

static UINT g_LightCounter = 0;

class CZenLight : public CZenObject
{
public:
        CZenLight();
        ~CZenLight();

// Variables
public:
        D3DLIGHT8 m_Light;

protected:

        int m_ID;            // The lights index
        BOOL m_bIsOn;        // Is the light on?

// Functions:
public:
        // Sets the light's color properties
        void SetDiffuselater( float r, float g, float b );
        void SetSpecular( float r, float g, float b );
        void SetAmbient( float r, float g, float b );
```

```
        // Turns the light on or off
        void Enable( BOOL bEnable );
        // Returns the status of the light
        BOOL IsOn(){ return m_bIsOn; }

        // Updates the status of the light
        HRESULT Render();

        // Returns the size of the light object (in bytes)
        int GetSize(){ return sizeof( *this ); }
protected:

};
```

Notice that global static variable called g_LightCounter just before the class definition? Well, I use that to generate the index for the light. Remember I was talking about the way that Direct3D looks after lights? It differentiates between them by giving each one a unique ID. You could implement a complicated unique number generator to make sure that every new light you have has a unique ID, but there is a much easier way: just create a counter variable and increment it every time a new light is created, and then set the ID of the light to the new value of the counter. That way, unless you happen to have more than 4,294,967,296 lights, the lights will never get an ID that is not unique. I'll show you more on this in a second.

As you can see, the class definition is based around only three member variables. m_Light is the D3DLIGHT8 structure that contains all the information about the light. m_ID is an integer that looks after the unique index ID of the light that I was describing in the last paragraph; it is set in the constructor. And finally, m_bIsOn is there to track the status of the light's activation. In other words, it is TRUE when the light is on and FALSE otherwise.

Have a look at the constructor to see how the unique ID is set for lights as they are created:

```
CZenLight::CZenLight()
{
        // Zero out the D3DLIGHT8 structure
        ZeroMemory( &m_Light, sizeof( D3DLIGHT8 ) );

        // Set the initial type to point
        m_Light.Type = D3DLIGHT_POINT;
```

```
        // Set the initial color to white
        m_Light.Diffuse.r = 1.0f;
        m_Light.Diffuse.g = 1.0f;
        m_Light.Diffuse.b = 1.0f;

        // Set the attenuation
        m_Light.Attenuation0 = 1.0f;

        // Set the initial range to 100 units
        m_Light.Range = 100.0f;

        // Set the index based on a static counter
        m_ID = g_LightCounter++;

        // Set the light status tracker to off
        m_bIsOn = FALSE;
}


CZenLight::~CZenLight()
{

}
```

NOTE

Don't forget that the ++ operator occurs *after* the assignment when it is placed as a suffix on the variable. In other words, the current value of g_LightCounter is copied into m_ID and *then* it is incremented. If I place the ++ operator as a prefix to the variable like this:

```
        m_ID = ++g_LightCounter;
```

it will increment the value of g_LightCounter and *then* copy its value into m_ID.

The Color of Light

For this class I create some helper functions to make it easier to set the color properties of the light. You can see this code here:

```
// Sets the ambient color of the light
void CZenLight::SetAmbient( float r, float g, float b )
{
```

```
        m_Light.Ambient.r = r;
        m_Light.Ambient.g = g;
        m_Light.Ambient.b = b;
}

// Sets the diffuse color of the light
void CZenLight::SetDiffuse( float r, float g, float b )
{
        m_Light.Diffuse.r = r;
        m_Light.Diffuse.g = g;
        m_Light.Diffuse.b = b;
}

// Sets the specular color of the light
void CZenLight::SetSpecular( float r, float g, float b )
{
        m_Light.Specular.r = r;
        m_Light.Specular.g = g;
        m_Light.Specular.b = b;
}
```

Turn on the Lights!

There comes a time in the life of every light where it reaches that point of no return, when it finally, after all the waiting, gets to be turned on. The code to turn on a light is surprisingly simple. You just have to make a call to IDirect3DDevice8::LightEnable() and pass a value of TRUE or FALSE telling it whether you want it on or off, respectively.

```
// Turns the light on or off
void CZenLight::Enable( BOOL bEnable )
{
        // Update the tracking variable
        m_bIsOn = bEnable;
        // Change the status of the light
        g_pDevice->LightEnable( m_ID, bEnable );
}
```

LightEnable() is one of those functions that is so simple you wonder if it was actually programmed by Microsoft or if they stole it off the Russians or something. I mean you just tell it what light you are talking about and then say whether you want it on or off. You don't need to tell it about the source country where the virtual copper for the wires came from, you don't need the ambient temperature of the conducting part of the bulb, you don't even need to know the average speed of electricity and how it varies in different parallel universes. Does this sound like Microsoft? I didn't think so either!

Anyway, for completeness here is the prototype for LightEnable():

```
HRESULT LightEnable(
    DWORD LightIndex,
    BOOL bEnable
);
```

LightIndex takes the index of the light of which you want to modify the status, and bEnable takes the TRUE or FALSE switch that determines if the light is going to be on or off.

Updating Lights with Direct3D

I prefer to use functions like those just discussed instead of filling in member structures because it is much more intuitive. So that's the easy stuff out of the way; let's get a little jiggy and check out the Render() function for the light.

```
// Puts the light at the same location as the parent frame
HRESULT CZenLight::Render()
{
        // The local matrix of the parent frame
        D3DXMATRIX ParentMatrix;
        // The position of this light = Center of frame.
        D3DXVECTOR3 Position = D3DXVECTOR3( 0, 0, 0 );

        if( m_pParentFrame )
        {
                // Get the position from the parent frame
                ((CZenFrame*)m_pParentFrame)->GetLocal( ParentMatrix );

                // Transform the light's position by the matrix
                D3DXVec3TransformCoord( &Position, &Position, &ParentMatrix );

                // Update the position
                m_Light.Position = Position;
```

```
        }
    else
    {
            // Set the light to be at the origin
            m_Light.Position.x = 0;
            m_Light.Position.y = 0;
            m_Light.Position.z = 0;

            SetError( "Light being rendered without a parent frame" );

    }


        // Update the light with Direct3D
        g_pDevice->SetLight( m_ID, &m_Light );

        return S_OK;
}
```

Lights are a little weird, and extremely annoying really, because when you set their positions with Direct3D it just decides that it is going to completely ignore any world coordinate data. Instead, you have to set the coordinates as raw world coordinates yourself. That is the reason for the call to CZenFrame::GetLocal(); the light needs to find out the position of the parent frame in order to have the correct coordinates. The way you calculate this is very simple. First set up a position vector that is at the location (0, 0, 0), which is essentially saying that light is positioned at the center of its parent frame. Then retrieve the local matrix for the parent frame and multiply it by the position vector. This automatically calculates where the light should be. I mean how hard would it be for Microsoft to insert those two lines of code into Direct3D and then put in some render state flag like D3DRS_LIGHTUSEWORLD-MATRIX? I have a funny feeling they will soon, and if they do, you know where they got the idea from!

Notice also that if the light is being rendered without first being inserted in a frame it outputs a debug error. Afterward I set the properties for the light with a call to IDirect3DDevice8::SetLight(), which has the following prototype:

```
HRESULT SetLight(
    DWORD Index,
    CONST D3DLIGHT8* pLight
);
```

The first parameter takes the index value for the light that you want to set the coordinates for, and the second takes the address of a D3DLIGHT8 structure that describes how you want the light to look. In this case, I just passed the light's ID and the member m_Light structure.

Ambient Lights

Well, CZenLight works nicely for all light styles (point, parallel, spot) except for the ambient light style. The ambient light for your scene is set with a function call to IDirect3DDevice8::SetRenderState(). To make it a little more intuitive to set the ambient light, I have created a small function to set the ambient light. Check out the code below.

```
void SetAmbientLight( D3DCOLOR AmbientColor )
{
        // Set the ambient light
        g_pDevice->SetRenderState( D3DRS_AMBIENT, AmbientColor );
}
```

Using CZenLight

As you know, lights come in a variety of shapes and sizes, but in Direct3D they only come in three types. Well, four actually, but ambient lights don't really count. To set the type of light you must set it manually in the D3DLIGHT8 structure. By default the light type is set to a point light. To create a new light is simple; just type

```
CZenLight g_Light;
```

and that's it. To change the color to red, you could make a call to one of the property functions, like this:

```
g_Light.SetDiffuse( 1.0f, 0.0f, 0.0f );
```

Lights need to be added to a frame before they can be used. So if you have a frame lying around you can type

```
g_Frame.AddObject( &g_Light );
```

And of course finally the light needs to be turned on if you want it to affect any of the objects in the scene.

```
g_Light.Enable( TRUE );
```

To make sure the light keeps in the place you want it to be in you need to call `Render()` on its parent frame.

```
g_Frame.Render();
```

You may remember that the constructor for `CZenLight` automatically sets the type of the light to be a point light (`D3DLIGHT_POINT`) by default. Following is an example of how to set the light to another type:

```
g_Light.m_Light.Type = D3DLIGHT _SPOT;
```

Advanced Synchronization

As you are brainier than most, I'm sure that you noticed throughout your trip through this book that the frame rate varies widely depending on what is within a scene, and also on the card being used to do the rendering. For instance, if you look back at some of the earlier screen shots you may see some frame rates as low as 15 fps while others are up over 300 fps. The slower rates are generally from when I was testing the code on older cards like an ATI 3D Rage Pro TURBO or an early Voodoo. The faster rates come from the newer GeForce2/3 cards and the Matrox Millennium G450 (my favorite—and not just because they are paying me to say it).

But what I'm getting at with all these figures is that the execution rate of your game will vary widely depending on scene complexity and the resources of the host machine. This variance leads to many problems. For instance, if you want to set the velocity of a character so that it moves 2 pixels every frame, then it will move 60 pixels a second on a computer running at 30 fps, but it will go at 800 pixels per second on a 400 fps system. Which is annoying because, as you know, you generally want to give players on differing systems a similar experience when playing your game.

There are two solutions to this problem, one more complex than the other, but with similar results. Basically, you need a scaling factor with which you can modify the speed of objects based on how fast the game is executed. This scaling factor can be computed by either computing the amount of time that has elapsed since the last frame or by measuring how far the frame rate has deviated from some norm, such as 25 fps. The time method gives superior results but can be restrictive and a pain to implement. So I am going to compute the value by comparing how far the frame rate has deviated.

It works like this: The deviance is computed by dividing the frame rate by 25.

$$Deviance = FrameRate / 25;$$

If the frame rate is 25 fps, then the deviance will be zero, so the velocities of objects will not need to be modified. However, if the frame rate rises to 50, then the deviance will be 2, and the velocities will need to be halved. Similarly, if the frame rate drops to 15, then the deviance will be 0.6, and the velocities will need to be increased.

Implementing this is very easy. Just declare a global floating-point variable called g_Frequency.

```
float g_Frequency = 0.0f;
```

And then add the computational code into the FrameCount() function, which gets called every frame anyway.

```
void FrameCount()
{
        INT64 NewCount = 0;              // The current count
        static INT64 LastCount = 0;     // The last count
        INT64 Difference = 0;           // The difference since the last count

        // Get the current count
        QueryPerformanceCounter( (LARGE_INTEGER*)&NewCount );

        // If the count is zero then this system does not have
        // high performance timers
        if( NewCount == 0 )
                SetError( "The system does not support high resolution timing" );

        // Increase the frame count
        g_FrameCount++;

        // Compute the difference since the last count
        Difference = NewCount - LastCount;

        // If more than a second has passed
        if( Difference >= g_Frequency )
        {
                // Record the number of elapsed frames
                g_FrameRate = g_FrameCount;
```

```
                // Reset the counter
                g_FrameCount = 0;

                // Update the last count
                LastCount = NewCount;
        }

        // Compute the deviance in the frame rate for synchronization
        g_FrameDeviance = (float)g_FrameRate / 25.0f;

}
```

You can then use g_FrameDeviance to compute a more realistic update value for your game objects.

Extending the Camera

I showed you a little bit of code two chapters ago that encapsulated the view matrix into a *camera* class. The code I showed you was great except for the fact that it was really bad. I mean it was fine for an introduction, but because you want to know how the pros do this stuff, you need to get a little bit more advanced. In this section, I am going to show you the CZenCamera class again, except that this time things are going to get really jiggy. You will probably find some of the code that I'm going to show you familiar, because it is quite similar to the code in the CZenFrame class. Let me start by showing you the new definition for CZenCamera:

```
// ------------------- class CZenCamera
// Encapsulates the View matrix into a 'camera' class

class CZenCamera : public CZenObject
{
public:
        CZenCamera();
        ~CZenCamera();

// Functions:
public:

        // Sets/Gets the up vector
```

```cpp
void SetUp( float x, float y, float z );
void GetUp( float& x, float& y, float& z );

// Sets/Gets the right vector
void SetRight( float x, float y, float z );
void GetRight( float& x, float& y, float& z );

// Sets/Gets the velocity
void SetVelocity( float x, float y, float z );
void GetVelocity( float& x, float& y, float& z );

// Sets/Gets Position
void SetPosition(float x, float y, float z );
void GetPosition( float& x, float& y, float& z );

// Sets/Gets the look point
void SetLookPoint(float x, float y, float z );
void GetLookPoint( float& x, float& y, float& z );

// Updates the position of the camera
void Update();

// Moves the camera
void Move(float x, float y, float z );

// Sets the roll, pitch, or yaw
void SetRoll( float Roll );
void SetYaw( float Yaw );
void SetPitch( float Pitch );

// Returns the roll, pitch, or yaw
void GetRoll( float& Roll );
void GetYaw( float& Yaw );
void GetPitch( float& Pitch );

// Resets the camera back to the origin
void Reset();

// Nor implemented
HRESULT Render();
```

```cpp
          // Returns the size (in bytes) of this object
          int GetSize(){ return sizeof( *this ); }
protected:


// Variables
public:


protected:

          // The roll, pitch, and yaw
          // for the camera's orientation

          float m_Roll;
          float m_Pitch;
          float m_Yaw;

          // The position
          D3DXVECTOR3 m_Position;
          // The look at vector
          D3DXVECTOR3 m_LookAt;
          // The up vector
          D3DXVECTOR3 m_Up;
          // The right vector
          D3DXVECTOR3 m_Right;

          // The camera's velocity
          D3DXVECTOR3 m_Velocity;
};
```

Stop complaining. I know it's long—but you're a Zen guru, right? Well, deal with it. I'll cover all this code in a second, and I think the best place to start is to get you oriented.

Camera Orientation

Yep, you got it—more information on the pitch, roll, and yaw. From now on, think of the camera as a person's head. As you know, any normal person has three arrows sticking out of his head. Well, they do here in Scotland, anyway. One arrow is called the *up vector,* and it points up, surprisingly. Or, in a more mathematical sort of way, it is a vector, which when normalized has the value <0, 1, 0>. You can use the up vector to figure out which direction is up. If you set the up vector to <0, −1, 0>, then everything the face sees will be upside down. Similarly, the face also has another arrow, or vector, sticking out to the right of it, called the *right vector,* which, surprisingly, lets you figure out which way is right <1, 0, 0>. And finally, there is also a *look at vector,* which tells you in which direction the face is looking. Using these three vectors you can set any orientation that you want for the camera (see Figure 15.10).

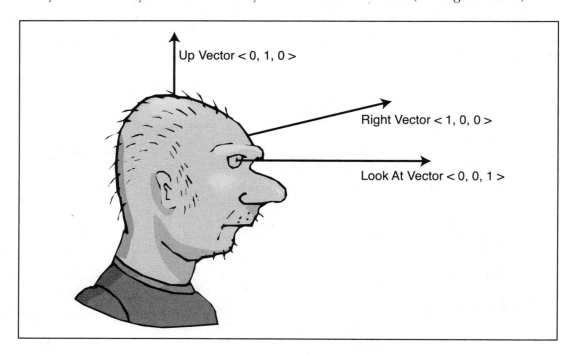

Figure 15.10

The up, right, and look at vectors

Recall from the introductory chapters that the view matrix exists so that you can translate and rotate all the objects in the scene so that they are straight down the positive z-axis. This allows the projection matrix to easily be set later on. So in other words, you want the view matrix to move every object in the scene inversely to the offset in orientation to the camera. For instance, if the camera has a pitch of 45° and a yaw of 20°, then you want the view matrix to rotate the pitch by −45° and the yaw by −20°. Previously, I glossed over the details of how you actually create this matrix and instead stuck in the just-left-of-useless function D3DXMatrixLookAtLH(). Don't get me wrong. The function is great for little sample applications, but when you want to get really advanced you need to learn how to program a view matrix yourself.

So with that in mind, I can introduce you to the member variables of your old friend CZenCamera. m_Pitch, m_Roll, and m_Yaw are there to hold the pitch, roll, and yaw of the camera. You'll recall from when I was talking about CZenFrame that this defines the rotations around the x-, z-, and y-axes, respectively. m_Position is the same as before—it holds the position of the camera in world coordinates. m_LookAt, m_Up, and m_Right are D3DVECTORs that hold the look at vector, up vector, and right vector that I mentioned a couple paragraphs ago. And finally, the m_Velocity vector looks after the velocity of the camera.

Let me show you the simple Get*/Set* code for this class before I show you the complicated stuff.

```
// Constructor
CZenCamera::CZenCamera()
{
        // Set the position
        m_Position      = D3DXVECTOR3( 0.0f, 0.0f,-1.0f );
        // Set the velocity to zero
        m_Velocity      = D3DXVECTOR3( 0.0f, 0.0f, 0.0f );

        // Set the look at vector to straight ahead
        m_LookAt        = D3DXVECTOR3( 0.0f, 0.0f,-1.0f );
        // Set the right vector to right
        m_Right         = D3DXVECTOR3( 1.0f, 0.0f, 0.0f );
        // Set the up vector to up
        m_Up            = D3DXVECTOR3( 0.0f, 1.0f, 0.0f );


        // Set the roll, pitch, and yaw to zero
        m_Roll = m_Pitch = m_Yaw = 0.0f;
}


// Destructor
CZenCamera::~CZenCamera()
{

}


// Moves the camera back to the origin
void CZenCamera::Reset()
{
```

```cpp
        m_Position      = D3DXVECTOR3( 0.0f, 0.0f,-1.0f );

        m_LookAt        = D3DXVECTOR3( 0.0f, 0.0f, 1.0f ); // z
        m_Right         = D3DXVECTOR3( 1.0f, 0.0f, 0.0f ); // x
        m_Up            = D3DXVECTOR3( 0.0f, 1.0f, 0.0f ); // y


        m_Roll = m_Pitch = m_Yaw = 0.0f;
}

// Moves the camera relative to its current position
void CZenCamera::Move( float x, float y, float z )
{

        m_Position.x += x;
        m_Position.y += y;
        m_Position.z += z;


}

// Sets the position of the camera
void CZenCamera::SetPosition( float x, float y, float z )
{
        m_Position.x = x;
        m_Position.y = y;
        m_Position.z = z;
}

// Gets the position for the camera
void CZenCamera::GetPosition( float& x, float& y, float& z )
{
        x = m_Position.x;
        y = m_Position.y;
        z = m_Position.z;
}

// Sets the roll of the camera
void CZenCamera::SetRoll( float Roll )
{
        m_Roll = Roll;
}
```

```cpp
// Gets the roll for the camera
void CZenCamera::GetRoll( float& Roll )
{
        Roll = m_Roll;
}


// Gets the yaw for the camera
void CZenCamera::GetYaw( float& Yaw )
{
        Yaw = m_Yaw;
}


// Sets the yaw for the camera
void CZenCamera::SetYaw( float Yaw )
{
        m_Yaw = Yaw;
}


// Gets the pitch for the camera
void CZenCamera::GetPitch( float& Pitch )
{
        Pitch = m_Pitch;
}


// Sets the pitch for the camera
void CZenCamera::SetPitch( float Pitch )
{
        m_Pitch = Pitch;
}


// Sets the point for the camera to look at
void CZenCamera::SetLookPoint( float x, float y, float z )
{
        m_LookAt.x = x;
        m_LookAt.y = y;
        m_LookAt.z = z;
}


// Gets the look vector
void CZenCamera::GetLookPoint( float& x, float& y, float& z )
{
```

```
        x = m_LookAt.x;
        y = m_LookAt.y;
        z = m_LookAt.z;
}


// Sets the up direction
void CZenCamera::SetUp( float x, float y, float z )
{
        m_Up.x = x;
        m_Up.y = y;
        m_Up.z = z;
}


// Gets the up vector
void CZenCamera::GetUp( float& x, float& y, float& z )
{
        x = m_Up.x;
        y = m_Up.y;
        z = m_Up.z;
}


// Sets the velocity
void CZenCamera::SetVelocity( float x, float y, float z )
{
        m_Velocity.x = x;
        m_Velocity.y = y;
        m_Velocity.z = z;
}


// Gets the velocity
void CZenCamera::GetVelocity( float& x, float& y, float& z )
{
        x = m_Velocity.x;
        y = m_Velocity.y;
        z = m_Velocity.z;
}


// Sets the right vector
void CZenCamera::SetRight( float x, float y, float z )
{
```

```
        m_Right.x = x;
        m_Right.y = y;
        m_Right.z = z;
}


// Gets the right vector
void CZenCamera::GetRight( float& x, float& y, float& z )
{
        x = m_Right.x;
        y = m_Right.y;
        z = m_Right.z;
}
```

As you can see, it is all pretty self-explanatory so far. All the code listed previously just updates member variables. The real code comes in the CZenCamera::Update() function, which recomputes the view matrix every frame depending on the camera's position.

Creating the View Matrix...the Hard Way

The main problem with the view matrix is that it can be tough to set up because of velocities and whatnot. Basically, from this moment on, you are no longer setting the position of the camera using a simple SetPosition() type of function. There are a few reasons for this. If you start at the origin, facing forward, and you want to move five units forward—you just add five to the z-coordinate. But what happens if you rotate to the right 45° and want to move forward two units? Well, you are going to need to move one unit in the x direction and one unit in the z direction if you want it to work properly. And it gets worse with other angles. The solution? Check out the code that follows, and then I will explain it.

```
// Updates the Direct3D view matrix
void CZenCamera::Update()
{
        // Update the x position
        m_Position.x += m_Velocity.x * m_Right.x;
        m_Position.y += m_Velocity.x * m_Right.y;
        m_Position.z += m_Velocity.x * m_Right.z;
```

```
// Update the y position
m_Position.x += m_Velocity.y * m_Up.x;
m_Position.y += m_Velocity.y * m_Up.y;
m_Position.z += m_Velocity.y * m_Up.z;

// Update the z position
m_Position.x += m_Velocity.z * m_LookAt.x;
m_Position.y += m_Velocity.z * m_LookAt.y;
m_Position.z += m_Velocity.z * m_LookAt.z;

D3DXMATRIX mPitch, mRoll, mYaw;

// Normalize and Regenerate the Look At, Right, and Up Vectors
D3DXVec3Normalize( &m_LookAt, &m_LookAt );
D3DXVec3Cross( &m_Right, &m_Up, &m_LookAt );
D3DXVec3Normalize( &m_Right, &m_Right );
D3DXVec3Cross( &m_Up, &m_LookAt, &m_Right );
D3DXVec3Normalize( &m_Up, &m_Up );

// Set up the y-axis rotation
D3DXMatrixRotationAxis( &mYaw, &m_Up, m_Yaw );
D3DXVec3TransformCoord( &m_LookAt, &m_LookAt, &mYaw );
D3DXVec3TransformCoord( &m_Right, &m_Right, &mYaw );

// Set up the x-axis rotation
D3DXMatrixRotationAxis( &mPitch, &m_Right, m_Pitch );
D3DXVec3TransformCoord( &m_LookAt, &m_LookAt, &mPitch );
D3DXVec3TransformCoord( &m_Up, &m_Up, &mPitch );

// Set up the z-axis rotation
D3DXMatrixRotationAxis( &mRoll, &m_LookAt, m_Roll );
D3DXVec3TransformCoord( &m_Right, &m_Right, &mRoll );
D3DXVec3TransformCoord( &m_Up, &m_Up, &mRoll );

D3DXMATRIX mView;

// Init the view matrix to an identity
D3DXMatrixIdentity( &mView );
```

```
        // Fill in the view matrix
        mView(0,0) = m_Right.x;
        mView(0,1) = m_Up.x;
        mView(0,2) = m_LookAt.x;

        mView(1,0) = m_Right.y;
        mView(1,1) = m_Up.y;
        mView(1,2) = m_LookAt.y;

        mView(2,0) = m_Right.z;
        mView(2,1) = m_Up.z;
        mView(2,2) = m_LookAt.z;

        mView(3,0) = - D3DXVec3Dot( &m_Position, &m_Right );
        mView(3,1) = - D3DXVec3Dot( &m_Position, &m_Up );
        mView(3,2) = - D3DXVec3Dot( &m_Position, &m_LookAt );

        // Set the view matrix
        g_pDevice->SetTransform( D3DTS_VIEW, &mView );
}
```

I think there is one word to describe that bad boy, and my editors won't let me print it. So instead of cursing, I'm going to run through it and explain it step by step.

Translating the Camera Position

Here is the first piece of code

```
// Update the x position
m_Position.x += m_Velocity.x * m_Right.x;
m_Position.y += m_Velocity.x * m_Right.y;
m_Position.z += m_Velocity.x * m_Right.z;

// Update the y position
m_Position.x += m_Velocity.y * m_Up.x;
m_Position.y += m_Velocity.y * m_Up.y;
m_Position.z += m_Velocity.y * m_Up.z;

// Update the z position
m_Position.x += m_Velocity.z * m_LookAt.x;
m_Position.y += m_Velocity.z * m_LookAt.y;
m_Position.z += m_Velocity.z * m_LookAt.z;
```

The first 100 times I looked at this code, and variations on it, I just could not for the life of me figure it out. No matter how many explanations I was given, or by whom, I just could not grasp what was going on. Until a couple of weeks later I woke up and just thought, "This morning is a good morning. Not only did I remember to take out my contact lenses before going to bed, but I also understand how the velocity updates the position of the camera in relation to the way it is pointing." To celebrate I had a shower, put in my contacts, and went back to sleep for a while, happy that I was genius.

I'm sure you can see what is going on in terms of the multiplications and so on. But here is where I keep my promise from Chapter 1. I'm going to explain the *why* bit. Because you want the camera to move the way it is pointing, that's why. When you press the Up button on the keyboard you don't mean "Hey game dude, move the camera down the z-axis." What you mean is "Hey game dude, move the camera a number of units in the direction that the camera is pointing." The code works by accumulating all the movements in the direction of the camera and then updating the main position coordinates (see Figure 15.11).

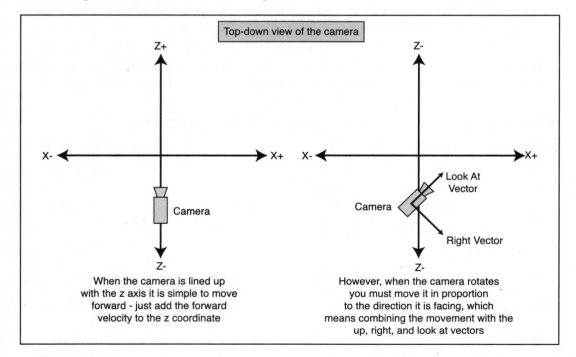

Figure 15.11

Moving the camera when its orientation is modified

Regenerating the Vectors

One of the problems with programming games on computers is that a lot of the time quality is sacrificed for speed. For instance, you could implement the latest ray-traced rendering techniques, but the speed would be so slow that you wouldn't be able to play anything very well at all. So instead, you make do with gouraud shading, which is fast but not very realistic. Another example is with floating point numbers. Unfortunately, there is just not enough precision in standard floating point numbers to make everything work properly all the time. This makes itself very obvious when dealing with camera coordinates. Basically, errors start to accumulate because of the rounding off that the processor has to do with low resolution floating point numbers. The result is that you get an up vector, a right vector, and a look at vector that are not perpendicular to each other, which can lead to interesting visual artifacts after a while (see Figure 15.12). The solution is to recompute the base vectors every update so that they are definitely perpendicular to each other, and that is exactly what the second piece of code achieves.

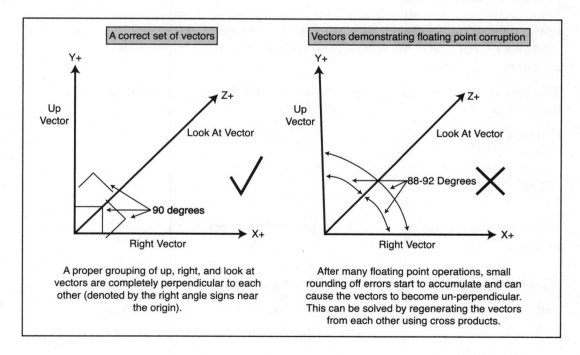

Figure 15.12

Regeneration of vectors is important to avoid corruption

```
// Normalize and Regenerate the Look At, Right, and Up Vectors
D3DXVec3Normalize( &m_LookAt, &m_LookAt );
D3DXVec3Cross( &m_Right, &m_Up, &m_LookAt );
D3DXVec3Normalize( &m_Right, &m_Right );
D3DXVec3Cross( &m_Up, &m_LookAt, &m_Right );
D3DXVec3Normalize( &m_Up, &m_Up );
```

Notice also how the vectors are all normalized so that they have a magnitude of 1. This is standard practice when dealing with vectors for the view matrix, as well as in many other cases. The function to normalize a vector that I use here is D3DXVec3Normalize(), and its prototype is as follows:

```
D3DXVECTOR3* D3DXVec3Normalize(
   D3DXVECTOR3* pOut,
   CONST D3DXVECTOR3* pV
);
```

pOut is a pointer to a D3DXVECTOR3 structure that receives the result of the operation. pV is the input vector that you want to normalize. By specifying the same vector for both parameters, you are telling Direct3D to normalize a vector and save the result in the same structure. By the way, the D3DXVECTOR3 structure is exactly the same as a D3DVECTOR except that it has some enhanced C++ functionality, such as overridden assignment operators.

The function to achieve a cross product is D3DXVec3Cross(). Its prototype is listed here.

```
D3DXVECTOR3* D3DXVec3Cross(
   D3DXVECTOR3* pOut,
   CONST D3DXVECTOR3* pV1,
   CONST D3DXVECTOR3* pV2
);
```

pOut takes the output from the cross product between the two D3DXVECTOR, pV1 and pV2.

Setting Up the Orientation

Setting up the orientation is an interesting process involving nine steps.

1. Create a yaw rotation matrix by figuring out the rotation of the camera around the y-axis.
2. Multiply the yaw matrix by the look at vector.

3. Multiply the yaw matrix by the right vector.
4. Create a pitch rotation matrix by figuring out the rotation of the camera around the x-axis.
5. Multiply the pitch matrix by the look at vector.
6. Multiply the pitch matrix by the up vector.
7. Create a roll rotation matrix by figuring out the rotation of the camera around the z-axis.
8. Multiply the roll matrix by the right vector.
9. Multiply the roll matrix by the up vector.

The code pretty much follows those steps to the letter. Check it out:

```
// Set up the y-axis rotation
D3DXMatrixRotationAxis( &mYaw, &m_Up, m_Yaw );
D3DXVec3TransformCoord( &m_LookAt, &m_LookAt, &mYaw );
D3DXVec3TransformCoord( &m_Right, &m_Right, &mYaw );

// Set up the x-axis rotation
D3DXMatrixRotationAxis( &mPitch, &m_Right, m_Pitch );
D3DXVec3TransformCoord( &m_LookAt, &m_LookAt, &mPitch );
D3DXVec3TransformCoord( &m_Up, &m_Up, &mPitch );

// Set up the z-axis rotation
D3DXMatrixRotationAxis( &mRoll, &m_LookAt, m_Roll );
D3DXVec3TransformCoord( &m_Right, &m_Right, &mRoll );
D3DXVec3TransformCoord( &m_Up, &m_Up, &mRoll );
```

There are a few new functions that you may not have seen before. First up is D3DXMatrixRotationAxis(). You use this function by passing it an axis that you want to rotate a point around; pass it an angle, and it will construct a matrix for you. Here is the prototype:

```
D3DXMATRIX* D3DXMatrixRotationAxis(
  D3DXMATRIX* pOut,
  CONST D3DXVECTOR3* pV,
  FLOAT Angle
);
```

pOut, the first parameter, gives you the matrix that you wanted it to create. pV is the axis that you want to rotate around, and Angle is the angle about the axis.

Another *really* useful function is D3DXVec3TransformCoord(). It is so useful that I even put "really" in italics. That important. What the function does is to multiply a vector by a matrix and give you the result in a new vector. You could program this stuff yourself if you want, but hey, if it's already done for you, and done well, why bother? The function has the following prototype:

```
D3DXVECTOR3* D3DXVec3TransformCoord(
  D3DXVECTOR3* pOut,
  CONST D3DXVECTOR3* pV,
  CONST D3DXMATRIX* pM
);
```

As you can see, the parameters are very similar to D3DXMatrixRotationAxis(). pOut takes a pointer to a D3DXVECTOR3 structure, which will be filled with the result of the operation. pV is the source vector that you want to multiply by the source matrix, which is called pM.

Creating the View Matrix

Now that all—well, almost all—the calculations are complete, the next step is to just fill in the view matrix with the required information and tell Direct3D about it. A view matrix looks like this

$$
\begin{bmatrix}
\text{Right X,} & \text{Up X,} & \text{Look At X,} & 0 \\
\text{Right Y,} & \text{Up Y,} & \text{Look At Y,} & 0 \\
\text{Right Z,} & \text{Up Z,} & \text{Look At Z,} & 0 \\
-(\text{Right} \cdot \text{Position}), & -(\text{Up} \cdot \text{Position}), & -(\text{Look At} \cdot \text{Position}), & 1
\end{bmatrix}
$$

Right is the right vector, Up is the up vector, Look At is the look at vector, and Position is the position of the camera. The code to fill in the matrix in this fashion is as follows:

```
D3DXMATRIX mView;

// Initialize the view matrix to an identity
D3DXMatrixIdentity( &mView );
```

```
// Fill in the view matrix
mView(0,0) = m_Right.x;
mView(0,1) = m_Up.x;
mView(0,2) = m_LookAt.x;

mView(1,0) = m_Right.y;
mView(1,1) = m_Up.y;
mView(1,2) = m_LookAt.y;

mView(2,0) = m_Right.z;
mView(2,1) = m_Up.z;
mView(2,2) = m_LookAt.z;

mView(3,0) = - D3DXVec3Dot( &m_Position, &m_Right );
mView(3,1) = - D3DXVec3Dot( &m_Position, &m_Up );
mView(3,2) = - D3DXVec3Dot( &m_Position, &m_LookAt );
```

One thing to note here is the this-is-so-Microsoft feature of the D3DXMATRIX structure, and in particular its C++ extensions. You would think that since every single mathematician in the world since the dinosaurs has indexed into matrices starting at 1. For instance, the very upper-left entry in a matrix is (1, 1) and the lower-right entry of a 4 x 4 is (4, 4). Even Microsoft follows this principle in D3DMATRIX. To get to entry (1, 1) you type

```
Matrix._11 = 5
```

Simple, right? Well, with D3DXMATRIX Microsoft decided to go for a 1-based index if you are indexing through the structure (for example, like the code snippet above), but went for a 0-based index for the C++ extensions. So depending on who you're talking to, in D3DXMATRIX (0, 0) means (1, 1), (3, 3) means (4, 4), and (4, 4) will cause a memory protection error (see Figure 15.13)! If you want more information look it up, uhhmmm. . . nowhere, because I discovered this myself the hard way, along with everyone else. Anyway, all that ranting and raving is the reason that the code doesn't quite match the instructions. So now you know.

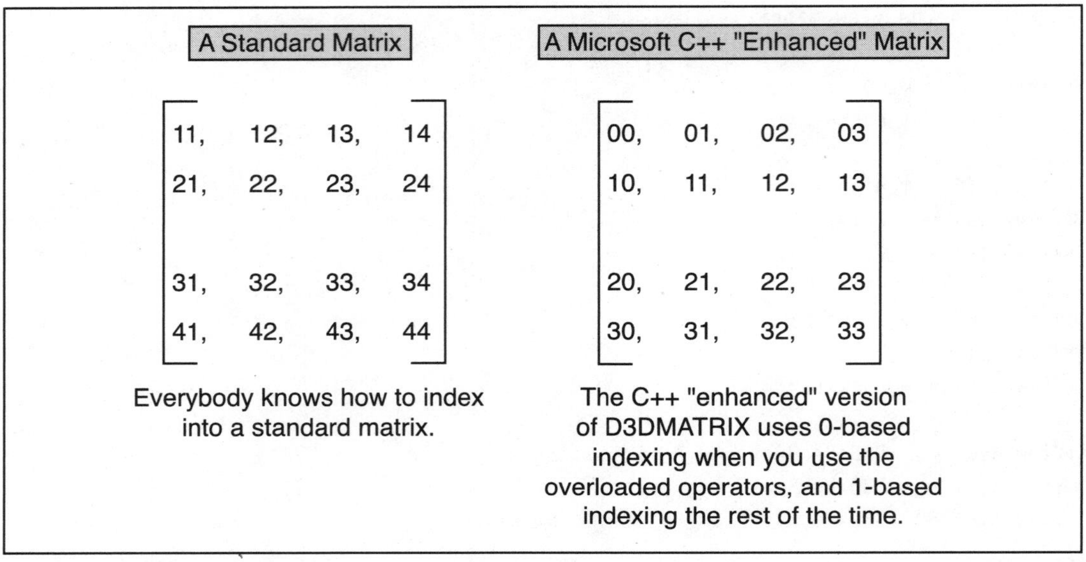

A Standard Matrix					A Microsoft C++ "Enhanced" Matrix			
11,	12,	13,	14		00,	01,	02,	03
21,	22,	23,	24		10,	11,	12,	13
31,	32,	33,	34		20,	21,	22,	23
41,	42,	43,	44		30,	31,	32,	33

Everybody knows how to index into a standard matrix.

The C++ "enhanced" version of D3DMATRIX uses 0-based indexing when you use the overloaded operators, and 1-based indexing the rest of the time.

Figure 15.13

Be careful with C++ enhanced Microsoft matrices—they may not behave like you expect.

There is also a new function that popped up. D3DXVec3Dot() is a simple function that computes the dot product of two functions. Here is the prototype

```
FLOAT D3DXVec3Dot(
  CONST D3DXVECTOR3* pV1,
  CONST D3DXVECTOR3* pV2
);
```

The parameters, pV1 and pV2, are the two source vectors for which you want to compute the dot product. The result of the operation is returned as the return value from the function.

Setting the View Matrix...Finally!

Well, this next bit of code should be a relief. It is only one line long, and you have already seen it in use before:

```
// Set the view matrix

g_pDevice->SetTransform( D3DTS_VIEW, &mView );
```

I would insert my usual "And that's it!" phrase here except, man, how much work was that?

Oh, Yes—Connecting the Camera to DirectInput

There comes a time in the life of every Zen engine when it wants to break out of its shell. And this is that time. All the technologies start to grow and grow until they can be connected up to be greater than the sum of their parts. Okay, maybe I'm exaggerating a little, but that's what happens when you type for 90 days solid without sleep. My beard keeps getting in the way of the keyboard.

Back to the code...so what have you got? A well-implemented and well-structured keyboard and mouse class, and also an easy-to-use camera object. What you need to complete now is the linkage of a new function, called `HandleInput()`, that is called every frame from the main `GameLoop()` function. This new function will look after acquiring any input from the input devices, and then notifying the relevant parts of the game that something needs doing. For now I'm just going to show you how to hook the camera up to the mouse, because it is the most convenient form of movement.

What we need for this is the global camera declared, as I discussed before.

```
CZenCamera g_Camera;
```

And then initialize the camera to some start position, if you want to.

```
g_Camera.SetPosition( 0, 5, 20 );
```

Then you need to make a call to the new `HandleInput()` function down in `GameInit()`.

```
int GameLoop()
{
        if( !g_bActive )
                return S_OK;

        FrameCount();

        HandleInput();

        Render();

        return S_OK;
}
```

Think about the kind of behavior you want your camera to have. You can always change it later, but at this stage it's a bad idea to think about implementing a terrain-tracking camera. For instance, a camera that does collision detection for walls, floors, stairs, etc., is something that you would implement much later on in the development process, after you had completed your collision detection code.

For now I just want to implement a simple camera. You may know from game level editing programs like QuakeEd or WorldCraft that a kind of "standard" exists for mouse-related camera movement. Generally, when you move the mouse forward or backward, the camera also moves forward or backward. Moving the mouse left or right causes the yaw of the camera to be changed; that is, moving the mouse left rotates the camera left, and moving the mouse right has the opposite effect. When you hold down the right mouse button the behavior changes so that moving forward or backward moves the camera up and down, and moving the mouse left or right moves the camera left or right, as opposed to rotating.

Check out the following code, which implements this functionality:

```
HRESULT HandleInput()
{
        if( g_Keyboard.IsKeyDown( DIK_ESCAPE ) )
             PostQuitMessage( 0 );

        float CameraX = 0.0f;
        float CameraZ = 0.0f;

        // Retrieve the current state of the mouse
        g_Mouse.Poll();

        // Scale the mouse movement so it moves slower
        CameraX = ((float)g_Mouse.GetMousePos().x / 8.0f);
        CameraZ = ((float)g_Mouse.GetMousePos().y / 8.0f);

        // If the right mouse button is down...
        if( g_Mouse.IsButtonDown( 1 ) )
        {
                // Move the camera up/down and left/right
                g_Camera.SetVelocity( CameraX, -CameraZ, 0 );
        }
        else
        {
                // ...Or if the right mouse button is up
                // move the camera forward/backward and
                // rotate the camera left/right
```

```
                float Yaw = 0.0f;
                Yaw = CameraX / 100.0f;

                // Set the Yaw
                g_Camera.SetYaw( Yaw );
                // Set the velocity
                g_Camera.SetVelocity( 0, 0, -CameraZ );
        }

        // Update the camera
        g_Camera.Update();

        return S_OK;
}
```

And that is all you need to be able to move around a 3D world with ease.

Miscellaneous Items

There are a few more things I want to cover that don't seem to fit in anywhere but that I think you may find useful when you start programming your own engines. The first is how to render GDI text efficiently onto a Direct3D render target.

Rendering Real Fonts

I showed you way back in the 2D chapters how to create your own bitmap-based font engine. However, there are times when you just want to render normal GDI text onto a Direct3D render target, without going through all the GDI copying nonsense. The guys at Microsoft must have thought this as well, because they have come up with an entire COM interface to make it simple to output text, using any Windows font to a surface.

The interface is called ID3DXFont, and as you can see from its name it's a member of the Direct3D utility library. It's really useful for rendering text to the screen, without bothering with the GDI. The font is based around the concept that you use one font object for each font that you want to output, if you get me. For instance, say you want to output three strings, each in a different font. To do this, you would create three font objects—one for each font—and then call DrawText() on each object that represents the correct font to output the right text for you to the screen. As with all DirectX COM objects, they are messy to deal with in their raw form, so I created a simple C++ class to encapsulate the functionality.

The CZenFont Class Definition

Check out the class definition that follows:

```cpp
// -------------- class CZenFont

class CZenFont
{
public:
        CZenFont();
        ~CZenFont();

// Variables
public:
        D3DCOLOR m_FontColor;

        int m_Align;

protected:
        LPD3DXFONT m_pFont;
        RECT m_FontRect;

        BOOL m_bInitialized;

// Functions:
public:
        HRESULT Initialize( HFONT hFont, D3DCOLOR FontColor );
        HRESULT OutputText( char* pString, int x, int y );
protected:

};
```

m_pFont is a pointer to the ID3DXFont object that this class encapsulates and, is created in the Initialize() function, which I will show you very shortly. m_FontColor is, you guessed right again, the color of the font, which is also set in the Initialize() function. m_Align is kind of interesting; it allows you to set the format for the way that the text aligns itself. By default I set it to DT_LEFT, which aligns the text to the left of the rectangle at which you specify for the text to be drawn. Other options include DT_RIGHT and DT_CENTER. m_FontRect holds the rectangle into which you want to render the text into. I'll show you how to calculate that bad boy in two ticks of an Apple G4 processor (about five minutes). And finally, m_bInitialized looks after the initialization status of the class, since it just won't work without being initialized. For your reference, here is the constructor and destructor for the class:

```
CZenFont::CZenFont()
{
        m_pFont = 0;

        // Set the default font color to red
        m_FontColor = D3DCOLOR_XRGB( 255, 0, 0 );

        // The object has not been initialized yet
        m_bInitialized = FALSE;

        // Align font to the left by default
        m_Align = DT_LEFT;
}


CZenFont::~CZenFont()
{
        // Release the font if it has been created
        if( m_pFont )
                m_pFont->Release();
}
```

Font Initialization

As I mentioned, the CZenFont object must be initialized before it will function properly. The Initialize() member function is shown below; it takes a handle to a Windows font that you want to render with, and also a color for the font. Then it takes this information and does all the rest of the dirty work for you.

```
HRESULT CZenFont::Initialize( HFONT hFont, D3DCOLOR FontColor )
{
        HRESULT r;

        // Release the font if it has already been created
        if( m_pFont )
        {
                m_pFont->Release();
                m_pFont = 0;
        }
```

```
        // Create the font
        r = D3DXCreateFont( g_pDevice, hFont, &m_pFont );
        if( FAILED( r ) )
        {
                SetError( "Could not create font" );
                return E_FAIL;
        }

        // Save the color
        m_FontColor = FontColor;

        // Set initialization flag to true.
        m_bInitialized = TRUE;

        return S_OK;
}
```

The first part of the code releases the font object, if it already exists. You have probably noticed code like this in a lot of the other code that I have created. When
dealing with resources such as DirectX COM objects, it is a good idea to take a pre-
vention-is-better-than-cure approach to memory leaks. After that, I create the
ID3DXFont with a call to D3DXCreateFont(), which has the following prototype:

```
HRESULT D3DXCreateFont(
  LPDIRECT3DDEVICE8 pDevice,
  HFONT hFont,
  LPD3DXFONT* ppFont
);
```

For those of you who like pain, there is also an associated function called
D3DXCreateFontIndirect(). However, D3DXCreateFont() is easy and does everything that
you could ever want it to, so I'll just stick with it. It takes three parameters: a
pointer to your device object, a handle for the font that you want to use, and finally
the address of a pointer that will be filled with the address of the newly-created font
object.

After the D3DXCreateFontIndirect() call, Initialize() moves on to save the color of the
font in a member variable and sets the m_bInitialized flag to TRUE. Notice that the
m_FontColor variable has public status, so you can change the color of the font at any
time, and the changes will take effect the next time you render it.

Rendering with CZenFont

Rendering is really simple, except that, in typical Microsoft fashion, it requires some totally pointless steps. All the code for rendering text to the screen is held in the function CZenFont::OutputText(). It is a very simple function that just takes the string you want to render and an x, y coordinate of where on the screen you want the text to appear.

```
HRESULT CZenFont::OutputText( char* pString, int x, int y )
{
        // Return if the class has not been initialized yet
        if( !m_bInitialized )
                return E_FAIL;

        HRESULT r;

        // Fill in the rect structure with the dest coords
        // for the font
        RECT FontRect = { x, y, 0, 0 };

        // Tell the font we are about to begin rendering
        m_pFont->Begin();

        // Calculate the rectangle for the string
        m_pFont->DrawText( pString, -1, &FontRect, DT_CALCRECT, 0 );

        // Render the string to the screen
        r = m_pFont->DrawText( pString, -1, &FontRect, m_Align, m_FontColor );

        // We are done rendering
        m_pFont->End();

        return r;
}
```

The code starts with the usual behavior of quitting, if it has not been initialized yet, because trying to render with a COM object that doesn't exist is really hard. Stay with me here; as I was saying, this is Microsoft territory. The first thing you need to do is create a RECT structure and fill in the x, y coordinates for where you want the text to appear—into the left and top members, respectively. Now here is where it gets really interesting. First you have to call ID3DXFont::Begin() so that the font can know that it is about to be used. Next you need to call the function `ID3DXFont::DrawText()` and tell it to calculate the rectangle on the screen that the string is going to take up. *Then* you need to call `DrawText()` again and tell *it* the rectangle (the one it just figured out for you) that the string is going to take up so that it can draw it properly. Don't ask me. Finally, you need to call `End()` so the font knows that for the time being it won't be used anymore. No, you are not watching the *Outer Limits*. This is the real world—well, the real Matrix anyway.

Using CZenFont Is Easy As Pie

To use your new font object, you follow the same pattern as for all the other code that I've written. You should try to follow this Zen philosophy as well—it is written in the ancient Buddhist scripts in Tibet: "Programmer who make everything work in kind of same way find it easier to sleep well at night and not wonder what go in McDonald's burger."

So if you want to output the text "I love San Francisco" in yellow, at the coordinates (10, 10), then you would implant the following code into the main `Render()` function:

```
// Declare a new CZenFont object
CZenFont Font;
// Initialize the font
Font.Initialize((HFONT)GetStockObject( SYSTEM_FONT ), D3DCOLOR_XRGB( 255, 255, 0 ) );

// Output the text
Font.OutputText( "I love San Francisco", 10, 10 );
```

Like I was saying, easy as pie. There are a couple of things to note about using `CZenFont`. The first is that you must *only* make calls to output text with `CZenFont` in between the main calls in `Render()` to `IDirect3DDevice8::BeginScene()` and `IDirect3DDevice8::EndScene()`. Otherwise, nothing will be output to the screen.

The other thing to note is that this class is not meant to *compete* with the alphabet functionality that I showed you before. The previous code relating to text output had to do with creating your own bitmap-based font engine. This code is just outputting standard Windows text to the screen. However, the really great thing about this class is that it can be used to output really classy TrueType fonts. I'm not going to show you how to do this because it's way off topic, but if you happen to be reading a "how to program windows" book then they will tell you how to create a TrueType font. When you have the font created, you can pass the handle for the font to the CZenFont object through its Initialize() function.

Direct3D Sprites

I showed you before how to create an entire sprite class from the ground up, but you may find it useful to know about the Direct3D sprite COM interface. I'm not going to develop this as far as the last sprite class—for instance, it won't support animation of images or indexing into bitmaps that hold more than one image—but you should find it really easy to extend it if you wanted, using the code from the previous class. Just to let you know, the performance of the Direct3D sprite class is pretty much the same as my software implementation, even though mine contains almost no optimizations. However, the Direct3D version does support some really useful functionality like rotation, scaling, and translation of the sprites. But enough introductions, let's get moving with the code.

First off, I have entitled the class I am about to show CZenSprite; this is opposed to the other sprite class, which you probably remember was called CSprite. Anyway, CZenSprite is based around the functionality of ID3DXSprite. This is a really simple COM interface that only has five functions, which I have listed in Table 15.1.

Table 15.1 Member Functions for ID3DXMesh

Function	Description
Begin()	Informs the sprite that you are about to start drawing
Draw()	Renders the sprite to the screen
DrawTransform()	Renders the sprite to the screen after applying a transform matrix that you supply
End()	Informs the sprite that you are finished rendering
GetDevice()	Retrieves the device that is being used to draw this sprite

The CZenSprite Class

The COM version is great, but as usual I'm going to encapsulate it into a `CZenSprite` so that it is easier to use and maps better to the functionality of the rest of the engine . Following is the definition for the class:

```
// ------------ class CZenSprite

class CZenSprite : public CZenObject
{
public:
        CZenSprite();
        ~CZenSprite();

// Variables:
public:
        // The center of rotation
        D3DXVECTOR2 m_RotCenter;
        // The translation factor
        D3DXVECTOR2 m_Translation;
        // The scaling factor
        D3DXVECTOR2 m_Scaling;
        // The angle of rotation
        float m_Rotation;

        // The color to modulate with the sprite
        D3DCOLOR m_ModulateColor;

protected:
        // The ID3DXSprite
        LPD3DXSPRITE m_pSprite;

        // The image to use for the sprite
        LPDIRECT3DTEXTURE8 m_pTexture;

        // The initialization status of the class
        BOOL m_bInitialized;

// Functions
public:
```

```
        // Initializes the sprite with an image from disk
        HRESULT Initialize( char* TexPathName );
        // Initializes the sprite with a texture already in memory
        HRESULT Initialize( LPDIRECT3DTEXTURE8 pTexture );

        // Renders the sprite
        HRESULT Render();

        int GetSize(){ return sizeof( *this ); }
protected:

};
```

As you can see, there are some interesting members for this class. First are those three vectors. Notice that they are of the type D3DXVECTOR2, which means that they are 2D vectors. That is, they have only two components: x and y. Images obviously have no third dimension, so there is no point including a z-coordinate.

m_RotCenter contains the coordinates that you want to use for the position that you want to rotate the image around—that is, if you choose to rotate the image. For instance, the point (0, 0) would mean you wanted to rotate the sprite around the upper-left corner of the image. m_Translation contains the translation for the image, or, in other words, how much you offset it from the upper-left corner of the screen. m_Scaling also contains a scalar value specifying by how much you want to scale the image. A value of (0.5, 0.5) would cause the image to shrink by 50 percent. m_Rotation contains a value specifying the angle by which you want to rotate the image.

m_ModulateColor is kind of interesting. This is a color that will be modulated, or combined with, the source image in order to change its appearance. The result is that the image retains its visual appearance but maps all its colors to be very similar to the modulation color. For instance, if you had a blue texture representing water and you modulated it with the color red, then you would get a texture that looked very much like lava. You can use this technique on the fly to create other interesting effects as well. For instance, if you were to quickly flash a player sprite with the color red as he was getting shot, it would be a good visual indicator for the player to move out of the way of the bullets. Hey, some people don't know that bullets are bad.

Don't forget that all the previous members have public member status so you can change them at any time and the changes will be updated the next time you render the sprite. So if you want to change the rotation, just go ahead and modify the member variable. You won't break anything—don't worry!

m_pSprite is just a pointer to the ID3DXSprite object that I was talking about before. This pointer is initialized in the ever famous Initialize() function.

m_pTexture is a pointer to the texture that you want to use to render for the sprite. At the moment it only supports a single image that is set during initialization. However, this could easily be expanded to read into larger texture files like I did in CSprite.

Following is the code for the constructor and destructor:

```
// Constructor
CZenSprite::CZenSprite()
{
        m_pSprite = 0;
        m_pTexture = 0;

        m_bInitialized = FALSE;

        m_RotCenter.x = 0.0f;
        m_RotCenter.y = 0.0f;

        m_Translation.x = 0.0f;
        m_Translation.y = 0.0f;

        m_Scaling.x = 1.0f;
        m_Scaling.y = 1.0f;

        m_ModulateColor = D3DCOLOR_XRGB( 255, 255, 255 );

        m_Rotation = 0.0f;
}
```

This code initializes the pointers to 0, sets the center of rotation to the center of the image, sets the translation to 0, and sets the scale factor to one, which causes it not be scaled at all. And finally, the modulation color is set to white, which leaves the images as they are.

```
// Destructor
CZenSprite::~CZenSprite()
{
        // Release the ID3DXSprite if it exists
        if( m_pSprite )
                m_pSprite->Release();
```

```
        // Release the texture if it exists
        if( m_pTexture )
                m_pTexture->Release();
}
```

The destructor releases the sprite and texture object, if they exist, to avoid memory leaks.

Initialization

You may have noticed from the class definition that I created two different versions of the initialization function: one that loads an image from the disk, and another that uses an image that already exists in memory. Let's look at the disk version first:

```
// Initializes the sprite with an image from the disk
HRESULT CZenSprite::Initialize( char* TexPathName )
{
        HRESULT r = 0;

        // Load the texture from disk into memory
        r = D3DXCreateTextureFromFile( g_pDevice, TexPathName, &m_pTexture );
        if( FAILED( r ) )
        {
                SetError( "Couldnt load texture for sprite.  Pathname is" );
                SetError( TexPathName );
                return E_FAIL;
        }

        // Create a new ID3DXSprite object
        r = D3DXCreateSprite( g_pDevice, &m_pSprite );
        if( FAILED( r ) )
        {
                SetError( "Failed Sprite Creation" );
                return E_FAIL;
        }

        m_bInitialized = TRUE;

        return S_OK;
}
```

This function is pretty simple, as you can see—it just loads an image from disk into a texture and then creates a new sprite object with a call to D3DXCreateSprite(), which has the following prototype:

```
HRESULT D3DXCreateSprite(
    LPDIRECT3DDEVICE8 pDevice,
    LPD3DXSPRITE* ppSprite
);
```

The first parameter is a pointer to the device that you want to use to render the device. You can just set this to the device that you use for everything else. The second parameter takes the usual address of a pointer that will be filled the address of the newly created sprite.

Now let me show you the second version of the Initialize() function:

```
// Initializes the sprite with an image already in memory
HRESULT CZenSprite::Initialize( LPDIRECT3DTEXTURE8 pTexture )
{
        HRESULT r = 0;

        // Return if the texture is invalid
        if( !pTexture )
                return E_FAIL;

        // Keep a copy of the texture
        m_pTexture = pTexture;
        // Add a reference texture
        pTexture->AddRef();

        // Create the sprite object
        r = D3DXCreateSprite( g_pDevice, &m_pSprite );
        if( FAILED( r ) )
        {
                SetError( "Failed Sprite Creation" );
                return E_FAIL;
        }

        // Set the initialization flag to true
        m_bInitialized = TRUE;

        return S_OK;
}
```

It is pretty much the same except for the first two steps. First it makes sure that the parameter passed to it in the formal parameter is correct. If it is not, then it just returns failure because there is no point in rendering a sprite that doesn't have an associated image—it would be invisible! Next the code makes a copy of the pointer to the texture and saves it as a member variable. Since this is a COM object, I make another call to increase the reference count of the object. This is *very* important because if you do not increase the reference count, and then the original pointer is released, there is a very high chance the texture will be removed from memory. That would mean that the next time your sprite tried to access its texture, you would cause a memory fault, which as I've said before is a total bummer, dude. The rest of the function follows the same pattern as the first version of Initialize().

Rendering with CZenSprite

Rendering is really simple, since this class has only minimum functionality; it just renders an image at a certain point, possibly with scaling, translation, and rotation. Considering that Microsoft produced the rendering code, it's surprisingly simple to follow. There are three main steps.

1. Call ID3DXSprite::Begin() so that Direct3D knows you are about to start rendering the sprite.
2. Call ID3DXSprite::Draw() to perform the actual rendering of the sprite.
3. Call ID3DXSprite::End() to inform Direct3D you are finished rendering this sprite.

Have a quick look at the code to see the steps in action:

```
// Renders the sprite to the screen
HRESULT CZenSprite::Render()
{
        // Return if not initialized
        if( !m_bInitialized )
                return E_FAIL;

        HRESULT r = 0;

        // Tell sprite it is about to be rendered
        m_pSprite->Begin();
```

```
        // Draw the sprite
        r = m_pSprite->Draw( m_pTexture, NULL, &m_Scaling, &m_RotCenter,
                                        m_Rotation, &m_Translation,
m_ModulateColor );
        if( FAILED( r ) )
        {
                SetError( "Failed to render CZenSprite" );
        }

        // End drawing with this sprite
        m_pSprite->End();

        return S_OK;
}
```

After making sure that the class has been initialized, the code moves on to make the initial call to Begin(). Then the rendering of the sprite is made with a call to Draw(), which has the following prototype:

```
HRESULT Draw(
  LPDIRECT3DTEXTURE8 pSrcTexture,
  CONST RECT* pSrcRect,
  CONST D3DXVECTOR2* pScaling,
  CONST D3DXVECTOR2* pRotationCenter,
  FLOAT Rotation,
  CONST D3DVECTOR2* pTranslation,
  D3DCOLOR Color
);
```

As you can see, it's big fish. Table 15.2 gives the parameters.

Table 15.2 Draw() Parameters

Perameter	Definition
pSrcTexture	Takes the address of a texture with which you want to use to render. For this class I specify the member texture that was created during initialization.
pSrcRect	Takes the address of a RECT structure identifying the rectangle in the source texture that contains the section of the image that you want to render. This is where you could implement the functionality to index into a large image that contains multiple images.
pScaling	Takes the address of a D3DXVECTOR2 2D vector structure that identifies how much you want to scale the sprite.
pRotationCenter	Takes another D3DXVECTOR2 structure identifying where you want the center of the rotation to be, with (0, 0) indicating the upper-left corner.
Rotation	Contains the value that you want to rotate the image by, or just set it to zero if you don't want rotation.
pTranslation	Takes yet another pointer to a D3DXVECTOR2, although this time it specifies how far you want to translate the image from the origin.
Color	Takes the color that you want to modulate with the sprite. I talked about the modulation color a few pages ago when I was explaining the class definition for CZenSprite.

CZenSprite in Action

CZenSprite is another really easy-to-use object for the Zen engine. To use it you must follow these steps:

1. Create a new instance of CZenSprite.
2. Initialize the object with an image file that you want to use.
3. Render the sprite.

Or in a more C++ kind of way, you could do it like this:

```
// Create a new sprite
CZenSprite Sprite;

// Initialize the sprite with an Image
Sprite.Initialize( "Sprite.bmp" );

Sprite.Render()
```

Pretty easy, huh? I hope that short introduction to `ID3DXSprite` helped you. Actually, I say "short introduction," but as I think about it, I just showed you absolutely everything there is to the `ID3DXSprite`, except for animation and indexing.

The Vsync

I found with some of the code in this chapter that I was getting some annoying visual artifacts, such as flickering and tearing, on the screen, particularly at high frame rates. I want to show you a little piece of code that you can implement to get rid of them, in case you are getting them too. You'll recall that it's the computer updating the screen faster than the monitor can keep up that causes this problem. The solution is to just tell the computer to wait until the vertical retrace is in progress before it updates the screen. Unfortunately, this does effectively restrict your frame rate to whatever the monitor is running at, but this is still very fast.

The changes take place in the original `InitDirect3DDevice()` function that I showed you hundreds and hundreds of pages ago. Here is the current implementation:

```
// Initializes the Direct3D device
int InitDirect3DDevice( HWND hWndTarget, int Width, int Height, BOOL bWindowed,
        D3DFORMAT FullScreenFormat, LPDIRECT3D8 pD3D, LPDIRECT3DDEVICE8* ppDevice )
{
        // Structure to hold information about the rendering method
        D3DPRESENT_PARAMETERS d3dpp;
        // Structure to hold information about the current display mode
        D3DDISPLAYMODE d3ddm;

        HRESULT r = 0;

        if( *ppDevice )
                (*ppDevice)->Release();

        // Initialize the structure to zero
        ZeroMemory( &d3dpp, sizeof( D3DPRESENT_PARAMETERS ) );
```

```cpp
// Get the settings for the current display mode
r = pD3D->GetAdapterDisplayMode( D3DADAPTER_DEFAULT, &d3ddm );
if( FAILED( r ) )
{
        SetError( "Could not get display adapter information" );
        return E_FAIL;
}


// The width of the back buffer in pixels
d3dpp.BackBufferWidth = Width;
// The height of the back buffer in pixels
d3dpp.BackBufferHeight = Height;
// The format of the back buffer
d3dpp.BackBufferFormat = bWindowed ? d3ddm.Format : FullScreenFormat;

// The number of back buffers
d3dpp.BackBufferCount = 1;

// The type of multisampling
d3dpp.MultiSampleType = D3DMULTISAMPLE_NONE;
// The swap effect
d3dpp.SwapEffect = D3DSWAPEFFECT_COPY;

// The handle to the window that we want to render to
d3dpp.hDeviceWindow = hWndTarget;
// Windowed or fullscreen
d3dpp.Windowed = bWindowed;

// Let Direct3D manage the depth buffer
d3dpp.EnableAutoDepthStencil = TRUE;
// Set the depth buffer format to 16 bits
d3dpp.AutoDepthStencilFormat = D3DFMT_D16;

// Use the default refresh rate available
d3dpp.FullScreen_RefreshRateInHz = D3DPRESENT_RATE_DEFAULT;

// Present the information as fast as possible
d3dpp.FullScreen_PresentationInterval = bWindowed ? 0 :
                        D3DPRESENT_INTERVAL_IMMEDIATE;
// Allow the back buffer to be accessed for 2D work
d3dpp.Flags = D3DPRESENTFLAG_LOCKABLE_BACKBUFFER;
```

```
        // Acquire a pointer to IDirect3DDevice8
        r = pD3D->CreateDevice( D3DADAPTER_DEFAULT, D3DDEVTYPE_HAL,
                hWndTarget, D3DCREATE_SOFTWARE_VERTEXPROCESSING, &d3dpp, ppDevice );
        if( FAILED( r ) )
        {
                SetError( "Could not create the render device" );
                return E_FAIL;
        }

        // Save global copies of the device dimensions
        g_DeviceHeight = Height;
        g_DeviceWidth = Width;

        // Save a copy of the present params for use in device validation later
        g_SavedPresParams = d3dpp;

        return S_OK;
}
```

To make the code wait for the vertical retrace, you need to make the following changes:

```
// Initializes the Direct3D device
int InitDirect3DDevice( HWND hWndTarget, int Width, int Height, BOOL bWindowed,
        D3DFORMAT FullScreenFormat, LPDIRECT3D8 pD3D, LPDIRECT3DDEVICE8* ppDevice )
{
        // Structure to hold information about the rendering method
        D3DPRESENT_PARAMETERS d3dpp;
        // Structure to hold information about the current display mode
        D3DDISPLAYMODE d3ddm;

        HRESULT r = 0;

        if( *ppDevice )
                (*ppDevice)->Release();

        // Initialize the structure to zero
        ZeroMemory( &d3dpp, sizeof( D3DPRESENT_PARAMETERS ) );

        // Get the settings for the current display mode
        r = pD3D->GetAdapterDisplayMode( D3DADAPTER_DEFAULT, &d3ddm );
        if( FAILED( r ) )
        {
```

```
            SetError( "Could not get display adapter information" );
            return E_FAIL;
        }


        // The width of the back buffer in pixels
        d3dpp.BackBufferWidth = Width;
        // The height of the back buffer in pixels
        d3dpp.BackBufferHeight = Height;
        // The format of the back buffer
        d3dpp.BackBufferFormat = bWindowed ? d3ddm.Format : FullScreenFormat;

        // The number of back buffers
        d3dpp.BackBufferCount = 1;

        // The type of multisampling
        d3dpp.MultiSampleType = D3DMULTISAMPLE_NONE;
        // The swap effect
        d3dpp.SwapEffect = D3DSWAPEFFECT_COPY_VSYNC;

        // The handle to the window that we want to render to
        d3dpp.hDeviceWindow = hWndTarget;
        // Windowed or fullscreen
        d3dpp.Windowed = bWindowed;

        // Let Direct3D manage the depth buffer
        d3dpp.EnableAutoDepthStencil = TRUE;
        // Set the depth buffer format to 16 bits
        d3dpp.AutoDepthStencilFormat = D3DFMT_D16;

        // Use the default refresh rate available
        d3dpp.FullScreen_RefreshRateInHz = D3DPRESENT_RATE_DEFAULT;

        // Present the information as fast as possible
        d3dpp.FullScreen_PresentationInterval = bWindowed ? 0 :
D3DPRESENT_INTERVAL_ONE;
        // Allow the back buffer to be accessed for 2D work
        d3dpp.Flags = D3DPRESENTFLAG_LOCKABLE_BACKBUFFER;

        // Acquire a pointer to IDirect3DDevice8
        r = pD3D->CreateDevice( D3DADAPTER_DEFAULT, D3DDEVTYPE_HAL, hWndTarget,
                    D3DCREATE_SOFTWARE_VERTEXPROCESSING, &d3dpp, ppDevice );
```

```
if( FAILED( r ) )
{
        SetError( "Could not create the render device" );
        return E_FAIL;
}

// Save global copies of the device dimensions
g_DeviceHeight = Height;
g_DeviceWidth = Width;

// Save a copy of the pres params for use in device validation later
g_SavedPresParams = d3dpp;

return S_OK;
}
```

Let me start by warning you that this code will *not* work on all machines. In particular, it will not work on any cards that don't support the reporting of vsync status. If you are one of these unfortunate people you will know it, because the program will crash out almost as soon as you press Execute. For instance, one card on which I know it definitely doesn't work is my ATI 3D Rage Pro TURBO PCI. But that is a really old card these days, so yours probably should work. It works just fine on my dual-head Matrox Millennium G450.

Now let's look at the changes. The first is to change the SwapEffect member of D3DPRESENT_PARAMETERS to be equal to D3DSWAPEFFECT_COPY_VSYNC. This lets the Direct3D device know that you want it to monitor the status of the vsync. The second change is to tell Direct3D how you want it to react to the vsync. It can either ignore it, wait for the vsync before it copies, wait for two vsyncs, wait for three, or wait for four, before it copies. To achieve this change in behavior you need to set the FullScreen_PresentationInterval member of the structure to one of the values in Table 15.3.

Table 15.3   FullScreen_PresentationInterval Values

Flag	Description
D3DPRESENT_INTERVAL_DEFAULT	The back buffer will be presented to the primary surface at the device's default rate. This parameter must be set for windowed mode. It is equal to zero.
D3DPRESENT_INTERVAL_IMMEDIATE	The back buffer will be presented to the primary surface as quickly as possible, regardless of the vsync.
D3DPRESENT_INTERVAL_ONE	The back buffer will not be presented until one screen refresh has occurred.
D3DPRESENT_INTERVAL_TWO	The back buffer will not be presented until two screen refreshes have occurred.
D3DPRESENT_INTERVAL_THREE	The back buffer will not be presented until three screen refreshes have occurred.
D3DPRESENT_INTERVAL_FOUR	The back buffer will not be presented until four screen refreshes have occurred.

Personally, I can't really see any reason to use any of the flags except for the first three. The rest you could use for testing, I guess, but I can say that I have honestly never had any cause to even think about delaying for more than a single vsync. If you do, then be sure to let me know!

Conclusion

We have covered *a lot* of new stuff, ranging all the way from how to use materials, lights, and frames up to how to advanced timing, take advantage of the vsync, advanced Direct3D sprites, and how to render with Windows fonts!

You can call yourself a Zen guru even if you have only grasped half of what I have been bantering on about up to this point in the book. In the next chapter I'm going to show you how to advance frames so that you can start to create really advanced movement systems, and then move on to some examples to demonstrate the power of what you have created. And it *is* powerful—as of this chapter there are more than five thousand lines of code developed for the engine. As they say in *Quake III—Impressive!*

But don't start feeling all high and mighty just because you're a Zen guru. You still have far too much work for that. You only get to feel high and mighty when you're overworked after toiling away on a 1.5-year game project that is overbudget and mismanaged, plus your marriage is falling apart. (Not me, by the way. I'm not even married—I've just heard the horror stories. About the game industry, that is, not marriage!)

CHAPTER 16

Advanced Graphics Techniques

I went back in time the other day to hang out with Siddhartha Gautama. He was chillin' with some of his homeboys in da hood and he said, "Peter, as someone who spreads the ways of Zen graphics, you must put 110 percent into your work." So from now on I will put in 5 percent effort on Monday, 25 percent on Tuesday, 40 percent on Wednesday, 25 percent on Thursday, and maybe around 10–15 percent on Friday.

You will probably love this chapter because there is so much cool stuff that I'm going to show you, such as

- creating an extremely advanced frame-based hierarchical object-management system (phew!).
- how to implement frames efficiently with a really cool trip to the Zen solar system example program.
- using Direct3D to implement custom mouse cursors.
- how to implement bilinear filtering to get rid of the jaggies.
- how to implement scene antialiasing.
- Hhw to use the Direct3D texture utility to create alpha-blended surfaces and DDS files.

Frames are what set the immortals from the boys in terms of game engines, so I think they are definitely the best place to start.

Developing an Advanced Frame-Based Hierarchy System

I gave you quite a large introduction to frames in the last chapter, so you should now have a good knowledge of the theory behind why they are useful. But what have you got right now? Not much, compared to what you will have at the end of this section. At the moment you have a frame class that is capable of acting as a management container for objects. In other words, it is able to maintain a list of member objects, which can be anything from meshes to lights, and it can also modify the properties of its members. For instance, if you set the position or orientation for the frame, it will automatically read into its *child objects* and update them appropriately.

That's fantastic, but it doesn't really do much more than if you had just programmed the positioning logic straight into `CZenObject`. And that's what you are going to solve in this chapter. What you need to add to the frames is not just the ability to manage objects, but also to manage *child frames* as well. So a frame can be a parent of an object *and* a parent of a frame, which could also be a parent to another entire list of frames. It sounds really complex, and it kind of is, but frames are so great that your brain will absorb them easily. Fingers crossed.

A list of child frames is really useful because it allows you to create a tree of additive transformations. But what else would be good? How about a way to hook up the frames to advanced movement controls and AI hooks? For instance, say you have a frame that is used to hold the model of a bird that you want to fly in a large figure eight pattern in the sky. You could program this manually, but what about if two levels later you want to put in another bird? Programming all that code again would be a total waste of time. The solution? Allow the frame to be hooked up to an independent behavior control function. If you want the frame to be a bird you just "plug in" the bird program. And if you want it to be a fish, then you plug in the fish program. It's kind of like in *The Matrix*, except that you completely control the personality of the object.

Unfortunately, as much as I want to at this moment, I can't actually show you some of the amazing effects that you can create with this stuff because I just don't have room. That's bordering on physics and AI, and this is a graphics book. Tell you what—if you get enough of your friends to buy this book and sales are *really* high, I'll write a second volume that gets more advanced, while staying interesting, than any other book on the market. But don't despair, I'll show you some basic behavior routines and then you can go pick up a physics or AI book and implement the advanced behavior code yourself. But you will be amazed at what you can achieve with relatively little code. I know I sound like a marketing employee, but when you add all of the benefits of frames together they almost always form something greater than the sum of the parts.

Getting Changed

So what changes need to be made? Well, first is the change in structure to the class. It's going to need resources to hold information about the list of its child frames, not to mention its parents. Then the `Update()` and `Render()` functions are going to need modifications as well. And the frame needs to get some pointers added so that it can be used easily in a list. As you move through this section, try to get the terminology that relates to frames into your head because it is very important. Pay attention to how I use all the child and parent stuff in sentences and you will get a better understanding of everything that is going on.

Take a look at the new class definition that follows. The updates are in bold.

```
// ---------------- class CZenFrame
class CZenFrame;
typedef int (*FRAME_MOVEMENT_CALLBACK)( CZenFrame* pFrame, void* Parameter );


class CZenFrame
{
public:
        CZenFrame();
        ~CZenFrame();

// Variables
public:
        void* m_pParameter;

protected:
        // The local matrix for this frame
        D3DXMATRIX m_mLocal;

        // The position of this frame
        D3DXVECTOR3 m_vPosition;
        // The velocity of this frame
        D3DXVECTOR3 m_vVelocity;

        // The orientation of this frame
        float m_Yaw, m_Pitch, m_Roll;

        // The list of objects in this frame
        CZenObject* m_pObjectList;

        // Pointer to the next frame in the list
        CZenFrame* m_pNext;

        CZenFrame* m_pChildFrameList;
        CZenFrame* m_pParentFrame;
```

```cpp
        FRAME_MOVEMENT_CALLBACK m_pfnCallback;
        BOOL m_bCallback;



// Functions
public:
        HRESULT SetCallback( FRAME_MOVEMENT_CALLBACK pfnCallback );

        void SetVelocity( float x, float y, float z );
        void GetVelocity( float& x, float& y, float& z );

        void SetPosition( float x, float y, float z );
        void GetPosition( float& x, float& y, float& z );

        // Returns the local matrix for this frame
        void GetLocal( D3DXMATRIX& pMatrix );

        void SetYaw( float Yaw ){ m_Yaw = Yaw;  }
        void GetYaw( float& Yaw){ Yaw = m_Yaw; }

        void SetPitch( float Pitch ){ m_Pitch = Pitch;  }
        void GetPitch( float& Pitch){ Pitch = m_Pitch; }

        void SetRoll( float Roll ){ m_Roll = Roll;  }
        void GetRoll( float& Roll){ Roll = m_Roll; }

        // Update the position of this object
        void Update();

        // Add an object to the frame
        HRESULT AddObject( CZenObject* pNewObject );

        // Render the objects
        HRESULT Render();

        // Set/Get the next pointer for use in the list
        void SetNext( CZenFrame* pNext ){ m_pNext = pNext; }
        CZenFrame* GetNext(){ return m_pNext; }

        // Add a child frame to this frame
        HRESULT AddFrame( CZenFrame* pNewFrame );
```

```
protected:

        void SetParent( CZenFrame* pParent ){ m_pParentFrame = pParent; }
        CZenFrame* GetParent(){ return m_pParentFrame; }
};
```

See that bit of code just before the class is declared? It looks a little like this:

```
class CZenFrame;
typedef int (*FRAME_MOVEMENT_CALLBACK)( CZenFrame* pFrame, void* Parameter );
```

That is the definition for the "pluggable" behavior control device that you can attach to this frame. It's basically a function pointer type declaration that says that the function that you can attach to the frame has to (a) pass a pointer to the frame that you want to modify the behavior of and (b) pass a pointer to the parameters for the function, which are dependent on the function's behavior. I'll explain this in much more detail shortly.

Now for the class changes. There are five new member variables. m_pNext is used for the frame lists; it is basically a pointer to the next frame in the list. More on this soon. m_pChildFrameList is used to construct a list of child frames to this frame. A child frame relies on the transformations applied to its parent frame to help compute its own position. Again, more on this soon. m_pParentFrame is a pointer to this frame's parent frame, which may or may not exist. m_pfnCallback is a pointer to the pluggable behavior function that I was talking about in the preceding paragraph and will elaborate on later. And finally, m_bCallback is a BOOL variable that monitors whether a behavior function has been assigned or not.

There also are a few new functions for the class. SetNext() and GetNext() are just simple functions for maintaining the list of frames. AddFrame() is the function that, in a bizarre twist of fate, is used to add a child frame to the list of frames. Following is the new constructor, which has a few new bits and pieces added, but nothing too important:

```
CZenFrame::CZenFrame()
{
        // Set the orientation to zero
        m_Yaw = 0.0f;
        m_Pitch = 0.0f;
        m_Roll = 0.0f;
```

```
        // Set the position and velocity to zero
        m_vPosition = D3DXVECTOR3( 0.0f, 0.0f, 0.0f );
        m_vVelocity = D3DXVECTOR3( 0.0f, 0.0f, 0.0f );

        // Initialize the local matrix to an identity
        D3DXMatrixIdentity( &m_mLocal );

        // Zero out the object list
        m_pObjectList = 0;

        m_pNext = 0;
        m_pChildFrameList = 0;
        m_pParentFrame = 0;

        m_pfnCallback = 0;
        m_bCallback = FALSE;
}


CZenFrame::~CZenFrame()
{


}
```

Just your usual assign everything to 0 routine. Let's move on into the depths of frames....

Adding Child Frames

This is pretty easy, and it is really similar to the code that I showed you in the last chapter that was used to add objects to the frame. Follow the steps below to add a frame.

1. Call AddFrame() on the frame that you want to add the child to, and pass the pointer of the child to the parent.
2. In AddFrame() make sure that the pointer to the child is a valid pointer.
3. Tell the new child frame that it has just been adopted! Or, basically, just give the child a pointer to its new parent.
4. Add the new child frame to the list of child frames. If the list has not yet been created, then set the new frame as the start of the list.

And that's it. Check out the following code:

```cpp
// Adds a new child frame to this frame
HRESULT CZenFrame::AddFrame( CZenFrame* pNewFrame )
{
        // Make sure the new frame is valid
        if( !pNewFrame )
        {
                SetError( "Failed in attempt to add an invalid child frame" );
                return E_FAIL;
        }

        // Tell it who's da daddy
        pNewFrame->SetParent( this );

        // If the child frame has not been created yet...
        if( !m_pChildFrameList )
        {
                // ...Set this new frame as the first in the list
                m_pChildFrameList = pNewFrame;
        }
        else
        {
                // ...The list already exists

                // Get a pointer to the start of the list
                CZenFrame* pTempFrame = m_pChildFrameList;

                // Find the last entry in the list
                while( pTempFrame->GetNext() )
                        pTempFrame = pTempFrame->GetNext();

                // Add this frame to the end of this list
                pTempFrame->SetNext( pNewFrame );
        }

        return S_OK;
}
```

In fact, the only difference between this code and the code for
CZenFrame::AddObject() is that the pointers are to CZenFrame rather than to CZenObject.

Dealing with Additive Transformations

Recall when I said, about a hundred times, that the location of a frame depends on the location of its parent? Also remember in the last chapter's implementation that the frames called a function entitled `CZenFrame::Update()` to update the world transform matrix before they rendered their child objects? Well, you need to make some changes to the `Update()` function so that it takes account of its parents position.

Check out the code that follows; the additions are in bold:

```
// Updates the frame's position and orientation
// taking into account the properties of the
// parent frame.
void CZenFrame::Update()
{
        // Call the behavior plugin if one has been assigned
        if( m_bCallback )
                m_pfnCallback( this, m_pParameter );

        // Create some temporary matrices for the
        // rotation and translation transformations
        D3DXMATRIX mRotX, mRotY, mRotZ, mTrans, mRotTemp;

        // Update the position by the velocity
        m_vPosition.x += m_vVelocity.x;
        m_vPosition.y += m_vVelocity.y;
        m_vPosition.z += m_vVelocity.z;

        // Set the translation matrix
        D3DXMatrixTranslation( &mTrans, m_vPosition.x, m_vPosition.y, m_vPosition.z
);

        // Set the rotation around the x-axis
        D3DXMatrixRotationX( &mRotX, m_Pitch );
        // Set the rotation around the y-axis
        D3DXMatrixRotationY( &mRotY, m_Yaw );
        // Set the rotation around the z-axis
        D3DXMatrixRotationZ( &mRotZ, m_Roll );
```

```
// Concatenate the y-axis and x-axis rotation matrices
D3DXMatrixMultiply( &mRotTemp, &mRotX, &mRotY );
// Concatenate the x- and y-axes and z-axis rotation matrices
D3DXMatrixMultiply( &mRotTemp, &mRotZ, &mRotTemp );
// Concatenate the x-, y-, and z-axes and translation matrices
D3DXMatrixMultiply( &mTrans, &mRotTemp, &mTrans );

// Update the copy of the local matrix
m_mLocal = mTrans;

// If this frame is a child of another frame...
if( GetParent() )
{
        // ...Then we need to get the parent's transform matrix

        // Matrix to hold the parent's matrix
        D3DXMATRIX mParent;

        // Get the parent's local to world transform matrix
        GetParent()->GetLocal( mParent );

        // Concatenate the parent's matrix with this frame's matrix
        D3DXMatrixMultiply( &m_mLocal, &m_mLocal, &mParent);
}


// Set the new world matrix
g_pDevice->SetTransform( D3DTS_WORLD, &m_mLocal );

}
```

The first thing to look at is the call to the behavior plug-in at the start of the function. You may be starting to build up a picture in your mind of how the plugin functionality works by now; if not then don't worry—I will be covering them very shortly. So let me just gloss over them for now and move on to the new code at the bottom of the function.

You can see that the function makes a call to check if a parent frame exists. If the parent frame does exist, then it needs to get the parent's transform matrix and combine it with its own. Don't forget that the parent may have already combined its matrix with its parent's matrix, and that matrix with its parent, and so on. In fact, this frame could be a thousand frames deep in the chain, and it will still only take about five lines of code to resolve all the differences. That's the fantastic thing about frames. After the matrices are combined Direct3D is informed about the change to the world matrix so that the changes can take effect.

You may be wondering what happens when this frame has finished its update and returns control to the parent. I mean now that the child frame has changed the world matrix, won't the parents be all screwed up because the world matrix now reflects the status of the child and not the parent? Well, as you will soon see, the parent frame resets the world matrix after it has finished dealing with its children so that everything works out all hunky-dory. You never have to call this `Update()` function yourself externally, by the way; it is automatically called from the `Render()` function, which I will show you now....

Rendering with Frame Trees and Object Lists

Rendering gets substantially more complex than it was in the last chapter. I mean, when you see the code you may think, "Dude, that's, like, not so bad." I say it is more complex because there is a lot going on, and it all has to happen in the right order. And I can guarantee you that when you start developing your own frame engines, this is the point where the most bugs will make themselves known. With that in mind, let's look at the steps that have to be performed:

1. Call `CZenFrame::Render()` on the frame that you want to render.

2. Call `CZenFrame::Update()` to recompute the local to world transform matrix for this frame, and possibly combine it with the parent frame's matrix, if one exists. And make a copy of the matrix so it doesn't have to be recomputed later.

3. Call `CZenFrame::Render()` on each child frame. Yes, this is the same function that you are in now. What this does is recursively traverse the tree, calling `CZenFrame::Render()` on each frame, which subsequently calls `CZenObject::Render()` on every object in every frame. Think about it for a bit, and then it will click. It took me about a week!

4. Now that all the child frames have completed this function, you are only halfway through. There is nothing I hate more than trying to explain recursions! It's kind of like a fault in the space-time continuum. Anywho, now you need to check if this object has any member objects to render. If it does, then go to step 5; otherwise you can just return control to the parent frame.

5. Get a pointer to the start of the object list.

6. *Don't forget this step.* Remember that those little delinquent child frames have been messing around with the world transform matrix, so you need to reset it to the correct matrix for this frame. Don't worry though; help is at hand since you saved a copy of the local matrix in the call to Update earlier. I am making this point because *everybody*—yes, even me—forgets to reset the world matrix the first time. If they deny it, they are lying!

7. Now loop through every object that this frame is looking after and call CZenObject::Render() on it so that the objects can paint themselves to the screen.

8. Go get a beer (or refreshing nonalcoholic beverage of your choice) and relax after all that hard work.

After all that explanation you are probably expecting a function that is a few hundred lines long. Well, it is way short of that, running all of 13 lines not including comments! I told you frames were great! Try to map the steps above to what is going on in the code. Here it is:

```
HRESULT CZenFrame::Render()
{

        // Update the position and orientation of the frame
        // and set the new world transform matrix
        Update();

        // Get a pointer to the child frame list
        CZenFrame* pFrame = m_pChildFrameList;

        // Loop for every child frame in the list
        while( pFrame )
        {
                // Render this child frame
                pFrame->Render();
                // Iterate to the next frame
                pFrame = pFrame->GetNext();
        }


        // Return if this frame has no visuals to render
        if( !m_pObjectList )
                return S_OK;
```

```
        // Get a pointer to the start of the list
        CZenObject* pObject = m_pObjectList;

        // Reset the transform in case those pesky children modified it
        g_pDevice->SetTransform( D3DTS_WORLD, &m_mLocal );

        // Loop for each object in the list
        while( pObject )
        {
                // Render the object
                pObject->Render();

                // Increment to the next object in the list
                pObject = (CZenObject*)pObject->GetNext();
        }

        // Success!
        return S_OK;


}
```

Programming Pluggable Frame Behavior Modification Routines

As I was saying before, the reason you want to have pluggable behavior modification routines is so that you can

- avoid hard coding behavior logic to a specific frame.

- gain the ability to increase the modularity and reusability of your code.

- be able to use ridiculously long strings of words in front of your friends and sound intelligent!

Enough justification for their use—how do they work? Well, you'll recall that any function that is going to be used in this way with a frame *must* follow a certain pattern. For instance, in this case I set the prototype for the function definition to look like this:

```
class CZenFrame;
typedef int (*FRAME_MOVEMENT_CALLBACK)( CZenFrame* pFrame, void* Parameter );
```

By the way, a little note before I go on. You may be wondering why I declared a prototype for the class before the function pointer definition. This is because the function is used in the class, and the class is used in the function declaration, so you get into a which-one-do-I-declare-first situation. The solution is to just put the name of the class first with a semicolon, effectively saying, "Yo, compiler man, there's a class with this name below and although you haven't seen it yet you can totally trust me, dude. So give me any trouble in the next line when I refer to it and I'll give you a fistful of Drachma."

Also remember that in the class definition for CZenFrame I included the following code snippet:

```
    .
    .
    .
protected:
    .
    .
    .

        FRAME_MOVEMENT_CALLBACK m_pfnCallback;
        BOOL m_bCallback;


// Functions
public:
        HRESULT SetCallback( FRAME_MOVEMENT_CALLBACK pfnCallback );
    .
    .
    .
```

As I said before, m_pfnCallback holds the pointer to the behavior function's location, and m_bCallback is a flag indicating whether or not a function has been attached yet. You may also notice that both of these have protected status, so from where oh where do they get set? The answer is behind door number three....

Attaching a Behavior Modifier

The behavior modifier is attached with the SetCallback() function:

```
// Sets the callback behavior function for this frame
HRESULT CZenFrame::SetCallback( FRAME_MOVEMENT_CALLBACK pfnCallback )
{
```

```
                // If a valid pointer was not specified
                // (or if the user wants to disable all plugins)...
                if( !pfnCallback )
                {
                        // Set the callback status flag to FALSE
                        m_bCallback = FALSE;
                        // Set the callback pointer to NULL
                        m_pfnCallback = NULL;
                        // Return failure. If the caller is disabling
                        // callbacks on purpose then it can just
                        // ignore the failure return.
                        return E_FAIL;
                }

                // Set the callback pointer to the new function
                m_pfnCallback = pfnCallback;

                // Set the callback presence flag to TRUE
                m_bCallback = TRUE;

                return S_OK;
        }
```

SetCallback() is a little function that does some verification that a valid function is
being attached and then updates the member variables. The only parameter it
takes is the pointer to the new behavior routine, which must be of the FRAME_MOVE-
MENT_CALLBACK type. By the way, I know all this function pointer stuff is an absolute
nightmare to understand, so if you are having trouble getting this you can either
take the boring option and look them up in a C++ book or do what I would do:
smile, nod, and just be happy it works.

Notice that the function takes a pointer to the frame that needs updating, and also
a void pointer to something called a parameter. The frame pointer is needed
because you obviously want the function to know which frame it is supposed to be
updating. The parameter function is a cool little concept that I added in. It allows
you pass information that is specific to the frame you are moving.

Maybe an example would be the best way to explain this. Say you have a behavior
modifier that is controlling the path of some clouds in the sky, but you want the
higher clouds to move more slowly than the lower clouds. You could program three
versions of the modifier and call them MoveFast(), MoveMed(), and MoveSlow(),

but if they all do the same thing this is a waste of time. Wouldn't it be better if you could just program one modifier and then pass a parameter to it containing the speed at which you want the clouds to move? I thought so, too. But you never know how many parameters a modifier is going to need ahead of time, so I made the only parameter a void pointer. Using some intelligent casting, this lets you pass anything from a simple single variable to an entire class or structure to the modifier.

You set the parameter right into the frame. So if you have your frames called HighClouds, MidCouds, and LowClouds, you could set the speed like in the pseudocode that follows:

```
float g_Fast = 10.0f, g_Med = 5.0f, g_Slow = 2.0f;

HighCloud.m_pParamter = &g_Slow;
MidCloud.m_pParamter = &g_Med;
LowCloud.m_pParamter = &g_Slow;

LowCloud.SetCallback( MoveClouds );
```

Then in the modifier that moves the clouds, you would have some code that extracted the floating point speed through the void pointer parameter, which is passed to it automatically by the frame that it is attached to.

Don't worry if this is a little up in the air—I'm about to show you a real-life modifier. I've told it not to bite, so you should be fine.

I'm Too Jiggy for My Bemodies

Actually, programming one of these bad boys is probably much simpler than you think. Despite how much I go on about how great they are and the length of their name, they can be only a few lines long and reproduce very advanced behavior. And speaking of those silly names, I should have thought of this earlier: behavior modifiers can be shortened to *bemodies*. Much better!

Bemodies have a few properties that you should keep in mind as I describe them. Firstly, once you program one you can assign it to as many frames as you like. Secondly, once you assign a bemodie to a frame it is called automatically every time the frame is rendered, until you disable it by either setting a new bemodie or passing NULL as the new bemodie. And finally, bemodies must be either global in scope or static members of a class. You can probably get other function types to work if you try, but I can see so many problems possibly showing up that it's just not worth being a messer.

Following is a real-life bemodie:

```
int FC_RotateYaw( CZenFrame* pFrame, void* pParameter )
{
        // Return if a valid frame was not specified
        if( !pFrame )
                return E_FAIL;

        // Get the speed from the pointer
        float speed = *((float*)pParameter);

        // Set the yaw for this frame to rotate
        pFrame->SetYaw( timeGetTime() / speed );

        return S_OK;
}
```

Interesting, huh? Can you see what it does? The function rotates a frame around the y-axis. The pParameter contains a void pointer that can be cast so that the speed of the rotation can be retrieved. For this function the higher the value is, the slower the rotation will be. The FC prefix on the function name is there to remind me that the function is a bemodie specifically meant for frames and not something else. It can get confusing in more advanced implementations. The FC stands for *frame callback*.

Now let me show you how to connect it to a frame. Say you have a planet mesh in a frame that you want to rotate. The following code will do that for you:

```
g_PlanetFrame.SetCallback( FC_RotateYaw );
```

And that's it! All you have to do is call CZenFrame::Render() as you did before from the main Render() function, and the rotation will occur automatically. I will show you a really cool example in just a second, but first you need to make a few more minor structural changes to the engine.

Bringing Structure to the Zen Engine

Up until now I have been showing you objects and then rendering them in the main Render() function. Well, all that has got to change now. As a game engine becomes more developed you need to start making constructive decisions about how data is going to flow through your game. And here is the first decision that will change the way the rest of the engine is constructed: from now on all 3D data, from meshes to points to lines, will be rendered only if it is part of a frame. Of course this is a voluntary code of conduct, but it will help you if you stick to it.

What this means is that you are now basing everything around the frame instead of a wide collection of differing objects. In other words, the frame is going to *bind* everything together so that it comes under a simple manageable interface. Most games are developed with a *root frame*, which is at the top of the frame hierarchy. Nothing can be higher than the root frame. The root frame is generally referred to as the *scene frame*, or just the *scene*. If you want to add an object to the game, you first add it to its own frame and then add that frame to the scene. So *all* objects, no matter how far down the chain they are, must be able to trace back to the scene frame.

You may be wondering what the point of doing this is. Well, I'll tell you, because I am just that nice. It means that to render every single 3D object in your entire game, no matter how complex, you only have to make a *single* call to render the scene and everything else will be rendered automatically by the tree traversal routines. Which means that you have a nice uncluttered main Render() function that can be used to render the user interface and deal with the player.

To implement this is very simple. All you need is a global CZenFrame that you know is going to be there for the entire game. I declare mine like this:

```
CZenFrame g_Scene;
```

It is also a good idea to add two more main functions called InitScene(), which is called from GameInit() and DestroyScene(), which is called from GameShutdown(). Neither of these functions takes any parameters, but they are good because you can package away all your scene initialization code into InitScene() and keep GameInit() clear for the more technical stuff.

Here's what they look like when they are empty:

```
HRESULT InitScene()
{
        return S_OK;
}

HRESULT DestroyScene()
{
        return S_OK;
}
```

And the final change is to add a call to the main `Render()` function to render the root scene frame, like so:

```
g_Scene.Render();
```

Obviously, you want to make that call between the calls to `IDirect3DDevice8::BeginScene()` and `IDirect3DDevice8::EndScene()`. Note that the "scene" bit of those device function calls has nothing to do with a scene, as in the frame type. It just tells the display adapter that rendering is about to begin and end, respectively.

Everything in Action...Finally!

This is a really cool example, and everyone who sees it running on my computer just has to stop by and ask about it. It's kind of like a sports car, but not quite as impressive to the ladies. It is basically a reconstruction of the Zen solar system, a system not unlike our own, but cooler! I'm not going to list out all the code for it because it gets quite long, but I will show you everything important.

> **TIP**
>
> Peruse the code on the CD for this example to see how everything fits together.

Let me start by explaining how this example is constructed. First there is the sun, which rotates. Added to that are four frames for the four planets in the Zen system. Each of these, because they are added to the sun's frame, also rotates. In the frame for the planet that looks like earth there is another subframe holding a moon that rotates around the earth. In fact, I programmed this so well that it even exhibits the "dark side of the moon" behavior. Except I made the earth spin the wrong way. Oops. And finally there is another frame holding the light for the sun that is positioned inside the sun's mesh.

When you are looking at the code, notice how I applied a material to the sun to make it look like it is giving out light. I achieved this by setting the emissive components of the material to their highest value. Also pay attention to how I changed the range of the light. The first part of the code is just the main declaration of variables and so on:

```cpp
class CPlanet
{
public:
        CPlanet()
        {
                Speed = 0.0f;
        }

        // The planet's mesh
        CZenMesh Mesh;
        // The planets frame
        CZenFrame Frame;
        // The speed of rotation (higher=slower)
        float Speed;
};

// The frame for the sun's lights
CZenFrame g_LightFrame;

// The light for the sun
CZenLight g_SunLight;

// The mesh for the sun
CZenMesh g_SunMesh;

// The frame for the sun
CZenFrame g_SunFrame;

// The material for the sun
CZenMaterial g_SunMaterial;

// The 4 planets of the zen system
CPlanet g_Planets[4];

// The planet class for the moon
CPlanet g_EarthMoon;

// The frame for the moon
CZenFrame g_MoonFrame;
```

```
// The speed of rotation for the moon
float g_MoonSpeed = -600.0f;

// The sun's speed of rotation
float g_SunSpeed = 1500.0f;

// The starry background bitmap
LPDIRECT3DSURFACE8 g_pBackground = 0;
```

Notice how I kept all the information for the planets inside the CPlanet class. I haven't gone class crazy, don't worry. CPlanet was originally a struct, but I turned it into a class to make sure the speed was always set to 0 by default. So sue me! Anyway, here is the interesting code, from InitScene():

```
HRESULT InitScene()
{
        // Load the background bitmap
        LoadBitmapToSurface( "ex1Background.bmp", &g_pBackground, g_pDevice );

        // Load the sun model
        g_SunMesh.LoadXFile( "ex1sun.x" );

        // Add the sun mesh to the sun frame
        g_SunFrame.AddObject( &g_SunMesh );
        // Set the speed for the sun
        g_SunFrame.m_pParameter = (void*)&g_SunSpeed;
        // Set the behavior modifier for the frame
        g_SunFrame.SetCallback( FC_RotateYaw );
        // Set the material to very bright
        g_SunMaterial.SetEmissive(1,1,1);
        // Attach the material to the sun
        g_SunMesh.SetMaterial( &g_SunMaterial );
        // Set the light to be at the center of the sun
        g_LightFrame.SetPosition( 0, 0, 0 );
        // Turn on the light
        g_SunLight.Enable( TRUE );
        // Make sure the light reaches all the planets
        g_SunLight.m_Light.Range = 400.0f;
        // Add the light to the frame
        g_LightFrame.AddObject( &g_SunLight );
```

```cpp
// Load the moon mesh
g_EarthMoon.Mesh.LoadXFile( "ex1Moon.x" );
// Sets the moon's rotation speed
g_EarthMoon.Speed = 1500.0f;
// Set the speed into the frame
g_EarthMoon.Frame.m_pParameter = &g_EarthMoon.Speed;
// Insert the moon mesh into the frame
g_EarthMoon.Frame.AddObject( &g_EarthMoon.Mesh );
// Attach the behavior modifier
g_EarthMoon.Frame.SetCallback( FC_RotateYaw );
// Set the moon to be outside the earth
g_EarthMoon.Frame.SetPosition( 10.0f, 5.0f, 0.0f );

// Set the moon frame to be at the center of the earth
g_MoonFrame.SetPosition(0,0,0);
// Set the speed of rotation
g_MoonFrame.m_pParameter = &g_MoonSpeed;
// Attach the behavior modifier
g_MoonFrame.SetCallback( FC_RotateYaw );
// Add the moon frame to the earth frame
g_MoonFrame.AddFrame( &g_EarthMoon.Frame );
// Add the moon frame to the moon rotation frame
g_Planets[0].Frame.AddFrame( &g_MoonFrame );

// Load the  mesh
g_Planets[0].Mesh.LoadXFile( "ex1Earth.x" );
// Set the rotation speed
g_Planets[0].Speed = 1500.0f;
// Insert the speed into the frame
g_Planets[0].Frame.m_pParameter = &g_Planets[0].Speed;
// Add the  mesh to the frame
g_Planets[0].Frame.AddObject( &g_Planets[0].Mesh );
// Attach the behavior modifier
g_Planets[0].Frame.SetCallback( FC_RotateYaw );
// Set the position of the frame
g_Planets[0].Frame.SetPosition( 50.0f, 0.0f, 0.0f );

// Load the  mesh
g_Planets.Mesh.LoadXFile( "ex1Mars.x" );
// Set the rotation speed
g_Planets.Speed = 1000.0f;
```

```cpp
    // Insert the speed into the frame
    g_Planets.Frame.m_pParameter = &g_Planets.Speed;
    // Add the  mesh to the frame
    g_Planets.Frame.AddObject( &g_Planets.Mesh );
    // Attach the behavior modifier
    g_Planets.Frame.SetCallback( FC_RotateYaw );
    // Set the position of the frame
    g_Planets.Frame.SetPosition( 0.0f, 0.0f, 100.0f );

    // Load the  mesh
    g_Planets.Mesh.LoadXFile( "ex1Jupiter.x" );
    // Set the rotation speed
    g_Planets.Speed = 2500.0f;
    // Insert the speed into the frame
    g_Planets.Frame.m_pParameter = &g_Planets.Speed;
    // Add the  mesh to the frame
    g_Planets.Frame.AddObject( &g_Planets.Mesh );
    // Attach the behavior modifier
    g_Planets.Frame.SetCallback( FC_RotateYaw );
    // Set the position of the frame
    g_Planets.Frame.SetPosition( 150.0f, 0.0f, 150.0f );

    // Load the  mesh
    g_Planets.Mesh.LoadXFile( "ex1Neptune.x" );
    // Set the rotation speed
    g_Planets.Speed = 1400.0f;
    // Insert the speed into the frame
    g_Planets.Frame.m_pParameter = &g_Planets.Speed;
    // Add the  mesh to the frame
    g_Planets.Frame.AddObject( &g_Planets.Mesh );
    // Attach the behavior modifier
    g_Planets.Frame.SetCallback( FC_RotateYaw );
    // Set the position of the frame
    g_Planets.Frame.SetPosition( -220.0f, 0.0f, 220.0f );

    // Add all the frames to the main sun frame
    g_SunFrame.AddFrame( &g_Planets[0].Frame );
    g_SunFrame.AddFrame( &g_Planets.Frame );
    g_SunFrame.AddFrame( &g_Planets.Frame );
    g_SunFrame.AddFrame( &g_Planets.Frame );
```

```
// Add the sun frame to the scene
g_Scene.AddFrame( &g_SunFrame );
// Add the sunlight to the scene
g_Scene.AddFrame( &g_LightFrame );


    return S_OK;
}
```

I suppose you want to see what all the code does? Well, have a look at Figure 16.1. The figure doesn't do it justice though. Go on, load that puppy up and see it in color. You can run around like you're onboard the *Starship Enterprise*. You can even go inside the sun if you want! That's what they call in Microsoft a *feature*. Only joking—keep the leashes on your lawyers, Bill.

Figure 16.1

The Zen solar system, utilizing materials, lights, textures, meshes, and surfaces

Bilinear Filtering and Scene Anti-aliasing

These are two terms that you may have heard before; I'll start with *bilinear filtering*. This technique is used to eliminate the two visual artifacts that show up a lot in texture-mapped games: shimmering and pixelization. *Shimmering* occurs when the image you are using is so far in the distance that the amount of pixels on the monitor being used to display the image is not large enough to display as much texture as the algorithm would like. The result is that light variations of the texture's pixels are used each frame, which creates an effect that looks like heat rising off the ground. *Pixelization* is a much more obvious problem, particularly in older games. You know what happens when you walk up quite close to a textured wall, and then the blockiness of the pixels in the texture becomes very obvious. It's called *pixelization*.

For an example of pixelization, take a look at Figure 16.2.

Figure 16.2

Pixelization because of poor texture filtering

Now check out bilinear filtering in Figure 16.3. See the difference? That is a much nicer image.

Figure 16.3

Bilinear filtering to the rescue

To implement this is really easy. It only takes two lines of code and should be supported by just about every card on the market. It works on all of mine anyway. By the way, if you happen to be looking up how to do this in the DirectX 8 documentation, be careful because their code is wrong; it is meant for DirectX 7 and will not compile. You can fix it by using my version below, which I suggest you add to your main GameInit() function:

```
g_pDevice->SetTextureStageState( 0, D3DTSS_MAGFILTER, D3DTEXF_LINEAR );
g_pDevice->SetTextureStageState( 0, D3DTSS_MINFILTER, D3DTEXF_LINEAR );
```

What you are doing here is setting the magnification and minification filters for the texture stage 0, which is the one being used for textures at the moment.

Another option that you can turn on to improve the quality of the rendered images is *edge antialiasing,* which reduces the amount of jaggies that show up between faces that are not exactly horizontal or vertical. Be aware that antialiasing is not available on all cards. To turn it on you just have to add the following line of code to the GameInit() function:

> **Magnification is when the image is too close, or blocky, and *minification* occurs when the image is too far away. The code requests that in these cases a linear blend of pixels take place, which results in a nice blurred image.**

```
g_pDevice->SetRenderState( D3DRS_EDGEANTIALIAS, TRUE );
```

Using the Direct3D Texture Utility to Create Advanced Textures

As you learn more advanced texturing techniques you may find that your average image editor just doesn't cut it anymore. Even Photoshop does not give you enough control to create some of the texture types that you need. For instance, it is very hard to combine a 24-bit RGB image with an 8-bit alpha channel image unless you are very educated on the package. For those reasons, and because a lot of people just can't afford Photoshop, Microsoft created a tool called the DirectX Texture Tool. Though it has a few bugs, it's really good for what it's designed for. And the best thing is that it's a fully visual program, unlike that Conv3DS.exe nonsense. Watch out for future releases of programs such as Photoshop, because as DirectX becomes more engrained in the game development world, you may see support for its file formats seep into other packages.

To start the Texture Tool, go to Start, Programs, DirectX 8.0 SDK, DirectX Utilities, DirectX Texture Tool. You can see an editor in Figure 16.4.

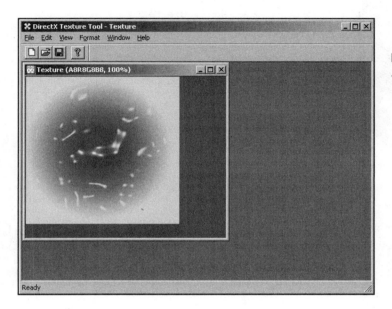

Figure 16.4

The DirectX Texture Tool

Later on in the chapter I will show you how to use Direct3D to create your own custom mouse cursor, which is really cool. However, Direct3D requires that the image for the mouse be in a certain format; it must be a 32-bit ARGB image and the alpha channel must be set to either 1.0, for fully opaque, or 0.0, for fully transparent. Alpha values in between are not accepted. The alpha channel lets you specify which parts of the cursor are transparent. Another requirement is that both the width and height must be a power of two, such as 32 x 64.

Now that's all fine and dandy, but how do you create that from a standard bitmap? Well, let's take it in steps. First you get the image that you want to use as the mouse pointer, which in this case is the Super Zen Cursor shown, enlarged, in Figure 16.5.

Figure 16.5

The Super Zen Cursor!

So now you have a cursor, but what about the alpha value? Well, the easiest thing to do is to just create a new 8-bit grayscale image and fill in the parts of it with black and white until you get the right mask. This is really easy to do with the magic selection wand in most image editors. In Figure 16.6 is the alpha channel for the cursor, enlarged for clarity.

Figure 16.6

The alpha channel for the cursor

Now comes the interesting part: combining both images.

1. Open the 24-bit cursor image into the Texture Tool.
2. Go to File, Open onto Alpha channel of this file in the Texture Tool.
3. Open the 8-bit alpha channel.
4. Confirm that the alpha mask fits properly. You should see the original image, and anything transparent will have changed color to something like green.
5. Go to File, Save As and save the image as a DDS file.

You have just successfully created your first DDS file in the Texture Tool. (DDS stands for *DirectDraw Surface*.) You can easily load and save DDS files with utility functions like `D3DXLoadSurfaceFromFile()` and others. Most Direct3D image-loading functions support the DDS format.

Using Custom Mouse Cursors

There are a lot of times in games when you want the user to be able to use the mouse to select options from some sort of user interface. However, there are some really big problems with this, because Direct3D in full-screen mode does not get on well with the standard Windows GDI when it is trying to display the mouse cursor. In fact, it generally doesn't work at all. The second problem, or more of an issue really, is that the regular Windows cursor doesn't look very cool. It is just a white arrow with a black background. I mean how much cooler is the Super Zen Cursor, I ask you?

You may or may not have the experience of programming a mouse cursor yourself in a gaming environment, but if you haven't, know that it is something that I would compare to having a root canal. Hand it over to someone who enjoys pain. Anyway, since every programmer under the sun was wasting days of valuable programming time developing custom cursor software, Microsoft decided to just build the functionality right into the device in release 8.

And since I already developed a class to encapsulate the mouse back when we were dealing with DirectInput, I decided to just implement all this cursor stuff straight into `CZenMouse`. Don't worry—there are only minor changes (shown in bold). Have a look at the new definition:

```
class CZenMouse
{
```

```cpp
public:
        CZenMouse();
        ~CZenMouse();

// Variables
public:

protected:
        LPDIRECTINPUTDEVICE8 m_pMouseDev;
        LPDIRECT3DSURFACE8 m_pCursorSurf;

        BOOL m_bInitialized;
        BOOL m_bShowCursor;

        DIMOUSESTATE m_MouseData;

        // The cursor position
        POINT m_Position;
// Functions
public:
        HRESULT Initialize();
        HRESULT Poll();

        POINT GetMousePos();
        BOOL IsButtonDown( int Button );

        // Handles the WM_SETCURSOR message
        BOOL HandleSetCursor();
        // Toggles cursor display
        void ShowCursor( BOOL bShow ){ m_bShowCursor = bShow; }
        // Sets the position of the cursor
        void SetCursorPosition( int x, int y );
        // Gets the position of the cursor
        void GetCursorPosition( int& x, int& y );
        // Moves the position of the cursor.
        void MoveCursor( int x, int y );
        // Update the cursor position
        // based on mouse movement
        void UpdateCursorPos();
protected:

};
```

The new member variable, m_Position, looks after the position of the mouse in *screen coordinates*. This is opposed to the DIMOUSESTATE structure, which holds mouse coordinates as relative distance since the previous poll event.

Now let's move on to those functions, starting with HandleSetCursor(). This function is there to handle the WM_SETCURSOR message that is sent to the WndProc() function. In the window procedure you connect it to the mouse like this:

```
case WM_SETCURSOR:
{
        return g_Mouse.HandleSetCursor();
}
```

The code for the function is as follows:

```
// Handles the WM_SETCURSOR message
BOOL CZenMouse::HandleSetCursor()
{
        // Return if the mouse hasn't been initialized yet
        if( !m_bInitialized )
                return FALSE;

        // If the cursor is set to be visible...
        if( m_bShowCursor )
        {
                // Turn off standard cursor
                SetCursor( NULL );
                // Show the zen cursor
                g_pDevice->ShowCursor( TRUE );

                // Return TRUE, which prevents
                // Windows from messing with the
                // cursors anymore
                return TRUE;
        }

        // Return FALSE to let Windows do
        // its thing if our cursor is not visible
        return FALSE;

}
```

The function just figures out exactly what the heck the mouse is set to do at the moment and then returns TRUE or FALSE to WndProc(). The function returns TRUE if the Direct3D cursor is meant to be visible, which causes Windows to bow out gracefully and stop attempting to change the cursor settings. Returning FALSE indicates to Windows that it is free to do whatever it wants with the cursor.

Initialization

Have a look at the changes, shown in bold, to the initialization code for the mouse:

```
// Initializes the mouse
HRESULT CZenMouse::Initialize()
{
        HRESULT r = 0;

        // Return if the DirectInput object does not exist
        if( !g_pDI )
                return E_FAIL;

        // Release the mouse device if it has already been created
        if( m_pMouseDev )
                m_pMouseDev->Release();

        // Create the mouse device
        r = g_pDI->CreateDevice( GUID_SysMouse, &m_pMouseDev, NULL );
        if( FAILED( r ) )
        {
                SetError( "Unable to create mouse device" );
                return E_FAIL;
        }

        // Set the data format for the mouse
        r = m_pMouseDev->SetDataFormat( &c_dfDIMouse );
        if( FAILED( r ) )
        {
                SetError( "Unable to set the mouse data format" );
                return E_FAIL;
        }

        // Set the cooperative level for the mouse
        r = m_pMouseDev->SetCooperativeLevel( g_hWndMain,
                        DISCL_EXCLUSIVE | DISCL_FOREGROUND );
        if( FAILED( r ) )
        {
```

```
            SetError( "Unable to set the cooperative level for the mouse" );
            return E_FAIL;
     }


     // Acquire the physical mouse into the device
     r = m_pMouseDev->Acquire();
     if( FAILED( r ) )
     {
            SetError( "Unable to acquire mouse" );
            return E_FAIL;
     }


     // Create a new surface for the mouse pointer image
     g_pDevice->CreateImageSurface( 32, 64, D3DFMT_A8R8G8B8, &m_pCursorSurf );
     // Load the image file from disk
     D3DXLoadSurfaceFromFile( m_pCursorSurf, 0, 0,
                    "ZenCursor.dds", 0, D3DX_FILTER_NONE, 0, 0 );
     // Set the hotspot for the cursor
     g_pDevice->SetCursorProperties( 0, 0, m_pCursorSurf );


     // Set the initialization flag to true
     m_bInitialized = TRUE;


     return S_OK;
}
```

It is pretty easy to initialize the mouse cursor—just create an image surface for the
cursor image, then load the image from the disk onto the surface, and finally set
the hotspot for the cursor. The *hotspot* is the area that is clickable. For instance, on
the standard arrow the hotspot is at (0, 0), or in other words at the end of the
arrow on the upper-left corner of the cursor image.

Positioning the Mouse

To set the position of the cursor to some point on the screen, you can use the function SetCursorPosition():

```
// Set the position of the cursor, in screen coords
void CZenMouse::SetCursorPosition( int x, int y )
{
```

```
        // Make sure the point stays within the screen
        if( x < 0 )
                x = 0;

        if( y < 0 )
                y = 0;

        if( x > g_DeviceWidth-1 )
                x = g_DeviceWidth-1;

        if( y > g_DeviceHeight-1 )
                y = g_DeviceHeight-1;

        // Update the position tracker
        m_Position.x = x;
        m_Position.y = y;

        // Tell Direct3D about the new position
        g_pDevice->SetCursorPosition( x, y, 0 );
}
```

It is important to make sure that the mouse stays within the bounds of the screen because otherwise the tracking functions, which I haven't shown you yet, get all screwed up. Or you can also move the cursor relative to its current position with the MoveCursor() function.

```
// Moves the cursor relative to its current position
void CZenMouse::MoveCursor( int x, int y )
{
        m_Position.x += x;
        m_Position.y += y;

        g_pDevice->SetCursorPosition( x, y, 0 );
}
```

To retrieve the position of the mouse you can call GetPosition().

```
// Returns the current position of the cursor
void CZenMouse::GetCursorPosition( int& x, int& y )
{
        x = m_Position.x;
        y = m_Position.y;
}
```

It was kind of annoying having to program this function myself. I mean, they put a SetPosition() function into the device, why couldn't they put in a GetPosition() as well?

Updating the Cursor Position

Have a look at the following code, which shows you how to update the position of the Direct3D mouse cursor on the screen.

```
// Sets the mouse cursor position
// by tracking how far it has moved
// since the last update.
void CZenMouse::UpdateCursorPos()
{
        // Get the relative movement
        // out of the DIMOUSESTATE structure
        m_Position.x += m_MouseData.lX;
        m_Position.y += m_MouseData.lY;

        // Make sure the point is within screen bounds
        if( m_Position.x < 0 )
                m_Position.x = 0;

        if( m_Position.y < 0 )
                m_Position.y = 0;

        if( m_Position.x > g_DeviceWidth-1 )
                m_Position.x = g_DeviceWidth-1;

        if( m_Position.y > g_DeviceHeight-1 )
                m_Position.y = g_DeviceHeight-1;

        // Set the new position into the device
        g_pDevice->SetCursorPosition( m_Position.x, m_Position.y, 0 );
}
```

This function should be called right after you call Poll() if you want it to track the position properly. I'll show you how to implement it shortly. The function starts by adding the relative movements into the m_Position absolute screen-coordinate movement-tracking structure. Again, the coordinates are checked to make sure they are within bounds. Finally, the position of the cursor is updated into the device.

Using CZenMouse and the Custom Cursor

Using a custom cursor couldn't be easier. The whole unit is pretty much self-contained, so all you have to do, when you want to start using the cursor, is to make a call to toggle the display of the cursor on. For instance, I put the following code into the main `GameInit()` function:

```
g_Mouse.ShowCursor( TRUE );
```

And then I put two calls into the main `HandleInput` function to track the movement of the mouse. In the following code fragment I have removed all the 3D camera related code for simplicity:

```
HRESULT HandleInput()
{
        if( g_Keyboard.IsKeyDown( DIK_ESCAPE ) )
                PostQuitMessage( 0 );

        // Retrieve the current state of the mouse
        g_Mouse.Poll();

        // Move the cursor
        g_Mouse.UpdateCursorPos();
}
```

And don't forget the call to handle the `WM_SETCURSOR` message that I showed you before. And that's it. You now have a working mouse cursor. And not just any cursor—but a Super Zen Cursor! Check out Figure 16.7. Tell me if you think I'm getting a little carried away with this whole cursor thing....

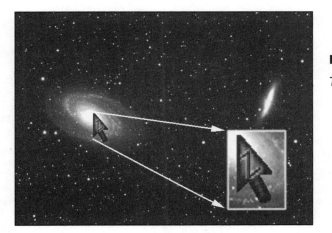

Figure 16.7

The Super Zen Cursor in action

Conclusion

And that, ladies and gentlemen, is where I sign off. I hope the tricks and techniques that you have learned prove valuable to you in your future endeavors as a Zen-guru-interactive-entertainment-engineer. It's been a long journey, for both of us! My poor hands will never function properly again after all this typing.

I think I got to discuss nearly everything I wanted to. Although as I write this, I keep thinking of 100 other things that I could put in. That's the problem with game development—the more you know, the less you know.

I think the next best step for you to take from here would be to start looking into AI and physics, so that you can really enhance the graphical technology that you now understand. If you want resources on where to go to improve your knowledge, check out http://www.gamedev.net. That's one of the most useful sites I've ever seen for game development resources, and it's not just for programmers.

Please feel free to contact me at mrzen@msn.com if you have any questions or comments, and I will try my best to get back to you.

With that in mind...

ZZZZZZZZZZZZZzzzzzzzzzzzz Britney, is that you? ZZZzzzzzzzz ZZZzzz

-Peter Walsh

Stardate 30-04-2001

May The Zen Be With You

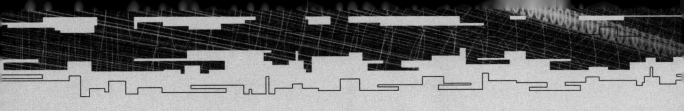

Part Five

Appendices

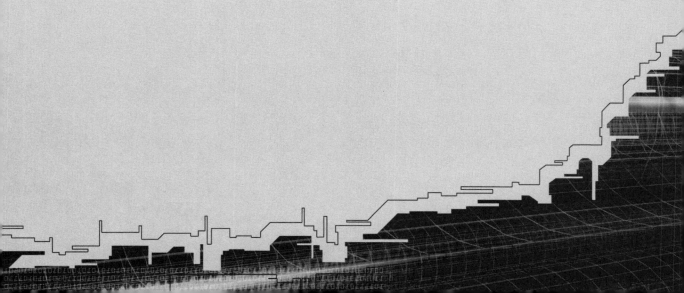

APPENDIX A

C++ PROGRAMMING 101

-by Jim Bulvan

Welcome to C++ Programming 101. This chapter serves as a fundamental introductory course to the C++ programming language for those who have some familiarity with straight C. I say "fundamental," because this appendix is not meant to turn you into a master C++ programmer. Rather, the following pages will introduce you to many features of C++ and give you the knowledge you need to understand and write your own C++ programs with confidence. To accomplish this, I will cover

- the theory behind object-oriented programming.
- the features new to C++.
- how to implement C++ features in your own programs.
- other miscellaneous topics that you will need to know to effectively grasp C++.

With that in mind, let's get moving....

C, C++: What's the Difference?

A lot of programmers are introduced to C first, or sometimes more basic "learning languages" such as Pascal or BASIC. If you learned programming at a school or a university, then you probably know what I am talking about. Having learned C, you may have seen some C++ every so often and wondered, "What the heck is the difference between C and C++?" I know I used to wonder that way back when I was learning. You may have seen some C++ jargon, like *polymorphism*, and wondered what it meant. Don't worry. You have come to the right spot. I'm going to show you everything you need to be a competent C++ programmer. Let's start at the beginning and look at the philosophies at the heart of C++, which is *object-oriented programming*.

If you take a look around you, you'll probably see many objects. I see a computer system, a TV, a chair, etc. The TV has different states: on or off. It can also be tuned to different channels and different levels of volume. The chair I mentioned is actually a bar stool, which has a swivel capability. In other words, every *object* has *properties* and the ability to perform certain tasks. An *object-oriented language* is a language that was built with object modeling in mind. Now you may be thinking, "But I can model objects in C." You are absolutely correct. However, the object-oriented design of C++ allows for a much better representation of those objects in code form. This is because C++ has the following object-oriented features:

- Classes
- Inheritance
- Polymorphism

That's not too much information to grasp, so let's get to it!

Classes

Let's start with *classes*. In C, data representations are usually encapsulated within a structure. Structures hold data representing an object. Any functions manipulating this object would be written outside the structure declaration. Check out Figure A.1. Notice how the code that operates on the data is external to the structure. So how are classes better? Well, with C++, the data and the functions manipulating that data are contained within a class. The data and the functions are brought together under one roof, giving the feeling of unity. See how in Figure A.1 the code that operates on the data is now internal to the object? With C, the data and the functions are separated, which makes it seem like they don't really go together. With C++, the data and functions are part of the same object. This technique of combining the data in one place is called *encapsulation*. All of the object's data and code to manipulate that data are encapsulated in the class.

Struct TV

Data
int channel
int volume
boo1 power

•

•

•

Functions in another
code section

Functions
Power()
ChangeChannel()
ChangeVolume

•

•

•

In C, the functions that
operate on date are external
to the structural definition.

Class TV

Data
int channel
int volume
boo1 power

•

•

•

Functions
Power()
ChangeChannel()
ChangeVolume

•

•

•

In C++, the functions that operate
on the object's data are included in
the class definition. This helps to
represent the object as a whole,
which is more akin to the way
humans think.

A.I

*Comparison of a C structure
and a C++ class.*

Inheritance

The second advantage with C++ is *inheritance*. Inheritance allows you to form relationships between classes. That is, you can create one class, called the *base class* (or *parent class*) and then create child classes from the parent class. The child classes *inherit* the properties from the parent class. Take a look at Figure A.2. GameDeveloper is the parent class, here. You can see that this branches down into two more specific types of GameDeveloper, the Programmer and Artist. Programmer and Artist inherit GameDeveloper's data members, because every Programmer and Artist is a GameDeveloper. On the other hand, GameDeveloper would not inherit anything from Programmer or Artist if you decided to expand the functionality of these classes. If you wanted to get even more specific, you could create new classes from Programmer, maybe AIProgrammer and GraphicsProgrammer. The idea here is that, with inheritance, you can start with something general and create more specific implementations from that. When you create a class based on another class, the technical term is that you are *deriving* one class from another.

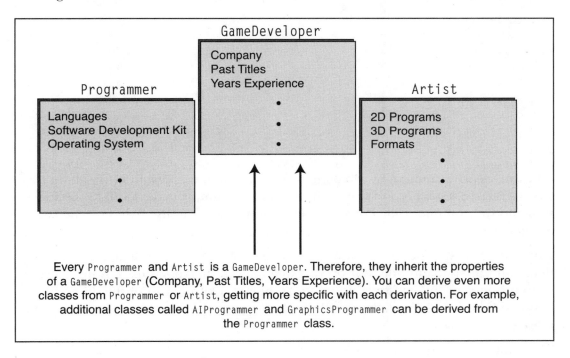

A.2

Inheritance: forming relationships between classes.

Polymorphism

The third feature to object-oriented programming is *polymorphism*. *Poly* means "many" and *morph* means "form." So, using a lot of brainpower, you can see that polymorphism means *many forms*. What this boils down to is that in C++, things don't always have to do what they are meant to do. They can take on other forms. For instance, usually the + operator is used to add two types together. However, in C++ it is possible to rewrite the + operator to actually make it subtract! How crazy is that? This is actually known as *operator overloading*, which I will discuss later in the chapter.

Another example of polymorphism is called *function overloading*. With function overloading, you can have two different functions with the same name! Why? Well, check this out:

```
int Add(int x, int y)
{
//   Insert code here
}

float Add(float x, float y)
{
//   Insert code here
}
```

Can you see why function overloading is useful? You don't have to worry about the type of variables you are working with. Instead, you simply make a call to the function and the compiler will choose which version it needs to use based on the parameters you provided.

Don't worry if you don't fully understand these concepts yet. I will go into further detail on function and operator overloading later in the appendix. For now, just keep this idea of "many forms" in mind. So now you know most of the differences between C and C++. Virtually everything that you'll learn about C++ has to do with these three concepts.

Well, you finished the theory behind C++, so let's get jiggy and check out some implementation tactics!

The Basics of Implementing C++

There isn't much difference between C and C++ from an implementation standpoint, once you figure out all C++'s intricacies. However, let's make sure that everything is covered and start at the beginning. It all begins with Speakin' Da English...

Comments

Comments are every programmer's best friend, right? As long as you remember to include the comment operator, whatever follows will never generate any errors. Let's start with the C comment operator /* */. You know how these work, but I'll just put them here for comparative purposes.

```
/* Hello, I am a C comment */

/*
    Hey!
    Me
    Too
*/
```

I don't know about you, but there have been many times when I have forgotten to close my comment off when using this style. I especially find it a pain to add that extra */ to the end of the comment when it is only a single line. Now although some of you may be die-hard fans of this style of commenting, you may find the new C++ way of commenting more productive in many situations. You will be happy to know that there is nothing wrong with this old-school style of commenting. In fact, you can still use this style in your C++ programs. However, check out the new C++ comment operator //.

```
// Hello, I am the new single-line C++ comment
```

As you can tell from the comment above, the // operator only comments out a single line. The downside to this is when your comment is several lines long, you have to add the forward slashes in front of each line. The bonus is that you don't have to worry about closing the comment. A good rule of thumb to follow is to use the C++ way if your comment is around one to three lines long. If your comment is anything longer, then it is probably more efficient to go with the original C method.

True Constants

Let's pretend that you are writing a game in which the screen resolution is always the same size, meaning there is no option for higher or lower resolutions. Say 640 x 480. Now the resolution will never change, so obviously it is best to make it a constant. How would you go about doing this in C? You would probably do something like this bad boy:

```
#define SCREEN_WIDTH   640
#define SCREEN_HEIGHT 480
```

Problem solved, right? Well, not exactly. Is SCREEN_WIDTH an integer? A floating point number? How about the size of SCREEN_WIDTH? Honestly, I have no clue, and neither does the compiler. In your program, when the compiler comes across the #define directive, it will basically think of SCREEN_WIDTH as a symbol to mean 640. So anywhere you use `SCREEN_WIDTH` in your program, the compiler will replace it with 640. The problem is that it doesn't replace it with the *integer* 640, but the *text* "640." Obviously, this isn't what you want. So let's try something else:

```
int SCREEN_WIDTH  = 640;
int SCREEN_HEIGHT = 480;
```

Well, now you know that both variables are integers, and the compiler can do type checking to avoid mistakes. But they aren't really constants, which means that their value may accidentally be changed during run time in your game. As you can probably guess, this could lead to bad situations. But don't give up just yet—C++ provides a handy new type that goes by the name of `const`. And yes, you guessed it, `const` is short for *constant*. This makes it a lot easier to create read-only variables. Check it out:

```
const int SCREEN_WIDTH  = 640;
const int SCREEN_HEIGHT = 480;
```

Clever, huh? Now you can use these two variables anywhere in your program and not be afraid of them being overwritten. Furthermore, you know they are integers and the compiler can do type checking!

Creating Variables

One feature I find really handy in C++ is the ability to create variables almost anywhere. No longer are you limited to creating variables at the global or functional level as you were with C. Take a look at the following C code to see exactly what I mean:

```
void InitializeData()
{
        int Index;
        // Initialize some stuff here...

        // Initialize enemy energy
        for( Index = 0; Index < 100; Index++)
                enemy[Index].energy = 100;

        // initialize some other things...

} // end InitializeData
```

This code is fine and will get the job done, but what isn't obvious about this example is the declaration and scope of index. Usually in C, variables are declared at the beginning of a function and they remain in scope until the function exits. Take a look at how that very same loop could be done in C++.

```
// initialize enemy energy
for(int index = 0; index < 100; index++)
        enemy[index].energy = 100;
```

Isn't that awesome? You now have a lot more freedom for variable creation. Instead of defining index at the top of the function, you can define it right when you want to use it. Expanding on this same idea, you can create code blocks to define the scope of your variables.

```
void main()
{
        int x = 5, y = 10;

        printf("\nGlobal Scope: x = %d, y = %d",x,y);

        // Now move Inside another block with Isolated variable scope
        {
                int x = 10, y = 15;
                printf("\nScope Block: x = %d, y = %d",x,y);
        }

        printf("\nAfter Scope Block: Global Scope: x = %d, y = %d",x,y);

}// end main
```

This code would output the following:

```
Global Scope: x = 5, y = 10
Scope Block: x = 10, y = 15
After Scope Block: Global Scope: x = 5, y = 10
```

If you look closely, you will see that I have declared two different versions of x and y. The first pair is global to main() and would normally be seen anywhere within main(). However, I used parentheses to create a code block. When I declared a new x and y in my scope block, the global pair immediately went out of scope. Then when I close off the code block, the global pair came back into scope. This is an easy way to localize your variables and keep them "hidden" from other code blocks.

This new variable scoping thing is really cool. However, your code can get harder and harder to read and debug if you overuse it. So don't get carried away, especially if other people need to read your code. Generally you will find that most programmers hardly, if ever, use this feature other than for loop counters, but it's always good to know about it in case it comes up sometime.

Passing Variables by Reference

Sometimes you may want a function to change the value of a variable that you pass to it. C++ makes it really easy for you to do this with reference variables. You remember how the only way to pass a variable in C, other than by direct value, was to use its address like this:

```
int EatApple(int *pApple)
{
        (*pApple)--;
        int NewCount = *pApple;

        return NewCount;
}

int main()
{
        int Apples = 100;
        Apples = EatApple( &Apples );

        return 0;
}
```

Well, that's not really hard, but I don't want to go through all that trouble just to eat an apple. And then if I forget to add the & in front of apple when calling the function, I'll be eating an error instead! So let's look to C++ for an easier way of eating apples.

```
int EatApple(int &Apple)
{
        Apple--;
        return Apple;
}

int main()
{
```

```
        int Apples = 100;
        Apples = EatApple( Apples );

        return 0;
}
```

How about them apples! Isn't that easier? Now you don't have to worry about adding the & when calling your function. Basically what happens when you call EatApple() is that Apple will point to the same memory space as the variable passed, in this case it's Apples. In other words, whatever you do to Apple, you do to Apples!

To get a better understanding of reference variables, look at the following example:

```
int John;
```

```
int &Mike = John;
```

This is the same thing you saw in the previous example, except this time it's from outside of a function. The & in front of Mike simply assigns it the same memory space that John has. In other words you are assigning the address of the integer variable Mike to be the same as John. So whatever happens to John happens to Mike. And vice versa.

Streaming Input and Output

Moving ahead swiftly, you come to input and output. I'm sure you know the printf() function—it is used for formatted text output like in the following example:

```
printf("\nHippos like mud!");
```

This code will output the following to the screen:

```
Hippos like mud!
```

Well, that's easy enough. But what about when you have to output variables? Don't you just love all the format specifiers (%x, %d, %f, etc.)? I sure don't. I have a hard enough time remembering them all! C++ gets rid of these problems with its new output command, cout (most people pronounce it *see out*). Here is a comparison of these two output commands in action:

```
int   number = 99;
float decimal = 99.9f;
char  character = 'A';
char  string[9] = "A string";
```

```
// normal C output
printf("\nDid Mary really have a little lamb?");

// normal C++ output
cout << "\nNo, it's all a conspiracy!";

// integer output in C
printf("%i\n", number);

// integer output in C++
cout << number;

// decimal output in C
printf("%g", decimal);

// decimal output in C++
cout << decimal;

// character and string output in C
printf("%c, %s", character, string);


// in C++
cout << character << ", " << string;
```

And this would output the following:

```
Did Mary really have a little lamb?
No, it's all a conspiracy!
99
99
99.9
99.9
A, A string
A, A string
```

Well, that is much nicer than C, isn't it? Notice how cout automatically figures out the type of variable that you want to output. That is *so* much easier than remembering all those character codes. The only thing that might be causing confusion is the last example. You can output several variables with one cout statement, but after each one, you have to add another <<. If you find this hard to grasp, try writing it this way:

```
cout << character
        << ", "
        << string;
```

Moving on to input, there is a new `cin` command (pronounced *see in*). Let's try a few examples:

```
int number;
char character;
char string[10];

// integer input in C
printf("\nWhat is your favorite number?");
scanf("%d", &number);

// C++
cout << "\nWhat is your favorite number?";
cin >> number;

// character and string input in C
printf("What is your first name and middle initial?");
scanf("%s %c", string, &character);

// in C++
cout << "What is your first name and middle initial?";
cin >> string >> character;
```

Jeez, C++ is a lot easier to deal with. Notice how you don't have to worry about the & operator in C++ input. The only thing that I get mixed up is which way to point the arrows for `cin` and `cout`.

TIP

Try to think of the functions as the devices themselves and that will help you point the arrows the right way. For instance, if `cout` is the monitor, then you are outputting text *to* the monitor and therefore you point the arrows toward it. Similarly, you are getting data *from* the keyboard so you want the arrows to point away from `cin`. Pretend the data is following the arrows and all will be cool!

These new input and output commands are really neat, but before you can take advantage of them you have to include iostream.h in your program. Of course, there are a million other functions included with iostream.h, but the ones covered here are the most important.

Managing Memory

C++ gives you the option of using two new operators to help with memory management. These are the new and delete operators. These new operators aren't that much different from malloc() and free(). However, as with C++ stream I/O, these new operators know the type of data that is being dealt with. In other words, in C where you would have to do something like this...

```
int *x = (int*)malloc(100*sizeof(int));
```

you could accomplish the same task in C++ like this:

```
int *x = new int[100];
```

As you can see, the type casting is not needed in C++. The code is also much easier to read. But now that you've created the memory, how do you release it? Well, in C, it would go like this:

```
free(x);
```

And in C++, you would do this:

```
delete x;
```

There really isn't that much difference, except for the new operator. You can use whichever style you are more comfortable with, but don't play mix and match. Use either the C method or the C++ method.

Classes

Finally, you've made it to the heart of C++: classes. It's time for the discussion on object-oriented programming features of C++. Well, I don't know about you, but I'm excited.

Data Representation in the Dark Ages

Let me just take a moment to nail down how to model objects in C. Usually it looks like this:

```
struct Rectangle
{
        int length;
        int width;
};
```

Then you can create an object of this structure by doing this:

```
struct Rectangle r1;
```

However, many C programmers don't like typing `struct` every time they want to create an object, so they use the handy keyword `typedef`, like this:

```
typedef struct Rectangle_tag
{
int length;
int width;
}Rectangle;
```

Then when you want to instantiate the structure, you simply type this:

```
Rectangle r1;
```

You know all this, so let's get jiggy and get to what you want to see—how to create a simple class!

A Basic Class

The basic class definition looks almost exactly like a `struct` definition in C, with the exception of the `class` and `public` keywords. Take a look here:

```
class CRectangle
{
        public:
        int m_Length;
        int m_Width;
};
```

Not too bad, huh? The keyword `public` basically describes how the variables can be accessed (more on that later). The way you create an instance of this class and access its data is exactly the same way you do it with a `struct`.

The class definition above is really just that, a definition. To use it you need to create an object based on the class definition. The technical term for this is *instantiation*. It is one of those simple concepts that has a complicated name. Basically, all you are doing is declaring a variable based on the class, as in the following:

```
CRectangle r1;

r1.m_Length = 5;
r1.m_Width  = 10;
```

Or for pointers:

```
CRectangle *r1;

r1->m_Length = 5;
r1->m_Width  = 10;
```

> **NOTE**
>
> It is a popular programming convention to place a capital "C" before the name of your class. This makes class objects easy to identify when reading code. So whenever you see something like `CRectangle`, you can be sure it's a class object. Also take a moment to take note of the `m_` that is in front of the member variables, which signifies that the variable is a member variable and not a standard variable. You don't have to do this, but it is really good programming practice and will keep other programmers happy when they have to read your code.

If you think that is an awful lot like `struct`s, then you are right. Classes are really just `struct`s with extra functionality added, which you will see very soon.

Accessing Class Data Elements

Let's take another look at the class definition from above:

```
class CRectangle
{
public:
        int m_Length;
        int m_Width;
};
```

Notice once again the use of the keyword `public`. This is used to describe how the member variables and member functions of the class can be accessed. Besides `public`, you can choose either `private` or `protected`. So what does each one mean?

The keyword `public` is used when you want anybody who uses your class to have access to your member variables and member functions. Basically, you can access the member variables just as you would in a `struct`. In other words, it is perfectly legal to do something like this:

```
CRectangle   r1;
r1.m_Length = 2;
r1.m_Width   = 4;
```

However, there are times when you may not want everybody to have access to your data and member functions. Typically, this is done when you are creating a black box class where you don't want anybody messing with certain variables. Here is how you would set this up:

```
class CRectangle
{
public:      //anybody can mess with these variables
        int m_Top, m_Bottom;
        int m_Left, m_Right;

private:     // the following variables are "untouchable" by any code outside the
class definition
        int m_Length;
        int m_Width;
};
```

In this case, if you tried to do something like this...

```
CRectangle r1;
r1.m_Length = 5;    //  WRONG!!!
```

you would get an error! The only way to access private member variables is through member functions. I will get to those in just a second. First let's talk about what a `protected` member variable is. In most respects, protected members are just like private members. However, derived classes have direct access to protected members of their parent class as well.

All this accessing variables stuff is probably a little bit up in the air right now because it is so new, but don't worry, it should solidify in your mind as you read through the rest of the appendix. In the meantime, mark this page and you can come back to it if you get confused. So try and keep the following in your head:

- **Public** functions and variables can be accessed by code from anywhere in your program.
- **Protected** functions and variables can only be accessed from code that is part of the class itself or part of a derived class.
- **Private** functions and variables can only be accessed from code within the class. External code and code from derived classes are denied access to the code.

With that in mind, let's move on to encapsulated code.

Member Functions

With all that talk about member functions, you're probably dying to know what they are. If you remember in the beginning of the chapter, I discussed how classes contain data and the functions that operate on that data. Well, *member functions* are what I was talking about, and here's how you would create one:

```
class CRectangle
{
public:     //  these members can be seen by everyone
        int m_Top, m_Bottom;
        int m_Left, m_Right;
```

```
        void Dimensions(int x, int y)
        {
                m_Length - x;
                m_Width  - y;
        }

private:      // member functions
have access to these variables
        int m_Length;
        int m_Width;
};
```

Check out the bolded member function, `Dimensions()`. Member functions are simply functions that you declare right inside the class. Of course, you don't go declaring just any function inside the class. Only those that deal with the manipulation of the object you are modeling. Also, usually you don't define the function inside the class, unless the function is only a few lines. Typically, you only include the function prototype inside the class declaration. However, defining a member function outside of the class definition is a bit tricky, so I'll save that for later.

Okay, now you have a member function that manipulates your private members, but how do you use it? Simple, just like you access member variables of a class.

```
CRectangle r1;

//sets private members (m_Length, m_Width) to 5 and 10
r1.Dimensions(5,10);
```

Or do the same through a pointer:

```
CRectangle *r1;

//sets private members (m_Length,m_Width) to 5 and 10
r1->Dimensions(5,10);
```

In a real program, you may not want to declare `m_length` and `m_width` as private members. I just did it here for illustrative purposes. Also, member functions aren't only used to manipulate private members. For example, you could write a member function to rotate the rectangle based on its public members (m_Top, m_Bottom, m_Left, m_Right).

At this point, you should start to see the importance of the private keyword. There will be times when you create a class and have certain elements that other programmers shouldn't have access to, usually when accessing them has the potential to cause problems. In your rectangle class, the only way the private members can be changed is by a call to Dimensions(). And even then, all you can do is set the private variables' values to an integer. It's like security for member variables.

Constructors and Destructors

Now here is one really cool feature of C++. In short, *constructors* are functions you can write that will be automatically called when you create an object. They are used to initialize the data in your class. *Destructors,* on the other hand, are functions that are automatically called when your object goes out of scope. They are used to free any resources that were acquired during the lifetime of the object. These are both optional features of C++, but they come in very handy. To see their real power, let's go over the C way of initializing a struct.

```
typedef struct Enemy_tag
{
        int x, y;     // enemy position
        int health;  // enemy health
        char *name; // in case we need to allocate memory
}Enemy;

Enemy monster[10];
```

OK, now we need to initialize all 10 monster structures:

```
for(int index=0;index<10;index++)
{
        monster[index].x = rand()%640;
        monster[index].y = rand()%480;
        monster[index].health = 100;
        monster[index].name = NULL;
}
```

Well, that isn't too bad. But what if you forget to initialize the structures? Or even worse, what if you allocate memory to the structures and forget to free it? You would run into some major run-time problems that could cause memory leaks, crashes, slow performance, and a bunch of other stuff that is usually found only in poor programs. This is where constructors and destructors come in very handy.

Creating a Constructor

Let's just jump right in and create a constructor:

```
class CEnemy
{
public:
        int m_x, m_y;
        int m_Health;
        char *m_strName;

        // this is our constructor
        CEnemy()
          {
                m_x = rand()%640;
                m_y = rand()%480;
                m_Health = 100;

                m_strName = NULL;
          }
};
```

There are two rules to follow when creating constructors.

- They must have the same name as the class.
- They must never return a value.

You may also have noticed that there aren't any parameters in this constructor. When a constructor doesn't have any parameters, it is called the *default constructor*. The term comes from the fact that it is default and is therefore called automatically by the compiler. To use a default constructor, you simply do this:

```
CEnemy monster[10];
```

That's pretty nice, isn't it? You don't have to do *anything* to invoke the default constructor. It's automatically called when you create the object. All 10 monsters will be initialized without your doing anything! Never again will you forget to initialize your objects! How slick is that?

Let's write another constructor now, except this time you will add parameters to it. This is an example of function overloading that I talked about in the beginning of this appendix.

```cpp
class CEnemy
{
public:
        int m_x, m_y;
        int m_Health;
        char *m_strName;

        //our default constructor
        CEnemy()
        {
                m_x = rand()%640;
                m_y = rand()%480;

                m_Health = 100;
                m_strName = NULL;
        }

        // another constructor, but with parameters
        CEnemy(int x, int y, int Health, char *strName)
        {
                m_x = x;
                m_y = y;

                m_Health = Health;
                m_strName = new char[strlen(strName)+1];
                strcpy(m_strName, strName);
        }
};
```

You may be thinking, "What do I need two constructors for?" Well, maybe you'll want to create a unique monster at some point instead of the generic monster created by the default constructor. For example, let's create a super monster!

```cpp
CEnemy SuperMonster(100, 100, 5000, "Super Monster");
```

And of course, you can still create a generic monster:

```cpp
CEnemy monster;
```

Can you see what is happening? If you declare the class normally, then the default constructor is called automatically. However, if you want to you can quickly initialize the class, then you can declare the new object with parameters and the appropriate constructor will be called. There are a few more types of constructors, but the two kinds I showed you here are enough to get you started in C++. If you want some more, albeit complex, information on constructors, check out *MSDN for Visual C++ 6.0 / Visual C++ Documentation / Reference / C++ Language and Libraries / C++ Language Reference / Special Member Functions / Constructors / Constructors.*

Creating the Destructor

As I mentioned earlier, destructors are the opposite of constructors. Their primary purpose is to free up any memory allocated after the object is no longer required. Unlike constructors, there is only one type of destructor, and the syntax is as follows:

```
~Classname();
```

There are no parameters or return types. The only thing special about them is the ~ (known as a tilde) in front of the class name. Let's create a destructor for the CEnemy class:

```
class CEnemy
{
        public:
        int m_x, m_y;
        int m_Health;
        char *m_strName;

        //The default constructor
        CEnemy()
        {
                m_x = rand()%640;
                m_y = rand()%480;

                m_Health = 100;
                m_strName = NULL;
        }// end default constructor
```

```
        // another constructor, but with parameters
        CEnemy(int x, int y, int Health, char *strName)
        {
                m_x = x;
                m_y = y;
                m_Health = Health;

                m_strName = new char[strlen(strName)+1];
                strcpy(m_strName,strName);

        }// end constructor(int,int,int,char*)

        // destructor
        ~CEnemy()
        {

                delete m_strName;

        }// end destructor
};
```

With destructors, you will never have to worry about freeing up memory that was used by your objects. Whenever your object is done being used, the compiler automatically calls the destructor for you. Hence, no memory leaks!

Scope Resolution

Remember I told you that member functions are usually defined outside the class? This is mainly for readability. There will be times when you create a class that will have several member functions, some of which may be several lines long. Obviously, your class definition will start to get cluttered. Previously, all of the functions you've been using for your classes were defined within the class definition, including your constructors and destructor. Well, get ready, because now I'm going to show you how to define class functions outside your classes!

C++ has yet a new operator, called the *scope resolution operator* (::). This is used to show the compiler that certain functions or variables belong to a class. Check out the funky syntax:

```
ReturnType ClassName::FunctionName(Parameters)
{
// implementation
}// end function_name
```

It's not bad. Just think of the :: like the possessive "'s" used in English. For instance, take the phrase "Joanna's house is big." You can see that the 's shows that the house belongs to Joanna. It is the same in C++. `ClassName::FunctionName()` simply means that the function `FunctionName()` belongs to `ClassName`. A good tip is to read the declaration in an English sort of way. For instance, "`ClassName's FunctionName` performs this operation." You just have to remember to add the class name and scope resolution operator to the beginning of the function name. Let's give it a try:

```
class CEnemy
{
        int m_x, m_y;
        int m_Health;
        char *m_strName;

        //our default constructor
        CEnemy();

        // another constructor, but with parameters!
        CEnemy(int x, int y, int Health, char *strName);

        // destructor
        ~CEnemy();
};

// Now define the functions.  Outside the class!!!
// DEFAULT CONSTRUCTOR

CEnemy::CEnemy()
{
        m_x = rand()%640;
        m_y = rand()%480;

        m_Health = 100;
        m_strName = NULL;
}// end default constructor
```

```
// ANOTHER CONSTRUCTOR

CEnemy::CEnemy(int x, int y, int Health, char *strName)
{
        public:
        m_x = x;
        m_y = y;
        m_Health = Health;

        m_strName = new char[strlen(strName)+1];
        strcpy(m_strName, strName);
}// end constructor(int,int,int,char*)

// DESTRUCTOR

CEnemy::~CEnemy()
{
        delete m_strName;
}// end destructor
```

Take a look at how clean your class definition looks now. Yippy Skippy!

Friend Functions

Another type of function that you have available in your C++ arsenal is the *friend* function type. These are special functions that are given access to a class's private member variables. However, friend functions are not members of the class, so an object of the class does not activate them. They are ordinary functions that need access to private members. Here is how you can create a friend function:

```
class CStuff
{
public:
        int m_Garbage;

        //a friend function
        friend void StealSecrets(CStuff &government);

private:
        int m_SecretStuff;
};
```

Notice the use of the keyword friend. That is all there is to creating friend functions. This is how you would implement StealSecrets();

```
void StealSecrets(CStuff &government)
{
        government.m_SecretStuff += 5;
}
```

The definition is just like any normal function you would write. The only difference is that it can access the private members of class CStuff.

Well, there I go talking about what can and can't access the different members of a class. If you are having trouble with this, take a look at Table A.1. This table should help clarify things for you. It really isn't that bad.

> **TIP**
>
> If a function needs access to the private members of a class, you should first consider providing the access via a member function. If this is somehow inconvenient or unacceptable, then you may grant friendship to an external standard function.

Table A.1   Access Specifiers for Classes

	Public Members	Private Members	Protected Members
Class Member Functions	Have Access	Have Access	Have Access
Normal Functions	Have Access	Don't Have Access	Don't Have Access
Friend Functions	Have Access	Have Access	Have Access
Derived Classes	Have Access	Don't Have Access	Have Access
Main Program	Have Access	Don't Have Access	Don't Have Access

Got it? OK, let's keep truckin'...

Function and Operator Overloading

Function overloading is when you have two or more functions with the same name but different parameter lists. Take a look at the following example:

```
int Add(int x, int y)
{
        return(x + y);
}

float Add(float x, float y)
{
        return(x + y);
}
```

This would be a big no-no in C, but in C++ it is just fine. Both of the functions above have the same name, but they each take different parameters and return a different type. This is a nice feature because you don't have to worry about whether you are working with integers or floats. You simply make a call to Add() and plug in the variables. The compiler will call the correct version of the function automatically.

```
int x = 5;
int  y = 6;
int z;

float a = 7.0f;
float b = 9.5f;
float c;

z = Add(x,y);      //  calls the integer version of add

c = Add(a,b);      //  calls the floating point version of add
```

The other type of overloading that you can do with C++ is called *operator overloading*. With operator overloading, you can define a new meaning for an operator. For example, you can overload the binary operators (==, !=, <, >, <=, >=) and the input and output operators (>>, <<). Altogether, there are something like 44 operators you can overload. In order to overload an operator, you have to define a function to tell it what to do. As an example, let's use the first class you created:

```
class CRectangle
{
public:
        int m_Length;
        int m_Width;
};
```

And say you fill in that bad boy like this:

```
CRectangle r1, r2, r3;

r1.m_Length = 5;
r1.m_Width = 10;

r2.m_Length = 10;
r2.m_Width = 15;
```

Now say you want to set r3 equal to the sum of r1 and r2. In other words, you want r3.length to equal the sum of r1.length and r2.length, and you want r3.width to equal the sum of r1.width and r2.width. You couldn't just do this:

```
r3 = r1 + r2;   // This will not work!!!
```

If you did this, you would get an error! The compiler doesn't understand the type CRectangle, so you have to redefine the $\pm$ operator to tell the compiler what to do when it sees that line above. You have to change your class definition to look like this:

```
class CRectangle
{
public:
        int m_Length;
        int m_Width;

        // operator overload
        CRectangle operator+(CRectangle &rect)
        {
                CRectangle sum;
                sum.m_Length = m_Length + rect.m_Length;
                sum.m_Width  = m_Width + rect.m_Width;
                return(sum);
        }// end operator+
};
```

Now, when you write a statement like this...

```
r3 = r1 + r2;
```

...you get exactly what you wanted! That's pretty cool, huh?

The syntax for overloading an operator is pretty weird, especially because there is only one parameter. However, this is basically how it is done. If you want some more detailed information on operator overloading, then check out *MSDN Library for Visual C++ 6.0 / Visual C++ Documentation / Reference / C++ Language and Libraries / C++ Language Reference / Overloading / Overloading*. There is a ton of information there on the subject, although it is quite complex.

Conclusion

Congratulations! You have just completed this crash course in C++. If you made it this far, then you should now have a fairly good understanding of the fundamentals of C++. What you need to do now is get out and put those skills to work! If you need more information on C++, then check out the language reference in MSDN, where there is more information than you can imagine on the subject. However, Microsoft's documentation has a reputation for being overly complex and without much direction, so you may find it more useful to purchase a book on the subject.

Two excellent sources of information on C++ are *Beginning Visual C++ 6* by Ivor Horton, published by Wrox Press, and *1001 Visual C++ Programming Tips* by Charles Wright, published by Prima Publishing.

APPENDIX B

Direct3D
Advanced
Reference

Welcome to Appendix B, your home for all important information concerning Direct3D. I have included a reference to all the functions, methods, and interfaces that are either important or occurred throughout the book. There are a few conventions you should know about in this reference. Beside each of the parameters is a small icon, which is labeled *in, out,* or *both.* These icons reflect how the parameter is to be used by Direct3D. If the icon is *in,* then Direct3D is expecting information from you. Conversely, if the icon is *out,* Direct3D will be providing you with information. And as you can probably guess, *both* means that Direct3D will take information from you and then give you back information through the same parameter.

I would suggest not reading this appendix from cover to cover because you may just die of boredom. I know I did about six times while writing it, but I had the cheats turned on so I came back to life. The appendix is arranged alphabetically and is meant to be used when you are typing out code and can't be bothered to install the Help files from the SDK—you can just flip through these pages instead. Man, I am such a nice guy.

C++ Functions

Direct3DCreate8()

Purpose

The creation of the main IDirect3D8 object, which is subsequently used for the creation of all other Direct3D objects.

Prototype

```
IDirect3D8* Direct3DCreate8(
  UINT SDKVersion
);
```

Parameters

 SDKVersion: The version of the Direct3D object that you want to create. Set this to `D3D_SDK_VERSION`.

COM Interfaces

IDirect3D8

CheckDepthStencilMatch()

Purpose

Determines whether or not the format of the depth/stencil buffer is compatible with the format of the target render device.

Prototype

```
HRESULT CheckDepthStencilMatch(
  UINT Adapter,
  D3DDEVTYPE DeviceType,
  D3DFORMAT AdapterFormat,
  D3DFORMAT RenderTargetFormat,
  D3DFORMAT DepthStencilFormat
);
```

Parameters

 **Adapter:** The index number for the adapter that you are enquiring about.

 DeviceType: A `D3DDEVTYPE` enumeration member identifying the device type.

 AdapterFormat: A `D3DFORMAT` enumeration member identifying the display mode that the device will be placed in.

 RenderTargetFormat: A `D3DFORMAT` enumeration member identifying the format of the render target surface on the adapter that will be tested.

 DepthStencilFormat: A `D3DFORMAT` enumeration member identifying the format of the depth and stencil buffer that will be tested.

CheckDeviceFormat()

Purpose

Determines whether or not a surface format is available for use as a texture, depth, or stencil buffer, a render target, or a combination of all options.

Prototype

```
HRESULT CheckDeviceFormat(
  UINT Adapter,
  D3DDEVTYPE DeviceType,
  D3DFORMAT AdapterFormat,
  DWORD Usage,
  D3DRESOURCETYPE RType,
  D3DFORMAT CheckFormat
);
```

Parameters

IN **Adapter:** The index number for the adapter that you are enquiring about.

IN **DeviceType:** A D3DDEVTYPE enumeration member identifying the device type.

IN **AdapterFormat:** A D3DFORMAT enumeration member identifying the display mode that the device will be placed in.

IN **Usage:** Flag, which can be either D3DUSAGE_DEPTHSTENCIL (for a depth or stencil buffer) or D3DUSAGE_RENDERTARGET (for a render target), specifying the use of the surface.

IN **RType:** A D3DRESOURCETYPE enumeration member identifying the resource type that will be used with the requested format.

IN **CheckFormat:** A D3DFORMAT enumeration member identifying the format of the surfaces that can be used.

CheckDeviceMultiSampleType()

Purpose

Figures out whether or not a multisample technique is available on a device.

Prototype

```
HRESULT CheckDeviceMultiSampleType(
  UINT Adapter,
  D3DDEVTYPE DeviceType,
  D3DFORMAT SurfaceFormat,
  BOOL Windowed,
  D3DMULTISAMPLE_TYPE MultiSampleType
);
```

Parameters

IN **Adapter:** The index number for the adapter that you are enquiring about.

IN **DeviceType:** A D3DDEVTYPE enumeration member identifying the device type.

IN **SurfaceFormat:** A D3DFORMAT enumeration member identifying the multisample technique that you want to request for the surface.

IN **Windowed:** A BOOL value that specifies whether you are enquiring about full-screen or windowed multisampling.

IN **MultiSampleType:** A D3DMULTISAMPLE_TYPE enumeration member identifying the multisampling technique that you want to test for.

CheckDeviceType()

Purpose

Determines if a type of device, such as HAL or HEL, can be used with this device and also what, if any, hardware acceleration is available on the device.

Prototype

```
HRESULT CheckDeviceType(
  UINT Adapter,
  D3DDEVTYPE CheckType,
  D3DFORMAT DisplayFormat,
  D3DFORMAT BackBufferFormat,
BOOL Windowed
);
```

Parameters

IN **Adapter:** The index number for the adapter that you are enquiring about.

IN **DeviceType:** A D3DDEVTYPE enumeration member identifying the device type that you want to check.

IN **DisplayFormat:** A D3DFORMAT enumeration member identifying the display mode format that you want to check.

IN **BackBufferFormat:** A D3DFORMAT enumeration member identifying the format of the back buffer to be tested.

IN **Windowed:** A BOOL value that specifies whether you are enquiring about full-screen or windowed mode.

CreateDevice()

Purpose

Creates a COM IDirect3DDevice8 object that is used to represent a hardware device.

Prototype

```
HRESULT CreateDevice(
  UINT Adapter,
  D3DDEVTYPE DeviceType,
  HWND  hFocusWindow,
  DWORD BehaviorFlags,
  D3DPRESENT_PARAMETERS* pPresentationParameters,
  IDirect3DDevice8** ppReturnedDeviceInterface
);
```

Parameters

IN **Adapter:** The index number for the adapter that you are enquiring about.

IN **DeviceType:** A D3DDEVTYPE enumeration member identifying the device type that you want to check.

IN hFocusWindow: HWND handle to the window that will be associated with the new device.

IN BehaviorFlags: A creation flag, which can be one of the flags listed in Table B.1, specifying how you want the device to behave.

Table B.1   CreateDevice() Behavior Flags

Flag	Explanation
D3DCREATE_FPU_PRESERVE:	The application needs either double precision FPU or FPU exceptions disabled.
D3DCREATE_HARDWARE_VERTEXPROCESSING:	The device will process vertices independent of the main CPU.
D3DCREATE_MIXED_VERTEXPROCESSING:	The device and the CPU will process vertices.
D3DCREATE_SOFTWARE_VERTEXPROCESSING:	The main CPU will process vertices.
D3DCREATE_MULTITHREADED:	Requests that Direct3D is multithread safe, slightly degrading performance but increasing stability.
D3DCREATE_PUREDEVICE:	The device will not support any functions that return data about the device that can be stored in state blocks and will not provide any emulation functionality.

IN OUT pPresentationParameters: Pointer to a D3DPRESENT_PARAMETERS structure, which contains information about presentation behavior. The BackBufferCount member of the structure may be changed.

OUT ppReturnedDeviceInterface: Returns pointer to a new IDirect3DDevice8.

EnumAdapterModes()

Purpose

Enumerates through all of the display modes that a device supports.

Prototype

```
HRESULT EnumAdapterModes(
  UINT Adapter,
  UINT Mode,
  D3DDISPLAYMODE* pMode
);
```

Parameters

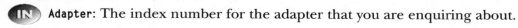 **Adapter:** The index number for the adapter that you are enquiring about.

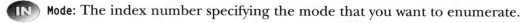 **Mode:** The index number specifying the mode that you want to enumerate.

pMode: Pointer to a D3DDISPLAYMODE structure that will be filled with information about the display mode.

GetAdapterCount()

Purpose

Returns the number of display adapters installed in the host system.

Prototype

```
UINT GetAdapterCount();
```

Parameters

NA

GetAdapterDisplayMode()

Purpose

Retrieves the display mode that the display adapter is currently set to.

Prototype

```
HRESULT GetAdapterDisplayMode(
  UINT Adapter,
  D3DDISPLAYMODE* pMode
);
```

Parameters

 Adapter: The index number for the adapter that you are enquiring about.

 pMode: Pointer to a D3DDISPLAYMODE structure, which is filled with information about the current display mode.

GetAdapterIdentifier()

Purpose

Gets information about the adapters that were installed in the system when IDirect3D8 was instantiated.

Prototype

```
HRESULT GetAdapterIdentifier(
  UINT Adapter,
  DWORD Flags,
  D3DADAPTER_IDENTIFIER8* pIdentifier
);
```

Parameters

 Adapter: The index number for the adapter that you are enquiring about.

Flags: Usually set to zero, but you can set it to D3DENUM_NO_WHQL_LEVEL to speed up the loading process by stopping Direct3D messing around with WHQL certification dates.

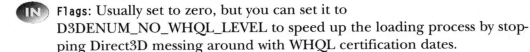 **pIdentifier:** Takes the address of a D3DADAPTER_IDENTIFIER structure that will be filled with information about the display adapter.

GetAdapterModeCount()

Purpose

Returns the number of display modes that the display adapter supports.

Prototype

```
UINT GetAdapterModeCount(
  UINT Adapter
);
```

Parameters

 Adapter: The index number for the adapter that you are enquiring about.

GetAdapterMonitor()

Purpose

Returns the handle of the monitor associated with the Direct3D object.

Prototype

```
HMONITOR GetAdapterMonitor(
  UINT Adapter
);
```

Parameters

 Adapter: The index number for the adapter that you are enquiring about.

GetDeviceCaps()

Purpose

Retrieves information about a display adapter.

Prototype

```
HRESULT GetDeviceCaps(
  UINT Adapter,
  D3DDEVTYPE DeviceType,
  D3DCAPS8* pCaps
);
```

Parameters

IN Adapter: The index number for the adapter that you are enquiring about.

IN DeviceType: A D3DDEVTYPE enumeration member identifying the device type that you want to check.

OUT pCaps: Pointer to a D3DCAPS8 structure that will be filled with information about the device.

RegisterSoftwareDevice()

Purpose

Registers a pluggable software device, such as a software rasterizer, with Direct3D.

Prototype

```
HRESULT RegisterSoftwareDevice(
  void* pInitializeFunction
);
```

Parameters

IN pInitializeFunction: Pointer to the initialization function that you want to register.

IDirect3DDevice8

ApplyStateBlock()

Purpose

Applies an existing state block to a rendering device.

Prototype

```
HRESULT ApplyStateBlock(
  DWORD Token
);
```

Parameters

 Token: Handle to a device-state block that you want to execute. You retrieve this from a previous call to IDirect3DDevice8::EndStateBlock().

BeginScene()

Purpose

Informs Direct3D and the display adapter that you are about to start rendering 3D objects.

Prototype

```
HRESULT BeginScene();
```

Parameters

NA

BeginStateBlock()

Purpose

Tells Direct3D to start recording a state block.

Prototype

```
HRESULT BeginStateBlock();
```

Parameters

NA

CaptureStateBlock()

Purpose

Updates the values in a state block that already exists to match the values to the device.

Prototype

```
HRESULT CaptureStateBlock(
  DWORD Token
);
```

Parameters

 Token: Handle to the state block that the device state will be captured into.

Clear()

Purpose

Clears the viewport to a specified RGBA color, clears the depth buffer, and clears the stencil buffer.

Prototype

```
HRESULT Clear(
   DWORD Count,
   CONST D3DRECT* pRects,
   DWORD Flags,
   D3DCOLOR Color,
   float Z,
   DWORD Stencil
);
```

Parameters

 Count: The number of rectangles in the array pointed to by pRects. If you set pRects to NULL then this must be set to zero.

 pRects: Contains an array of D3DRECT structures that contain information about the array you want to clear.

 Flags: Specifies which surfaces you want to clear. It can be set to any of the values in Table B.2.

Table B.2　Clear Flags for IDirect3DDevice8::Clear()

Flag	Explanation
D3DCLEAR_STENCIL:	Clears the stencil buffer to the value held in Stencil.
D3DCLEAR_TARGET:	Clears the render target surface to the value in Color.
D3DCLEAR_ZBUFFER:	Clears the depth buffer to the value held in Z.

IN Color: An ARGB color to which you want to clear the render target to.

IN Z: A floating point value to which you want to clear the depth buffer to.

IN Stencil: An integer to which you want to clear the stencil buffer to.

CopyRects()

Purpose

Copies rectangular areas of pixels from one surface to another.

Prototype

```
HRESULT CopyRects(
   IDirect3DSurface8* pSourceSurface,
   CONST RECT* pSourceRectsArray,
   UINT cRects,
   IDirect3DSurface8* pDestinationSurface,
   CONST POINT* pDestPointsArray
);
```

Parameters

IN pSourceSurface: Pointer to the source IDirect3DSurface8.

IN pSourceRectsArray: Pointer to an array of rectangles that you want to copy. If you set this parameter to NULL, then the entire surface will be copied.

IN cRects: Integer containing the number of rectangles in the array.

IN pDestinationSurface: Pointer to the destination IDirect3DSurface8.

IN pDestPointsArray: Pointer to an array of POINT structures that contains the upper-left destination coordinates for each rectangle in pSourceRectsArray.

CreateAdditionalSwapChain()

Purpose

Creates an additional swap chain so that you can render in multiple views.

Prototype

```
HRESULT CreateAdditionalSwapChain(
  D3DPRESENT_PARAMETERS* pPresentationParameters,
  IDirect3DSwapChain8** ppSwapChain
);
```

Parameters

IN pPresentationParameters: Pointer to a D3DPRESENT_PARAMETERS that contains information about the new swap chain.

OUT ppSwapChain: Address of a pointer to an IDirect3DSwapChain8 interface.

CreateCubeTexture()

Purpose

Creates a cube texture.

Prototype

```
HRESULT CreateCubeTexture(
  UINT EdgeLength,
  UINT Levels,
  DWORD Usage,
  D3DFORMAT Format,
  D3DPOOL Pool,
  IDirect3DCubeTexture8** ppCubeTexture
);
```

Parameters

IN **EdgeLength:** The size of the edges, in pixels, of all the top-level faces for the cube texture.

IN **Levels:** The number of mip levels for the cube texture. If you set this to zero, then Direct3D will generate mip levels for you if the hardware supports it.

IN **Usage:** Flag describing how the new texture will be used. You can set this to either D3DUSAGE_DEPTHSTENCIL or D3DUSAGE_RENDERTARGET.

IN **Format:** A D3DFORMAT enumeration member identifying the format for all the levels of the new texture.

IN **Pool:** A D3DPOOL enumeration member, describing where in memory the texture should be placed.

OUT **ppCubeTexture:** Address of a pointer to the newly created IDirect3DCubeTexture8 object.

CreateDepthStencilSurface()

Purpose

Creates a new depth or stencil buffer.

Prototype

```
HRESULT CreateDepthStencilSurface(
  UINT Width,
  UINT Height,
  D3DFORMAT Format,
  D3DMULTISAMPLE_TYPE MultiSample,
  IDirect3DSurface8** ppSurface
);
```

Parameters

IN **Width:** The width of the surface, in pixels.

IN **Height:** The height of the surface, in pixels.

IN Format: A D3DFORMAT enumeration member identifying the format for the new surface.

IN Multisample: A D3DMULTISAMPLE_TYPE enumeration member, identifying the type of multisample buffer to use with this surface.

OUT ppSurface: A pointer to the newly created IDirect3DSurface8 object.

CreateImageSurface

Purpose

Creates a new image surface.

Prototype

```
HRESULT CreateImageSurface(
  UINT Width,
  UINT Height,
  D3DFORMAT Format,
  IDirect3DSurface8** ppSurface
);
```

Parameters

IN Width: The width of the image surface, in pixels.

IN Height: The height of the image surface, in pixels.

IN Format: A D3DFORMAT enumeration member identifying the format for the new surface.

OUT ppSurface: A pointer to the newly created IDirect3DSurface8 object.

CreateIndexBuffer()

Purpose

Creates a new index buffer.

Prototype

```
HRESULT CreateIndexBuffer(
  UINT Length,
  DWORD Usage,
  D3DFORMAT Format,
  D3DPOOL Pool,
  IDirect3DIndexBuffer8** ppIndexBuffer
);
```

Parameters

IN **Length:** The length of the new index buffer, in bytes.

IN **Usage:** Flags describing how the buffer will be used. Can be one of the flags shown in Table B.3.

Table B.3   Usage Flags for CreateIndexBuffer()

Flag	Explanation
D3DUSAGE_DONOTCLIP:	The contents of the index buffer will never require clipping.
D3DUSAGE_DYNAMIC:	The index buffer requires dynamic memory usage.
D3DUSAGE_RTPATCHES:	The index buffer will be used to draw high-level primitives.
D3DUSAGE_NPATCHES:	The index buffer will be used to draw n-patches.
D3DUSAGE_POINTS:	The index buffer will be used to draw point sprites or indexed point lists.
D3DUSAGE_SOFTWAREPROCESSING:	The buffer will be used with software vertex processing.
D3DUSAGE_WRITEONLY:	The application will only write to the buffer and never read. This can be used to increase performance. Reading from a buffer with this flag set can degrade performance.

CreatePixelShader()

Purpose

Creates a pixel shader.

Prototype

```
HRESULT CreatePixelShader(
  CONST DWORD* pFunction,
  DWORD* pHandle
);
```

Parameters

 pFunction: Pointer to the pixel shader array of function tokens.

 pHandle: Pointer to the newly created pixel shader's handle.

CreateRenderTarget()

Purpose

Creates a render target surface.

Prototype

```
HRESULT CreateRenderTarget(
  UINT Width,
  UINT Height,
  D3DFORMAT Format,
  D3DMULTISAMPLE_TYPE MultiSample,
  BOOL Lockable,
  IDirect3DSurface8** ppSurface
);
```

Parameters

 Width: The width of the surface, in pixels.

 Height: The height of the surface, in pixels.

 Format: A D3DFORMAT enumeration member identifying the format for the new surface.

IN **Multisample:** A `D3DMULTISAMPLE_TYPE` enumeration member, identifying the type of multisample buffer to use with this surface.

IN **Lockable:** You can only lock the render target if you specify `TRUE` for this flag, which may incur a performance degradation on some hardware.

OUT **ppSurface:** Pointer to the newly created `IDirect3DSurface8`.

CreateStateBlock()

Purpose

Creates a new state block that contains all the information relating to the device, vertex, and pixel states.

Prototype

```
HRESULT CreateStateBlock(
    D3DSTATEBLOCKTYPE Type,
    DWORD* pToken
);
```

Parameters

IN **Type:** A `D3DSTATEBLOCKTYPE` enumeration member identifying the type of state data that you want to capture.

OUT **pToken:** The handle to the state block.

CreateTexture

Purpose

Creates a new texture resource.

Prototype

```
HRESULT CreateTexture(
    UINT Width,
    UINT Height,
    UINT  Levels,
    DWORD Usage,
```

```
  D3DFORMAT Format,
  D3DPOOL Pool,
  IDirect3DTexture8** ppTexture
);
```

Parameters

IN **Width:** The width of the top-level texture, in pixels.

IN **Height:** The height of the top-level texture, in pixels.

IN **Levels:** The number of mip levels in the texture.

IN **Usage:** Flag, which can be D3DUSAGE_DEPTHSTENCIL, D3DUSAGE_RENDERTARGET, or both, specifying how the surface will be used.

IN **Format:** A D3DFORMAT enumeration member identifying the format.

IN **Pool:** A D3DPOOL enumeration member identifying the memory usage of the new texture.

OUT **ppTexture:** Pointer to the newly created IDirect3DTexture8 object.

CreateVertexBuffer()

Purpose

Creates a new vertex buffer.

Prototype

```
HRESULT CreateVertexBuffer(
  UINT Length,
  DWORD Usage,
  DWORD FVF,
  D3DPOOL Pool,
  IDirect3DVertexBuffer8** ppVertexBuffer
);
```

Parameters

IN **Length:** The length of the new vertex buffer, in bytes.

IN **Usage:** Flags specifying how the new vertex buffer will be used. These can be any of the values specified in Table B.3.

IN **FVF:** A combination of FVF (flexible vertex format) flags specifying what format the vertices in the buffer will take.

IN **Pool:** A D3DPOOL enumeration member identifying the memory usage of the new buffer.

OUT **ppVertexBuffer:** Pointer to the newly created IDirect3DVertexBuffer8.

CreateVertexShader()

Purpose

Creates a new vertex shader and sets it as the current shader if the call is successful.

Prototype

```
HRESULT CreateVertexShader(
    CONST DWORD* pDeclaration,
    CONST DWORD* pFunction,
    DWORD* pHandle,
    DWORD Usage
);
```

Parameters

IN/OUT **pDeclaration:** Pointer to the token array for the vertex shader declaration.

IN/OUT **pFunction:** Pointer to the token array for the vertex shader function.

IN/OUT **pHandle:** Pointer to the returned vertex shader handle.

IN **Usage:** Usage flag for the shader, which can be set to D3DUSAGE_SOFTWAREPROCESS-ING or NULL.

CreateVolumeTexture()

Purpose

Creates a volume texture.

Prototype

```
HRESULT CreateVolumeTexture(
    UINT Width,
    UINT Height,
    UINT Depth,
    UINT Levels,
    DWORD Usage,
    D3DFORMAT Format,
    D3DPOOL Pool,
    IDirect3DVolumeTexture8** ppVolumeTexture
);
```

Parameters

IN **Width:** The width of the top-level volume texture, in pixels.

IN **Height:** The height of the top-level volume texture, in pixels.

IN **Depth:** The depth of the top-level volume texture, in pixels.

IN **Levels:** The number of mip levels in the texture.

IN **Usage:** Must be set to zero.

IN **Format:** A D3DFORMAT enumeration member identifying the format for the levels in the texture.

IN **Pool:** A D3DFORMAT enumeration member identifying the memory usage for the texture.

OUT **ppVolumeTexture:** Pointer to the newly created volume texture.

DeletePixelShader()

Purpose

Deletes a pixel shader.

Prototype

```
HRESULT DeletePixelShader(
  DWORD Handle
);
```

Parameters

 Handle: Handle to the pixel shader that you want to delete.

DeletePatch()

Purpose

Deletes a cached high-order primitive.

Prototype

```
HRESULT DeletePatch(
  UINT Handle
);
```

Parameters

 Handle: Handle to the patch that you want to delete.

DeleteStateBlock()

Purpose

Deletes a previously recorded device-state block.

Prototype

```
HRESULT DeleteStateBlock(
  DWORD Token
);
```

Parameters

 Token: Handle to the device-state block that you want to delete.

DeleteVertexShader()

Purpose

Deletes the vertex shader and its associated resources.

Prototype

```
HRESULT DeleteVertexShader(
  DWORD Handle
);
```

Parameters

 Handle: Handle to the vertex shader that you want to delete.

DrawIndexedPrimitive()

Purpose

Renders a geometric primitive by indexing into an array of vertices.

Prototype

```
HRESULT DrawIndexedPrimitive(
  D3DPRIMITIVETYPE Type,
  UINT MinIndex,
  UINT NumVertices,
  UINT StartIndex,
  UINT PrimitiveCount
);
```

Parameters

 Type: A D3DPRIMITIVETYPE enumeration member identifying the type of primitive you want to render.

 MinIndex: The lowest index to use in the buffer for this call.

IN **NumVertices:** The number of vertices used in the buffer for this call.

IN **StartIndex:** Location in the index buffer to start reading vertices.

IN **PrimitiveCount:** The number of primitives to render.

DrawIndexedPrimitiveUP()

Purpose

Renders a primitive using data that is at a location specified by a memory pointer.

Prototype

```
HRESULT DrawIndexedPrimitiveUP(
  D3DPRIMITIVETYPE PrimitiveType,
  UINT MinIndex,
  UINT NumVertices,
  UINT PrimitiveCount,
  CONST void* pIndexData,
  D3DFORMAT IndexDataFormat,
  CONST void* pVertexStreamZeroData,
  UINT VertexStreamZeroStride
);
```

Parameters

IN **Type:** A D3DPRIMITIVETYPE enumeration member identifying the type of primitive you want to render.

IN **MinIndex:** Start vertex index that will be used during this call.

IN **NumVertices:** Number of vertices that will be used in this call.

IN **PrimitiveCount:** Number of primitives that you want to render.

IN **pIndexData:** Pointer to the index data.

IN **IndexDataFormat:** A D3DFORMAT enumeration member identifying the format for the vertex data. It can be either D3DFMT_INDEX16 or D3DFMT_INDEX32.

DrawPrimitive()

Purpose

Renders a sequence of primitives.

Prototype

```
HRESULT DrawPrimitive(
  D3DPRIMITIVETYPE PrimitiveType,
  UINT StartVertex,
  UINT PrimitiveCount
);
```

Parameters

IN **Type:** A D3DPRIMITIVETYPE enumeration member identifying the type of primitive you want to render.

IN **StartVertex:** Index of the first vertex that you want to load.

IN **PrimitiveCount:** Number of primitives that you want to render.

DrawPrimitiveUP()

Purpose

Renders primitive data that is provided by a user pointer.

Prototype

```
HRESULT DrawPrimitiveUP(
  D3DPRIMITIVETYPE PrimitiveType,
  UINT PrimitiveCount,
  CONST void* pVertexStreamZeroData,
  UINT VertexStreamZeroStride
);
```

Parameters

 Type: A D3DPRIMITIVETYPE enumeration member identifying the type of primitive you want to render.

 PrimitiveCount: The number of primitives that you want to render.

DrawRectPatch()

Purpose

Draws a rectangular patch using the currently set streams.

Prototype

```
HRESULT DrawRectPatch(
  UINT Handle,
  CONST float* pNumSegs,
  CONST D3DRECTPATCH_INFO* pRectPatchInfo
);
```

Parameters

 Handle: Handle to the path that you want to draw.

 pNumSegs: Pointer to the value identifying the number of segments that each edge of the primitive should be divided into when tessellated.

 pRectPatchInfo: Pointer to a D3DRECTPATCH_INFO structure, which identifies the patch that you want to draw.

DrawTriPatch()

Purpose

Draws a patch using the currently set streams.

Prototype

```
HRESULT DrawTriPatch(
  UINT Handle,
  CONST float* pNumSegs,
  CONST D3DTRIPATCH_INFO* pTriPatchInfo
);
```

Parameters

 Handle: Handle to the patch that you want to draw.

 pNumSegs: Pointer to the value identifying the number of segments the primitive should be divided into.

 pTriPatchInfo: Pointer to a D3DTRIPATCH_INFO structure, describing the patch that you want to draw.

EndScene()

Purpose

Ends a scene.

Prototype

```
HRESULT EndScene();
```

Parameters

NA

EndStateBlock()

Purpose

Tells Direct3D to stop recording a device-state block.

Prototype

```
HRESULT EndStateBlock(
  DWORD* pToken
);
```

Parameters

 pToken: Pointer to a variable to fill with the handle to the completed device-state block.

GetAvailableTextureMem()

Purpose

Fetches an estimate of available texture memory.

Prototype

```
UINT GetAvailableTextureMem();
```

Parameters

NA

GetBackBuffer()

Purpose

Gets a back buffer from the swap chain.

Prototype

```
HRESULT GetBackBuffer(
  UINT BackBuffer,
  D3DBACKBUFFER_TYPE Type,
  IDirect3DSurface8** ppBackBuffer
);
```

Parameters

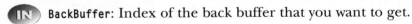 **BackBuffer:** Index of the back buffer that you want to get.

IN **Type:** You can only set this to D3DBACKBUFFER_TYPE_MONO.

OUT **ppBackBuffer:** Takes the address of a pointer that will be filled with the address of the newly created IDirect3DSurface8.

GetClipPlane()

Purpose

Gets the coefficients of a user-defined clipping plane for the device.

Prototype

```
HRESULT GetClipPlane(
  DWORD Index,
  float* pPlane
);
```

Parameters

 Index: This is the index of the clipping plane for which the plane equation coefficients are retrieved.

 pPlane: Pointer to a four-element array of values that represent the coefficients of the clipping plane in the form of the general plane equation.

GetClipStatus()

Purpose

Gets the clip status.

Prototype

```
HRESULT GetClipStatus(
  D3DCLIPSTATUS8* pClipStatus
);
```

Parameters

 pClipStatus: Pointer to a D3DCLIPSTATUS8 structure, which describes the clip status.

GetCreationParameters()

Purpose

This obtains the creation parameters of the device.

Prototype

```
HRESULT GetCreationParameters(
  D3DDEVICE_CREATION_PARAMETERS* pParameters
);
```

Parameters

 pParameters: Pointer to a D3DDEVICE CREATION PARAMETERS structure, explaining the device's creation parameters.

GetCurrentTexturePalette()

Purpose

This gets the current texture palette.

Prototype

```
HRESULT GetCurrentTexturePalette(
  UINT* pPaletteNumber
);
```

Parameters

 pPaletteNumber: Pointer to a value that's returned that identifies the texture palette.

GetDepthStencilSurface()

Purpose

Gets you the depth-stencil surface owned by the Direct3DDevice object.

Prototype

```
HRESULT GetDepthStencilSurface(
  IDirect3DSurface8** ppZStencilSurface
);
```

Parameters

 ppZStencilSurface: Takes the address of a pointer that will be filled with the address of an IDirect3DSurface8.

GetDeviceCaps()

Purpose

Gets the capabilities of the rendering device.

Prototype

```
HRESULT GetDeviceCaps(
  D3DCAPS8* pCaps
);
```

Parameters

 pCaps: Pointer to a D3DCAPS8 structure, explaining the device returned.

GetDirect3D()

Purpose

This gets the interface to the instance of the Direct3D object that created the device.

Prototype

```
HRESULT GetDirect3D(
  IDirect3D8** ppD3D8
);
```

Parameters

 ppD3D8: Takes the address of a pointer that will be filled with the address of the IDirect3D8 object.

GetDisplayMode()

Purpose

Gets the display mode's spatial resolution, color resolution, and refresh frequency.

Prototype

```
HRESULT GetDisplayMode(
  D3DDISPLAYMODE* pMode
);
```

Parameters

 pMode: A pointer to a `D3DDISPLAYMODE` structure holding data about the display mode of the adapter.

GetFrontBuffer()

Purpose

This creates a copy of the device's front buffer and places the copy in a system memory buffer produced by the application.

Prototype

```
HRESULT GetFrontBuffer(
  IDirect3DSurface8* pDestSurface
);
```

Parameters

 pDestSurface: This is a pointer to the `IDirect3DSurface8` interface that receives a copy of the contents of the front buffer.

GetGammaRamp()

Purpose

Fetches the gamma correction ramp for the swap chain.

Prototype

```
void GetGammaRamp(
  D3DGAMMARAMP* pRamp
);
```

Parameters

 pRamp: Pointer to an application-supplied `D3DGAMMARAMP` structure to fill with the gamma correction ramp.

GetIndices()

Purpose

Gets the index data.

Prototype

```
HRESULT GetIndices(
  IDirect3DIndexBuffer8** ppIndexData,
  UINT* pBaseVertexIndex
);
```

Parameters

 ppIndexData: Takes the address of a pointer that will be filled with the address of a `IDirect3DIndexBuffer8`.

 pBaseVertexIndex: A pointer to a UINT value, storing the value of the returned base for vertex indices.

GetInfo()

Purpose

Gets information about the rendering device.

Prototype

```
HRESULT GetInfo(
  DWORD DevInfoID,
  VOID* pDevInfoStruct,
  DWORD DevInfoStructSize
);
```

Parameters

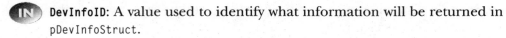 **DevInfoID:** A value used to identify what information will be returned in `pDevInfoStruct`.

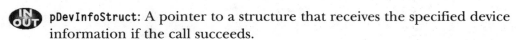 **pDevInfoStruct:** A pointer to a structure that receives the specified device information if the call succeeds.

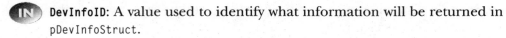 **DevInfoStructSize:** Is the size of the structure at `pDevInfoStruct`, in bytes.

GetLight()

Purpose

Gets the set of lighting properties that this device uses.

Prototype

```
HRESULT GetLight(
  DWORD Index,
  D3DLIGHT8* pLight
);
```

Parameters

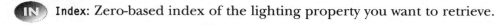 **Index:** Zero-based index of the lighting property you want to retrieve.

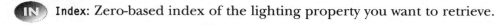 **pLight:** A pointer to a `D3DLIGHT8` structure containing the retrieved lighting-parameter set.

GetLightEnable()

Purpose

Gets the activity status-enabled or disabled-for a set of lighting parameters inside a device.

Prototype

```
HRESULT GetLightEnable(
  DWORD Index,
  BOOL* pEnable
);
```

Parameters

 Index: A zero-based index of the lighting parameters that are the target of this method.

 pEnable: A pointer to a variable that can be filled with the status of the lighting parameters.

GetMaterial()

Purpose

This returns the current material properties for the device.

Prototype

```
HRESULT GetMaterial(
  D3DMATERIAL8*pMaterial
);
```

Parameters

 pMaterial: A pointer to D3DMATERIAL8 that can be filled with the material properties.

GetPaletteEntries()

Purpose

Gets the palette entries.

Prototype

```
HRESULT GetPaletteEntries(
  UINT PaletteNumber,
  PALETTEENTRY* pEntries
);
```

Parameters

 PaletteNumber: An index value identifying the particular palette to retrieve.

 pEntries: This is a pointer to a PALETTEENTRY structure, representing the returned palette entries.

GetPixelShader()

Purpose

Retrieves the currently set pixel shader.

Prototype

```
HRESULT GetPixelShader(
    DWORD* pHandle
);
```

Parameters

 pHandle: Address of the handle for the returned pixel shader.

GetPixelShaderConstant()

Purpose

Retrieves the current values that are set in the pixel constant array.

Prototype

```
HRESULT GetPixelShaderConstant(
    DWORD Register,
    void* pConstantData,
    DWORD ConstantCount
);
```

Parameters

IN **Register:** Address of the register that you want to start retrieving data from the pixel constant array.

IN OUT **pConstantData:** Pointer to the data block that will hold the retrieved values from the constant array. Set the size to (ConstantCount * 4 * sizeof(float))

IN **ConstantCount:** Number of constants that you want to retrieve, each of which comprises four floating-point values.

GetPixelShaderFunction

Purpose

Gets the pixel shader function.

Prototype

```
HRESULT GetPixelShaderFunction(
    DWORD Handle,
    void* pData,
    DWORD* pSizeOfData
);
```

Parameters

IN **Handle:** Handle to the pixel shader that you want to retrieve the function for.

OUT **pData:** Pointer to an allocated buffer that will be filled with the code for the function.

IN OUT **pSizeOfData:** Address of a DWORD value, which holds the size of the buffer that you gave the address for in pData.

GetRasterStatus()

Purpose

Gets information for you regarding the raster status for the monitor to which the swap chain is presenting.

Prototype

```
HRESULT GetRasterStatus(
  D3DRASTER_STATUS* pRasterStatus
);
```

Parameters

 pRasterStatus: Address of a D3DRASTER_STATUS structure that contains information about the raster status of the monitor.

GetRenderState()

Purpose

Gets the current render state value from the device.

Prototype

```
HRESULT GetRenderState(
  D3DRENDERSTATETYPE State,
  DWORD* pValue
);
```

Parameters

 State: The state variable that you want to retrieve, which can be any of the D3DRENDERSTATETYPE enumeration members.

 pValue: Pointer to a variable that receives the value of the variable about which you are asking.

GetRenderTarget()

Purpose

Gets a pointer to the surface that is the current render target.

Prototype

```
HRESULT GetRenderTarget(
  IDirect3DSurface8** ppRenderTarget
);
```

Parameters

ppRenderTarget: Takes the address of a pointer that will receive the address of the render target.

GetStreamSource()

Purpose

Gets the vertex buffer that is currently connected to the data stream specified.

Prototype

```
HRESULT GetStreamSource(
   UINT StreamNumber
   IDirect3DVertexBuffer8** ppStreamData,
   UINT* pStride
);
```

Parameters

 StreamNumber: The index number of the stream that you are querying about.

 ppStreamData: Takes the address of a pointer to an IDirect3DVertexBuffer8 interface, which will be filled with the address of the vertex buffer that you want to retrieve.

 pStride: Pointer to an integer that will receive the stride of the buffer.

GetTexture()

Purpose

Gets a texture from a texture stage that you specify.

Prototype

```
HRESULT GetTexture(
  DWORD Stage,
  IDirect3DBaseTexture8** ppTexture
);
```

Parameters

 Stage: Index for the texture stage that you want to retrieve the texture from, ranging from zero to 7.

 ppTexture: Address of a pointer to a texture that will be filled with the address of the texture that you want to retrieve.

GetTextureStageState()

Purpose

Gets the state value for one of the assigned textures.

Prototype

```
HRESULT GetTextureStageState(
  DWORD Stage,
  D3DTEXTURESTAGESTATETYPE Type,
  DWORD* pValue
);
```

Parameters

IN **Stage:** Number identifying the stage of the texture that you want to receive state information about, which can range from zero to 7.

IN **Type:** A D3DTEXTURESTAGESTATEYPE enumeration member identifying which state you want to get.

OUT **pValue:** Address of a DWORD that will be filled with the information you want to get.

GetTransform

Purpose

Gets a matrix from one of the main transform matrices, such as the world matrix.

Prototype

```
HRESULT GetTransform(
  D3DTRANSFORMSTATETYPE State,
  D3DMATRIX* pMatrix
);
```

Parameters

IN **State:** The state that you want to retrieve the matrix for. This is usually set to D3DTS_WORLD, D3DTS_VIEW, or D3DTS_PROJECTION.

OUT **pMatrix:** Returns the address of the matrix that you want to retrieve.

GetVertexShader()

Purpose

Gets the currently set vertex shader.

Prototype

```
HRESULT GetVertexShader(
  DWORD* pHandle
);
```

Parameters

 pHandle: Retrieves a pointer to the vertex shader handle.

GetVertexShaderConstant

Purpose

Gets the values in the vertex constant array.

Prototype

```
HRESULT GetVertexShaderConstant(
    DWORD Register,
    void* pConstantData,
    DWORD ConstantCount
);
```

Parameters

 Register: Register address that you want to start receiving data from.

 pConstantData: Pointer to a data block that will hold the received data. The size will be (`ConstantCount * 4 * sizeof( float ) `).

 ConstantCount: The number of constants that you want to retrieve from the constant array.

GetVertexShaderDeclaration()

Purpose

Retrieves the vertex shader declaration array of tokens.

Prototype

```
HRESULT GetVertexShaderDeclaration(
    DWORD Handle,
    void* pData,
    DWORD* pSizeOfData
);
```

Parameters

 Handle: Handle to the vertex shader that you want to get the declaration for.

 pData: Pointer to a previously allocated buffer that will be filled with the declaration that you want to retrieve.

 pSizeOfData: Pointer to a DWORD that contains the size of the buffer specified in pData.

GetVertexShaderFunction()

Purpose

Gets the vertex shader function.

Prototype

```
HRESULT GetVertexShaderFunction(
    DWORD Handle,
    void* pData,
    DWORD* pSizeOfData
);
```

Parameters

 Handle: Handle to the vertex shader that you want to retrieve the shader for.

 pData: Pointer to a previously allocated buffer that will be filled with the code for the function.

 pSizeOfData: Pointer to a DWORD value that contains the size of the buffer specified in pData.

GetViewport()

Purpose

Retrieves the viewport for the currently set device.

Prototype

```
HRESULT GetViewport(
   D3DVIEWPORT8* pViewport
);
```

Parameters

 pViewport: Pointer to a D3DVIEWPORT8 structure that will be filled with information about the currently set viewport.

LightEnable()

Purpose

Enables or disables a specific light index.

Prototype

```
HRESULT LightEnable(
   DWORD LightIndex,
   BOOL bEnable
);
```

Parameters

 LightIndex: Index of the light that you want to modify the enable status for.

 bEnable: Boolean value identifying whether you want to enable the light or not.

MultiplyTransform

Purpose

Multiplies a world, view, or projection matrix by another supplied matrix.

Prototype

```
HRESULT MultiplyTransform(
   D3DTRANSFORMSTATETYPE State,
   CONST D3DMATRIX* pMatrix
);
```

Parameters

IN **State:** Flag, which can be set to either D3DTS_WORLDMATRIX, D3DTS_VIEW, or D3DTS_PROJECTION, identifying the transform matrix that you want to modify.

IN **pMatrix:** Address of the D3DMATRIX that you want to concatenate with the transform matrix.

Present()

Purpose

Presents the contents of the back buffer to the primary surface.

Prototype

```
HRESULT Present(
    CONST RECT* pSourceRect,
    CONST RECT* pDestRect,
    HWND hDestWindowOverride,
    CONST RGNDATA* pDirtyRegion
);
```

Parameters

IN **pSourceRect:** Pointer that can be either NULL for the entire surface to be copied, or the address of a rectangle that you want to copy. Only specify a rectangle if you specified D3DSWAPEFFECT_COPY or D3DSWAPEFFECT_COPY_VSYNC when creating the swap chain.

IN **pDestRect:** Can be either NULL or the address of a destination rectangle, which can only be specified if the conditions in pSourceRect are met.

IN **hDestWindowOverride:** Either NULL to render to the default window, or the handle to a window that you want to render to instead.

IN **pDirtyRegion:** Not used and must be set to NULL.

ProcessVertices()

Purpose

Applies the vertex shader processing to a set of data streams and combines them into a single interleaved stream in the destination vertex buffer.

Prototype

```
RESULT ProcessVertices(
  UINT SrcStartIndex,
  UINT DestIndex,
  UINT VertexCount,
  IDirect3DVertexBuffer8* pDestBuffer,
  DWORD Flags
);
```

Parameters

IN **SrcStartIndex:** Index for the first index that you want to load.

IN **DestIndex:** Index into the destination buffer where the results should be placed.

IN **VertexCount:** The number of vertices that you want to process.

IN **pDestBuffer:** Pointer to a destination vertex buffer that will be filled with the processed vertices.

IN **Flags:** Set this flag to either NULL or to D3DPV_DONOTCOPYDATA to prevent the copying of vertices that are not affected by the processing.

Reset()

Purpose

Resets type, size, and format of the swap chain.

Prototype

```
HRESULT Reset(
  D3DPRESENT_PARAMETERS* pPresentationParameters
);
```

Parameters

pPresentationParameters: Pointer to a `D3DPRESENT_PARAMETERS` structure that contains information for how you want to reset the device.

ResourceManagerDiscardBytes()

Purpose

To give the programmer RSI because of the length of its name! No, seriously, it invokes the resource manager to free memory.

Prototype

```
HRESULT ResourceManagerDiscardBytes(
  DWORD Bytes
);
```

Parameters

Bytes: The number of bytes to discard, or specify zero to discard all bytes.

SetClipPlane()

Purpose

Sets the values for the view plane coefficients.

Prototype

```
HRESULT SetClipPlane(
  DWORD Index,
  CONST float* pPlane
);
```

Parameters

 Index: Index of the clipping plane that you want to set the coefficients for.

 pPlane: Address of a four element `float` array containing the new coefficients.

SetClipStatus()

Purpose

Sets the clip status.

Prototype

```
HRESULT SetClipStatus(
  CONST D3DCLIPSTATUS8* pClipStatus
);
```

Parameters

 pClipStatus: Pointer to a D3DCLIPSTATUS8 structure describing the status of the clipper.

SetCurrentTexturePalette()

Purpose

Sets the current texture palette.

Prototype

```
HRESULT SetCurrentTexturePalette(
  UINT PaletteNumber
);
```

Parameters

PaletteNumber: Value that identifies which texture to set the current texture palette to.

SetCursorPosition

Purpose

Sets the cursor position and associated options.

Prototype

```
void SetCursorPosition(
  UINT XScreenSpace,
  UINT YScreenSpace,
  DWORD Flags
);
```

Parameters

IN **XScreenSpace:** The new x-coordinate for the cursor in screen space.

IN **YScreenSpace:** The new y-coordinate for the cursor in screen space.

IN **Flags:** Sets the update options for the cursor. Currently you can only set this to D3DCURSOR_IMMEDIATE_UPDATE.

SetCursorProperties

Purpose

Sets the properties for the cursor.

Prototype

```
HRESULT SetCursorProperties(
  UINT XHotSpot,
  UINT YHotSpot,
  IDirect3DSurface8* pCursorBitmap
);
```

Parameters

IN **XHotSpot:** The x-coordinate index into the cursor image that is considered to be the center (e.g., the end of the arrow on the standard Windows cursor).

IN **YHotSpot:** The x-coordinate index into the cursor image that is considered to be the center.

IN **pCursorBitmap:** Pointer to a surface.

SetGammaRamp()

Purpose

Sets the gamma correction for the implicit swap chain.

Prototype

```
void SetGammaRamp(
  DWORD Flags,
  CONST D3DGAMMARAMP* pRamp
);
```

Parameters

 Flags: Specifies whether you want to apply gamma correction or not, with D3DSGR_CALIBRATE or D3DSGR_NO_CALIBRATION, respectively.

 pRamp: Pointer to a D3DGAMMARAMP structure, which identifies the gamma correction that you want to set for the swap chain.

SetIndices()

Purpose

Sets the index data.

Prototype

```
HRESULT SetIndices(
  IDirect3DIndexBuffer8* pIndexData
  UINT BaseVertexIndex
);
```

Parameters

 pIndexData: Pointer to an index buffer for which you want to set the data.

 BaseVertexIndex: Base value for the vertex index, which is added to all future index values. Usually just set it to zero.

SetLight()

Purpose

Sets the properties for a light index.

Prototype

```
HRESULT SetLight(
  DWORD Index,
  CONST D3DLIGHT8* pLight
);
```

Parameters

 Index: Index of the light that you want to set the properties for.

 pLight: Pointer to a D3DLIGHT8 structure that contains information that you want to set for the light at Index.

SetMaterial()

Purpose

Sets the material properties for the device.

Prototype

```
HRESULT SetMaterial(
   CONST D3DMATERIAL8* pMaterial
);
```

Parameters

 pMaterial: Pointer to a D3DMATERIAL8 structure containing information about the new material that you want to set.

SetPaletteEntries()

Purpose

Sets the palette entries.

Prototype

```
HRESULT SetPaletteEntries(
  UINT PaletteNumber,
  CONST PALETTEENTRY* pEntries
);
```

Parameters

 PaletteNumber: Index of the palette that you want to modify.

 pEntries: Pointer to a PALETTEENTRY structure containing 256 entries for the new palette.

SetPixelShader()

Purpose

Sets the pixel shader to a previously created shader.

Prototype

```
HRESULT SetPixelShader(
  DWORD Handle
);
```

Parameters

 Handle: Handle to the pixel shader that you want to set.

SetPixelShaderConstant()

Purpose

Sets the values in the pixel shader constant array.

Prototype

```
HRESULT SetPixelShaderConstant(
  DWORD Register,
  CONST void* pConstantData,
  DWORD ConstantCount
);
```

Parameters

IN `Register`: The register address at which you want to start loading data.

IN `pConstantData`: Pointer to a data block holding the values that you want to load into the constant array.

IN `ConstantCount`: Number of constants that you want to load into the constant array.

SetRenderState()

Purpose

Sets a render state parameter.

Prototype

```
HRESULT SetRenderState(
  D3DRENDERSTATETYPE State,
  DWORD Value
);
```

Parameters

IN `State`: A `D3DRENDERSTATE` enumeration member specifying which parameter you want to modify.

IN `Value`: The new value for the parameter specified in `State`.

SetRenderTarget()

Purpose

Sets a new render buffer, depth buffer, or both for the device.

Prototype

```
HRESULT SetRenderTarget(
  IDirect3DSurface8* pRenderTarget,
  IDirect3DSurface8* pNewZStencil
);
```

Parameters

IN **pRenderTarget:** A pointer to the new render target buffer, or NULL if you want to retain the existing render target.

IN **pNewZStencil:** Pointer to the new depth buffer, or NULL if you want to retain the existing depth buffer.

SetStreamSource()

Purpose

Connects a vertex buffer to a device data stream.

Prototype

```
HRESULT SetStreamSource(
  UINT StreamNumber,
  IDirect3DVertexBuffer8* pStreamData,
  UINT Stride
);
```

Parameters

IN **StreamNumber:** The index for the stream to which you want to connect the vertex buffer.

IN **pStreamData:** Pointer to the vertex buffer that contains the data that you want to connect to the stream.

IN **Stride:** The stride, in bytes, of the vertex buffer. The stride is the length of each component.

SetTexture()

Purpose

Assigns a texture to a texture state for the device.

Prototype

```
HRESULT SetTexture(
  DWORD Stage,
  IDirect3DBaseTexture8* pTexture
);
```

Parameters

IN **Stage:** Index for the stage to which you want to assign the texture.

IN **pTexture:** Pointer to an IDirect3DBaseTexture8 interface, which holds the texture that you want to set.

SetTextureStageState()

Purpose

Sets the state value for a texture stage.

Prototype

```
HRESULT SetTextureStageState(
  DWORD Stage,
  D3DTEXTURESTAGESTATETYPE Type,
  DWORD Value
);
```

Parameters

IN **Stage:** The index for the stage for which you want to change the state information.

IN **Type:** A member of the D3DTEXTURESTAGESTATETYPE enumeration identifying which stage state you want to modify.

IN **Value:** The new state value to set.

SetTransform()

Purpose

Sets a transform matrix for the device.

Prototype

```
HRESULT SetTransform(
  D3DTRANSFORMSTATETYPE State,
  CONST D3DMATRIX* pMatrix
);
```

Parameters

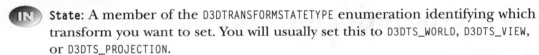 **State:** A member of the D3DTRANSFORMSTATETYPE enumeration identifying which transform you want to set. You will usually set this to D3DTS_WORLD, D3DTS_VIEW, or D3DTS_PROJECTION.

 **pMatrix:** Pointer to the new transform matrix that you want to set.

SetVertexShader()

Purpose

Sets the current vertex shader to a previously created vertex shader.

Prototype

```
HRESULT SetVertexShader(
  DWORD Handle
);
```

Parameters

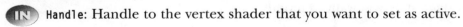 **Handle:** Handle to the vertex shader that you want to set as active.

SetVertexShaderConstant()

Purpose

Sets the values for the vertex shader's constant array.

Prototype

```
HRESULT SetVertexShaderConstant(
   DWORD Register,
   CONST void* pConstantData,
   DWORD  ConstantCount
);
```

Parameters

 Register: Register address that you want to start loading data into.

 pConstantData: Pointer to a data block containing the values that you want to load into the constant array.

 ConstantCount: The number of constants that you want to load into the array.

SetViewport()

Purpose

Sets the viewport parameters to the device.

Prototype

```
HRESULT SetViewport(
   CONST D3DVIEWPORT8* pViewport
);
```

Parameters

 pViewport: Pointer to a D3DVIEWPORT8 structure containing the new viewport specifications.

ShowCursor()

Purpose

Sets whether the cursor is visible or not.

Prototype

```
BOOL ShowCursor(
  BOOL bShow
);
```

Parameters

 bShow: Sets the cursor as either visible or not visible if the value is set to TRUE or FALSE, respectively.

TestCooperativeLevel()

Purpose

Tells you about the current status of the device.

Prototype

```
HRESULT TestCooperativeLevel();
```

Parameters

NA: The function will return either D3D_OK, D3DERR_DEVICELOST, or D3DERR_DEVICENOTRE-SET.

UpdateTexture()

Purpose

Updates a dirty portion of a texture.

Prototype

```
HRESULT UpdateTexture(
  IDirect3DBaseTexture8* pSourceTexture,
  IDirect3DBaseTexture8* pDestinationTexture
);
```

Parameters

 pSourceTexture: Pointer to the source texture, which must be in system memory.

 pDestinationTexture: Pointer to the destination texture, which must be in the default memory pool.

ValidateDevice()

Purpose

Tells you if the device can render with the current texture blending operations and arguments in a single pass.

Prototype

```
HRESULT ValidateDevice(
  DWORD* pNumPasses
);
```

Parameters

 pNumPasses: Returns the number of passes that the effect will take to complete with multipass rendering.

IDirect3DIndexBuffer8

GetDesc()

Purpose

Gets a description of the index buffer resource.

Prototype

```
HRESULT GetDesc(
  D3DINDEXBUFFER_DESC* pDesc
);
```

Parameters

OUT **pDesc:** Pointer to a D3DINDEXBUFFER_DESC structure, which contains the information you requested about the index buffer.

Lock()

Purpose

Locks a range of data in the buffer and gets a pointer to the memory.

Prototype

```
HRESULT Lock(
   UINT OffsetToLock,
   UINT SizeToLock,
   BYTE** ppbData,
   DWORD Flags
);
```

Parameters

IN **OffsetToLock:** The starting offset into the buffer, in bytes, that you want to lock.

IN **SizeToLock:** The amount of memory, in bytes, that you want to lock.

OUT **ppbData:** Pointer to the memory that has been locked.

IN **Flags:** Flags indicating how you want the lock to occur, which can be any of the values in Table B.4.

Table B.4   Flags for Lock()

Flag	Definition
D3DLOCK_DISCARD:	Indicates that you plan to rewrite the *entire* buffer, which allows Direct3D to increase performance slightly.
D3DLOCK_NOOVERWRITE:	Indicates that you plan to only append the buffer, rather than modify the contents, which can increase performance.
D3DLOCK_NOSYSLOCK:	Causes Direct3D not to bother performing a systemwide critical section, which guarantees no display mode changes will occur. This flag increases performance.
D3DLOCK_READONLY:	Indicates that you will not modify the contents of the buffer.

Unlock()

Purpose

Unlocks the index buffer, or section of the buffer.

Prototype

```
HRESULT Unlock();
```

Parameters

NA

IDirect3DSurface8

FreePrivateData()

Purpose

Frees the private data that is connected with the surface.

Prototype

```
HRESULT FreePrivateData(
  REFGUID refguid
);
```

Parameters

 refguid: Reference to (C++) or address (C) of the GUID that is associated with the private data that you want to free.

GetContainer()

Purpose

Gets access to the parent cube texture or mipmap texture, if the texture is a child of another object.

Prototype

```
HRESULT GetContainer(
  REFIID riid
  void** ppContainer
);
```

Parameters

 riid: The reference identifier of the container that you want to get access to.

 ppContainer: Address of a pointer that will be filled with the address of the container.

GetDesc()

Purpose

Gets information about a surface.

Prototype

```
HRESULT GetDesc(
  D3DSURFACE_DESC* pDesc
);
```

Parameters

 pDesc: Pointer to a D3DSURFACE_DESC structure that gets filled with information describing the surface.

GetDevice()

Purpose

Gets the device that was used to create this surface.

Prototype

```
HRESULT GetDevice(
  IDirect3DDevice8** ppDevice
);
```

Parameters

 ppDevice: Address of a pointer to a device that will be filled with the address of the device associated with this surface.

GetPrivateData()

Purpose

Makes a copy of the private data associated with the device into a buffer.

Prototype

```
HRESULT GetPrivateData(
  REFGUID refguid,
  void* pData,
  DWORD* pSizeOfData
);
```

Parameters

 refguid: Reference (C++) or address (C) of the GUID associated with the private data to which you want to get access.

 pData: Pointer to a previously allocated buffer that will be filled with the private data.

 pSizeOfData: Pointer to the size of the buffer specified in pData.

LockRect()

Purpose

Locks a rectangle within a surface.

Prototype

```
HRESULT LockRect(
  D3DLOCKED_RECT* pLockedRect,
  CONST RECT* pRect,
  DWORD Flags
);
```

Parameters

OUT pLockedRect: Pointer to a D3DLOCKED_RECT structure that includes a pointer to the locked memory and an integer describing the pitch of the surface.

IN pRect: Pointer to a RECT that you want to lock.

IN Flags: Flags, which can be set to any of the values in Table B.4 except for D3DLOCK_NOOVERWRITE, identifying how you want to lock the surface.

SetPrivateData()

Purpose

Associates user-defined data with the surface. The data is not used by Direct3D.

Prototype

```
HRESULT SetPrivateData(
  REFGUID refguid,
  void* pData,
  DWORD SizeOfData,
  DWORD Flags
);
```

Parameters

IN `refguid`: Reference(C++) or address(C) of a GUID that identifies the private data.

IN `pData`: Pointer to a buffer that contains the information that you want to associate with the surface.

IN `SizeOfData`: The size, in bytes, of the buffer that you specified in `pData`.

IN `Flags`: Set this either to `NULL` or to `D3DSPD_IUNKNOWN` if the data you are setting is part of a COM IUnknown interface.

UnlockRect()

Purpose

Unlocks a rectangle within the surface.

Prototype

```
HRESULT UnlockRect();
```

Parameters

NA

IDirect3DTexture8

AddDirtyRect()

Purpose

Adds a dirty region to a texture.

Prototype

```
HRESULT AddDirtyRect(
  CONST RECT* pDirtyRect
);
```

Parameters

 pDirtyRect: Set this either to NULL, to specify the entire surface as dirty, or to a pointer to a RECT structure identifying the rectangle that you want to set as dirty.

GetLevelDesc()

Purpose

Gets a description of a texture at a specified level.

Prototype

```
HRESULT GetLevelDesc(
  UINT Level,
  D3DSURFACE_DESC* pDesc
);
```

Parameters

 Level: Specifies the level of the texture for which you want to get a description.

 pDesc: A pointer to a D3DSURFACE_DESC that will be filled with information about the surface.

GetSurfaceLevel()

Purpose

Gets the surface level for a texture.

Prototype

```
HRESULT GetSurfaceLevel(
  UINT Level,
  IDirect3DSurface8** ppSurfaceLevel
);
```

Parameters

IN **Level:** Specifies the level of the texture that you want to get.

IN **ppSurfaceLevel:** Takes the address of a pointer to a surface that will be filled with the address of the surface you are trying to get.

LockRect()

Purpose

Locks a rectangle within a texture.

Prototype

```
HRESULT LockRect(
  UINT Level,
  D3DLOCKED_RECT* pLockedRect,
  CONST RECT* pRect,
  DWORD Flags
);
```

Parameters

IN **Level:** Specifies the level of the texture that you want to lock.

OUT **pLockedRect:** Pointer to D3DLOCKED_RECT structure, which contains a pointer to the locked data, and information about the pitch of the texture.

IN **pRect:** Pointer to a RECT that holds information about the rectangle that you want to lock. Specify NULL to lock the entire texture.

IN **Flags:** Flags, which can be set to any of the values in Table B.4 except for D3DLOCK_NOOVERWRITE, identifying how you want to lock the surface.

UnlockRect()

Purpose

Unlocks a locked texture.

Prototype

```
HRESULT UnlockRect(
  UINT Level
);
```

Parameters

 Level: The level of the texture that you want to unlock.

IDirect3DVertexBuffer8

GetDesc

Purpose

Gets a description of the vertex buffer.

Prototype

```
HRESULT GetDesc(
  D3DVERTEXBUFFER_DESC* pDesc
);
```

Parameters

 pDesc: Pointer to a D3DVERTEXBUFFER_DESC structure that will be filled to contain information about the vertex buffer.

Lock()

Purpose

Locks a range of vertex data and gets a pointer to the buffer memory.

Prototype

```
HRESULT Lock(
  UINT OffsetToLock,
  UINT SizeToLock,
  BYTE** ppbData,
  DWORD Flags
);
```

Parameters

IN `OffsetToLock`: Starting offset into the buffer that you want to lock.

IN `SizeToLock`: Size of the vertex buffer that you want to lock, in bytes.

OUT `ppbData`: Address of a pointer that will be filled with a pointer to an array of `BYTE` values.

IN `Flags`: Flags that describe how the lock will behave. They can be set to any of the values in Table B.4.

Unlock

Purpose

Unlocks a locked vertex buffer.

Prototype

```
HRESULT Unlock();
```

Parameters

NA

INDEX

X-Z

License Agreement/Notice of Limited Warranty